INDUSTRY STRUCTURE, STRATEGY, AND PUBLIC POLICY

The HarperCollins Series in Economics

INDUSTRY STRUCTURE, STRATEGY, AND PUBLIC POLICY

F. M. Scherer

Harvard University
John F. Kennedy School of Government

HarperCollins*CollegePublishers*

Executive Editor: John Greenman
Project Editor: Ellen MacElree
Cover Designer: John Callahan
Text Designer: Laura Leever
Cover Photograph: Copyright © 1994 by Pete Saloutos/The Stock Market.
Art Studio: ElectraGraphics, Inc.
Electronic Production Manager: Su Levine
Desktop Administrator: Laura Leever
Manufacturing Manager: Willie Lane
Electronic Page Makeup: Interactive Composition Corporation
Printer and Binder: R. R. Donnelley & Sons Company
Cover Printer: New England Book Components

Industry Structure, Strategy, and Public Policy

Library of Congress Cataloging-in-Publication Data

Scherer, F. M. (Frederic M.)
    Industry structure, strategy, and public policy / F. M. Scherer.
        p. cm.
    Includes index.
    ISBN 0-673-99289-6
    1. Industrial concentration--Government policy--United States--Case studies.
2. Industrial policy--United States--Case studies. 3. Industrial organization--
United States--Case studies. I. Title.
HD2795.S25 1996
338.973--dc20
                                                          95-41498
                                                           CIP

99 9 8 7 6 5 4 3 2

CONTENTS

PREFACE

In the fall of 1970, the first edition of my textbook *Industrial Market Structure and Economic Performance* appeared in print. The book contained most of what I knew about the theory of industrial organization ("I-O") and the systematic evidence illuminating it. This posed a problem. Since there were few competing texts at the time, how would I teach the subject matter in the future? To regurgitate what was in my book would be incredibly dull both for my students and myself. This dilemma became the mother of invention. For the term beginning in January 1971, I initiated a new undergraduate course that sought to teach "I-O" through a series of in-depth industry case studies. Since then I have used the case-study approach at the undergraduate and masters levels approximately twenty times. That case-oriented offering has without doubt been the most successful of my courses during more than three decades of teaching. Blending real-world industrial history, theory, and policy is a powerful way to convey to students what industrial organization economists know.

This book crystallizes my experience in a way that I hope will be stimulating to teachers and students alike. It contains nine industry case studies carefully selected and sequenced so that most of the basic theoretical tools emerge naturally in the process of analyzing real-world industry structure and conduct. The assumed prerequisite is a solid introductory microeconomics course. Those who use the book in their teaching can elaborate on the core concepts to whatever extent their interests and the ability of their students dictate. Because the chosen industries have at one time or another posed difficult problems for policy makers, the case studies also illuminate the uses and limitations of diverse public policies toward business, including some not normally treated in industrial organization texts. My intention for the future is to bring the book up to date on both policy issues and data through fairly frequent revisions.

My knowledge of the industries has accumulated through reading others' work (including papers written by my students), my own research, my two-year stint as a Federal Trade Commission official implementing antitrust policy and supervising a program of industry studies, and my work as a consultant on policy questions involving the industries. I owe a huge debt to the many unnamed practitioners who have educated me on one or another aspect of the nine industries, as well as to the scholars (almost always cited) and students (occasionally cited) who have done research on them.

Helpful critical comments on the outline and particular chapters were received from William S. Comanor, William W. Hogan, Tarun Khanna, John E. Kwoka, Jr., Richard Langlois, Anita McGahan, Ashish Nanda, Erin Page, Subi Rangan, and Raymond Vernon, among others. Substantial parts of the manuscript were constructively critiqued by Samuel Baker, Gary Biglaiser, Joseph I. Daniel, Mark E. McBride, Richard L. Manning, James W. Meehan, Jr., David E. Mills, Irene Powell, John J. Siegfried, Lawrence White,

Richard L. Wobbekind, and a friend of long standing who, perhaps to avoid guilt by association, chose to remain anonymous. Substantial parts of the manuscript were tested on two cohorts of Kennedy School students, some of whom called errors to my attention. Research assistance specific to the manuscript was provided by David Cope and Pasha Mahmood. I am grateful to all.

Needless to say, they are not responsible for errors; I am. This limited warranty applies only for three years. After that, responsibility shifts to those who have detected errors and not communicated them to the author.

The book is dedicated to my wife Barbara, who has sustained me through nearly four decades of learning-by-doing about industrial organization.

F. M. Scherer

Industry Structure, Strategy, and Public Policy

1

INTRODUCTION

This book offers a deeply intuitive introduction to the field of economics known as *industrial organization* or, in Europe, as *industrial economics*. It does so through nine case studies of important industries. It differs from the many other useful case study volumes by continuously and cumulatively interweaving three main strands—history, theory, and policy.

The case studies are for the most part organized historically in the belief that real-world industries are complex organisms whose evolution can be understood only through careful attention to the historical dynamics. An historical approach is adopted also to help readers avoid the trap of which George Santayana warned: that those who fail to learn the lessons of the past condemn themselves to repeat its errors.

Equally vital to understanding industry behavior and performance, including the strategy choices of individual participants, is the mastery of appropriate theoretical tools, static and dynamic. The development of those tools is tightly integrated with the industry histories. Indeed, the industries were chosen not only because they are interesting and significant, but also because, to be appreciated fully, each requires a particular set of tools. The case studies are ordered so that a comprehensive theoretical structure unfolds in a logical and cumulative sequence.

We begin with two primary commodity industries, grain farming and crude oil. After rounding out the crude oil study with an analysis of petroleum refining and marketing, we move on to undifferentiated and then highly differentiated producers' goods: steel, semiconductors, and computers. The sequence continues with a durable consumer goods industry, automobiles, and two nondurable consumer goods industries, pharmaceuticals and beer brewing.

Another consideration in selecting the industries is that their histories illustrate well the principal public policies governments apply to influence industry performance and the strategic responses of industry members to those governmental initiatives. Excluded by conscious design from the case study sample are the traditional "regulated" industries. Yet we shall see that there has been pervasive governmental intervention into most of the chosen industries, revealing that although the United States has no coordinated industrial policy, it pursues a host of ad hoc industry-specific policies with profound positive and negative consequences.

The case studies emphasize the structure, conduct, and performance of U.S. industries. Most of the industries, however, have been subjected to significant competitive challenges from enterprises with home bases outside the United States, and some—wheat, crude oil, and semiconductors—are unambiguously worldwide in scope. We therefore explore carefully the international context within which each industry has functioned.

THE STRUCTURE-CONDUCT-PERFORMANCE PARADIGM

Our investigation will be influenced by an approach to industry analysis known as the structure-conduct-performance (S-C-P) paradigm. It is illustrated schematically by Figure 1.1.

FIGURE 1.1
The Structure-Conduct-Performance Paradigm

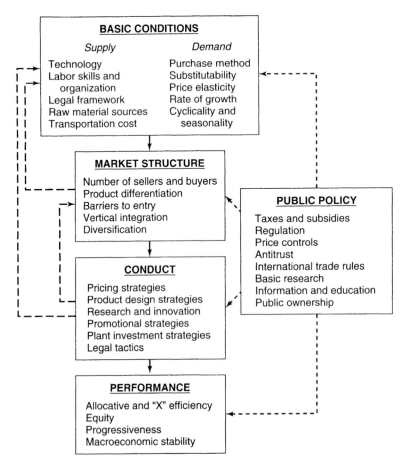

Good performance is what a nation's citizens ultimately seek from their industries. The component dimensions of industrial performance include distortion-free responsiveness to consumer demands (i.e., allocative efficiency), frugal resource use in satisfying demands (so-called X-efficiency[1]), an equitable distribution of income among resource providers and consumers, the swift exploitation of opportunities afforded by advances in science and technology to improve products and production processes (i.e., technical progressiveness), and adaptation to emerging challenges in ways that sustain macroeconomic stability (including reasonably full employment) and harmonious relationships among nations. These goals, we shall see, sometimes conflict, and so trade-offs are required.

According to the S-C-P paradigm, the ultimate performance of industries depends (as shown by the direction of solid arrows in Figure 1.1) upon their members' *conduct* along a number of dimensions, including the pricing strategies pursued, company policies toward product design and durability, the innovative efforts firms undertake, how they advertise and promote their products, whether they anticipate or lag demand in their plant capacity investments, and the legal tactics they adopt on such matters as the enforcement of intellectual property rights and the attempted exclusion of competitors, foreign and domestic.

Industry members' conduct is said in turn to depend upon the structure of the markets within which they operate. Key aspects of structure include the number and relative sizes of producing firms and their customers; the extent to which products are differentiated one from another by variations in function, design, and image; and the ease or difficulty of entry into the market by new competitors (characterized under the rubric "barriers to entry"). Other dimensions of market structure include the extent to which producers are vertically integrated—for example, from mining or growing raw materials to the wholesale and retail distribution of products—and the extent to which producers specialize in only a few related products, as contrasted to diversifying their efforts over a broad array of products.

At a still more fundamental level, market structures are affected by a host of basic conditions, of which Figure 1.1 illustrates some especially important elements. On the supply side are such variables as product and production process technology; the level of employee skills and the degree to which workers are organized, as in unions; the complex framework of laws and other public policies within which corporations operate; the ubiquity and location of raw materials; and whether industry products are relatively expensive or cheap to transport from factories to the loci of consumption. On the demand side are consumer buying methods (e.g., impulse purchasing, comparison shopping, or the solicitation of competitive bids); the extent to which functional substitutes for firm and industry products exist; the price elasticity of consumer demand; whether demand is growing rapidly or stagnant; whether

---

[1]On the concept of X-efficiency, see Harvey Leibenstein, "Allocative Efficiency vs. X-Efficiency," *American Economic Review*, vol. 56 (June 1966), pp. 392–415.

products are purchased repetitively or only occasionally; and the extent to which there are cyclical or other time patterns in consumer purchases.

The S-C-P paradigm is sometimes erroneously interpreted as implying that the chain of causation runs in only one direction—that is, from basic conditions to market structure to conduct to performance. In truth, feedback effects (shown by the dashed vertical arrows in Figure 1.1) are equally significant. Companies' pricing and product strategies, as we shall see, often have a powerful impact in shaping market structures. Firms' investments in research and technological innovation affect technology, production and transportation cost conditions, the viability of raw material sources, the extent of product differentiation, and barriers to the entry of new rivals. Company legal tactics can affect the framework of laws and public policies (e.g., through successful lobbying) and the ability of rivals to enter or remain in the market. Many concrete illustrations will follow.

Finally, industries' structure and conduct are influenced by a host of general and specific public policies. At an extreme that will seldom be encountered in this volume, publicly owned enterprises may displace or compete with performance by private sector companies. Taxes and subsidies are often tailored to the conditions of individual industries. Through explicit regulatory intervention, government agencies determine which firms are allowed to offer particular products and set more or less detailed rules for companies' conduct. Several of the industries studied in this volume have been subjected on occasion to governmental price controls of varying pervasiveness. Antitrust enforcement influences market structures (e.g., by breaking apart firms with large market shares under Section 2 of the Sherman Act and preventing certain mergers under Section 7 of the Clayton Act). It also establishes rules (e.g., Sherman Act Section 1's prohibition against collusion) to which sellers' conduct must conform. International trade policies—that is, those within the General Agreement on Tariffs and Trade (GATT) framework—permit injured firms to seek protection against the competition of international rivals and limit the kinds of subsidies that governments can bestow upon their clients. Through their support of basic research, education, and the provision of information, governments help both producers and consumers respond more intelligently to market opportunities.

THE PRINCIPAL MARKET STRUCTURES

The S-C-P paradigm is useful not only because some organizing principle is necessary in such a complex field, but also because economic theory predicts systematic differences in sellers' conduct with variations in market structure.

Figure 1.2 offers a simple but useful two-way typology. The columns array industries according to the number of significant sellers they harbor; the rows according to whether products are homogeneous or differentiated in functionality, locational convenience, and image. As the number of sellers increases from one through "a few" to many, the most basic market structure variants—

FIGURE 1.2
The Principal Sellers' Market Structure Types

	Number of Sellers		
	One	A Few	Many
Homogeneous products	Pure monopoly	Homogeneous oligopoly	Pure competition
Differentiated products	Multiproduct monopoly	Differentiated oligopoly	Monopolistic competition

monopoly, oligopoly, and atomistic competition—are delineated. Variants proliferate for diverse degrees of product differentiation, culminating with the most recent addition to the standard nomenclature—the case of "monopolistic competition" first explored by Edward H. Chamberlin during the 1930s.[2]

Unadulterated examples of pure monopoly are rare in the real world. In this volume we will encounter approximations in Standard Oil's position during the late nineteenth century, many current petroleum pipeline routes, some semiconductor products, and certain unique pharmaceuticals. Cases of pure competition are somewhat more prevalent. Grain farming will provide the closest approximation among the industries studied here. Monopolistic competition occurs in microcomputers, drug retailing, and (at least in the larger cities) gasoline marketing, among others. The intermediate few-sellers case of oligopoly is common, both among the industries scrutinized here and in the broader world. Homogeneous oligopolies include crude oil, the refining of most petroleum products, some retail gasoline market structures, steel, and dynamic random-access memory chips. Among the differentiated oligopolies are numerous semiconductor products, mainframe computers and minicomputers, automobiles, most pharmaceutical products, and beer.

Diverse quantitative indices are used to characterize market structures in terms of the number of sellers. The simplest is a count of the number of independent firms vying to peddle their wares. It is really too simple, because most industries contain "fringes" of numerous very small firms, each too small to have any appreciable influence on the industry's performance. A somewhat better measure, and the only one for which extended historical data exist, is the so-called concentration ratio, or to emphasize a more specific example of the genus, the four-firm sales concentration ratio.[3] It is found by

---

[2]E. H. Chamberlin, *The Theory of Monopolistic Competition* (Cambridge: Harvard University Press, 1933).

[3]For a discussion of other concentration and monopoly power measures, see, e.g., F. M. Scherer and David Ross, *Industrial Market Structure and Economic Performance* (Boston: Houghton Mifflin, 1990), pp. 70–79; and Leslie Hannah and John A. Kay, *Concentration in Modern Industry* (New York: Macmillan, 1977).

arraying all members of a meaningfully defined industry, from largest in terms of sales volume to smallest, and then computing:

$$CR4 = \frac{\text{Sales of the largest four companies}}{\text{Sales of all industry members}} \, 100$$

The index can vary from slightly above zero to 100, with a value near zero characterizing "atomistic competition" and a value near 100 a structure ranging from "tight" oligopoly to complete monopoly. (If concentration ratios were computed for only the single largest seller, a value approaching 100 would connote pure monopoly.)

The most comprehensive information on industry concentration comes from periodic compilations conducted by national census authorities (e.g., in the United States, every five years by the Bureau of the Census for the economy's manufacturing sector). Unfortunately, systematic concentration statistics for other sectors (such as agriculture, mining, transportation, banking, and the various service industries) are much rarer, if available at all.

Figure 1.3 shows the distribution of four-firm sales concentration ratios for the 459 "four-digit" manufacturing industry categories into which the U.S. Census Bureau subdivided its data for the year 1987. "Four-digit" industries are identified by a four-digit code in the U.S. Standard Industrial Classification—for example, 2082 for beer, 2911 for petroleum refining, and 3674 for semiconductors. Tightly oligopolistic industries—that is, those with concentration ratios in the 60–100 percent range—are relatively uncommon in manufacturing, although their incidence is seen to be higher when measured by the fraction of total manufacturing sector value added that they originate rather than by a simple count of the number of industries encom-

FIGURE 1.3
Incidence of Industry Four-Firm Concentration Ratio Ranges

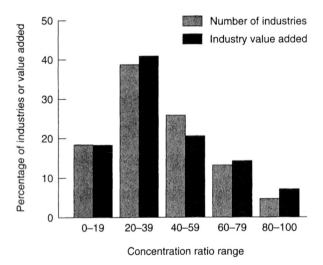

passed. Roughly 40 percent of all manufacturing industries, both by number and value added, have concentration ratios in the 20–39 percent range, which marks a border zone between the atomistic structures of pure or monopolistic competition and loose oligopoly. Some of these industries would be found to be more clearly oligopolistic if one took into account qualitative differences in product offerings within the four-digit definitional categories and the tendency of some producers (such as petroleum refiners) to serve geographic areas smaller than the whole national expanse. Thus, from Figure 1.3 and supplemental information, one might conclude that approximately half of U.S. manufacturing sector activity is best characterized as occurring under oligopolistic conditions.

STRUCTURE TO PERFORMANCE LINKS IN ECONOMIC THEORY

Microeconomic theory offers sharply focused predictions concerning the differences in performance between the two polar cases of pure competition and pure monopoly. We review the most basic concepts here.

PURE COMPETITION

Figure 1.4 illustrates the standard competitive case. At the industry level (left-hand panel), the demand curve D arrays consumers' valuations of incremental product units, beginning with that first unit for which some consumer would be willing to pay the very high price OZ rather than forgo its consumption,

FIGURE 1.4
Equilibrium Under Pure Competition

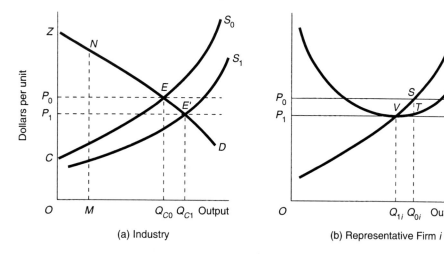

(a) Industry   (b) Representative Firm i

progressing downward over units such as the Mth, for which the consumer's marginal valuation or *reservation price* is MN, and continuing to descend through less and less highly valued units. The supply curve S_0 similarly arrays the units of output sellers are willing to supply in ascending order of the marginal cost of producing and delivering them—for example, from OC for the first unit supplied through units of increasing marginal supply cost. Market equilibrium occurs at price OP_0, where the quantity demanded by consumers equals the quantity supplied by producers.

In a purely competitive industry,[4] each supplying firm is such a small atom relative to the total supply that it perceives its output decisions—that is, whether to produce nothing, some intermediate quantity, or all its capacity permits—to have no appreciable effect on the ruling market price. To a competitive firm, the price of its product is a *parameter* fixed outside its control by the impersonal forces of supply and demand. Therefore, the ith individual competitive firm (right-hand panel) sees its demand curve as the horizontal line P_0P_0' set at level OP_0 in the industry-wide marketplace. To maximize its profits, the firm expands production until its marginal cost MC_i rises into equality with parametric price (i.e., at output OQ_{0i}).

If firm i is representative, however, price OP_0 is inconsistent with long-run industry equilibrium because the firm is earning supranormal unit profits measured by the vertical distance ST between its price line and the ordinate of its average total cost curve ATC at output OQ_{0i}. "Supranormal" means that profits are received above and beyond what is necessary to attract the firm's invested capital away from alternative uses—for example, above the return that could be earned investing in a diversified common stock portfolio. If many suppliers realize supranormal profits, they will find it worthwhile to expand their plants or build additional new plants, and outsiders will be induced to construct their own new plants and enter the industry. The industry supply function will shift outward to S_1, displacing the industry equilibrium (left-hand panel) from point E to E' and forcing the price down to OP_1. That new and lower price, projected over to firm i's situation (right-hand panel), will lead firm i to contract its output to OQ_{1i}. This is just sufficient to eliminate all supranormal profits at point V, where the price line and marginal cost intersect. If firm i is representative, the industry will have attained long-run equilibrium, with no tendency toward either net new entry or net exit of existing suppliers.

At the long-run equilibrium of a purely competitive industry, three conditions hold simultaneously:

---

[4]The terms "pure" and "perfect" are often interchanged carelessly in discussions of competition. "Pure" competition is used here to imply numerous sellers, homogeneous products, and easy entry. "Perfect" competition entails further assumptions about the quality of information available to sellers and buyers and the divisibility of resources.

1. Each supplier's marginal cost *MC* is equal to the ruling price.
2. Each representative firm realizes zero supranormal profits.
3. Each firm is operating at minimum average total cost *ATC*.

Condition 1 holds whenever competitive firms are maximizing their profits. Conditions 2 and 3 hold because the marginal cost curve cuts the average total cost curve ATC at its minimum, and so if the price equals both marginal cost and (for zero supranormal profits) average total cost, ATC must be at its minimum. Minimum-cost condition 3 satisfies an X-efficiency performance goal; that is, competitive firms use their resources frugally. Condition 2 satisfies an equity goal, for firms receive no greater reward than what is required to draw their services from alternative occupations. To understand the broader performance implications of condition 1, we must examine the alternative monopoly case in which it does not hold.

PURE MONOPOLY

Figure 1.5 contrasts the equilibria resulting under pure competition (left-hand panel) and pure monopoly (right-hand panel), assuming otherwise identical cost and demand conditions. The monopolist, unlike the purely competitive firm, originates a sufficiently large fraction of total industry output (in the limiting case, all of it) that it recognizes the impact of changes in its supply on the market price. To sell more, it must reduce its price. But unless it can practice a sophisticated form of price discrimination, which we provisionally rule out at this stage of the exposition, the monopolist's gain in physical unit sales and hence revenue from reducing price is offset at least in part by the revenue

FIGURE 1.5
Comparison of Competitive and Monopoly Equilibria

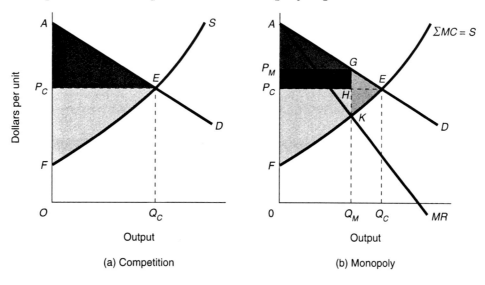

(a) Competition

(b) Monopoly

lost from charging lower prices to customers who otherwise would have purchased in any event at the prereduction price. Revenue gains are balanced against losses from price reductions sufficient to sell incremental units by constructing marginal revenue function *MR* in the right-hand panel of Figure 1.5.[5] The monopolist expands output only to the point where marginal revenue falls into equality with marginal cost (summed across all of the firm's production facilities). The monopoly price OP_M is greater than the corresponding competitive price OP_C; the monopoly output OQ_M is therefore less than the competitive output OQ_C.

Under competition (left-hand panel), consumers realize consumers' surplus—that is, the surplus of what they are willing to pay (read off the demand curve) over the price they actually pay—measured by darkly shaded area AEP_C. To cover their fixed costs, competitive sellers realize a producers' surplus above their marginal costs measured by the lightly shaded area $P_C EF$. Under monopoly (right-hand panel), consumers' surplus shrinks to area AGP_M. Some of what was consumers' surplus, measured by rectangular area $P_M GHP_C$, is appropriated as producer's surplus or, somewhat less precisely, monopoly profit. Gaining that surplus is the main point of monopoly price-raising. Furthermore, output $Q_M Q_C$ that would have been produced under competition is not produced under monopoly. The value to consumers of each such unit, read off the demand curve, is greater than its production cost, read off the summed marginal cost curve. By leaving those $Q_M Q_C$ units unproduced, the monopolist causes a *dead-weight loss* measured by triangle GEK.[6] Roughly half of that dead-weight loss entails the disappearance of what

---

[5]The price received by a monopolist is an inverse function $P(Q)$ of the quantity sold. Total revenue *TR* to the monopolist is price $P(Q)$ times quantity Q. Marginal revenue is the derivative of total revenue with respect to Q; that is,

$$MR = \frac{dTR}{dQ} = Q\,\frac{dP}{dQ} + P(Q)$$

The first term on the right-hand side (carrying a negative sign) is the reduction in revenue obtained from customers who would have bought even at the higher price; the second term is the gain in revenue from supplying one more unit of output at the reduced price.

In the case of straight-line demand functions, $P = a - bQ$ and $TR = Q(a - bQ) = aQ - bQ^2$. Marginal revenue is the derivative $a - 2bQ$, with the same vertical intercept as the demand function but twice its slope. Because the geometric relationships are so simple, we frequently assume straight-line monopoly demand curves in what follows when no sacrifice of realism is imposed.

[6]To where are the resources that would have been used to produce output $Q_M Q_C$ reallocated? The standard assumption is that they flow into producing other competitively supplied goods and services at prices equaling costs at the margin, so that little or no new surplus is created to replace the surplus lost under monopoly. If this assumption does not hold, complexities analyzed under the *theory of second best* arise. See, for example, Scherer and Ross, *Industrial Market Structure and Economic Performance*, pp. 33–38.

would have been consumers' surplus under competition; the other half represents a sacrifice of producer's surplus, given up by the monopolist in order to raise prices and hence capture the larger surplus P_MGHP_C. Because monopolistic price-raising and output restriction cause dead-weight surplus losses, we say that resources are *allocated inefficiently* under monopoly. This inefficiency occurs whenever production stops short of the output at which price equals marginal cost—that is, whenever condition 1 associated with competitive pricing is not satisfied.

MONOPOLISTIC COMPETITION AND OLIGOPOLY

One consequence of monopoly, then, is a distortion of output decisions. In addition, equity may suffer. Figure 1.6 provides a more detailed view. The monopoly's demand curve is now D_1, its marginal revenue function MR_1, the profit-maximizing price OP_1, and the monopoly output OQ_1. The dead-weight loss is measured by the area of triangle *MEL*. At output OQ_1, the price is well above average total cost (read from point *A*), so supranormal profits of *MA* per unit, or the area of rectangle P_1MAC in total, are realized. That the monopoly commands profits beyond those needed to call forth its services may be deemed inequitable. In addition, if the monopoly's owners are among the wealthier members of society, the inequality of income distribution will increase, which may also offend equity norms.[7] We say "may" here because

FIGURE 1.6
Profits Under Monopoly and Monopolistic Competition

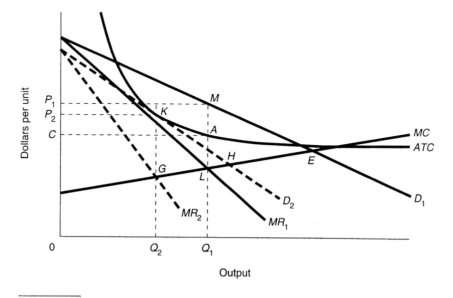

[7]See, for example, William S. Comanor and Robert H. Smiley, "Monopoly and the Distribution of Wealth," *Quarterly Journal of Economics*, vol. 89 (May 1975), pp. 177–194.

equity questions require value judgments over which reasonable (not to mention self-aggrandizing) individuals often disagree.

If entry into the monopolized market is not barred, supranormal profits are likely to attract new entrants who cannibalize some of the original monopolist's demand. When sellers face downward-sloping demand curves but entry by small rivals is easy, monopoly gives way to the case of monopolistic competition. Entry then shifts the original monopolist's demand curve to the left until the supranormal profits are squeezed out, i.e., with (dashed) demand curve D_2 in Figure 1.6. At this monopolistic competition equilibrium, the firm's demand curve is tangent to its average total cost curve (at point K). The best the "monopolist" can do now is to produce output OQ_2, where marginal cost equals (shifted) marginal revenue MR_2, setting a price OP_2 at which supranormal profits are precisely zero. Thus, it is entirely possible for pricing to be monopolistic, giving rise inter alia to dead-weight losses (e.g., triangle KHG), without yielding monopoly profits. A further characteristic of long-run equilibrium under monopolistic competition is that firms operate at outputs too small to minimize average total cost, violating condition 3 of purely competitive equilibrium. However, under monopolistic competition prices tend to be lower than they would be under pure monopoly. In addition, monopolistic competitors are likely to offer a wider diversity of products differentiated by design, quality level, and accompanying service, satisfying better than a single seller would consumers' desires for variety.

Between the one-seller case of pure monopoly and the many-sellers cases of pure or monopolistic competition is the few-sellers case of oligopoly. Under oligopoly, each seller is sufficiently large relative to its rivals that its pricing, output, product design, and service actions have a perceptible and significant impact on the demand and profits of the rival firms. The hallmark of oligopoly is interdependence of the several sellers' fortunes. Each oligopolist must therefore make strategic decisions that attempt to take into account likely rival reactions and counteractions. Because of this strategic interdependence, it is difficult to predict the outcome of oligopolistic rivalries with any confidence. Pricing outcomes, for example, can range from the high prices associated with pure monopoly to the low prices associated with pure competition or even to lower "warfare" levels. Economists have struggled with the oligopoly problem for more than a century without achieving a unified behavioral theory. In this book the question is approached inductively. We strive to learn as much as we can through a constant interplay between theorizing and observing how real-world oligopolists behave.[8]

---

[8]For more comprehensive theoretical treatments, both inductive and deductive, see one or more of the leading industrial organization textbooks—for example, Scherer and Ross, *Industrial Market Structure and Economic Performance;* Dennis W. Carlton and Jeffrey M. Perloff, *Modern Industrial Organization* (Glenview, IL: Scott, Foresman, 1989); Stephen Martin, *Advanced Industrial Economics* (Oxford, England: Basil Blackwell, 1993); and Jean Tirole, *The Theory of Industrial Organization* (Cambridge: MIT Press, 1988). See also Richard Schmalensee and Robert D. Willig, eds., *Handbook of Industrial Organization* (2 volumes) (Amsterdam: North-Holland: 1989).

STATIC AND DYNAMIC TRADE-OFFS

The allocative inefficiencies associated with monopoly pricing could be mitigated if for some reason monopolists conducted their operations at lower cost than competitors. Costs might be lower because monopolists are able to realize economies of scale more fully, because they can control market risks and therefore attract capital at lower interest rates, or because they have hired superior managers. For these or other reasons, the marginal cost curve under monopoly MC_M in Figure 1.7 might lie below the summed marginal cost curve MC_C (i.e., the supply curve) under competitive industry organization. As the curves are constructed, output under monopoly OQ_M will still be lower, and the price OP_M will be higher, than under competition (OQ_C and OP_C). There will still be a dead-weight loss from the monopolist's price-raising—in this instance, measured by the darkly shaded trapezoidal area $MCHG$. (Triangle CEH is not included because, although the monopolist could feasibly reach equilibrium point E, competitive producers cannot, and so surplus is not forgone relative to the benchmark competitive case.) But on the (smaller) output OQ_M that the monopolist does produce, there are cost savings measured by the lightly shaded area between the two cost curves $JFGK$. Thus, the monopoly causes dead-weight loss $MCHG$ by its pricing, but saves $JFGK$ by virtue of its superior X-efficiency. Under the assumptions embodied in Figure 1.7, the gains from monopolization outweigh the dead-weight losses, although the trade-off is a close one. But with a smaller cost saving, the balance could tip in the other direction. Whether operating costs are in fact significantly lower under monopolistic industry organization (e.g., because of scale economies) is an empirical question. We address it repeatedly in our industry case studies.

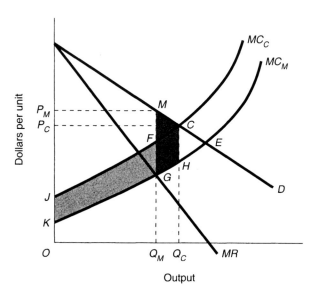

FIGURE 1.7
Trade-off of Monopoly Cost Savings Against Dead-Weight Losses

In principle, no trade-off need exist. Monopolies might operate at higher rather than lower costs. The security and generous profits from a monopoly position may permit managers to relax their efforts to run a tight ship and to spend money on superfluous amenities. "Monopoly . . . is a great enemy to good management," Adam Smith warned two centuries ago.[9] Or as J. R. Hicks observed, "The best of all monopoly profits is a quiet life."[10] We will find empirical support for these caveats in some of our case studies.

Industrial organization is a discipline that requires multiarmed economists.[11] On the one hand, monopoly restricts output and imposes dead-weight allocative inefficiencies. On another hand, monopoly may reduce operating costs. But arriving on the third hand is a set of hypotheses most closely associated with the writings of Joseph A. Schumpeter.[12] Whatever merits monopoly may or may not possess in the short run, Schumpeter argued, what really matters for human welfare is not static allocative and operating efficiency, but the long-run consequences of technological progress. If under monopoly an economy's output is lower by 10 percent today because of static inefficiencies, that handicap will be overcome in just 10.6 years if the monopolistic economy can increase its output at an annual rate of 3 percent per year when its competitive counterpart grows at only a 2 percent rate. And if the monopolistic economy continues to grow more rapidly, it will, after overtaking the competitive economy, exhibit ever-increasing material superiority.

Schumpeter went on to argue that technological progress and hence the rate of output growth would in fact be more rapid under monopoly than under competition. Monopolists could afford to devote more resources to research, development, and innovation than their competitive counterparts; they could hire superior R&D talent; and they could realize economies of scale and risk-pooling in their R&D laboratories. And indeed, the output restrictions and high profits associated with monopoly could be lures that spur firms to seek their own monopolies through innovation, displacing existing monopolists in a process Schumpeter called "creative destruction." He summed up his argument:[13]

---

[9]Adam Smith, *An Inquiry into the Nature and Causes of the Wealth of Nations* (New York: Modern Library edition of the 1776 original, 1937), p. 147.

[10]"Annual Survey of Economic Theory: The Theory of Monopoly," *Econometrica*, vol. 3 (January 1935), p. 8.

[11]Dismayed by economists whose answers to his questions were often prefaced by "On the one hand . . . but on the other hand," President Harry S. Truman is said to have exclaimed, "Get me a one-armed economist!"

[12]J. A. Schumpeter, *Capitalism, Socialism, and Democracy* (New York: Harper, 1942).

[13]*Capitalism, Socialism, and Democracy*, p. 106.

What we have got to accept is that [the large-scale establishment or unit of control] has come to be the most powerful engine of . . . progress and . . . long-run expansion of total output not only in spite of, but to a considerable extent through, this strategy which looks so restrictive when viewed in the individual case and from the individual point in time. In this respect, perfect competition is not only impossible but inferior, and has no title to being set up as a model of ideal efficiency.

Whether Schumpeter was right—that is, whether technological progress is significantly more rapid under monopoly than under competition—is a question on which economists have devised elaborate theories, but which at bottom must be settled empirically.[14] It too will be a continuing focus in the case studies that follow. One reason why most of the industries chosen for analysis in this volume belong to the manufacturing sector is that roughly 95 percent of the American economy's industrial research and development is performed by manufacturers, who transmit the new technology they have developed to other sectors through their sales of new products.[15] Thus, manufacturing plays a central role in generating the technological changes that underlie economic growth. In our effort to discern the validity of the Schumpeterian hypotheses, we will analyze some of the most technologically dynamic industries alongside others of much less impressive dynamism.

REPRISE

Our agenda is set. We seek to understand how nine important U.S. industries are structured, how and why their structures have evolved over time, the rationale of behavioral strategy choices taken by members of those industries, and how in the end the level of economic performance has been affected. Economic theory provides some guidance, both normatively and in identifying the questions that must be asked and answered. But in pursuing our inquiry, we shall have to develop much new theory and test it against the observed facts.

---

[14]For reviews of the literature, see William L. Baldwin and John T. Scott, *Market Structure and Technological Change* (Chur, Switzerland: Harwood Academic Publishers, 1987); Jennifer F. Reinganum, "The Timing of Innovation," in Schmalensee and Willig, eds., *Handbook of Industrial Organization*, vol. I, pp. 849–908; and Wesley M. Cohen and Richard C. Levin, "Empirical Studies of Innovation and Market Structure," *Handbook of Industrial Organization*, vol. II, pp. 1059–1107.

[15]See F. M. Scherer, "Interindustry Technology Flows in the United States," *Research Policy*, vol. 11 (August 1982), pp. 227–245.

2

GRAIN FARMING

The textbook model of purely competitive price-setting and resource allocation applies unusually well in grain farming. But because resources, and especially labor, are relatively immobile, the agricultural industries have experienced significant problems—notably price instability, chronic poverty of farm owners and workers, and, more recently, low returns on farmers' investments. Because farmers are politically powerful, the government has intervened in complex ways to support prices and incomes. Analyzing those interventions will require us to stretch the competitive model to extract numerous new insights. Among other things, the role of competitive world trade and the impact of the 1994 Uruguay Round international trade treaty must be taken into account.

INTRODUCTION

The various agricultural industries have structures that approximate the conditions characterizing pure competition about as closely as one can realistically encounter. There are large numbers of sellers, the products are homogeneous, and entry is relatively easy.

Because many farms serve as the homes of people who earn their main living elsewhere, it is difficult to determine the exact number of farms in the United States. The official U.S. Census count for 1991 was 2.1 million farms, among which 326,000 with sales of $100,000 or more gained 77 percent of the gross cash income of all U.S. farms.[1] To be sure, the number of farms producing individual commodities is smaller. In 1981, a single corporation, Tenneco, originated 15 percent of the nation's table grapes, 25 percent of the California

---

[1] U.S. Bureau of the Census, *Statistical Abstract of the United States: 1993* (Washington, DC: USGPO, 1993), p. 658.

almonds, and 40 percent of the pistachio nuts.[2] But these cases are exceptional. Corn is grown by nearly a million farms, wheat and soybeans by several hundred thousand, cotton by 67,000, and sugar beets by roughly 8,000, each grower holding a market share too small to have a perceptible influence on the market price.[3]

Individual agricultural products are also not strictly homogeneous. There are several standard wheat varieties—for example, durum (used mainly for pasta), hard red, soft red, and white—each with special uses. Corn and wheat vary in their protein content, sugar cane in the fraction of extractable sugar. But the products are readily classified by grade and sell at well-recognized price differentials. For any given grade, there are many sellers.

Entry conditions also vary from product to product. One can enter tomato farming with a small plot in a good-sized backyard. The typical Illinois corn, soybean, and livestock farm, on the other hand, encompassed 350 or more acres at an average 1990 value per acre of $1,400.[4] In addition to the implied investment in land and buildings of nearly $500,000, the Illinois corn farmer is likely to have machinery valued at well above $100,000 plus another $100,000 invested in working capital to cover seeds, livestock, and stored grain. But the lion's share of such investments can be financed with bank and other loans, and as a result, old farms can be purchased and (land conditions permitting) new farms can be started. Certainly, the million-dollar investment required to enter farming on a commercial scale is much smaller than the entry antes for other industries studied in this volume. The skills needed to enter commercial farming are also widely accessible—for example, through training at universities, which turned out more than 10,000 baccalaureate graduates in agricultural sciences per year during the 1980s.

THE FARM PROBLEM: PAST AND PRESENT

That farming is characterized by pure competition does not mean that it is without significant economic problems. In fact, farming in the United States (and Europe too) has experienced a seemingly unending series of problems that have precipitated massive governmental interventions. These problems can be grouped under four main headings: unstable prices, an historical tendency toward poverty, wide swings in the financial fortunes of farm enterprises, and new problems introduced by the government in its attempts to solve the first three problems.

---

[2]"Tenneco's Corporate Farming," *New York Times*, April 1, 1981, p. D1.

[3]Bruce L. Gardner, "Causes of U.S. Farm Commodity Programs," *Journal of Political Economy*, vol. 95 (April 1987), p. 297.

[4]A square mile comprises 640 acres. Most of the world measures land according to hectares, with one hectare equaling 2.47 U.S. acres.

PRICE INSTABILITY

That agriculture differed from other sectors of the economy in the way prices responded to changing demand conditions was suggested vividly by the experience of the Great Depression, which reduced real U.S. gross national product by 18 percent between 1929 and 1932. The percentage changes in prices and physical outputs over that three-year period for selected commodities were as follows:[5]

	Price Change (percent)	*Output Change (percent)*
Wheat	−63	+14
Cotton	−61	−12
Hogs	−53	+0.5
Potatoes	−71	+12
Apples	−56	+8.7
Steel rails	−1.4	−85
Portland cement	−32	−55
Ford Model A standard coupe	−12	−46
Phosphate rock (for fertilizer)	+0.7	−45
Electric power	+11	−14

For farm products, large price declines were the norm, accompanied in some instances by output increases despite depressed demand conditions. In the other sectors, output tended to decline much more, while prices fell by smaller amounts or (in two cases) actually rose.

We advance two preliminary hypotheses for the observed differences in pricing behavior. Price-setting in agriculture was unambiguously competitive, whereas in at least some of the other industries, there were important elements of monopoly power and/or cartelization. Chapter 5 will examine the cartellike pricing in steel; Chapter 8 covers the position of Ford. Electric power was an extreme case, regulated as a natural monopoly. Under the price-setting rules accepted by regulators at the time, the first block of kilowatt-hours consumed carried a much higher price than additional blocks, and so

---

[5] The sources are U.S. Bureau of the Census, *Historical Statistics of the United States: Colonial Times to 1957* (Washington, DC: USGPO, 1960), pp. 123, 289, 295–296, 303, 416, 506, and 511; Jesse W. Markham, *The Fertilizer Industry* (Nashville: Vanderbilt University Press, 1958), pp. 35 and 120; Samuel M. Loescher, *Imperfect Collusion in the Cement Industry* (Cambridge: Harvard University Press, 1959), pp. 168–171; and Allan Nevins and Frank E. Hill, *Ford: Expansion and Challenge, 1915–1933* (New York: Scribner, 1957), pp. 468–477 and 570–586. The Ford data are for 1929 through August 1931, when Model A production was discontinued to retool for new four- and eight-cylinder models. The assumed Model A quantity decline conservatively compares total 1931 production to two-thirds of 1929 production.

as consumption declined, the user's average rate rose. Also, legal mandates required regulators to approve rates that covered the electric utilities' full costs. With declining demand, overhead cost per kilowatt-hour rose, precipitating regulated rate increases.

Even where price-setting was competitive, there may have been systematic differences in the supply and demand conditions facing farmers as compared to manufacturers. Because people must eat to survive, the short-run price elasticity of most farm commodities is quite low. Demand for manufactured goods may be more price-elastic. Also, and more importantly, short-run supply curves in agriculture are almost surely more price-inelastic than those in most manufacturing and mining industries. Manufacturers incur substantial variable costs for materials and labor, imparting significant elasticity to their supply curves at below-capacity output levels. For farmers, on the other hand, the cost of variable inputs such as seed and fuel is modest in relation to normal selling prices, and because farmers have few alternative employment opportunities, the implicit cost of their labor was more fixed than variable. Figure 2.1 shows how inelastic supply and demand functions imply greater price swings in the face of a demand shock than more elastic functions. Figure 2.1a approximates conditions in farming; Figure 2.1b, those in manufacturing. A demand decline from D_0 to D_1 is introduced. At the initial price OP_0, the demand curve shifts leftward by the same absolute and percentage magnitudes in both panels. (Measurement may be required to overcome an optical illusion and persuade the viewer that horizontal-shift distances *GH* and *KM* are equal.) However, with more elastic supply and demand in manufacturing, the price decline is much smaller, being mitigated by more contraction of output (along the supply function) and more expansion of demand (along the demand function) for a given price decrease.

FIGURE 2.1
Effect of an Equal Demand Shock in Agriculture and Manufacturing

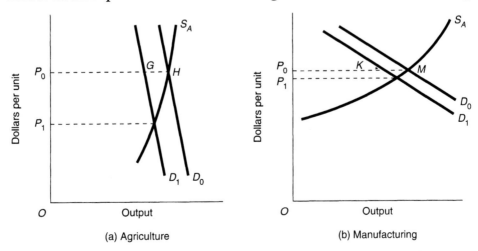

(a) Agriculture

(b) Manufacturing

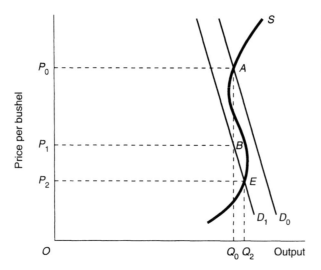

FIGURE 2.2
Backward-Bending
Supply Response in
the Great Depression

It is possible that under the unusual conditions of the early 1930s, farmers had paradoxical but theoretically plausible backward-bending supply curves, as illustrated in Figure 2.2.[6] Before the depression began, farmers operated at a normal supply-demand equilibrium point such as A, with price OP_0 and output OQ_0. But the decline in demand drove their prices down to OP_1 before any supply response was possible (i.e., vertically from A to B), after which they struggled to keep body and soul together by *increasing* their planting and harvesting efforts, leading to a new low-price (OP_2) equilibrium at E with a higher output OQ_2 than under preshock, high-price conditions.

Inelastic demand and supply lead to instability not only when a depression occurs, as in the early 1930s, but also with weather-induced supply shocks. Figure 2.3 provides illustration. S_0 assumes "normal" growing conditions, S_1 approximates the drought conditions that plagued much of the United States during 1983 and again in 1988. The drought shifts the supply function to the left by 22 percent relative to its normal position at price OP_0. Because both demand and supply are inelastic, and hence relatively unresponsive to changes in price, a near doubling of prices is required to restore market equilibrium.

Basic farm product prices have been unstable because of demand fluctuations, such as during the Great Depression, and (more frequently) as a consequence of weather-related and similar shocks. Figure 2.4 provides a 46-year perspective from 1947 through 1993, comparing the current-dollar average annual price of hard red winter wheat per bushel in the United States with the price index (calibrated to 1947 = 1.00) for the most popular product manufactured from wheat, white pan bread.[7] Bread prices fluctuate little on average

---

[6]The theory underlying backward-bending supply functions is illustrated more completely in the next chapter (Figure 3.6).

[7]Hard red winter wheat is used mainly to produce the flour for white bread and rolls.

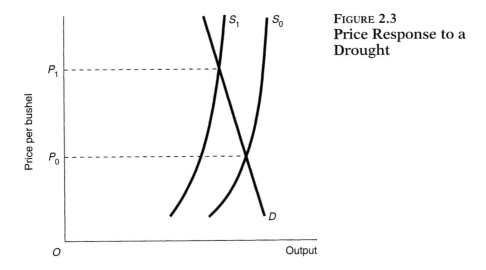

FIGURE 2.3
Price Response to a Drought

FIGURE 2.4
Trends in Hard Red Winter Wheat and White Bread Prices

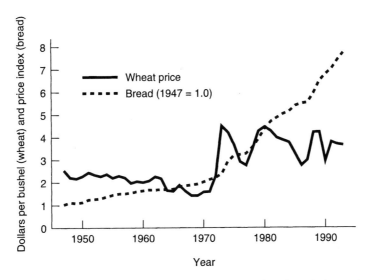

Sources: U.S. Department of Agriculture, *Agricultural Statistics*, various years; U.S. Department of Agriculture, Economic Research Service, *Wheat Yearbook* (WHS–1995), February 1995, p. 43; and U.S. Department of Labor, Bureau of Labor Statistics, special compilation.

from year to year. Wheat prices exhibit much larger fluctuations (which, however, are damped in Figure 2.4 by the use of annual averages). Bread prices move relentlessly upward, mirroring more general economic inflationary trends. The trend in wheat prices is strikingly different. Between 1947 and 1971, there is a clear downward trend, even though price levels generally in the U.S. economy (measured by the gross national product deflator) increased

94 percent. During the early 1970s, a shock (described more fully later) hit the wheat market (and with a lag, bread markets), driving prices sharply upward, after which there was considerable instability, but a slight downward trend from the 1973 peak. Meanwhile, the gross domestic product (GDP) deflator was trebling between 1973 and 1993.

Figure 2.4 poses a twofold challenge for the analysis that follows. First, we must go beyond our consideration of price elasticities to understand more fully the forces that lead to farm product price instability. And second, we must explore the causes and consequences of the longer-term downward price trends during the 1950s and 1960s and again in the 1980s. How, in particular, could wheat farmers sell their product at declining current-dollar prices when most other goods and services were becoming more expensive?

THE RACE BETWEEN SUPPLY AND DEMAND

The answer is found most fundamentally through supply and demand analysis. Farm prices are the result of a race between shifting demand curves and shifting supply curves.[8] Here we observe the race over two long intervals: 1950 to 1970, and 1970 to 1990.

The demand for food grows with population and consumers' affluence. In the 1950–1970 period, U.S. population grew at an average annual rate of 1.49 percent per year; in the 1970–1990 period, at the slower rate of 1.02 percent per year.[9] Ignoring age structure variations, we assume that food consumption rises linearly with population.

Engel's law, derived from research by the nineteenth-century Prussian statistician Ernst Engel, states that consumption rises less than proportionately with increasing family income. Further work has shown that the income elasticity of food consumption at the farm level declines as people become increasingly prosperous—for example, from just below unity in very poor nations to roughly 0.2 in nations as wealthy as the United States. It might be surprising that in an affluent society there is *any* continuing relationship between incremental income and the quantity of food consumed. There are two main reasons. First, as real income rises, consumers demand more processing of their food. This leads to substantial income elasticities at the food processing industry level, but not necessarily at the farm level. Second, as income rises, consumers (at least until recently) have changed their diet to take more nutrition in the form of meat and less in the form of grain products. Producing a net pound of meat in 1989 required feed grain inputs of 13 pounds for beef, 6 pounds for pork products, or 2.7 pounds for broiler chick-

---

[8]For a predecessor to this approach, see Willard W. Cochrane, *Farm Prices: Myth and Reality* (Minneapolis: University of Minnesota Press, 1958), Chapter 5.

[9]Most of the data for this analysis are taken from the *Economic Report of the President*, February 1991, pp. 317, 321, 396, and 397; augmented with data from the February 1992 report. Rates of growth assume continuous compounding.

ens. This explains both the existence of positive income elasticities among well-fed populations and why chicken is less expensive than beefsteak.[10]

Given this, food demand at the farm level appears to rise by approximately 0.2 percent for each percentage point increase in real income per capita.[11] Real disposable income per capita in the United States grew at an average rate of 2.22 percent per annum from 1950–1970 and 1.73 percent in the 1970–1990 period. To illustrate how the income and income elasticity effects are combined, we convert growth percentages to ratios and obtain for 1950–1970 an annual per capita food consumption growth factor of $1 + (0.0222 \times 0.2) = 1.00444$. Similarly, for 1970–1990, we have $1 + (0.0173 \times 0.2) = 1.00346$. These are multiplied by the annual population growth factors, yielding the demand shift estimates:

1950–1970: $1.00444 \times 1.0149 = 1.0194 = 1.94\%$ per year.

1970–1990: $1.00346 \times 1.0102 = 1.0137 = 1.37\%$ per year.

The supply of food depends upon the quantity of inputs into food production and the productivity, or output per unit of input, of those inputs. For consistency, we focus on labor inputs and labor productivity, or output per unit of labor input.

As we shall see in greater detail shortly, farmers and farm workers have been exiting almost continuously from farming since World War II and indeed earlier. Between 1950 and 1970, the number of farm family members working on farms declined at an average rate of 4.1 percent per year and the number of hired hands fell at a rate of 3.42 percent. Weighting the two inputs by their relative magnitudes, we find that labor input into farming decreased at an average rate of 3.93 percent per year during the 1950–1970 period. From 1970 to 1990, it fell at an average rate of 2.28 percent per year.

These figures alone would imply declining food supply. But the productivity of farm labor has been rising—at an average rate of 6.07 percent per year from 1950 to 1970 and 3.26 percent per annum in the 1970–1990 period. These are extraordinarily high productivity growth rates. The comparable average for all manufacturing industries between 1960 and 1990 was 2.83 percent. In achieving productivity growth, agriculture has been a superstar. Agriculture's outstanding productivity record is in large measure the result of countless technological innovations—improved hybrid seeds; increasingly intensive use of fertilizers,[12] herbicides, and pesticides; and a dazzling array of labor-saving machinery. The typical farm is far too small to invent or develop such innovations on its own, but seed, chemical, and machinery suppliers

---

[10]U.S. Department of Agriculture, *Agricultural Statistics: 1991* (Washington, DC: USGPO, 1991), p. 57.

[11]See Cochrane, *Farm Prices,* p. 86; and A. Desmond O'Rourke, *The Changing Dimensions of U.S. Agricultural Policy* (Englewood Cliffs, NJ: Prentice-Hall, 1978), p. 114.

[12]Between 1950 and 1984, fertilizer nutrient content usage increased by a factor of 5.4.

compete vigorously to offer superior new products to farmers,[13] who adopt the latest technology with alacrity thanks to their considerable education in agricultural science[14] and the information they receive from county technical advisory staffs. Rapid technical advance has been supported by research at U.S. land grant universities, whose evolution began with the Morrill Act, passed in 1862.[15] In 1991, U.S. universities conducted research and development in the agricultural sciences valued at $1.46 billion, of which $379 million was financed by the federal government.[16]

With output per unit of labor input growing at 6.07 percent per year in the 1950–1970 period and labor inputs being withdrawn from agriculture at the rate of 3.93 percent, the net rightward shift of aggregate farm product supply functions was 6.07 – 3.93 = 2.14 percent per year. In the 1970–1990 period, the net shift was 3.26 – 2.28 = 0.98 percent per year.

Figure 2.5 brings these calculations together in the form of demand and supply function shifts over time. To recapitulate, the net annual changes were:

	1950–1970	*1970–1990*
Demand shift	1.94%	1.37%
Supply shift	2.14%	0.98%
Supply less demand	+0.20%	−0.39%

In the earlier period, supply was shifting out more rapidly than demand, leading to a declining price trend, consistent with the wheat price pattern observed in Figure 2.4. In the later period, demand shifted out more rapidly than supply, which implies rising prices, also consistent with the wheat experience in Figure 2.4. We shall see that government policy and export market complications also had a bearing. But Figure 2.5 and its underlying data provide a good first approximation to the pricing relationships in U.S. agriculture during the second half of the twentieth century.

---

[13]See F. M. Scherer, "Interindustry Technology Flows in the United States," *Research Policy*, vol. 11 (August 1982), pp. 227–245, which shows that in 1974, manufacturing industry research and development expenditures of more than a half billion dollars were targeted toward agricultural industry uses.

[14]In 1981, 12.1 percent of the 1.07 million farmers and farm managers covered by a Census of Population survey had completed four or more years of college education. Ten percent had between one and three years in college. U.S. Bureau of the Census, Current Population Reports Series P–20, no. 390, *Educational Attainment in the United States: March 1981 and 1980* (Washington, DC: USGPO, 1984), p. 53.

[15]See Vernon W. Ruttan, *Agricultural Research Policy* (Minneapolis: University of Minnesota Press, 1962), pp. 76–83.

[16]U.S. National Science Board, *Science & Engineering Indicators: 1993* (Washington, DC: USGPO, 1993), p. 396.

FIGURE 2.5

Price Trends with Differentially Shifting Supply and Demand Functions, 1950–1990

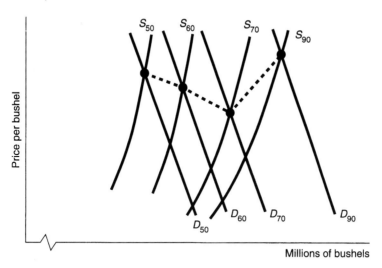

FARM POVERTY

The general fall in farm prices during the 1950s and 1960s and the move to a new plateau in the 1970s had a significant impact on the welfare of farmers. However, some additional considerations must be taken into account.

For a long time, the relative poverty of farmers was considered to be an important component of "the farm problem." Figure 2.6 places the problem in historical perspective, tracing the relationship of the average income of individuals and families living on farms to the incomes of nonfarm (i.e., city and other rural) inhabitants.[17] From the 1930s (and also earlier decades) through the 1960s, the average income per capita of farm occupants was substantially lower than that of nonfarm residents. Farm dwellers' income rose to 60 percent or more of nonfarm income in good times, for example, during World War II and its aftermath and again during the 1960s, but fell to half or less during the 1930s and 1950s. In the early 1960s, farming was singled out as a principal locus of poverty in the United States.[18] Farm family income, for which less complete data exist, exhibited the same general pattern,

---

[17]For similar data extending back to 1910, see Cochrane, *Farm Prices: Myth and Reality*, p. 22.

[18]See Michael Harrington, *The Other America: Poverty in the United States* (New York: Macmillan, 1962), Chapter 3; James N. Morgan, M. H. David, W. J. Cohen, and H. E. Brazer, *Income and Welfare in the United States* (New York: McGraw-Hill, 1962), pp. 194–217; and *Economic Report of the President: 1964*, Chapter 2 (which foreshadowed President Lyndon Johnson's war on poverty).

FIGURE 2.6
Trends in Farm Income Compared to Nonfarm Income, 1934–1989

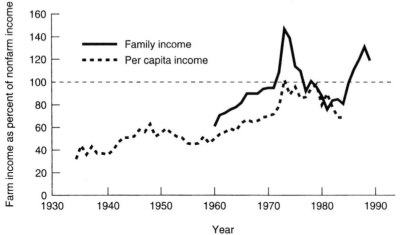

Source: Bruce L. Gardner, "Changing Economic Perspectives on the Farm Problem," *Journal of Economic Literature,* vol. 30 (March 1992), pp. 78–79, combining diverse Department of Agriculture estimates.

although farm families fared somewhat better relative to city dwellers in the whole-family comparison, partly because farm families were somewhat more likely to have three or more children in residence (e.g., 25 percent vs. 22 percent in 1965).[19]

During the 1960s, important changes began to materialize. Farm incomes rose relative to nonfarm incomes, and when wheat (and other farm product prices) exploded during the early 1970s (compare Figure 2.4), farm incomes moved for the first time in modern U.S. history above nonfarm norms. They fell back with the decline of farm prices during the second half of the 1970s, but in the 1980s, farm family incomes fluctuated around the average for their nonfarm counterpart. The problem of relative farm poverty seemed to have ebbed or even disappeared.

If farm dwellers' economic fortunes were so much less attractive than those of city dwellers, why were farmers slow in exiting from farming to embrace more lucrative urban job opportunities? Three answers can be provided immediately; others must follow in due course. First, over a still longer historical perspective, exit from farming has not in fact been slow. The fraction of the U.S. labor force engaged in farming declined from 72 percent in 1820 to 53 percent in 1870, 27 percent in 1920, 11.5 percent in 1950, 4.2 per-

---

[19]*Statistical Abstract of the United States: 1970,* p. 39.

cent in 1970, and 2.6 percent in 1990.[20] In absolute terms, the number of persons engaged in farming fell from 7.2 million in 1950 to 3.2 million in 1990. This is an extraordinary record of exit, equaled in few other nations around the world. Second, especially when unemployment rates were high, farmers were reluctant to leave their farms for uncertain prospects in the city. On the farm, at least, they had food and shelter. Many low-income farmers, unlike the operators of commercial-size farms, had completed only meager schooling, which limited their urban job opportunities and made them more reluctant to exit. Third, despite the humble existence marginal farmers were able to eke out, farming offered a certain measure of independence, fresh air, and other pleasures of field and fen. In other words, to at least some individuals, farming offers intangible benefits compensating in part for the higher monetary incomes available in the city. That farm incomes do not converge on 100 percent of urban incomes should not be surprising.

Much of the exodus from the farm to urban occupations entailed moving to a new residence, often at considerable distance. The construction of the interstate highway system during the 1950s and 1960s made the shift from farming easier. With improved transportation routes to market, manufacturers and other employers moved to rural areas, where wages were lower and work attitudes were unsullied by the temptations of urban life. By 1988, Table 2.1 reveals, a majority of U.S. farm operators earned more income from nonfarm pursuits than from farming. The smaller the farm, the more its operator

TABLE 2.1

Net Cash Income of Farm Operators from Farming and Off-Farm Activities by Farm Size: 1988

Value of Farm Sales in 1988	Number of Farms	Net Income from Farming ($ billions)	Off-Farm Income ($ billions)	Off-Farm Income as Percent of Total Income
Less than $40,000	1,555,000	3.1	41.1	93.0%
$40,000 to $99,999	321,000	8.1	4.7	36.7
100,000 to $249,999	216,000	13.9	3.8	21.5
$250,000 to $499,999	76,000	11.7	1.2	9.3
$500,000 or more	30,000	23.2	0.8	3.3
All farms	2,198,000	59.9	51.7	46.3%

Source: U.S. Bureau of the Census, *Statistical Abstract of the United States: 1990* (Washington, D.C.: USGPO, 1990), p. 648.

---

[20]*Historical Statistics of the United States,* pp. 70–72; and *Economic Report of the President,* February 1992, p. 332. Minor inconsistencies in the data series do not alter the broad picture.

tended to depend upon off-farm employment and income. For farms with sales of less than $40,000, the average net income per farm was $28,422, of which all but $1,988 came from off-farm activities. Although those smaller farm operators did not exit physically from farming, in the most meaningful economic sense they had exited, leaving 81 percent of the net income from farming to be earned by the 322,000 farms with sales of $100,000 or more.

With these changes and the rise of average farm incomes as a fraction of urban incomes, poverty per se was no longer a pressing farm problem. But new problems took its place. One was instability. The price fluctuations revealed by Figure 2.4 and the net income fluctuations shown in Figure 2.6 made it difficult for farmers to meet debt obligations. The price and income surge of the early 1970s induced many farmers to expand, buying nearby farm land at values inflated owing to the greater returns it appeared land would yield. When prices fell again during the late 1970s and early 1980s, those expectations proved incorrect. At the same time, the Federal Reserve Board's efforts to squeeze inflation out of the U.S. economy drove average new mortgage interest rates up from 9.0 percent in 1975 to 15.1 percent in 1982.[21] The prime rate paid on short-term financing rose from 7.9 percent to 14.9 percent. Farmers who expanded during the 1970s were caught in a squeeze between falling income and rising finance costs. Between 1980 and 1988, despite an array of federal government initiatives to increase mortgage and short-term credit to farmers, an estimated 200 to 300 thousand farmers were driven into bankruptcy, or financial restructurings with consequences similar to bankruptcy.[22] These arid statistics cannot convey the personal anguish farmers experienced as they lost the farms to which they and in many cases their forbears had devoted their lives.[23] Rural banks were also imperiled by loan delinquencies that reached $20.6 billion in 1986—roughly 17 percent of total farm loans outstanding.[24] Between 1981 and 1989, 311 commercial banks serving largely agricultural clienteles failed. As land values fell and loans were restructured, the total recorded value of U.S. farm real estate declined from a peak value of $852 billion in 1981 to a trough of $613 billion in 1986. The value of farmers' net equity in their farming operations dropped from $894 billion in 1981 to $681 billion in 1986.[25] In five years, U.S. farmers lost $213 billion, or 24 percent, of their net worth.

---

[21]*Economic Report of the President,* February 1992, p. 378.

[22]U.S. Department of Agriculture, Economic Research Service, Report no. 645, *Farm Financial Stress, Farm Exits, and Public Sector Assistance to the Farm Sector in the 1980s,* April 1991, pp. 2 and 14–19.

[23]See "Emotional Erosion Imperils the Farm Family," *New York Times,* November 21, 1984, p. 1; and "What Five Families Did After Losing the Farm," *New York Times,* February 4, 1987, p. 1.

[24]*Farm Financial Stress,* p. 38.

[25]U.S. Department of Agriculture, *Agricultural Statistics: 1991* (Washington, DC: USGPO, 1991), p. 362.

Farmers who avoided financial failure during the 1980s, and especially those who had consistently shunned heavy borrowing, emerged from these developments wealthy—at least on paper. In 1988, the average value of assets recorded by farms in diverse sales classes were as follows:[26]

Farm Sales Class	Average Assets
$500,000 and over	$3,666,667
$250,000–$499,999	$1,603,947
$100,000–$249,999	$889,815
$40,000–$99,999	$506,875
$20,000–$39,999	$309,562

The average farm in 1988 had debt obligations amounting to 15.5 percent of its assets—a much more conservative financial structure than that prevailing for the typical industrial corporation. Thus, farmers operating at commercial scales possessed net worth—that is, residual claims on assets—far above those enjoyed by the average city dweller. But although farmers were on average asset-rich, most were cash-poor. Averaging net farm income (including the imputed value of dwelling rent and home-grown food consumption) over 1987 through 1989, one finds that the average net income return on farmers' 1988 net worth of $808 billion was 5.4 percent[27]—a return lower than the risk-free interest rate on short-term U.S. Treasury notes at the time. But the net income for which that return percentage is calculated had to compensate farmers' labor as well as a return on the capital they had invested in their farm enterprise. If one counts only the 643,000 farms with sales of $40,000 or more in 1988 and assumes conservatively that the opportunity cost of the average operator-manager's labor was $30,000 per year, the net return after deduction of imputed labor wages on farmers' equity investment turns out to be 3.0 percent. In that sense, U.S. farmers continued to face what they, at least, considered to be a poverty problem.

IMPROVING FARMERS' WELFARE

Farmers, like all producers, would like to sell their products at prices higher than those with which competitive markets confront them. Because extreme price fluctuations make planning difficult (mitigated to some extent by

[26]*Statistical Abstract of the United States: 1990,* p. 646.

[27]*Agricultural Statistics: 1991,* pp. 362 and 392.

recourse to futures markets) and lead, as in the 1930s and 1980s, to widespread bankruptcies, farmers tend also to prefer relatively stable to unstable prices.

For consumers, stable food prices also facilitate menu and budgetary planning. It is less obvious whether consumers should be willing to sacrifice the bargains they can enjoy in times of agricultural abundance to escape the high prices charged when food products are relatively scarce. There is a substantial theoretical literature analyzing whether consumers and producers are better off when prices are stabilized by cartellike government interventions, or whether their welfare (measured in terms of consumers' and producers' surplus) is higher on average when prices fluctuate in response to demand and supply shocks. The conclusions are sensitive to assumptions about the exact shapes of supply and demand curves (linearity is usually presumed) and how the curves shift over time. They also depend critically on how markets are made to clear when prices do not perform the clearance function automatically and whether (e.g., under so-called buffer stock cartels) output is stored during periods of excess supply and returned to the market when demand exceeds supply at the stabilized price. The theoretical analyses are too complex and difficult to be presented here.[28] A brief summary of the conclusions must therefore suffice.

When prices are stabilized at a level reflecting the *average* of fluctuating demand and/or supply conditions, and assuming no risk aversion, consumers realize higher average consumers' surplus with freely fluctuating competitive prices if supply shocks are the cause of fluctuations. But when fluctuations result from demand shocks and when rationing mechanisms allocate scarce supplies to demanders with the highest reservation prices—a feat difficult to accomplish in practice—consumers could be better off on average with mean-stabilized prices. The sum of consumers' plus producers' surpluses is higher on average under buffer stock cartels than under cartels in which producers equate marginal cost to the stabilized price in times when the price would otherwise be high, but have their output restrained by outside authorities when the stabilized price is higher than the price that would prevail under competition. Producers gain higher average profits (or more precisely, producers' surplus) with competitively fluctuating prices than with stabilized prices under a buffer stock cartel when demand shifts are the cause of fluctuations, but fare better under a mean-price quoting buffer stock cartel when supply shifts underlie price fluctuations. In the supply shift case, which is more important than the demand shift case in agriculture, producers may favor cartelization because it can yield higher average profits when prices are stabilized at the mean, because they are risk-averse, and because it may be possible to stabilize prices at levels higher than those that would result on average from competition.

---

[28]For a moderately transparent geometric approach and a survey of the literature, see F. M. Scherer and David Ross, *Industrial Market Structure and Economic Performance,* 3rd ed. (Boston: Houghton Mifflin, 1990), pp. 298–306.

FARMER-ORGANIZED CARTELS

To combat the perceived problems of inadequate and unstable prices, U.S. farmers have on occasion attempted to organize price-raising cartels. During 1967, for example, the National Farmers Organization (NFO), a self-help group competing with organizations such as the American Farm Bureau Federation for membership, organized "milk strikes" under which dairy farmer members were urged to ship no milk to market and to spill the unmarketed milk onto the ground in order to raise prices by two cents per quart.[29] Although the NFO officially disavowed violence, supporters tried to elicit cooperation by stationing riflemen along rural roads to rain fire upon milk trucks traveling to processing plants in defiance of the strike. Similarly, during the late 1970s another self-help group, the American Agricultural Movement (AAM), urged wheat farmers to reduce their plantings by 50 percent to raise what were considered to be insufficient prices.[30]

The basic logic of the NFO and AAM initiatives is illustrated in Figure 2.7. In Figure 2.7a the competitive industry equilibrium entails a price of OP_C and

FIGURE 2.7
Dairy Farm Cartelization and the Incentive to Chisel

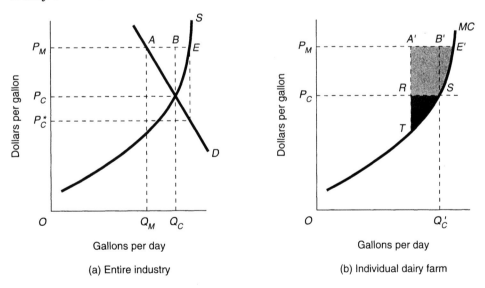

(a) Entire industry

(b) Individual dairy farm

---

[29]See "Milk Is Withheld by Farmer Group," *New York Times*, March 16, 1967, p. 22; "Milk Is Dumped in Pricing Drive," *New York Times*, March 17, 1967, p. 28; "Terror Charged in Milk Campaign," *New York Times*, March 21, 1967, p. 22; "4 Milk Trucks Shot at in Jersey in Farmers' Drive to Raise Price," *New York Times*, March 22, 1967, p. 32; and "Milk Plentiful and Price Firm Despite Dumping," *New York Times*, March 28, 1967, p. 30.

[30]"Despite Strike, Most Farmers Will Reap Full Crop," *New York Times*, February 4, 1978, p. 6.

output of OQ_C. Each farm is asked to cut back its output by, say, one-seventh, leading to a collective output restriction of $Q_M Q_C = AB$. Given the low price elasticity of demand, this restriction causes a sharp increase in the price to OP_M, and for the average farmer (Figure 2.7b) an increase in profits equal to rectangular area $P_M A'RP_C$ minus the small darkly shaded area RST. But the efforts of NFO and AAM were unsuccessful. Collectively, farmers very much wanted their peers to cooperate with the output restriction schemes, because if they did, all would be better off. But as a small atom in the sea of suppliers, each individual farmer viewed his own milk or wheat deliveries as having an imperceptible impact on the ultimate market price. "My little bit won't hurt— or help," the typical farmer was bound to reason. By "chiseling" on the scheme and raising his own output until the cartel-supported price equaled his marginal cost at point E', the farmer could augment his profits by a bit less than shaded area $A'E'T$. Or even if the cartel functioned imperfectly and raised prices above OP_C to some value less than OP_M, the individual farmer could make a smaller but still attractive gain by opting out or chiseling. The temptation to chisel was irresistible. As a result, virtually all chiseled and tried to "free ride" on the anticipated price-raising efforts of others, and so the cartels broke down. Indeed, the more successful the price-raising efforts were initially, the greater was the incentive to chisel, and hence (e.g., if farmers collectively increased their output to point E in the left-hand panel) the deeper prices plunged (e.g., to OP_C^*) before all farmers ceased participating, everyone realized that the cartel was defunct, and prices returned to the competitive level OP_C.

THE GOVERNMENT AS PRICE-MAKER

Recognizing that it was virtually impossible to regiment the members of an atomistically structured industry into effective price-raising cartels, farmers' self-help organizations directed their efforts elsewhere—to the federal government as de facto cartel broker and enforcer. At the grassroots level, they brought pressure to bear on local congressional representatives and senators to enact laws that would enhance farm prices. And on occasion, to make their resolve known more broadly, they had their members drive tractors to the District of Columbia and parade en masse down Pennsylvania Avenue to Capitol Hill. In these political efforts they have been highly successful, because a majority of the states harbor at least one important food crop,[31] and legislators from the farm-oriented states were able to swap favors with (i.e., logroll) their peers from urban states to elicit their assent to price support legislation.

---

[31]In 1990, only 14 of the 50 states had cash receipts from farm products of less than $1 billion, and only 19 had receipts of less than $2 billion. *Agricultural Statistics: 1991*, p. 393.

When farm prices collapsed following a World War I boom, bills were introduced repeatedly into Congress seeking to have the federal government undertake price support actions.[32] At first they came to naught, but in 1927 and again in 1928 bills that would support the prices of wheat, cotton, rice, corn, and hogs were passed by both houses, only to be vetoed by President Calvin Coolidge. When Herbert Hoover took office in 1929, he signed a newly passed Agricultural Marketing Act. Among other things, the act established a $500 million fund with which the newly created Federal Farm Board was to finance cooperative associations that would purchase surplus crops when prices were low, holding them and returning them to the market only when prices moved up again. At the time $500 million was not a piddling sum; total federal tax receipts in 1929 amounted to $2.94 billion. Soon thereafter the Great Depression was under way and farm prices declined at an accelerating rate. The Federal Farm Board pursued its mandate to intervene conscientiously, but in 1931 it ran out of funds and ceased taking crops off the still-falling market. In 1932 it began liquidating its accumulated surpluses. The supplies it added to an already distressed market drove prices even lower. Its effect can be analyzed using Figure 2.7a. To support prices at OP_M (that is, above the market-clearing level OP_C) the FFB had to accumulate surplus production AE. When AE was dumped into the market, prices fell to OP_C^*, well below the competitive equilibrium value. In the course of its unsuccessful price-stabilizing efforts, the FFB lost more than two-thirds of its $500 million endowment.

As the depression deepened and the Roosevelt administration took office, the Agricultural Adjustment Act (AAA) of 1933 was passed, inaugurating a new and more aggressive era of federal government farm price support efforts. Like the Agricultural Marketing Act of 1929, but on a more systematic basis, the AAA sought to stabilize prices by setting generous (so-called "parity") floors for the prices of basic agricultural commodities, lending money to farmers who stored crops that could not be sold at the floor price levels, and acquiring surplus output when farmers proved unwilling to keep it in storage. But AAA went much farther. While millions of unemployed Americans were standing in breadlines, the farm product price problem was seen (in technical, if not humanitarian, terms, correctly) as a problem of surplus production. To avoid incessant accumulation of surpluses, the Achilles' heel of the 1929 law, the government intervened also to curb farmers' production. This it did by paying farmers to plow under crops already planted (in 1933), not to plant cash crops on a substantial fraction of their acreage (after 1933), to turn over to the government surplus pigs and grain for poor relief or for destruction,

---

[32]For useful histories, see Walter W. Wilcox and Willard W. Cochrane, *Economics of American Agriculture* (Englewood Cliffs, NJ: Prentice-Hall, 1951), Chapter 30; and Clifton B. Luttrell, *The High Cost of Farm Welfare* (Washington, DC: Cato Institute, 1989), Chapters 1–3.

and to limit the quantity of certain specified products they brought to market. At first the payments to farmers were financed by a tax on processors. When the tax was ruled unconstitutional by the Supreme Court in 1936,[33] alternative means of accomplishing the same result using general federal revenues and referendum votes by affected farmers were devised.[34]

The Agricultural Adjustment Acts of 1933 and 1938 set a basic pattern, varied in myriad details, for federal government price support efforts in decades to come. We return for a thoroughgoing analysis shortly. First, however, some other federal initiatives must be mentioned more briefly.

During the 1930s the federal government stimulated demand for food products in part by channeling some surplus production to out-of-work citizens. More recently, school lunch programs, food stamps (since 1961), and the direct distribution of cheese and other surplus milk products to welfare recipients have had similar demand-enhancing effects.[35] Food surpluses have been exported to less-developed and disaster-impacted nations under the "Food for Peace" program initiated in 1954—a subject to which we return later. Some payments to farmers to take land out of cultivation were aimed primarily at reducing surplus crop supplies, but others have fostered reforestation, drainage improvement, soil stabilization, and other genuinely conservationist objectives. The government insures crops against hail, droughts, floods, and other natural disasters at highly subsidized rates.[36] And since 1916, Washington has intervened to make working capital and then mortgage loans available to farmers on favorable terms.[37] The most prominent federal credit supplier, the Farmers Home Administration, had $29 billion in loans outstanding at the start of 1990.[38]

Beginning with the Agricultural Adjustment Act of 1933 and continuing under extensions of the 1937 Marketing Agreement Act, the federal government has intervened to help make agricultural producer cartels work when they would collapse if left to their own devices. This help materializes through federal enforcement of so-called "marketing orders," which have been emplaced in dozens of product lines including milk, citrus fruits, olives, avoca-

---

[33]U.S. v. Butler, 297 U.S. 1 (1936).

[34] The constitutional issues became less important after new justices more tolerant of active governmental intervention to regulate interstate commerce joined the Supreme Court.

[35]See, for example, "Food Stamps Become New 'Currency,'" *New York Times*, August 25, 1963, p. 1; and "Handouts of Cheese, Milk and Rice Face 50% Cut Next Year," *New York Times*, November 17, 1987, p. 1.

[36]But see "Expanded Crop Insurance Fails to Curb High Disaster Costs," *New York Times*, December 29, 1989, p. A23; and "Two Reports Describe Widespread Abuse in Disaster Aid for Farmers," *New York Times*, October 3, 1994, p. B12.

[37]*Farm Financial Stress*, pp. 36–43.

[38]*Agricultural Statistics: 1991*, p. 411.

dos, cranberries, almonds, and much else. Typically, groups of producers organize themselves into cooperative associations, which are accorded substantial immunity from antitrust law under the Capper-Volstead Act of 1922. (Prominent examples include Sunkist Growers, Inc., Associated Milk Producers, Inc., and Ocean Spray Cranberries Inc.) Working with processors (called "handlers") and Department of Agriculture staff, they formulate marketing orders—that is, restrictions on the marketable quantity or price of their products. If a two-thirds (or in some cases, three-fourths) majority of the growers approve the restrictions, they become legally binding upon the handlers (who are typically few in number and therefore more easily monitored). The handlers must ensure that the output limits and other restrictions are observed. In principle, the enabling legislation requires the Department of Agriculture to ensure that cooperatives' prices are not unduly enhanced. However, this oversight responsibility has been exercised at best lackadaisically.[39] Associations with marketing orders cannot restrain entry into their product category or prevent the formation of competing associations. They may therefore find it difficult to sustain monopoly prices over the long run. Nevertheless, when entry in response to enhanced prices generates excess capacity and raises producers' unit costs, discouraging further entry, or when associations aggressively merge with their principal competitors, prices may be held above the level that would prevail under competition.[40]

WHEAT AND FEED GRAIN PRICE SUPPORT MECHANISMS

On other staple agricultural commodities, the federal government takes a more active role in setting and stabilizing prices. The principal programs operating in 1990 covered wheat, corn, barley, sorghum, oats, rye, rice, cotton, tobacco, peanuts, sugar, and soybeans.[41] Conspicuously absent are the

---

[39] Thus, in a 1976 meeting with Federal Trade Commission officials, the secretary of agriculture conceded that his agency had never attempted to determine whether marketing order prices were unduly enhanced and that it lacked criteria for making such judgments.

[40] For various views, see Gardner, *The Governing of Agriculture*, pp. 49–56; Paul W. MacAvoy, ed., *Federal Milk Marketing Orders and Price Supports* (Washington, DC: American Enterprise Institute: 1977); Ananth Madhavan, Robert T. Masson, and William Lesser, "Cooperation for Monopolization? An Empirical Analysis," *Review of Economics and Statistics*, vol. 76 (February 1994), pp. 161–175; Willard F. Mueller, Peter G. Helmberger, and Thomas Paterson, *The Sunkist Case* (Lexington, MA: Lexington Books, 1987); and Thomas M. Lenard and Michael Mazur, "Harvest of Waste: The Marketing Order Program," *Regulation*, May/June 1985, pp. 19–26.

[41] For details, see *Agricultural Statistics: 1991*, pp. 390–391; and the *Situation and Outlook Reports* issued periodically for diverse commodities by the Economic Research Service of the U.S. Department of Agriculture.

various species of livestock, whose storage is problematic. Since many hog and beef cattle producers also grow at least some of their own feed grain, they receive indirect support. Beef prices are also enhanced by import limitations. The marketing orders in which dairy farmers participate differentiate between Class I milk for direct fluid consumption, whose quantity is limited, and (physically indistinguishable) Class II milk, which is diverted into the manufacturing of butter, cheese, and other products and whose prices are supported by a federal government program.

The staple food programs use widely varying methods to achieve their objectives. Their detailed provisions often change every two to five years as the implementing legislation is renewed. The sugar program, for example, has operated since 1982 by adjusting sugar imports to maintain prices above a specified floor; the tobacco and edible peanut programs by limiting imports and assigning each authorized acre of domestic land a marketing poundage quota (which in effect prevents the shift of production to other land). Here we focus on the programs for two of the most important staples, wheat and (typifying several feed grains) corn (to Europeans, maize).

PRICE SUPPORT THROUGH NONRECOURSE LOANS

The wheat and feed grain programs stand upon three main pillars: loan prices, acreage controls, and target prices. Each will be analyzed in turn.

Since 1933, some sort of price floor, called a support price or loan price, has existed for staple grains. In principle, price floors could be created, as in the European Common Market, by having the government acquire grain whenever actual market prices fall below the announced support price. In the United States, beginning with the cotton and corn programs and then spreading to other commodities, a more decentralized system was implemented. The federal government offers farmers the opportunity to put their grain into storage when it is harvested and receive from the U.S. Commodity Credit Corporation (CCC) a *nonrecourse loan*, whose cash value is equal to the number of bushels stored times the official *loan price* (e.g., in the 1990 crop season, $1.95 per bushel for wheat and $1.57 per bushel for shelled corn). The stored grain is security for the loan. If at the end of the loan period (usually nine months initially, but renewable for as long as three years under the "Farmer-Owned Reserve" program) the market price is less than the loan price, the farmer can default on the loan and surrender the stored grain to the CCC.[42] There are no

---

[42]But see "Government Halts a Corn Reserve Program, Touching Off a Protest," *New York Times*, January 30, 1991, p. A16.

A new provision was added under the 1990 agriculture law, giving farmers an option to pay off wheat and feed grain loans at the world market price, which is often lower than the domestic loan price, as long as the payoff price did not fall below 70 percent of the loan price.

further consequences; the CCC has no recourse to other assets of the farmer, hence the name "nonrecourse" loan. Thus, the farmer receives at minimum the loan price for his grain. If the market price is below the loan price at harvest time, the grain will almost surely be stored under loan. If during the period of storage the market price rises above the loan price, the farmer can choose an opportune moment, take the grain out of storage, sell it, repay the loan plus an interest charge pegged to the government's short-term borrowing rate, and retain the surplus cash. To limit speculation and ensure that stored supplies come onto the market when prices are high, nonrecourse loans can be called (i.e., payment is demanded) when market prices exceed some trigger value—for example, during the late 1970s, 175 percent of the loan price for wheat and 140 percent of the loan price for corn.

Grain storage under these programs usually takes place on the farms where the grain is harvested. Anyone who has driven through the farming country of the American Midwest has observed numerous squat cylindrical structures made of corrugated steel. Those are the storage bins, whose construction was probably subsidized by the Department of Agriculture. For storage beyond nine months in the so-called Farmer-Owned Reserve, the farmer receives a per-bushel storage fee (e.g., during the late 1970s, 25 cents per bushel of wheat stored per year).

The effects of the nonrecourse loan program depend upon the level of loan prices established by Congress and (within some discretionary band) the secretary of agriculture. If loan prices are set at approximately the level to which an unfettered market would gravitate, averaging good years and bad, the program acts as a public-spirited buffer stock cartel. It follows the example Joseph, son of Israel, initiated more than three millennia ago:[43]

> Seven years are coming, bringing great plenty to the whole land of Egypt, but seven years of famine will follow them, when all the plenty . . . will be forgotten, and famine will exhaust the land. . . . Pharaoh should take action and appoint supervisors over the land, and impose a tax of one-fifth on the land of Egypt during the seven years of plenty. . . . They will store the corn in Pharaoh's name, and place the food in the towns and hold it there. This food will serve as a reserve for the land during the seven years of famine . . . and so the land will not be destroyed by the famine.

Typically, however, political pressures have pushed loan prices above long-run average market-clearing levels. From the 1930s into the 1960s, Congress tried to satisfy farmers' demands for prices at or near "parity" (i.e., the average crop prices realized in the relatively prosperous 1909–1914 period, inflated by an index of the prices farmers had to pay for their inputs, but not adjusted for productivity gains). Because the parity-based loan prices were often above market-clearing levels, a surplus problem emerged, as illustrated

---

[43]*Genesis* 41: 29–36, from *The Jerusalem Bible* (New York: Doubleday, 1966), p. 64.

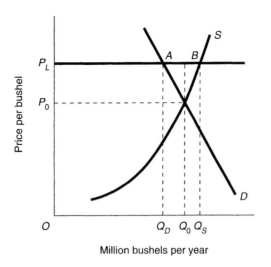

FIGURE 2.8
Accumulation of Surpluses with High Loan Prices

in Figure 2.8. With supply and demand curves S and D characterizing average crop year conditions, the average free-market price will approximate OP_0. If the loan price is set higher at OP_L, some consumption will be choked off—that is, to level OQ_D. Production will be stimulated so that the average output is OQ_S, leaving an annual surplus of $Q_D Q_S = AB$. Initially, that surplus will pile up in farmers' storage bins. But as farmers default on their loans, the surplus will move to governmental storage facilities and accumulate there.

Figure 2.9 traces movements in the current-dollar value of Commodity Credit Corporation loans outstanding, mostly for crops stored by farmers, and the commodities held by CCC, usually following loan defaults by farmers. The cycles evident in Figure 2.9 reflect changes in policy as well as in the general supply-demand balance. Large surpluses accumulated during the 1930s were worked off as a result of the resource constraints and prosperity associated

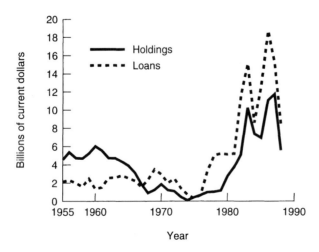

FIGURE 2.9
CCC Crop Holdings and Loans Outstanding, 1955–1988
Source: U.S. Bureau of the Census, *Statistical Abstract of the United States*, various years.

with World War II. The Korean War also helped alleviate, but did not eliminate, a rebounding surplus problem. Policy changes and disastrous harvests elsewhere in the world led to the price explosion in the early 1970s so prominent in Figure 2.4. With a return to more normal conditions, surpluses again mounted, first in the form of crops stored on loan and then, as loans were defaulted, in rapidly rising CCC holdings. Further policy changes, we shall see, explain the decline in holdings during the late 1980s.

One means of reducing surpluses without driving domestic prices down and angering farmers is to dump them in overseas markets. This is done, we shall see, but usually cautiously, because nations such as Canada, Australia, New Zealand, and Argentina depend significantly upon grain and cattle exports for their international trade balances, and maintaining their good will requires reticence. A less obtrusive solution was Public Law 480, first enacted in 1954, which initiated what became known as the "Food for Peace" program. The program operates by delivering agricultural products to nations lacking hard-currency reserves—usually, less-developed nations—free of charge, for payment through long-term loans on favorable conditions, or in exchange for the inconvertible currencies of the recipient nations. The "soft" currencies received in this way are spent on other forms of development assistance and U.S. consular functions in the recipient nations. By targeting nations without the funds to make large commercial purchases in international markets, the Food for Peace program lessened (but did not eliminate altogether) the adverse impact on competing grain exporters. In the first two decades of its existence, the program exported commodities valued at an average of $1.2 billion per year. Twenty-two percent of the transactions occurred under dollar loans, 41 percent under soft-currency repayment arrangements, and the remainder through gifts.[44] More recently, the emphasis has shifted to subsidized convertible currency sales and long-term dollar loans. Despite its good intention of helping others while alleviating U.S. surplus problems, the program has tended to depress basic food prices in recipient nations, weakening incentives for the development of indigenous crop production.

ACREAGE RESTRICTIONS

The surplus problem has also been attacked by efforts to curb the production of price-supported commodities, usually by requiring farmers to limit the number of acres they plant. Farmers have been induced to accept these restraints by making the receipt of loans and other government benefits conditional upon acreage limitations and, in some years, through direct cash or in-kind payments for each acre "set aside" up to some percentage limit. The amount of land idled under set-aside programs has waxed and waned with the severity of surplus problems and the vigor of policies chosen to combat them. On the approximately one billion acres devoted to farming in the United States, 250 to 350 million of which might in a typical year be devoted to crops

---

[44]*Statistical Abstract of the United States: 1976*, p. 656.

FIGURE 2.10
Effects of a 20 Percent Acreage Restriction

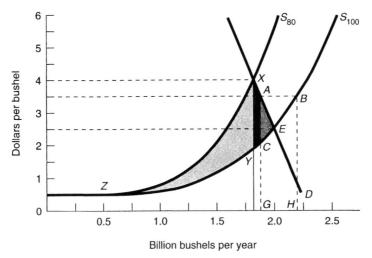

covered by support programs, set-asides averaged 24 million acres in 1956–1960, 52 million in 1961–1965, 54 million in 1966–1970, 25 million in 1971–1975, 6 million in 1976–1980, 35 million in 1981–1985, and 66 million during the late 1980s.[45]

Figure 2.10 provides a first approximation to the welfare economics of wheat price supports combined with acreage controls. It adopts the time frame of a full crop year, before fields have been tilled, seeds planted, and fertilizer applied. Under these assumptions, no output would be forthcoming at all if the price were much less than 50 cents per bushel. (Once the crop is planted, the supply function becomes less elastic at all prices.) Under unfettered supply (S_{100}) and demand conditions, output would be 2.0 billion bushels and the price $2.50 per bushel. If the loan price is set at $3.50 per bushel but there are no acreage restrictions, farmers will move to point *B*, producing 2.2 billion bushels, and a surplus of *AB* (= 350 million bushels) will emerge. The increased price and reduced domestic consumption cause a conventional dead-weight welfare loss defined by shaded triangle *AEC*. But the true welfare loss will be much larger, because the surplus production will be diverted to uses whose value (read off some unidentified overseas demand curve) is much less than the marginal cost of production (read off the supply curve). Alternatively, the surplus output may be allowed to rot, in which case its marginal value is zero and the dead-weight loss equals trapezoid *GCBH*

---

[45]D. Gale Johnson et al., *Agricultural Policy and Trade* (New York: New York University Press, 1985), p. 67; and Gardner, "Changing Perspectives," p. 86.

(the cost of the surplus) plus the upper portion of triangle *AEC* (consumers' surplus foregone because of the high price).

Now assume that wheat farmers' acreage is limited to 80 percent of the acreage that would be used with S_{100}. The supply function shifts leftward to S_{80}, the price is driven up to $4 per bushel, and because the new price is above the loan price, no surplus materializes. But there are further dead-weight loss repercussions. The high price chokes off additional consumption whose value (read off the demand curve) exceeds its cost (read off the S_{100} supply curve). Dead-weight loss triangle *AEC* is augmented by the more darkly shaded loss trapezoid *XACY*. In addition, the leftward supply curve shift is tantamount to an upward shift, which means that some acres are diverted whose production cost per bushel is less than the cost of the marginal acres still cultivated in less fertile areas. The higher costs resulting from this reallocation give rise to a further dead-weight loss of lightly shaded horn *ZXY*. Whether that loss is greater or less than the loss from accumulating surplus production without acreage restraints cannot be determined without additional information on supply and demand function shapes and the value of alternative uses to which the surplus is put.

Figure 2.10 probably exaggerates the output reduction from a 20 percent acreage set-aside, and hence the amount of the resulting dead-weight efficiency loss.[46] Farmers will naturally set aside their least productive acres, so the output reduction at any given price is less than the assumed 20 percent. In the early years of U.S. price support policy, they planted the diverted acres with other crops. To the extent that the other crops were substitutes for the controlled crop, the increased substitute output and concomitant price decrease caused a leftward shift in the demand curve for the controlled crop, making it more difficult to support the controlled product's price. It is said also that farmers react to acreage set-aside mandates by fertilizing their remaining acres more vigorously, although the economic rationale of this response is puzzling.[47]

---

[46]See, for example, Gardner, *The Governing of Agriculture*, pp. 26–29 and 32; and Luttrell, *The High Cost of Farm Welfare*, pp. 23 and 31.

[47]Profit maximization demands that fertilizer be applied to any given cultivated acre until the value of the fertilizer's marginal product falls into equality with the marginal cost of application. See, for example, Carl Fox, Statement, in U.S. Congress, Joint Economic Committee, *Policy for Commercial Agriculture* (Washington, DC: USGPO, 1957), pp. 423–424, who estimates that on a representative Iowa farm during 1955, the profit-maximizing application of fertilizer was approximately 170 pounds per acre at a corn price of $1.00 per bushel and 250 pounds at a corn price of $1.40 per bushel. This behavioral rule should hold, whether or not other acres belonging to the farmer are set aside. It is possible that increased fertilization occurs because tighter acreage restraints are expected to raise prices (which would be true only if the support price is exceeded). Or acreage restrictions might reduce the perceived opportunity cost of the time spent by the farmer in applying fertilizer.

Farmers' efforts to circumvent the restraints sought through acreage set-asides have elicited bewilderingly complex Department of Agriculture regulations.[48] Set-aside requirements must be met on all covered crops in order to receive diversion payments, loans, or other support on any given crop. There are rules (apparently honored frequently in the breach) defining the physical characteristics of tracts that can be set aside. On some diverted acres, no cash crops can be grown; the land must be left fallow. But on other (so-called "flex") acres, other supported crops can be planted if acreage limits are satisfied for the aggregate of the farm's productive area.

Heavy-handed regimentation of farmers' decision making is politically unpopular. It could also draw constitutionality challenges, as did the 1930s program to finance output restriction subsidies through a processor tax.[49] Programs have therefore been democratized in two main ways. In some cases, as in wheat until the mid–1960s, farmers voted in referenda whether to accept output or acreage restrictions in exchange for price supports. As under marketing orders, a two-thirds vote was required to implement the support program. A key test came in the thirteenth wheat referendum, covering the 1964 crop.[50] Farmers were asked to vote whether they favored a mandatory 10 percent wheat acreage cut, in exchange for which they would receive $2 per bushel on 80 percent of their normal production. The alternative was said to be a decline in prices. The conservative American Farm Bureau Federation urged farmers to vote against the restraints, asking rhetorically, "Who will run the farms of America? Will it be the farmers or political bureaucrats?"[51] Fifty-two percent of the wheat growers voted against the restraints. As the AFBF's leaders predicted, with a national election coming, Congress reacted ten months later by setting the loan price at $2 and making loans available to farmers who *voluntarily* accepted announced acreage reductions. The volun-

---

[48]See, for example, U.S. Department of Agriculture, Economic Research Service, *Wheat Situation and Outlook Report*, November 1991, pp. 4–5; and "Crop Subsidies: Help and Headaches," *New York Times*, July 5, 1994, p. D1.

[49]See Dale E. Hathaway, "Agricultural Policy and Farmers' Freedom: A Suggested Framework," *Journal of Farm Economics*, vol. 35 (November 1953), pp. 496–510.

[50]See "Wheat Control Plan Beaten by Farmers in Blow to Kennedy," *New York Times*, May 22, 1963, p. 1; and "Farmers' Defeat of Wheat Curbs Arouses Capital," *New York Times*, May 23, 1963, p. 1.

[51]"How To Shoot Santa Claus," *Time*, September 3, 1965, p. 24. Reflecting on his experience, the Department of Agriculture economist who spearheaded the referendum attributed his defeat to "distressingly low" economic literacy among farmers. Willard W. Cochrane, "Some Observations of an Ex Economic Advisor: or What I Learned in Washington," *Journal of Farm Economics*, vol. 47 (May 1965), p. 456. A better explanation is that farmers understood more about congressional politics than he.

tary approach has dominated food and feed grain support programs since then.

TARGET PRICES AND DEFICIENCY PAYMENTS

In order to induce voluntary compliance, the Department of Agriculture must offer farmers a package from which they expect higher profits than they would obtain planting their acreage without restrictions and accepting the market price on their larger output. If loan prices and acreage restrictions were the only instruments at hand, this would mean setting loan prices above free-market-clearing levels, stimulating added production and hence precipitating mounting surpluses or more stringent acreage set-asides. However, the third main pillar of U.S. food and feed grain policy—target prices and deficiency payments—provides an additional instrument.

It also helps solve another problem. Unless farm products are to be sold overseas at prices substantially below their domestic price—a practice known as dumping, which contravenes the spirit if not the letter of the 1947 General Agreement on Tariffs and Trade (GATT)[52]—high crop loan prices raise the price of grain in export markets and limit, perhaps greatly, U.S. sales in those markets. This situation is unfortunate, because the United States is one of the world's most efficient grain and livestock producers, and by virtue of its superior natural endowments and acquired technology, it should enjoy comparative advantage in exporting such commodities. Deficiency payments make it possible to have one's cake and eat it—that is, to have low domestic grain prices but to maintain farmers' incomes at levels to which they would like to become accustomed.

A deficiency payment system was proposed unsuccessfully by Charles Brannan, secretary of agriculture in the last years of President Harry S Truman's administration, and then by Ezra Taft Benson, President Eisenhower's agriculture secretary. Thus, it has often been called the Benson-Brannan plan. Elements of the plan were accepted during the 1960s and gained further ground in the 1970 Agriculture Act. The system was fully implemented for wheat and feed grains in 1973 and has persisted with diverse amendments since then.

The deficiency payment mechanism begins with the setting of a target price—ostensibly, a price sufficient to cover the full crop production cost per bushel, including a return on the farmer's investment, but more realistically, the result of a bargaining process in Congress. To illustrate, consider the experience of Farmer Smith, a wheat grower, during the 1991–1992 growing year.

---

[52] The 1947 GATT agreement excluded agricultural products from its antidumping and subsidy provisions; hence, only the "spirit" of GATT is breached. In the Marrakesh Treaty of 1994, a process was begun to bring agricultural products within GATT's ambit. More will be said on this subject later.

The target price was $4.00 per bushel. The loan price was $2.04 per bushel, and the average price realized by farmers on the market was $3.00 per bushel.[53] Because the market price fell short of the target price, there was a *deficiency* in Farmer Smith's wheat revenue realization. Having complied with relevant acreage restrictions, Farmer Smith received from the Department of Agriculture a *deficiency payment* reflecting, as a first approximation, the target price less the market price, or $1.00 per bushel. Had the market price been lower than the loan price (which was not the case in 1991–1992), the deficiency payment would have been the difference between the target price and the loan price, or $1.96.

This calculation sets the payment per bushel. On how many bushels is the payment made? For this there is a formula. The total deficiency payment *TDP* is:

$$TDP = \text{(Target price} - \text{market price) per bushel} \times \text{base acreage} \times \text{program}$$
$$\text{yield (in bushels per acre)}$$

The base acreage was not the actual number of acres used in 1991 for wheat production, but a measure based upon Farmer Smith's historical experience, adjusted for required acreage diversions and set-asides. Since 1973, the calculation normally began with a five-year moving-average of the acreage devoted to wheat production. If, for example, Smith planted wheat on 360 acres in 1986, 380 acres in 1987, 320 in 1988, 350 in 1989, and 400 in 1990, his moving average acreage would be 362 acres. This is then adjusted downward to reflect mandated and "flex" acreage set-asides, say, 20 percent, leaving an adjusted base acreage of $0.8 \times 362 = 290$ acres. Since 1985, farmers have been able to include in their historical base land they were required to leave fallow or divert to other crops as well as the acres actually planted in wheat.

If Farmer Smith's adjusted base acreage in 1991–1992 was 290 acres, the deficiency per bushel $1.00, and his program yield 38 bushels per acre, Smith would receive a deficiency payment check of $290 \times \$1.00 \times 38 = \$11,020$.

But how is the program yield set? On this it is difficult to make a general statement, because the authorizing laws have changed over time, the laws typically give the secretary of agriculture considerable discretion in their implementation, and county program committees have in turn exercised some discretion in setting individual farm yields. In 1978, program yields in Will County, Illinois, were fixed as the average number of bushels grown per acre by all participating farmers in the county—*not* as the number grown by Farmer Smith. Since 1985, historical yields have been emphasized, and the secretary has not exercised the discretion given him by Congress to set yields on the basis of current-year production. Thus, Farmer Smith's program yield

---

[53]For purposes of program administration, the average market price is determined from the average price realized during the first five months after harvest.

for 1991 was based upon the number of bushels he harvested per acre in 1986, five years earlier, with the further proviso that if 1986 yields were 10 percent or more lower than 1985 yields, the 1985 figure would be substituted.[54] Earlier in the 1980s, moving average historical yields were used; e.g., the program yield for Smith in 1984 would have been the five-year moving average of his realizations in 1979 through 1983.

The details of these program yield calculation provisions are enormously important. If the program yield is Farmer Smith's *actual* wheat yield, the deficiency payment system in effect raises Smith's price realization up to the target price level ($4.00 in 1991) for every bushel he markets, stimulating him to equate his marginal cost with that price and produce the corresponding quantity. But suppose the yield is set as the average output realized by all wheat growers in Smith's county, or as Smith's own yield many years ago. Then Smith's output decision is essentially *decoupled* from the level of the target price. Asking the standard profit-maximizing question, "How much will I receive if I grow one more bushel of wheat?" Smith must realize that his marginal revenue is not the target price, but the price he obtains selling that extra bushel on the market—that is, in 1991–1992, approximately $3.00. By decoupling farmers' marginal revenue from the target price, the deficiency payment system can add to farmers' incomes without encouraging excessive production and the accumulation of unwanted surpluses. In other words, when the program yield is based upon broad-sweeping county averages or past decisions that cannot be altered, the deficiency payment becomes a lump-sum transfer to the farmer with no (or at least, a minimal) influence on output. Indeed, at the other output extreme, even if Smith grows *no* wheat on his land (e.g., because a hailstorm has wiped out the entire crop, or because he began converting the land into a housing development at the start of the crop year), he will still receive the deficiency payment implied by the historical formula—declining, to be sure, over time as his moving average base acreage falls.

Figure 2.11 illustrates this case for the U.S. wheat growing industry under 1991–1992 conditions. The supply function, adjusted for acreage limitations, is S. The demand function is D. The loan price is $2.04 per bushel—too low to pull much grain into storage or otherwise influence the market price. If the target price of $4.00 were paid on every bushel marketed, producers would move to supply curve intersection point Z and produce an output of OQ_T, of which $YZ = Q_E Q_T$ bushels would move into the market and drive the market price down to the $2.04 loan price, leaving a small surplus in storage. But with program yields decoupled from individual farmers' current output, the deficiency payment becomes a lump-sum transfer measured by, say, cross-hatched rectangle *FGHK*. The rectangle's horizontal dimension is essentially arbitrary, that is,

---

[54]See U.S. Department of Agriculture, Economic Research Service, Agriculture Information Bulletin No. 624, *Provisions of the Food, Agriculture, Conservation and Trade Act of 1990* (Washington, DC: 1991), pp. 35–36.

FIGURE 2.11
Market Equilibrium with Decoupled Deficiency Payments

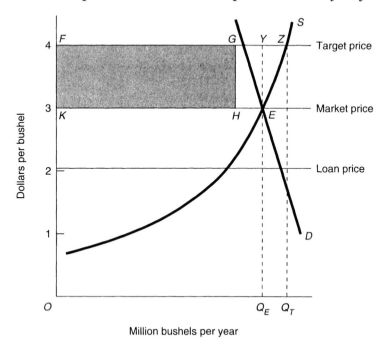

Million bushels per year

unrelated to current supply and demand conditions, but set instead by acreage diversion requirements, historical acreage, and historical or other producers' output per acre. Given this situation, market equilibrium is left to be established by the forces of supply and demand, generating a price of $3.00, which becomes the marginal revenue influencing farmers' output choices. Equilibrium occurs at point E, with an output of OQ_E and no surplus accumulation.

The rules by which deficiency payments are calculated have made this decoupling process less than perfect, so it would be inaccurate to say that the target prices have *no* influence on current output. There are at least two links. For one, consider the historical moving-average system used to set program yields in some jurisdictions. The number of bushels harvested from an acre in year T by Farmer Smith would not affect year T's deficiency payment receipts. However, by producing an extra bushel per acre in year T, Smith increases the program yield by $\frac{1}{5}$ bushel in year $T + 1$, by $\frac{1}{5}$ bushel in year $T + 2$, and so on, out through year $T + 5$. If the deficiency payment per program yield bushel is expected to be $1 in each of the next five years, the discounted present value of *future* deficiency payment increments from producing an extra bushel per acre this year is approximately 78 cents, assuming a 10 percent interest rate.[55] The output stimulus is not as great as with a $1 deficiency payment for every bushel of wheat marketed currently, but it is not trivial. By fixing program yields for all time at some historical value or by tying them to countywide output averages, surplus-increasing output stimuli can be minimized. It is doubtful whether most legislators voting on farm bills understand this crucial subtlety.

The deficiency payment system may also affect output by influencing farmers' decisions on how many acres to plant in a covered crop. By planting more acres this year, they increase under the moving average formula their base acreage in future years, and hence the size of their future deficiency payments, assuming that acreage set-aside mandates are met. Thus, farmers are likely to allocate their land toward crops with particularly attractive target prices and away from those with little or no target price support.

Eligibility for target payments (and also for crop loans) is contingent upon complying with all acreage restrictions announced by the Department of Agriculture. Farmers do not have to participate; they can opt out. Figure 2.12 analyzes the individual farmer's opt-out decision. Like Figure 2.11, it assumes 1991–1992 wheat program parameters. If all farmers comply, the supply for wheat will be S_{80} (Figure 2.12a), the market price will be $3.00 per bushel, and a lump-sum deficiency payment given by the lightly shaded rectangle *FGHK* will be paid to the cohort of wheat growers. Beginning from this aggregate picture, Farmer Smith examines his own situation in Figure 2.12b. If he participates in the program, his marginal cost curve (with restricted acreage) will be MC_{80}; if he opts out, it will be MC_{100}. If he participates and the market price is $3.00, he will produce at $MC_{80} = $3.00 intersection point *X*, realizing $3.00 per bushel times *OS* bushels from marketing plus a deficiency payment of *F'G'H'K'*. If he opts out, he can use his full production capacity, moving to $MC_{100} = $3.00 intersection point *R* and realizing an additional surplus of sales revenue over production costs measured by the lightly shaded area *XRN*. (The trapezoid *NRTS* is additional production cost.) In addition, with no restraint on land use, his marginal cost is lower on any given bushel produced, so on the output he would have produced with acreage restrictions, he saves costs measured by the darkly shaded horn-shaped area *MXN*. His total incremental gain from opting out is the darkly shaded horn-shaped area *MXR*; his sacrifice is the deficiency payment *F'G'H'K'*. For the assumptions taken, the gains from participating exceed the gains from opting out, so Farmer Smith will participate. However, if the target price were reduced to $3.50, halving the size of rectangle *F'G'H'K'*, opting out would be the more profitable decision.

But suppose the target price were only $3.50 and the typical wheat grower opted out. Then the collective supply curve would approach S_{100}, total output

---

[55]That is,

$$\sum_{T=1}^{5} \$1 \times \frac{1}{5} \times \frac{1}{(1 + 0.1)^T}$$

Figure 2.12
Deficiency Payments, Acreage Restrictions, and the Farmer's Opt-Out Decision

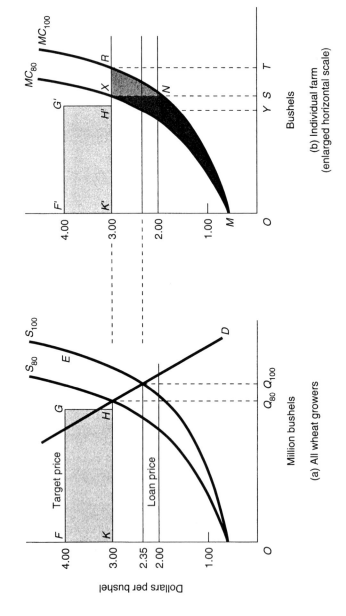

(a) All wheat growers

(b) Individual farm
(enlarged horizontal scale)

would increase toward OQ_{100}, and the market price would drop toward $2.35. Now the deficiency payment will rise to $3.50 − $2.35 = $1.15, more than with a $4.00 target price and total acreage set-aside compliance. With the lower market price, the sales revenue gains from opting out will fall. Much of area XRN in Figure 2.12b will be lost, and with a smaller output OY, some of the darkly shaded excess production cost from restricting acreage will be avoided. Meanwhile, the base on which deficiency payments are calculated will not change at all, and with a $1.15 payment per bushel, the total deficiency payment will be larger than $F'G'H'K'$. Now opting out is not profitable after all. We have what macroeconomists call a problem in rational expectations. It is more profitable for an individual farmer to opt out if other farmers do not, but if all farmers reason in this way, they will opt out too, contradicting the expectations on which they acted, which in turn increases the profitability of complying with acreage restrictions, and so on.[56] Under the circumstances, wide year-to-year gyrations in program compliance—for example, from 48 percent of eligible wheat acreage in 1982 to 88 percent in 1988[57]—should not be surprising.

CHANGES IN PROGRAM MIX

Further complexity is introduced by occasional changes in the mix of instruments with which Congress has attempted to influence farmers' prices, incomes, and crop stockpiles. The history of loan and target price policy since 1970 is traced in Table 2.2.[58]

High loan prices caused surpluses to accumulate during the late 1950s and early 1960s. At first the government attempted to solve the surplus problem through tight acreage restrictions. When the wheat referendum of 1963 was rejected, loan prices were reduced and deficiency payments were added to make up the difference. By 1970, loan prices were quite low relative to target prices (not yet called by that name), especially for wheat, and U.S. grain became highly competitive on world markets. This precipitated among other things huge purchases in 1972 (440 million bushels of wheat and 394 million bushels of corn in one month alone) by the Soviet Union, which had experienced a series of bad harvests.[59] U.S. grain stockpiles were depleted, and

---

[56] There is probably an equilibrium level of compliance, but reaching it is likely to be difficult, given the complexity of the circumstances affecting individual farmers' profitability.

[57] U.S. Department of Agriculture, Economic Research Service, *Wheat Situation and Outlook Report*, February 1994, p. 42; and (on feed grains) *Feed Situation and Outlook Yearbook*, October 1994, p. 48.

[58] For earlier data that are not completely comparable, mixing loan and target prices, see Luttrell, *The High Cost of Farm Welfare*, pp. 141–142.

[59] See James Trager, *The Great Grain Robbery* (New York: Ballantine, 1975).

TABLE 2.2

History of U.S. Crop Loan and Target Price Policy

Year	Wheat Program			Corn Program		
	Loan Price (dollars)	Target Price (dollars)	Loan-to-Target Ratio	Loan Price (dollars)	Target Price (dollars)	Loan-to-Target Ratio
1971	1.25	2.93	0.43	1.05	1.35	0.78
1972	1.25	3.02	0.41	1.05	1.41	0.74
1973	1.25	3.39	0.37	1.05	1.64	0.64
1974	1.37	2.05	0.67	1.10	1.38	0.80
1975	1.37	2.05	0.67	1.10	1.38	0.80
1976	2.25	2.29	0.98	1.50	1.57	0.96
1977	2.25	2.90	0.78	2.00	2.00	1.00
1978	2.35	3.40	0.69	2.00	2.10	0.95
1979	2.50	3.40	0.74	2.10	2.20	0.95
1980	3.00	3.63	0.83	2.25	2.35	0.96
1981	3.20	3.81	0.84	2.40	2.40	1.00
1982	3.55	4.05	0.88	2.55	2.70	0.94
1983	3.65	4.30	0.85	2.65	2.86	0.93
1984	3.30	4.38	0.75	2.55	3.03	0.84
1985	3.30	4.38	0.75	2.55	3.03	0.84
1986	2.40	4.38	0.55	1.92	3.03	0.63
1987	2.28	4.38	0.52	1.82	3.03	0.60
1988	2.21	4.23	0.52	1.77	2.93	0.60
1989	2.05	4.10	0.50	1.65	2.84	0.58
1990	1.95	4.00	0.49	1.57	2.75	0.57
1991	2.04	4.00	0.51	1.62	2.75	0.59
1992	2.21	4.00	0.55	1.72	2.75	0.63
1993	2.45	4.00	0.61	1.72	2.75	0.63
1994	2.58	4.00	0.65	1.89	2.75	0.69

Source: U.S. Department of Agriculture, *Agricultural Statistics: 1991,* pp. 390–391, and the same table for earlier years.

prices soared. See Figure 2.4. As conditions returned toward normal and grain prices fell, loan prices were raised sharply beginning with the 1976 crop year. A new farm policy law in 1977 continued the movement toward high loan rates relative to (rising) target prices.[60] Large numbers of farmers opted out of acreage restraint programs. Despite direct government transfers to still-participating farmers of $1.3 billion in 1980, $1.9 billion in 1981, and $3.5 billion in 1982, mainly for acreage set-asides and deficiency payments, surpluses continued climbing to crisis levels. See Figure 2.9.

In 1983, when loan prices reached an all-time high, the government's response to the surplus problem was a new initiative, the payment-in-kind (PIK) program.[61] Under it, farmers were asked to effect acreage reductions of up to 50 percent. In compensation, they were given grain, rice, or cotton from U.S. surplus stockpiles up to 80 percent of the normal yield on the acres they idled, along with a 10 percent cash bonus.[62] The results were dramatic. Wheat plantings were reduced by 33 percent and corn plantings by 26 percent relative to normal levels. The depletion of corn stockpiles was "helped" by drought conditions in much of the Midwest. Cotton farmers cut their acreage by half, requiring so much PIK cotton that the Agriculture Department exhausted its stockpiles and fell short by 17 percent on the cotton it had agreed to distribute.[63] To make up the shortfall in the face of rapidly rising cotton prices, the government called its nonrecourse cotton loans, compelling farmers to surrender the cotton they had stored at relatively low loan prices, much of which they had already sold forward at higher prices. Total direct payments to farmers in support of agricultural programs during 1983, including the accounting value of surplus crops delivered for payments in kind, amounted to a record-breaking $9.3 billion, or two-thirds of the unusually low net income of all U.S. farms in that year.

Although PIK programs continued on a more modest scale following the 1983 debacle, the government struggled for a new approach to agricultural policy. The solution embodied in the 1985 agriculture law was essentially a

---

[60]A bill introduced by Senator Robert Dole in 1978 would have increased wheat target prices to $5.04 and corn targets to $2.45 per bushel, contingent upon acreage reductions of up to 50 percent. It was rejected in the Senate. "Senate Votes Rise in Farmer Subsidies for Grain and Cotton," *New York Times*, March 22, 1978, p. 1.

[61]See "Reagan Proposes Offering Farmers Grain as Payment," *New York Times*, December 10, 1982, p. 1; "Farmers Looking to a Top Nonharvest," *New York Times*, April 25, 1983, p. 10; "How PIK Is Poisoning Farm Policy," *Business Week*, August 8, 1983, pp. 62–66; and "Corn Crop Down 49% in Year, U.S. Says," *New York Times*, October 13, 1983, p. D2.

[62]In Iowa the program inspired a widely circulated joke: "A man goes into a shoe store and asks for a pair of loafers. He comes out carrying a farmer under each arm."

[63]"'Payment in Kind' in Cotton Backfires," *New York Times*, July 11, 1983, p. 10.

reversion to the policy mix adopted during the early 1970s.[64] In an effort to make U.S. crops more competitive in export markets and reduce surplus accumulations, loan prices were cut sharply and then pegged by formula to be 75 to 85 percent of average domestic market prices in the preceding five years. Annual reductions, however, were limited to not more than 5 percent. The expectation was that the loan prices would no longer serve to enhance farmers' income year-in and year-out. Rather, they would be a floor under true market-determined prices, encouraging the accumulation of reserves during years of abnormally low prices and returning them to the market when prices were high. Target prices were initially held at existing levels, but it was planned that (unless Congress changed its mind again, as it did with the 1990 agriculture law) they would be progressively phased down so that, in the long run, the market could replace government in determining farmers' incomes.

INCOME DISTRIBUTION IMPLICATIONS

To sum up, three main instruments have been used in proportions varying widely over time to raise the incomes of U.S. grain farmers: loan programs that set a floor under prices, acreage restrictions to raise prices and limit surplus output, and deficiency payments to supplement market prices deemed insufficient. Whether these interventions are warranted or whether they attempt to solve a farm poverty problem that has long since faded to insignificance continues to be debated vigorously. If there is a case for intervention, it rests on the belief that unfettered competitive markets are efficient but cruel masters, depressing the return on agricultural assets unable or reluctant to find other uses and subjecting farmers' incomes to wild fluctuations with changes in weather, domestic economic conditions, and the state of world food markets. Certainly, the productive performance of U.S. farmers cannot be faulted. The agriculture sector has been a technological superstar, exhibiting high productivity and rapid productivity increases. The average American engaged in farming during 1991 fed 77 fellow citizens and exported a considerable surplus to help feed the inhabitants of other nations.

Whatever the merits, the benefits from government income supports in agriculture are unequally distributed. Table 2.3 summarizes the evidence for 1991, a relatively prosperous year for farmers, on *direct* government payments to farmers—that is, for deficiency payments, acreage diversion subsidies, and storage charges—by farm product sales classes. From the second-to-last column, we see that 57.3 percent of all direct government payments went to the

---

[64]See "Block Says Reagan's Farm Bill Seeks 'Revolutionary' Changes," *New York Times,* January 23, 1985, p. A11; "Farm Bill: Its Impact," *New York Times,* December 15, 1985, p. A16; "Congress Votes Sweeping Change in Government Support for Farms," *New York Times,* December 19, 1985, p. 1; and Joseph C. Wakefield, "Federal Farm Programs for 1986–90," *Survey of Current Business,* April 1986, pp. 31–34.

TABLE 2.3

Distribution of Farm Income and Direct Government Payments by Farm Size Class: 1991

1991 Farm Product Sales	Number of Farms (000)	Net Cash Income per Farm (dollars)	Average Government Payment per Farm	Percent of Total Government Payments	Government Payments as Percent of Farms' Cash Receipts
Less than $20,000	1,229	−81	651	9.8	11.6
$20,000 to $39,999	240	9,167	2,500	7.3	8.7
$40,000 to $99,999	309	24,595	6,796	25.6	10.4
$100,000 to $249,999	215	60,465	10,698	28.0	6.9
$250,000 to $499,999	69	131,884	17,391	14.6	5.0
$500,000 to $999,999	26	250,000	30,769	9.8	4.4
$1,000,000 and over	16	1,225,000	25,000	4.9	0.7
Total	2,105	27,553	3,895	100.0	4.9

Source: U.S. Bureau of the Census, *Statistical Abstract of the United States: 1993* (Washington, DC: USGPO, 1993), p. 658.

326,000 farms with sales of $100,000 or more.[65] Less than 10 percent of the payments went to the 1.2 million quite small farms whose net income from farming (after deducting expenses) was negative, but whose occupants earned their living more from off-farm work than from farming. Government payments comprised the next largest fraction of total receipts from farming (last column) for the 309,000 farms with sales of $40,000–100,000. These were farms of modest size run mostly by full-time farmers—perhaps the closest approximation to the yeoman farmers legislators claim to be helping. But much larger average *absolute* payments (fourth column) went to fully commercial farms with sales of more than $100,000 per year.

Table 2.3 probably underestimates the share of benefits from government support programs accruing to the largest, most prosperous farmers, because it covers only direct government payments and not the benefits realized indirectly as farmers sell their crops at prices above free market-clearing levels. Because large farms produce more output of a given crop per acre on average than small farms, larger farmers gain relatively more from price supports, whereas smaller farmers do best under acreage set-aside and similar pro-

---

[65] The situation was little different during the 1960s. See the testimony of James T. Bonnen in U.S. Congress, Joint Economic Committee, Report, *The Analysis and Evaluation of Public Expenditures: The PPB System* (Washington, DC: USGPO: 1969), vol. I, p. 440. See also Luttrell, *The High Cost of Farm Welfare*, pp. 117–118.

grams linked to acreage rather than output. Also, many of the farms with sales of $1 million or more were cane sugar plantations. Under the sugar program prevailing since 1982, the federal government makes almost no direct payments to farmers, but through import restrictions holds the domestic price well above world market levels, thereby conferring large indirect benefits upon sugar growers.[66]

During the late 1960s it became known that some large farms were receiving enormous subsidies under the various government programs. Thus, in 1970, nine farms received direct government payments exceeding $1 million, and 23 received at least $500,000.[67] Among the leading recipients was a plantation owned by Senator James O. Eastland, member of the Senate Committee on Agriculture. In response to a storm of criticism, Congress included in the 1970 Agriculture Act provisions limiting the subsidy on any given crop to $55,000 annually per farm. The limitation was later changed to $50,000 per farm for all crops, although complex exceptions have been allowed for payments in kind, export subsidies,[68] and gains on the repayment of nonrecourse loans at preferred rates. Farm owners reacted to these constraints by subdividing their farms into smaller parcels transferred to relatives or leased to outsiders.[69] In continuing amendments to the agriculture laws Congress has attempted to close such loopholes by articulating stringent ownership rules, but human ingenuity has outrun the legislators' drafting skills. Thus, although most farmers and farmland owners receive modest government support payments, a few continue to gain disproportionately.

Important distributional questions also arise on the side of those who ultimately pay for farm income supports. High loan prices and stringent acreage restrictions imply high food prices, placing the burden of farm income support on food consumers. Under an approach emphasizing deficiency payments, the burden is shifted primarily to taxpayers. Members of the U.S. Congress (and also legislators in other industrialized nations) dislike the deficiency payment approach because it reeks of outright subsidy and because it requires either increased taxes or larger government budget deficits. To reduce deficiency payment obligations, they have tended therefore to couple them with price-raising acreage restraints. Under either approach, the citizens pay. But there is a distributional difference. Because the income elasticity of food demand at the farm level is well below unity, poor families devote a significantly larger fraction of their household budgets to food pur-

---

[66]See F. M. Scherer, "The United States Sugar Program," John F. Kennedy School of Government case study, Harvard University, January 1992.

[67]See "9 Topped Million in Farm Subsidies," *New York Times*, April 8, 1971, p. 12; and "The Best Crop," *New York Times*, July 22, 1971, p. 32.

[68]See "U.S. Gives Millions to 10 Farms," *New York Times*, June 9, 1987, p. D2.

[69]See Tom Wicker, "Down on the Farm," *New York Times*, July 15, 1971, p. 31; and "Limits on Subsidies to Big Farms Go Awry, Sending Costs Climbing," *New York Times*, June 15, 1987, pp. 1 and B11.

chases than do rich families. Thus, the incidence of high loan price and acreage restriction programs falls disproportionately upon relatively poor citizens. This regressive effect is attenuated to some extent by the fact that farmers' sales account for only 30 percent of the retail value of food products, the other 70 percent being expended for processing, transportation, and marketing.[70] Deficiency payments, on the other hand, are financed by federal income taxes, whose rate structure is progressive. Therefore, the burden of deficiency payments falls disproportionately upon more affluent citizens. This point seems to have escaped the attention of both politicians and journalists.

INTERNATIONAL TRADE REPERCUSSIONS

Despite its distaste for direct subsidy payments, the U.S. Congress shifted in 1970 and again in 1985 from policies emphasizing high grain prices to low-price policies under which deficiency payments played a prominent role. The reason in both cases was the recognition that high support prices made it more difficult for U.S. agricultural products to compete in world markets, despite the vast expanses of fertile, well-watered land and the advanced technology that confer comparative advantage in world trade upon American farmers.[71] In years of both high and low grain support prices, total U.S. exports of farm products exceeded imports by a considerable margin—that is, by a ratio of 1.9 to 1 from 1971 through 1990.[72]

Whether the United States gains more in world trade from high-price or low-price domestic policies is not readily answered. If the world demand for U.S. agricultural exports is price-elastic, total agricultural export revenues are likely to be larger under a low-price policy, all else equal. If, in contrast, world demand is price-inelastic, as it probably was when the former Soviet Union sold off its once-large gold reserves to buy grain to augment deficient domestic harvests, U.S. export revenues are likely to be larger under a high-price policy. The evidence on this crucial point is mixed and inconclusive,[73] probably because elasticities vary by commodity and because the answer depends

---

[70]*Agricultural Statistics: 1991*, p. 378.

[71]See Leo Sveikauskas, "Science and Technology in United States Foreign Trade, *Economic Journal*, vol. 92 (September 1983), pp. 542–554.

[72]The export balance was larger on average in years of high wheat price supports, although the chain of causation that might lead to such a surprising correlation remains in doubt.

[73]See Gardner, "Changing Economic Perspectives on the Farm Program," pp. 65–67; and Colin A. Carter and Walter H. Gardiner, eds., *Elasticities in International Agricultural Trade* (Boulder, CO: Westview, 1988) (which explicitly addresses the rationale of the 1985 U.S. grain price policy change).

upon whether world supply-demand balances are tight or slack and how rival nation exporters react to U.S. pricing and credit term initiatives.

The choice of U.S. grain export pricing strategies has been complicated by the agricultural policies pursued by European Common Market member nations, who have become an important participant in international grain markets. During the first decade after the Common Market's formation in 1957, national and European Community officials struggled to shape what eventually came to be called the Common Agricultural Policy (CAP).[74] Uniform marketwide food prices were one objective, and to reconcile conflicting French and German interests, mechanisms were created to support a wide array of basic products—much wider than the U.S. system covers—at prices well above customary world market levels. For wheat and similar grain products, Common Market authorities set a *target price* at the level they wish to see attained and, slightly below it, an *intervention price* (i.e., OP_T and OP_i in Figure 2.13a). Both are well above the price OP_F that would prevail in an autarkic free European market. If the internal market price falls below the intervention

FIGURE 2.13
Operation of European Common Market Wheat Market Interventions

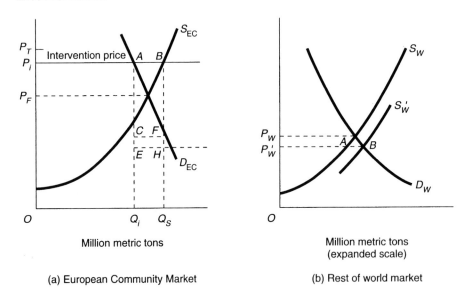

(a) European Community Market

(b) Rest of world market

---

[74] This section draws upon Johnson et al., *Agricultural Policy and Trade,* pp. 99–111; D. Swann, *The Economics of the Common Market* (New York: Penguin, 1970), pp. 78–94; OECD, *National Policies and Agricultural Trade* (Paris: OCED, 1987); and Brian Hill, "Agriculture," in Peter Johnson, ed., *European Industries* (Hants, UK: Edward Elgar, 1993), pp. 27–51.

price, national or Common Market authorities intervene to buy supplies and take them off the market, driving the price upward. This approach differs from U.S. practice in bypassing on-farm storage loans and having the EC take direct possession of surplus supplies—that is, quantity *AB* in Figure 2.13a.

Like any high-price, surplus-stimulating policy, the CAP for wheat creates two new problems while solving one (supporting farmers' income). First, with European prices pegged well above world prices, foreign grain must be excluded to protect the internal price level. This is done by setting a variable tariff. The prices at which foreign wheat is offered, delivered to European ports, are scrutinized daily. Transportation costs from entrepôts to Duisburg, Germany—a Rhine River city relatively distant from European grain-growing areas—are subtracted from the internal intervention price to arrive at what is called a *threshold price*. Each day the variable tariff levy is adjusted to bring import prices plus internal transport costs up to the threshold price so that foreign wheat competes on essentially equal terms with indigenous wheat. Ignoring internal transport costs and assuming (provisionally) the world price (Figure 2.13b) panel to be OP_W, the tariff is set at *AC* per metric ton (Figure 2.13a). This approach plus the convenience of buying from local sources ensures that little wheat will be imported.

Second, the stimulating effect of high internal prices, combined with technological changes adopted throughout the industrialized world, moved Common Market member nations from being net importers of grain in the 1950s to substantial net exporters in the 1970s and 1980s.[75] Internal prices well above world market levels make European grain (and many other foods) uncompetitive in export markets. Some of the surplus (*AB* in Figure 2.13) is sold under soft currency or credit conditions analogous to those used by the U.S. Food for Peace program. But in addition, large quantities are simply "dumped" into world commercial markets at prices well below the internal European price.[76] This is done by refunding to exporters a "restitution"—the cash difference between the internal intervention price, net of transport costs to a port, and the world price. In the first instance, the export restitution amounts to *BF* per ton of wheat exported (left-hand panel). But the addition of subsidized European wheat to the world market shifts the world supply function from S_W to S'_W (panel b). The world price is depressed from OP_W to OP'_W, requiring an increase in the export subsidy from *BF* per ton to *BH* along with a comparable increase in the import levy.

---

[75] "Why Wheat Is Coming Out of Our Ears," *The Economist*, June 6, 1987, p. 69; and "EEC Farm Policy: Just Offal," *The Economist*, December 17, 1988, p. 52.

[76] This practice is pursued for many commodities in addition to wheat. For example, in 1987 and 1988, Community authorities sold 1.7 million tons of milk products from their famous surplus "butter mountain" to the Soviet Union, recording losses of approximately $4 billion relative to original acquisition prices. See "EEC Farm Surpluses: Lakes Deep, Mountains High," *The Economist*, August 6, 1988, p. 42.

Subsidized exports distort international trading patterns. Under the General Agreement on Tariffs and Trade (GATT), ratified in the late 1940s, signatory nations are permitted to take stringent measures to combat injurious subsidized imports. However, at the insistence of the United States, primary agricultural products were exempted from the agreement as long as subsidies are "not applied in a manner which results in [a] contracting party having more than an equitable share of world export trade in that product."[77] European Union authorities insist that they allocate export subsidies so as to avoid excessive world market impacts. This rationalization from a trading bloc that imported grain before the Common Agricultural Policy took effect has been received skeptically by traditional grain exporters such as the United States, Canada, Argentina, Australia, and New Zealand.

When it reduced loan prices in 1985 to increase the competitiveness of American grain in world markets, the U.S. Congress also created a new Export Enhancement Program (EEP) authorizing subsidies for food and feed grain exports to combat "unfair" trade practices by other exporting nations—with the European Common Market members as a prime target.[78] The subsidies were in the first instance to be in-kind allocations from government surplus stockpiles, but when stocks are short, cash subsidies can also be awarded. The program was implemented aggressively.[79] Figure 2.14 traces the average wheat subsidies per ton awarded quarterly under EEP (dashed line) and their corresponding European Union "restitutions" (dot-dash line) between 1987 and 1993. Also shown (solid line) to reflect broader world market conditions is the average Canadian price per metric ton for wheat exported through the St. Lawrence Seaway. When world wheat prices fell, making wheat priced at European and U.S. domestic levels less competitive, export subsidies rose; when wheat prices rose, the subsidies fell. The correlation between the European subsidy and Canadian price series was −0.91. Between Canadian prices and U.S. export subsidies, the correlation was a weaker −0.38. Because U.S. internal prices were much lower than those in Europe, U.S. wheat could be rendered competitive at substantially lower subsidy rates, and perhaps also with less consistent intervention, than European wheat.

This subsidy "war," with grain replacing bullets as ammunition, brought the European Union, the United States, and other affected grain-exporting nations to the bargaining table to seek a less disadvantageous solution.

---

[77]General Agreement on Tariffs and Trade, Article XVI, Section B, quoted at greater length in Johnson et al., *Agricultural Policy and Trade*, p. 27.

[78]Grain export subsidies were also provided during the late 1960s and early 1970s, but were halted when grain prices soared following massive subsidized Soviet Union purchases.

[79] "U.S. Wheat Subsidies Are 'Message' to Europe," *New York Times*, September 3, 1992, p. D2. But see "Abuses Plague Programs to Help Exports of Agricultural Products," *New York Times*, October 10, 1993, p. 1.

FIGURE 2.14
Wheat Prices and Export Subsidies, 1987–1993

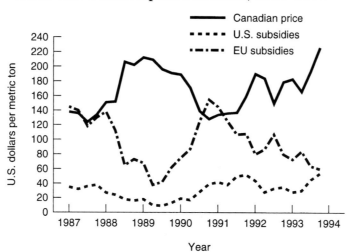

Source: U.S. Department of Agriculture, Economic Research Service, *Wheat Situation and Outlook Report,* November 1991, p. 13; and May 1994, p. 18.

Extending the antidumping and antisubsidy provisions of GATT to agricultural products was given high priority in the Uruguay Round negotiations, initiated in 1986. The Europeans were in any event receptive to reforms, since subsidies to agriculture constituted a heavy burden, averaging 70 percent of total European Community budgetary expenditures during the 1970s and 65 percent in the 1980s.[80] Nor were the EC and the United States alone in distorting world trade patterns by maintaining high prices at home, keeping imports out, and providing subsidies that sometimes worked their way into exports. Japan and Korea protected their rice growers with prices set far above world levels, Switzerland sheltered its dairy producers, and others engaged in similar practices. Perhaps the most remarkable case of all was Saudi Arabia. Hardly blessed with verdant prairies, it pegged irrigated domestic wheat prices at ten times the world price and in 1988 exported more than 700,000 tons of surplus wheat.[81] An analysis covering the years 1979–1981 found that on average, producers of agricultural staples in 24 OECD member nations realized direct and (from price supports) indirect subsidies amounting to 32

[80]Hill, "Agriculture," p. 45.

[81]"Saudis Report Wheat Export," *New York Times,* September 15, 1988 (from a Reuters dispatch).

percent of the value of the products they sold.[82] Japan had the highest average subsidy level (at 59 percent) of the nations studied; Australia and New Zealand the lowest levels. For the United States, the average subsidy level across 11 commodity classes was 16 percent. It was 17 percent in wheat and 13 percent in coarse grains.

The Uruguay Round negotiations, seeking changes in the rules governing international trade in farm products and a wide array of other commodities, broke down repeatedly owing to disagreements between the United States and European Union members on the magnitude of farm subsidy cuts. Prospects for agreement improved in 1992 when European Union member nations accepted the so-called MacSharry Plan for reforming Common Market agricultural policy.[83] Central to the reforms were planned 29 percent grain price reductions by 1997, 15 percent acreage reductions, and the initiation of deficiency payments to compensate farmers for the attending income losses. Thus, EU policies began converging toward their U.S. counterparts.

Renewed Uruguay Round negotiations yielded an agreement in December of 1993 under which, among other things, the European Union would reduce the volume of farm exports receiving subsidies by 21 percent between the years 1994 and 2000.[84] Subsidized European wheat exports were expected eventually to fall from 25.5 million to 13.5 million tons per year.[85] The United States agreed in turn to end its physical restraints on the importation of price-supported farm commodities and to replace them with tariffs that would (through future negotiations) decline over time. Other nations pledged to reduce (typically modestly) the extent to which key domestic crops were protected from imports; for example, Japan and Korea would shift from the outright prohibition of rice imports to token imports and later to high but eventually declining tariffs. After a brief but heated debate, the U.S. Congress ratified the Uruguay Round agreement in December 1994. How its implementation will affect the fortunes of U.S. farmers will be watched with intense interest.[86] Because deficiency payments were decoupled from farmers' output, they were not deemed export-distorting under the new GATT agreement, and so the United States

---

[82]OECD staff, *National Policies and Agricultural Trade* (Paris: OECD, 1987), p. 117. See also Robert E. Lipsey and Birgitta Swedenborg, "The High Cost of Eating: Agricultural Protection and International Differences in Food Prices," National Bureau of Economic Research working paper no. 4555 (December 1993).

[83]See Hill, "Agriculture," p. 49; and "EC Farm Policy: Getting Better," *The Economist*, May 23, 1992, p. 55.

[84]"After 7 Years, Nations Near Pact That Would Slash Many Tariffs but Would Omit Some Key Markets," *Wall Street Journal*, December 15, 1993, p. A7.

[85]One metric ton is equivalent to approximately 37 U.S. bushels.

[86]For an optimistic prognosis, see U.S. Department of Agriculture, Economic Research Service, *Effects of the Uruguay Round Agreement on U.S. Agricultural Commodities* (March 1994).

could continue to subsidize farmers through the target price approach. Because most of the European subsidized export reductions were backloaded to the year 2000, U.S. grain exports were expected to receive continuing subsidies under the Export Enhancement Program for a considerable period.

POLICY DEVELOPMENTS IN 1995

During the closing months of 1995, a budget-cutting U.S. Congress debated proposals for a new farm price and income support law. The House and Senate Agriculture Committees rejected a "Freedom to Farm" bill proposed by Rep. Pat Roberts of Iowa. It would have eliminated the ties between deficiency payments, crop prices, and acreage restraint compliance, granting farmers lump-sum income subsidies whose magnitude depended only upon past program participation histories. The subsidies were to be phased down over time, with a decision on their eventual retention or elimination deferred to the year 2000. At the time this book went to press, it seemed probable that grain price and income support programs would follow the pattern established in the 1985 and 1990 laws, except that eligible acreage would be reduced and farmers would gain greater flexibility in their choice of crops to plant on qualifying acreage.

FUTURE CHALLENGES

The Uruguay Round agreements will by no means end the problems faced by U.S. agricultural policymakers. Several important challenges remain for the future.

As we have seen, U.S. agriculture has enjoyed outstanding increases in productivity since the 1930s. Figure 2.15 traces the trends in two productivity measures: output per hour of on-farm work (i.e., labor productivity), and total factor productivity, or output relative to all measured inputs (including land, hybrid seeds, machinery, and chemicals as well as labor). Given the logarithmic vertical scale, a constant productivity growth rate would be manifested by straight-line trends. There are clear signs of retarded growth in the labor productivity series, but not the total factor productivity series, suggesting that substituting technologically advanced machinery and chemicals for labor inputs may be becoming more difficult.[87] Absent a return to higher past labor productivity growth rates, the exodus of labor from farming will have to decline, and/or the United States will find it difficult to feed its own slowly growing population and at the same time export a substantial fraction of its agricultural output.

Productivity growth could be retarded further in the very long run if continuing erosion depletes the growing powers of U.S. farms' soil. Under prevailing

---

[87]For an earlier and somewhat more optimistic view, see the National Academy of Sciences report, *Agricultural Production Efficiency* (Washington, DC: USGPO, 1975).

FIGURE 2.15
Trends in U.S. Agricultural Productivity

Source: *Economic Report of the President*, February 1992, p. 406.

high-yield cultivation practices, 8.1 tons of soil are lost per year through water and wind erosion on the average cropland acre.[88] For all but the most vulnerable farms, erosion is not likely to impair output significantly until late in the twenty-first century. Under a series of government programs, farmers have been given subsidies to remove erosion-prone acreage from cultivation or to adopt soil conservation measures. By 1990, 61 million acres were covered by Soil Conservation Service protective measures.[89] In other cases, farmers have adopted "no-till" and other soil-conserving practices without government inducement.[90] Thus, a crisis is hardly imminent, but a farsighted approach is needed, since lost topsoil could take centuries to regenerate.

Global warming is a potential threat on an even longer time scale. There is considerable disagreement over the rate at which it is proceeding and its likely effects on agriculture. The best-accepted projections suggest that rising

---

[88]But see "Scarcities To Force a Leaner Diet, Experts Say," *New York Times*, February 18, 1995, p. 22. National Research Council, Committee on Conservation Needs and Opportunities report, *Soil Conservation: Assessing the National Resources Inventory*, vol. I (Washington, DC: 1986), p. 8. See also Paul Faeth, *Paying the Farm Bill: U.S. Agricultural Policy and the Transition to Sustainable Agriculture* (Washington, DC: World Resources Institute, 1991).

[89]*Agricultural Statistics: 1991*, pp. 456–457.

[90]See "Erosion-Wary Farmers Are Spurning Traditional Plow," *New York Times*, May 11, 1982, p. 19; and "Farmers Are Learning New Tricks from Mother Nature," *Business Week*, November 6, 1989, pp. 76–88.

temperatures will be accompanied by added precipitation, which could be favorable for growing certain crops while adversely affecting others.[91] But the rainfall is likely to be unevenly distributed. Some highly productive U.S. agricultural areas could be turned into deserts, and the oscillation between drought and excessive rain may become more pronounced in other areas. No one knows with confidence what the net impact will be.

In other parts of the world, and especially in Asia, the "Green Revolution" has dramatically raised rice and wheat yields by introducing improved hybrid seeds along with new fertilization and irrigation methods and, in China, more effective incentives. As a result, the periodic crises against which U.S. Food for Peace supplies were marshaled became milder and less frequent. Nevertheless, the future balance remains precarious. The growth of food output in Asia has outstripped population growth by only a slender margin, the poor in Asia continue to be undernourished, and Africa remains famine-prone.[92]

The United States and a few other nations such as Canada, Australia, and Argentina have traditionally been the world's granaries of last resort, drawing upon their reserves to help alleviate the worst consequences of sudden famine in other nations. Recently, however, concern over the high budgetary cost of crop loan and surplus purchase programs has led to U.S. and European Union policies aimed at reducing surpluses. In the United States, for example, surplus-shedding policies caused the annual carryover of wheat stocks on June 1 to decline from an average of 1.43 billion bushels, or enough to cover domestic usage for 1.41 years, between 1980 and 1987 to 504 million bushels between 1988 and 1993.[93] With smaller reserves, it will be more difficult to make emergency supplies available to areas of large population suffering unusually unfavorable growing conditions, and staple crop prices on world markets are likely to become more volatile. What responsibility does the United States have, as a rich and highly productive food producer, to carry reserves that will help avert other nations' misfortunes? Should there be international agreements to distribute the burden of reserve holding and to avoid the price-depressing effect of reserve shedding in normal years?[94] Such questions call for the wisdom of a biblical Joseph.

---

[91]See Robert Mendelsohn, William D. Nordhaus, and Daigee Shaw, "The Impact of Global Warming on Agriculture," *American Economic Review,* vol. 84 (September 1994), pp. 753–771.

[92]See Sartaj Aziz, *Agricultural Policies for the 1990s* (Paris: OECD, 1990); and Hans Singer, John Wood, and Tony Jennings, *Food Aid: The Challenge and the Opportunity* (New York: Oxford University Press, 1987).

[93]*Agricultural Statistics: 1991,* p. 4; and *Wheat Situation and Outlook Report,* May 1994, p. 23.

[94]See Philip H. Trezise, *Rebuilding Grain Reserves: Toward an International System* (Washington, DC: Brookings, 1976).

3

CRUDE OIL

During its early decades, crude oil supply was competitively structured. The instability associated with large new discoveries and the business cycle precipitated government interventions to raise U.S. crude oil prices, enhance the after-tax returns to well drilling, and inhibit competitive imports. The depletion of U.S. reserves and the growing power of OPEC changed world supply and demand relationships dramatically, providing insight into the conditions under which cartels are successful in restricting output and raising prices. The United States reacted to OPEC's price-raising by imposing price control and taxation measures whose analysis requires further extensions of the standard competitive model.

EARLY HISTORY

Petroleum (from the Greek, rock oil) has been known for at least three millennia. It was skimmed from the surface of ponds and scooped from trenches dug into natural outcroppings to make medicines, caulking material, fiery weapons, and illuminants. The modern petroleum era began as an economic response to the pull of demand. During the 1850s, the whale oil used by many as a lamp fuel became increasingly expensive when the intensive whaling efforts portrayed in Melville's *Moby Dick* (1851) depleted the population of whales. A lower-cost substitute was desired. Work by chemists in Europe and America (including Yale University's Benjamin Silliman, Jr.) revealed that with appropriate purification, the kerosene distilled from crude petroleum would serve. What was needed was a means of producing petroleum in sufficiently large quantities.

Well-known techniques used to drill for salt solved the problem. The first significant success was achieved at Oil Creek near Titusville, in northwest

Pennsylvania.[1] In August 1859, Colonel Edwin L. Drake's primitive well filled with pumpable oil after penetrating 69 feet into the earth. Word of the discovery spread rapidly, and Titusville became the first of many oil boomtowns, imitated in nearby Pennsylvania towns and then in Ohio, California, Texas, Oklahoma, Louisiana, and other parts of the United States.

Other nations, in some of which oil had long been extracted by low-volume methods, slowly but surely emulated Drake's approach. Huge reserves were struck through drilling in Russia's Caucasus during 1871. Shortly thereafter, Sweden's Nobel family took a leading role in their development. Important successes were achieved in Sumatra by the predecessor of the Shell Company in 1885; in Rumania by local interests during the 1890s; in Persia by the predecessor of British Petroleum in 1908; in Mexico by U.S. and British wildcatters during 1910; in Venezuela by Shell in 1922; in Iraq by a multinational consortium in 1928; in Bahrain by Standard Oil of California in 1932; in Kuwait by Gulf Oil and British Petroleum and in Saudi Arabia by Texaco and Standard of California in 1938; in Nigeria by Shell and British Petroleum and in Algeria by Elf-Arap of France during 1956; along with others.

World crude oil production grew from nearly a million tons per year in 1870 to 20 million tons in 1900 and 3 billion tons in 1980.[2] On average, annual output doubled every 11 years during the first 80 years of the twentieth century.

The industry that achieved this growth is commonly characterized in terms of four vertical stages—crude oil exploration, development, and production; transportation (notably, pipelines and seafaring tankers); refining; and marketing (i.e., terminal distribution and retailing). Each has its own distinctive structure and conduct record. We focus in this chapter on the crude oil stage, whose market, we shall see, has become global in scope, dominated by OPEC (the Organization of Petroleum Exporting Countries). Refining, transportation, and marketing will follow in Chapter 4.

During the closing decades of the nineteenth century, crude petroleum production in Russia expanded more rapidly than in the United States. By 1900, Russia had edged out the United States as world supply leader. Soon thereafter the United States regained its lead, and as late as 1950, it originated more than half of the world's crude oil output.[3] Middle Eastern and other supply sources then grew by leaps and bounds. In 1970 the U.S. share of total world output had fallen to 21 percent. By 1990 it had dropped to 12 percent.[4]

---

[1]For a highly readable history of the petroleum industry, see Daniel Yergin, *The Prize* (New York: Simon & Schuster, 1991).

[2]John Evans, *OPEC, Its Member States and the World Energy Market* (New York: Longman, 1986), p. 12.

[3]Ibid., p. 12.

[4]U.S. Department of Energy, Energy Information Administration, *Annual Energy Review: 1992* (Washington, DC: USGPO, June 1993), p. 275.

THE EVOLUTION OF U.S. PETROLEUM POLICY

Throughout its first seven decades the U.S. petroleum industry lurched between periods of glut and scarcity. Between the late 1870s and 1911, the domestic industry was dominated by the Standard Oil Company. Standard, however, devoted most of its energies to refining and marketing, in which its market share was as high as 90 percent. Until broken into 34 pieces under an antitrust judgment in 1911, about which we will learn much more in the next chapter, it preferred to obtain most of its crude oil feedstocks from the large number of independent well operators. It had considerable power as a monopsony (single) buyer of crude, and it was often able to buy on very favorable terms. Despite its attempts to impose stability upon the industry, the pricing of crude was volatile over time. There were two main reasons.

For one, the size distribution of crude oil reservoirs is extremely skew.[5] That is, there are hundreds of thousands of crude oil agglomerations under the earth's surface. Most are quite small, but a few, accounting for a large fraction of the total reserve volume, are huge. When an important new reservoir was discovered, supply outraced existing demand, and so prices temporarily plummeted.

Also, new sources of supply tended to be developed very rapidly under the freewheeling laissez-faire conditions prevailing in the United States (but not in many other nations, where exclusive mineral rights encompassing sizable areas were often granted to a single entity by national authorities).[6] When a large reservoir was discovered, hundreds of prospectors would try to buy drilling rights above it and sink their wells into it, draining it as quickly as they could. Indeed, petroleum extraction provides the classic example of what economists call the "common-pool" problem. Within a pool, oil flows toward the segments that have been evacuated. When many individuals have the right to draw oil from the pool, the faster they extract, the more oil they capture not only from the deposits lying directly below their property, but also from the deposits that would otherwise be available to their neighbors. If they do not deplete the oil quickly, the fear that others will seize the prize intensifies their incentive for speed. This behavior has three adverse consequences. First, the rapid depletion of a reservoir's reserves may bring oil onto the market more quickly than it can be absorbed, aggravating price swings. Second, draining a pool too quickly reduces the pool's internal gas pressure, making it less likely that all of the pool's oil will flow to wells. It therefore reduces the total amount of oil that can be recovered (unless costly secondary and tertiary recovery measures are taken—e.g., injecting water and emulsifiers under pressure).

---

[5]See Morris A. Adelman, *The World Petroleum Market* (Baltimore: Johns Hopkins University Press, 1992), pp. 34–39.

[6]*Ibid.*, pp. 43–44.

Third, the proliferation of wells is wasteful in its own right, since the maximum long-run yield of a reservoir might be achieved with far fewer wells, each producing a larger total volume at lower cost per meter drilled.

Measures were under way to alleviate these problems (with at best middling success) when two shocks struck the industry almost simultaneously. In 1929, the U.S. economy plunged into the worst recession in its history. Unemployment soared to 16 percent of the labor force in 1931 and 24 percent in 1932, reducing inter alia the demand for petroleum products. In October 1930, oil began gushing from a wildcat well drilled in east Texas by Columbus "Dad" Joiner. The reservoir soon proved to be the largest one found in America to date, more than 100 square miles in area. Within a year a thousand wells had been drilled, extracting oil at a rate that exceeded a third of total U.S. 1929 production. Nationwide average wellhead prices plunged from $1.27 per (42-gallon) barrel in 1929 to $1.19 in 1930 and 65 cents in 1931.[7] In east Texas, oil seeking transportation to distant refineries sold for as little as ten cents per barrel.

Something, the oil industry and its host states insisted, had to be done. Several of the oil-producing states had established commissions to regulate oil production, in part to minimize common pool wastes by encouraging or mandating that reservoirs be "unitized," or subjected to common management. The Texas Railroad Commission was one such agency, although its powers frequently proved insufficient for the task. After a more potent authorizing law was passed in 1932, east Texas production cutbacks were ordered, and Texas Rangers were dispatched to enforce the orders. The effort succeeded in relieving some of the pressure on prices. However, many producers cheated on their output quotas and smuggled oil (so-called "hot oil") over state borders. Once it had passed into interstate commerce, it lay beyond state commission jurisdiction. This plus generally depressed market conditions kept nationwide average prices at 87 cents per barrel in 1932 and 67 cents in 1933.

Then, in October 1933, oil production was brought under the compulsory provisions of the National Industrial Recovery Act, a law recommended by President Franklin D. Roosevelt and passed in June 1933 by Congress in the hope of "reflating" the economy. The basic NIRA idea was to raise wages by encouraging collective bargaining with strong unions and, to support those wages, to raise prices through the widespread cartelization of industry.[8] As an instrument of macroeconomic policy the program failed, largely because industry was quick to cartelize, so prices rose, but wages increased more

---

[7]U.S. Bureau of the Census, *Historical Statistics of the United States: Colonial Times to 1957* (Washington, DC: USGPO, 1960), p. 360.

[8]See Ellis W. Hawley, *The New Deal and the Problem of Monopoly* (Princeton, NJ: Princeton University Press, 1966).

slowly, so real purchasing power fell rather than rising as hoped. For oil, among other commodities, the intended price-raising occurred. State oil regulators cooperated with each other and with federal administrators to set individual well production quotas (called "prorationing" assignments), and the interstate shipment of "hot oil" (i.e., oil in excess of the quotas) was ruled illegal. The NIRA was declared to be unconstitutional in January 1935, but Congress quickly filled the gap by passing the Connally Hot Oil Act, which explicitly prohibited interstate shipment of oil produced in excess of state prorationing quotas.[9] Nationwide average wellhead prices dipped to 97 cents per barrel in 1935 but rose then and remained above a dollar throughout the remainder of the 1930s.

Supported by the Connally Act, prorationing continued in most of the major oil-producing states (excepting California and Wyoming) until the 1970s.[10] Under it, the Federal Bureau of Mines made monthly estimates of crude oil demand, assuming prevailing prices. The regulatory commissions of major oil-producing states met to discuss informally (without binding force) how to divide up the national projection, and the state commissions adjusted individual well production quotas upward or downward to match supply with demand at the prevailing price.[11] Typically, "stripper" wells extracting only a few barrels per day were exempted from the restraints, so the bulk of output restriction was borne by the largest wells, which produced at lower marginal cost per barrel than stripper wells. Consequently, even more so than with *uniform* percentage acreage restrictions in grain crop farming, supply functions were shifted upward and to the left, so that any given amount of (restricted) output was produced at higher cost than it would be if the lowest-cost wells were allowed to expand their output until marginal cost equaled price. The result was a considerable amount of excess cost, estimated from Henry Steele's computations at roughly $750 million per year under 1965 conditions.[12]

While prorationing was restricting output, another federal policy instrument was encouraging investment in the discovery and development of new wells. From 1918 to 1975, U.S. crude oil producers were allowed to use a special accounting procedure, *percentage depletion*, in computing their federal

---

[9] Not surprisingly, the sponsor, Senator Tom Connally, was a Texan.

[10] The low point in the post–World War II period was 1962, when the Texas Railroad Commission allowed prorationed wells to operate at only 27 percent of maximum annual output.

[11] See Gary D. Libecap, "The Political Economy of Crude Oil Cartelization in the United States, 1933–1972," *Journal of Economic History*, vol. 49 (December 1989), pp. 833–855.

[12] Testimony of Henry Steele in U.S. Senate, Committee on the Judiciary, Subcommittee on Antitrust and Monopoly, Hearings, *Governmental Intervention in the Market Mechanism* (Washington, DC: USGPO, 1969), Part 1, pp. 219–229.

income tax liability.[13] During most of this period, they could deduct as an arbitrary depletion allowance 27.5 percent of the wellhead price or half of the pretax income from selling their oil, whichever was less. To illustrate, consider a well whose oil was selling in 1969 at $3.10 per barrel, and whose production cost was $1.35 per barrel. Assume a federal income tax rate of 52 percent. The accounting for a barrel of oil sold would proceed as follows:

Normal Tax Accounting			*Depletion Accounting*	
		Allowance		
Price	$3.10	$0.8525	Price	$3.10
Less cost	1.35		Operating cost	−1.35
Net income	$1.75	$0.875		
			Lower allowance	−0.8525
			Income net of allowance	$0.8975
52% income tax	0.91			0.4667
Income after tax	$0.84			$1.2833

Without percentage depletion, after-tax income would be 84 cents per barrel. With a depletion allowance taken for costs not actually incurred out of pocket, after-tax income would be the true pretax income of $1.75 minus the $0.4667 tax = $1.2833, or 44.33 cents more per barrel than without the allowance. Since the allowance made oil production more profitable than it otherwise would have been, there was an added incentive to invest in finding oil.[14]

Another stimulus was provided by the price structure maintained through prorationing. Prices stabilized during the 1930s and then, following the relaxation of World War II controls, stair-stepped upward. See Figure 3.1.[15] But this created another problem. Vast new oil reserves were being developed in the Middle East and elsewhere. At first the pricing of foreign oil was pegged to U.S. prices, but as the supply of Middle East oil soared, its price fell relative to U.S. prices, making it attractive to import oil into the United States. This situation threatened to undermine the domestic price structure. To protect domestic oil producers, the federal government imposed "voluntary" limits on oil imports beginning in 1957 and made them mandatory in 1959.

Initially, imports were limited to 9 percent of domestic demand. Subsequent technical revisions and adjustments (mostly upward) occurred to

---

[13]Percentage depletion was eliminated from the tax law for all but stripper wells in 1975.

[14]Percentage depletion also led refiners to proliferate retail gasoline stations—a phenomenon addressed in Chapter 4.

[15]The "real" prices are contemporary (i.e., current-dollar) prices divided by a wholesale price index (1947 = 1.0) for all commodities.

FIGURE 3.1
Trends in Crude Oil Prices, 1900–1970

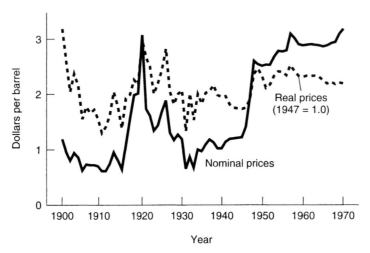

Sources: U.S. Bureau of the Census, *Historical Statistics of the United States: Colonial Times to 1957* (Washington, DC: USGPO, 1960), pp. 360–361; and U.S. Department of Energy, Energy Information Administration, *Annual Energy Review: 1992* (Washington, DC: USGPO, June 1993), p. 157.

reflect changing supply and demand conditions. Since most inland refineries were not physically able to receive imported oil except at very high cost, an ingenious system was devised to spread the benefits of the import restraints. Each refinery received "tickets" to import a quantity of foreign oil more or less proportional to its prior month's crude oil throughput. (More precisely, reflecting Congress's favoritism toward "independent" refiners, small refineries received larger proportional ticket allocations than large refineries.) The value of a ticket to import a barrel of oil depended upon the difference between the price of domestic crude and the cost of imported crude. To illustrate, consider the situation typical in 1969. Oil could be purchased in Iran at $1.40 per barrel. Tanker freight to the East Coast refineries best positioned to use imports from the Middle East added about 75 cents per barrel to the landed cost, and an import tariff added another 11 cents. Thus, the landed cost of Iranian crude at Philadelphia was $1.40 + $0.75 + $0.11 = $2.26 per barrel. Equivalent Texas crude cost $3.10 at the wellhead plus 30 cents transportation to Philadelphia, or $3.40 per barrel. Since the refinery saves $3.40 − $2.26 = $1.14 by using imported crude rather than domestic crude, the value of a barrel's import ticket was approximately $1.14. The tickets could not be bought and sold. But they could be bartered, and so, for instance, a Chicago area refinery with tickets would trade them to an East Coast refinery and agree in exchange to provide gasoline of equal value to the East Coast refin-

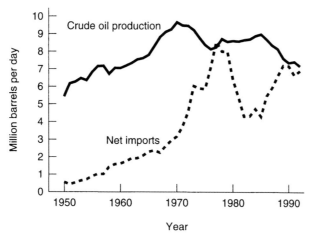

FIGURE 3.2

Trends in U.S. Crude Oil Output and Imports

Source: U.S. Department of Energy, Energy Information Administration, *Annual Energy Review: 1992*, p. 125.

ery's midwestern marketing organization. In this way, the refineries best positioned to use imported oil received it, but all refiners shared in the benefits from its contrived scarcity.

Thus, during the 1960s the United States had deployed four major policy instruments to benefit oil producers: prorationing and the Connally Act, to keep domestic prices high; import quotas, to prevent the high prices from being undermined; and percentage depletion, complementing the incentive from high prices to encourage exploration and drilling for oil. The combination of the four can be characterized as a "Drain America First" policy, since it encouraged production from finite domestic reserves and discouraged reliance upon abundant supplies overseas.

Drain it did. Gradually, the roster of attractive oil drilling prospects was depleted. Domestic crude oil production peaked at 9.64 million barrels per day in 1970 and then declined. See Figure 3.2.[16] The addition of massive Alaskan north slope supplies beginning in 1977 was unable to restore output to earlier peak levels. Meanwhile, demand continued to rise. By the early 1970s, the prorationing authorities were allowing most wells to operate at full sustainable capacity.[17] But to fill a growing gap, import restraints had to be relaxed, and so by 1973, 35 percent of the nation's petroleum product demand was satisfied through crude oil and/or refined product imports. This set the stage for dramatic changes in the functioning of world petroleum markets.

---

[16] The output series includes crude oil and lease condensates, but excludes natural gas plant liquids. Net imports include imported crude oil and petroleum products, deducting exports of the same.

[17] There were exceptions. In 1981, the Texas Railroad Commission was still limiting output in the huge Yates Field of west Texas to levels less than those desired by its owners.

OPEC AND WORLD PETROLEUM

To understand those changes, we must drop back to assimilate some earlier history. Many of the primitively industrialized nations in which huge oil reserves were discovered awarded exclusive exploration and production franchises to the companies, or groups of companies, that made the initial discoveries. A few companies grew to massive size by virtue of their discoveries, or by aggressively seeking new franchises. The winners began working together to maintain their privileged positions. World War I demonstrated that control of petroleum resources was vital to national security, so governments took an active interest in ensuring that their national oil company champions were well treated. Among other things, the wartime victors wished to ensure that they benefited and that German and Turkish oil interests were held back.

Oil had been flowing in Persia (Iran) since 1908. It was believed that large untapped reserves remained in other parts of the Middle East. After years of negotiation, representatives of what is now British Petroleum, Royal Dutch Shell, the leading French company, and a consortium of six U.S. companies plus Armenian entrepreneur Calouste Gulbenkian signed in June 1928 what was called the "Red Line Agreement."[18] It settled two points. First, the reserves in what is now Iraq would be shared equally by four national groups, with Gulbenkian retaining a residual 5 percent interest. Second, the companies agreed that they would cooperate in developing new oil operations throughout the former Turkish empire, including the Arabian peninsula, which Gulbenkian had encircled on a map with a red line. Although there would be many disputes and alterations in the future, the basic structure of the Middle Eastern crude oil industry was established.

As events evolved, the industry came to be dominated by a group of seven companies known as the "Seven Sisters." They included three of the main participants in the Red Line Agreement: British Petroleum, which had discovered oil in Iran, Shell (jointly owned by Dutch and British interests), and Standard Oil of New Jersey (now Exxon). The other members were American companies: Standard Oil of California and Texaco, which had jointly discovered oil in Saudi Arabia; Gulf Oil, which had pioneered in Kuwait; and Mobil. In 1948, Exxon, Texaco, California Standard, and Mobil formed a joint venture,

---

[18]See Yergin, *The Prize*, pp. 184–206; and U.S. Senate Committee on Foreign Relations report, *Multinational Oil Corporations and U.S. Foreign Policy* (Washington, DC: USGPO, 1975), pp. 34–36. The original U.S. participants, included at the insistence of the U.S. Secretary of State, were Standard Oil of New Jersey (now Exxon), Texaco, Gulf, Standard Oil of Indiana, Atlantic, and Sinclair. Some dropped out later and others were added.

Aramco (the Arabian-American Oil Company), to exploit the extraordinary reserves found in Saudi Arabia.

PRICES, PROFITS, AND TAXES

In 1951 the major companies drawing oil from the Middle East began announcing "posted prices," which determined among other things the payment received by host governments for the oil taken from their territory. At first the posted prices were a good approximation to the prices at which Middle Eastern oil actually changed hands. But in the late 1950s, as new fields were opened and output rose dramatically, substantial amounts of oil began to be sold to third parties at "arm's-length prices" below the posted prices. This development had important implications.

To understand them, we must examine more carefully how the host governments were paid. Consider the situation for heavy Kuwait oil in December of 1968. The posted price was $1.59 per barrel. The agreement prevailing at the time was that host governments would be paid a 12.5 percent royalty on oil removals—a typical royalty rate for landowners—*plus* a 50 percent tax on the oil company's accounting profit. Payments per barrel to the Kuwait government, indicated with an asterisk, were therefore calculated as follows:[19]

Posted price	$1.59
Less: OPEC discount	−.10
Less: operating costs	−.06
Less: 12.5% royalty to Kuwait	−.20*
Accounting profit	$1.23
50% tax to Kuwait	$0.615*

Thus, the total payment to Kuwait was 20 cents plus 61.5 cents = 81.5 cents.

This only begins the story, however. At the time, the prices actually received at the wellhead on arm's-length sales (e.g., about $1.15 per barrel) were lower than the posted prices.[20] Gulf Oil's accounting of its profits therefore proceeded as follows on page 74:

---

[19]See the exhibits prepared by John M. Blair in U.S. Senate, *Governmental Intervention in the Market Mechanism*, pp. 171–173.

[20]Note that the arm's-length price here is lower than the $1.40 Iranian oil price used in our earlier import ticket value example. The reason is that Kuwait oil was heavier than Iranian oil, and heavy oil sells at a discount.

Actual arm's-length price	$1.15
Less: operating costs	−.06
Less: royalty to Kuwait	−.20
Less: tax to Kuwait	−.615
Actual profit	$0.275

Thus Gulf's actual profit was considerably less than the 61.5 cent profit implied in the accounting for its payments to Kuwait. It nevertheless provided a substantial return on investment for oil that cost only 6 cents to remove from the earth.

Moreover, such profits enjoyed a special U.S. income tax advantage. Beginning in 1951, the United States government agreed to let American oil companies treat the severance taxes paid to foreign nations as income taxes.[21] This was more than a mere exercise in semantics. If the severance tax had been treated as a royalty, it would have been deducted from revenues, as above, leaving income per barrel of 27.5 cents taxable in the United States. But as an "income" tax paid to a foreign sovereign, it could be *credited* dollar-for-dollar against any U.S. income tax obligation from foreign oil operations. Thus, in its accounting to the Internal Revenue Service, Gulf would report as follows:

Actual arm's-length price	$1.15
Less: operating costs and royalty	−.26
Taxable income	$0.89
52 percent U.S. income tax	0.4628
Offset: credit for tax paid to Kuwait	0.615
Due Internal Revenue Service	0.000

Because their calculated U.S. income tax obligations were fully shielded by overseas tax credits, U.S. oil companies paid little or no income tax to the U.S. federal government on their highly profitable overseas crude oil operations.

Why did the U.S. government (and later the home governments of other major international oil companies) agree to this tax revenue sacrifice? Harmonious relationships with Middle Eastern governments were considered vital to the U.S. national interest, especially in view of the possibility that they might otherwise join hands with a menacing Soviet Union. Forgoing U.S. income taxes on companies' overseas oil profits was considered an effective but inconspicuous means of inducing the companies to be generous to their

---

[21]U.S. Congress, *Multinational Oil Corporations and U.S. Foreign Policy*, pp. 81–87.

foreign hosts, and hence to keep the governments of the oil-producing lands happy and anticommunist.

THE FORMATION AND ASCENDANCE OF OPEC

Petroleum companies, like other business enterprises, do not gladly sacrifice substantial profits. As output surged and arm's-length prices dropped below posted prices, the international companies found themselves squeezed by their posted price-based payments to host nations. To achieve a closer approximation to arm's-length prices, they announced in two steps during 1959 and 1960 a reduction in their posted prices—for example, for light Arabian crude, from $2.08 to $1.80 per barrel. This action of course reduced both the royalty and "income" tax payments to host governments. The host governments were outraged. Led by Venezuela, several of the leading host governments—Saudi Arabia, Kuwait, Iraq, and Iran—met in Baghdad during September of 1960 to form a countercartel, the Organization of Petroleum Exporting Countries, or OPEC. The companies in response rescinded most of the posted price reductions. OPEC had scored its first victory.

Although other oil-exporting nations joined,[22] OPEC made little further progress during the next decade. It tried twice to establish prorationing systems like those administered in the United States, but its members could not agree on how to share any output restrictions needed to raise prices. And because new reserves were forthcoming in great abundance, markets remained loose, unpropitious to price-raising. Among other things, if an OPEC member tried to squeeze the companies operating within its boundaries, the companies could obtain alternative supplies from the substantial excess capacity existing in the United States.

Gradually this situation changed. Demand rose relative to available production capacity, shifting the advantage to the host nations. Perhaps as important was an historical accident.

Oil was discovered in Libya by Exxon in 1959. In 1965, a newcomer to the international oil game, Occidental Petroleum (Oxy) of Los Angeles, won the franchise to drill in what had previously been considered an unpromising part of Libya. In 1966, it struck large deposits. In 1969, King Idris of Libya was overthrown in a coup led by Colonel Muammar Qadaffi. Qadaffi sought to obtain a better deal for Libya by insisting that Exxon and Occidental renegotiate their contracts. His hand was strengthened by fortuitous developments. In 1967, the so-called "six days' war" broke out in and around Israel. As a consequence of the conflict, no ships could traverse the Suez Canal until 1975. A 1970 accident also interrupted shipments on the Trans-Arabian pipeline (Tapline), extending from Saudi Arabia to a Mediterranean terminal in

---

[22]Other members include Algeria, Gabon, Indonesia, Libya, Nigeria, Qatar, and the United Arab Emirates. Ecuador exited in September 1992.

Lebanon. Because of these blockages, oil from Saudi Arabia and the Persian Gulf had to be transported great distances around the horn of Africa to its principal European markets, rather than by short pipelines or Suez Canal routes reaching the Mediterranean more directly. See Figure 3.3. Tanker rental rates soared. Libyan oil was spared these additional costs, and so the locational premium it already enjoyed was magnified. Qadaffi demanded to participate in the form of a 40-cent price increase. Exxon could resist his demands because Libyan crude provided only a small fraction of its worldwide requirements. But Oxy was almost totally dependent upon Libyan crude,

FIGURE 3.3
Changes in Shipping Distances Caused by Closure of the Suez Canal and Tapline

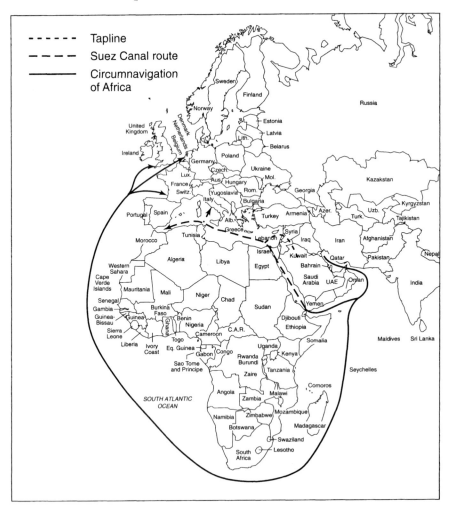

and in the summer of 1970, Qadaffi ordered a 360,000-barrel reduction in daily output. Given the legacy of antipathy toward newcomers originating in the Red Line Agreement, the major oil companies, and particularly Exxon, refused to supply on favorable terms the oil Oxy needed to meet its contractual commitments.[23] Occidental was forced to accept a 30-cent-per-barrel posted price increase, from $2.23 to $2.53, and an increase in Libya's "tax" on Oxy's accounting profits from 50 percent to 58 percent.

These concessions whetted the appetites of the Persian Gulf oil countries, who demanded similar price increases. Their officials met with representatives of the principal international oil companies in Teheran during February of 1971 and agreed to a 35 cent per barrel increase in posted prices, future annual escalations of 2.5 percent of the posted price plus 5 cents, and a rise in the "tax" rate from 50 to 55 percent.[24] The negotiations ended with a smug declaration that oil prices would be stable in the foreseeable future. But soon thereafter, Libya and Algeria secured a further 65-cent increase on oil shipped from Mediterranean ports. And in October 1971, Libya began a campaign that led within two years to full nationalization or majority ownership in the petroleum operations within its borders. Other nations followed suit, sometimes paying significant compensation for their takings, sometimes not.[25] Saudi Arabia took a 25 percent ownership share in Aramco's crude oil concession rights in 1972, added 35 percent more in 1974, and assumed full ownership in 1980. It paid the companies the accounting value of their investments, not the much higher market value. The international oil companies became tenants or at best partial owners of their petroleum operations outside the industrialized world, receiving fees (e.g., of 20 to 30 cents per barrel extracted) for their technical and managerial services.[26]

Price stability did not in fact endure. Oil sales were (and continue to be) denominated in U.S. dollars. When the dollar was allowed to "float" in December of 1971, it declined in value—for example, by 24 percent relative to the West German Mark by 1973. With their purchasing power eroded by this

---

[23]See Armand Hammer, *Hammer* (New York: Perigree, 1988), pp. 338–339 and 344–347.

[24]"5-Year Accord Is Reached in Iran by 23 Companies," *New York Times*, February 15, 1971, p. 1. The U.S. company delegates were accorded special exemptions from the U.S. antitrust laws to collaborate in the price negotiations.

[25]"Oil-Producing Lands Weigh Nationalization," *New York Times*, June 6, 1972, p. 55. On how Occidental Petroleum extracted compensation from Libya for its takeover, see *Hammer*, pp. 350–352.

[26]On the assumption of full Saudi Arabian management over its oil operations, see "Successors Ready, U.S. Oilmen Bow Out of Their Saudi Empire," *New York Times*, April 1, 1989, p. 4.

change, the OPEC nations insisted that the Teheran agreement be renegotiated. As discussions proceeded inconclusively in 1973, virtually all of the world's industrialized nations were experiencing an unusual synchronized boom that raised the demand for petroleum products and left markets extraordinarily tight. As OPEC officials prepared to negotiate in Vienna with oil company representatives over large further price increases, Egypt and Syria on October 6 invaded disputed territories occupied by Israel. The Vienna meeting was disbanded, but as the "Yom Kippur" war continued, delegates from six Persian Gulf nations met in Kuwait City and unilaterally seized control of the price-posting process. The price increases they quoted were unprecedented (e.g., on Saudi Arabian light marker crude oil, from $2.93 per barrel to $5.11 per barrel). Soon thereafter, they announced planned output cutbacks of 5 percent each month until their objectives were attained and a total embargo on shipments to nations that supported Israel in the war—notably, as events transpired, the United States and the Netherlands. The embargoes were ineffective, because ships leaving Arabian ports for nonboycotted locations were simply redirected in midvoyage. But the output cutbacks in an already strained market worked, spot petroleum prices soared, and by January 1974, the official price of Saudi Arabian marker crude had been raised to $11.65 per barrel.

In 1973, OPEC member nations averaged 31 million barrels of crude oil production per day—56 percent of total world output. The price increases of late 1973 and early 1974 redistributed nearly 9 dollars of purchasing power per barrel from consuming nations to OPEC members—that is, approximately $100 billion in total per year. "Petrodollars" flowed to OPEC nations much more rapidly than they could be respent. Merchant ships queued for weeks outside congested Persian Gulf ports, waiting to unload cargos ranging from air conditioners to Caterpillar tractors. The transfer of such large sums to OPEC reduced aggregate demand in the industrialized nations.[27] That plus central bank efforts to combat the inflation resulting from oil and other commodity price increases (see Figure 2.4 in Chapter 2) triggered a sharp worldwide recession beginning in 1974 and 1975. It was without doubt the worst macroeconomic shock ever precipitated by the microeconomics of cartel pricing. From January 1974 to June 1975, unemployment in the United States alone increased by 3.5 million persons.

Eventually, the OPEC nations found ways to respend their newly won wealth on goods imported from industrialized nations, restoring aggregate demand. Petrodollars also flowed into international banks, from which they

---

[27]By a standard identity, GNP = Consumption + investment + government spending + exports – imports. An increase in the dollar volume of imports without a commensurate increase in exports reduces aggregate demand.

FIGURE 3.4
Output and Prices of OPEC Nations, 1968–1992

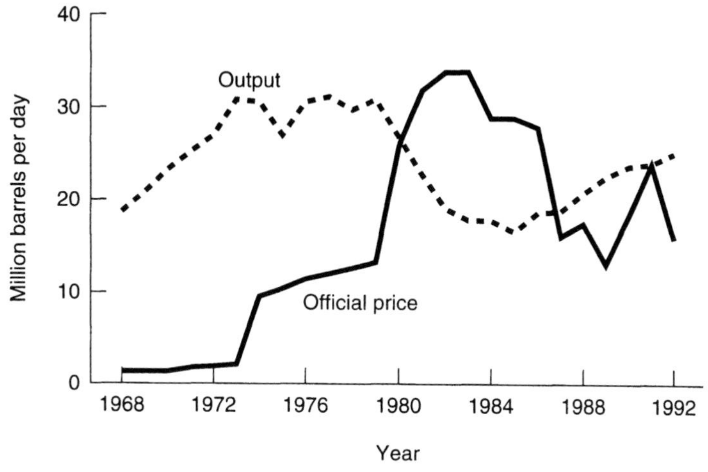

Source: U.S. Department of Energy, Energy Information Administration, *Annual Energy Review: 1992,* pp. 275 and 281.

were loaned out, often to support investment projects in Third World countries without significant oil resources. A Third World investment boom occurred, but it collapsed during the early 1980s in the wake of further oil price increases, central bank efforts to combat the accompanying inflation, and recession. New elements of instability had infiltrated the world economy.

THE IRANIAN CRISES

The recession of the mid–1970s reduced the demand for OPEC oil, and partly as a result, nominal oil prices remained relatively stable for several years. See Figure 3.4.[28] But as growth resumed in the world economy, oil demand strengthened and markets tightened again. This interacted with another political event—the Iranian revolution of 1979—to initiate an even more dramatic round of price increases.

---

[28]The source is U.S. Department of Energy, *Annual Energy Review: 1992,* pp. 275 and 281. The prices are the "official" prices for 34° Saudi Arabian light crude f.o.b. Ras Tanura. Arm's length prices sometimes departed significantly from the "official" prices—above them in periods of tight supply, below them in slack markets.

Oil and politics had long been an explosive mixture in Iran.[29] In April 1951 Prime Minister Mohammed Mossadegh declared that the Anglo-Iranian Oil Company, British Petroleum's operating unit, was being nationalized without compensation. BP shut down the company's export operations and obtained help from both friendly governments and other oil companies, who pooled supplies to cover shortfalls caused by the loss of Iranian output. With its principal source of foreign exchange cut off, the Iranian economy plunged into economic crisis. American CIA and British MI–6 operatives orchestrated a plot to overthrow Mossadegh, securing inter alia the complicity of Shah Reza Pahlavi. When Mossadegh learned of an impending dismissal order from the Shah, he counterattacked, causing the Shah to flee to Rome. But with probable encouragement from the CIA, demonstrators filled the streets of Teheran on August 18, 1952, and when police and military elements joined in, Mossadegh fled. The Shah returned, and a new oil company consortium (with American, Dutch, and French participation) assumed de facto control of Iranian oil operations, even though ownership of the oil fields and equipment was shifted nominally to the Iranian government.

During the closing months of 1978, strikes and rioting escalated in protest against political repression and perceived departures from Shiite fundamentalist principles by the Iranian government. Strikers invaded the oil consortium's facilities, disrupting operations and insisting that output be cut, since, the intruders argued, the consumers in Western nations should lead more spartan lives. Beginning on December 25 and continuing for 69 days, exports ceased altogether. Iran had been exporting 4.5 million barrels of oil per day— 15 percent of OPEC's total 1978 production. Other OPEC nations had little spare capacity. Prices began to rise, and panic buying drove spot oil prices up from the $13 level that had prevailed during much of 1978 to $40 per barrel. After continuing debate over the right strategy, OPEC announced a series of official price increases converging by October 1981 to $34 per barrel.[30] The wealth transfer shock to the world economy was even larger than during the mid–1970s. The U.S. Federal Reserve concurrently initiated two waves of money supply tightening. Both industrialized and oil-poor developing nations lapsed into the most severe recession since the 1930s.

This time, however, OPEC overstepped the world economy's tolerance for price increases. The price level of $12 to $13 reached in 1974 had already hastened the development of major new non-OPEC oil such as Prudhoe Bay in Alaska and the North Sea between Scotland and Norway. Supplies from

---

[29]See Yergin, *The Prize*, pp. 450–478, from which this summary is drawn.

[30]"OPEC Meets in Secret on Prices, Cuts in Output," *New York Times*, Feb. 20, 1981, p. 1; "OPEC Price Agreement Is Considered Unlikely," *New York Times*, May 11, 1981, p. D1; and "OPEC's New Unity: How Durable Is It?" *New York Times*, November 2, 1981, p. D1.

sources other than OPEC and the Soviet Union increased from 19.2 million barrels per day in 1978 to 25.8 million barrels in 1985.[31] Recessions meanwhile curbed demand. OPEC production dropped from 31 million barrels per day in 1979 to 23 million in 1982, 18 million in 1984, and 16.6 million in 1985. See Figure 3.4. OPEC members tried to defend the price level by establishing national output quotas, but adherence was erratic. At first slowly and then dramatically, downward price adjustments were compelled. For a few months during mid–1986, until more rigid quotas were set, OPEC oil was selling in the range of $6 to $8 per barrel. OPEC's halcyon days had passed. Or at least, so it was believed.

MODELS OF CARTEL BEHAVIOR

To make sensible predictions about the future of OPEC, one must understand in greater detail how it has behaved in the past. On this, as on so many things, economists are not of a single mind. There are at least five contending theories of OPEC behavior: the competitive model, a "property rights" theory, the "target revenue" model, the cartel model (with many variants), and the "crutch" theory. We examine each with appropriate brevity.[32]

THE COMPETITIVE MODEL

The competitive model views oil as a depletable resource and assumes that oil resource holders have full information about both the size and cost of all potential reservoirs.[33] They then maximize the discounted present value of their profits over all time, assuming that their individual output decisions have no appreciable impact on price.[34] In its starkest form, the theory assumes that in year zero, all present and future sources can be arrayed on a

---

[31]See Adam Seymour, *The Oil Price and Non-OPEC Supplies* (Oxford, UK: Oxford Institute for Energy Studies, 1990).

[32]A much more thorough exploration is found in the collection edited by James Griffin and David Teece, *OPEC Behavior and World Oil Prices* (London: Allen & Unwin, 1982).

[33]The theory is attributable to Harold Hotelling, "The Economics of Exhaustible Resources," *Journal of Political Economy*, vol. 39 (April 1931), pp. 137–175.

[34]The theory also holds with minor modifications for monopolists. See Joseph E. Stiglitz, "Monopoly and the Rate of Extraction of Exhaustible Resources," *American Economic Review*, vol. 66 (September 1976), pp. 655–661. The equilibrium price trajectory under monopoly is higher in initial years and lower (because more oil reserves remain unexploited) in later years.

FIGURE 3.5
Shifting Supply Curves with Competitive
Extraction of Crude Oil

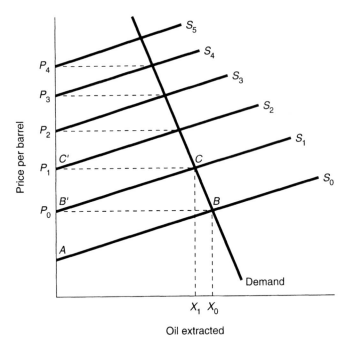

long-run oil supply curve S_0 (Figure 3.5), with the lowest-cost sources com-
prising the curve's most southwesterly segments, and with other sources
entailing progresssively increasing cost per barrel of oil extracted. Because a
million dollars of profit in the distant future is worth less than a million dollars in year zero—that is, future returns are discounted—the lowest-cost
sources are exploited first. (Demand is assumed only for simplicity to be
unchanging over time.) Thus, in year zero, output will be X_0, where supply S_0
meets demand, and the price will be P_0. As a result, segment AB of the supply
curve is gone forever. The remainder of the supply array (representing the
segment located to the right of point B) is shifted over to the zero output vertical, so that in period 1, the supply curve is $B'S_1$. The output will be X_1, sold at
price P_1. Segment $B'C$ of the supply curve is now exhausted, so the relevant
curve in period 2 is $C'S_2$, with still higher price P_2 and lower output X_2, and so
forth. The key point is that prices will tend to rise over time as the lower-cost
reservoirs are depleted.

The foresight assumed by this model is much more than what can be
exercised in the real world, but the essence of the matter can be grasped by
assuming that, with possible deviations due to forecasting errors and other
shocks, the prices of depletable resources tend to rise over time. Then a
profit-maximizing resource holder can be viewed as making a series of sim-

ple annual decisions: whether to extract the resource today, or wait and reassess the situation a year hence. We assume for simplicity that the real marginal cost of extraction will be the same (e.g., MC per barrel) in either case. The resource holder knows today's price and makes a prediction about next year's price. A real (i.e., constant-purchasing-power) dollar a year hence is worth less than a dollar today. Appropriately discounted, it is worth only $1/(1 + r)$, where r is the real rate of interest. Assume that prices are expected to rise at $100g$ percent per year, so oil that brings P_0 dollars today will yield $P_0 (1 + g)$ dollars a year hence. Our resource holder now compares:

$$P_0 - MC \quad vs. \quad \frac{P_0 (1 + g) - MC}{1 + r}$$

If the marginal extraction cost is zero and prices are rising at a rate exceeding the rate of interest, the resource holder keeps its oil in the ground; if they are rising at a rate less than the rate of interest, the oil will be extracted today. With positive extraction cost, similar logic applies, except that the decision may be tipped toward deferred extraction at lower interest rates; the more so, the higher MC is in relation to P_0.

The aggregate of all such extraction decisions affects the market price of oil. If, for example, many resource holders defer production because they expect large price increases, today's prices will rise, causing at least some resource owners to change their minds. The market attains equilibrium when:

$$(P - MC)_0 = \frac{(P - MC)_1}{(1 + r)} = \cdots = \frac{(P - MC)_t}{(1 + r)t}$$

where $(P - MC)_t$ is the (expected) difference between price and marginal cost in year t, and so on. The larger t is, the larger the denominator $(1 + r)^t$ will be, and so the more price must rise over time to keep the market in balance. If marginal extraction costs rise over time, prices must increase all the more to maintain equilibrium.

How might this theory explain the oil market events of the 1970s and 1980s? If some shock occurred, causing oil resource holders to expect either augmented future demand for their oil, or a markedly reduced rate of new resource discovery, producers would hold back their supplies to take advantage of higher future prices, thereby driving current prices higher. Even though demand was usually (but temporarily) strong in 1973 and 1979, there is no evidence of a change in expectations sufficiently large, and sufficiently sudden, to induce the output and price swings actually observed. Nor does it seem plausible that between 1982 and 1986 OPEC members came to believe that the rate of resource discovery would be appreciably higher than previously expected in the foreseeable future, warranting reduced prices. Indeed, in that interval, Alaskan and North Sea reserve accretions were ebbing, and there were signs of depletion even in the massive Saudi Arabian fields.[35] Over the very long run of decades or even centuries, oil resource holders must sooner or later bring their decisions into accord with the competitive model. But predictions of impending oil reserve shortfalls have been wrong sufficiently often in the past to warrant skepticism whether the full-information competitive theory holds, or at least has held, even over the very long run.[36]

PROPERTY RIGHTS

The property rights theory is much simpler. The events in Iran during 1951 and 1952 warned the international petroleum companies that their tenure was uncertain. During the early 1970s, extensive further nationalizations occurred. The nations who took total or majority control of their oil reserves, unlike the oil companies, presumably had more secure tenure. (We temporarily ignore the prominent counterexample of Kuwait in 1990 and 1991.) With more secure tenure, the oil-producing nations might reasonably apply lower discount rates to the future, and hence conserve more oil for the future. The oil companies, on the other hand, might have been well advised to extract as much oil as they could before they received their marching orders.[37] Thus, nationalization in the early 1970s led to production cutbacks, which precipitated a violent price rise.

Despite intrinsic plausibility, the theory's overall predictive power is weak. The second great price surge, in 1979–1981, is difficult to reconcile with the timing of most nationalizations. Nor can the theory explain the price collapse that followed. There is also evidence that in the period *before* nationalization, the host nations often complained about the slow rate at which the companies were producing and selling their oil—the opposite of what the theory asserts.[38] Thus one must seek other explanations.

TARGET REVENUE

The target revenue model asserts in commonsense terms that once a certain living standard is reached, individuals may react to income-raising wage or price increases by supplying less work or output, not more. Figure 3.6 illus-

---

[35]"Aramco's Tough Oil Search," *New York Times*, February 10, 1982, p. D1. On the resurgence of non-OPEC production in the 1990s, see "OPEC Rivals Curb Cartel Impact," *New York Times*, December 27, 1994, p. D1.

[36]See Morris A. Adelman, "Mineral Depletion, with Special Reference to Petroleum," *Review of Economics and Statistics*, vol. 72 (February 1990), pp. 1–10.

[37]See, for example the quotation from an unnamed Saudi Arabian economist: "Aramco is a foreign beast here just to exploit our wealth. . . . Its only concern is to produce as much oil as possible, as rapidly as possible, at the least possible cost." "Aramco's Tough Oil Search," p. D7.

[38]See Adelman, "Mineral Depletion," p. 7.

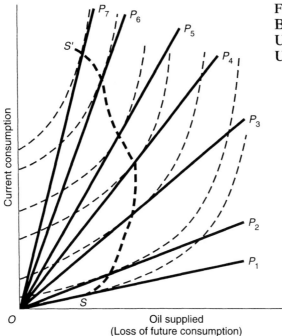

FIGURE 3.6
**Backward-Bending Supply
Under Target Revenue
Utility Maximization**

trates the underlying theory. It depicts the preferences of an oil-producing nation's citizens whose income depends entirely upon the sale of petroleum or its products. The horizontal axis measures the quantity of oil supplied this year, the vertical axis this year's consumption of goods and services (paid for with the money received from selling oil). Supplying more oil this year means that there will be less oil to supply in future years, and hence less future consumption, all else equal. Oil supply is a "bad," not a "good." Consumption is perceived as a good. Thus, the nation's collective indifference curves (light dashed lines) have the general northeast-sloping convex downward shape shown in the diagram. Oil is sold at a fixed price per barrel. Revenue supporting consumption is zero if no oil is sold and rises linearly with the amount sold (solid lines from the origin). The higher the price per barrel of oil, the steeper the revenue line. For a given price and hence revenue line, the oil-producing nation tries to reach the highest possible indifference curve—that is, at a tangency point. The locus of tangents SS' (heavy dashed line) is the nation's supply curve. It reveals that at low prices, an increase in the price leads to more output. But at high prices, when the nation enjoys great affluence this year, further price increases induce lower, not higher, supply. This, of course, is what happened in the aggregate with the price increases of 1973–1974 and 1978–1981.

A sufficiently rapid diminution of the marginal utility from current consumption assures that the pattern depicted will hold. Sharply diminishing

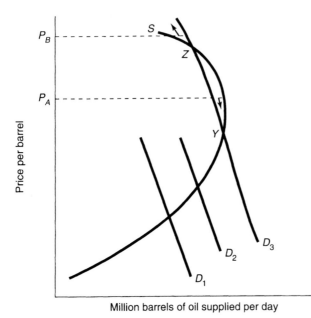

FIGURE 3.7
Price Instability with a Backward-Bending Supply Curve for Crude Oil

marginal utility seems especially plausible in ascetic societies—for example, those in which Muslim fundamentalist instincts are strong. However, the theory holds much better for a few nations (e.g., Libya, post-Khomeini Iran, and Saudi Arabia) than for others. The citizens of very poor, overpopulated nations such as Nigeria and Indonesia plainly had not reached target income levels. Even in sparsely populated, oil-rich Saudi Arabia and Kuwait, high levels of consumption appear to be addictive. The leaders of Iraq, Iran, and even Libya exhibited virtually insatiable demand for weapons, if not for consumer goods. And the theory fits poorly with evidence of most member nations' demands, in OPEC meetings, for increased oil output quotas during the high-price, low-output years of the 1980s.

To the extent that the choice pattern suggested by Figure 3.6 holds with any generality, the supply curve for oil may be backward-bending.[39] This phenomenon can lead to unusual market dynamics, illustrated in Figure 3.7. The supply curve is given by S. Demand grows over time. At some moment it shifts to D_3, which yields two equilibrium points Y and Z. If for some reason the price is set too high (e.g., through miscalculation), at OP_A, the quantity supplied will exceed the quantity demanded, so the price will fall and restore

---

[39] There are indications of backward-bending supply curves in U.S. agriculture during the early 1930s, as plantings increased with a sharp fall in prices. (See Figure 2.2 on page 20.)

equilibrium. Well and good. But if a big error is made and the price is set at OP_B, the quantity demanded exceeds the quantity supplied, and the price must rise even more in a possible disequilibrium spiral. One might argue that this happened during the late 1970s. However, constraining forces not shown in the diagram probably exist. In particular, at some high price demand becomes much more elastic, as the experience of the early 1980s suggests. The demand curve may then bend backward more than the supply curve, restoring equilibrium.

CARTEL THEORIES

One can hardly deny that OPEC is a cartel. Its members meet regularly to discuss how they can coordinate their actions toward the objective of achieving high prices and profits. From those discussions, decisions are made.[40] The discussions reflect an awareness that the OPEC members' actions are constrained by the reactions of non-OPEC oil sources and consumers to their decisions. Thus, one key question is how much monopoly power OPEC collectively enjoys. Also, when the national oil ministers return home from OPEC conferences, they do not always do what they agreed to do. Instead, they "chisel" on the agreements in a variety of ways. Given this, can OPEC be said to be an *effective* cartel?

OPEC is plainly not the only supplier of oil. Its share of the world's oil consumption ranged from 56 percent in 1973, the year in whose closing months dramatic price increases began, down to 31 percent in 1985, the year preceding sharp but temporary price decreases. In 1978–1981, when an Iranian crisis triggered a second round of major price increases, its share averaged 48 percent. Evidently, its power is correlated at least to some extent with supplying a considerable fraction of the world's needs.

At least as important from a long-run strategic perspective is OPEC's share of the world's proven crude oil reserves—approximately 77 percent in 1992.[41] Thus, barring major structural shifts, OPEC will continue to be in a strong position. Indeed, unless new reserves are discovered at a vastly disproportionate rate outside OPEC, the larger the non-OPEC share of world oil supply is in any given year, the greater will be the market share OPEC members can expect to hold in future years as nonmember nations exhaust their reserves more rapidly than OPEC does.

---

[40]Do the activities of OPEC violate U.S. antitrust laws prohibiting collusion? In a suit following the 1973–1974 price hikes, a U.S. appellate court ruled that OPEC's actions were "acts of state" beyond the reach of the U.S. courts. International Association of Machinists and Aerospace Workers v. OPEC et al., 649 F. 2d 1354 (1981).

[41]U.S. Department of Energy, *Annual Energy Review: 1992*, p. 271. The share of the United States, Canada, and Mexico combined was 8.2 percent.

FIGURE 3.8
How the Incentive to Chisel Varies with Demand at
a Fixed Cartel Price

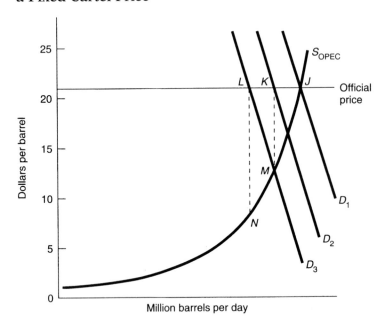

Like all cartels, OPEC is vulnerable to "chiseling" by its members. Figure 3.8 repeats in the oil context the lesson we have already learned from agriculture. S_{OPEC} is the supply curve for OPEC oil. Much of it lies in the range of $1 to $5 per barrel, because most Middle Eastern oil comes from large, relatively shallow wells with very low production costs. Assume that OPEC has set an average price of $21 per barrel. If the demand for OPEC oil (after subtracting out the supply of non-OPEC sources[42]) is strong at that price (i.e., D_1), OPEC will have no difficulty maintaining price discipline. Indeed, its producers can function as independent competitors, setting marginal cost equal to price, and the market will clear. But if demand is weaker at D_2, OPEC members will have to restrict their output by the amount KJ relative to the quantity they would supply equating marginal cost with price. Now an incentive to chisel arises. For the average OPEC member, the gap between the $21 price and the cost of producing an additional barrel of oil is KM, or about $8 per barrel. There is a real temptation to chisel and sell some above-quota output at a price a dollar or so below the official price. If demand is even weaker at D_3, the incentive to chisel increases to LN, or about $13 per barrel. The temptation may at this level become irresistible. Quite generally, the more OPEC members collec-

---

[42]The relevant theory will be presented more fully in Chapter 5.

tively restrict their output below the $P = MC$ point or, slightly inaccurately, the more excess capacity they have, the stronger will be the incentive to chisel. Even with very weak demand D_3, that tendency can be suppressed by cutting the official price—that is, to $8 per barrel. But this would entail enormous collective losses for the OPEC members. It is far more sensible for them to use some mechanism—whose instruments could range from moral suasion to war—to keep chiseling within tolerable bounds.

Complicating the members' coordination problem is the fact that crude petroleum is not a homogeneous commodity. Lighter crudes (those with relatively *high* gravity numbers, on the order of 34 to 37) yield more gasoline, or a given fraction of gasoline with less costly refining, and therefore command a price premium. For similar reasons, low-sulfur oils (e.g., from Nigeria and the North Sea) command a price premium over high-sulfur oils (e.g., from Venezuela). Oil located near major markets (as in Libya) is more valuable than, say, oil in Kuwait. This is well understood, but it is hard to get the differentials right. They vary with the time of year (the demand for gasoline, and hence light oil, is relatively stronger in the summer), the availability of transportation media, and the like. During the 1970s and early 1980s, OPEC members quarreled incessantly about them at their meetings.[43] The difficulty of solving the differential problem is a principal reason why OPEC shifted its emphasis in 1983 from setting a benchmark price (for Arabian 34° light crude at the Ras Tanura port) to individual member physical production quotas.[44]

Even more difficulty comes from the great differences in aspirations of the various OPEC members. Some are sparsely populated but quite rich. For them the target revenue model may serve as a first approximation. Others are densely populated and relatively poor. Some have abundant oil reserves, others meager reserves. The relatively poor countries tend in OPEC discussions to support high prices and to insist that they be accorded generous output quotas. During the 1970s Iran, led by a shah with grandiose dreams of empire for his large and relatively poor population, was a strong advocate of high prices. Saudi Arabia, with much higher oil revenues per capita, favored price restraint. Analyses it had commissioned with U.S. consulting firms suggested (in hindsight, correctly) that if the price were elevated much above $18 or $20, OPEC would lose sales rapidly to other energy sources and conservation. With reserves that were expected to last 100 years at its current output levels, Saudi Arabia was in a good position to take the long view. During the 1980s, nations (such as Iran and Iraq) bearing enormous war expenses consistently supported high prices and large output shares for themselves. Difficult compromises had to be made.

So great were the differences among the OPEC members that some were willing to go to war over them. The invasion of Kuwait by Iraq is the case in

---

[43]See, for example, "A Threat to OPEC's Unity," *Business Week,* January 26, 1976, p. 91; and "The Nigerian Oil Price Battle," *New York Times,* April 9, 1982, pp. D1 and D3.

[44]"Communique by OPEC," *New York Times,* March 15, 1983, p. D22.

point. Iraq had two widely publicized grievances against Kuwait. One was the Rumaila oil field, an oval-shaped 50-mile long reservoir extending on a north-south axis, with its southern tip stretching across the border into Kuwait. Kuwait was draining the field at a rate Iraqis considered excessive—a classic example of the common-pool problem. Second, during the 1980s Kuwait had used some of its oil-based wealth to integrate vertically "downstream," building refining capacity at home and buying two additional refineries and 4800 retail gasoline stations in Europe.[45] To keep these operations supplied, it insisted that it needed to produce 1.5 million barrels of crude oil per day. At an OPEC meeting during the first week of June 1989, Kuwait was assigned a quota of only 1.09 million barrels, which it subsequently exceeded by a wide margin. Deeply in debt after a debilitating eight-year war with Iran, Iraq viewed Kuwait's actions (and also those of the United Arab Emirates) as a threat to price stability, and hence to Iraq's revenues. On July 15, 1990, Iraq moved several divisions of its Republican Guards to its border with Kuwait, and on July 17, President Saddam Hussein threatened military action against Arab nations that did not curb their production. He is quoted as saying:[46]

> Iraqis will not forget the saying that cutting necks is better than cutting means of living. . . . O God almighty, be witness that we have warned them. If words fail to protect Iraqis, something effective must be done to return things to their natural course and to return usurped rights to their owners.

Sixteen days later Iraq invaded Kuwait, touching off a brief war in which the Iraqi army was routed by allied U.S., European, and several Middle Eastern national forces.

More frequently, the members of OPEC tried to limit their chiseling to levels that would provoke neither military nor economic retaliation. The conduct of Nigeria is illustrative. Its production capacity was somewhat in excess of 2 million barrels per day. It was often accused, no doubt correctly, of chiseling, but between 1982 and 1987, its average daily output was 1.37 million barrels per day. During this period Nigeria was under heavy pressure from the World Bank to reform its economy, among other things to reduce a large balance of payments deficit. By chiseling on a widespread scale, it could have sold an additional 600,000 barrels of oil daily. At average 1984–1987 prices of $23 per barrel, it could have added nearly $5 billion annually to its exports. But it chose not to. Asked why, a Nigerian economist explained to the author, "If we heavily discount our oil sales, the other OPEC nations cannot help but match our discounts, and then we will all end up selling our oil for less." This attitude epitomizes the thinking of a reasonably loyal cartel member.

---

[45]"Kuwait's Oil Industry: Tomorrow the World," *The Economist*, June 24, 1989, p. 82.

[46]"Iraq Threatens Emirates and Kuwait on Oil Glut," *New York Times*, July 18, 1990, p. D1.

OPEC was also strengthened by the willingness of some members to sacrifice for the greater good of the cartel. Saudi Arabia is the most important example. Throughout the 1970s and 1980s, OPEC's total oil-producing capacity was approximately 30 million barrels per day, while Saudi Arabia's varied between 9 and 11 million barrels—by far the largest share of any member. Saudi Arabia seldom reached that level of output, and when the OPEC price structure was threatened by excess capacity and chiseling, it reduced its own output to relieve the pressure. Thus, during the OPEC-induced recession of 1975, it cut its production from 8.5 to 5.6 million barrels per day.[47] When demand recovered, it returned to higher output levels.

As Figure 3.4 reveals, the events of the late 1970s and early 1980s led to a much more serious drop in OPEC demand. Saudi Arabia resisted the move to $34 price levels for long-run strategic reasons, but it provided key support in 1981 by effecting a 10 percent output reduction.[48] It continued making disproportionate cuts as the imbalance worsened—to an average of 6.5 million barrels per day in 1982, 5.1 million in 1983, 4.7 million in 1984, and 3.4 million in 1985. During the summer of 1985, it was producing only slightly more than 2 million barrels per day and running a significant national government budget deficit (including oil revenues). But then it changed policy visibly, doubling its output in the closing months of 1985.[49] There were two reasons. First, its industrial infrastructure needed the by-product natural gas resulting from producing at least 4 million barrels of oil per day. But second and probably more important, it had decided to act as disciplinarian to the cartel. Prices dropped from an average of $25 per barrel in 1985 to roughly $10 in mid–1986. Through its actions as well as its words, Saudi Arabia communicated to its fellow members, "Unless we all cooperate and restrict output, we are doomed to sell at low prices." The message was received, and at a special OPEC meeting in August, new and more stringent output quotas were accepted. Prices rose briskly into the $14–$16 range. However, Saudi Arabia's efforts aroused so much antipathy both at home and abroad that its oil minister was fired from his job.[50] He was replaced by a new minister committed to keeping the nation's output above 4.3 million barrels per day. Saudi Arabia continued to threaten output increases if other members did not adhere to

---

[47]"Excerpts from Sheik Yamani's news conference at OPEC Meeting," *New York Times,* December 18, 1976, p. 32.

[48]"Unified Price Eludes OPEC,"*International Herald-Tribune,* August 22, 1981, p. 1.

[49]See, for example, "Saudi Arabia Plays High-Stakes Game," *New York Times,* January 24, 1986, p. D1; "Belt-Tightening by Saudis," *New York Times,* January 28, 1986, p. D1; "Why the Saudis Keep Talking the Price of Oil Down," *Business Week,* March 17, 1986, p. 52; and "OPEC Panel To Tackle Pricing," *New York Times,* November 14, 1986, p. D1.

[50]"Yamani Caught in a Crossfire," *New York Times,* October 31, 1986, p. D1.

their quotas.[51] Nevertheless, as the Kuwait-Iraq dispute shows, deviations persisted.

Following the war of 1990–1991, Saudi Arabia announced plans to increase its oil extraction and storage capacity.[52] These were said to be components of a Saudi effort to stabilize oil prices at levels sufficiently restrained to preserve OPEC's role as the world's paramount petroleum supplier. They also reflect the increased need of Saudi Arabia for oil revenues to service its large Iraqi war debt and perhaps greater disillusion with the behavior of its fellow Arab nations. Because of these changes, an important pillar supporting OPEC's ability to sustain elevated prices was weakened.

THE CRUTCH THEORY

Still another interpretation of history argues that OPEC would not have succeeded in its efforts to raise oil prices, especially during the early 1970s, without the active support of the integrated international oil companies. This "crutch" theory is illustrated for the case of Exxon in Figure 3.9. Exxon had numerous oil-producing concessions from foreign governments, including a 30 percent interest in Aramco. It also owned outright substantial crude oil reserves in the United States and elsewhere. Crude oil must move through elaborate transportation channels to refineries, of which Exxon was a major operator, in the United States, Europe, and Asia. As a transporter and refiner–purchaser of oil, Exxon might behave in either of two ways toward the oil of its foreign hosts. It could play one government off against the others, trying to bargain prices down and get the best deal possible for its refineries. Or it could cooperate to ensure that oil flowed to the refineries with a minimum of disruption, including disruption to the price structure.

It is easy to see in the structure of Figure 3.9 powerful incentives for choosing the minimum-disruption strategy. In 1970, for example, Exxon owned in the United States and Canada alone 6.6 billion barrels of proven crude oil reserves.[53] The OPEC price actions of 1973–1974 raised the value of owned reserves by approximately $9 per barrel. Thus, ignoring extraction tim-

---

[51]"Saudi Threat To Raise Oil Output," *New York Times*, October 5, 1988, p. D1; and "The Saudis Use 'Pain' To Pressure OPEC," *New York Times*, November 3, 1988, p. 1.

[52]"Saudis Increasing Oil Storage," *New York Times*, September 4, 1991, p. D1; and "Saudis Say They'll Lift Oil Output," *New York Times*, November 27, 1991, p. D1. The program was phased down when capacity reached 10 million barrels per day. "Saudi Arabia: ARAMCO Poised for Upstream Development Cuts," *Weekly Petroleum Argus*, October 25, 1993, p. 3. Before nationalization of its concession began in 1970, Aramco had developed plans to expand its production capacity from 12 to 20 million barrels per day by 1983. With 8 million barrels more per day of capacity, OPEC would have had much greater difficulty sustaining high prices.

[53]Federal Trade Commission staff report, *Concentration Levels and Trends in the Energy Sector of the U.S. Economy* (Washington, DC: USGPO, March 1974), p. 39.

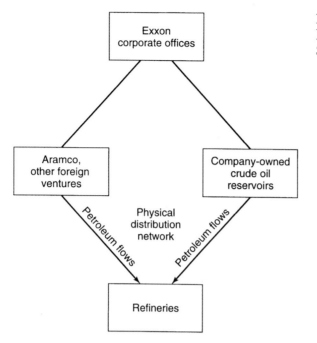

FIGURE 3.9
Exxon's Vertical Structure

ing complications, the price increases conferred upon Exxon a windfall capital gain of approximately 9×6.6 billion = $59.4 billion. Who could resist cooperating in such an arrangement?

We will probably never know whether Exxon and other companies consciously adhered to the logic of the crutch theory.[54] The most one can say is that there are counterarguments, both logical and factual. The major oil companies had an incentive to cooperate with their national hosts to avoid nationalization on unfavorable terms and to maintain in tight markets their access to crude oil, vital for efficient refinery operation, as well as to enhance the value of their owned reserves. The oil companies visibly defied Arab nations' boycott of the United States and the Netherlands during the Yom Kippur war of 1973. In 1982 the Aramco partners shifted substantial purchases away from Saudi Arabia because they considered Saudi oil too high-priced.[55] In 1983 they again threatened to reduce their Saudi purchases unless prices were reduced.[56] And even if the companies did generally cooperate to support high prices, it

_____

[54]Knowledge on such matters is not easily obtained. The head of a Federal Trade Commission task force investigating the international petroleum cartel during the early 1950s was found dead by mysterious causes in a New York subway station.

[55]"Shift Seen in Oil Sales by Saudis," _New York Times,_ August 16, 1982, p. D1.

[56]"Narrowing Options for Saudi Oil Policy," _Business Week,_ January 17, 1983, p. 35. The force of the example is blunted by the fact that the companies also asked Saudi Arabia to stabilize prices by cutting production and sustaining price floors.

might be argued that theirs was not an indispensable crutch, since the OPEC nations could (and later did) develop their own channels of distribution to the refinery market. Indeed, as the example of Kuwait suggests, the nations' vertical integration into refining and marketing may, while providing more secure market access for individual nations, make it more difficult to avoid quota chiseling and sustain collective OPEC pricing discipline.[57]

CONSUMING NATIONS' REACTIONS TO OPEC

Although we know a considerable amount about what makes OPEC tick, we do not know enough to apportion precise weights to the contending behavioral theories. Clearly, the cartel theory goes a long way toward explaining OPEC's successes and failures.[58] Among other things, it emphasizes as a critical variable the tightness or slackness of the crude oil market. If demand rises to press hard against available production capacity, OPEC will remain strong. There is also some intrinsic and evidentiary support, albeit less compelling, for other theories. Truth probably lies in some complex explanatory amalgam.

Having come as far as we can toward understanding OPEC, we must now examine how consuming nations, and especially the United States, responded to its economic challenges.

A few responses must be reported only summarily. Since the United States had become critically dependent upon imports, the import quotas were ended. In 1975, percentage depletion tax allowances were terminated for all but stripper wells. In 1976 the United States Senate considered a series of bills that would divest the refining and marketing operations of the largest U.S. petroleum companies from their crude oil activities.[59] The bills were offered in the belief that large, vertically integrated petroleum companies contributed to monopolistically high prices by acting as a "crutch" for OPEC and by making it difficult for smaller independent refiners and marketers to secure crude oil and gasoline supplies. A divestiture bill was voted out of subcommittee but went no further.[60] Even before the first OPEC shock, the Federal Trade Com-

---

[57]See "Refined Accent," *The Economist*, October 17, 1987, p. 81; "Why the Kings of Crude Want to Be Pump Boys," *Business Week*, March 21, 1988, p. 110; and "Merger Unleashes New Powerhouse," *Financial Times*, June 17, 1993.

[58]In a statistical analysis covering the years 1971–1983, James M. Griffin tests the cartel, competitive, target revenue, and property rights models and finds the strongest support for the cartel hypothesis. "OPEC Behavior: A Test of Alternative Hypotheses," *American Economic Review*, vol. 75 (December 1985), pp. 954–963.

[59]See "Hill Unit Votes Oil Breakup," *Washington Post*, April 2, 1976, p. A23; and U.S. Senate Committee on the Judiciary, Subcommittee on Antitrust and Monopoly, Hearings, *The Petroleum Industry* (Washington, DC: USGPO, 1976), Parts 1–3.

[60]A similar antitrust action in Canada was also dismissed. See the Restrictive Practices Commission's *Report on Competition in the Canadian Petroleum Industry* (Ottawa: RPC, June 1986).

mission brought an antitrust action alleging collective monopolization of the petroleum industry by the eight largest U.S. petroleum companies. The suit was eventually abandoned for lack of sufficient evidence.

PRICE CONTROLS

Price controls received much more emphasis during the 1970s. Beginning in August 1971, the U.S. government implemented a series of economywide price control measures in an effort to combat mounting inflationary pressures. The controls were phased out for most industries in 1973, but they were retained for petroleum. While a new control program was being developed, OPEC raised its prices in the wake of the Yom Kippur war. This threatened to elevate U.S. prices apace, since in a freely functioning market, domestic producers would not choose to offer their crude oil at prices less than those being paid to import substantial quantities of OPEC oil.

The situation in the U.S. petroleum market as 1973 gave way to 1974 can be characterized by Figure 3.10. Without the OPEC shock, crude oil would have been selling in the United States at prices averaging $5 per barrel. This was insufficient to satisfy domestic demand, so the balance had to be made up by imported oil. The domestic supply curve is given by S_{DOM} and domestic demand, quite inelastic in the short run, by D. Had demand been satisfied

FIGURE 3.10
Changing Crude Oil Import Prices and Windfall Profits to Domestic Oil Producers

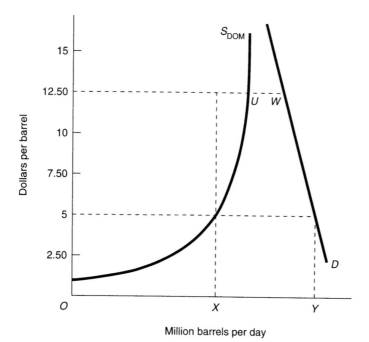

Million barrels per day

autarkically (i.e., entirely from domestic sources), the price would have risen to unknown but very high levels. Imports filled the gap, however, so that the market could be served at $5, with *OX* being drawn from domestic wells and *XY* as imports. As OPEC prices rose to approximately $11, and adding transportation charges of roughly $1.50, the U.S. market would clear at a price of $12.50. In the short run, some small expansion of domestic supply from existing wells would occur, and demand would be curbed owing to the substantial price elevation. Thus, imports would be reduced to *UW*. But here is the crucial point: On the quantity of oil *OX* domestic wells would have supplied in any event at the old $5 price, a new price of $12.50 is realized. The difference of $7.50 per barrel is called (pejoratively) a windfall profit. The quantity *OX* works out to approximately 3.3 billion barrels of domestic crude per year. Thus, the annual income windfall (before taxes) to U.S. crude oil resource owners because of the OPEC shock was on the order of $7.50 × 3.3 billion = $25 billion. The cry arose, why should already wealthy oil producers realize such a huge windfall due to the actions of a foreign cartel? And wasn't the windfall even more objectionable if the major petroleum companies had acted as a crutch for OPEC in implementing the price increases?

Another consideration argued in the opposite direction. The United States (and other nations) were dependent upon OPEC and were being exploited by it. Should they not try to become less dependent? One way to do so was to find and produce additional domestic oil. But confiscating the windfall by putting a ceiling on domestic oil prices would reduce the incentive to discover more domestic oil. In this respect, price controls were counterproductive.

To resolve this dilemma, federal government policymakers implemented in late 1973 a complex and ingenious scheme called "two-tier" price controls.[61] Under it, oil from domestic wells was divided into two main categories.[62] "Old oil" was oil from wells that were already developed and flowing by December 31, 1972. "New oil" included oil from wells brought onstream after then, oil from "stripper" wells producing less than 10 barrels per day, and increments of output above 1972 levels from old oil wells. The price of old oil was fixed at modest preshock levels (e.g., as the controls program stood in 1975, at $5.03 per barrel).[63] But the price of new oil was allowed to float up to world market levels (e.g., approximately $12.50). The

---

[61]The theoretical analysis here is based upon Calvin T. Roush, Jr., *Effects of Federal Price and Allocation Regulations on the Petroleum Industry*, Federal Trade Commission Bureau of Economics staff report (Washington, DC: December 1976); and Joseph P. Kalt, *The Economics and Politics of Oil Price Regulation* (Cambridge: MIT Press, 1981).

[62]The actual classifications changed over time in complex ways.

[63]Prices varied by geographic location and gravity. We use here the values reported in Kalt, *The Economics and Politics of Oil Regulation,* rather than the slightly different values in Roush, *Effects of . . . Regulations.*

FIGURE 3.11
Two-Tier Crude Oil Price Controls, 1975

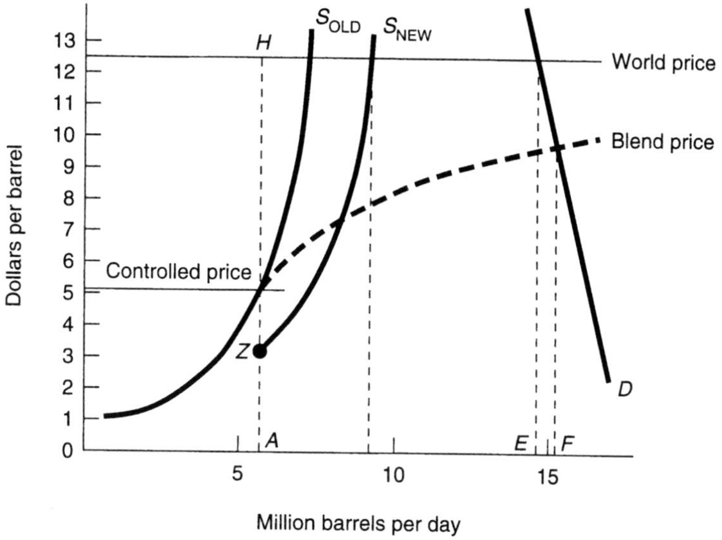

Million barrels per day

low price for "old oil" captured windfall profits; the high price for "new oil" left incentives in place for investments to enhance domestic supply.[64]

Figure 3.11 illustrates how the controls system worked as of 1975. D is the demand curve (derived from product demand, and subtracting out refining and marketing costs) for all crude petroleum utilized in the United States. The domestic supply side has to be characterized in terms of two curves, one for old oil S_{OLD} and one for new oil S_{NEW}. At the controlled price of $5.03 per barrel, 5.7 million barrels of old oil per day will be supplied. The first unusual feature of the diagram comes in the placement of the new oil supply curve. Its zero point is the point Z at which the supply of old oil ends—that is, along the vertical line AH. The curve lies generally higher than the old oil supply curve because smaller, deeper, and offshore sources predominate. The new oil's price floats up to the delivered world price level of $12.50. At that price, approximately 3.5 million barrels of new oil (including oil from old stripper wells) are supplied in 1975. The remaining demand is supplied by imported oil—that is, approximately 6 million barrels per day.

Windfall profits are captured by suppressing the price of old oil. Who benefits, if not domestic oil producers? The government's initial intent was to force the savings out into the hands of consumers by requiring the refiners

---

[64]It also created incentives to misclassify old oil as new oil. On the most elaborate scheme, see "Rich Case Snares Clarendon," *New York Times*, October 29, 1983, p. D1.

who buy the oil to set *their* prices in such a way as to cover only the $5.03 controlled price on any old oil they use, while costing out new and imported oil at the market price of $12.50. They did this by computing a *blend price*, which is given by:

$$\text{Blend Price} = \frac{(Q_{OLD} \times \$5.03) + [(Q_{NEW} + Q_{IMPORT}) \times \$12.50]}{Q_{OLD} + Q_{NEW} + Q_{IMPORT}}$$

where Q_{OLD} is the quantity of old oil, Q_{NEW} the quantity of new oil, and Q_{IMPORT} the quantity of imported oil processed by the refinery. If nothing but old oil is processed, the refinery's oil cost will be $5.03 per barrel. Once new or imported oil is used, the blend price rises, to a limit of $12.50 per barrel. The blend price is a weighted average of the prices of the crude inputs. It is shown by the dashed line marked "Blend Price" in Figure 3.11. Because a substantial quantity of old oil is included in the blend at the point where the blend price curve intersects the market demand curve, the price confronting the demanders of oil (ultimately, after accounting for refining costs, consumers) is approximately $9.72 per barrel—well below the world price of $12.50. Consumers respond to the bargain by consuming more oil products than they would if all oil were sold at the world market price of $12.50. Total consumption rises then by the amount *EF* in Figure 3.11.

There remained a complication which became evident soon after the two-tier price controls system was implemented. Consider an integrated petroleum company that owns reserves of both old and new crude oil, operates refineries, and supplies a chain of gasoline stations carrying its brand name. What oil will it channel to its own refineries? The cheap old oil, of course, because, after the savings are passed down the line, that gives its retail stations a strategic advantage. And to whom will it transfer any extra new or imported oil it might have? To independent refiner customers, of course. Thus, in February of 1974, the refineries of major integrated companies such as Exxon, Gulf, and Texaco reported average input blend prices of $8.20 per barrel, while large independent refiners such as Clark, Hess, and Murphy lacking their own crude oil sources averaged $10.50. Traditionally, independent refiners' gasoline was priced at retail 2 to 3 cents below major companies' prices. The crude oil input cost disadvantage, amounting to more than 5 cents per gallon of refined product, forced independents to raise their product prices *above* those of the majors. Needless to say, the independents complained bitterly to Washington.

Consequently, the crude oil *entitlements* program was initiated in November 1974. Under it, as a first approximation, each refinery was entitled to price-controlled old oil in proportion to overall national usage of old oil. In 1975, for example, 37.6 percent of the refinery inputs were of old oil, and that was, barring certain complications, the fraction to which a given refinery was entitled. But the old oil was not physically located in such a way that this equality of usage could occur. To appreciate what was done, consider two cases. One is an Oklahoma refinery processing 100,000 barrels of oil per day, 80 percent of it old oil. It is entitled to 37,600 barrels of old oil and exceeds its entitlement by 42,400 barrels. Using an extra barrel of old oil at $5.03 in place of a barrel of new or imported oil at $12.50, it saves $7.47—the value of a barrel-per-day entitlement. So at the end of the month it must write a check to the Department of the Interior for $7.47 times 42,400 times the number of days in the month to compensate for its excess usage of price-controlled oil. Now consider a refinery at Marcus Hook, Pennsylvania, processing 100,000 barrels per day, all of it imported. It is entitled to but does not process 37,600 barrels of price-controlled oil per day. So at the end of the month, the Department of the Interior *sends* it a check for $7.47 times 37,600 times the number of days in the month. In this way, the costs of oil per barrel, after all checks changed hands, were equalized across refineries.

Congress seldom leaves matters so simple, however—not, at least, in the oil patch. Because small, typically independent refiners customarily sold their products at lower prices than did the large major companies, Congress considered them especially important to maintaining competition in the petroleum industry. Old oil entitlements were therefore awarded on a sliding scale—the smaller the refinery, the larger the fraction of its throughput was entitled to be of price-controlled oil. The excess value of these preferential entitlements amounted to approximately $9 million per year in 1978 for a refinery with a throughput of 30,000 barrels per day.[65] Even though there was excess capacity in the refining industry, entrepreneurs reacted by building new "teakettle" refineries too small to be efficient, but able to thrive on the value of their preferential entitlements. Later, in the six years after the entitlements system was phased out, a correction occurred. One hundred ten refineries, mostly with capacities below 30,000 barrels per day and mostly built after 1973, were closed.[66]

The basic objective of the petroleum price control program was to capture the windfall profits crude oil owners would have received owing to OPEC's actions and to pass them on to more worthy recipients—notably, American petroleum product consumers. Economists who have analyzed the program disagree on the extent to which consumers actually benefited. Some claim that the price controls on refiners were largely ineffective, so refiners captured most of the windfalls.[67] However, this view is almost surely wrong. The

---

[65]Kalt, *The Economics and Politics of Oil Price Regulation*, p. 59.

[66]Neil Lloyd, "The Impact of the Small Refiner Bias on the Structure of the U.S. Petroleum Industry," econometrics seminar paper, Swarthmore College, 1986.

[67]Among other things, refiner-level price controls were ended in 1976 on heavy and intermediate (i.e., home heating) oils. But even without controls, refiners might have been under sufficient pressure from petroleum product imports that their price-raising was constrained. The contending arguments are reviewed in Kalt, *The Economics and Politics of Oil Price Regulation*, Chapter 4. Kalt's best-guess statistical estimate is that 40 percent of the windfalls was passed through to consumers. However, better-specified statistical analyses suggest passthrough rates nearer 100 percent. See the testimony of William Hogan in U.S. Department of Energy, *In the Matter of Stripper Well Exemption Litigation*, transcript, pp. 3300–3363 (September 1984).

controls accompanied by the entitlement system reduced crude oil costs, both average and marginal, below world oil prices for virtually all refiners. As a result, they encouraged refiners to expand output beyond the level they would have set if all crude oil input prices floated up to equal world prices.

Considering the 1975 data presented earlier, the blend price was $9.72, or 22 percent less than the corresponding world price. Because refiners may have trapped some of the gains, that is a maximum estimate of the price reduction. The short-run elasticity of demand for crude oil is on the order of –0.1.[68] A 22 percent price reduction at that elasticity implies a 2.2 percent increase in the quantity demanded, or about 330,000 barrels per day. Over the longer run of several years, as consumers acquire fewer gas-guzzling automobiles, install insulation, and make other complementary durable goods adjustments, the elasticities may rise to as much as –0.6, implying demand augmentation approaching 2 million barrels per day. The actual effect of the 1970s controls probably lay within that range. The additional oil needed to supply that incremental demand did not come from the United States. If anything, despite good intentions, the price controls probably discouraged domestic petroleum production marginally. Rather, the oil came from imports, including imports from OPEC. Thus, the controls program *increased* the dependence of the United States upon OPEC. If consumption increased toward our upper-bound estimate, the world supply-demand balance could have been tightened sufficiently to strengthen appreciably OPEC's hand during the Iranian crisis of 1979–1981, permitting larger OPEC price increases than would have occurred in a looser market. But here we approach the limits of defensible counterfactual speculation.

FROM CONTROLS TO TAXATION

By 1975, the two-tier controls program's tendency to spur oil consumption, discourage domestic crude oil development, increase dependence upon OPEC, and stimulate inefficient investment in "teakettle" refineries was well understood. Efforts to end the program were defeated in Congress. But in a 1975 law renewing and amending the program, among other things bringing some new oil under price controls, the U.S. president was given the authority to begin phasing the controls out in 1979. President Jimmy Carter announced a 30-month phaseout beginning in May 1979. As the phaseout's final stages approached, oil well owners ceased producing oil still under controls to await the higher postcontrols price. Thus, when President Reagan announced an early end to the program on January 28, 1981, there was hardly any old oil to be had and hence hardly any to decontrol.

---

[68]See William W. Hogan, "OECD Oil Demand Dynamics: Trends and Asymmetries," *Energy Journal*, vol. 14 (1993), pp. 125–157.

Phaseout did not terminate concern with windfall profits, however. Indeed, rapid crude oil price increases caused by the Iranian crisis heightened congressional concern. To replace the petroleum price controls, President Carter recommended, and the Congress passed, a complex windfall profits tax law.[69] Like the previous controls, the new law distinguished among various types of oil wells, depending upon their age and productivity. There were three main categories. On "lower-tier" oil, from wells already flowing by December 31, 1978, any surplus of the actually realized price over $12.89 per barrel (escalated over time at the general inflation rate) was subjected to a 70 percent tax. On "upper-tier" oil, from new wells, a 30 percent tax would apply on the surplus of the actual price over $16.55 per barrel, the latter escalated at the general inflation rate plus two percent. Surplus revenues from "tertiary" oil—oil produced from old wells in excess of historical yield profiles as a result of enhanced recovery methods—were also subjected to a tax of only 30 percent. Alaskan north slope oil was exempted from the tax, and "stripper" oil was accorded complex special preferences, including the retention of percentage depletion.

The new law provided for automatic phaseout beginning in January 1988 or in the month after a cumulative total of $227 billion of windfall profit taxes had been received, whichever came later. This tax revenue target was based upon the assumption that prices, already high because of the Iranian crisis, would continue to rise. But as Figure 3.4 shows, OPEC prices, and hence U.S. crude oil prices, peaked in 1982 and then declined, at first gradually and then sharply. Meanwhile, inflation raised the thresholds above which windfall profits were to be taxed (e.g., in April 1988, to $19.50 for lower-tier oil and $28 for new oil). As a result, actual prices were below the recapture prices, no taxes were being collected, and cumulative revenue, far from reaching the $227 billion target anticipated in 1980, had mounted to only $80 billion.[70] To end substantial continuing administration costs, the law was repealed in 1988.

The windfall profits tax program placed a tax on, and hence reduced the net revenues from, newly discovered oil as well as old oil. In this respect, it impaired incentives for seeking new oil to a greater degree than did the two-tier price controls of the 1970s. However, drilling activity was much more sensitive to the general level of, and expectations concerning, crude oil prices than to the marginal impact of windfall profits taxes. The number of exploratory oil and gas wells drilled in the United States peaked in 1981 and declined precipitously after 1985 with the collapse of OPEC prices. See Figure

---

[69]See "Oil Compromise Opens Way for Final Tax Action," *New York Times*, January 23, 1980, p. D1; and "Oil-Profits Bill Contains Variety of Compromises," *New York Times*, February 25, 1980, p. D1.

[70]"Carter Oil Tax Hangs by a Thread," *New York Times*, April 11, 1988, p. D10.

FIGURE 3.12
**Trends in U.S. Exploratory Oil and Gas Well
Drilling, 1960–1992**

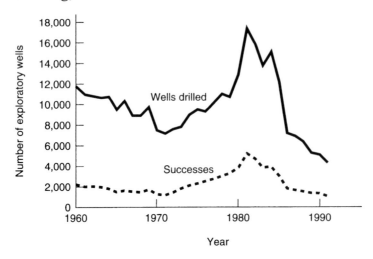

Source: American Petroleum Institute, *Basic Petroleum Data Book*
(Washington, DC: API, September 1992), Section III, Table 1a.

3.12.[71] Similar movements are evident in the number of successful
exploratory wells. The end of windfall profits taxation brought no discernible
increase in drilling.[72] Due to the relatively low level of exploratory drilling and
the depletion of existing fields, U.S. crude oil production also declined during
the 1980s (recall Figure 3.2), and the United States once again became
increasingly dependent upon imported oil.

STRATEGIC PETROLEUM RESERVES

Spot crude oil prices rose rapidly at the onset of the Iranian crisis in
1978–1979 in part because of panic buying precipitated by temporary shortages. To reduce U.S. vulnerability to international crises, the federal govern-

---

[71]Because one never knows whether oil or gas (or both) will be discovered, wells seeking both are counted. On the 1981 turning point, see also "U.S. Oil Rush Begins To
Slow," *New York Times*, March 30, 1982, p. 31.

[72]Compare Charles J. DiBona, "The 'Windfall' Tax Should Blow Away," *New York
Times*, September 3, 1987, p. A27; and "Few Texas Oil Gushers for Bush," *New York
Times*, August 22, 1992, p. 33.

ment began in 1977 to accumulate a strategic petroleum reserve, storing the oil in abandoned salt wells and other reservoirs, from which it could be pumped if international supplies were suddenly reduced or cut off. By 1990, the reserve had grown to 585 million barrels, or the equivalent of 82 days imports.[73] The United States also led the way in 1974 to the creation of the International Energy Agency, housed in Paris, to encourage stockpiling by 21 industrialized member nations and to coordinate the release of reserve supplies in times of crisis.

The strategic reserve system's first test came with Iraq's invasion of Kuwait on August 2, 1990. Kuwait's supply ceased, and Iraq's oil was boycotted by most other nations. Spot prices soon doubled to more than $30 per barrel. There were two reasons for the increase: uncertainty as to whether other OPEC nations would choose to make up the supply shortfall from their reserve capacity, and fear that Iraq's sizable air force might disrupt further supplies by bombing key Persian Gulf ports and the pipelines that feed them. The first uncertainty abated on August 29 when OPEC members (excluding Iraq and Kuwait, and with Iran dissenting) agreed to abandon previous quotas. In the ensuing months, the United States sold 21 million barrels (three days' imports) from its Strategic Petroleum Reserve on an experimental basis,[74] while delegates to the International Energy Agency debated whether to authorize worldwide reserve releases. Finally, on January 28, IEA members agreed to a release. But the decision came too late, because twelve days earlier the air war began, revealing within a few hours that the forces allied against Iraq had overwhelming air superiority. Thus, the threat to supply lines was minimized, and the reserve release program ended on March 7.

CONCLUSION

In the remaining pages we shall encounter no industries with as turbulent a history as crude oil. For the better part of a century following the development of commercial extraction methods, the United States was the world's leading petroleum supplier. More recently, however, its share of world production has dropped to less than 12 percent, and it has become critically dependent upon cartel-controlled foreign oil to keep its industry and transportation systems running. Government policy toward the petroleum industry has lurched from extremes of protecting domestic oil producers at the expense of consumers to capturing scarcity rents from producers for the ostensible benefit of consumers. The policies have induced many inefficiencies.

---

[73]U.S. Department of Energy, *Annual Energy Review: 1992*, p. 155.

[74]On the U.S. debate over whether to do so, see "On Tapping Oil Reserve," *New York Times*, August 9, 1990, p. D1.

Military force has been used to facilitate their implementation. And perhaps most important, since the 1960s, the policies have strongly favored consumption rather than conservation, aggravating the nation's dependence upon foreign sources and setting the stage for future crises. They have not lacked ingenuity. It is hard to conceive of a market intervention more elaborate, and more effective in achieving its questionable objectives, than the two-tier price control program. Only the agricultural price support system rivals it. Yet one might have hoped for a more astute choice of objectives, a longer time perspective, and more coherence among the chosen instruments.

4

PETROLEUM REFINING AND MARKETING

*Late in the nineteenth ce   Company
achieved a near monopoly   e United
States. We analyze the p   strategies
through which Standard (s monopoly position, only to lose i   antitrust
case. To understand the in   examine
the sources of scale economies, the a   een scale
economies and transportation costs, and the basic logic of oligopolistic pricing rivalry in situations characterized by a "prisoners' dilemma." We then investigate how changes in crude oil
supply conditions and in U.S. policies toward the petroleum
industry precipitated a restructuring of retail gasoline markets.*

INTRODUCTION

Slaking the thirst of U.S. consumers and business firms for petroleum products engages a vast network of refineries, transport media, wholesalers, and retail outlets. In 1987 the "downstream" industry included 187 refineries, 168,000 miles of pipelines, and 137,000 retail gasoline stations. At the refining stage, where crude petroleum is transformed into gasoline, jet aircraft fuel (i.e., kerosene), diesel and heating oil, lubricants, petrochemical feedstocks, asphalt, and other products, the four largest companies accounted for 32 percent of 1987 industry sales; the eight largest originated 52 percent.[1] Thus, ignoring for the moment regional disparities, the structure of the domestic refining industry can be characterized as loosely oligopolistic.

---

[1]U.S. Bureau of the Census, *1987 Census of Manufactures*, MC87-S–6, "Concentration Ratios in Manufacturing" (Washington, DC: USGPO, 1992), p. 22.

THE ASCENT AND DECLINE OF STANDARD OIL

This was not always the case. During the last two decades of the nineteenth century and the first decade of the twentieth, the industry was dominated by one company: Standard Oil.

When crude oil was discovered in northwestern Pennsylvania, Cleveland, Ohio, became the nation's leading kerosene refining center. The city enjoyed a natural advantage through its proximity to the oil fields and its excellent rail and water transportation facilities. By 1871, the number of petroleum refineries in Cleveland had grown to somewhere between 25 and 40. (Frequent closures made an exact count difficult.) Among these were the two refineries of the Standard Oil Company, incorporated in 1870, whose operations were initiated by John D. Rockefeller and a partner in 1862. By constructing unusually large refining facilities (including the world's largest unit to date, with a capacity of 1500 barrels per day) and through rigorous quality control and tight-fisted cost reduction, Standard Oil had by 1870 become the nation's largest refiner, with about 10 percent of nationwide capacity.[2]

Rapidly expanding crude oil production and concomitant price declines led Rockefeller and his colleagues to conclude that Standard should undertake an aggressive campaign to bring "order" to the new industry. The first step was the acquisition of nearly all competing refineries in the Cleveland area, along with foothold refining interests on the East Coast. In its quest to consolidate the industry, Standard Oil enjoyed two initial advantages in addition to sheer ambition. Its low-cost operations yielded superior profits to which the company could point in persuading rivals to exchange their equity for Standard's stock: "Join us and you will be wealthier." But more important, Standard exploited the bargaining power derived from its substantial volume and advantageous location to play off the three main-line railroads connecting the East Coast and the Cleveland area—the New York Central, the Pennsylvania, and the Erie—one against the other, extracting from them freight rate concessions or "rebates" ranging from 10 to 50 percent of the rates charged Standard's competitors. At times during the 1870s, Standard also received from Cleveland area railroads "drawbacks," that is, rebates to Standard for the oil and kerosene shipped by *competing* oil companies. Although other refiners also received rebates on occasion, Standard's were larger and more consistent.

---

[2]Authoritative sources on the early history of Standard Oil include Harold W. Williamson and Arnold R. Daum, *The American Petroleum Industry: The Age of Illumination, 1859–1899* (Evanston, IL: Northwestern University Press, 1959); Allan Nevins, *Study in Power: John D. Rockefeller* (New York: Scribner, 1953); Ralph and Muriel Hidy, *Pioneering in Big Business* (New York: Harper, 1955); and the three-volume report of the U.S. Bureau of Corporations, *Report of the Commissioner of Corporations on the Petroleum Industry* (Washington, DC: 1907 and 1909).

These were crucial to Standard's superior cost and profit position, for during the early 1870s, refining costs (excluding the cost of crude oil inputs) varied in the range of 0.5 to 1.5 cents per gallon of kerosene, while a rail shipment of crude oil or products from northwestern Pennsylvania or Cleveland to New York cost from 0.5 to 2.7 cents, depending upon competitive conditions.[3]

In these and especially subsequent acquisitions, Standard is said to have used "predatory" pricing to stimulate its rivals' willingness to sell out, or to induce them to sell at distress prices. "Predatory" must be enclosed in quotation marks, because there is no universally accepted definition. Sometimes the term refers to the intent of a firm to injure or destroy its rivals, but often to selling below some measure of the alleged predator's unit costs—that is, below average total cost or (most commonly) marginal or average variable cost.[4] Given the widely differing definitions, it should not be surprising that there is controversy among scholars as to whether, or how much, Standard engaged in predation.[5] Most of the time, rivals probably sold out voluntarily because they recognized Standard's superior cost position and hoped to share in or capitalize on its monopoly gains. But the historical record is clear that Standard did occasionally use sharply focused price warfare to "sweat" recalcitrant rivals (Rockefeller's term) and induce them to sell. To avoid having to reduce its prices across the board, it created among other things "bogus" subsidiaries which quoted bargain prices only to the customers served by targeted rivals, while branches doing business under the "Standard" name maintained their higher prices.[6] Its ability to target rivals for price cuts was enhanced by an elaborate intelligence network, tapping inter alia the shipping invoices of rivals provided to it by friendly railroads.

Until the late 1880s, Standard Oil showed little interest in finding and owning crude oil reserves. It believed that it could control crude oil markets by being the dominant refiner-buyer of crude oil. This control was facilitated by acquiring and later building pipelines that connected the oil fields with railroad junction points. In 1878, Pennsylvania oil producers attempted to break free from Standard's control by building the Tidewater pipeline, connecting

---

[3]See Eliot Jones, *The Trust Problem in the United States* (New York: Macmillan, 1921), pp. 48–55; and Alfred Chandler (with Takashi Hikino), *Scale and Scope: The Dynamics of Industrial Capitalism* (Cambridge: Harvard University Press, 1990), p. 25.

[4]See Joseph F. Brodley and George A. Hay, "Predatory Pricing: Competing Economic Theories and the Evolution of Legal Standards," *Cornell Law Review*, vol. 66 (April 1981), pp. 738–803.

[5]Compare John S. McGee, "Predatory Price Cutting: The Standard Oil (N.J.) Case," *Journal of Law & Economics*, vol. 1 (October 1958), pp. 137–169; and Randall Mariger, "Predatory Price Cutting: The Standard Oil of New Jersey Case Revisited," *Explorations in Economic History*, vol. 15 (October 1978), pp. 341–367.

[6]See Daniel Yergin, *The Prize* (New York: Simon & Schuster, 1991), pp. 42–43.

the oil fields to a major railroad junction in central Pennsylvania. The venture was unprecedented both in its length—109 miles, compared to the previous maximum of 30 miles—and its success in crossing the Allegheny Mountains. Standard quickly retaliated in four ways. First, it secured unusually low rates from the railroads traversing parallel routes. Second, it bought out most of the East Coast refineries to which the Tidewater pipeline was to deliver its oil, thereby depriving the pipeline of its best markets. Third, it commenced a crash program to construct its own pipelines from the oil fields to Philadelphia and Bayonne, New Jersey, as well as to Pittsburgh, Cleveland, and Buffalo. And finally, it succeeded in obtaining first a minority interest in Tidewater's stock and later (in 1883) full control.

By 1880, through acquiring more than 100 competitors along with its own refinery and pipeline building programs, Standard came to control approximately 90 percent of U.S. petroleum refining capacity. It retained an 85 to 90 percent share for the next 20 years. It continued to receive rebates and discriminatorily favorable freight rates from the railroads at least through 1906, even though the Interstate Commerce Act of 1887 sought to outlaw discrimination in favor of individual shippers. More important to its continuing dominance was its control of pipelines, which provided much lower-cost crude oil transportation than the railroads. At the height of the contest between Standard and the Tidewater pipeline, for example, rail rates from northwestern Pennsylvania to the New York harbor were reduced from $1.15 per barrel to 20 cents for Standard and 30 cents for other shippers, but oil could be transported over the same route by pipeline at a cost of less than 17 cents.[7] Standard attempted to prevent the construction of competing pipelines by opposing their petitions seeking eminent domain and paying premiums for crude oil originating in the producing areas they sought to serve. Although required by the Hepburn Act of 1906 to behave as a common carrier, letting rivals ship over its pipelines, it prevented them from doing so by quoting extremely high rates, quoting no rates at all to the most attractive destinations, and imposing minimum shipment quantities too large for most crude oil shippers to meet.[8]

Gradually, however, Standard's market share began to ebb. Because of handicaps imposed by the Texas antitrust laws,[9] Standard failed to dominate the purchase of oil from the 1901 Spindletop discovery, permitting Gulf, Texaco, and Shell to gain strong footholds. It was also slow in recognizing the potential of California oil fields, allowing Union Oil (now Unocal) to become

----

[7]Jones, *The Trust Problem*, p. 55.

[8]Jones, *The Trust Problem*, pp. 66–72.

[9]Joseph A. Pratt and Mark E. Steiner, " 'An Intent To Terrify': State Antitrust in the Formative Years of the Modern Oil Industry," *Washburn Law Journal*, vol. 29 (Winter 1990), pp. 270–289.

established. In the East, several independent refining companies banded together to form a viable Pure Oil Company.

To control their increasingly far-flung operations, Standard Oil's principal owners brought their various affiliates under the umbrella of a trust created in 1882 under Ohio law. Thus emerged the first of the great market-dominating "trusts," giving a name (often inconsistent with the actual legal structure) to all big businesses of the time and, in 1890, to a new federal law, the Sherman Antitrust Act, passed to rein them in. Challenged under Ohio state antitrust laws, the Ohio Standard Oil trust was dissolved, and in 1899 it was reorganized as a holding company under the more permissive laws of New Jersey.

The Sherman Act was passed as a reaction to public concern over the new and monopolistic, but poorly understood, business forms epitomized by Standard Oil and emulated in diverse ways by other enterprises. It contained two main substantive provisions. Section 1 outlawed contracts, combinations, and conspiracies in restraint of trade, which presumably included both loose-knit price-fixing and other restrictive agreements and also mergers and trusts that permanently eliminated competition. Section 2 prohibited "monopolization" and attempts to monopolize any part of interstate or international trade or commerce, leaving imprecisely defined exactly what the word "monopolization" meant.

At first the new law was enforced in desultory fashion. Key precedents articulated during the late 1890s suggested that it had more clout against price-fixing agreements among supposedly independent competitors than against the mergers through which competitors became permanently joined in common cause. This real or perceived bias helped trigger the most sweeping merger wave in U.S. history between 1899 and 1904, fusing the leading firms in dozens of industries into new enterprises that dominated the markets they served.[10]

With the ascent of Theodore Roosevelt to the presidency in 1901, enforcement of the antitrust laws took a much more vigorous turn. A major investigation of Standard Oil was launched by the newly formed Bureau of Corporations, and in November 1906, a suit was brought accusing Standard Oil of monopolizing the petroleum industry. Standard Oil lost at the circuit court level in 1909, and in May of 1911, the Supreme Court concurred.[11] Establishing a "rule of reason" approach to determining whether monopolization had

---

[10]See, for example, Jesse W. Markham, "Survey of the Evidence and Findings on Mergers," in the National Bureau of Economic Research conference report, *Business Concentration and Price Policy* (Princeton, NJ: Princeton University Press, 1955), pp. 141–212; Ralph L. Nelson, *Merger Movements in American Industry* (Princeton, NJ: Princeton University Press, 1959); and Naomi R. Lamoreaux, *The Great Merger Movement in American Business: 1895–1904* (New York: Cambridge University Press, 1985).

occurred, it recited the many competition-excluding practices of which Standard was accused and concluded:

> [W]e think no disinterested mind can survey the period in question without being irresistibly driven to the conclusion that . . . [the] acts and dealings [were] wholly inconsistent with the theory that they were made with the single conception of advancing the development of business power by usual methods, but which, on the contrary, necessarily involved the intent to drive others from the field and to exclude them from their right to trade. . . .

The Court ordered that the Standard holding company be broken into 34 separate companies within six months, with the stock in those companies distributed pro rata to shareholders of New Jersey Standard Oil.[12] Among the 33 corporations whose stock interests had to be divested were 12 refining and/or marketing companies—Atlantic (now Arco), Continental Oil (Conoco, now a subsidiary of Du Pont); Standard of California; Standard of Indiana (now Amoco); Standard of New York (now Mobil); Standard of Ohio (acquired by British Petroleum in 1987); Solar (acquired in 1931 by Standard of Ohio); Standard of Kansas (liquidated in 1948, after its refining assets were acquired by Standard of Indiana in 1932); Standard of Kentucky (acquired by Standard of California in 1961); Standard of Nebraska (acquired by Indiana Standard in 1939); Vacuum (acquired by Standard of New York in 1931); and Waters-Pierce (whose fate is unknown). Also divested were four subsidiaries producing crude oil (one of which became Marathon Oil, acquired in 1982 by United States Steel), ten pipeline companies, and Standard's British affiliate. Standard Oil of New Jersey (renamed Exxon in 1972) retained sizable refineries in New Jersey, Texas, West Virginia, and Louisiana; and most of its overseas subsidiaries, including the Imperial Oil Company of Canada.

At first the breakup did little to increase competition in petroleum refining and marketing. The principal divested Standard Oil companies were organized along regional lines, and divestiture left each company with a dominant position in its natural geographic market. Each was at first reluctant to interpenetrate others' markets, perhaps in part because John D. Rockefeller and his associates still controlled a majority interest in each of the divested companies' shares. Rockefeller alone owned 25 percent. Also, despite the 1906 law declar-

---

[11]U.S. v. Standard Oil Company of New Jersey et al., 221 U.S. 1 (1911).

[12]The next several paragraphs are drawn from William S. Comanor and F. M. Scherer, "Rewriting History: The Early Sherman Act Monopolization Cases," *International Journal of the Economics of Business*, vol. 2 (July 1995), pp. 266–269.

ing them to be common carriers, the divested pipeline compani es continued to shun or charge high rates to independent petroleum companies.[13]

Gradually, however, the divested fragments began to compete. The ownership position of the Rockefeller family and the other founding fathers declined as large amounts of stock were transferred to philanthropic trusts, which diversified or liquidated their holdings, and as new public stock offerings were floated to support the expansions needed to meet the burgeoning demand for automotive fuel and to achieve greater balance between crude oil and refining operations. At first slowly, but during the 1920s at an expanding rate, the refining and marketing companies spread out from their traditional territories into adjacent and later more distant states. Surveying the situation in 1927, the Federal Trade Commission found that "a considerable degree of competition" had emerged among the spin-off companies, with no Standard company achieving as much as 50 percent of the sales in its home territory.[14] By 1955, at least three successor companies were selling in each state of the United States.[15]

The explosive growth of demand and the discovery of vast new crude oil sources outside Pennsylvania and Ohio also created opportunities for the entry and growth of non-Standard companies. Standard's petroleum product market share slipped from 90 percent in 1899 to 87 percent in 1904 and 80 percent before the breakup in 1911. The combined market share of Standard's spin-off companies declined at an accelerated rate between 1910 and 1920. See Figure 4.1. This decrease was apparently not attributable to disruptions caused by divestiture, since there was little evidence of organizational problems. Indeed,

---

[13] The newly named president of three divested pipeline companies had his initial post divestiture office in the Manhattan headquarters of New Jersey Standard Oil! George S. Gibb and Evelyn H. Knowlton, *The Resurgent Years: 1911–1927* (History of Standard Oil Company) (New York: Harper, 1956), p. 18.

Pipeline access and pricing problems eased as the pipelines achieved greater independence from their former parent and new lines were built. But even after more stringent pricing and access rules were negotiated in a 1941 consent decree, problems remained. See U.S. Senate, Committee on the Judiciary, Subcommittee on Antitrust and Monopoly, Staff Report, *Oil Company Ownership of Pipelines* (Washington, DC: USGPO, 1978); Edward J. Mitchell, ed., *Oil Pipelines and Public Policy* (Washington, DC: American Enterprise Institute, 1979); and U.S. Department of Energy, Energy Information Administration, *Oil Pipeline Symposium* (Washington, DC: USGPO, October 1980). Regulatory responsibility was transferred from the Interstate Commerce Commission to the Federal Energy Regulatory Commission in 1977.

[14] U.S. Federal Trade Commission, *Petroleum Industry: Prices, Profits, and Competition*, Senate Document 61, 70th Congress, 1st sess. (Washington, DC: USGPO, 1928), pp. 263–265.

[15] Simon N. Whitney, *Antitrust Policies*, vol. I (New York: Twentieth Century Fund, 1958), p. 106.

FIGURE 4.1

Trends in the Combined Market Shares of
Standard Oil and Its Spin-Offs

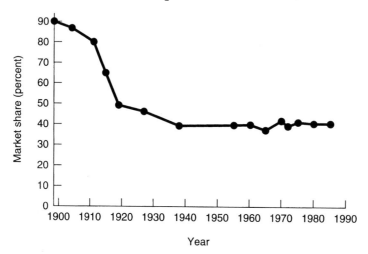

Sources: Oil industry histories, annual compilations by the Department of Interior under the oil import program, and (after 1975) *Oil and Gas Journal* refinery capacity estimates.

a new generation of Standard managers seems to have thrived on the postdivestiture challenges.[16] Rather, there were two main causes: the doubling of U.S. crude oil output between 1911 and 1920, and the tendency of the regional Standard companies to set their prices relatively high, holding an umbrella that encouraged the expansion of rivals into their territories.[17] Gradually, however, as the Standard fragments began competing more aggressively for market position, the rate of market share decline slowed, and after 1938, the combined share of the (now independent) spin-off companies stabilized at approximately 40 percent.

[16]See Comanor and Scherer, "Rewriting History."

[17]See Melvin G. de Chazeau and Alfred E. Kahn, *Integration and Competition in the Petroleum Industry* (New York: Yale University Press, 1959), pp. 457–459; and Edmund P. Learned with Catherine C. Ellsworth, *Gasoline Pricing in Ohio* (Boston: Harvard Business School Division of Research, 1959), pp. 23–24.

TECHNOLOGY, ECONOMIES OF SCALE, AND MARKET STRUCTURE

By 1987, to reiterate, the four leading U.S. petroleum refiners originated 32 percent of domestic output. The largest seller, Standard of California, which had taken over industry leadership from Exxon (successor to the original New Jersey Standard Company) by acquiring Gulf Oil in 1984, accounted for 11 percent.[18] To what extent is this degree of seller concentration, modest though it may be, required to achieve the cost savings stemming from economies of scale?

A petroleum refinery is a plumber's dream—an assortment of processing vessels connected by intricate piping and valves, all controlled from an elaborately instrumented operations center. Crude oil normally reaches the refinery by tanker ship or pipeline. After blending and other preliminary treatment, the crude oil is heated under vacuum conditions until it evaporates. The vapor flows into a distillation tower—usually the largest single processing unit in a refinery—where it condenses in stages, the most volatile fractions (e.g., propane, natural gasoline, and naphtha) condensing at the top, intermediate fractions (kerosene and heating oil) condensing at lower levels, and the heaviest fractions (residual fuel oil, tar, and asphalt) settling to the bottom. Gasoline comprises roughly 16 to 24 percent of the resulting distillate, with light crudes yielding a higher gasoline fraction than heavy crudes. This amount is not enough to satisfy U.S. consumers' craving for gasoline, which averaged 42 percent of total petroleum distillate yields during the 1980s.[19] Thus, further processing is necessary to transform heavier fractions into gasoline and also to increase the octane rating of natural gasoline. These processes include cracking, in which heavy molecules are broken into lighter ones under pressure and heat in the presence of catalysts; alkylation, in which light gaseous molecules are fused into high-octane gasoline; hydrogenation, in which hydrogen is added to molecules to lighten them; and various catalytic re-forming steps that alter the molecular structure to yield either gasoline or petrochemical feedstocks. The black, sticky residue that remains may be used directly as asphalt for road and roof construction, or it may be processed in a coking unit to obtain more volatile fractions and carbon coke. As a rule, the higher a refin-

---

[18]Conventionally calculated concentration ratios overstate the true degree of concentration, since petroleum product imports from a diversity of sources amounted to 12 percent of domestic output.

[19] The fraction of petroleum products consumed as gasoline is higher in California and the South, where fuel oil is demanded less, and lower in New England, where much home heating is done using fuel oil. The "traditional" western European refinery produced relatively little gasoline and much fuel oil, but that has changed with growing automobile ownership and greater availability of natural gas for heating.

ery's yield of gasoline and other volatile distillates, the greater the refinery's capital cost, holding overall crude oil processing capacity constant.

The vessels in which petroleum products are refined are mostly cylindrical or spherical in shape. From high school geometry, the reader may recall that the volume of a sphere or cylinder increases with the two-thirds power of the object's surface area. The cost of constructing a petroleum or chemical processing vessel, including the cost of materials, forming, and welds, is roughly proportional to the vessel's surface area. But the vessel's capacity is proportional to its volume. These relationships give rise to the so-called "two-thirds rule" used extensively by engineers in estimating petroleum and other processing plant costs:

$$\text{Construction cost} = k \text{ (throughput capacity)}^{2/3}$$

where k varies with the particular technology being implemented. The two-thirds rule implies the existence of significant scale economies, since capital costs rise less than proportionately with capacity as plants of increasingly large capacity are built. In principle, these economies of large-scale construction might persist out to indefinitely large sizes. But in practice, processing unit sizes encounter metallurgical, fabrication, and materials flow constraints. These are often relaxed as technological knowledge advances. Thus, in 1870, the largest distillation unit operated by Standard Oil had a daily capacity of 1500 barrels. A century later, best-practice distillation units processed 200,000 barrels per day. For any given state of technology, there is usually a maximum practical size at which the cost-saving opportunities from building and fully utilizing larger-scale units are exhausted. This maximum defines, sometimes in a complex way when processing units of differing scales must be dovetailed, the *minimum efficient scale* or *MES* of a processing plant—that is, the scale at which average cost per unit of output first reaches its minimum value. For petroleum refineries, the MES is usually governed by the size of a least-cost distillation tower, which has stabilized at roughly 200,000 barrels of crude oil processing per day during the past several decades.[20] The investment required in 1990 to build a fully equipped 200,000-barrel-per-day refinery ranged from $800 million to $2 billion, depending upon location and the richness of the gasoline yield.

Unit processing costs depend not only upon the capital servicing costs of the equipment used, but also upon the costs of day-to-day operation—for example, for labor, supplies, and the like. Here too, economies of large-scale operation are found. Energy requirements commonly rise less than proportionately with the size of processing vessels. In some materials processing situ-

---

[20] There may be slight cost savings from even larger refineries—for example, from building and operating port facilities that can handle supertankers. See F. M. Scherer, *Economies of Scale at the Plant and Multi-Plant Levels: Detailed Evidence* (compendium deposited at selected U.S. research libraries, 1975), pp. 15–19.

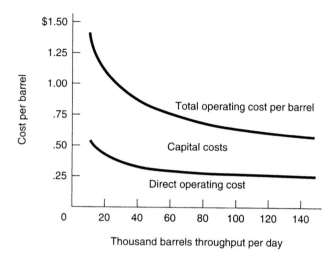

FIGURE 4.2
Unit Processing Costs for a Cracking Refinery, Circa 1960
Sources: Adapted from Gunnar Ribrant, *Stordrifts-fördelar inom industripro-duktionen* (Stockholm: Statens offentliga utred-ningar, 1970), p. 250; draw-ing in turn upon C. H. Gamer, "A Modern Refin-ery," and C. A. Heller, "Eco-nomics of Refining," in United Nations Inter-regional Seminar on Tech-niques of Petroleum Devel-opment, Proceedings, *Techniques of Petroleum Development* (New York: UN, 1962), pp. 184–201.

ations, a crew can operate a large facility with little or no augmentation above what is required to operate a small one, so the labor cost per unit of output produced falls with the quantity of output.[21] Here too, however, there are lim-its. Large plants are harder to manage than small plants and, at some scale, cost increases attributable to the growing complexity of management out-weigh the cost savings from operating larger, or additional, processing units.[22]

There have been many studies of scale economy relationships in petroleum refining. Those that are in the public domain are relatively old, but the techno-logical relationships have changed only slightly since their publication. Figure 4.2 reproduces the unit cost-scale relationships for a high-gasoline-yield, or cracking, refinery, analyzed at a 1962 United Nations symposium.[23] Scale economies persist out to the size of the largest refinery investigated. Larger scale leads to unit cost savings in both the carrying costs of the required capital investment (i.e., interest and depreciation) and operation, with somewhat stronger economies in the former than the latter. A refinery designed to oper-

---

[21]See Lawrence J. Lau and Shuji Tamura, "Economies of Scale, Technical Progress, and the Nonhomothetic Leontief Production Function," *Journal of Political Economy,* vol. 80 (November/December 1972), pp. 1167–1187.

[22]See W. L. Nelson, "Costs of Major Refiners Compared with Those of the Indepen-dents," *Oil and Gas Journal,* December 2, 1974, pp. 98–101.

[23]The throughout data have been converted here from tons to barrels per day.

ate at 30,000 barrels per day (i.e., just beyond "teakettle" status) could process its crude oil at a total cost slightly below $1 per barrel. With a 140,000-barrel-per-day design, unit costs fall to 58 cents per barrel. If the curves were to be extrapolated, one would find continuing—but more modest—unit cost decreases out to a volume of 200,000 barrels per day.

Do such economies of scale compel a high concentration of industry output in the hands of few producers, if minimum-cost operation is to be achieved? The answer is, it depends upon the size of the relevant market. The United States market for petroleum products is huge—in 1990, 13.6 million barrels per day, excluding refined product imports. Thus, the U.S. market could accommodate 13.6 million/200,000 = 68 refineries of minimum efficient scale—enough, as a first approximation, for competition approaching that of the atomistic model. For a small nation like Sweden, on the other hand, a difficult trade-off between achieving scale economies and a competitive market structure is posed. Sweden's petroleum products consumption in 1990 was 280,000 barrels per day, enough for only one and a half efficient-scale refineries.

This discussion, however, has only scraped the surface of a complex subject. Shipping costs limit the market that can be served by a refinery, and there are even more compelling economies of scale in the transportation of crude oil or petroleum products. Within the United States, pipelines are commonly the lowest-cost bulk transportation medium. The throughput capacity of a pipeline is proportional to its cross-sectional area. The construction cost is roughly proportional to the pipe's circumference. Because circumference varies linearly with a pipe's radius ($C = 2\pi R$) but cross-sectional area varies by the square ($A = \pi R^2$), construction cost rises roughly with the square root of the pipeline's capacity, implying even greater scale economies than under the two-thirds rule. This concept is illustrated in Figure 4.3, which plots as of 1969 the short-run average total costs (continuous lines designated by letters) for pipelines of given design capacity and the envelope of long-run cost possibilities presented by building pipelines of varying capacity. For a pipeline of given capacity, costs are much lower when it is operated at its design capacity rather than at substantially lower or higher throughputs. But, more important for our present purposes, there are huge savings from building a large pipeline as compared to a small one, provided that the volume needed to keep it busy exists. With 10.75-inch-diameter pipeline A, whose design capacity was 50,000 barrels per day, it cost a bit more than 40 cents under 1969 conditions to transport a barrel of crude oil 1000 miles. With 48-inch pipeline H—the largest size constructed then or now—a barrel of crude oil could be transported 1000 miles for 8 cents. But to achieve that low cost, it would be necessary to ship more than a million barrels of oil per day. There are relatively few origin-destination pairs over which such a large volume flows. Crude oil pipelines with daily capacities of a million barrels or more exist between the north slope of Alaska and Valdez and from the Louisiana gulf coast to south central Illinois. A prod-

FIGURE 4.3

Average Cost of Transporting Crude Oil by Pipeline, 1969

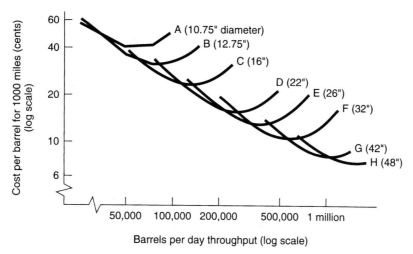

Source: Adapted from D. J. Pearl and J. L. Enos, "Engineering Production Functions and Technological Progress," *Journal of Industrial Economics*, vol. 24 (September 1975), p. 61.

uct pipeline of comparable size links southeastern Texas to northern Virginia and (with somewhat reduced capacities) points north. Except under the most extraordinary market conditions, pipelining is a *natural monopoly*—that is, a situation in which unit costs fall out to the largest throughput the market can accommodate.

Most petroleum product shipments within the United States occur under conditions requiring a sacrifice of scale economies. Then diverse shipping media may come into play, with the 1966 cost of transporting a barrel of product 1000 miles varying as follows:[24]

---

[24]Adapted by the author from Michael Hubbard, "The Comparative Cost of Oil Transport to and Within Europe," *Journal of the Institute of Petroleum*, vol. 54 (January 1967), pp. 1–23.

Transportation Medium	Dollar Cost
150,000-ton ocean tanker (3000-mile trip)	$0.04
30,000-ton ocean tanker (3000-mile trip)	.06
42-inch-diameter pipeline	.10
12-inch-diameter pipeline	.51
Inland barge (500-mile trips)	.52
Rail (500-mile trips)	1.54
25-ton payload tank truck (50-mile trips)	4.42
15-ton payload tank truck (50-mile trips)	5.11

Given this pattern, crude oil is usually transported from the oil fields to refineries by tanker ship or pipeline. Petroleum products move from the refineries to tank farm terminals by ship (for coastal terminals),[25] pipeline, barge, or (infrequently) rail, depending upon the circumstances. Products move from the terminals to wholesale bulk stations and retail gasoline stations by tank truck.

Transportation costs constrain the sizes at which refineries are built and operated. The larger a refinery's output, the more widely the refinery must reach out to find customers for its products, all else (such as population density and market share) held equal. The wider the shipping radius, the higher the outbound transportation costs will be. This gives rise to the trade-off illustrated in Figure 4.4. Owing to economies of scale, unit processing costs (UPC) decline with increased refinery output. But to sell a larger output, rising unit transportation costs (UTC) must be incurred. Average *total* cost ATC is the vertical sum of the two curves. It is minimized at an output smaller than the output at which unit processing costs alone are minimized. This trade-off (along with the small-refiner entitlements bias discussed in Chapter 3) has led petroleum companies to maintain numerous refineries much smaller than the

---

[25]Transportation patterns to coastal locations are affected in important ways by the Jones Act of 1920, as periodically amended, which requires that water shipments between locations in the United States must be made in vessels constructed in the United States and staffed by U.S. crews. Relative to international alternatives, this regulation more than doubles shipping costs. As a result, even though it could be less expensive to ship products from the Gulf coast to the Northeast coast by water, pipelines are used. And because New England is poorly served by pipelines, it is often cheaper to import products than to ship them in U.S. "bottoms" from domestic refineries.

Water shipment is also inhibited by the inability of ports on the U.S. East and Gulf coasts to accomodate tankers of more capacity than about 80,000 deadweight tons, despite continuing economies of scale out to at least 200,000 tons. See "No Superports for Supertankers," *Business Week*, May 20, 1972, pp. 108–110. For crude oil, offshore unloading to pipeline terminals partially solves the problem on the Texas Gulf coast.

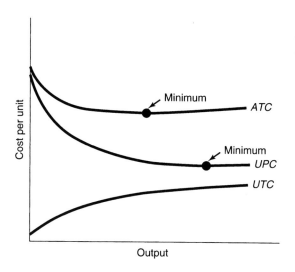

FIGURE 4.4
Trade-off Between Production and Transportation Costs

200,000-barrel-per-day capacity identified here as the minimum efficient scale, especially in sparsely populated sections of the United States.[26] In 1984, for example, the distribution of U.S. refinery sizes was as follows:[27]

Refinery Capacity (barrels per day)	Number of Refineries	Percentage of Total Capacity
200,000 or more	19	39.3
100,000–199,999	30	28.4
50,000–99,999	33	16.1
20,000–49,999	51	12.6
Less than 20,000	86	3.5

Because of the constraining effect of transportation costs, large petroleum companies serve the geographically vast U. S. market from a network of dispersed refineries, not from central locations reaping maximum processing scale

---

[26]For a generalization to 12 industries in six nations and an analysis of the (typically modest) scale economies that stem from operating multiple plants, see F. M. Scherer et al., *The Economics of Multi-Plant Operation: An International Comparisons Study* (Cambridge: Harvard University Press, 1975), chapters 2 and 3.

[27]Drawn from James E. Hibdon and Michael J. Mueller, "Economies of Scale in Petroleum Refining, 1947–1984," *Review of Industrial Organization*, vol. 5 (Fall 1990), p. 38.

economies. In 1990, for example, the leading U.S. refiner, Chevron (i.e., Standard of California), had refineries with locations and capacities as follows:[28]

Port Arthur, Texas	329,000 bbl/day
Pascagoula, Mississippi	295,000
El Segundo, California	286,000
Richmond, California	270,000
Philadelphia, Pennsylvania	175,000
Perth Amboy, New Jersey	80,000
El Paso, Texas	66,000
Salt Lake City, Utah	45,000
Kenai, Alaska	22,000
Portland, Oregon	15,000
Seattle, Washington	5,000

Exxon, the second-largest refiner, had a more compact refinery structure:

Baytown, Texas	426,000
Baton Rouge, Louisiana	421,000
Linden, New Jersey[29]	130,000
Benicia, California	128,000
Billings, Montana	42,000

Petroleum companies with widespread retail distribution also economize on transportation costs by swapping gasoline with more conveniently located rivals. Exxon, for example, might obtain gasoline supplies for its retail outlets in the North Central states (where it has no refinery) from Amoco's Whiting, Indiana, refinery, supplying Amoco with comparable quantities in the San Francisco area, where Amoco has no refinery. Such swaps have a compelling cost-saving rationale. However, they also engender among ostensibly competing companies rich mutual-dependence relationships whose behavioral implications are poorly understood.

Further implications follow. The unavailability of low-cost transportation media isolates some regions of the United States, making it prohibitively costly for refiners located elsewhere to compete in those regions. As a result, the mar-

---

[28]The source is the *Oil and Gas Journal Data Book: 1991* (Tulsa: PennWell, 1991).

[29]Reduced from 265,000 bbl/day in the early 1980s, and sold off in 1992 to Tosco Corporation.

ket for petroleum products, meaningfully defined, is less than nationwide, contrary to the implications of structural statistics (such as concentration ratios) defined at the national level. Two levels of subtlety must be penetrated to obtain more meaningful market definitions.

First, broad regions of the United States are either linked by crude oil and product pipelines or are deficient in such linkages. Caribbean Gulf Coast and South Central refineries enjoy especially rich product pipeline and tanker connections to the eastern seaboard, so those two areas are in a broad sense a common market. The Midwest is poorly linked to the East Coast and mountain states by low-cost transportation media, and it is better served by crude oil than product pipelines from the Gulf Coast. As a consequence, its refiners are at least partially isolated. The western Mountain states and Pacific Coast states are also isolated, both from each other and other parts of the nation. They too should therefore be viewed as separate and distinct petroleum product markets. When concentration ratios for the top four and eight petroleum refining companies in 1981 are defined regionally, figures higher than the nationwide values result, suggesting a somewhat tighter form of oligopoly than the national statistics imply:[30]

Region	*Concentration Ratios*	
	Four-Firm	*Eight-Firm*
East Coast and South Central	35.0%	55.0
Midwest	37.4	60.0
Mountain states	48.0	75.3
Pacific Coast	54.4	76.5
Entire United States	29.0	49.1

Second, the principal locus of wholesale price decisions for gasoline and heating oil is not the refinery, but several hundred pipeline and port terminals scattered throughout the United States, usually near metropolitan areas. There the petroleum companies quote "terminal rack" prices that vary with local supply and demand conditions by as much as several cents per gallon of

---

[30]The source of regional concentration estimates (based upon actually operating capacity) is U.S. Federal Trade Commission, *Mergers in the Petroleum Industry* (Washington, DC: September 1982), pp. 184–185. The national data are drawn from the record of *Marathon Oil Co. v. Mobil Corporation et al.*, 530 F. Supp. 315 (1981).

gasoline.[31] The refiner without storage facilities at a terminal, or lacking equivalent swap arrangements, is often precluded from being an active participant in the surrounding territory, since shipping products in by low-volume, high-cost media such as rail or tank trucks from more distant terminals can be prohibitively costly. Thus, in a more fine-grained sense, the markets for petroleum products are localized, and meaningful concentration ratios are even higher than those observed at the broad regional level. Oligopolistic structure prevails.

GASOLINE PRICING: THEORY AND EVIDENCE

As we begin analyzing how prices are set for gasoline, the principal petroleum product, another structural characteristic must be taken into account. Key pricing decisions are made not only at wholesale terminals, but at the retail gasoline station level. Pricing at the wholesale and retail levels is closely linked, because petroleum refiners adjust their terminal prices to reflect conditions in the retail markets they serve, and when gasoline price wars emerge, as they have with some frequency in the past, narrowly targeted "competitive allowances" (i.e., discounts from the posted terminal rack price) have been granted to affected retailers.[32] Thus, we focus our analysis initially on pricing at the retail level.[33]

Gasoline is provided to U.S. motorists by more than 100,000 retail outlets. Traditionally, most gasoline stations have been operated as independent businesses whose head obtains a franchise to sell the branded products of a major petroleum refiner. Sometimes the station's land and structures are owned by the franchisee, but more frequently for single-unit stations, the refining company owns the property and leases it to the retailer. The larger franchised retailers pick up their gasoline supplies at a terminal and pay the terminal rack

---

[31]See F. M. Scherer, "Merger in the Petroleum Industry: The *Mobil-Marathon* Case," in John Kwoka and Lawrence J. White, ed., *The Antitrust Revolution* (Glenview, IL: Scott, Foresman, 1989), pp. 24–34.

[32]See, for example, Learned and Ellsworth, *Gasoline Pricing in Ohio*, pp. 27–28, 76–83, and 106–108; and U.S. Department of Energy, Assistant Secretary for Policy and Evaluation, *The State of Competition in Gasoline Marketing*, final report (Washington, DC: January 1981), Book I, p. 6; and Book II, p. 13.

[33]Since the repeal in 1975 of federal laws exempting resale price maintenance from antitrust price-fixing prohibitions, refiners have not been able to stipulate the prices at which their independent retailers sell.

price, but smaller units characteristically purchase through a "jobber," who delivers the gasoline to stations at a higher "tank wagon" price. To this general pattern there are several significant exceptions. For one, jobbers often operate their own retail chains in addition to, or instead of, delivering gasoline to individual franchised retailers. Sometimes the jobbers' stations display their supplier's principal brand (e.g., Exxon, Amoco, or Chevron); sometimes they use their own brand (e.g., U-Pay-Less). Second, to an increasing extent, refining companies have operated their own "company stores"—that is, retail stations staffed by the refiner's own employees rather than by franchisees.[34] Third, it is customary to distinguish between "major" petroleum refining companies, notably, the larger companies that among other things advertise their brands extensively, and the "independent refiners," who are smaller and/or support less advertising. There are also fully "independent" retail distribution chains that purchase gasoline from diverse refiners, large and small, and sell it under their own (typically local) brand names. In 1979, the distribution of the 28 largest (mostly "major") U.S. refiners' sales to various retail distributor classes was as follows:[35]

Dealers supplied directly by refiner	39.1%
Jobbers selling refiner's brand	29.7%
Company stores	11.7%
Unbranded sales to independents	19.5%

As a first approximation, retail gasoline markets fall into the *monopolistic competition* structural category. In the typical larger metropolitan area, there are many retail outlets. Entry and exit are relatively easy. Individual stations' services are differentiated by the relative convenience of their location and often by brand reputation, the repair and credit card services offered (or not offered), long-standing personal relationships with customers, and the like. As a closer approximation, however, the assumption that each retailer is so small

---

[34]Company outlets were also common in the early days of gasoline retailing, mainly as an assurance of otherwise uncertain quality. By the 1920s, however, quality had become more uniform and brand names were accepted as signals of good quality. The petroleum companies then found that franchised operators were more efficient and responsive to local market conditions than were company-owned stores. See Thomas F. Hogarty, "The Origin and Evolution of Gasoline Marketing," American Petroleum Institute Research Study 022, October 1981.

[35]U.S. Department of Energy, *The State of Competition in Gasoline Marketing*, Book I, p. 111. Bulk sales to end users are excluded. The distinction between jobbers selling under their own brand and independent unbranded outlets is blurred in the data.

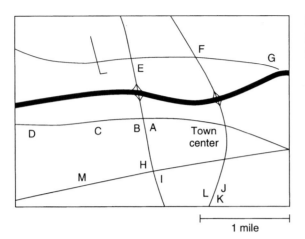

FIGURE 4.5
Gasoline Station Locations

that it can ignore the pricing actions of rivals is wrong. Rather, gasoline retailing is better described as a differentiated *chain oligopoly*. Figure 4.5 illustrates with a skeletal street map part of a typical medium-size city. (Smaller connecting streets are omitted.) The city is bisected by a limited-access highway (heavy line). Most of the individual stations designated by the letters A through M are located along arterial streets (lighter lines) or at intersections of those streets. Stations facing one another across intersections (such as A and B, H and I, and J, K, and L) view one another as head-to-head direct rivals, each of whose pricing decisions has a direct and significant impact on the other's fortunes. Stations located some distance away on the same artery have a perceptibly less potent effect, while those on "the other side of town" interact only weakly.

OLIGOPOLY AND THE PRISONERS' DILEMMA

The direct interaction between adjacent stations A and B can be used to illustrate at the most basic level the fundamental problem of oligopoly pricing, or in this instance, *duopoly* pricing. Figure 4.6 simplifies the matter to its essence. Each panel in the figure is a *payoff matrix*. The upper panel shows how the daily volume of gasoline pumped by stations A and B depends upon the unleaded regular gasoline prices each posts at the start of the day's activity. We assume for simplicity that only two alternative prices, or *strategies*, are considered: a low price of $1.099 per gallon and a high price of $1.149. The entries within the matrix indicate gallons sold per day as a function of the prices posted by A and B, with A's gallonage before the commas and B's after the commas. If both post the high price of $1.149, each sells 2500 gallons. If both post the lower price of $1.099, each sells more, drawing some patronage from stations C, D, E, and so forth. If A quotes a low price of $1.099 and B quotes $1.149, A will capture the lion's share of the two stations' business, 3500 gallons, whereas B is left serving only its most loyal customers.

FIGURE 4.6
Gasoline Pricing "Prisoners' Dilemma"

Station B's prices

		$1.149	$1.099
Station A's prices	$1.149	2500, 2500	1800, 3500
	$1.099	3500, 1800	3000, 3000

Gallonage matrix

Station B's prices

		$1.149	$1.099
Station A's prices	$1.149	$497.50, $497.50	$358.20, $521.50
	$1.099	$521.50, $358.20	$447.00, $447.00

Daily gross profit margin

The lower panel translates these gallon sales into daily gross profits (before deduction of rent and the operator's residual income), assuming that the variable cost of gasoline, taxes, and temporary hired help is 95 cents per gallon.

This profit payoff matrix structure is identical to that of a classic game theory metaphor, the so-called prisoners' dilemma game. In the prisoners' dilemma, the district attorney interrogates in separate rooms two individuals suspected of grand larceny. If both confess (analogous to both stations quoting a low price), both are sent to jail for three years. If neither confesses (analogous to both stations quoting a high price), each is jailed six months for possessing stolen merchandise. If one testifies against the other (quotes a low price) and the other does not confess (maintains a high price), the squealer is set free (gains maximum profits) while the informed-upon is jailed for eight years (receives minimal profits).

Consider now station A's price-posting problem from the perspective of game theory. If B posts a price of $1.149, A will receive a gross profit of $497.50 if it quotes the same high price and $521.50 if it quotes the low price. A is better off posting the low price. If B posts the low price of $1.099, A receives $358.20 if it quotes the high price and $447.00 if it posts the low price. Again, A is better off posting the low price. Since the low price yields higher gross profit to A, whichever strategy B chooses, it is said to be a *dominant strategy* for A. Because the payoff matrix is symmetrical, the same logic holds for B. There seems to be a compelling rationale for each to quote the low price, so each will realize gross profits of $447 per day. However, if the station operators could see their way clear so that each quoted the high price of $1.149, each would realize gross profits of $497.50—that is, $50 more per day. That is the dilemma of both the prisoners and oligopolists: there are powerful incentives to behave in self-aggrandizing ways that lead to outcomes sacrificing profit compared to what could be obtained if the participants cooperated toward securing more lucrative outcomes. Oligopolistic rivalries are "games" that mix rivalrous instincts with incentives to cooperate.[36] The outcome of the game depends upon which force is stronger.

ESCAPE FROM THE DILEMMA

The rivalry as characterized thus far is sufficiently oversimplified that it is easy to see ways out of the dilemma. One obvious escape route is collusion. Station A's operator can walk across the street to her counterpart and observe, "This $1.099 price business is crazy; we're killing one another. Why don't you post the $1.149 price and I'll do the same, and we'll keep it that way until we get together again over a beer and agree on an even more profitable change."

There are two problems with this solution. First, it has been recognized since the time of the ancient Greeks that collusion can lead to monopoly prices. Monopoly prices injure consumers and misallocate resources. To combat them, most industrialized nations' laws declare collusion to be illegal. Indeed, under Section 1 of the U.S. Sherman Act, the unvarnished collusion described in our simple example is illegal per se—that is, without any consideration of whether the prices set are "fair" or not. Since the late 1950s, stiff prison sentences and fines have been meted out to individuals and business firms caught violating the law. Collusion persists, perhaps especially among small business operators (such as gasoline station franchisees) too small to attract the attention of antitrust enforcers or to hire lawyers warning them of the risks.[37] But the law has become a potent deterrent.

Also, as we have seen in our analysis of OPEC's price-setting efforts, firms often "chisel" on their agreements even when they agree to set high prices. Chiseling is more likely, the more prices are raised above the competitive level, and the larger the number of participants in a price-elevating arrangement.[38] Even if stations A and B abide by their agreements, other links in the chain C, D, . . . , M may behave differently and drain off enough business to undermine the willingness of A and B to persist in maintaining high prices. More on this shortly.

---

[36]A seminal development of these and many other notions is Thomas C. Schelling, *The Strategy of Conflict* (Cambridge: Harvard University Press, 1960).

[37]See, for example, Ralph Cassady, Jr., *Price Making and Price Behavior in the Petroleum Industry* (New Haven: Yale University Press, 1954), pp. 246–248.

[38]Important insights into this "*N*-firm" problem include Antoine A. Cournot, *Récherches sur les principes mathématiques de la théorie des richesses* (Paris: 1838), Chapter VII; Edward H. Chamberlin, *The Theory of Monopolistic Competition* (Cambridge: Harvard University Press, 1933), chap. III; and George J. Stigler, "A Theory of Oligopoly," *Journal of Political Economy*, vol. 72 (February 1964), pp. 44–61.

An alternative means for setting oligopoly prices above the competitive level is through price leadership. In our gasoline station example, station A might by tradition be recognized as the price leader. Every morning it posts prices at levels that will benefit both itself and other sellers, and the other stations follow suit without actually discussing the matter. Pricing in this case becomes interdependent and cooperative through an accepted time sequence, rather than simultaneous and independent, as assumed with the prisoners' dilemma.

Three distinct types of price leadership—dominant-firm, collusive, and barometric—are commonly recognized.[39] Dominant-firm leadership occurs when one firm has such a large market share—for example, upwards of 40 percent—that it literally dominates price-setting in its industry. We examine its theoretical underpinnings in Chapter 5. Collusive leadership functions when by tacit consent the members of a tightly oligopolistic industry consistently match the prices announced by a leading member, recognizing that by doing so they can sustain prices above competitive equilibrium values. Although it is hard to draw a precise line, barometric leadership is a weaker variant under which there is less universal acceptance of the leader (whose identity may change from time to time) and the prices set by the leader. The leader is said to act as a "barometer" whose price announcements reflect or formalize prevailing market supply and demand conditions.

There is a long tradition of price leadership in the sale of gasoline at both wholesale and retail.[40] The leaders have more often than not been fragments of the original Standard Oil Company—for example, Exxon or Arco (previously Atlantic) in the middle Atlantic seaboard area, Amoco in Indiana and adjoining states other than Ohio, Sohio in Ohio, Chevron in the Far West, and so on. The leadership institutions are typically characterized as barometric. The pricing of Standard Oil of Ohio (Sohio, now a subsidiary of British Petroleum) has been studied particularly thoroughly. Discussing his company's leadership on downward terminal rack price moves, a Sohio vice president observed:[41]

> The major sales executives of all companies watch carefully the number and size of subnormal markets. . . . If the number of local price cuts increases, if the number and amount of secret concessions to commercial consumers increase, if the secret unpublicized concessions to dealers increase, it becomes more and

---

[39]The trichotomy was proposed by Jesse W. Markham, "The Nature and Significance of Price Leadership," *American Economic Review*, vol. 41 (December 1951), pp. 891–905.

[40]See, for example, Learned and Ellsworth, *Gasoline Pricing in Ohio*, pp. 4–7; Cassady, *Price Making and Price Behavior*, chap. 6; and U.S. Department of Energy, *The State of Competition*, part II, p. 13.

[41]Statement of S. A. Swensrud, quoted in George J. Stigler, "The Kinky Oligopoly Demand Curve and Rigid Prices," *Journal of Political Economy*, vol. 55 (October 1947), p. 445.

more difficult to maintain the higher prices. . . . Finally, some company, usually the largest marketer in the territory, recognizes that the subnormal price has become the normal price and announces a general price reduction throughout the territory.

Raising prices requires stronger leadership, as another Sohio management statement reveals:[42]

> [I]n our own interest we must usually take the lead in attempting higher price levels when we believe that conditions will permit. Having a substantial distribution in our market we are confronted with the fact that few marketers, especially those with a lesser consumer acceptance, can take the lead in increasing prices. Upward moves . . . are made by us only when, in our opinion, general prices and the economic pressure from industry costs are such that our competitors in their own interest will follow. It is notorious that when we guess wrong, or when we advance our market too far, immediate market disintegration sets in.

It would appear to follow that price increases can be achieved with barometric leadership that might not be accomplished, or would have been delayed, if no leadership institutions existed. Still the leader's discretion may be narrowly constrained.

Although most price moves attributable to leadership occur at the local or regional market level, there are exceptions. One of the most important spanned the late 1960s. In March 1965, following a "price war" that had become nationwide, Texaco took the lead in announcing that it would no longer grant competitive allowances (i.e., discounts) to impacted dealers in any part of the United States.[43] At the time, Texaco was the nation's largest gasoline marketer, with especially uniform coverage of the lower 48 states. Other refiners followed suit, and prices rose. Erosion then set in, but at an uneven pace across metropolitan areas. Howard Marvel's statistical analysis suggests that the erosion was most rapid in cities served by numerous refiners.[44] Three to five years later, prices continued to be higher in urban markets where the leading companies held particularly large market shares.

Another feature helping gasoline retailers and marketers escape from the prisoners' dilemma is the repetition of the pricing game day after day. Meeting in smoke-filled rooms to communicate price strategies is illegal. But posting

---

[42]Learned and Ellsworth, *Gasoline Pricing in Ohio*, p. 25.

[43]A similar action was taken by Texaco in February 1972, but its impact was blunted by pervasive price controls.

[44]Howard P. Marvel, "Competition and Price Levels in the Retail Gasoline Market," *Review of Economics and Statistics*, vol. 60 (May 1978), pp. 252–258. See also Robert T. Masson and Fred C. Allvine, "Strategies and Structure: Majors, Independents, and Prices of Gasoline in Local Markets," in Masson and P. D. Qualls, eds., *Essays on Industrial Organization in Honor of Joe S. Bain* (Cambridge: Ballinger, 1976), p. 174.

prices for all the world to see is also a form of communication. If station A undercuts station B today, station B can signal its displeasure by posting an equally low, or perhaps even lower, price tomorrow. After a burst of such price competition, station A can sue for peace by posting a price increase. If station B follows suit (along with other affected outlets), prices may return to stable, higher levels.

How the participants in repeated games having a prisoners' dilemma structure communicate with one another through their responses and counterresponses has been studied extensively under simulated experimental conditions.[45] Some of the most interesting insights have come from two tournaments in which 14 and then 63 game theorists participated by submitting computerized strategies for playing an indefinitely repeated prisoners' dilemma duopoly pricing game.[46] The strategies ranged in complexity from four to 152 BASIC or FORTRAN statements. Each strategy was juxtaposed by computer against the strategies of every other entry, and scores (equivalent to profits) were summed across all the encounters. Remarkably, the entry that accumulated the highest score in both tournaments was the simplest, with only four BASIC statements. Called Tit-for-Tat, it had the following characteristics:

1. Begin by playing the high-price strategy.
2. If the rival chooses the high-price strategy, continue doing so.
3. If the rival plays the low-price strategy, retaliate on the next move by choosing the low price.
4. If the rival shifts to the high-price strategy, follow suit on the next move and continue as in 1.

As a solution to prisoners' dilemma situations, Tit-for-Tat has four compelling merits.[47] It avoids unnecessary conflict by choosing high prices as long as rivals follow suit. It is quickly provoked into retaliating against uncooperative behavior. It forgives quickly when the rival returns to a cooperative stance. And it is simple and clear, so rivals can adapt to it and at the same time recognize that they cannot exploit it.

Using the "extensive form" of game-theoretic analysis, embodied in a so-called "game tree," Figure 4.7 illustrates the diverse courses a duopolistic rivalry can take when player A adheres to a Tit-for-Tat strategy through three sets of moves, or "stages." It assumes the two alternative gasoline pricing strategies of Figure 4.6; that is, the rivals can quote either the "high" $1.149

---

[45]See Charles R. Plott, "Industrial Organization Theory and Experimental Economics," *Journal of Economic Literature*, vol. 20 (December 1982), pp. 1485–1527; and Plott, "An Updated Review of Industrial Organization: Applications of Experimental Methods," in Richard Schmalensee and Robert D. Willig, eds., *Handbook of Industrial Organization*, vol. II (Amsterdam: North-Holland, 1989), pp. 1111–1176.

[46]See Robert Axelrod, *The Evolution of Cooperation* (New York: Basic Books, 1984).

[47]Axelrod, p. 20.

FIGURE 4.7
**Extensive Form of Price-Setting Rivalry with Firm A Playing a
Tit-for-Tat Strategy**

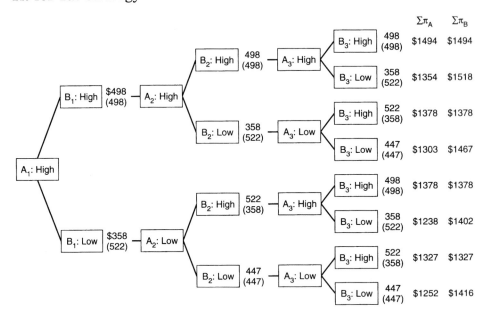

			$\Sigma\pi_A$	$\Sigma\pi_B$
B_3: High	498 (498)		$1494	$1494
B_3: Low	358 (522)		$1354	$1518
B_3: High	522 (358)		$1378	$1378
B_3: Low	447 (447)		$1303	$1467
B_3: High	498 (498)		$1378	$1378
B_3: Low	358 (522)		$1238	$1402
B_3: High	522 (358)		$1327	$1327
B_3: Low	447 (447)		$1252	$1416

price or the "low" $1.099 price, summarized in Figure 4.7 as "high" or "low."
Strategy choices are boxed, with the game's stage identified by a subscript to
the player's identifying letter (e.g., B_2 is firm B's choice in the game's second
stage). Following each pair of choices within a stage are the profit payoffs
(rounded to the nearest dollar)—first firm A's, and then below it, in parentheses, firm B's. Unlike more complex game trees, there is no branching of firm
A's choice set in the next stage following B's prior choice. Rather, A responds to
B's choice with the unique Tit-for-Tat sequitur—for example, a high price for
B's prior high price choice and a low price for B's prior low price choice. A is
assumed to have the first move (leftmost node), offering, consistent with the
Tit-for-Tat rules, the cooperative high price. The summed profits $\Sigma\pi_A$ and $\Sigma\pi_B$
for each three-stage "branch" of the game tree are presented in the two right-
most columns.

In this three-stage game, unlike the single-stage prisoners' dilemma game,
no clearly dominant strategy emerges. The symmetric low-price strategy dominant when the rivalry occurs only once yields only the fourth best of eight
alternative summed outcomes ($1416) for firm B and the seventh-best out-
come for firm A ($1252) when the game is repeated three times. B's best payoff
($1518) occurs when B plays the cooperative high-price strategy during the
first two stages, defecting to a low price on the third stage. But defection by B
in the third stage makes sense only when the game is terminated then. If the
game is repeated indefinitely (extending beyond the bounds of Figure 4.7), a

more cooperative stance is advisable. B's second-best payoff ($1494) comes from choosing the high price three times in a row. This in turn yields A's best outcome. Thus, in repeated two-player rivalries, there are much stronger incentives than in single-play games to cooperate by adopting consistent high-price strategies.

The standard prisoners' dilemma game is much simpler than real-world pricing rivalries in several respects. The payoff structure is symmetric, clearly stated, and unchanging, whereas real-world oligopolists operate under ever-changing, imperfectly perceived, and frequently asymmetric cost and demand conditions. In the standard example, the player chooses from only two discrete strategy options, whereas oligopolists must select from an infinitely variable array of price alternatives.[48] And perhaps most importantly, the tournaments won by the Tit-for-Tat strategy were duopolies—that is, with only two contestants facing one another in any given game. Other experiments, mimicking reality, have shown that cooperation breaks down with larger numbers of participants. Nevertheless, the experiments reveal what intelligent oligopolists have long known: that by using the repeated rounds of their rivalry to signal intent, displeasure, and satisfaction, mutually disadvantageous price cuts can often be avoided. Margaret Slade's detailed analysis of retail gasoline pricing in Vancouver, British Columbia, reveals interfirm reactions approximating those of the Tit-for-Tat model, although with more consistent reactions to price cuts than to price increases.[49]

PRECARIOUS STABILITY AND PRICE WARS

Threats of retaliation are insufficient to deter price-cutting consistently. They may not be believed. Or they may be ignored or misunderstood, especially when supply or demand conditions are changing rapidly, or when there is no consensus among sellers as to the "right" price. All these complications are encountered in gasoline pricing, which has tended to lurch between periods of precarious stability and price warfare.[50]

---

[48]But complexity is often reduced by confining one's choice set to a relatively few round-number or traditional "focal point" prices. See F. M. Scherer, "Focal Point Pricing and Conscious Parallelism," *Antitrust Bulletin*, vol. 12 (Summer 1967), pp. 495–503. This is probably why gasoline retailers quote prices ending with nine-tenths of a cent.

[49]Margaret E. Slade, "Interfirm Rivalry in a Repeated Game: An Empirical Test of Tacit Collusion," *Journal of Industrial Economics*, vol. 35 (June 1987), pp. 499–516; and "Vancouver's Gasoline-Price Wars: An Empirical Exercise in Uncovering Supergame Strategies," *Review of Economic Studies*, vol. 59 (April 1992), pp. 257–274.

[50]On the price war phenomenon generally, see Learned and Ellsworth, *Gasoline Pricing in Ohio;* Cassady, *Price Making and Price Behavior,* chap. 15; Masson and Allvine, "Strategies and Structure;" and Harold M. Fleming, *Gasoline Prices and Competition* (New York: Appleton-Century-Crofts, 1966), chaps. 4 and 5.

Gasoline retailing's geographic structure plays a prominent role in these fluctuations. Price-cutting often begins in one neighborhood, or a few, triggered by a handful of outlets on heavily traveled arteries. As the price cutters gain volume at the expense of more distant stations, it spreads like a chain reaction, and if undamped, it may engulf whole metropolitan areas or (more rarely) the entire United States.

The clustered arrival of more supply than the market can absorb is one plausible precipitating factor. Jobbers or retail chains burdened by heavy inventories may choose to dump them at distress prices, especially when their financial resources are meager.[51] A triggering mechanism of this sort is suggested inter alia by the price-cutting episodes observed at seemingly random intervals, with an average incidence of eight weeks, in Los Angeles during the late 1960s.[52]

Independent marketers appear to play a systematic and important role. They have been a persistently aggressive force in gasoline marketing since the 1940s.[53] Their gasoline is advertised less than that of the typical "branded" refiner outlet;[54] they frequently accept only cash, not credit; and until self-service stations proliferated during the 1970s, they characteristically provided less service. To compensate for these elements of product differentiation, the "major" brands have sold at a premium relative to the prices of the "independents"—normally 2 or 3 cents, but rising on occasion to as much as 5 cents. Price wars have broken out when an independent refiner or marketer attempted to gain market share by enlarging the spread between its price and that of the major sellers, and the shift of patronage became sufficiently large that the majors chose to fight back. These actions and reactions frequently originate in only one section of an urban market. But because of the geographic linkages among the various retail outlets, they spread to other parts of the city and perhaps to other metropolitan areas.

---

[51]When major petroleum refiners adopted independent refiners as "dancing partners" during the depressed 1930s to acquire their surplus gasoline and dispose of it in a way that did not disrupt the market, the U.S. Supreme Court ruled the arrangement a per se violation of the Sherman Act. The Court ruled inter alia that "Congress . . . has not permitted the age-old cry of ruinous competition to be a defense to price-fixing conspiracies." *U.S.* v. *Socony-Vacuum Oil Co. et al.*, 310 U.S. 150 (1940). See also D. Bruce Johnsen, "Property Rights to Cartel Rents: The *Socony-Vacuum* Story," *Journal of Law & Economics*, vol. 34 (April 1991), pp. 177–203.

[52]Rick Castanias and Herb Johnson, "Gas Wars: Retail Price Fluctuations," *Review of Economics and Statistics*, vol. 75 (February 1993), pp. 171–174. Lacking data on causal factors, the authors advance a more mechanical explanation.

[53]On their history, see Fred C. Allvine and James M. Patterson, *Competition, Ltd.: The Marketing of Gasoline* (Bloomington: Indiana University Press, 1972), chap. 3.

[54]Compared to other consumer goods industries we will encounter later, petroleum refiners allocated only a small fraction of their sales receipts to media advertising—in the mid–1970s, between two- and three-tenths of a cent per sales dollar.

There has been considerable "Who struck John?" debate over whether it is independent price cuts, or the reactions of major brands to independent inroads, that precipitate price wars. The best evidence suggests that it is the independents who cut first, but that price wars erupt only when the independents gain volume sufficiently large to provoke aggressive retaliation by major branded stations.[55] Aggressive reactions are encouraged when the major supplying refiners offer impacted retailers "competitive allowances," characteristically, a discount of seven-tenths of a cent for each cent by which branded retailers reduce their pump prices to thwart the independent inroads. To retard the spread of a price war, the majors "feather" their allowances, providing the full discount only in the immediate war zone, smaller cuts for nearby retailers, and none for retailers located some distance from the action. By announcing an end to its allowances, the local price leader attempts to quench the war, but individual price-raising efforts appear to be rebuffed at least as frequently as they succeed.

There have also been allegations that in their support of price wars during the 1960s and 1970s, the major refiners were in effect predating upon the independents, attempting to drive them from the market or at least to slow their growth.[56] The truth of the matter is more complex. Although sometimes retarded temporarily, the independents continued to capture a growing share of retail gasoline sales—for example, for refiners defined as "independents," from 23 percent of U.S. gasoline sales in 1969 to 35 percent in 1980.[57] Rather, the price wars were symptoms of a struggle to make the structure of petroleum marketing more efficient. To that subject we now turn.

CHANGES IN THE STRUCTURE OF GASOLINE RETAILING

During the 1970s and early 1980s, the structure of gasoline retailing was radically reshaped. In 1972, according to the U.S. Census of Retail Trade, there were 183,400 outlets specializing in the retail sale of gasoline, counting only stations with paid employees other than the owner. By 1982, the comparable count stood at 116,188—a decline of 37 percent. Tens of thousands of street corners where gasoline outlets once stood were converted to fast-food stores,

---

[55]See, for example, Learned and Ellsworth, *Gasoline Pricing in Ohio*, p. 108; and (on British Columbia gasoline price wars) Margaret Slade, "Conjectures, Firm Characteristics, and Market Structure," *International Journal of Industrial Organization*, vol. 4 (December 1986), pp. 347–367.

[56]See, for example, Masson and Allvine, "Strategies and Structure," pp. 169–173; and U.S. Department of Energy, *The State of Competition in Gasoline Marketing*, Book I, chap. I.

[57]Federal Trade Commission, *Mergers in the Petroleum Industry*, p. 278.

offices, and (in many cases) abandoned wastelands. How this change happened is of considerable interest.

From the 1920s through the 1960s, the major petroleum companies pursued a strategy of proliferating a dense network of retail gasoline outlets. A majority of these outlets' sites and physical facilities were, as we have seen, owned by the refining companies and leased to independent franchisees. Making the operator the residual profit or loss recipient encouraged initiative and efficiency. Most of the outlets offered full service, including automobile repair bays. They charged relatively high markups above their wholesale gasoline cost. They typically did not erect signs advertising their prices unless they were participating in a price war. Because customers whose autos they serviced were relatively loyal, their high prices were sustainable even when low-price gasoline was available elsewhere in the city. The high prices, however, constrained volume, as did the high density of nearby competing stations. Consequently, the average Exxon brand station pumped 27,400 gallons of gasoline per month in 1972 (i.e., 70 gallons per hour, assuming 14-hour days six and one-half days per week).[58] Meanwhile, low-price low-service outlets were selling more than 100,000 gallons per month.

There are several hypotheses as to why the major companies chose this low-volume station strategy. It was probably what most motorists wanted under the prevailing conditions. There is consensus also that the major companies were motivated to proliferate small outlets, even when their retailing investments yielded low or negative returns, as they in fact did, to increase their sales of highly profitable crude oil from domestic wells and franchises in the Middle East.[59] The choice was undoubtedly encouraged by anomalies fostered by the percentage depletion tax break given domestic oil producers.[60] To see this, consider the crude oil pricing decision in 1959 of a vertically integrated petroleum refiner filing separate federal income tax returns for its crude and refining-marketing operations. Assume the initially prevailing price to be $3.00 per barrel. The question is, how profitable would a 20-cent crude oil price increase be, assuming that it is followed by other producers at the crude oil stage but not at the product stage? The federal income tax on that extra 20 cents of profit is 0.52 (the corporate tax rate) times (20 cents minus 27.5 percent percentage depletion of 5.5 cents), or 7.54 cents. The increase in after-tax income per barrel is therefore 20 − 7.54 = 12.46 cents. At the refining

---

[58]Hogarty, "The Origin and Evolution," p. 60. See also "The Oil Giants Fight the Independents," *Business Week*, May 13, 1972, pp. 135–144.

[59]See U.S. Department of Energy, *The State of Competition*, Book II, pp. 10–13, quoting internal strategy documents subpoenaed from eight petroleum companies; and "The Oil Majors Retreat from the Gasoline Pump," *Business Week*, August 7, 1978, pp. 50–51.

[60]See Chapter 3, pp. 68–69 supra; and de Chazeau and Kahn, *Integration and Competition*, pp. 221–225, from which the example that follows is drawn.

stage, its costs are increased, and gross profits are reduced, by 20 cents, but if profits are still positive, after-tax income is reduced only by 9.6 cents (20–0.52 × 20). If the refining company is fully self-sufficient in oil, or even, it can be shown, if 77 percent or more of the oil it uses is from its own tax-preferred wells, the loss at the refining-marketing stage is more than compensated by the gain at the crude oil stage, even when, as assumed in the example, product prices are not raised at all! Thus, petroleum companies had an incentive to take their profits at the crude oil stage by setting high crude oil prices, and arguably also by expand'ng their distribution networks to sell more of the high-profit crude oil.

To be sure, they could have sold their crude oil or gasoline to others, including independent refiners and marketers, as well as pushing the products through their own vertically integrated channels. Some major petroleum companies did so. But this strategy entailed costs and risks. The more they sold to independents, and especially to independent marketers, the larger the independents' disruptive influence in product markets was likely to be. It appeared preferable to direct the oil through "safe" company channels less likely to trigger price wars. The exceptions in this case prove the rule. The leading eight integrated petroleum companies did sell or swap crude oil to independent refiners, but they sold virtually no gasoline to independent marketers; indeed, most had explicit policies to that effect.[61] Most of the gasoline flowing from integrated companies to independent marketers came from the smaller integrated refiners, whose market shares were sufficiently small that they were inclined not to concern themselves with preserving refined product pricing discipline, in effect "chiseling" on the industry consensus.

During the 1970s, a dramatic change in the major companies' retail marketing policies became apparent. Low-volume outlets were no longer encouraged, the development of high-volume channels was stressed, and quite generally, company leaders began insisting that the profitability of refining and especially marketing operations had to be raised. Subsidization of marketing by crude oil was no longer tolerated. Each stage of the vertical structure was expected to meet stringent return-on-investment goals.

The majors' new stress on low-cost marketing coincided in time with the renewal of franchise expropriation measures in the Middle East (e.g., Libya in 1971, Saudi Arabia in 1972) and the termination of percentage depletion tax treatment in the United States (in 1975). These events, which reduced the profitability of crude oil operations and hence the incentive to sell as much crude as possible, may have contributed to the majors' change of heart. But more importantly, by the early 1970s, the large integrated companies realized that

---

[61]U.S. Senate, Committee on Government Operations, Permanent Subcommittee on Investigations, *Investigation of the Petroleum Industry* (Washington, DC: USGPO, July 1973), pp. 6–11; and Federal Trade Commission, *Mergers in the Petroleum Industry*, pp. 266–267.

the independent marketers' way of doing business not only delivered gasoline to consumers at lower cost, but satisfied better than the majors' high-cost system the demands of a steadily growing plurality of consumers.[62] If the majors did not respond in kind, the independents would continue to increase their share of the market and undermine even more the integrated companies' refining and marketing profits.

There were several reasons for the changes in consumer preferences. As automobiles became more reliable and required less frequent servicing, consumers were less closely tied to their gasoline vendors for regular maintenance. Gradually it became known that the gasoline dispensed by independents was equal in quality to that of the major branded stations, often emerging from the same refineries and (except for last-minute additives) the same terminal storage tanks. Octane rating disclosure standards were unified under a 1972 Federal Trade Commission regulation, further reducing perceived differences in product quality. The sharp increases in product prices induced by OPEC in 1973–1974 and 1979 made consumers more price-conscious. Greater price sensitivity in turn led consumers to embrace self-service—a concept implemented more economically with the pump layouts of independent stations than in the traditional small full-service station. State laws and fire insurance codes had been changed in the late 1960s and early 1970s to eliminate barriers to self-service. In 1974, only 6 percent of all retail gasoline outlets offered self-service. The fraction soared to 68 percent in 1978.[63] By 1985, 87 percent of all stations had self-service pumps, and 46 percent offered only self-service.[64]

The major petroleum companies implemented numerous measures to increase their marketing channel efficiency. They chose not to renew the franchises of low-volume outlets at their annual expiration dates. They began charging a percentage fee for credit card services,[65] and, more important, sharply raised franchisee's rents—in one reported case, from $7,300 per year in 1970 to $60,000 in 1992.[66] They closed down their own-brand marketing operations altogether in whole sections of the country where their market shares were considered too small to sustain profitability, retrenching to regions in which their position was stronger. Thus, Texaco, which had previously prided

---

[62]See U.S. Department of Energy, *The State of Competition*, Book I, pp. 191–205, and Book II, pp. 14–21 (drawing upon subpoenaed company strategy papers); and "The Oil Giants Fight the Independents," *Business Week*, May 13, 1972, pp. 135–144.

[63]Hogarty, "The Origin and Evolution of Gasoline Marketing," pp. 50–55. See also Allvine and Patterson, *Competition, Ltd.*, pp. 95–100.

[64]"Big Shift in Gasoline Retailing Is Changing Buying Patterns," *New York Times*, May 28, 1985, p. 1.

[65]See "Shell Upsets a Credit Tradition," *Business Week*, June 17, 1972, p. 28.

[66]"Gas Station Owner Takes on the Giants," *Brookline TAB* (Brookline, MA), July 6, 1992.

itself on being the only petroleum company with outlets in all 50 states, withdrew from six upper midwestern states in 1978.[67] Exxon exited in 1982 from Kentucky, Ohio, Vermont, and parts of other northeast states.[68] Chevron abandoned Arkansas and adjacent parts of Tennessee and Kentucky in 1993 and sold off all of its company-owned stations to jobbers in seven other states while increasing its investment in Gulf Coast state retailing.[69]

While retrenching on the franchised retailer front, some major companies, especially the medium-size firms, increased the number, size, and aggressiveness of their company-operated outlets. The share of gasoline sold at retail by the 28 largest marketers rose from 7.3% in 1972 to 11.7% in 1979.[70] Some offered company store gasoline at cut-rate prices under "fighting" brand names, e.g., Alert for Exxon, Sello and Big-Bi for Mobil, and Gastown and Speedway for Marathon. Others sold the company's principal brand at rigorously competitive prices from modern high-volume self-service stations. Because the new company stores lacked service bays and other complications, they were relatively simple to manage, making the effort and initiative of a franchised owner-manager less essential. New company outlets were typically located on heavily traveled urban traffic arteries, where they could satisfy two objectives: meeting the competition of independents head-to-head, and maintaining pressure on the refining company's smaller franchised dealers, who might otherwise be inclined to set relatively high prices and sacrifice volume.[71]

Needless to say, this price competition from company-owned outlets infuriated smaller franchised operators selling the same brand. At least as galling was the competition from stations owned by jobbers. Under the "dual distribution" system used by most petroleum companies, jobbers buy directly from terminals at rack prices, sell to small franchised retailers at tank wagon prices, and also sell at retail through their own stations, sometimes using the refiner's brand and sometimes their own brand.[72] Jobber-owned outlets tended to favor low-price high-volume strategies much more strongly than small franchised

---

[67]"Sales Shift in Coastline Industry," *New York Times,* May 22, 1978, p. D1; and "Texaco Strategy: Sacrificing Pawns But Still in the Game," *National Petroleum News,* June 1978, pp. 46–52.

[68]"Exxon Will Close 850 Gas Stations," *New York Times,* August 26, 1982, p. A1.

[69]"Chevron Dealers Feel Orphaned," *New York Times,* May 29, 1993, p. D1.

[70]U.S. Department of Energy, *The State of Competition,* Book I, p. 111.

[71]The high-price proclivity of small franchised outlets was bolstered by federal government controls between 1974 and 1980, since the amount of gasoline individual gasoline operators could obtain was governed by rigid quantity allocation rules. If Figure 4.6 is recast so that very little more can be sold at low prices than at high prices, one finds that the high-price strategy becomes dominant.

[72]That such arrangements were not illegally discriminatory if they represent a good-faith response of refiners to competition for jobbers' business was settled by the U.S. Supreme Court in *Federal Trade Commission* v. *Standard Oil Co.,* 355 U.S. 396 (1958).

operators. If the spread between rack and tank wagon prices widens to exceed the jobber's wholesaling costs, the inherent conflict between jobbers and their franchised customers is intensified. In a competitive situation, jobbers can cut into their wholesaler's margin to sell gasoline at retail for less—perhaps even less than the tank wagon price paid by their franchised dealer customers. The testimony of a franchised Phillips dealer in Atlanta is illustrative:[73]

> [At some point in 1974] I noticed my gallons started dropping. I looked around to see what was happening. About a mile-and-a half behind me was a Phillips 66 station, flying the colors, using the credit cards, the whole works, posting a price on the street . . . that was 2 cents below my dealer tank wagon costs. We talked to Phillips about this. . . . What they were doing was selling gasoline to a jobber, a so-called jobber. He was a retailer. He was selling gas at retail using his jobber buying bracket in order to do this. So consequently, we could get nothing done about it.

There were at least two reasons why these conflicts arose. For one, when the gasoline industry was subject to thoroughgoing federal controls between 1974 and 1981, the regulations probably froze jobbers' wholesale margins at levels sufficiently generous to put retailers too small to buy direct from refiners at a significant disadvantage. Jobbers were also subjected to less-stringent quantity allocation rules than individual franchised outlets.[74] Between 1972 and 1979, the share of the 28 largest U.S. refiners' gasoline sales made directly to franchised dealers dropped from 56.1 percent to 39.1 percent. Meanwhile, sales to branded jobbers rose from 23.1 to 29.7 percent, and unbranded gasoline sales increased from 12.9 to 19.5 percent.[75] But second, even after federal regulation ended, dealer-jobber conflicts persisted.[76] It seems probable that the refiners recognized the superior market retention potential of low-price jobber-owned stations. Therefore, they did little to discourage their jobbers from maintaining rack-to-tank wagon price spreads that squeezed small franchised outlets—perhaps into oblivion.

When the livelihood of 100 thousand small businessmen plying a single trade is jeopardized, political action cannot be far behind. In 1978, the dealers successfully lobbied for passage of the federal Petroleum Marketing Practices Act, informally called the "Dealer Day in Court" law. The statute specified the conditions under which refiners could unilaterally terminate their dealer franchises—for example, only for a lack of good-faith efforts to carry out the franchise terms (including reasonable volume quotas), or when the refiner was

---

[73]U.S. Department of Energy, *The State of Competition*, Book I, p. 230.

[74]See *The State of Competition*, Book I, pp. 125–135 and 213–232.

[75]*The State of Competition*, Book I, pp. 111 and 172–177.

[76]See "Gasoline Wholesalers and Dealers Are Locked in a Battle for Profits," *Philadelphia Inquirer*, August 20, 1989.

abandoning the relevant market area altogether.[77] This almost surely heightened companies' incentives to withdraw from regions in which their market shares were low. Some states, such as Maryland and Connecticut, passed laws banning company-owned gasoline outlets.[78] A few states banned self-service stations or limited the conditions under which full-service outlets could be converted to self-service. In 1984, thirteen major petroleum companies settled a private antitrust suit by agreeing to let their more than 50,000 nonowner franchised dealers sell other refiners' gasoline, as long as the pumps are clearly marked to let consumers know that an alternative brand is being supplied.[79]

During the 1980s, the exodus from gasoline retailing slowed. The number of stations with employees fell from 116,188 in 1982 to 114,748 in 1987 and then to 105,335 in 1992.[80] Whether these laws were the reason, or whether the industry's structure had approached a reasonably efficient new equilibrium, is unclear.

It is also unclear whether the petroleum companies succeeded in their efforts to raise the profitability of their refining and marketing operations. Federal Trade Commission surveys revealed the following ratios of pre-tax operating income to assets for the combined refining and marketing operations of from 27 to 29 large petroleum companies:[81]

Year	Return on Assets (percent)
1974	−0.6
1975	0.4
1976	3.7
1977	11.2

Plainly, the companies' profitability increased enormously during the period when the restructuring of retailing was at its peak. (Between 1972 and 1977,

---

[77]*The State of Competition*, Book I, Appendix A, pp. 7–9.

[78]See John Barron and John Umbeck, "A Dubious Bill of Divorcement: The Case of Oil Refiners and Gas Stations," *Regulation*, vol. 7 (January/February 1993), pp. 29–33. On proposed federal legislation, see "House Panel Ponders Bills to Curb Distribution Practices by Refiners," *BNA Antitrust and Trade Regulation Report*, vol. 61 (September 1991).

[79]"13 Refiners Agree Stations May Sell Any Brand of Gas," *New York Times*, September 25, 1984, p. 1.

[80]The most recent figures are from a CD/ROM preliminary version of the 1992 Census of Retail Trade.

[81]Federal Trade Commission, *Statistical Report: Annual Line of Business Report* (Washington, DC: various years).

the number of gasoline stations declined by 50,000.) Whether restructuring was the main cause, or whether the returns for 1974 were unusually severely impacted by the OPEC shock, recession, and government price controls, is less certain. Noncomparable Department of Energy surveys covering 26 companies' domestic refining and marketing operations show net income as a percentage of assets at 7.1 percent in 1977 (compared to 11.2 percent in the FTC survey), and averaging 6.4 percent, with no significant time trend, between 1977 and 1991.[82] During the same 1977–1991 period, the companies' domestic crude oil and natural gas production operations averaged a return of 11.1 percent on assets, with a marked downward trend after 1982. Indeed, between 1987 and 1991, refining and marketing averaged 7.2 percent while oil and gas production averaged 4.7 percent. It would appear that the companies succeeded in raising refining and marketing profits and in making the refining-marketing tub rest on its own bottom, even if absolute profitability goals were not attained because of excess capacity and continuing competition.

One thing is clear. By 1992, petroleum refining and marketing had been transformed radically relative to the state in which John D. Rockefeller Sr. left it. Competition, though imperfect, has become widespread and relentless. We suspect that Mr. Rockefeller frowns disapprovingly from his exalted position in Entrepreneurs' Heaven.

AFTERWORD

Changes over time in the structures of crude oil, refining, and petroleum products markets have given us examples of pricing behavior ranging from predation through coordination by a cartel to coordination among oligopolists by means of institutions such as price leadership and Tit-for-Tat strategies. Pricing behavior varies with the structure of the market, which is influenced among other things by the logic of scale economies. Market structures in turn have been shaped by the strategies sellers adopt. A host of governmental interventions have also had important effects on both structures and strategy choices. In the next chapter we extend our investigation into these reciprocal relationships.

---

[82]U.S. Department of Energy, Energy Information Administration, *Annual Energy Review: 1992* (Washington: USGPO, June 1993), pp. 88–91.

5

STEEL

In 1901 the United States Steel Corporation achieved through a gigantic merger a dominant position in the steel industry. We analyze the pricing strategy problem of firms that dominate their markets, finding that under the conditions faced by U.S. Steel, a policy of gradually surrendering market share to rivals maximized long-run profits. Price leadership in the steel industry was best characterized at first by the dominant-firm model, then by a formula-based collusive model, and much later by a barometric model. We explore how maturing of the steel industry's growth led to slow technological innovation, which, combined with ill-starred labor relations choices, increased the U.S. industry's vulnerability to import competition. That development requires an analysis of dumping in international trade and the logic and effects of import-barring policies adopted by the U.S. government. A crisis experienced during the 1980s led to industry restructuring and the restoration of international competitiveness.

INTRODUCTION

More millennia ago than there is written history, families ringed their cooking and heating fires with locally gathered orange-colored rocks. As the heat became intense, a shiny gray viscous mass oozed from the rocks. With some experimentation, the procedure was replicated under better-controlled conditions, and the resulting metal was beaten into swords, tools, and vessels. Thus began the iron age, whose traces persist today in the form of a large and endlessly controversial industry.

TECHNOLOGICAL DEVELOPMENT AND SCALE ECONOMIES

Iron and its higher-technology derivative, steel, come from naturally abundant iron ore, which is simply iron oxide. The trick learned in ancient times was burning charcoal to strip off the oxygen and form carbon dioxide, leaving iron and various contaminants. Gradually it was discovered that the process worked more economically when the iron ore and charcoal (and later, limestone) were mixed and heated in a relatively tall furnace, at the bottom of which a blast of air is introduced. The resulting "pig iron" settles to the bottom and can be drawn off through a tap. From this evolved the modern blast furnace, which in German and French is still called a "tall furnace."

During the sixteenth and seventeenth centuries, the production of iron was held back in many parts of Europe by dwindling supplies of timber to make charcoal. Sweden, with rich iron ore deposits and abundant forests, became by a substantial margin the world's leading producer of iron and (after further refining) steel. In the early 1700s England's Abraham Darby Sr. was the first of numerous experimenters to succeed in firing a blast furnace with coke made from coal. His son advanced the art by devising a means to remove silicone from the pig iron. Further innovations followed—notably, using water power and then James Watt's steam engine to drive air bellows of improved design, and Henry Cort's radically superior puddling furnace for making wrought iron. By the late eighteenth century, England, with abundant coal supplies and rapidly advancing technology, had surpassed Sweden in iron production.[1]

The pig iron that emerges from a blast furnace contains a residue of 2.2 to 5 percent carbon from the oxygen-seizing charcoal or coke along with other impurities, and the resulting product is brittle. Stronger wrought iron products were achieved first by heating and hammering strips of pig iron, and later by rolling molten puddles of pig iron using Cort's furnace. The reheating burned off unwanted carbon, and the pounding helped dissipate other mineral contaminants. Steel with a very low carbon content and high strength was also made, at considerable cost, by melting pig iron in a ceramic-lined crucible.

Two further innovations greatly reduced the cost of making steel, permitting its use to expand enormously. Around 1856 England's Henry Bessemer developed a method of blowing heated air through a pool of molten pig iron enclosed in a ceramic-lined vessel. The air's oxygen burned off the remaining carbon, leaving low-carbon steel. This Bessemer process produced a "heat" of steel quickly, permitting a single converter to turn out unprecedented quantities of steel in a year's time. During the 1860s the Martin brothers of France brought William Siemens's regenerative furnace concept to bear on steelmaking. With the resulting Siemens-Martin open-hearth process, fiery heat is applied to the surface of molten pig iron for six to eight hours, burning off

---

[1]See T. S. Ashton, *Iron and Steel in the Industrial Revolution*, 2nd ed. (Manchester, UK: Manchester University Press, 1951); and Joel Mokyr, *The Lever of Riches* (New York: Oxford University Press, 1990), pp. 92–95.

unwanted carbon. The original Bessemer and open-hearth processes were unsuited to high-phosphorus iron ores, (e.g., ores from the Lorraine region of France), but that problem was solved by further innovations during the 1870s. Because the Bessemer process leaves nitrogen from its air blast dissolved in the steel, its product tends to be more brittle than open-hearth steel, so gradually the slower open-hearth method came to dominate the fast but lower-quality Bessemer process.

With these developments, the basic technology of low-cost steel production was in place. Subsequent improvements have for the most part been evolutionary, although three important exceptions warrant immediate attention. First, beginning in the 1950s, a new method of steel refining, the basic oxygen furnace (BOF) process, began to replace open-hearth furnaces. BOF is a variant on Bessemer converters, but instead of injecting air (with its high nitrogen content) at the bottom of the molten pig iron, a lance of pure oxygen is directed toward the surface of the melt. The violent ensuing reaction burns off residual carbon elements and at the same time stirs the steel to ensure uniform treatment. Second, the molten steel from Bessemer converters, open-hearth furnaces, or basic oxygen furnaces was traditionally poured into ingot molds. The poured ingots were allowed to cool, and then, at the appropriate time, they were reheated for reduction in primary rolling mills into either billets (elongated, roughly square, bars) or slabs (e.g., 8 inches thick, 48 inches wide, and 20 feet long). But more recently, the ingot–primary reduction mill sequence has been replaced by continuous casting, in which the newly refined, still-molten steel is poured into a casting mill that forms the steel directly into either billets or slabs. Third, the slabs or billets are then reheated and rolled in multistage mills into a host of final product shapes—for example, thin wide steel strip, thicker construction plates, construction angles and I-beams, heavy bars, thin concrete reinforcing bars, wire, and wire rods. There have been recurring improvements in rolling mill technology, the most important of which was the continuous strip mill, pioneered during the 1920s by the American Rolling Mill Company (later, Armco).

Figure 5.1 illustrates the layout in 1973 of a modern integrated steel works, Nippon Kokan's (NKK) Fukuyama works near Hiroshima. At the time Fukuyama was the world's largest single steelmaking facility, with an annual capacity of 12 million tons. Iron ore, coal, and limestone arrive at the plant's receiving docks (right-hand side). The coal is transformed to coke in coke ovens, and ore is converted into more easily processed pellets in sintering ovens. These raw materials are fed into the blast furnaces (middle of plant), whose pig iron moves to basic oxygen furnace shops. From there the steel flows to a continuous casting shop or (as ingots) to slabbing and billet mills. The resulting slabs and billets are carried to a secondary reduction mill, such as a hot strip mill, a plate mill, or a large shape mill. Coils of strip steel may be processed further in a cold strip mill and galvanizing mills before moving into warehouses and then by water transportation to market.

Important economies of large-scale operation exist at several stages of the steelmaking sequence. As early as the eighteenth century, it was recognized that costs could be reduced by building larger blast furnaces, if diverse physical constraints could be overcome. As in building petroleum refineries, the

FIGURE 5.1

Layout map of NKK Corporation's Fukuyama Steelworks, 1973

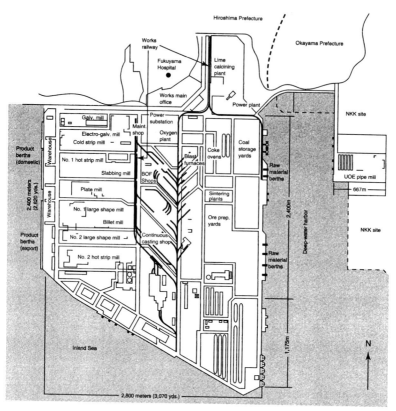

Source: NKK Corporation, reproduced with permission.

two-thirds rule holds approximately. Figure 5.2 depicts the state of the art as of 1962.[2] The horizontal scale shows annual output of pig iron (in millions of metric tons); the vertical axis total investment cost in U.S. dollars per ton of annual capacity.[3] The thin solid line traces the envelope cost curve for single-furnace shops of increasing capacity. For a shop operating one blast furnace with a hearth diameter of 3.5 meters (11 feet), the investment cost was $43 per ton. As the hearth diameter was increased to 10.0 meters (33

---

[2]The cost data, originally presented in West German DM, were converted to U.S. dollars at the then-prevailing 4-to-1 exchange rate.

[3]To transform investment costs per annual ton to annual investment carrying costs, one multiplies the former by two factors—an annual depreciation rate and an annual interest or cost of capital rate—and adds the results.

FIGURE 5.2
Investment Cost Per Annual Ton of Blast Furnace Capacity, 1962

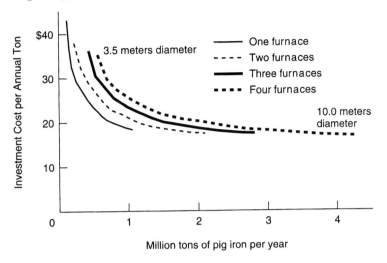

Source: Adapted from Hermann Schenck and Hans Küppersbusch, *Baukosten und Leistungsfähigheit von Hochofenanlagen* (Düsseldorf: Verlag Stahleisen, 1966), p. 42.

feet), raising annual capacity to roughly 1 million tons per year, investment cost per ton fell to $18.25. Because of better infrastructure equipment usage and a smoother flow of metal during furnace relining periods, investment costs per ton for furnaces of any given hearth diameter were lower when the shop includes two furnaces (light dashes), three furnaces (solid line), or four furnaces (heavy dashes). The savings from multifurnace operation, however, were much more modest than the savings from building large as compared to small individual furnaces.

Anyone examining Figure 5.2 during the early 1960s would have seen that it is incomplete. Unit costs continued to decline up to the point at which 10-meter hearth diameter furnaces—the best state of the art at the time—were constructed. One suspects that extrapolation would yield even lower unit costs. This proved to be the case. During the next 10 years furnace capacities were extended from 1 million to 3.8 million tons per year. It was found, however, that the largest units encountered internal fluid dynamics problems, and little was saved by moving to that size from furnaces of roughly 2.5 million tons annual capacity. On this we shall have more to say later.

Scale economies are even more compelling in a BOF shop. Because of the violent reaction occurring when the oxygen lance strikes the molten iron's surface, the furnace's ceramic tile lining wears out quickly and must be replaced every 25 to 40 days. In a two-furnace shop, one is typically shut down for relining while the other operates. With furnaces of 250-ton capacity,[4] the shop's annual output is approximately 3 million tons. If a third furnace is added, however, two can operate while the third is relined. Output is doubled to 6 million tons per year, but capital and operating labor costs are increased by less than 50 percent.

Because BOF shops commonly include 25 to 30 percent scrap steel along with pig iron in their heats, a single 6-million-ton BOF shop requires roughly 4.3 million tons of pig iron inputs per year. One blast furnace provides too little pig iron to meet this requirement; two produce too much. Better balance is achieved in an integrated steel works with two optimal BOF shops—with 12 million tons of raw steel capacity, supplied by three blast furnaces, each with a capacity of 3 million tons.

Before BOF and large blast furnace technology came to the forefront, the minimum efficient scale for an integrated steel works was more apt to be governed by the size of the largest product rolling mills. Now, however, the "hot metal" side of the operation dominates. The largest product mill in widespread use is a hot strip mill with 10 pairs of rollers, extruding thin steel sheets 80 inches in width at a rate of roughly 4 million tons per year. A modern integrated works of minimum efficient scale is likely to require several rolling mills of diverse types to process its voracious output of hot metal.

These relationships are being rent asunder by the encroachment of still another technological and managerial innovation—the electric arc furnace "minimill."[5] Electric arc furnaces were used to refine top-quality steel in the early years of the twentieth century. During the 1950s and 1960s, however, the process was extended to make steel of commercial quality in large quantities at competitive costs. No iron ore is used; one begins with steel scrap as an input, saving several steps and much expense relative to traditional integrated steelmaking methods. Minimum efficient scales in both the hot metal and rolling mill departments have remained below 1 million tons per year—much less than the MES of an integrated works. With the smaller size of minimills have come managerial innovations, stressing lean staffing and high employee productivity.[6] The spread of minimills was limited by two constraints. First, if the input requirements of minimills outrun the supply of scrap steel (to be sure, a receding constraint in mature economies), scrap prices can rise to render the process uneconomic.[7] Second, scale limitations and impurities

---

[4]The first nonexperimental BOF furnaces had capacities of 35 tons per heat. There too, optimal sizes have increased greatly as the technology has advanced. But beyond 250 tons, inflexibilities limit further cost savings.

[5]See Donald F. Barnett and Robert W. Crandall, *Up from the Ashes: The Rise of the Steel Minimill in the United States* (Washington, DC: Brookings, 1986).

[6]See "The Big Threat to Big Steel's Future," *Fortune*, July 15, 1991, pp. 106–108.

[7]This happened in 1973–1974 and again in 1993–1994. See "Big Steel's Big Opportunity," *Business Week*, January 10, 1994, p. 74.

remaining in the refined scrap confined minimills to relatively simple products such as concrete reinforcing bars and small structural shapes. During the late 1980s, however, the electric arc process was successfully extended to produce heavy structural members (e.g., I-beams) and thin strips up to 53 inches in width.[8] By continuously casting the molten steel into 2-inch-thick slabs rather than the 10-inch slabs customary in integrated works, the minimill process is able to roll thin strips with only four roller sets rather than ten, saving capital cost at the rolling mill stage as well as at the hot-metal stage. Minimills are still unable to yield the blemish-free wide steel sheets needed for automobile bodies, washing-machine cases, and the like. But they were moving in that direction, thereby threatening the last bastions defended exclusively by integrated steel works.

In 1992 electric arc furnaces accounted for 35 percent of U.S. production of ordinary carbon steel products (excluding the much more expensive special alloy and stainless varieties), which totalled 82.5 million tons. Electric furnaces were also used to produce virtually all of the stainless steel (2 million tons in 1992) and more than half of the other special alloy steels (8.5 million tons).[9]

GROWTH AND RESTRUCTURING OF THE U.S. STEEL INDUSTRY

After a century of world leadership, British steelmakers failed to exploit aggressively the opportunities opened up by the Bessemer and open-hearth processes, and as a result, their growth lagged. Responding inter alia to the rapidly expanding demand for railroad rails and rolling stock, the United States surged forward and seized the world steel production lead during the 1880s. Germany took second place ahead of England during the 1890s. Total U.S. production of steel ingots and castings grew by decades as follows (in million tons):[10]

---

[8]See "Nucor's Thin-Slab Casting Decision," Harvard Business School case study N9–391–109 (April 1992); "U.S. Minimills Launch a Full-Scale Attack," *Business Week*, June 13, 1988, p. 100; and "Nucor: Rolling Right into Steel's Big Time," *Business Week*, November 19, 1990, pp. 76–77.

[9]American Iron and Steel Institute, *Annual Statistical Report: 1992* (Washington DC: AISI, 1993), p. 70.

[10]U.S. Bureau of the Census, *Historical Statistics of the United States: Colonial Times to 1957* (Washington, DC: USGPO, 1960), pp. 416–417. Pig iron production was 1.67 million tons in 1870 and 3.84 million tons in 1880. Peter Temin, *Iron and Steel in Nineteenth-Century America* (Cambridge: MIT Press, 1964), p. 266.

1870	0.08
1880	1.39
1890	4.79
1900	11.41
1910	29.22
1920	47.19
1930	45.58
1940	66.99
1950	96.84

As production advanced at a 10 percent annual rate in the early 1890s, the U.S. steel industry consisted of hundreds of small, geographically dispersed producers. Most were not integrated vertically; that is, some specialized in producing pig iron from purchased ore, some in converting the pig iron to steel ingots, and still others in rolling rails, construction angles, sheet, or wire. Price-fixing agreements or "pools" were common, but there was extensive chiseling on the agreements (except perhaps in steel rails), and the industry gravitated on occasion toward price competition viewed (with considerable exaggeration) by its participants as "cutthroat" or "ruinous."[11] During the 1890s, numerous competitors joined forces in a series of mergers, giving rise to relatively integrated companies such as Federal Steel (from a five-company merger) and (mainly without merger) Carnegie Steel (producing 18 percent of the nation's steel ingots in 1900), and also to firms holding dominant market shares within their specialties, such as American Sheet Steel (the sheet steel trust), Shelby Steel Tube (the seamless-tube trust), and American Tin Plate (the tin-plated steel trust).[12]

At the turn of the century these newly consolidated enterprises began contemplating further growth through vertical integration. American Steel and Wire, for example, planned to erect new blast furnaces and steel refining facilities to replace ingots it purchased from Carnegie and Federal; and Carnegie investigated the construction of a major pipe and tube plant at Conneaut Harbor on Lake Erie. Some industry members, including Carnegie's president, Charles Schwab, believed that these expansions would create considerable excess capacity, threatening the relatively high prices that had been secured during the late 1890s. Schwab presented his arguments to the leading

---

[11]Compare Temin, *Iron and Steel,* pp. 174–189; Arthur T. Hadley, "Private Monopolies and Public Rights," *Quarterly Journal of Economics,* vol. 1 (October 1886), pp. 30–44; Eliot Jones, "Is Competition in Industry Ruinous?" *Quarterly Journal of Economics,* vol. 34 (May 1920), pp. 497–502; and Ida M. Tarbell, *The Life of Elbert H. Gary* (New York: Appleton, 1925), pp. 98–106.

[12]See Eliot Jones, *The Trust Problem in the United States* (New York: Macmillan, 1920), pp. 188–200.

financier of the time, J. Pierpont Morgan, who had previously arranged several earlier steel company consolidations. Morgan resolved to create a "consolidation of consolidations."

The result was the United States Steel Corporation (USS), which at its formation in February 1901 originated 66 percent of the nation's steel ingots and castings, 73 percent of the tin plate supply, 78 percent of the wire rods, 83 percent of all seamless-tube output, and much else.[13] The principal companies merged were Carnegie Steel, Federal Steel, National Tube, Shelby Steel Tube, National Steel, American Sheet Steel, American Steel and Wire, American Tin Plate, American Steel Hoop, American Bridge Company, and Lake Superior Consolidated Iron Mines.[14] The resulting organization included at least 177 manufacturing plants, 42 iron ore companies, numerous coal mines, more than 1000 miles of railroad, and much else.[15] The Carnegie Company was the largest and (as the industry's most aggressive competitor) key acquisition. To induce Andrew Carnegie to sell out, Morgan tendered Carnegie shareholders stocks and bonds valued at $332 million and assumed preexisting bond obligations of $160 million.[16] Altogether, the securities issued to float the United States Steel Corporation were valued at $1.37 billion—more than twice the estimated market value of the acquired companies before they sold out. It was the first billion-dollar industrial corporation in U.S. history, capitalized at 14 times the book value and twice the market value of Standard Oil.[17] For its efforts, the Morgan underwriting syndicate realized a net promoter's profit estimated at $62.5 million.[18]

Following its initial consolidation, USS acquired several smaller iron and steel interests. Two other moves were more important. In January 1907, it signed a long-term lease covering most of the vast Mesabi Range iron ore deposits held by the Great Northern Railroad. In November 1907, it acquired the Tennessee Coal and Iron Company, which produced 4.3 percent of the

---

[13]Jones, *The Trust Problem*, p. 207.

[14]John Moody, *The Truth About the Trusts* (New York: Moody, 1904), p. 153.

[15]Moody, *The Truth*, pp. 142–147.

[16]Moody, *The Truth*, p. 155. Meeting Morgan on a Transatlantic liner after the transaction was completed, Carnegie observed that "I should have asked you another hundred million for those Carnegie properties." "If you had, I should have paid it," Morgan replied. According to a later *Wall Street Journal* account, Carnegie "was so soured in his soul that he could take no more toast and marmalade." Andrew Sinclair, *Corsair: The Life of J. Pierpont Morgan* (Boston: Little, Brown, 1981), p. 126.

[17]See Moody, *The Truth*, pp. 200–204, who takes a skeptical view of U. S. Steel's true value and infers that its securities were "watered"—that is, sold to the public at prices exceeding their value. See also Jones, *The Trust Problem*, pp. 207–208.

[18]See "The Corporation," *Fortune*, March 1936, p. 65. In 1990 purchasing power equivalents, $62.5 million translates to approximately $800 million. There was no federal income tax in 1901.

nation's steel rails and owned more than half of the rich iron ore deposits in Tennessee and northern Alabama. The acquisition was ostensibly made, with the consent of President Theodore Roosevelt, to restore investor confidence during a stock market panic. But the Great Northern lease and the Tennessee acquisition left the Corporation (as it was called) controlling most of the best iron ore deposits in the United States, including a share of commercially available Lake Superior district ores variously estimated between 75 and 90 percent.[19]

UNITED STATES STEEL'S PRICING STRATEGY

Having acquired a dominant position in most facets of the American steel industry, the United States Steel Corporation was confronted with the problem of how best to exploit that position for the benefit of its stockholders.

Within the USS board of directors, there was intense debate over pricing strategy. On one side was Charles Schwab, the newly appointed president, who favored the policies of Andrew Carnegie: "hard driving," or running the steel works at their maximum capacity, and pricing as aggressively as was necessary to sell the resulting output. On the other side was attorney and (briefly) judge Elbert H. Gary, former president of Federal Steel and then chairman of the USS board. Judge Gary abhorred unfettered price competition, which he believed was ruinous. He argued that USS should instead exercise its leadership to set "reasonable" prices, publicize them, and abide by them unless compelled to respond by recalcitrant rivals. Before a U.S. House of Representatives committee in 1911 he observed:[20]

> The general policy of Mr. Carnegie, no doubt, whatever may be shown in exceptions, if there were any, was to keep his mills busy, and if he could not keep them busy by selling at one price he sold at another price, and at times he sold at prices which were ruinous to his competitors, because down to about his cost was very much below the cost of others. In my opinion, that was a very bad policy.

Gary's arguments carried the day, and in 1903, Schwab resigned as president to lead a much smaller consolidation, Bethlehem Steel.

---

[19]See Jones, *The Trust Problem*, pp. 222–233; and Donald O. Parsons and Edward J. Ray, "The United States Steel Consolidation: The Creation of Market Control," *Journal of Law & Economics*, vol. 18 (April 1975), pp. 194–201.

[20]Testimony before the Stanley Committee, quoted in Parsons and Ray, "The United States Steel Consolidation," p. 209.

DOMINANT FIRM LEADERSHIP VERSUS LIMIT PRICING

The pricing strategy alternatives confronting USS can best be characterized, at least as a first approximation, in terms of dichotomous alternatives: dominant-firm price leadership or limit pricing.

Figure 5.3a illustrates the standard dominant-firm price leadership case. The demand curve for steel in the United States is given by D_T (the T denoting total demand). United States Steel Corporation can produce as much or as little steel as it wishes at $17 per ton (including a competitive return on its invested capital), implying a horizontal marginal cost curve $LRMC_{USS}$.[21] Because it is confronted by a fringe of competitors, USS must take their supply into account. Assuming them to accept the price set by USS as given and react to it in a profit-maximizing way (that is, equating their marginal cost with the announced price), the behavior of the competitive fringe is characterized by short-run supply function KS_F. It is shown for geometric simplicity as a straight line, although in actuality it almost surely had curvature like the right-hand half of a "U." As KS_F is drawn, some fringe firms have lower supply costs than USS, others have higher costs. What happens next is crucial. To obtain its own *residual demand curve* D_{USS}, USS subtracts from the total market demand curve D_T the amount supplied by the fringe (read off KS_F) at each possible price. At a price of $13 per ton, the fringe supplies nothing, and so the corresponding point on USS's residual demand curve is *J*. At a price of $41.50 per ton, the fringe supplies all the steel the market will demand (i.e., at point *N*), leaving no residual demand for USS. Other points on the residual demand curve are interpolated linearly between these extremes, assuming linearity of supply and market demand functions. Given its residual demand curve, USS as dominant firm derives the corresponding marginal revenue function—that is, with a vertical-axis intercept at $41.50 and twice the slope of the residual demand curve. To maximize profits, USS increases output until its marginal revenue falls into equality with the $17 marginal cost—that is, at point *Z*. Its output then is 14 million tons, sold at a price (read off the *residual* demand function) of $29 per ton. Its profits (ignoring any fixed costs) are $12 per ton times 14 million tons, or $168 million. At the $29 price, the fringe will supply the remainder of the 23-million-ton market demand, or roughly 39 percent of total demand, leaving 61 percent for USS. Note that by geometric construction, *AB*, or the fringe output indicated by the fringe supply curve at the $29 price, equals *EF*, the amount of market demand *not* satisfied by United States Steel.

This is the situation at a moment in time—say, 1905. Unless fringe producers have costs much higher than the $17 cost of USS, they too are likely to earn appreciable profits under the price umbrella hoisted by USS. If they do,

---

[21]See Temin, *Iron and Steel*, p. 143. For purposes of determining pricing *strategy*, the curve should be the long-run, rather than the short-run, marginal cost curve.

FIGURE 5.3
Profit Maximization by a Dominant Firm

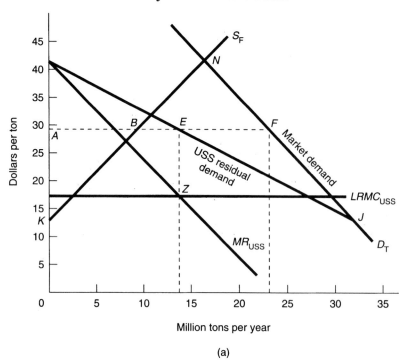

(a)

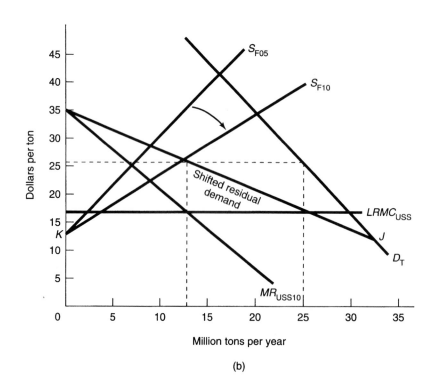

(b)

they will expand their plants, and other fringe firms will enter the industry. When this happens, the fringe supply curve for, say, 1910, swings to the right—that is, in Figure 5.3b from KS_{F05} to KS_{F10}, as shown by the arrow. USS as dominant firm must construct a new and more elastic residual demand curve and the corresponding marginal revenue curve MR_{USS10}. Equating marginal revenue with marginal cost, it sets a new, lower, price of $26 per ton and produces a smaller (52 percent) share of the expanded total market demand of 25 million tons.

As additional entry and fringe firm expansion are induced by the still-high prices set by the dominant firm, the fringe supply will swing ever more to the right, leading the dominant firm to set progressively lower prices, secure an increasingly small share of total industry sales, and realize diminishing profits.

Before inquiring whether there is a strategy that avoids this fate, we must pause for a reality check. Figure 5.4 shows the market share of United States Steel Corporation, measured in terms of steel ingot supply, between its formation in 1901 and 1988. The evidence of decline—at first rapidly, and then somewhat more slowly—is unmistakable. USS began with a 66 percent ingot market share. Despite the acquisition of Tennessee Coal and Iron and other smaller firms, its share declined to 54 percent in 1910. It declined further to 46 percent in 1920, 41 percent in 1930, 28 percent in

FIGURE 5.4
United States Steel Corporation Market Share Trends

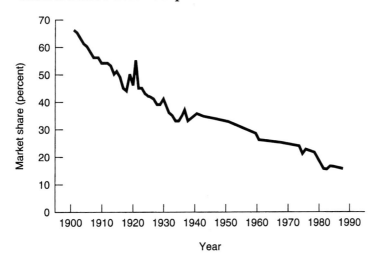

Sources: Thomas K. McCraw and Forest Reinhardt, "Losing To Win: U.S. Steel's Pricing, Investment Decisions, and Market Shares," *Journal of Economic History,* vol. 49 (September 1989), p. 598; and (after 1938) numerous contemporary accounts.

FIGURE 5.5
Comparison of Dominant-Firm Pricing and Limit Pricing Profit Trajectories

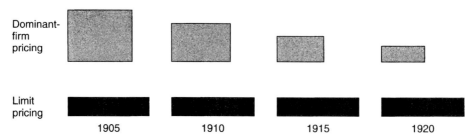

1960, and so on. In this respect, the declining dominant-firm model's predictions fit the facts.[22]

How might decline have been avoided? An alternative to dominant-firm price leadership would be some variant of a limit pricing strategy—that is, pricing to limit the entry and expansion of fringe competitors. Suppose that new entrants into the steel industry, or plant expansions carried out by competitors already in the industry at the formation of USS, could produce steel at a full cost of no less than $23 per ton. Then by setting a demand-expanding price of $22.95 per ton, USS could discourage all such entry and expansion, retain its market position, and (ignoring for the moment market growth) continue to earn profits above and beyond a "normal" return on capital of ($22.95 − $17.00) × 20 million tons = $119 million per year in perpetuity.

Figure 5.5 compares the two alternative strategies. Because the dominant-firm strategy of Figure 5.3a is the short-run profit-maximizing choice for a company in the structural position of United States Steel at a moment in time, profits under the dominant-firm strategy (upper panel) are necessarily higher at first than profits under the limit pricing strategy (lower panel). But with the dominant-firm strategy, entry erodes profits over time, and sooner or later, USS's profit rectangle under dominant-firm pricing shrinks to less than the constant level of profits retained under limit pricing.

THE CHOICE BETWEEN STRATEGIES

Which strategy is preferred depends upon three key variables: the magnitude of the cost advantage enjoyed by the dominant firm, the rate at which entry erodes the dominant firm's profits, and the discount rate (derived, finance theorists teach, from the market cost of capital) with which the firm compares future against current earnings.

---

[22]For support from a careful econometric study, see Hideki Yamawaki, "Dominant Firm Pricing and Fringe Expansion: The Case of the U.S. Iron and Steel Industry, 1907–1930," *Review of Economics and Statistics*, vol. 67 (August 1985), pp. 429–437.

Taking the variables in reverse order, if the dominant firm discounted future profits at the 15 percent rate commonly applied by large corporations during the 1970s and 1980s, the value of a dollar's profit gained or lost in 1920, seen from a 1901 vantage point in time, would be $1/(1 + 0.15)^{19} = 7$ cents. Very little weight would be accorded to future as opposed to present profits, favoring the high-initial-profit dominant-firm strategy. But if profits 19 years into the future were discounted at the 7 percent rate USS paid on the $550 million in preferred stock it issued in 1901, a dollar of profit in 1920 would have a discounted present value of 27.6 cents in 1901, making it hard to ignore altogether the long-term profit sacrifice implied by the declining dominant-firm strategy.

Second, the strategy choice depends in part upon the rate at which entry occurs with a high umbrella price strategy, and hence on the rate at which the profit rectangles in the upper panel of Figure 5.5 erode. Entry with modern steelmaking facilities was not easy. It was not necessary to build at the scale of United States Steel's Gary, Indiana, works, completed in 1912 with a capacity of 2.2 million ingot tons at an estimated cost of $62 million.[23] But entry at less than a third of that scale was likely to sacrifice scale economies.[24] Obtaining the requisite capital in financial markets dominated by the J. P. Morgan interests required entrepreneurial flair. Financing plant expansions through the plowback of internal earnings could be slow. And, most important, United States Steel had acquired the lion's share of known high-quality iron ore reserves, so entrants had to make do with lower-quality supplies, reach out to such distant locations as Cuba, Chile, and Sweden (as Bethlehem Steel did), or buy ore from USS on its terms and at the volume it chose to provide. All of this means that a torrent of entry was not to be expected, even if prices were set at levels well above USS costs.

The third and crucial variable was the unit cost of entrants as compared to the cost of the dominant firm. Figure 5.5 assumes that would-be entrants' costs were $23, or $6 more per ton than those of United States Steel. But this is contradicted by the evidence. Although *some* of the Corporation's plants may have had lower costs, on average, USS could pour and shape steel at costs no lower than those of its rivals, actual or potential. After assuming the helm at Bethlehem Steel, Charles Schwab testified that mill costs at Gary and Pittsburgh—the best plants of USS—did not differ materially from costs at his best Bethlehem mill.[25] Schwab's successor as president of USS enumerated 14 steel companies the Corporation could not put out of business "without committing financial suicide."[26] If USS had to set its ingot price below $17 to limit

---

[23]Jones, *The Trust Problem*, p. 209.

[24]Jones, *The Trust Problem*, p. 218 note.

[25]Jones, *The Trust Problem*, p. 219.

[26]*Ibid.*, citing testimony in an antitrust trial to be discussed shortly. Similarly, a much smaller rival testified that if the Corporation were to set prices so that there was no profit for it, there would be nothing left for USS.

or exclude the entry of rivals, its profit rectangles in the lower panel of Figure 5.5 would have zero height. And zero supranormal profits, sustained over however long a time period, are not an attractive alternative. Thus, it would appear that the umbrella pricing strategy was the only alternative that would yield significant monopoly profits.

This conclusion oversimplifies in one respect. USS did have a significant cost advantage over many of its rivals, and especially over would-be new entrants: its control of the high-grade iron ore reserves and the railroads needed to transport them from the mines to lake shipping facilities. But here we must recognize a point that is as important as it is subtle. The Corporation could derive high profits from its ore cost advantage by shipping ore at bargain prices to USS plants and taking the profit at the steel mills, or by selling ore at high prices, either to captive mills or to competitors. Because the option of selling ore at high prices to competitors existed, the opportunity cost of ore was high. USS management apparently recognized this and chose to take its profits at the ore stage, selling at prices well above mining costs both inside and outside. Paying opportunity cost prices, its steel mills had no cost advantage, and so letting its steelmaking market share erode maximized profits. But in its domestic ore supply operations, where it did have a cost advantage, its market share declined very little—to 45.3 percent in 1902, 44.2 percent in 1910, 40.0 percent in 1920, and (despite considerable depletion of Mesabi Range holdings) 41.9 percent in 1948.[27]

ELABORATION: THE DYNAMICS

Two further theoretical complications must be considered. For one, Figures 5.3b and 5.5 show the dominant firm's share declining over time in a market of constant size. Steel output in the United States, however, grew rapidly—for example, as we have seen earlier, from 10 million tons in 1900 to 26 million tons in 1910, 42 million tons in 1920, and 56 million tons in 1929 (the last year before the Great Depression). Dominant-firm umbrella pricing does not imply a necessary decline in absolute size, but only in the leader's relative share of the market. In fact, the ingot capacity of USS (seldom utilized fully) rose from 10.6 million tons in 1901 to 20 million in 1910, 25 million in 1920, and 27 million in 1929.[28] What is crucial is that USS grew at a considerably slower rate than the market, while its rivals grew commensurately more rapidly. Indeed,

---

[27]Parsons and Ray, "The United States Steel Consolidation," p. 202; and U.S. Federal Trade Commission, Report to the Senate Committee on the Judiciary, Subcommittee on Antitrust and Monopoly, *Control of Iron Ore* (Washington, DC: USGPO, December 1952), pp. 33–36, 82, and 150–153. For 1948, production by mining companies in which USS had a partial share interest was allocated according to its ownership share.

[28]Gertrude C. Schroeder, *The Growth of Major Steel Companies, 1900–1950* (Baltimore: Johns Hopkins Press, 1953), p. 216.

when rivals choose to take advantage of the profit opportunities created by umbrella pricing and expand more rapidly than the market, it is the fate of the dominant firm to grow more slowly, because if it kept pace, its additional output would force prices down to less profitable, or even unprofitable, levels. This is what happened to Saudi Arabia when it attempted to maintain high crude oil prices in the early 1980s and to the refining spin-offs of Standard Oil after 1911 when they tried to keep gasoline prices high in their home market territories.

Second, dynamic considerations widen the array of options available to the dominant firm. Suppose the rate of competitive fringe firm expansion and entry depends upon the price set by the leader: the higher the price, the more rapid the entry. This tendency could arise because existing fringe firms' expansion rate depends upon their ability to plow back cash from profits, which is greater at high prices than at lower prices.[29] Or outsiders may be stimulated more strongly to risk entry when the pricing lure is irresistible. Then the dominant firm faces a trade-off: Higher prices mean more profits today, but more rapid entry and hence more erosion of profits tomorrow. It may no longer be rational for the dominant firm to raise its price all the way to the short-run profit-maximizing level of $29 shown in Figure 5.3a. Rather, articulating a theory of optimal *dynamic* limit pricing that substitutes differential equations for the calculus of static monopoly theory, Darius Gaskins proved that normally it is *not* rational to seek maximum short-run profits.[30] Prices will be held down enough to slow the rate of entry and raise future prices until some long-run profit-maximizing balance is struck. This insight almost surely represents a closer approximation to the United States Steel Corporation's actual strategy. It did not charge prices that by any standard could be called outrageously exploitative. It merely announced prices that yielded handsome profits to itself and its rivals, encouraging their moderate but not pell-mell expansion.

The Gaskins analysis yields important further insights. It shows that for any given constellation of dominant firm cost advantages, discount rates, and rates of entry response to price-cost differentials, there is a long-run profit-maximizing market share for the dominant firm. If the dominant firm has no cost advantage at all over its actual and potential rivals, its strategy, as we have seen, will be to keep prices above rival unit costs until entry has eroded

[29]See Kenneth L. Judd and Bruce C. Petersen, "Dynamic Limit Pricing and Internal Finance," *Journal of Economic Theory*, vol. 39 (August 1986), pp. 368–399.

[30]Darius W. Gaskins, Jr., "Dynamic Limit Pricing: Optimal Pricing Under Threat of Entry," *Journal of Economic Theory*, vol. 3 (September 1971), pp. 306–322; and "Optimal Pricing by Dominant Firms," Ph.D. dissertation, University of Michigan, 1970. See also Morton I. Kamien and Nancy L. Schwartz, "Limit Pricing and Uncertain Entry," *Econometrica*, vol. 39 (May 1971), pp. 441–454; and Norman J. Ireland, "Concentration and the Growth of Market Demand," *Journal of Economic Theory*, vol. 5 (October 1972), pp. 303–305.

its position so much that it no longer possesses price-setting power—that is, at a relatively small market share. If it has a modest cost advantage and it begins with a large market share, it will set price above rival costs and encourage entry for a while, but when its market share has fallen to the optimal value, it will shift to a strict limit pricing strategy, setting a price so close to rivals' unit costs that they neither expand nor contract. When it has a large cost advantage and rivals currently possess a sizable market share, it is likely to cut prices well below rivals' unit costs and perhaps even below its own costs (i.e., "predating"), driving the rivals out of business and expanding its own market share.

We see now why it was rational (i.e., long-run profit-maximizing) for John D. Rockefeller's Standard Oil and Gary's United States Steel to behave quite differently. In most parts of the country, Standard had a substantial cost advantage by virtue of its freight rebates and pipeline control. When rivals gained substantial local market shares and refused to sell out, Rockefeller cut prices sharply to drive them out.[31] But when he controlled most of the market, he set limit prices that kept his share near the desired 85 to 90 percent value. United States Steel, however, had no appreciable cost advantage in steelmaking, so it opted for high-price, market share–yielding policies.

OLIGOPOLISTIC FACILITATING PRACTICES

Some additional complications must now be addressed. It is debatable whether the "fringe" rivals of USS were of such inconsequential size that they behaved as classic price-takers, accepting the Corporation's price as given and responding accordingly on their competitive supply curves (collectively, S_F in Figure 5.3). At times they chiseled below the price set by USS, suggesting something short of atomistic competition. And during periodic recessions, some restricted their output more than one might have expected of pure price-takers. Both patterns suggest structural relationships closer to those of oligopoly than pure competition.

Judge Gary recognized his oligopoly problem. In the initial years after 1901, he tried hard to establish a transparent price lead, but his rivals did not always follow, inducing the Corporation on occasion to undertake its own disciplinary price cuts.[32] Price chiseling became especially widespread during the "panic" of 1907. Gary's solution was to invite the heads of rival steelmak-

---

[31]As Rockefeller wrote to his associate H. A. Hutchins in 1881, "We want to watch, and when our volume of business is to be cut down by the increase of competition to fifty percent, or less, it may be a very serious question whether we had not better make an important reduction, with a view of taking substantially all the business there is." Allan Nevins, *Study in Power: John D. Rockefeller,* vol. II (New York: Scribner, 1953), p. 65.

[32]See Naomi R. Lamoreaux, *The Great Merger Movement in American Business, 1895–1904* (New York: Cambridge University Press: 1985), pp. 134–138.

ers, together holding (with USS) 90 percent of industry capacity, to join him for a series of dinners in his New York City mansion. There he lectured them on the evils of ruinous competition and on the benefits that would accrue to the whole industry if all cooperated and adhered to the prices set by the Corporation.[33] In 1909 some firms reverted to their chiseling ways, but after USS retaliated and further "Gary dinners" were held, all fell into line. Gary's own explanation in 1911 of what ensued from the Gary dinners was as follows:[34]

> We have something better to guide and control us in our business methods than a contract which depends upon written or verbal promises with a penalty attached. We, as men, as gentlemen, as friends, as neighbors, having been in close communication and contact during the last few years, have reached a point where we entertain for one another respect and affectionate regard. We have reached a position so high in our lines of activity that we are bound to protect one another; and when a man reaches a position where his honor is at stake, where even more than life itself is concerned, where he can not act or fail to act except with a distinct and clear understanding that his honor is involved, then he has reached a position that is more binding on him than any written or verbal contract.

That Gary's evangelism had won converts was declared by Bethlehem Steel's Schwab at a 1909 testimonial dinner for Gary:[35]

> I am thankful for this opportunity of saying one thing, Judge. You and I have been associated in business, or we were, for some years; we have had many differences, and I am glad of this opportunity to say publicly that with my bounding enthusiasm and optimism I was wrong in most instances—indeed in all instances—and you were right. The broad principles that you brought into this business were new to all of us who had been trained in a somewhat different school. Their effect was marvelous, their success unquestioned. It was a renaissance and a newness of things ... that were necessary and invigorating. ... I have been present at gatherings where men have been honored by reason of their operative ability in the manufacture of steel; but, sir, this is the first time in the history of the industry when the great heads of all the big concerns ... have gathered to do honor to a man who has introduced a new and successful principle in our great industry.

---

[33]The meetings were not secret. Gary wrote to the U.S. attorney general at the time that "We have endeavored to maintain a position between the ... extremes [of agreements to maintain prices and ... such competition as will result in the destruction of the business of competitors]. We are perfectly satisfied to limit the amount of our business to our proportion of capacity and to do everything possible ... to promote the interests of our competitors; and by frequent meetings and the interchange of opinions we have thus far been able to accomplish this result without making any agreements of any kind." In a noncommittal reply letter, the attorney general in effect acquiesced. Tarbell, *The Life of Elbert H. Gary*, pp. 212–213.

[34]Quoted from a U.S. antitrust brief by Jones, *The Trust Problem*, p. 228.

[35]Quoted in Tarbell, p. 217.

Despite occasional aberrations, the members of the steel industry adhered for decades to the Corporation's price leadership with a degree of discipline seen in few if any other U.S. industries.

To make its price leadership even more transparent, the Corporation continued a practice that the steel "pools" (i.e., cartels) had originated during the 1880s—the basing-point system. Delivery costs are appreciable in relation to the cost of making steel—for example, on an average shipment from Pittsburgh to Chicago in 1966, about 10 percent.[36] Until the 1950s, steel was sold in the United States almost uniformly with delivery included as part of the price. The prices USS publicly announced at regular intervals were for shipments from its Pittsburgh plants—the original seat of the Carnegie operations. To the Pittsburgh "base" price, the cost of rail freight from Pittsburgh to the actual delivery site was added. Therefore, the pricing system was called "Pittsburgh plus." If, for example, construction beams had a Pittsburgh basing-point price of $30 per ton and freight to Chicago was $3, the price quoted Chicago customers was $33. This was true whether the steel was shipped from Pittsburgh, Alabama, or from any of the several steel mills located at the south end of Lake Michigan. Mills located away from Pittsburgh in effect billed nearby customers for freight costs they did not incur; this is called "phantom freight." But although advantaged in this way on local sales, a mill located near Chicago had to "absorb" increasing amounts of freight on eastbound shipments. That is, the farther east it shipped, the higher was its freight cost, but the lower the Pittsburgh-plus price it received was. The system was immensely controversial.[37] It was claimed, although there are counterarguments, that Pittsburgh-plus delayed the expansion of steelmaking capacity in the heavily steel-using belt between Detroit and Chicago.[38] After a series of antitrust challenges that culminated in 1924, United States Steel shifted to a multiple basing-point system, with Chicago, Birmingham, Duluth, and later other locations added as points from which base prices were quoted.[39] Further challenges followed, and in 1948, steel producers agreed to abandon the

---

[36]See F. M. Scherer, *Industrial Market Structure and Economic Performance*, 2nd ed. (Boston: Houghton Mifflin, 1980), p. 325.

[37]See for example Fritz Machlup, *The Basing Point System* (Philadelphia: Blakiston, 1949); Carl Kaysen, "Basing Point Pricing and Public Policy," *Quarterly Journal of Economics*, vol. 63 (August 1949), pp. 289–314; George J. Stigler, "A Theory of Delivered Pricing Systems," *American Economic Review*, vol. 39 (December 1949), pp. 213–225; and Dennis W. Carlton, "A Reexamination of Delivered Pricing Systems," *Journal of Law & Economics*, vol. 26 (April 1983), pp. 51–70.

[38]Compare A. R. Burns, *The Decline of Competition* (New York: McGraw-Hill, 1936), pp. 340–345; and Walter Isard and William M. Capron, "The Future Locational Pattern of Iron and Steel Production in the United States," *Journal of Political Economy*, vol. 57 (April 1949), pp. 131–133.

[39]See Simon N. Whitney, *Antitrust Policies*, vol. I (New York: Twentieth Century Fund, 1958), pp. 260–264 and 276–287.

systematic quotation of delivered prices, shifting to an f.o.b. (free on board) system under which prices were quoted at the mill gate, with customers paying whatever freight was incurred to the point of delivery.

Because the set of freight rates from Pittsburgh and, a fortiori, multiple basing points to all possible steel delivery locations is extremely complex, USS and (later) the American Iron and Steel Institute published freight rate books listing the rail freight rates from basing points to all parts of the United States. Steelmakers using the Pittsburgh-plus system were exhorted to apply the published rates faithfully, even when they were inaccurate or temporarily out of date. Because the books covered only rail freight, there was a tendency also to ship steel to customers only by rail, even when other media might have been quicker or otherwise more economical. When steelmakers shifted from basing-point pricing to f.o.b. pricing, the share of steel deliveries by truck increased from almost zero in 1948 to 44 percent of tonnage shipped in 1963.[40]

The pricing of steel products is complicated not only by the vast number of geographic locations served, but also by the many deviations from standard product specifications requested by individual customers—for example, for special gauges, heat treating, packaging, and the like. The steel producer who delivers at standard prices products requiring costly special processing is in effect chiseling on industry price norms. To deal with this problem, steelmakers held covert meetings to agree on the pricing of "extras." These continued into the 1960s, until and perhaps even after they were attacked by the U.S. antitrust authorities.[41]

WAS THE CORPORATION'S PRICING STRATEGY PROFITABLE?

The pricing strategy of United States Steel Corporation can be summarized as follows: As price leader, it quoted prices that were by no means exorbitant, but that were sufficiently high to maintain a comfortable existence for its principal competitors. It urged them to follow its lead, and on rare occasions inflicted retaliatory punishment on chiselers who strayed from the fold. On matters of unusual complexity, it met with its rivals to discuss how to solve emerging problems. As a result of this strategy, rivals expanded more rapidly than USS did, and so its market share declined steadily over time. We ask now, was this a profitable strategy?

Because the Corporation lacked any appreciable steel processing cost advantage over its rivals, we have seen, there was no really attractive alternative to the declining dominant firm strategy chosen. But more can be said.

---

[40]Scherer, *Industrial Market Structure*, p. 332.

[41]See "Steel Gets Hit with the Big One," *Business Week*, April 11, 1964, pp. 27–28; and (on earlier practice) Jonathan B. Baker, "Identifying Cartel Policing Under Uncertainty: The U.S. Steel Industry, 1933–1939," *Journal of Law & Economics*, vol. 32 (October 1989), p. S72, note 87. On later pricing discipline breakdowns owing to such complications, see "The Mystery of Steel Prices," *Fortune*, March 1977, pp. 158–160.

The strategy was at least profitable, even if not the best of all possible strategies. In the first ten years of its existence, USS recorded net profits (after deduction of interest costs) totaling $1.2 billion—slightly more than the $1.1 billion (par value) of common and preferred stocks issued to finance the 1901 consolidation.[42]

Those who bought the common stock of United States Steel in 1901, unlike the investors in many turn-of-the-century consolidations, fared well. At first, and especially when the sharp recession of 1904 struck, USS shares lost more than half their initial market value.[43] But after the Gary dinners commenced and other steelmakers began following the Corporation's price leadership more assiduously, USS share values soared. By 1911, a 1901 investor in USS shares would have realized capital gains twice those from buying a balanced market portfolio. By 1924, a $10,000 investment in USS common stock accumulated in value to $101,039.[44] Life under the umbrella was good.

As the Corporation's market share continued to decline, and with other developments to be considered shortly, the profit picture changed. In 1980, before USS diversified into the petroleum industry by acquiring Marathon Oil, the total market value of outstanding USS common stocks varied between $1.4 billion and $2.3 billion—at the mean, a threefold increase over the value of common stocks issued in 1901. Between 1901 and 1980, average price levels increased by a factor of ten. Thus, in the long run, USS shareholders did not even keep pace with inflation. But in the long run, as John Maynard Keynes quipped, we are all dead.

THE ANTITRUST CHALLENGE

When Theodore Roosevelt became U.S. president in 1901, he injected vigor into what had been a lackadaisically enforced Sherman Act antitrust program. Standard Oil, we have seen, was one of the first targets. Judge Gary, the chairman of USS, maintained close social relations with President Roosevelt and consulted with him or his subordinates on key initiatives such as the Tennessee Coal and Iron acquisition and the Gary dinners. His intent both in those consultations and in the broad policies pursued by USS was to avoid antitrust censure.[45] In 1905, however, the Bureau of Corporations, an agency

---

[42]Jones, *The Trust Problem*, p. 212.

[43]Parsons and Ray, "The United States Steel Consolidation," p. 183.

[44]George J. Stigler, "The Dominant Firm and the Inverted Umbrella," *Journal of Law & Economics*, vol. 8 (October 1965), pp. 167–173.

[45]For an analysis that probably overstates the role of antitrust considerations in the choice of USS policies, see Thomas K. McCraw and Forest Reinhardt, "Losing to Win: U.S. Steel's Pricing, Investment Decisions, and Market Share, 1901–1938," *Journal of Economic History*, vol. 49 (September 1989), pp. 593–619.

created by Roosevelt to investigate the activities of big business, was asked to consider United States Steel. A highly critical three-volume report was issued in July of 1911—only six weeks after the Supreme Court handed down its precedent-setting *Standard Oil* decision.[46] In October 1911 the government filed an antitrust suit asking inter alia that the Corporation be broken up. Nine months before, the Gary dinners had been terminated, and on the day the antitrust suit was made public, USS announced that it would cancel its lease on the Great Northern Mesabi Range ore deposits.

The Corporation emphasized three themes in its antitrust defense. First, it claimed that it did not in fact possess monopoly power, as shown inter alia by its declining share of total steel shipments. Second, it differentiated its policies from those of companies such as Standard Oil that had predated on rivals and driven them from the market. Rival steel company executives were called to testify on its behalf at the antitrust hearing. They were effusive in their praise of the Corporation's conduct.[47] Third, it emphasized its substantial contribution to the nation's trade balance by establishing 60 sales agencies in all corners of the globe. During its first decade, it accounted for an estimated 83 percent of all American steel exports.[48] Less stress was placed on the fact that the exports occurred at realized prices well below domestic levels—for example, 16 percent lower on steel rails between 1901 and 1907.[49]

In 1915, United States Steel was acquitted of monopolization charges by a Federal district court. Hearing of the government's appeal to the Supreme Court was delayed by the U.S. entry into World War I. But in 1920, a four-to-three majority of the Supreme Court found in favor of the Corporation.[50] Citing the district court findings, the majority observed that:

> The Corporation . . . did not at any time abuse the power or ascendancy it possessed. It resorted to none of the brutalities or tyrannies that the cases illustrate of other combinations. It did not secure freight rebates; . . . it did not oppress or coerce its competitors—its competition, though vigorous, was fair; . . . it did not obtain customers by secret rebates or departures from its published prices; there was no evidence that it attempted to crush its competitors or drive them out of the market. . . . It did not have power in and of itself, and the control it exerted was only in and by association with its competitors.

---

[46]U.S. Commissioner of Corporations, *Report on the Steel Industry* (Washington, DC: 1911).

[47]See e.g. Tarbell, *The Life of Elbert H. Gary,* pp. 237 and 258–259.

[48]Compare Tarbell, *The Life,* p. 111; and Parsons and Ray, "The United States Steel Consolidation," pp. 184–190. Parsons and Ray show statistically that relative to pre–1901 export levels, the Corporation's impact on export increases was modest.

[49]Selling at lower prices in the foreign market than at home is called "dumping."

[50]United States v. United States Steel Corporation, 251 U.S. 417 (1920). Justices Brandeis and McReynolds did not participate in the decision, having taken positions critical of USS in the past.

The majority considered the Gary dinners and other meetings to have been a violation of the antitrust laws, but noted that they ended before the government brought suit. Seeing in the proposed dissolution of USS the risk of a "material disturbance . . . to the foreign trade," the majority concluded:

> The Corporation is undoubtedly of impressive size and it takes an effort of resolution not to be affected by it or to exaggerate its influence. But . . . the law does not make mere size an offense, or the existence of unexerted power an offense. It . . . requires overt acts. . . . It does not compel competition nor require all that is possible.

The United States Steel decision crystallized the U.S. law on monopolies for the next two decades. Aggressive competition, driving competitors out of the market, and perhaps even limit pricing transgressed the boundaries of what would be permitted if the company, like Standard Oil, retained a dominant market position. Soft competition, however—hoisting a price umbrella over competitors and urging them to cooperate and expand at the umbrella-holder's market share expense—would be tolerated. The decision provided, we shall see, dangerous guidance to powerful U.S. corporations.[51]

SUBSEQUENT PRICING DEVELOPMENTS

With its leader absolved of wrongdoing, the steel industry persisted in the behavioral patterns to which it had become accustomed. United States Steel continued to provide price leadership. Others followed for the most part, although there were occasional exceptions, such as during the severe depression of the 1930s, when the industry's capacity utilization rate averaged only 48.5 percent.[52] National Steel, a newcomer to the industry during the 1920s, was a special thorn in the price leader's side. It constructed a plant embodying innovative rolling mill technology near Detroit, chiseled regularly on prices, and achieved nearly full capacity utilization while others were struggling along at half capacity.[53] The Corporation bore more than its fair share of the

---

[51]See William S. Comanor and F. M. Scherer, "Rewriting History: The Early Sherman Act Monopolization Cases," *International Journal of the Economics of Business*, vol. 2 (July 1995), pp. 263–289.

[52]Walter Adams, "The Steel Industry," in Adams, ed., *The Structure of American Industry*, 3rd ed. (New York: Macmillan, 1961), p. 173. On steelmakers' pricing interactions during the depression, both under the cartelization encouraged by the National Recovery Act and after the act was declared unconstitutional in 1935, see Baker, "Identifying Cartel Policing Under Uncertainty," pp. S–47–76.

[53]"The Corporation," *Fortune*, March 1936, p. 191.

output restrictions required to sustain the prices it set, and as Figure 5.4 shows, its market share continued to decline.

Decline may have been both cause and effect of another problem afflicting United States Steel—its inability to manage effectively its far-flung network of plants. It lagged in introducing new products, its cost standards were below industry norms, and it expanded its capacity at a snail's pace—by 25 percent in the 1910s, 12.6 percent in the 1920s, *minus* 1.6 percent during the 1930s, and 15 percent in the booming 1940s.[54] In a highly critical 1936 analysis, the editors of *Fortune* magazine concluded:[55]

> The trouble with the U.S. Steel Corporation can be briefly stated: it has been too big too long. . . . [T]he chief energies of the men who guided the corporation were directed to preventing deterioration in the investment value of the enormous properties confided in their care. To achieve this, they consistently tried to freeze the steel industry at present, or better yet, past levels.

As its market share declined below 40 percent during the 1930s, the Corporation probably lost its ability to serve as a dominant firm price leader. The leadership pattern gravitated closer to what we have identified in Chapter 4 as the collusive model. There is reason to believe that United States Steel's price-setting became guided by a formula that yielded a return on stockholders' equity after taxes approximating 8.25 percent at 80 percent capacity utilization.[56] This return implies a good deal less than monopoly profits. During the 1950s, U.S. manufacturing corporations as a whole attained an average return on equity of 11.3 percent.[57] In the mid–1950s, the Corporation apparently tried to change the formula. Its plant and equipment were becoming increasingly antiquated. Its leaders proclaimed repeatedly that the steel industry needed to generate more profits to plow back into modernization. A regression of USS's after-tax return on stockholders' equity (ROE) over the years 1920–1960 (but excluding World War II and Korean War price control years) as a function of its rate of capacity utilization (Capacity) and a shift variable (Shift) for the years 1955–1960, is as follows:[58]

$$ROE = -7.35 + 0.195 \text{ (Capacity)} + 4.19 \text{ (Shift)}$$
$$(10.47)\ (20.41) \qquad\qquad (7.79)$$

---

[54]Schroeder, *The Growth of Major Steel Companies*, p. 217. See also Whitney, *Antitrust Policies*, vol. 1, p. 293.

[55]"The Corporation," pp. 169–170.

[56]See John Blair, *Economic Concentration* (New York: Harcourt Brace Jovanovich, 1972), pp. 640–642. and 470–476.

[57]Calculated from the Federal Trade Commission–Securities and Exchange Commission *Quarterly Financial Reports* series.

[58]A slightly less complete but similar regression is reported in Blair, *Economic Concentration*, p. 641. The data are from Blair and Adams, "The Steel Industry."

with $R^2 = 0.945$ and t-ratios given in subscripted parentheses. The Shift variable is highly significant statistically. It suggests that United States Steel tried to raise its rate of return by roughly four percentage points for any given level of capacity utilization.

Accompanying these pricing policy changes were alterations in the climate of the steel industry's wage bargaining. The industry had long resisted unionization. A broken strike at Andrew Carnegie's Homestead works in 1892 was one of the bloodiest episodes in U.S. labor relations history.[59] Favorable legislation during the 1930s led to the unionization of most steel plants, and following World War II, the principal steel companies and the United Steel Workers union chose to bargain on an industry-wide basis. That is, wage patterns were set for eight or so leading companies at a single negotiation. Smaller producers and their workers then accepted the pattern with only minor variations. If there was no agreement, the whole industry was struck and effectively ceased operation. In 1952 President Harry S Truman attempted to avert a strike that might jeopardize Korean War production by nationalizing the steel companies, but the seizure was ruled unconstitutional. Strikes lasted 41 days in 1949, 62 days (with two interruptions) in 1952, 34 days in 1956, and 115 days in 1960.[60] The bargains that were consummated either to end strikes or avert them during the 1950s led to significant increases in steelworkers' wages. Those wage increases were promptly passed on as price increases under U.S. Steel's cost-plus pricing formula.

Combined profit and wage increases translated into substantial steel product price increases. Between 1955 and 1958, the average wholesale price of finished steel products climbed by 22.8 percent while the comparable index for all commodities rose 7.7 percent. The price increases in steel were passed through into higher costs and ultimately higher prices in other industries. Using input-output tables to trace the impact of steel price changes on other industries, Eckstein and Fromm found that the U.S. wholesale price index would have risen by 40 percent less over the 1947–1958 period had steel prices risen no more rapidly than the wholesale prices of all other goods.[61] The steel industry was made a focal point in a congressional investigation of "administered prices," that is, prices that seemed to defy the normal workings of supply

---

[59]Paul Krause, *The Battle for Homestead, 1880–1892* (Pittsburgh: University of Pittsburgh Press, 1992).

[60]Leonard W. Weiss, *Case Studies in American Industry*, second ed. (New York: Wiley, 1971), pp. 302–303.

[61]Otto Eckstein and Gary Fromm, *Steel and the Postwar Inflation*, Study Paper No. 2 in the U.S. Congress, Joint Economic Committee, series, *Study of Employment, Growth, and Price Levels* (Washington, DC: USGPO, 1958), pp. 1–38.

and demand, occurring even when steel producers were operating in 1957 and 1958 at only 73 percent of average rated capacity.[62]

Under intense political pressure, United States Steel grew wary of exercising its traditional role as price leader. In 1958, in the trough of a recession, the eighth-largest steel producer, Armco, took the lead in announcing an across-the-board price increase, ostensibly to cover rising wage costs. Others, including USS, followed suit. With political attacks continuing, the industry effected no further general price increases for nearly four years. Then, shortly after President John F. Kennedy had intervened in bargaining between the steelworkers and the steel companies to achieve what was heralded as a "noninflationary" settlement, United States Steel announced a price hike averaging 3.5 percent. Furious, Kennedy marshaled his not insubstantial forces to combat the increase.[63] When two medium-sized steelmakers announced (following presidential suasion) that they would not follow, the price change was rescinded. After that episode, the character of price leadership changed dramatically.[64] The Corporation became increasingly reluctant to lead. Others, particularly the number two producer, Bethlehem, with a 15 percent market share, assumed a leading role.[65] Price increase announcements were not always followed. In many cases, one firm would announce an increase, but USS would respond with a smaller increment, around which others would then rally. Announcements often covered only part of the array of steel products, and when across-the-board changes were made, they commonly included price decreases on some products along with increases on others. In 1968, United States Steel was discovered to have offered a secret price cut to an important Bethlehem Steel customer—an action that defied decades of tradition. Bethlehem retaliated by announcing a punitive 22 percent price cut, after which three months of turbulent quoting and counterquoting followed before peace was restored at price levels higher than those prevailing before the start of the war.[66] The industry had moved to a barometric form of leadership, but one in which the signals sent by leaders and followers were taken seriously indeed.[67]

---

[62]U.S. Senate, Committee on the Judiciary, Subcommittee on Antitrust and Monopoly, Report, *Administered Prices: Steel* (Washington, DC: USGPO, March 1958).

[63]See Grant McConnell, *Steel and the Presidency, 1962* (New York: Norton, 1962).

[64]See F. M. Scherer and David Ross, *Industrial Market Structure and Economic Performance*, 3rd ed. (Boston: Houghton Mifflin, 1990), pp. 178–180.

[65]See "Why Bethlehem Acts That Way," *Business Week*, April 24, 1971, pp. 85–87.

[66]For a blow-by-blow account, see Scherer and Ross, *Industrial Market Structure*, p. 179.

[67]Compare Chapter 4, p. 127.

FIGURE 5.6
Trends in Hot-Rolled Steel Strip Prices, 1960–1990

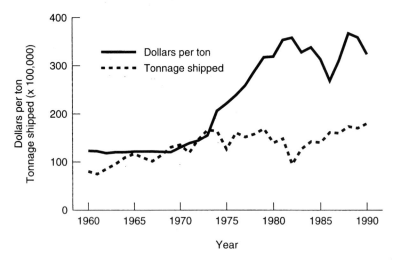

Source: U.S. Bureau of the Census, *Current Industrial Reports: Steel Mill Products,* various years.

With these changes, the industry was unable to sustain the profit target increases sought through USS's 1955–1960 pricing formula shift. The relationship between profit returns on stockholders' equity and capacity utilization fell to pre–1955 values, or perhaps even a percentage point below the historical pattern.[68]

Nevertheless, steelmakers continued to set prices that reflected mainly changes in cost and not changes in demand. Figure 5.6 illustrates by showing the trend in the average realized price per ton of one of the most important products, hot-rolled steel sheet and strip.[69] Prices (solid line) were stable during the 1960s, probably because of political pressure and the change in price leadership. They began to rise in 1970, continued to increase gradually under federal government price controls from August 1971 through April 1974, and then shot upward between 1974 and 1982. The dashed line series shows movements in tonnage (scaled in 100,000-ton units). There were recessions

[68]Blair, *Economic Concentration,* p. 641.

[69]The time series cover carbon steel hot-rolled and enameling sheet shipped to other companies—that is, excluding intracompany transactions on which arm's-length prices may not have been charged.

in steel sheet demand during 1966–1967, 1971, 1975, and 1980, but none precipitated a systematic decrease in the realized price.[70] We defer until later a discussion of the behavioral change that became evident in the 1980s.

IMPORT PROBLEMS

The rapid steel price increases during the late 1950s had unfortunate timing and consequences. European (especially German) and Japanese steelmakers had been devastated during World War II. By 1955, they had rebuilt enough capacity to meet their domestic needs, and from then on, they begin adding capacity sufficient to sustain increasingly vigorous export efforts. See Table 5.1. Japan, for example, more than doubled its output between 1955 and 1960, while the nations that had joined the European Community by 1975 increased their raw steel production by 25 million tons.

Some of this additional European and Japanese steel made its way into the U.S. market. Even at the peak of the Korean War mobilization in 1951, the United States had imported only 2.3 million tons of steel, and from 1950 through 1955, imports averaged 1.3 million tons per year. But as domestic steel prices rose, so did imports. See Table 5.2. In 1959, imports exceeded exports for the first time. In no subsequent year did exports regain the lead.

Imports rose abruptly in 1965, when steel users stockpiled supplies in anticipation of a strike that did not ensue, and again under similar circumstances in 1968. With imports amounting to one-sixth of domestic steel product consumption in 1968, the steel industry sought government protection. Invoking the provision of GATT (the General Agreement on Tariffs and Trade) that permits signatory nations to erect temporary trade barriers protecting severely distressed industries, the U.S. government persuaded the European Community and Japan to accept specific import tonnage quotas over the years 1969–1971. For 1969, the EC was allowed to import 5.57 million tons and Japan 5.75 million tons, with 5 percent annual increases in subsequent years. Up to that time, Japanese producers had been exporting mainly less

---

[70]Similarly, comparing a carefully collected set of actual transaction prices against list prices for the years 1957–1966, Stigler and Kindahl reported that "Neither index displays a noticeable cyclical movement in either expansion or contraction. . . . With the exception of three steel products [two of them from electric arc furnace shops]. . . we were not able to learn of any important and continuing departures from quoted prices." George J. Stigler and James K. Kindahl, *The Behavior of Industrial Prices* (New York: Columbia University Press, 1970), pp. 72–73. Compare Richard M. Duke, Richard L. Johnson, Hans Mueller, P. David Qualls, Calvin T. Roush, and David G. Tarr, *The United States Steel Industry and Its International Rivals*, Federal Trade Commission Staff Report (Washington, DC: November 1977), chapter 4, which marshals evidence of unsystematic price chiseling from the late 1960s on.

TABLE 5.1
Raw Steel Production of Principal Nations, 1950–1992

Year	World[a]	USA	Japan	EC	Rest of World
1950	207.1	96.8	5.3	53.4	51.6
1951	232.2	105.2	7.2	59.3	60.5
1952	234.2	93.2	7.7	65.6	67.7
1953	258.8	111.6	8.4	63.5	75.3
1954	246.5	88.3	8.5	69.2	80.5
1955	297.8	117.0	10.4	80.4	90.0
1956	312.9	115.2	13.2	85.9	98.6
1957	321.7	112.7	13.8	90.4	104.8
1958	298.9	85.3	13.3	86.0	114.3
1959	337.2	93.4	18.3	92.6	132.9
1960	381.6	99.3	24.4	107.9	150.0
1961	390.1	98.0	31.2	105.9	155.0
1962	394.1	98.3	30.4	103.6	161.8
1963	422.4	109.3	34.7	106.4	172.0
1964	479.0	127.1	43.9	121.2	186.8
1965	503.1	131.5	45.4	125.5	200.7
1966	519.1	134.1	52.7	121.5	210.8
1967	547.6	127.2	68.5	126.3	225.6
1968	582.5	131.5	73.7	138.2	239.1
1969	632.0	141.3	90.5	148.5	251.7
1970	654.2	131.5	102.9	151.7	268.1
1971	639.9	120.4	97.6	141.3	280.6
1972	694.5	133.2	106.8	153.4	301.1
1973	768.6	150.8	131.5	165.5	320.8
1974	782.8	145.7	129.1	171.5	336.5
1975	712.0	116.6	112.8	138.1	344.5
1976	753.1	128.0	118.4	148.1	358.6
1977	741.8	125.3	112.9	139.0	364.6
1978	790.6	137.0	112.6	146.2	394.8
1979	824.4	136.3	123.2	154.6	410.3
1980	790.4	111.8	122.8	140.8	415.0
1981	779.4	120.8	112.1	139.2	407.3
1982	710.7	74.6	109.7	122.7	403.7
1983	731.6	84.6	107.1	120.6	419.3
1984	782.6	92.5	116.4	132.5	441.2
1985	791.9	88.3	116.0	133.1	454.5
1986	784.8	81.6	108.3	135.9	454.0

TABLE 5.1 (CONTINUED)

Year	World[a]	USA	Japan	EC	Rest of World
1987	812.6	89.2	108.6	139.6	475.2
1988	859.2	99.9	116.5	151.9	490.9
1989	862.6	97.9	118.9	154.4	491.4
1990	848.8	98.9	121.7	150.9	477.3
1991	811.1	87.9	120.9	151.5	450.8
1992	810.2	92.9	108.2	146.1	463.0
1993	814.6	97.9	109.8	145.7	461.2

Source: American Iron and Steel Institute, *Annual Statistical Report,* various years.

[a]World output includes communist bloc nations.

sophisticated, low-price products such as concrete reinforcing bars, wire rods, and wire products.[71] Accepting a flat tonnage constraint, they shifted rapidly to top-of-the-line products such as stainless steel and flat-rolled sheets. The average value per ton of steel products imported into the United States from all sources rose from $109 in 1968, before the quotas, to $123 in 1969 and $146 in 1970.[72] United States firms producing high-priced stainless and specialty steels experienced particularly strong import competition growth.[73] Although the quotas were renewed for another three years in 1972, this time with more detailed product subdivisions, they faded to unimportance as world steel markets moved into a synchronized boom that drove prices outside the United States above (controlled) domestic prices and caused domestic steelmakers to ration deliveries to their customers.[74]

NEW LABOR RELATIONS STRATEGIES

Meanwhile, the steel industry acted on another front to deal with its import problem. Its perception was that much of the difficulty arose because domestic steel users turned to foreign sources when an industry-wide wage contract was about to expire—normally every three years. In anticipation of a strike,

---

[71]See Walter Adams and Joel B. Dirlam, "Steel Imports and Vertical Oligopoly Power," *American Economic Review,* vol. 54 (September 1964), pp. 626–655.

[72]Computed from Table 5.2 and import value data from the *Statistical Abstract of the United States,* various years. See also "Quota Backfires for Steelmakers," *Business Week,* September 12, 1970, p. 24.

[73]"Imports Bite into Specialty Steel," *Business Week,* July 31, 1971, p. 78.

[74]"Customers Scramble for Steel," *Business Week,* June 2, 1973, pp. 18–19.

TABLE 5.2
U.S. Steel Mill Product Exports and Imports

Year	Exports (million tons)	Imports (million tons)	Percent of Demand	Percent by National Origin Japan	EC	Other
1955	4.1	1.0	0.9	9.9	67.6	22.5
1956	4.3	1.3	1.2	3.5	84.2	12.3
1957	5.3	1.2	1.1	2.8	82.1	15.1
1958	2.8	1.7	2.0	14.6	75.5	9.9
1959	1.7	4.4	4.6	14.2	70.8	15.0
1960	3.0	3.4	4.8	17.9	68.7	13.4
1961	2.0	3.2	4.8	18.8	66.9	14.3
1962	2.0	4.1	5.6	26.1	57.0	16.9
1963	2.2	5.5	7.0	33.2	47.6	19.2
1964	3.4	6.4	7.3	38.0	44.6	17.4
1965	2.5	10.4	10.3	42.5	47.3	10.2
1966	1.7	10.8	10.9	45.1	42.7	12.2
1967	1.7	11.5	12.3	39.0	49.4	11.6
1968	2.2	18.0	16.7	40.6	46.8	12.6
1969	5.2	14.0	13.6	44.6	43.4	12.0
1970	7.1	13.4	13.8	44.4	40.4	15.2
1971	2.8	18.3	17.9	37.7	46.5	15.8
1972	2.9	17.7	16.6	36.4	44.0	19.6
1973	4.1	15.1	12.3	37.2	43.0	19.8
1974	5.8	16.0	13.4	38.6	40.2	21.2
1975	3.0	12.0	13.5	48.6	34.3	17.1
1976	2.7	14.3	14.1	55.9	19.4	24.7
1977	2.0	19.3	17.8	40.4	35.4	24.2
1978	2.4	21.1	18.1	30.9	35.4	33.7
1979	2.8	17.5	15.2	36.2	30.9	32.9
1980	4.1	15.5	16.3	38.7	25.2	36.1
1981	2.9	19.9	18.9	31.2	32.3	36.5
1982	1.8	16.7	21.9	31.2	33.5	35.3
1983	1.2	17.1	20.5	24.9	23.9	51.2
1984	1.0	26.2	26.5	25.4	24.2	50.4
1985	0.9	24.3	25.2	24.6	28.6	46.8
1986	0.9	20.7	23.0	21.3	31.7	47.0
1987	1.1	20.4	21.3	21.1	28.2	50.7

TABLE 5.2 (CONTINUED)

Year	Exports (million tons)	Imports (million tons)	Percent of Demand	Percent by National Origin Japan	EC	Other
1988	2.1	20.9	20.4	20.7	30.0	49.3
1989	4.6	17.3	17.9	21.2	32.4	46.4
1990	4.3	17.2	17.6	18.3	32.0	49.7
1991	6.3	15.8	17.9	17.8	29.6	52.6
1992	4.3	17.1	18.0	15.6	26.7	57.8
1993	4.0	19.5	18.7	9.1	35.0	55.9

Source: American Iron and Steel Institute, *Annual Statistical Report,* various years. All tonnage figures are for net finished products.

steel users built precautionary stockpiles. Steelmakers in the United States were flooded with orders they could not handle, and so the users turned abroad. Having found foreign prices and qualities agreeable, the steel users continued buying overseas, and so imports stabilized at a new plateau. See again Table 5.2, recalling that major contracts expired in 1956, 1959, 1962, 1965, and 1968.

To solve the problem, the companies and the United Steelworkers Union concluded an "Experimental Negotiating Agreement" in 1973. The agreement limited the union's right to strike, which, it was believed, would prevent steel users from turning abroad. In exchange, steelworkers were given a flat $150 bonus, a guaranteed 3 percent per year wage increase to reward productivity gains, and an escalator clause ensuring that most of any future cost-of-living increases would be passed on in the form of higher wages.

Again, the industry's timing was ill-starred.[75] Steel output per labor hour failed to increase at all on average during the next seven years, and so the 3 percent annual "productivity" increase exceeded actual productivity gains by 3 percent, causing essentially inflationary wage cost increases accumulating to 23 percent by 1980. Meanwhile, triggered by the first OPEC price shock and other commodity price increases, general inflation rates soared. The U.S. Consumer Price Index rose by 86 percent between 1973 and 1980. Indexed

[75]On subsequent developments, see Mary E. Deily, "Wages in the Integrated Steel Industry, 1970–1990," Lehigh University, Martindale Center, discussion paper no. 10 (June 1994).

FIGURE 5.7
**Cold-Rolled Steel Sheet Prices in the United
States, Japan, and the European Common Market**

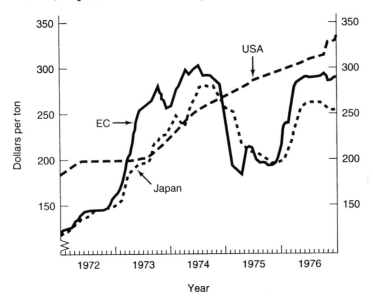

Source: U.S. Council on Wage and Price Stability, **Report to the President,**
Prices and Costs in the United States Steel Industry (Washington, DC:
USGPO, October 1977), pp. 64, 120, and 121.

against inflation much more fully than most other employees, the steelworkers enjoyed a rising wage differential relative to other manufacturing employees. In 1973, steelworkers earned $5.97 per hour on average plus $1.41 for
fringe benefits, compared to $4.15 and $0.67 for production workers in all
other manufacturing industries.[76] Thus, the steel differential, compensating
inter alia for the high skills required in many jobs and the above-average risks
of injury, amounted to 53 percent. By 1980, average wages plus fringes per
hour were $16.82 for steelworkers, compared to $8.68 for other manufacturing workers. The differential had risen to 94 percent. This growing labor cost
differential raised steelmaking costs in the United States relative to those of
other nations with lower differentials, exerting an upward cost-push on steel
prices.

The steel industry continued setting prices largely on the basis of its costs,
insensitive to demand and competitive pressures. Figure 5.7 provides a typical
illustration for cold-rolled steel sheets, a product that has been run through
one or two additional finishing steps beyond the hot-rolled sheets covered by

[76]Computed from U.S. Bureau of the Census, *Annual Survey of Manufactures,* for 1973
and 1980. The data are for Standard Industrial Classification code 331, which
includes separate cold-rolling, wire-drawing, and tube-extruding facilities.

Figure 5.6.[77] In the relatively weak markets of 1972, the export prices of European (solid line) and Japanese (short dashed line) cold-rolled sheet were lower than those of U.S. producers. In the boom market of 1973–1974, foreign sources' export prices shot above those of the United States, even though the latter rose rapidly after price controls expired. As an OPEC shock-induced recession set in during the closing months of 1974, foreign steel prices plummeted. But U.S. prices continued their rise, exceeding foreign export prices by nearly 50 percent at the trough of the recession. The U.S. market was once more rendered vulnerable to imports. Imports began rising again, exceeding during 1977 the levels experienced in 1968. When two mills in Youngstown, Ohio, were closed in late 1977, a congressional steel caucus formed to demand that President Carter intervene and protect the industry.

DUMPING AND IMPORT SUBSIDIES

In their petitions for succor, U.S. steelmakers asserted that they were being injured by foreign steel imports "dumped" in the U.S. market, often by foreign producers receiving substantial subsidies from their home governments. Dumping and trade-distorting governmental subsidies to specific industries are singled out by GATT as grounds for the erection of trade barriers by a signatory nation whose industries are materially injured. To understand the rationale of the positions taken by U.S. steelmakers and the U.S. government, one must explore why producers might dump and how dumping is defined.

The standard definition of dumping is selling a product abroad at a lower realized price, net of freight, than the price at which the product is sold at home. Dumping is thus a form of price discrimination. Price discrimination adds to profits only when there is some element of monopoly, or some similar imperfection, that leaves prices in the home market above marginal costs. Figure 5.8 illustrates a standard case. We assume that the foreign steelmaker holds a monopoly in its home market. It is not a particularly profitable monopoly, however. The profit-maximizing output OQ_M is much less than the output that minimizes average cost ATC, perhaps because a recession has occurred. The monopoly price OP_M is just sufficient (at point A) to cover average cost; only a normal return on invested capital is realized. Suppose now that the firm can export steel at the competitively ruling world price OP_W (which is well below the home price). Profits can be increased by increasing output to OQ_T, where marginal cost rises into equality with the world price. To maximize profits, marginal revenues must be equalized across the home and export markets. This is done by reducing home sales to OQ_H, sold at the increased home price OP_H, and selling the remaining output $Q_H Q_T$ in the world market. With the increase in output, average cost per ton falls to ATC_E. The accountants might report that a loss of GH is being incurred on exported steel, implying a total loss on exports given by the rectangle $FGHJ$. But this is faulty accounting, because each ton sold abroad brings more revenue (the

---

[77]The European and Japanese export prices are monthly; the U.S. prices are smoothed annual averages.

FIGURE 5.8
The Rationale for Dumping

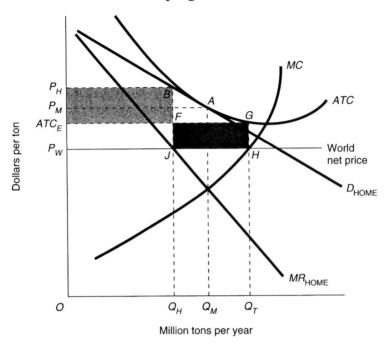

world price) than its marginal cost of production. From another perspective, the increased accounting profit at home given by lightly shaded rectangle $P_H BF\text{-}ATC_E$—some due to higher home prices, some to lower average costs—more than makes up for the accounting loss in the export market.

This is clearly enough dumping, and it is viewed with disfavor under GATT. But life is seldom so simple. The European Community (or technically, the European Coal and Steel Community) had authorized the existence of a two-price system for intra-Community steel trade.[78] Producers announce "base prices" at which they will ship steel from a given region (e.g., the steel-making center Duisburg in Germany). But they are allowed to "align" on lower prices when the base price plus freight from another producing region, either inside the Community or (with special rules) outside it, is lower than their own base price. During times of high demand, every producer tends to sell near home at base prices. But when demand is slack, some producers (notably, in Belgium and northern Italy) cut their base prices and begin shipping surplus steel to other parts of Europe. Other producers may choose to hold their base prices constant but align on the lower competitive prices whenever necessary. The more depressed business conditions are, the fewer

---

[78]See Klaus Stegemann, *Price Competition and Output Adjustment in the European Steel Market* (Tübingen: Mohr, 1977), chap. I.

transactions there are at maintained base prices and the more there are at alignment prices.

During the late 1970s and at many other times, the base prices of EC steelmakers' net of freight were well above U.S. prices, but the alignment prices were below U.S. prices. If EC producers are making substantial home market sales at alignment prices, which is "the" price against which dumping should be measured? U.S. steel producers, traditionally averse to cutting below their base prices in slumps, insisted that the base prices were those from which the existence of dumping was to be judged. Foreign steelmakers (including the Japanese, who had a similar but more complex multiprice system at home) insisted that their export prices should be measured relative to their alignment prices. And therein lay an international quarrel.

An escape from the dilemma was provided by another GATT provision. The original GATT treaty stated that in the absence of a comparable home price for the exporting nation's product, dumping could be found when the export price exceeded "the cost of production of the product in the country of origin plus a reasonable addition for selling cost and profit."[79] This criterion was incorporated into U.S. international trade law in 1974 as a "constructed-value" test. Specifically, the constructed value for an importer's products was to be found by adding to operating expenses (including allocated production and selling costs) per unit a fixed allocation for general, selling and administration costs of at least 10 percent, plus a profit margin of 8 percent on the sum of operating and overhead costs.[80] This essentially cost-plus test is illustrated in Figure 5.9. We assume that the 8 percent profit margin is built into the average total cost (ATC) curve. When demand is strong (D_{NORMAL}), the exporter can sell at a price as low as $150 per ton (point E) without running afoul of the constructed-value test. But during a recession (D_{SLUMP}), the test requires the exporter to raise its price to $160 (point F) when, under competitive pricing, the price would be set at $130 (point C). The constructed-value test in effect repeals the law of competitive supply and demand under recession conditions. But constructed value is the more authoritative law in U.S. trade jurisprudence, and so in a preliminary 1977 decision, Japanese steel producers were found to be dumping.[81]

Determining whether steel exports have been subsidized poses equally vexing problems. Some nations provide more generous unemployment, health, educational, and retirement benefits than others. Should the differences be considered subsidies? Under trade law, subsidies are actionable only

---

[79]General Agreement on Tariffs and Trade, signed at Geneva, October 30, 1947, Article VI, section 1(b)(ii).

[80]Tracy Murray, "The Administration of the Antidumping Duty Law by the Department of Commerce," in Richard Boltuck and Robert E. Litan, eds., *Down in the Dumps: Administration of the Unfair Trade Laws* (Washington, DC: Brookings: 1991), chap. 2.

[81]"U.S. Rules 5 Japanese Steel Exporters Dump Steel on American Market," *New York Times*, October 4, 1977, p. 1.

FIGURE 5.9
Constructed Value and Competitive Market Pricing

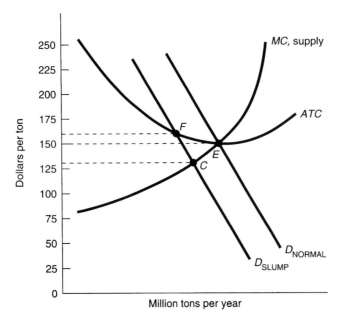

if they are industry-specific and not generally available, so such differences are not viewed as subsidies. Many nations chose to operate their steel industries, or parts thereof, as state-owned enterprises. How should subsidies be computed if capital is raised at interest rates lower than they would be without government guarantees? What if the state-owned company makes no profit on its (public) shareholders' net worth? What if losses are forgiven? What if the government imposes special burdens on its steel companies—for example, in Germany, requiring them to buy domestic coal at prices higher than they would pay for comparable coal in world markets? Wrestling with questions such as these, the Federal Trade Commission staff estimated in 1977 that specific subsidies per metric ton of steel ranged from $11.14 for the nationalized British Steel Corporation and $2.42 for Italy's publicly owned Finsider to as little 45 cents in Japan, zero in the Netherlands, and *negative* $3.49 in Germany.[82]

---

[82]Duke et al., *The United States Steel Industry*, chap. 6. See also Susan N. Houseman, *Industrial Restructuring in the European Community* (Cambridge, MA: Harvard University Press, 1994); "Europe: The Steel Community Tries To Stabilize Itself," *Business Week*, April 4, 1977, p. 36B; and "Britain: Steel Losses Race Toward $1 Billion," *Business Week*, November 28, 1977, p. 48. On later developments, see "Crying Foul: Europe's Steel Industry," *The Economist*, September 14, 1991, p. 85; and "Smelted," *The Economist*, October. 29, 1994, p. 80.

Attacking subsidies might also elicit unexpected national strategy responses. At least in the European Common Market, the most efficient steel-making operations tended to receive little or no subsidy, while the inefficient works were subsidized. In Italy, for example, state-owned Finsider, located in the high-unemployment Mezzogiorno region, received substantial subsidies, but it competed with highly efficient, unsubsidized privately owned companies (the Bresciani) in the North.[83] If the United States or some other significant steel-buying nation imposed countervailing duties against subsidized steelmakers, national or European Community authorities might arrange to have the unsubsidized works do all the exporting while subsidized works reallocated their output to the home market. The trade barriers would be circumvented, but nothing else would change.

RENEWED PROTECTION

From 1977 on, a cycle was repeated several times in the United States. Steel producers filed dumping and subsidy complaints with the U.S. authorities responsible for adjudicating international trade disputes. Seeking to avoid the complexities and jeopardy to foreign relations associated with levying punitive tariffs on offending importers, the U.S. president's trade representative negotiated "voluntary restraint agreements" (VRAs) with steel-exporting national governments, who in turn attempted to curb the exporting proclivities of their domestic steelmakers. If the VRAs proved ineffective or were about to expire, new dumping and subsidy complaints were filed, precipitating renewed or modified VRAs, and so forth.

The U.S. government's first response to the crisis of 1977 was to develop a "trigger price" system for identifying dumped steel imports. Using cost data provided by Japanese steelmakers, by then the lowest-cost producers in the world, the government published full-cost prices (including freight) that, if undercut by some imported steel shipment, would trigger an expedited antidumping action. The trigger prices were apparently effective in raising imported steel prices.[84] But there were problems. For one, the freight costs were set too high for steel delivered in the Chicago area, and as a result, shipments to Chicago were abruptly diverted to Houston. Also, some exporting steelmakers purchased steel warehouses in the United States, exported their steel at trigger prices to the warehouses, and then sold the steel to end customers at prices lower than the prices at which the steel was transferred to the warehouses. Dissatisfaction with the system led to its suspension in March 1980, reimplementation at higher price levels in September 1980, and termination in January 1982.

---

[83] "World Roundup: Italy," *Business Week*, October 31, 1977, p. 50.

[84] Robert W. Crandall, *The U.S. Steel Industry in Recurrent Crisis* (Washington, DC: Brookings, 1981), pp. 107–115. As a government official, Crandall participated in setting the first trigger prices.

Lacking what it considered to be adequate protection from imports and plunging into its worst recession since the 1930s, the U.S. steel industry deluged the government with dumping and subsidy petitions. Abandoning his election campaign promise to restore a free market to steel, President Ronald Reagan in late 1982 negotiated with the European Community (formally) and with Japan (informally) voluntary quotas limiting imports to specified percentages of total U.S. consumption (this time, heeding the lessons of 1969–1971, broken down into 40 narrow product classes).[85] Other nonsignatory nations, however, especially South Korea, Brazil, Argentina, and Mexico, were not bound by the quotas, and they expanded their steel exports rapidly. See the last column of Table 5.2. As a new crisis loomed, the U.S. government extended the VRA program for five years beginning in September 1984 and brought a total of 29 steel-exporting nations (but excluding Canada, Taiwan, and Sweden) under its web of quantity restraints. With expiration drawing near during the U.S. presidential election campaign of 1988, candidate George Bush promised, if elected, to extend the program again—as events transpired, to March 1992. When the quota system was ended in 1992, a surge of dumping and subsidy petitions again materialized. Once again, the steel industry found itself mired in a worldwide recession. As each firm sought to cope with deteriorating demand, all cut prices, and so, for example, the bemused steel-watcher saw U.S. steel companies accuse their Canadian brethren of dumping and Canadian authorities accuse U.S. firms of dumping.[86]

Why were steel-exporting nations willing to accept tonnage quota restrictions and trigger prices while they vehemently protested the imposition of import-limiting tariffs? Figure 5.10 explains. S_{DOM} is the domestic supply curve and D_{DOM} the domestic demand curve. If all imports were kept out, the domestic price would be $350 per ton. Conversely, if there is free trade and a highly elastic supply of imports at the world price of $270 per ton, the U.S. price will be competed down to $270, high-cost domestic mills will cease operating, domestic supply will be reduced to OQ_D, and imports amounting to $Q_D Q_I$ will cover the rest of the (expanded) domestic demand. Now suppose that to protect the domestic industry, a tariff of $30 per ton is imposed on imports. The world supply curve will shift upward by $30 to WS'. Domestic mills with costs between $270 and $300 will resume production, domestic supply will increase to OQ_D', the total quantity demanded will fall by $YR = Q_I'Q_P'$, and the quantity of imports will fall to $Q_D' Q_I'$. The large lightly shaded area represents increased producers' surplus for domestic steelmakers; the

---

[85]The European Community in turn imposed its own set of import quotas, fearing that steel, which otherwise might have been exported to the United States, would be diverted to European markets. In 1978, it had similarly instituted trigger prices in response to the U.S. initiative.

[86]"Canadian Steelmakers Aim to Dismantle Trade Barriers," *New York Times*, July 20, 1992, p. D3.

FIGURE 5.10
Distributional Consequences of Alternative Import Barrier Mechanisms

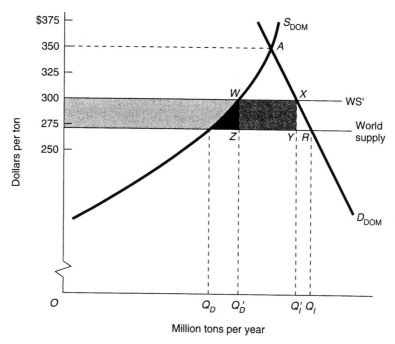

darkly shaded triangle, increased cost owing to the start-up of high-cost domestic mills; and the rectangle *WXYZ*, shaded to intermediate density, tariff revenues to the U.S. Treasury.

But suppose instead that an import quota of $Q'_D Q'_I$ is imposed—entailing the same quantity reduction induced by the tariff. Imports will be *WX*, and to close the gap between demand and supply, the price must again rise to $300.[87] Domestic output will expand to OQ'_D, as with the tariff. But who will capture the scarcity rent *WXYZ*? It will accrue in this case not to the U.S. Treasury, but to firms exporting to the United States at the higher market-clearing price of $300, rather than the $270 at which they were willing to supply. Although exporters suffer by selling fewer tons, they gain from the higher revenue realized per ton actually sold. *WXYZ* is in essence a bribe to exporters or their home governments to accept the trade restraints voluntarily and not complain

---

[87]This analysis assumes that domestic and imported steel of similar quality are perfect substitutes. But steel buyers are willing to pay premium prices for the security and quicker response time associated with buying from domestic sources. As they have gained experience procuring steel abroad, the premium has fallen—possibly to as little as $5 per ton.

to the GATT authorities. A trigger price of $300 has the same effect, since the domestic price will rise, domestic firms will expand their output, leaving less to be sold by importers, and importers will sell quantity WX at $300 instead of Q_DQ_I at $270.

OTHER REASONS FOR THE STEEL INDUSTRY'S PROBLEMS

Contributing to the domestic steel industry's difficulties in withstanding tough import competition was a multitude of problems the industry inherited from its halcyon days.

The most fundamental problem was the absence of growth. Industry steel ingot production reached an historic peak of 117 million tons in 1955.[88] See Table 5.1. That level was not exceeded until nine years later. Growth then resumed to a new peak of 151 million tons—29 percent above 1955 output—in 1973. In the meantime, 15 million tons of potential growth had been ceded to importers, along with an unknown quantity of potential growth to substitutes such as concrete, aluminum, and plastics. Growth in export markets was also sacrificed because domestic costs and prices were too high to sell in most foreign markets without provoking dumping allegations. But for the integrated works making rolled steel products from blast furnace pig iron, the problem was even more severe. Within the peak year output totals were 8 million tons of electric arc furnace production in 1955 and 28 million tons in 1973. Thus, the expansion of nonelectric steel production between 1955 and 1973 in the United States was only 14 million tons, or 12 percent in 18 years. During that same interval, Japan increased its steel output from 10.4 to 131.5 million tons, European Community nations added 85 million tons, and the rest of the world (including the Soviet Union and many less-developed nations) added 231 million tons.

Growth matters because expanding or (especially) building a completely new steelworks is the most opportune time for implementing new technologies, new plant layouts, and new locational strategies. Experiencing little growth, the integrated U.S. steelmakers lagged other nations in adopting important new technologies that appeared following World War II—notably, the basic oxygen furnace, continuous casting, and the giant blast furnace.

ADOPTION OF THE BASIC OXYGEN PROCESS

The basic oxygen furnace was developed and tested successfully by a state-owned Austrian steelmaker, VOEST, in 1949. Commercial-scale production commenced in 1952. The earliest commercial application in North America was by a Canadian firm, DOFASCO, in 1954. A relatively small Detroit-based firm, McLouth, also began operating a BOF shop in 1954. At first slowly and then at an accelerating pace, adoption of the process spread both within the pioneering nations and to other nations. Figure 5.11 traces the growing percentages

---

[88]The highest output during World War II was 90 million tons, in 1944.

FIGURE 5.11
The Diffusion of Basic Oxygen Steelmaking, 12 Nations, 1961–1978

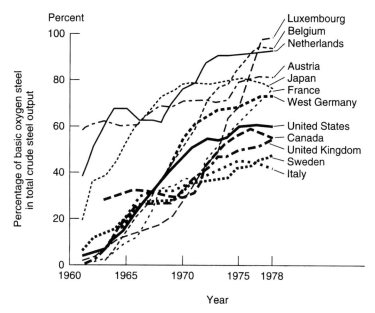

Source: Reproduced by permission from U.S. Office of Technology Assessment, Technology and Steel Industry Competitiveness (Washington, DC: USGPO, 1980), p. 130; drawing upon data from the Organization for Economic Cooperation and Development and the International Iron and Steel Institute. ©, OECD, 1980, Technology and Steel Industry Competitiveness.

of raw steel made using BOF in 12 nations over the years 1960 through 1978. Not surprisingly, Austria was the initial leader, followed in the early years by the Netherlands (with only one integrated steelworks), Canada, and Japan. The United States (heavy solid line) started slowly and by 1978 occupied a middling position. The fraction of U.S. raw carbon steel (i.e., excluding stainless and alloy steel) using the three main steelmaking processes at various benchmark years was as follows:[89]

Year	Basic Oxygen	Open Hearth	Electric
1960	3.7%	89.3%	5.7%
1965	18.7	73.6	7.2
1970	50.2	37.8	12.1
1975	64.6	19.7	15.7
1980	63.9	12.5	23.6
1990	62.1	3.7	34.2

---

[89]Based on periodic statistical reports of the American Iron and Steel Institute.

Basic oxygen gradually displaced the century-old Siemens-Martin open-hearth process, but in turn lost ground since 1975 to electric arc furnace production.

There has been furious debate in the economics literature as to whether United States steelmakers, or the subset of large integrated steelmakers, were delinquent in adopting the basic oxygen process.[90] The contending viewpoints are difficult to reconcile, since the technological parameters were changing rapidly over time, there was considerable uncertainty about them in the early years, the advantages of various furnace types depended critically upon the cost of scrap metal as compared to pig iron, and, as a result, explicit cost comparisons, when made at all, were for varying years and differed greatly. Among other things, as we have seen, there are massive scale economies in oxygen steelmaking, but steel producers mastered the technique of large furnaces only slowly. DOFASCO's first commercial-scale units held 35 tons of metal per heat. The largest furnace built during the 1950s (by Thyssen in Germany) had a capacity of 120 tons per heat; McLouth's early 110-ton furnaces were second in size. Pioneer VOEST in Austria did not install a furnace larger than 55 tons until 1973. Only in 1962 was what is now considered a full-scale furnace, holding 300 tons, inaugurated (by National Steel, in Detroit).

The cost comparisons between BOF and open-hearth furnaces that follow, synthesized from British and German sources,[91] attempt to reproduce the situation as U.S. steelmakers perceived it during the early 1960s. We assume that the iron inputs will be 67 percent newly smelted pig iron and 33 percent scrap—the highest proportion of scrap considered feasible in BOF shops at the time. In all but boom years scrap input prices tended to be slightly less than pig iron costs, but both clustered within a $30–$40 per ton range under U.S. market conditions during the early 1960s.[92] Scrap prices sufficiently low

---

[90]See, for example, Walter Adams and Joel Dirlam, "Big Steel, Invention, and Innovation," *Quarterly Journal of Economics*, vol. 80 (May 1966), pp. 167–189; G. S. Maddala and Peter Knight, "International Diffusion of Technical Change—A Case Study of the Oxygen Steelmaking Process," *Economic Journal*, vol. 77 (September 1967), pp. 531–558; Leonard Lynn, "New Data on the Diffusion of the Basic Oxygen Furnace in the U.S. and Japan," *Journal of Industrial Economics*, vol. 30 (December 1981), pp. 123–135; Sharon Oster, "The Diffusion of Innovation Among Steel Firms: The Basic Oxygen Furnace," *Bell Journal of Economics*, vol. 13 (Spring 1982), pp. 45–56; and Stephen Karlson, "Adoption of Competing Inventions by United States Steel Producers," *Review of Economics and Statistics*, vol. 68 (August 1986), pp. 415–422.

[91]British Iron and Steel Federation, Development Coordinating Committee, Stage 1 Report, *The Steel Industry* (London: BISF, July 1966), pp. 38–40; and Hermann R. Schenck et al., *Baukosten von Stahlwerken und betriebliche Verarbeitungskosten der Stahlwerksverfahren* (Düsseldorf: Verlag Stahleisen, 1970), pp. 552–591.

[92]See Myles G. Boylan Jr., *Economic Effects of Scale Increases in the Steel Industry: The Case of U.S. Blast Furnaces* (New York: Praeger, 1975), pp. 171–177; and Bela Gold et al.; *Technological Progress and Industrial Leadership* (Lexington, MA: Lexington Books, 1984), pp. 598 and 700.

to mandate higher scrap usage would favor either open-hearth (which could process heats with as much as 100 percent scrap) or, a fortiori, electric arc furnaces. Second, consistent with the lack of experience at the time operating larger BOF units, we assume a relatively small shop having two 100-ton furnaces, with one operating and one down for relining at any given time, producing 1.5 million tons of steel per year. The open-hearth works is of the same annual capacity. Third, annual interest and depreciation charges on fixed capital are assumed to be 16.5 percent. Fourth, costs denominated in West German DM are converted to dollars at an approximate purchasing power parity value of 3.2/1. Given these and other less crucial assumptions, the cost per ton of steel converted (excluding the cost of iron inputs, but including energy and oxygen inputs) was roughly as follows:

	Open Hearth	*Basic Oxygen*
Fuel and other energy	$4.48	$0.21
Oxygen	—	1.46
Other materials, wages, and repairs	5.81	6.58
Capital interest and depreciation	5.18	2.82
Total cost per ton	$15.47	$11.07

Clearly, basic oxygen was the superior choice. Or was it? Suppose the question was whether to replace existing and still functional open-hearth furnaces with new basic oxygen furnaces. This choice was faced repeatedly by U.S. steelmakers with sufficient capacity to meet slowly growing demand for their products. In such cases, the capital outlays for the open hearth furnaces already in operation had been sunk; there was no way to retrieve them. Therefore, the interest and depreciation costs of open hearth were also fixed and unavoidable. Only the *variable* costs of open hearth, totaling $4.48 plus $5.81 = $10.29 per ton, could be avoided if a decision were made to scrap the open hearths and install BOF. But to install BOF, the *full* costs of $11.07 per ton were incremental. Comparing the average variable cost per ton of $10.29 for open hearth against the full $11.07 cost of the BOF challenger, the rational decision maker would choose to continue operating its old open hearths. Only for capacity *expansions*, where existing open-hearth capacity was insufficient, would basic oxygen be the unambiguous choice. Because Japanese, European, and third world steelmakers were growing much more rapidly than U.S. integrated steel works, more of their decisions entailed capacity expansion, as contrasted to capacity replacement, than did those of U.S. integrated steelworks operators. Thus, the newest technology was more likely to be installed by producers experiencing rapid growth than by producers who faced static demand. Such is the tyranny of variable costs in a slow-growth environment.

Some complications must now be considered. The estimates above are for a BOF shop that fails to achieve all the scale economies eventually attained. And some early cost estimates assuming relatively small BOF shops found the full cost of BOF per ton to be lower than even the *variable* cost of open-hearth furnaces.[93] If this were the case, good open hearths should have been shut down to make way for basic oxygen. Or should they? As noted above, roughly a decade passed between the first practical BOF demonstration and the first installation of a BOF shop yielding all known scale economies. Rather than seizing the cost savings of early BOF units, a steelmaker might sensibly have waited at least until 1962 to secure even greater economies installing the most technologically advanced BOFs.

The passage of time favored BOF in other ways too (at least until the late 1970s). As the life of old open hearths was extended, ancillary equipment wore out and variable costs tended to rise, so that at some point, variable cost with the old process came to exceed the full cost of BOF. Thus, sooner or later, replacement became economic. Also, because open hearths, with their eight-hour heating cycle, are much more energy-intensive than BOFs, the oil price shock of 1973–1974 tilted replacement decisions strongly in favor of BOF (or electric furnaces) even in plants where continued operation of old open hearths had previously been justified. Replacement decisions were also hastened, especially during the 1960s, by pressure from state and local authorities to clean up the orange plume of iron oxide particulates characteristically emitted from the smokestacks of open-hearth shops. Doing so required the installation of electrostatic precipitators on each furnace chimney—in open-hearth shops with the same capacity as a modern BOF shop, on as many as 30 chimneys. With only three furnaces in a BOF shop, only three (larger) precipitators were needed. When cleanup was mandated, it suddenly became economical to scrap the open hearths and adopt BOF. Thus, during the late 1960s and early 1970s, BOFs replaced open hearths in large numbers throughout the United States.

Taking these complex considerations into account, how good was the U.S. industry's performance in adopting BOF? First, it seems clear that nations such as Japan installed basic oxygen more rapidly mainly because they were adding large amounts of new capacity and were therefore not held back by the tyranny of variable costs. Second, given the modest amount of integrated steelmaking capacity expansion they undertook after BOF's merits were proved, U.S. producers performed relatively well. A Federal Trade Commission study found that between 1956 and 1964, U.S. steelmakers added BOF capacity equal to 132 percent of their net capacity growth. Between 1964 and 1974, when replacement investment accelerated, their BOF additions amounted to 356 percent of net capacity growth. None of the 29 other nations covered by the analysis had a higher BOF/net capacity growth replacement

---

[93]Notably, Maddala and Knight, "International Diffusion," p. 535 (using South American data); and A. Cockerill, *The Steel Industry: International Comparisions of Industrial Structure and Performance* (Cambridge, UK: Cambridge University Press, 1974), p. 25 (comparing British furnaces of quite different capacities and vintage).

ratio—in part because few grew so slowly.[94] However, U.S. firms performed poorly relative to their Japanese counterparts during the early years of BOF on the subset of decisions involving clear-cut integrated works expansions. For such expansions, BOF had a strong full-cost advantage over open hearth. But of the 14 such integrated works expansions between 1954 and 1960 identified by Leonard Lynn, BOF was adopted four times and open hearth 10 times by U.S. steel companies.[95] In nine comparable Japanese expansions, BOF was adopted six times and open hearth three times. Finally, probably because they bore a disproportionate burden of restricting capacity growth to maintain prices, the largest U.S. steelmakers lagged behind their smaller rivals in the early adoption of BOF.[96]

OTHER TECHNOLOGY CHOICES

Modernization choices concerning other stages of the integrated steelmaking process have been less thoroughly investigated, but the histories were similar to those of basic oxygen furnaces. Figure 5.12 traces the rate at which continuous casting was adopted in 10 industrialized nations. Japan, expanding its steel output at an extraordinary pace, was the leader. Equipped with functioning slab and billet mills to satisfy their almost static output needs, U.S. firms (heavy solid line) were among the slowest adopters.[97] U.S. adoption rates accelerated noticeably after 1973, because one major advantage of "concast" is that the molten steel is transferred directly to continuous casters without being poured into ingots, cooled, and then reheated. Thus, there are substantial energy savings, and at the higher energy costs prevailing after the first OPEC price shock, the variable costs per ton of concast fell relative to those of slab and billet mills. Accelerated replacement continued in later years not covered by Figure 5.12. In 1978, the figure's terminal year, 12.5 percent of all raw

---

[94]Duke et al., *The United States Steel Industry and Its International Rivals,* Table 7.8. Particularly low BOF investment ratios were found, even when substantial capacity growth occurred, for Soviet Bloc nations. See also Madalla and Knight, "International Diffusion," pp. 549–550.

[95]Lynn, "New Data on the Diffusion," pp. 130–131.

[96]See, for example, Adams and Dirlam, "Big Steel," and Oster, "The Diffusion of Innovation." Compare Karlson, "Adoption of Competing Inventions," who argues that late adoption may have been rational because experience accumulated and scale economy frontiers expanded as the industry installed more units. After controlling for experience and scale effects, he finds that the larger firms did not lag significantly in the sense of failing to seek minimum costs.

[97]For a statistical analysis of variables influencing concast adoption through 1977, see Oster, "The Diffusion of Innovation," pp. 53–55.

FIGURE 5.12
The Diffusion of Continuous Casting, Ten Nations,
1962–1978

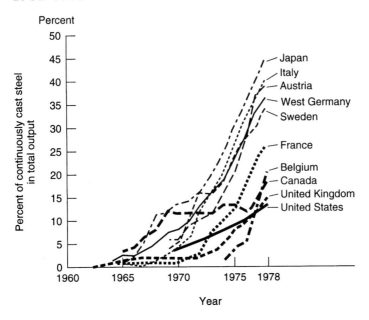

Source: Reproduced from U.S. Office of Technology Assessment, *Technology and Steel Industry Competitiveness*, p. 131, drawing upon data from the Organization for Economic Cooperation and Development.

steel produced in the United States was continuously cast. By 1982, adoption had increased to 29 percent; by 1992, to 79 percent.[98]

For similar reasons U.S. firms were slow to build blast furnaces taking advantage of the scale economy possibilities emerging during the 1960s. By 1968, blast furnaces producing 2.5 million tons of pig iron per year were operating in many parts of the world.[99] But the United States had none. At Gary, Indiana, the largest American steelmaking facility (with steel ingot capacity of

---

[98]From American Iron and Steel Institute, *Annual Statistical Report* (Washington, DC: AISI, 1985 and 1993).

[99]To ensure that steelmakers built blast furnaces of optimal scale, Japan's Ministry of Trade and Industry (MITI) administered a construction rotation program under which each blast furnace (and downstream facilities) project was scheduled so that its output did not arrive on the market concurrently with other firms' expanded output. MITI's power to implement this approach came from its control of the foreign exchange needed to buy additional supplies of imported iron ore. It ended during the late 1960s when Japan became a full member of the International Monetary Fund and had to relax its foreign exchange controls.

8.5 million tons), 12 furnaces were used to do the work that could be performed by two or three modern units. At the next three plants, ranked by capacity, the number of blast furnaces was as follows: Bethlehem Steel at Sparrows Point, Maryland, 10 blast furnaces; Inland Steel at Indiana Harbor, Indiana, eight furnaces; Bethlehem Steel at Lackawanna (near Buffalo), New York, six furnaces. Comparing the annual unit costs of 700,000-ton and 1.4-million-ton blast furnaces as of 1965, Myles Boylan found lower costs, as expected, with the larger furnace. But "When demand was not strong enough to support new capacity without abandoning or scrapping older and smaller furnaces, the cost figures indicate it would have been optimal to leave the blast furnace stock unchanged."[100] The first U.S. furnace of 2 million tons capacity was inaugurated in 1969 by Bethlehem Steel at its Burns Harbor, Indiana, plant—the only "green field" (i.e., completely new) pig iron–based steel works built in the United States during the 1960s and 1970s.[101] United States Steel Corporation followed with a 2.4-million-ton replacement furnace at Gary, Indiana, in 1974.

After Bethlehem's Burns Harbor plant was constructed, no American steel producer undertook a similar new project. At its formation in 1901, the United States Steel Corporation received from Andrew Carnegie a large tract on Lake Erie at Conneaut, Ohio (between Cleveland and Erie). Carnegie's proposal to build a new works there was the immediate impetus to the United States Steel consolidation. During the 1960s and 1970s, U.S. Steel repeatedly considered developing a new integrated works at Conneaut, but each study yielded the same negative conclusion—the plant would not be profitable, given stagnant demand and the company's abundance of older capacity, which could be expanded or modernized as needed at lower incremental cost.[102]

These decisions, though rational in the short term, had a significant long-run cost. Most of the pig iron–based steel works operated by U.S. companies during the 1960s and 1970s had been opened during the industry's period of rapid growth between 1885 and 1920. Growth was then achieved by installing additional furnaces, primary mills, and product mills wherever they fitted best into the existing plant layout. This growth was, in the words of one company's facilities planning director, "like Topsy"—that is, conforming to the

---

[100]Boylan, *Economic Effects of Scale Increases*, p. 174.

[101]Ironically, the Burns Harbor project was initiated after a U.S. federal court prevented (on antitrust grounds) Bethlehem Steel from acquiring the Youngstown Sheet & Tube Co. Bethlehem claimed that it needed to acquire Youngstown, which had an integrated works at the south end of Lake Michigan, in order to enter the Chicago area market. *U.S. v. Bethlehem Steel Corporation et al.*, 168 F. Supp. 576 (1958).

[102]For an extended discussion of those computations, see Crandall, *The U.S. Steel Industry in Recurrent Crisis*, chap. 4; and National Academy of Engineering, *The Competitive Status of the U.S. Steel Industry* (Washington, DC: National Academy Press, 1985), pp. 51–54.

necessities of the moment rather than to any coherent long-range plan.[103] As a result, materials flows were lengthy and complex, with hot metal circulating back and forth among the diversely located processing stages. The same executive estimated that in his company's largest plant, one of the most efficient integrated facilities in the United States, approximately one-fourth of all on-site costs were incurred for materials handling. In striking contrast was the typical new Japanese steel works of the 1960s and 1970s. Refer again to Figure 5.1. Raw materials entered on one side of the works, moving nearly minimal distances to blast furnaces, steel converters, casters and primary mills, and product mills before emerging on the plant's other side for shipment to customers.

The commitment of U.S. steelmakers to ancient locational choices had a further cost. Most of the industry's capacity had been sited to receive ore with an iron content averaging 50 percent from the Mesabi Range and other Great Lakes mines. Gradually, however, the reserves from those sources were depleted. The steel companies had to turn to lower-quality ores (e.g., Upper Michigan taconite, with an iron content of only 30 percent).[104] Meanwhile, Japanese, Korean, and other steel producers were locating their new greenfield plants at coastal ports capable of receiving large oceangoing ore freighters carrying 60 percent ores from Australia, Africa, and South America. Producers in the United States were unable to take advantage of these richer ore sources because of their inland locations. Only two integrated facilities—Bethlehem's plant at Sparrows Point, Maryland, and U.S. Steel's Fairless works near Trenton, New Jersey—were positioned to receive ores from locations outside North America without transshipping or a circuitous St. Lawrence Seaway voyage. American firms made the best of an inferior situation by developing methods of "beneficiating" taconite at the mine site to higher-quality blast furnace feeds. Nevertheless, their iron ore costs had risen by the 1970s to be significantly higher per ton of output than those of foreign rivals situated to receive ore from world market sources—for example, 39 percent higher than Japan's average ore costs in boom year 1973 and 58 percent higher in recession year 1975.[105]

Partially offsetting the disadvantages of high wages, older equipment, less efficient plant layouts, and expensive iron ore were certain advantages possessed by U.S. steelmakers. Most important, they were located much nearer their principal customers, so they incurred lower outbound freight costs and could respond more quickly to new orders. Also, the United States enjoys abundant reserves of high-grade coking coal. In many cases coal could be

---

[103]In an anonymous interview for F. M. Scherer et al., *The Economics of Multi-Plant Operation* (Cambridge: Harvard University Press, 1975).

[104]See, for example, Gold et al., *Technological Progress and Industrial Leadership*, pp. 309–317.

[105]Duke et al., *The United States Steel Industry and Its International Rivals*, chap. 3, Table 3.3.

delivered at relatively low cost to domestic coking ovens, whereas Japanese steelmakers were shipping coal across the Pacific Ocean from mines located in the northwestern United States and British Columbia. Overall, however, the costs of U.S. steelmakers were appreciably higher than those of their more efficient overseas rivals, especially those of Japan. Seven surveys found production cost per finished product ton to be 18.5 percent lower on average in Japan than in the United States during the mid–1970s.[106]

Sometimes U.S. producers complained that in addition to these technological and locational handicaps, they were forced to spend a higher fraction of their investment budgets than overseas rivals on pollution control. The assertion may have been true with respect to steel operations in some less-developed nations. But in Japan and the industrialized nations of Western Europe, pressures for pollution abatement were at least a strong as in the United States. A Federal Trade Commission study found that the share of capital expenditures earmarked for pollution control between 1973 and 1975 averaged 13.9 percent in the United States, 18.2 percent in Japan, and 13.8 percent in West Germany.[107]

One further handicap of the U.S. industry must be noted. Experiencing slow growth, it invested relatively less in new plant and equipment than its faster-growing overseas rivals, and as a result it lagged in introducing the most up-to-date technologies. Investment in capital goods research and development is stimulated by the demand for investment in new equipment.[108] With little demand for new technologies, the industry itself devoted only a small fraction of its revenues to research and development—for example, 0.33 percent in 1974 and 0.42 percent in 1977.[109] Even more importantly, the steel industry is supplied with new rolling mills, furnaces, and the like by firms specializing in the design of such equipment. With weak demand for their products, the equipment specialists spent relatively little on developing improved designs.[110] One major rolling mill supplier, Mesta, plunged into bankruptcy in 1985, and others diversified away from steel mill equipment. As a result, both the steel industry and its infrastructure suppliers fell behind technologically and no longer had command of the latest steelmaking techniques. The industry was slow to recognize this gap. Interviews conducted with steel company engineers during the early 1970s revealed that many had little familiarity with

---

[106]National Academy of Engineering, *The Competitive Status*, p. 47.

[107]Duke et al., *The United States Steel Industry and Its International Rivals*, Appendix Table A3.2. Weighted averages for the individual years have been taken.

[108]See Jacob Schmookler, *Invention and Economic Growth* (Cambridge: Harvard University Press, 1966); and F. M. Scherer, "Demand-Pull and Technological Innovation: Schmookler Revisited," *Journal of Industrial Economics*, vol. 30 (March 1982), pp. 225–238.

[109]Federal Trade Commission, *Statistical Report: Annual Line of Business Report*, for 1974 and 1977.

[110]See "Steel's Suppliers Feel the Blast," *Business Week*, October 25, 1982, pp. 114–118.

important developments pioneered abroad.[111] Gradually, however, U.S. steelmakers recognized their deficiency. They entered into technology-sharing arrangements with foreign steel producers, began buying major equipment units from foreign manufacturers, and in some cases offered minority or even majority stock interests to Japanese steel producers willing to transfer needed know-how.[112] In this way the technology gap was narrowed, though not completely eliminated.

RENAISSANCE

As the close of the 1970s approached, the U.S. steel industry was in serious trouble. Its costs had risen above those of overseas rivals in both industrialized and rapidly industrializing nations. Import pressure was mounting. Companies producing steel using blast furnace/converter methods were under heavy assault in the low-end lines from domestic minimill rivals, whose costs of refining scrap in electric furnaces (at least, under normal scrap price conditions) were substantially lower, and which did not conform to traditional industry pricing norms. What to do?

The integrated producers still maintained, albeit somewhat less faithfully, their traditions of price leadership and follow-the-leader discipline. But to what prices should the leader lead? The integrated producers lacked a cost advantage relative to foreign and domestic rivals. Under these circumstances, the logic of dynamic limit pricing theory teaches, deterring the entry and expansion of "outsiders" cannot be profitable. Rather, a tight-knit oligopoly will try to set prices sufficiently high to yield positive profits for its members and hope that entry is sufficiently slow to postpone the day of reckoning into the distant future. Competitive entry might be retarded by erecting entry barriers—in the case of steel, trigger prices and then quotas restraining import competition. The high-price plus import-limiting strategy is what the traditional steelmakers tried to implement.

Import barriers can have either of two basic rationales. They can provide a respite from intense import competition, permitting the domestic industry to enhance its cash flow and plow the funds gained thereby into modernization. This (plus belt-tightening measures) can reduce unit costs and permit the industry to meet its overseas rivals on more favorable terms in the future. Or they can serve as a narcotic, dulling the pain of decline while business-as-usual policies are pursued.

---

[111]The interviews were conducted for Scherer et al., *The Economics of Multi-Plant Operation.*

[112]See for example, "National Steel's New Game Plan Is Made in Japan," *Business Week*, June 3, 1985, p. 78; "Armco's Accord with Kawasaki," *New York Times*, April 6, 1989, p. D2; and (for domestic and foreign joint venture lists), William E. Scheuerman, "Joint Ventures in the U.S. Steel Industry," *American Journal of Economics and Sociology*, vol. 49 (October 1990), pp. 413–429.

To determine which of these alternatives better describes the U.S. industry's performance under import restraints, annual data for 1954–1988 on new capital investment outlays, raw steel output, import tonnage, cash flows, price level changes, and interest rates were collected for the three-digit Census industry category "blast furnace and basic steel products."[113] Using Census data, cash flow was measured as sales less materials purchases less payroll costs.[114] All dollar values were expressed in 1982 constant dollars using the GNP deflator for fixed nonresidential investment. The principal variables were as follows:

Invest   Plant and equipment investment outlays (millions of 1982 dollars).

Cashflow   Cash flow, as estimated above.

Output   Raw steel output (millions of tons).

Imports   Steel imports into the United States (millions of net tons).

Interest   Real interest rate (adjusted for current price inflation) on Baa corporate bonds.

Barriers   Dummy variable; zero if no import barriers in place; 1 in import barrier years (except 0.5 in 1980).

Figure 5.13 arrays the cash flow and investment data graphically. Investment (dash-dot line) appears to be lower in years of reduced cash flow (dashed line), although the correlation is imperfect. The years in which import barriers were in force are marked by a solid line elevated above the zero plane. Investment is clearly lower in barrier years, especially when one recognizes that the most pervasive quota scheme was in force between 1984 and 1988. Nevertheless, it is unclear whether barriers led to lower investment or whether barriers were imposed when cash flow and hence investment were impaired.

To probe the chain of causation more deeply, the impact of import barriers was estimated by a two-stage least-squares regression analysis . In the first stage, *Cashflow* was the dependent variable, with the following results:

$$\text{Cashflow} = -413 + 128 \, (\text{Output}) - 70 \, (\text{Imports}) - 502 \, (\text{Barriers})$$
$$\quad\quad\quad (0.20) \;\; (7.29) \quad\quad\quad (1.00) \quad\quad\quad (0.47)$$

---

[113]The data were used for a Kennedy School of Government exercise by first-year master's students in the applied economics and econometrics courses during April of 1981. The analysis here is the author's, but sensitivity was tested inter alia against the results achieved in student group analyses.

[114]Outlays for social security, unemployment compensation, health plans, and retirement benefits are not available for all years. They amounted to 19.6 percent of steel industry payrolls in 1970, 30.4 percent in 1980, and 36.7 percent in 1988. Estimating them nonlinearly for other years and deducting the estimates changes the results insignificantly.

FIGURE 5.13
The Relationship of Steel Investment to Cash Flows and Import Barriers

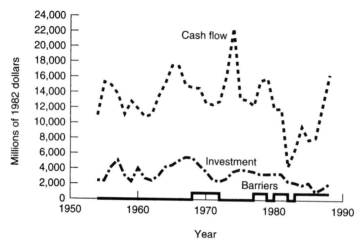

Source: U.S. Bureau of the Census, *Annual Survey of Manufactures,* various years.

with $R^2 = 0.652$ and *t*-ratios given in subscripted parentheses. The main variable influencing cash flow appears to have been the level of industry output. Imports affect cash flow negatively, but the effect is not statistically significant. The *Barriers* variable is negative but insignificant, either because import barriers were erected mainly during the years when the industry's finances were under heavy pressure or because the import restraints were not very effective. On this, more later.

For the second-stage analysis, *Invest* was the variable to be explained. The value of cash flow *Predflow* predicted by the equation above was used as an instrumental variable along with one- and two-year lagged values of *Cashflow* (because investment responds only with a lag), lagged real interest, and the *Barriers* dummy variable. The results were as follows:

$$\text{Invest} = 357 + 0.134 \ (\text{Predflow}) + 0.061 \ (\text{Cashflow}_{t-1})$$
$$(0.36) \ \ (1.96) \qquad\qquad (1.29)$$

$$+ \ 0.058 \ (\text{Cashflow}_{t-2}) - 20.1 \ (\text{Interest}_{t-1}) - 504 \ (\text{Barriers})$$
$$(1.64) \qquad\qquad (0.30) \qquad\qquad (1.66)$$

with $R^2 = 0.645$. With higher cash flow, more investment occurs, as expected. Earlier years' flows have less impact than current-year cash flow, suggesting fairly rapid adjustment of investment programs. Interest rates have the anticipated negative sign, but the effect is far from significant. Most important, having import barriers in place appears to have *inhibited* investment by an estimated $504 million per year, all else equal. The *Barriers* effect is significantly different from zero at the 88 percent confidence level in a two-tail test.

This last result suggests that the narcosis hypothesis describes steelmakers' behavior under import restraints better than the plowback and recoupment hypothesis. That having import barriers in place did not *enhance* investment, all else equal, emerges as a quite robust conclusion from many alternative econometric model specifications (not reported in detail here) investigating trade barrier–investment relationships.[115]

A corollary implication is that the various trade barriers, whatever their intent might have been, did not contribute much to the U.S. industry's cash flow. This is consistent with the statistical analyses of Crandall, who found that domestic steel prices rose much less than import prices in response to the quotas of 1968–1972 and the trigger prices of 1978–1980.[116] Figure 5.6 provides corroborating evidence for the 1980s. Something changed dramatically in that period. Previously, the average revenue realized per ton of hot-rolled strip had shown no tendency to fall in recessions, and during the inflationary 1970s, it moved relentlessly upward. But there was a pause in the upward trend during 1980, when the trigger price mechanism was suspended for six months. Then, in 1983, after quotas had been negotiated with the European Community and Japan, there was a distinct downward break, followed by even more severe erosion in the ensuing years despite extension of the quota agreement to many other nations.[117] Between 1982 (at the trough of a recession) and 1986, average prices fell by 25 percent. The transformation in pricing behavior is even more remarkable when two additional facts are taken

---

[115]In 25 diversely specified regression models, the estimated impact of generalized import barriers ranged from +$85 million to −$1655 million, with an average value of −$536 million. The positive cases all resulted from models in which some values of key explanatory variables were estimated by extrapolation; none came anywhere near statistical significance. In a model distinguishing between the 1969–1972 quotas, the 1978–1982 trigger prices, and the 1982–1988 quotas, only the 1967–1972 quotas were found to have a positive impact on investment.

[116]Crandall, *The U.S. Steel Industry in Recurrent Crisis*, pp. 107–113. See also U.S. Congressional Budget Office, *Has Trade Protection Revitalized Domestic Industries?* (Washington, DC: USGPO, November 1986), pp. 49–54.

[117]The break is attributable at least in part to a decision by United States Steel Corporation to cease acting as price leader and to match other firms' discounts. "Graham Is Trying to Forge a Tougher U.S. Steel," *Business Week*, October 10, 1983, pp. 104–106. A contributing factor may have been a change in the way General Motors purchased steel—from distributing its requirements among roughly 12 suppliers to awarding long-term contracts to a few low-price bidders. "Buyers' Market? Now Steel's Customers Are Taking Their Turn at Jolting the Industry," *Wall Street Journal*, May 21, 1982, p. 1.

into account. At the time, minimills had not yet extended their reach to strip products, so the competition they brought to bear in other product categories is absent from Figure 5.6. Second, during the period when the domestic strip producers' pricing discipline was eroding visibly, strip shipments were increasing—from 9.4 million tons in 1982 to 16.1 million tons in 1986. Evidently, the traditions inherited from the Gary dinners gave way at last.

While these pricing changes unfolded, the industry was plunged into crisis. Between 1982 and 1986, American steelmakers reported net after-tax losses totaling $11.6 billion—that is, 8.5 percent of their total sales and other revenues.[118] To stanch the hemorrhage, scores of high-cost plants were closed.[119] The industry's rated annual raw steelmaking capacity decreased from 154 million tons in 1982 to 112 million tons in 1987—a decline of 27 percent.[120] LTV Corporaton, which had acquired three second-tier steel companies—Jones & Laughlin, Youngstown Sheet & Tube, and Republic—reorganized under the bankruptcy laws. So did McLouth Steel and Wheeling-Pittsburgh. National Steel sold its Weirton, West Virginia, plant to its employees. The number of steel industry employees fell from 337,396 in 1977 to 198,477 in recession trough year 1982 and then to 120,865 in 1987—that is, by nearly two-thirds. With the closure of inefficient plants and massive layoffs, productivity (i.e., output per labor hour) soared. During the 1970s, it will be recalled, the growth of productivity was negative. Between 1980 and 1990, the average annual productivity growth rate was 5.2 percent per year.[121] Pressed by its customers to match the standards set by foreign competitors, and especially by Japanese steelmakers, the industry also exerted strenuous efforts to improve the quality of its products.[122]

Plant closures and layoffs in turn precipitated changes in the industry's labor bargaining practices. The 1980 industry-wide negotiation brought important deviations from the cost-of-living escalators and guaranteed productivity increase provisions accepted in previous bargains. As negotiations for the 1983 round began in 1982, an increasing number of smaller companies and

---

[118]American Iron and Steel Institute, *Annual Statistical Report: 1990* (Washington DC: AISI, 1991), p. 10. These figures are for the companies' steelmaking business segments, excluding financial data for other diversified lines of business. Because of their losses, the companies were able to claim income tax credits totalling $2.5 billion. Thus, their pre-tax loss was $14.1 billion.

[119]On the closure of Carnegie's famous Homestead Works, see William Serrin, *Homestead: The Glory and Tragedy of an American Steel Town* (New York: New York Times Books, 1992). See also more generally Mary E. Deily, "Exit Strategies and Plant-Closing Decisions: The Case of Steel," *RAND Journal of Economics*, vol. 23 (Summer 1991), pp. 250–263.

[120]American Iron and Steel Institute, *Annual Statistical Report: 1990*, p. 6.

[121]Ibid., p. 16. The calculation is between 1980 and 1990 end points, continuously compounded.

[122]See "Detroit's Call for Better Steel," *New York Times*, December 24, 1983, p. 29.

union locals bargained separately for concessions from the industry-wide pattern.[123] The imminent threat of plant closures changed the dynamic of bargaining. In the past, the perception of union leaders was that plants would remain open and that wage increases would threaten the jobs only of the workers with little seniority. A majority of the local members favored high wages. But when a whole plant might shut down, the majority found its employment at stake and favored concessions. As deviations from the general pattern spread, local union leaders twice rejected concessions incorporated into the provisional 1983 national bargain. On the third try, they accepted a national contract reducing wages immediately by $1.25 per hour, reducing other fringe benefits, forgoing past-due cost-of-living increases, and providing for future COL increases only if the inflation rate exceeded 4 percent.[124] Concessions at the local level continued to undercut the industry-wide contracts, and in 1985, the five companies that had persisted in bargaining jointly with the United Steelworkers abandoned their coordination efforts altogether.[125] Given the wage and fringe benefit concessions accepted in the now-fragmented bargains, the hourly compensation premium enjoyed by steelworkers relative to workers in other manufacturing industries narrowed:[126]

	Straight Wage Rate	*With Fringe Benefits*
1973	44%	53%
1980	78%	94%
1988	46%	62%

For wages per se, the differential returned to nearly the level at which it began with the Experimental Negotiating Agreement in 1973. The retreat for wages including fringe benefits was less because of substantial payments to laid-off workers.

Important relief came also from macroeconomic changes. Between 1981 and 1985, high domestic interest rates strengthened the U.S. dollar. On average over those years, a dollar could buy 237 Japanese yen or 2.61 West German DM. This made imports from those (and other) nations relatively

---

[123]See Deily, "Wages in the Integrated Steel Industry;" and "To Keep the Mills Open, Steelworkers Labor for Less," *Philadelphia Inquirer*, September 19, 1982, p. 10-G.

[124]See "A Costly Failure in Steel Bargaining," *Business Week*, August 16, 1982, pp. 22–23; "Steel's Outlook: Mutual Misery," *Business Week*, December 6, 1982, pp. 95–97; and "Steel Union Leaders Ratify Concessions," *New York Times*, March 2, 1983, p. A16.

[125]"End of Joint Steel Talks Laid to Union Decisions," *New York Times*, May 6, 1985, p. B11.

[126]The source is U.S. Bureau of the Census, *Annual Survey of Manufactures*, various years. Compare p. 174 supra.

cheap. Beginning in 1986, however, the dollar's value plummeted–e.g., on average between 1986 and 1990, to 145 Yen (a 39 percent devaluation) or 1.85 German Marks (a 29 percent devaluation). As foreign currency became more expensive, the dollar cost of foreign steel rose, *ceteris paribus.*

As a consequence of these several developments, the U.S. steel industry moved from a position of inferiority to being the lowest-cost supplier in its home market. By 1988, the average cost per ton for steel shipped to U.S. markets, including $70 to $80 inbound transportation charges, was estimated to be $491 from Great Britain (whose steel industry was restructured during the 1980s even more radically than the U.S. industry), $498 from South Korea, $527 from France, $545 from West Germany, and $632 from Japan.[127] The comparable average for U.S. steel makers (excluding shipping charges) was $484 per ton.

Table 5.2 shows that exports from the United States began rising, especially to Canada and Mexico, which can be reached with only modest outbound shipping charges. Despite the U.S. cost advantage, imports did not fall sharply. But the mix of import sources continued to change. Canada had become the leading importer, shipping in 4.2 million tons during 1992.[128] Japan was second with 2.7 million tons (disproportionately in high-value sheet and alloy products), Korea third with 1.6 million tons, Brazil fourth with 1.597 million tons, and France fifth with 0.95 million tons.[129]

We learned earlier that works processing scrap in electric arc furnaces increased their share of carbon steel output to 35 percent in 1992 and began to make inroads into flat-rolled sheet markets. The minimills' tradition of ignoring integrated steelmakers' price leadership, the broader breakdown of price leadership,[130] and the continued pressure of imports combined with worldwide recession between 1990 and 1993 to sustain vigorous price competition. Following two profitable years, U.S. steelmakers reported losses of $2.0 billion in 1991 and $3.8 billion in 1992.[131] Claims that foreign firms were

---

[127]"Did you say *de*-industrialising?" *The Economist,* December 17, 1988, p. 75. See also "An Industrial Comeback Story: U.S. Is Competing Again in Steel," *New York Times,* March 31, 1992, p. 1; and "Why American Steel Is Big Again," *New York Times,* July 21, 1994, p. D1.

[128]Steel trade between the United States and Canada was encouraged by the signing of a bilateral free trade agreement in 1988. But, in addition, there is reason to believe that trade was inhibited until the 1980s by implicit "you stay out of our market, we stay out of yours" understandings between Canadian and U.S. steel companies.

[129]American Iron and Steel Institute, *Annual Statistical Report: 1992* (Washington, DC: AISI, 1993), p. 53.

[130]See "America's Steel Industry: Protection's Stepchild," *The Economist,* May 16, 1992, p. 98.

[131]AISI, *Annual Statistical Report: 1992,* p. 8.

dumping and/or subsidizing their output escalated once more,[132] but the complaints were dropped when demand recovered and profits soared in 1993 and 1994.

Thus, even though the industry had become much more efficient—largely, it would appear, as a result of potent competitive pressures rather than from the protection provided by import quotas—its problems had by no means ended. It remains premature to conclude that, as Edward de Vere, the seventeenth earl of Oxfordshire, might have said, "All's well that ends well."

AFTERWORD

The steel industry provides a compelling example of how dominant firm and collusive pricing strategies that were at first highly profitable for industry members precipitated repercussions that unfolded like a Greek tragedy. High prices for steel products and the high wages paid to steelworkers rendered the U.S. industry vulnerable to increasing competition from importers. That competition, plus substitution away from steel induced by high prices and the general maturing of the industry, made it difficult to keep pace with new technological opportunities, which in turn magnified the industry's handicap relative to overseas rivals. Industry and government joined forces to address these problems by erecting import barriers, but in the end the protective efforts must be judged a failure. Only when the traditional pricing institutions broke down under the strain of both foreign and domestic competition did the needed large-scale restructuring occur, setting the stage for a more optimistic future.

---

[132]"Feeling Sorry for Steel," *The Economist*, October 3, 1992, pp. 69–70; and "Steel Mills Hope for Higher Prices," *New York Times*, October 15, 1992, p. D12.

6

SEMICONDUCTORS

The semiconductor industry is noteworthy for very rapid tech-nological change, large investments in research and develop-ment, and significant dynamic economies of scale realized through learning by doing. The uniquely aggressive pricing strategies chosen by firms to maximize learning curve advan-tages are analyzed. When similar pricing policies were pursued by Japanese firms, which were encouraged by their govern-ment's industrial policies to attain the technological frontier, a major international trade dispute erupted. Understanding that dispute requires additional insight into the economics of dumping and the consequences of import restraints. We then examine the policies that helped U.S. semiconductor makers regain world market leadership during the 1990s.

INTRODUCTION

Few industries have sustained more rapid technological progress than semi-conductors. Its products—microprocessors, memory cells, transistors, light-emitting diodes, solar cells, and so on—enhance the performance of comput-ers, compact disc players, point-and-shoot cameras, cellular telephones, automatic braking systems, guided missiles, and much else. In 1992, more than 800 U.S. semiconductor makers shipped products valued at approxi-mately $32 billion.[1] The leading four producers in 1987 originated 40 percent of domestic industry sales; the top eight 58 percent. Thus, the industry is oli-gopolistic, but its rapid technological changes and unusually differentiated products will require extensions to the oligopoly theories developed thus far.

---

[1]U.S. Bureau of the Census, *1992 Census of Manufactures,* Industry Series, MC92-I–36 (Electronic Components) (June 1995).

EARLY HISTORY

The industry had its genesis in the basic research section of Bell Telephone Laboratories, the research and development arm of AT&T, during the late 1940s.[2] Scientific knowledge concerning semiconducting materials (e.g., crystalline silicon or germanium, which would normally not conduct electricity, but in which electrons could flow under certain conditions when slight impurities were introduced) had advanced appreciably during the 1930s. Diode rectifiers, devices that allow electricity to flow in only one direction and thereby convert alternating into direct current, had been crafted from such materials. The electron tubes used in radios and coaxial cables at the time achieved amplification by adding a grid to a diode. It was believed that semiconducting materials could amplify currents, but the existing theory provided little guidance. The president of Bell Laboratories was also interested in developing more efficient switching (i.e., on-off) devices, since he foresaw a time, which actually arrived during the 1970s, when the growth of telephone networks would overwhelm the prevailing mechanical switch technology. As World War II activity drew to a close, a small team was assembled to explore the possibilities of semiconducting materials and the "solid-state" physical laws that governed their behavior.

The first deliberate attempts to create a semiconductor amplifier were unsuccessful, but almost by accident, it was discovered in late 1947 that amplification occurred when electrodes were placed in such a way as to form what is now called a point contact transistor. This discovery yielded new insights into the properties of semiconducting materials, which in turn suggested alternative, more efficient amplifier designs. From the continuing interaction between experimentation and theorizing during the next four years came a systematic theory of the behavior of electrons in semiconducting materials, plus practical amplifying, rectifying, and switching device designs along with new methods for producing them in quantity. For their published research on the theory of semiconducting materials, Bell Laboratories scientists William Shockley, Walter Brattain, and John Bardeen received the 1956 Nobel Prize in physics. The commercial prospects for semiconductors were disclosed to the industrial world at a 1951 symposium attended by representatives of 80 industrial firms along with government and university scientists.[3]

---

[2]See, for example, Richard R. Nelson, ed., "The Link Between Science and Invention: The Case of the Transistor," in the National Bureau of Economic Research conference report, *The Rate and Direction of Inventive Activity* (Princeton, NJ: Princeton University Press, 1962), pp. 549–583; and Richard C. Levin, "The Semiconductor Industry," in Richard R. Nelson, ed., *Government and Technical Progress* (New York: Pergamon, 1982), pp. 40–47.

[3]See John E. Tilton, *International Diffusion of Technology: The Case of Semiconductors* (Washington, DC: Brookings, 1971), p. 75.

At the time, AT&T offered to license its rapidly growing semiconductor patent portfolio to all interested applicants at modest royalty rates (reduced to zero in a 1956 antitrust settlement). In April 1952, 25 U.S. companies and 10 foreign companies paid a royalty advance of $25,000 each to attend an eight-day symposium imparting much of Bell Laboratories' accumulated semiconductor technology wisdom. The game was afoot.

Because one major advantage of semiconductor amplifiers over the prevailing electron tube technology was their much smaller size, it is hardly surprising that the first commercial use was for hearing aids, by the Sonotone Company in late 1952. A much larger-volume application to transistorized radios came in 1954. The pioneer was a small firm, Regency,[4] followed by a well-established radio maker, Emerson. In 1955 Sony, founded by Akira Morita in Japan following World War II, conceived a smaller (nearly pocket-size) model using semiconductors of its own design, and built its sales aggressively both at home and in the United States.[5] Other Japanese firms followed suit, and by the end of the 1950s, most of the portable transistorized radios seen in virtually every U.S. home and public meeting place had been imported from Japan. Sony and other Japanese electrical apparatus manufacturers obtained licenses from AT&T and other U.S. companies and rapidly accumulated the know-how needed to supply the transistors demanded by domestic radio assemblers.

Within the United States, the military establishment was keenly interested in semiconductor devices because of their smaller size, lower electric power usage, and their potentially greater ability to withstand the heat, cold, shock, and other conditions afflicting vacuum tubes' reliability. The first primitive transistors were too unreliable to be accepted for gruelling military applications. Thus, even though it had invented them, Bell Laboratories chose in 1953 not to include transistors in improved versions of the Nike Ajax antiaircraft missile system it had developed for the U.S. Army.[6] Nevertheless, military agencies provided $53 million of research and development support to fledgling U.S. semiconductor manufacturers between 1955 and 1960, and military orders accounted for 43 percent of the industry's sales (rapidly growing from $40 million in 1955 to $542 million in 1960) during that period.[7] A major

---

[4]Texas Instruments claimed in hindsight that its customer, the Idea Corporation, marketed the first such radio in 1954, but oral tradition gives Regency the nod.

[5]On the history at Sony, see Akira Morita, *Made in Japan: Akira Morita and Sony* (New York: Dutton, 1986), pp. 65–69 and 83–88. In his work on radio transistors, Sony scientist Leo Esaki invented the tunnel diode. For demonstrating the tunneling effect in semiconductors, he received the 1973 Nobel Prize in physics.

[6]F. M. Scherer, "The Development of the Nike Ajax Guided Missile System," unpublished Harvard Business School case study (1960), p. 158.

[7]Levin, "The Semiconductor Industry," pp. 60–69.

step forward occurred in 1958, when the U.S. Air Force decided to transistor-ize the guidance of its new Minuteman intercontinental ballistic missile sys-tem. To achieve its goals, it awarded contracts to 13 companies making, or proposing to produce, the needed semiconductor components.

While adopting accepted transistor designs for emerging weapon systems, the military procurement agencies also pushed hard to advance the state of the art. Although single-function transistors were much smaller than the elec-tron tubes they replaced, many military technical officers believed that giant steps toward miniaturization remained to be taken. During the late 1950s, each of the military agencies supported contract research programs to explore miniaturization possibilities.[8] The navy and one army laboratory asked con-tractors to connect numerous discrete transistors, each embedded separately on a single silicon platform. Another army laboratory stressed stacking dis-crete layers of semiconductor components and ceramic separators, with the various parts connected by exterior riser wires. The air force undertook the most radical approach in its "molecular electronics" program, awarding to RCA a contract to develop electronic devices "in which the basic building blocks will be electric field charges and spins, instead of the familiar resistor, capacitor, induction tube and transistor."[9] However, as events ensued, all of these dozen or so contract research programs were backing the wrong horses. The winning solution came from two companies aware of the government's demands, but without contracts under the military miniaturization programs.

One, Texas Instruments (TI), had entered the semiconductor business in 1953 by hiring away a key Bell Laboratories engineer. TI was the first, in 1954, to use silicon successfully instead of germanium to produce transistors. Because of its lower cost and greater heat resistance, silicon offered major advantages over germanium and soon became the preferred transistor mater-ial. Moving to the front ranks of semiconductor makers through that discov-ery, TI turned its attention to miniaturization. A key invention—what is now called the integrated circuit—was made by Jack Kilby between 1958 and 1959. Kilby's idea was to implant microscopic quantities of "doping" impurities at several locations on a single pure germanium chip, thereby creating multiple switching, amplifying, or resisting devices on that chip. The various devices were then laboriously connected by laying down metallic conductors to form a complete integrated circuit element.

Crucial complementary inventions came almost simultaneously from the Fairchild Semiconductor Company. In 1959 Fairchild's Robert Noyce devised an integrated circuit concept differing in some details from Kilby's—among

---

[8]See Levin, "The Semiconductor Industry," pp. 70–73; "New Techniques Shrink Avionics Size," *Aviation Week*, April 13, 1959, pp. 75–81; and "USAF Launches Molec-tronics Program," *Aviation Week*, April 27, 1959, pp. 54–62.

[9]"USAF Launches Molectronics Program," p. 54.

other things, using germanium as the semiconducting material and a layer of silicon oxide to insulate individual components within a circuit from one another. An advantage of silicon was that the much less labor-intensive planar method of production, invented by Fairchild's Jean Hoerni in 1958, could be adapted from single-function to integrated circuit wafer production. Together, the integrated circuit and planar process inventions precipitated a microeconomics revolution.[10]

Under the integrated circuit fabrication process in its ultimately implemented form, a highly polished wafer of pure silicon is coated with a thin protective layer of silicon oxide. The silicon oxide surface is coated in turn with a "photoresist" material which, when exposed to focused light patterns, can be developed like a photographic negative to expose only those microscopic segments of the silicon oxide and its underlying silicon plane upon which desired doping elements are to be deposited using a vacuum gas diffusion process invented at Bell Laboratories.[11] Further coating, light exposure, development, and diffusion iterations follow until the desired electronic functions are implanted. Conducting metals are then diffused onto the surface to connect up the electronic functions. On more complex chips, insulating material is then added and the process is repeated to form a new circuit layer—with as many as four layers on Pentium-class microprocessor chips. All the intricate work except attaching lead wires is done automatically,[12] without the intervention of human hands. In addition, as many as 200 complete integrated circuits can be laid down on a single 8 inch-diameter silicon wafer, to be diced into individual "chips" when processing is completed.

Although most of the military organizations backing alternative miniaturization concepts were at first skeptical, an air force laboratory quickly reacted by negotiating research and then production contracts with Texas Instruments. By 1961, work under those contracts demonstrated that the future belonged to integrated circuits.[13] Because their inventions were complementary, Texas Instruments and Fairchild became enmeshed in competing patent claims. But in 1966 they settled their dispute through a cross-licensing agreement that allowed either firm to license third parties to use the relevant technologies. This arrangement permitted many other companies to begin developing and producing their own integrated circuits.

---

[10]For a more detailed chronology of other early inventions, see Tilton, *International Diffusion of Technology*, pp. 16–17.

[11]The photolithographic approach had antecedents in earlier capacitor and resistor work done for the U.S. Army Signal Corps—an effort in which TI's Jack Kilby had participated. See Kenneth Flamm, *Mismanaged Trade? Strategic Policy and the Semiconductor Industry* (manuscript, Brookings Institution, 1993), chap. 1, note 33.

[12]Semifinished chips are often shipped to nations with low labor costs for lead attachment, testing, and final packaging.

[13]Levin, "The Semiconductor Industry," pp. 72–73.

Once the technology of integrated semiconductor circuits was firmly established, the trajectory along which further progress would occur became sufficiently clear that additional inventions, though requiring in some cases considerable ingenuity, were virtually inevitable.[14]

One obvious step was to substitute integrated circuits for the large numbers of discrete transistors wired to circuit boards to provide rapid-access memory for computers. The result was the dynamic random-access memory (DRAM) circuit. In 1967 Fairchild introduced a 256-bit memory device—that is, a single thumbnail-size chip with 256 on-off transistorized switches plus the circuitry to make them function. A new company, Intel, founded by refugees from Fairchild, is credited with introducing the first 1-kilobit (actually, $2^{10} = 1024$ bits) DRAM in 1970. From then on, DRAM chip capacities increased every three to four years by multiples of four—for example, to 4 kilobits (4K) in 1974, 16K in 1977, 64K in 1981, 256K in 1984, 1 million bits (1M) in 1986, 4M in 1990, 16M in 1993, and so forth.

During the late 1960s, numerous companies perceived the desirability of bringing together many or even all the functions of the computer's central processing unit on an integrated (microprocessor) circuit.[15] The first applications were for handheld calculators. Hewlett-Packard introduced a four-chip calculator in 1968. A horse race then ensued, with Texas Instruments, Bowmar of the United States, Busicom of Japan, and Casio of Japan all claiming laurels for the first single-chip calculators in 1971.[16] The microprocessors they used came from several semiconductor makers who also launched single-chip designs nearly simultaneously: Texas Instruments, National Semiconductor, Mostek, North American Rockwell, Intel, and (less certainly) Japanese sources. Led by Intel in 1971, several semiconductor firms brought out computer-oriented microprocessors, setting the stage for an escalation of capacity and speed analogous to the DRAM history, and making possible the development of personal computers.[17]

---

[14]See A. P. Usher, *A History of Mechanical Inventions*, revised ed. (Cambridge: Harvard University Press, 1954), chap. IV; Jacob Schmookler, *Invention and Economic Growth* (Cambridge: Harvard University Press, 1966), especially chaps. X and XI; and Richard R. Nelson and Sidney G. Winter, *An Evolutionary Theory of Economic Change* (Cambridge: Harvard University Press, 1982), pp. 255–262.

[15]See Lee Boysel, "Memory on a Chip: A Step Toward Large-Scale Integration," *Electronics*, February 6, 1967, pp. 93–97; and "LSI Poses Dilemma," *Electronic Design*, February 1, 1970, pp. 44–52.

[16]See "Single-Chip Calculator Hits Finish Line," *Electronics*, February 1, 1971, pp. 19–20; and "Calculator Roadsigns Difficult To Read," *Electronic News*, November 15, 1971, pp. 16 and 36.

[17]Ted Hoff of Intel, credited with inventing the microprocessor, is quoted as saying that if he had not made the invention, somebody else soon would have. "Modern Wonders: The Age of the Thing," *The Economist*, December 25, 1993, p. 47.

TABLE 6.1

U.S. Semiconductor Plant Sales by Device Type, 1987 and 1991

	Sales ($ millions)	
Device Type	1987	1991
Integrated microprocessors and microcontrollers	$6,646	$11,212
Integrated memory circuits	3,797	4,319
Other integrated circuits	1,864	3,611
Signal and power transistors	753	686
Diodes and rectifiers	734	623
Light-emitting diodes and related chips	221	360
Solar cells	48	37
Other semiconductor devices	109	809
Total	$14,172	$21,657

Source: U.S. Bureau of the Census, *1987 Census of Manufactures*, Industry Series 36E; and *Current Industrial Reports*, "Semiconductors, Printed Circuit Boards, and Other Electronic Components," MA36Q(91)–1 (October 1992).

As the technology advanced, the output of integrated circuits has grown to surpass by a wide margin the volume of semiconductors adhering to the single-function design concepts with which the industry began. Table 6.1 reports U.S. semiconductor plants' 1987 and 1991 sales classified by broad product class. Microprocessors and analogous microcontrollers led the list, with sales more than four times those of single-function power transistors and diodes.

CHANGING MARKET LEADERSHIP

Rapid technological change was accompanied by considerable turnover in the identity of industry-leading companies. Table 6.2 lists the five U.S. industry leaders, in descending market share order, at five milestone years between 1955 and 1978.[18] It includes only the companies classified as "mer-

---

[18] The source for 1955, 1960, and 1965 is Levin, "The Semiconductor Industry," p. 30. The rankings for 1974 and 1978 are drawn from U.S. Office of Technology Assessment, *International Competitiveness in Electronics* (Washington, DC: USGPO, 1983), pp. 131–143; Franco Malerba, *The Semiconductor Business* (Madison: University of Wisconsin Press: 1985), p. 159; and Michael G. Borrus, *Competing for Control: America's Stake in Microelectronics* (Cambridge: Ballinger, 1988), p. 16. There are minor differences in company rankings among the various sources.

TABLE 6.2

Ranking of the Five Leading Merchant Semiconductor Producers for Five Benchmark Years

1955	1960	1965	1974	1978
Hughes	Texas Instruments	Texas Instruments	Texas Instruments	Texas Instruments
Transitron	Transitron	Motorola	Motorola	Motorola
Philco	Philco	Fairchild	National	Nippon Electric[a]
Sylvania	General Electric	General Instrument	Semiconductor	Philips[a]
Texas	RCA	General Electric	Fairchild	National
Instruments			Toshiba[a]	Semiconductor
			Intel	Fairchild
				Intel

[a]Home base outside the United States.

chant" semiconductor producers—that is, those who sold most of their output on the open market. Western Electric, the manufacturing branch of industry pioneer AT&T, produced a substantial volume of semiconducting devices for internal telephone system use, but until restructured under an antitrust decree in 1982, it sold none of its output at arm's length. Even more important in this respect was IBM, whose internally consumed output in 1978 was sufficient to earn second rank among U.S. producers, had nonmerchant producers been included in the tabulation. Because non–U.S. companies became increasingly important actors on the world stage during the 1970s (and even more during the 1980s), the Table 6.2 rankings for 1974 and 1978 are by estimated world sales volume. Companies with a home base outside the United States are included (with a distinguishing superscript) along with the domestic top five.

Prominent among the industry leaders during the first decade were well-established electrical equipment companies such as Philco, Sylvania, General Electric, and RCA, which saw semiconductors as a natural extension of their electron tube product lines. At first they coexisted successfully with newcomers to the field: Texas Instruments, which added transistor work to its geophysical instrumentation business and moved to industry leadership through its silicon and, later, integrated circuit inventions; Hughes, which moved aggressively into semiconductors from a strong position in military electronic apparatus; and Transitron, an early start-up company established to implement the new technology. By the 1960s, however, the traditional electrical equipment makers receded when they failed to advance successfully into newer integrated circuit designs. So also did Transitron, which fell behind technologically, suffered severe losses during the late 1960s, and was gradually liquidated. Their places were taken by Motorola, an old-line radio manufacturer that diversified vigorously into semiconductors; Fairchild and General Instrument, which grew out of instrumentation companies by hiring top talent from other semiconductor producers; and start-up semiconductor specialists National Semiconductor and Intel. Quite generally, the firms that hired top talent and innovated aggressively thrived; those that did not dropped to lower ranks or exited altogether. Joining the list of world leaders during the 1970s were two broad-line Japanese companies, Toshiba and Nippon Electric, and the Dutch electrical equipment giant, Philips.

Accompanying the turbulence of company leadership positions was extraordinary mobility of highly talented semiconductor scientists and engineers. When their employers failed to back new technological concepts they considered promising, U.S. semiconductor designers evolved a tradition of packing their bags and seeking greener pastures, often in start-up companies.[19] Texas Instruments got off to a flying start by hiring Gordon Teal from Bell Laboratories. Teal extended the germanium crystal–growing techniques he had perfected at Bell to silicon crystals at TI. Fairchild moved to a leadership position by hiring away eight key persons in 1957 from Shockley Laboratories, founded by William Shockley, who had shared the Nobel Prize for his work at Bell Laboratories. After making crucial contributions, including the planar production process, Fairchild suffered massive defections, spawning the formation of such future industry leaders as Intel, National Semiconductor, and Advanced Micro Devices along with many other middling successes and also-rans.[20] By 1988 Fairchild, following an unsuccessful merger with Schlumberger of France, was sold to its own offspring, National Semiconductor.

ECONOMIES OF SCALE, STATIC AND DYNAMIC

Paralleling advances in semiconductor technology has been a dramatic change in the character of scale economies. In the industry's early days, a firm such as Transitron could rent an abandoned textile factory, install fairly rudimentary equipment, and begin producing transistors on a labor-intensive assembly line. Transitron's initial investment is reported to have been $1 million.[21] But as the density of functions packed onto a single chip increased, the costs of a

---

[19]See "Jobs: Scene in Silicon Valley Changes Fast," *Los Angeles Times*, September 11, 1990, p. D16, which observes that in Silicon Valley, "Leaving one firm to work for a competitor—considered disloyal or worse in most industries—became the thing most techies did."

[20]See Tilton, *International Diffusion of Technology*, pp. 51 and 77–81; Borrus, *Competing for Control*, pp. 80–81; "New Leaders in Semiconductors," *Business Week*, March 1, 1976, pp. 40–46; and "Fathers of Silicon Valley Reunited," *New York Times*, April 16, 1988, p. 41.

[21]Tilton, *International Diffusion of Technology*, pp. 87–88.

semiconductor fabricating plant—called a "fab" in the trade—rose apace. Because specks of dust, bacteria, or other unwanted contaminants can ruin the product, one must begin with a clean room, whose air purity and vibration avoidance standards have become increasingly stringent over time as circuit densities have risen.[22] The equipment needed to project ever-finer circuit details on photoresists—by the late 1980s, to less than 1 micron (one-thousandth of a millimeter, or one-hundredth the thickness of a human hair)—also became increasingly expensive, as did vacuum diffusion chambers and other apparatus. In 1972, a fully equipped high-volume integrated circuit production line required an investment of roughly $10 million. By 1980, the needed investment had risen to $100 million.[23] Constructing and outfitting plants for 4-megabit DRAM chips, produced experimentally in 1988, cost approximately $350 million.[24] A new plant producing Intel's 80486 microprocessor family, introduced commercially in 1989, is said to have cost $400 million.[25] Each 80486 chip contained the equivalent of 1.2 million transistors. Billion-dollar investments were made for "fabs" that processed 1990s–generation integrated circuits. Unless a high volume of output is achieved in these expensive plants, capital costs per unit of product will be prohibitively high.

Front-end investments in the research and development underlying the introduction of new semiconductor devices have risen commensurately. Complex circuit plans must be laid out—in the early days of integrated circuits, on room-size sheets of paper, but more recently, with computer programs that also check for erroneous interconnections. The circuit details must be reduced to a set of extremely precise photoresist masks, which for a single chip configuration in the 1990s cost approximately $100,000. New production methods must be worked out, and when the first experimental chips have been fabricated, extensive testing and (frequently) reworking of masks follow. Intel is said to have spent $10 million to develop its first 4-bit microprocessor during the early 1970s; $20 million on its 16-bit 8086 microprocessor (introduced in 1978), $100 million to develop its 32-bit 80386 microprocessor family (launched in 1985), and $250 million on the 80486 family.[26] The cost (ignoring interest charges) of amortizing the 80486 R&D investment across its life cycle would be $250 per chip if only a million chips could be sold, $25 per

---

[22]"Superchip Plants: Where 'Clean' Has a Whole New Meaning," *Business Week,* September 26, 1988, p. 77.

[23]U.S. Office of Technology Assessment, *International Competitiveness in Electronics,* p. 271.

[24]"The Costly Race Chipmakers Can't Afford To Lose," *Business Week,* December 10, 1990, p. 185.

[25]"Make It Fast—and Make It Right," *Business Week,* special Quality 1991 issue, p. 76.

[26]Richard N. Langlois et al., *Microelectronics: An Industry in Transition* (Boston: Unwin Hyman, 1988), p. 49; and "Make It Fast," *Business Week,* special Quality 1991 issue, p. 76.

chip with sales of 10 million, and $5 per chip if cumulative sales of 50 million could be achieved.[27]

To be sure, more flexible, lower-cost design methods have been embraced for special-purpose and other low-volume chips. But quite generally, the semiconductor industry has become one of the most R&D-intensive industries. In 1977, company-financed R&D expenditures averaged 6.1 percent of sales—the sixth-highest such ratio among 238 industry categories for which comparable data have been compiled.[28] Less comprehensive surveys for the late 1980s estimated the R&D/sales ratio in semiconductors to be between 11 and 13 percent.[29]

An equally important set of scale economies comes from the phenomenon known as "learning by doing." Solving the complex problems of producing a new semiconductor device entails much "art" accumulated by trial and error. When a new design embodying finer or more intricate circuit structures enters production, the manufacturing transition team is thankful if 2 percent of the chips pass quality control tests. Production must be halted to study why problems are emerging, and solutions must be tested and verified. Gradually, the team learns how to adjust the process parameters so that yields eventually rise as high as 90 percent. As the process comes under control, more chips can be squeezed onto a single wafer, and larger wafers—requiring no additional fabricating steps at the lithographing and deposition stages—can be used. Unit batch costs fall concurrently along what is called a *learning curve*. There is considerable evidence that until the production process matures, the decline of unit costs is well characterized by a learning curve that is linear in the logarithms of unit cost (on the vertical axis) and the *cumulative* number of units produced (on the horizontal axis), as illustrated in Figure 6.1. The "slope" of the typical semiconductor fabrication learning curve (solid line) appears to be approximately 28 percent, which means that unit costs fall by 28 percent on average with each doubling and redoubling of cumulative output.[30] Thus, the tenth unit produced (10^1) has a unit fabrication cost of

---

[27]In 1987, according to the Census of Manufactures, U.S. semiconductor plants shipped 133 million microprocessors. Between 1988 and 1991, Intel sold approximately 25 million 80386 chips. See "Intel's Chip Monopoly Is Facing Challengers," *New York Times*, September 5, 1990, p. D9.

[28]U.S. Federal Trade Commission, *Statistical Report: Annual Line of Business Report: 1977* (Washington: April 1985), p. 21.

[29]Flamm, *Mismanaged Trade?*, chap. 1.

[30]See Flamm, *Mismanaged Trade?*, chap 6. Although learning curves are often written as $UC = aQ_{CUM}^{-\beta}$, the "slope" as used in normal learning curve parlance is not β. Rather, β is the exponent to which the value 2 (reflecting a doubling of output) is raised to yield (1 minus the fraction by which unit cost is reduced).

Less steep learning curves prevail in the final "assembly" operations—as the wafers are diced into chips, lead wires are attached, and the chips are encapsulated in plastic or ceramic.

FIGURE 6.1
Semiconductor Learning Curve with 28 Percent Slope

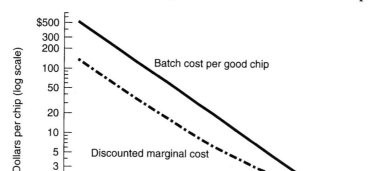

roughly $536; the hundredth unit, $180; the thousandth unit, $60.15; the ten-thousandth unit (10⁴), $20.15; the 500 thousandth unit, $3.14;[31] the millionth chip $2.26, and so forth. Only at some quite high cumulative output scale does the cost curve bottom out, with no further savings from learning. Until that scale is reached, chip production is, at least as a first approximation, a natural monopoly. Unit costs fall more or less continuously as output is increased to levels that may well exhaust the market's absorptive capacity.

When learning by doing occurs, the marginal cost of a batch is not simply the out-of-pocket cost incurred for producing that batch. Rather, the experience gained in producing the batch will help reduce costs on additional batches to be produced in the future. Thus, marginal cost is below, and possibly well below, current out-of-pocket cost (which in turn is below conventionally calculated average total cost because of the substantial investments sunk in research, development, and production facilities). Under certain limiting conditions, marginal cost in a learning curve environment can be viewed as the out-of-pocket cost incurred for the *last* unit to be produced—i.e., the unit at the foot of the learning curve.[32] But since the savings from learning accrue

---

[31]Technological progress in dynamic random access memory chips is sometimes characterized by what is called the "Pi rule." That is, no matter how high chip function density is, unit costs fall to approximately π = $3.14 when a substantial production volume has been achieved. See Flamm, *Mismanaged Trade?*, chap. 1.

[32]See A. Michael Spence, "The Learning Curve and Competition," *Bell Journal of Economics*, vol. 12 (Spring 1981), p. 51.

only in the future, their discounted present value at the moment when learning occurs is less, and hence the marginal cost at that moment is higher than at the learning curve's foot but converges eventually upon the terminal value. Also, the cumulative quantity that will eventually be produced is uncertain, and so also must be the terminal cost value. The undiscounted marginal cost curve (dashes) in Figure 6.1 assumes that production can end with equal probability at any output between the cumulative volume most recently attained and 5 million units. A zero time discount rate is assumed. The discounted marginal cost curve (dash-dot line) is a numerical approximation assuming DRAM output timing patterns estimated by Flaherty[33] and a 12 percent discount rate.

LEARNING CURVE PRICING

The existence of learning-by-doing scale economies may lead companies to engage in a dynamic form of limit pricing with crucial implications for the way market structures evolve. The first firm to race down the learning curve gains a cost advantage over its tardier rivals. The greater its lead, the larger is its cost advantage, all else equal. A cost advantage, we found in Chapter 5, is the sine qua non for limit pricing. If the advantage is sufficiently large, its possessor may choose to set prices so low as to deter the entry of other competitors. For example, in Figure 6.1, if one firm succeeds in reaching a cumulative volume of 1 million chips while its rivals are still at the 100,000 mark, the leader will enjoy batch costs of $2.30 per chip while rival costs are $6.52. By setting its price at, say, $3.00, the leader can realize an appreciable profit (ignoring fixed costs) while inflicting substantial losses upon its rivals, who may perceive their handicap to be insuperable and drop out of the race. This strategy choice can lead to an increasing asymmetry of positions and perhaps monopoly, at which point the remaining incumbent can sustain substantial profits without inducing new entry or reentry.[34]

There is more. Recognizing the advantage of being the first down the learning curve, firms have an incentive to lead the way in introducing the new product whose production entails learning by doing. And once they gain early production leadership positions, they may price their products aggressively to stimulate demand, thereby permitting more production and hence more

---

[33]Marie Therese Flaherty, "Manufacturing and Firm Performance in Technology-Intensive Industries: U.S. and Japanese DRAM Experience," *Review of Industrial Organization,* vol. 7 (1992), p. 283.

[34]See, for example, Kenneth Flamm, "Strategic Arguments for Semiconductor Trade Policy," *Review of Industrial Organization,* vol. 7 (1992), pp. 295–326; and David R. Ross, "Learning To Dominate," *Journal of Industrial Economics,* vol. 34 (June 1986), pp. 337–354.

learning, and also to win the lion's share of orders away from rivals, which again leads to more production and hence an enhanced cost advantage. Indeed, pricing can be so aggressive in the early learning stages that out-of-pocket losses are incurred. But if a monopoly position is the prize once a high cumulative production volume is attained, the early losses are a worth-while strategic investment in securing future monopoly profits.

These possibilities are interesting not only because learning by doing is so important in semiconductor device production, but also because Texas Instruments, the U.S. industry leader during the 1960s and 1970s, openly avowed its commitment to aggressive learning curve pricing strategies. TI's philosophy was described by its president in 1973 as follows:[35]

> Follow an aggressive pricing policy, focus on continuing cost reduction and productivity improvement, build on shared experience (gained in making related products), and keep capacity growing ahead of demand.

The ultimate goal was to be "No. 1 in each product field it enters."[36] It was advised in this strategy choice by the Boston Consulting Group, which preached passionately that seizing the low-cost position on what it called "experience curves" was the key to superior profitability.[37]

Carried to their logical conclusion, these policies could end with the first or most aggressive firm securing a monopoly position in the specific products it chooses to emphasize. However, three considerations may prevent such extreme outcomes.

First and perhaps most important, as products mature, learning curves sooner or later flatten out after most of the opportunities for further process improvement have been exploited. The best publicly available data on this point exist for aircraft production.[38] Semiconductor learning curve data are highly confidential, but there is reason to believe that the curves become less steep at cumulative volumes between 1 and 5 million good chips. The slopes probably continue to be negative—that is, some learning by doing continues—out to cumulative volumes as large as 50 million.

Second, the companies designing their electronic products around some key chip often insist upon a "second source" to ensure that supplies will not be interrupted by strikes, fires, or other plant-level catastrophes, and also to keep competitive pressure on the first source's pricing. Even when learning continues out to the last batch produced and second sourcing forces chip makers to forgo one last cumulative doubling of their output, costs may not

---

[35]"Selling Business a Theory of Economics," *Business Week,* September 8, 1973, p. 87.

[36]"Texas Instruments: Pushing Hard into the Consumer Markets," *Business Week,* August 24, 1974, p. 40.

[37]See Bruce D. Henderson, *The Logic of Business Strategy* (Cambridge: Ballinger, 1984), chaps. 2 and 3.

[38]See Harold Asher, *Cost-Quantity Relationships in the Airframe Industry,* RAND Corporation Study R–291 (Santa Monica: RAND Corp., July 1956), chaps. 4 and 7.

rise by the amount implied by the learning curve slope. There is evidence from the U.S. aircraft production experience during World War II that competition induces rivals to intensify their cost reduction efforts, and hence to steepen the learning curve slope.[39]

Finally, the learning achieved by the first producer may "spill over" to laggard rival firms—for example, as production engineers change jobs and bring with them the know-how they have acquired in the leader's plant, or as the engineers assigned by equipment suppliers to work within fabricating facilities, helping the chip makers iron out process difficulties, pass their insights on to other customers. How important such spillovers are in semiconductors is unknown. Although the turnover of Silicon Valley employees is extraordinarily rapid, a move by some key engineer to work on a directly competing product would probably provoke a lawsuit seeking to bar the job changer from assuming a position that jeopardizes trade secrets. And the insights gained by specialized equipment suppliers' on-site troubleshooters may be limited to only one fabrication process stage among the dozens used in producing a complex chip.

In addition to horizontal spillovers between companies producing similar semiconductor devices, there can also be intergenerational spillovers—that is, from one generation of semiconductor devices within a company to the next generation. Having patiently worked out the problems of producing one chip design probably reduces the initial unit cost of more advanced chips (after which a flatter learning curve slope follows), or it may accelerate progress down learning curves for the new generation. To the extent that this is true, the strategic advantage of being first down the learning curve on a new kind of semiconductor is amplified by its persistence into later generations.

Despite the attractions of aggressive learning curve pricing, its use may be constrained by capacity limitations. It takes time to "ramp up" the output of an integrated circuit production line to its full capacity. Until substantial learning occurs, yields are low, and equipment rigidities may permit output to increase only as rapidly as yields improve. If only a limited number of workable chips can be produced, cutting prices to stimulate the demand for additional chips will not increase sales, and hence will yield no incremental learning benefit. Thus, prices will be set at the market-clearing level.

Kenneth Flamm argues that pricing was in fact constrained mainly by supply-side rigidities in the early stages of DRAM production during the 1980s.[40] His analysis assumes, however, that the demand curve for new chips is smoothly convex downward, so that some demand would be forthcoming even at very high prices. The assumption is questionable. New chips must be priced low enough to induce substitution away from older-generation chips that have already progressed far down their learning curves. The aggressive strategies Texas Instruments and others adopted may have been motivated by

---

[39]F. M. Scherer, *The Weapons Acquisition Process: Economic Incentives* (Boston: Harvard Business School Division of Research, 1964), pp. 119–126.

[40]*Mismanaged Trade?*, chaps. 6 and 7.

the need to get the substitution process going as well as by the desire to achieve competitive advantage by moving more rapidly down learning curves. That producers consciously set early prices below market-clearing levels is shown by frequent "shortages" of new integrated circuits, which are rationed out to computer assemblers on nonprice bases during the first half year or so of their production. Also, there is evidence that "ramp-up" rates are not governed solely by rigid technological constraints. Some firms appear able to increase their output more rapidly than others. Japanese producers experienced particularly rapid ramp-up rates on the 64K DRAM generation.[41] Far too little is known, at least by economists, about the factors influencing ramp-up rates and in particular, about the role that "aggressiveness" (in either pricing or investment) plays.

Aggressive learning curve pricing also engenders a quite different set of problems. If one producer races down the learning curve ahead of its rivals, it (although perhaps not its consumers) will live happily ever after—or at least until the next technological generation takes over. But if several firms price aggressively in an effort to be the leader, a bloodbath may ensue. Contrary to their initial expectations in adopting the strategy, the rivals may end up sharing the market at costs too high, and prices too low, to repay their original investments in research, development, equipment, and learning.

Figure 6.2 arrays the principal alternative price histories that can unfold during an integrated circuit's life cycle, depending upon the strategies pursued by industry members. If one producer enjoys sufficiently powerful

FIGURE 6.2
Learning Curve Pricing Under Diverse Strategic Assumptions

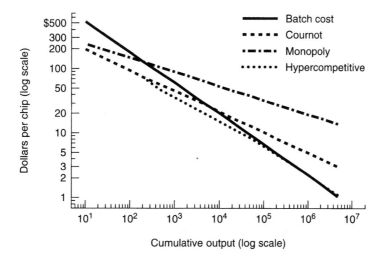

advantages that it remains a monopolist, prices will decline with learning, but only at a gradual rate, as shown by the dash-dot trajectory in Figure 6.2. If a few firms engage in oligopolistic price-setting, assuming others' prices to be parametric—that is, the so-called Cournot assumption—the steeper dashed line price trajectory ensues. After roughly 10,000 chips have been produced, prices move above the typical firm's current batch costs (solid line). The rivals begin recovering, and eventually more than recovering, their initial losses and sunk costs. If, however, several rivals each price aggressively in an effort to gain market leadership, the dotted "hypercompetitive" price trajectory materializes. Then prices may never ascend above current batch costs, and each rival ends the life cycle with substantial cumulative losses.

The hypercompetitive scenario best characterizes what happened in the early days of single-chip calculators. Texas Instruments sought to dominate the new, rapidly growing market.[42] At first its aggressive policies curbed the market shares of Japanese firms, which were having problems producing the needed microprocessors at home, but were not allowed by Japan's Ministry of Trade and Industry (MITI) to import enough U.S. chips to sustain their desired production rates.[43] In 1973 and 1974, however, the situation changed. Japanese companies improved their microprocessor yields and quality, and MITI's restraints on the importation of chips from the United States were relaxed. Equally important, the Japanese firms emulated the Texas Instruments strategy of pricing aggressively to sell their calculators in the U.S. market. As a result, their exports soared, prices plunged, and Texas Instruments found it necessary to close its Fort Walton, Florida, calculator plant, reporting calculator line write-offs of $16 million in early 1975. Both TI and Hewlett-Packard, another leading U.S. calculator supplier, exited from the low-price calculator business and retreated to a higher-price programmable calculator market niche.

Similar experiences followed in semiconductor lines and in TI's first venture into personal computers. In 1983, a leading business journal reported that "TI left its rivals with no option but to fight back with their own lower prices"—a practice that was said by an executive of a rival chip maker to have "wrecked the industry."[44] However, there is reason to believe that TI recognized the dangers of multifirm learning curve pricing and changed its strategy during the early 1980s, trying hard to avoid overly aggressive behavior.[45] The president of rival Intel stated in 1983 that "I don't think it's being applied as

---

[42]See F. M. Scherer, *International High-Technology Competition* (Cambridge: Harvard University Press: 1992), pp. 64–67.

[43]See Flamm, *Mismanaged Trade?*, chap. 2.

[44]"Chip Wars: The Japanese Threat, *Business Week,* May 23, 1983, p. 83.

[45]This inference was verified in a private conversation between the author and a TI executive.

broadly and with the same fervor as in the early 1970s. . . . We are all applying more business judgment now."[46]

However, Japanese semiconductor makers apparently persisted in the pursuit of learning curve pricing strategies. As the president of Nippon Electric Corporation's U.S. electronics subsidiary stated, "The Japanese perspective is that when you are still making inroads into a market, you can't afford the luxury of making money."[47] Japanese firms gained a 40 percent share of the 16K U.S. merchant DRAM market during the late 1970s and increased their share of 64K merchant DRAMS during the early 1980s to 70 percent.[48] In 1982 some U.S. companies complained of dumping to U.S. government trade authorities, but did not follow through when MITI intervened and apparently persuaded its wards to raise their export prices. But the Japanese advance continued. By 1985, Nippon Electric had displaced Texas Instruments as the world merchant sales leader. TI fell to third rank, behind Motorola but still ahead of Hitachi and Toshiba. By 1986, NEC, Hitachi, and Toshiba held first, second, and third ranks worldwide, and Japanese producers collectively surpassed U.S. companies for the first time ever in world merchant semiconductor sales volume, capturing 46 percent of the estimated world total.[49] Profits turned negative for many U.S. manufacturers,[50] and the crisis-ridden industry again asked Washington for protection.

JAPANESE INDUSTRIAL POLICY

We return in due course to the events of 1986. Now, however, we pause to ask how Japanese semiconductor makers came from behind to a position of world leadership during the mid 1980s. And in particular, we must explore the role played by the government of Japan. Did an enlightened industrial policy make the difference, as some have suggested?

The industrial policies of Japan toward industries such as semiconductors have been multifaceted. They have also changed significantly over time.

One much-acclaimed facet is "targeting," that is, seeking to identify high-growth industries and actively encouraging their development. Semiconductors and the electronics industry more generally were not among the industries—notably, coal, steel, shipbuilding, and electric power—designated by

[46]"Chip Wars," p. 83.

[47]*Ibid.*

[48]"The Selling of the 256K RAM," *New York Times*, June 3, 1983, p. D1.

[49]Flamm, *Mismanaged Trade?*, Figure 1–5; and David B. Yoffie, "The Global Semiconductor Industry, 1987," Harvard Business School case 9–388–052 (1987), pp. 18–21.

[50]See "The Bloodbath in Chips," *Business Week*, May 20, 1985, p. 63; and "2 Chip Makers' Losses Widen," *New York Times*, October 11, 1986, p. 39.

MITI during the early 1950s as "strategic." The success of companies such as Sony in radios and later television apparently came as somewhat of a surprise to MITI officials. However, that success was soon recognized as fitting well with the broad economic development strategy chosen by Japan—to disregard the prescriptions of neoclassical trade theory, which would emphasize low-wage industries in which Japan had immediate comparative advantage, and instead to move toward the technological frontier in modern high-technology fields.[51] As Japanese electronics manufacturers experienced early successes, their efforts were accorded increasing governmental priority. When energy prices rose briskly during the early 1970s, jeopardizing the competitiveness of energy-intensive industries such as steel, the "information industries" were given top priority.

A second industrial strategy component was to protect newly emerging domestic industries against foreign competitors who commanded the most advanced technology and who had already plumbed the lower segments of production learning curves. In this Japan explicitly embraced the "infant industry" philosophy of Germany's Friedrich List and his mentor, the first U.S. treasury secretary, Alexander Hamilton.[52] The basic idea was to give domestic producers a protected home market until they could gain sufficient experience to let them compete with foreign rivals on relatively equal terms. This was done in at least three ways. First, when Japan agreed to reduce many of its tariffs in GATT negotiations during 1961, it *raised* tariffs on electronic computers and components deemed "to have a good prospect of development in the future."[53] Tariffs on discrete transistors, in whose production Japanese manufacturers were already well established, were 6 percent during the 1970s, whereas integrated circuit tariffs were held at 12 percent until liberalization occurred in 1982. Second, MITI used its control over scarce foreign exchange (until the early 1970s) and moral suasion thereafter to limit the kinds of goods that could be imported. There were fierce internal battles over import limitations on integrated circuits, with calculator and computer makers arguing for liberal importation and semiconductor specialists for strict limits.[54] Those favoring protection of the semiconductor makers carried the day until 1973, when more open policies were adopted in response to U.S.

[51]See Martin Fransman, *The Market and Beyond: Cooperation and Competition in Information Technology Development in the Japanese System* (Cambridge University Press: 1990), pp. 24–25; and Christopher Freeman, *Technology Policy and Economic Performance: Lessons from Japan* (London: Pinter, 1987), pp. 34–35.

[52]Alexander Hamilton, *Report on the Subject of Manufactures* (Washington: 1791); and Friedrich List, *The National System of Political Economy* (1841), English translation by Sampson S. Lloyd (London: Longmans, Green, 1916).

[53]Fransman, *The Market and Beyond*, p. 25.

[54]Flamm, *Mismanaged Trade?*, chap. 2.

pressures. Third, Japanese chip users, and especially the powerful state-owned Nippon Telegraph and Telephone Company (NTT), accorded explicit or implicit preference to domestic sources in their procurement decisions.

To preserve the home market as an environment within which domestic semiconductor makers could learn by doing, direct investment in Japan by foreign semiconductor manufacturers was stringently restricted until 1974. Texas Instruments was the only U.S. corporation that successfully hurdled barriers against majority-owned foreign investments during the 1960s. It succeeded where others had failed by threatening not to license its extensive patent portfolio to Japanese electronics firms unless it was permitted to produce in Japan.[55]

Such market-closing policies carry a grave danger: that domestic producers will remain fat and lethargic, secure behind their wall of protection. In this realm the Japanese government pursued vacillating and sometimes contradictory policies that in the end, perhaps inadvertently, achieved an effective compromise between protection and competition. On one hand, it provided financial support (on which more later) to numerous companies and insisted that foreign technology licenses be widely shared among domestic enterprises so that no single producer obtained a decisive advantage. On the other hand, MITI proposals were floated during the early 1970s to merge the three largest computer makers into a single national champion and to form a cartel among integrated circuit makers, letting each firm specialize in specific types and hence take maximum advantage of learning curve economies.[56] These proposals were strenuously resisted by the Japanese electronics manufacturers, and so more than a dozen semiconductor makers continued to vie for mastery of the rapidly changing technology. A constant during the debate over structural policy was the government's insistence that the electronics firms move as quickly as possible to a level of technical competence and efficiency at which they could successfully export.

Because they began with a substantial technical handicap, it was essential that the Japanese electronics manufacturers obtain licenses to foreign (notably U.S.) technology. Foreign enterprises were allowed to invest in Japanese ventures (usually with no more than a minority equity position) only when they agreed to license their patents and know-how. MITI used its control over foreign exchange to constrain license payments. When a domestic company petitioned for the funds to pay license fees, MITI would often insist that the amount was excessive, sending the petitioner back for further negotiations with an additional argument favoring moderation. Nevertheless, the

---

[55]See Flamm, *Mismanaged Trade?*, chap. 2; and Tilton, *International Diffusion of Technology*, pp. 146–147.

[56]Flamm, *Mismanaged Trade?*, chap. 2. A similar cartel was operated during the 1970s in the ball bearing industry.

royalties paid by Japanese integrated circuit makers to U.S. patent holders during the late 1960s amounted to 10 percent of total chip sales.[57]

Technological development was also encouraged through governmental and quasi-governmental research and development subsidies. There were two main sources of support. The state-owned telephone service monopoly, NTT, built into its procurement contracts with outside equipment suppliers appreciable sums to support the development of new components. It also maintained a sizeable internal research and development laboratory, which took pains to ensure that the new technologies on which its R&D staff worked were rapidly disseminated to its domestic suppliers. In the early years of the semiconductor industry, direct R&D subsidies from the government were modest. The U.S. experience differed in this respect because the Department of Defense had an intense interest in semiconductors, whereas Japanese production was mainly for civilian products. As the Japanese government began to see greater strategic significance in computers and related electronic technologies, R&D subsidies to semiconductor makers were gradually increased— for example, from less than $1 million per year in 1963 to $30 million in the early 1970s.[58]

A much more important government intervention, the VLSI (very-large-scale integration) programs, began in the mid–1970s. There were two precipitating factors: the government's belief that information technologies were crucial to Japan's industrial future, but that Japan had not yet reached the rapidly shifting frontiers; and the relaxation of barriers to integrated circuit imports, for which semiconductor makers were to receive as a quid pro quo increased R&D subsidies. NTT led off in 1975 with a three-year, $65-million R&D project to develop computer chips jointly with Fujitsu, Hitachi, and Nippon Electric, with 64K DRAMs as the principal focus. In that same year MITI announced its own VLSI project and committed approximately $300 million, to be spent over the years 1976–1979 by a consortium of five companies—Fujitsu, Hitachi, Toshiba, Mitsubishi, and NEC—working to develop the technology needed to produce 1-megabit DRAMs by 1985.

The MITI-sponsored VLSI project is without doubt the most widely acclaimed cooperative R&D venture in modern Japanese history. It was unusual not only for its magnitude, but also in several other respects.[59] For one, cooperation was to be achieved not by having participating companies' R&D staff visit each other to exchange findings, but by reassigning the core staff members to a single new laboratory facility opened by MITI. Second, the

---

[57] Tilton, *International Diffusion of Technology*, p. 148. See also Flamm, *Mismanaged Trade?*, chap. 2.

[58] Flamm, *Mismanaged Trade?*, Fig. 2–6.

[59] The account here draws upon Flamm, *Mismanaged Trade?*, chap. 2; Fransman, *The Market and Beyond*, chap. 3; and Donna L. Doane, *From Technological Catchup to Frontier Innovation: Interfirm Cooperation, Groups, and the Government-Industry Relationship in Japan* (book manuscript, forthcoming).

project directors were MITI staff, not representatives chosen through political give-and-take among the cooperating companies. Third, the MITI laboratory director drew upon his extensive personal acquaintances to ensure that the companies assigned top talent to the joint laboratory, not the less-talented personnel commonly assigned to cooperative projects. Fourth, much of the project's effort was directed toward developing infrastructure technology rather than specific chip designs. Thus, subcontracts were issued to Canon and Nikon for work on the "steppers" by which mask images are projected repeatedly (literally, step-by-step) onto the silicon wafer photoresist; to Kyocera and NGK Spark Plug for work on ceramic chip packages; and to five silicon wafer manufacturers to perfect their silicon-refining techniques. Fifth, even when they were assigned to work in a common building, technical staff from the participating companies tended to remain within the sublaboratories dominated by their home company, and, fearful of compromising their employer's competitive advantage, exchanged information only reluctantly with other companies' representatives. Recognizing this situation, the laboratory director had the doors removed from the sublaboratories and organized intercompany symposia, parties, and sports events to make it clear that full cooperation was expected.

It is impossible to know how history would have been rewritten had there been no VLSI projects. What is clear, however, is that Japanese semiconductor makers moved in a very short time to world leadership, at least in the memory circuit field. They achieved chip yields much higher than those of their U.S. counterparts through much of the 64K, 256K, and 1M DRAM generations. And in that sense, the government's interventions must be judged successful.

Japanese companies also benefited from an abundance of low-cost capital. In the semiconductor industry's early years, they obtained loans at subsidized interest rates from the Industrial Bank of Japan. But even loans from private-sector banks were made at interest rates lower on average than those paid by U.S. corporations, in part because of Japan's much higher macroeconomic saving rate—for example, for net household saving, 18 percent of disposable household income in Japan between 1960 and 1986, compared to 8.8 percent for the United States.[60]

Japanese companies' financing advantage was enhanced, at least up to the 1980s, by leveraging their capital structure.[61] That is, borrowing accounted

[60]Organization for Economic Cooperation and Development, *Historical Statistics: 1960–86* (Paris: OECD, 1988), p. 70.

[61]The financing cost advantage of Japanese companies eroded considerably during the late 1980s as capital outflow constraints were relaxed, causing home interest rates to converge toward world rates, and as firms chose to reinvest substantial profits and build their equity positions instead of borrowing. Compare George N. Hatsopoulos and Stephen H. Brooks, "The Gap in the Cost of Capital," in Ralph Landau and Dale Jorgenson, eds., *Technology and Economic Policy* (Cambridge: Ballinger, 1986), pp. 221–280; and W. Carl Kester and Timothy A. Luehrman, "The Myth of Japan's Low-Cost Capital," *Harvard Business Review*, May–June 1992, pp. 130–138.

for a much higher fraction of corporate capital in Japan than in the United States—for example, with 80 percent debt financing in Japan during the 1970s compared to 33 percent in the United States. High leverage is advantageous because in both Japan and America, corporate interest payments are tax deductible, whereas dividend payments are not, and so more before-tax cash flow must be raised to service a given amount of capital under equity financing than under debt financing. An example will help illustrate the advantage of debt leveraging. Suppose that servicing debt requires a 6 percent before-tax return on capital invested, whereas common stock equity, lacking tax preferences and with only residual claims to corporate assets, requires a 20 percent return. If the corporation's capital structure has 80 percent debt and 20 percent equity, the average cost of capital will be $0.2 \times 20 + 0.8 \times 6 = 8.8$ percent. If the mix is one-third debt and two-thirds equity, the average capital cost will be $0.67 \times 20 + 0.33 \times 6 = 15.3$ percent. To be sure, borrowing carries risks of financial embarrassment or even default if serious setbacks occur, and for this reason U.S. corporations tended to keep their debt obligations low (at least until the "junk bond" craze of the 1980s). But Japanese enterprises were able to have their cake and eat it. By leveraging heavily, they had low capital costs. However, if they experienced a crisis, Japan Inc. came to their rescue. Lenders (often affiliated with the borrower through cross-stockholdings) restructured loans, and the government could be counted upon to authorize recession cartels, erect import barriers, or intervene in other ways to prevent the crisis from escalating into financial collapse.

Low capital costs probably played an appreciable role in the rise of Japanese corporations to world semiconductor sales leadership. Consider, for example, a $100 million investment in research and development spread over three years, the payoffs for which will accrue in equal increments over a period of five years following completion of the R&D. If the firm's cost of capital, and hence discount rate, is 8.8 percent, annual net cash inflows exceeding $28.3 million will make the project worthwhile.[62] If the cost of capital is 15.3 percent, however, the annual net cash inflow must be $36.4 million, or 28 percent more, to make the investment worthwhile. Thus, projects will be undertaken by companies with low capital costs that would not be approved at higher capital costs. Also, as we saw in Chapter 5, one key variable in determining whether limit pricing is profitable is the firm's discount rate, which is based upon its cost of capital. Aggressive learning curve pricing is more likely to be attractive to a semiconductor maker if its cost of capital is low. Among other things, as Figure 6.1 suggests, marginal costs in a learning curve environment are higher, the higher the firm's discount rate is.

Whether these objective economic and government policy variables suffice to explain the aggressive investment and pricing behavior of Japanese

---

[62]Continuous compounding is assumed. The R&D outlays accumulate to a value of $114.4 million at the time of their completion. To have a discounted present value of $114.4 million, inflows must be $28.3 million per year for five years.

semiconductor manufacturers during the 1970s and 1980s is uncertain. A quite different hypothesis holds that the "corporate culture" of Japanese firms has been different from that of their U.S. counterparts. Matched surveys administered during the early 1980s to 1031 top managers in Japan and 1000 in the United States revealed that the U.S. managers ranked return on investment first, higher stock prices second, market share third, and improving products and introducing new products fourth among eight listed goals. The Japanese managers' rankings on the same goals were third, eighth, second, and first respectively.[63] Thus, Japanese managers apparently placed much more emphasis on technological innovation and high market shares for their own sake, and much less on short-run profitability.

There may also be international differences in the focus of R&D efforts, which can emphasize either product innovation and improvement or the perfection of production processes. Surveying 100 matched Japanese and U.S. corporations, Edwin Mansfield found that the average Japanese company devoted 64 percent of its R&D budget to process development and improvement, while the average U.S. company allocated only 32 percent to process activity and the remainder to product-oriented work.[64] One reason for the Japanese bias may be the longer job tenure of Japanese scientists and engineers and hence more willingness patiently to perfect production methods. Observing that progress in memory chips was measured not in huge intellectual breakthroughs but in shaving off tenths of microns, the head of a Japanese 64-megabit DRAM development project mused:[65]

> I have many friends in the U.S. . . . but every time I meet them their job is changed. My job has not changed for 18 years. My staff stays with me; they do not jump to other jobs or companies. I think that lifetime employment in Japan is very suitable for memory-chip making.

By extension, comparative advantage in the United States may lie in carrying out the rapid design changes associated with application-specific chips and (less clearly after early generations) the software concept advances embodied in microprocessors.

We must not conclude that favorable business value systems and industrial policies were solely responsible for the great leap forward achieved by Japanese semiconductor makers during the late 1970s and early 1980s. There were also complementary U.S. failures. Most important, while Japanese firms

---

[63]Tadao Kagawa et al., "Strategy and Organization of Japanese and American Corporations," summarized in M. J. Peck, "The Large Japanese Corporation," in John R. Meyer and James M. Gustafson, *The U.S. Business Corporation* (Cambridge: Ballinger, 1988), pp. 35–36.

[64]Edwin Mansfield, "Industrial R&D in Japan and the United States: A Comparative Study," *American Economic Review*, vol. 78 (May 1988), pp. 223–228. A 1994 survey that corrected for semantic problems revealed that the product vs. process ratio difference between nations may be much smaller.

[65]"Hitachi's Quest for Super Chips," *New York Times*, September 10, 1990, p. D1.

invested aggressively in integrated circuit research and production facilities during the 1970s, U.S. merchant firms held back. In addition to relatively high capital costs, there was a further reason. The combination of still-aggressive learning curve pricing and sharp recession in 1974–1975 significantly crimped U.S. semiconductor manufacturers' profits and cash flows, as the following Federal Trade Commission Line of Business survey data show:[66]

Year	Operating Income as Percent of Assets	Rank Among 234 Industries	R&D as Percent of Sales
1974	4.5	197	6.0
1975	−3.7	233	7.1
1976	4.2	214	6.1
1977	4.3	221	6.1

For four years running, the semiconductor industry was one of the least profitable among the 234 manufacturing industries surveyed by the Federal Trade Commission. Its return on assets was consistently below the return one could obtain investing in risk-free government securities. As a result, investment in capacity lagged. Company-financed R&D spending was kept roughly constant in relation to sales while foreign competition intensified. When the demand for 16K DRAMs soared during the late 1970s, U.S. companies were ill prepared to satisfy it, and so chip users turned to Japanese suppliers to fill their requirements. Also, some U.S. DRAM producers purchased additional chips from Japanese companies or named them as their second sources, simultaneously complaining to the U.S. government about rising imports. With the experience they accumulated making 16K chips and through the VLSI projects, and possessing abundant capacity, the Japanese firms were even better positioned to meet the early 1980s demand for 64K and later-generation chips.

THE 1986 INTERNATIONAL TRADE AGREEMENT AND ITS SEQUEL

The continuing ascent of Japanese chip makers' world market shares and a cyclical decline of integrated circuit demand interacted to plunge the semiconductor industry into crisis during 1985 and 1986. Intel, National Semiconductor, and Mostek announced that they were exiting from DRAM produc-

---

[66]Federal Trade Commission, *Statistical Report: Annual Line of Business Survey,* various years. Unfortunately, the survey was discontinued after 1977, and so there are no comparable later data segregated by line of business within companies that are often highly diversified.

tion. Others followed suit, so that by mid–1986, only three U.S. companies (Texas Instruments, Micron Technology, and, mostly for internal use, AT&T) continued to produce DRAMs for the merchant market. Japanese companies reported losses along with their U.S. counterparts.[67] Responding to formal and informal complaints alleging Japanese dumping and denial of market access, the U.S. International trade authorities initiated dumping and Section 301 investigations, first on 64K DRAMs and then on the relatively new 256K DRAMs and EPROMs (erasable programmable read-only memories).[68] Although Japanese firms reduced their exports and raised their prices, intergovernmental negotiations continued during the first half of 1986.

It is important to recognize exactly what the dumping allegations entailed. The main charge was not that Japanese producers were selling at lower prices in the U.S. market than at home, for they almost surely were not, at least, not on direct contract sales.[69] Rather, they were said to be selling their chips at less than "constructed value"—i.e., fully allocated production cost, including the amortization of R&D and plant outlays, plus 10 percent general selling and administration overhead, plus 8 percent profit.[70] Again, as we observed in Chapter 5, the U.S. trade laws attempt in this respect to repeal the law of supply and demand, for one would not expect competitive producers to maintain an 8 percent profit margin during a recession. Learning by doing, which was still occurring at a rapid rate on the 256K chips introduced commercially only in 1984, complicated matters further. Even without aggressive learning curve pricing, a rational profit-maximizing firm will almost always set its prices below its out-of-pocket batch costs in the early stages of production.[71] If it did not do so, new products would be too high-priced to displace technologically inferior substitutes that had progressed far down their learning curves. Thus, "constructed value" is a nonsensical test in learning curve situations. As Dickens's Mr. Bumble would have appreciated, there was only one ground for its application to the semiconductor dispute: It was the law.

In July 1986 the trade officials of the United States and Japan reached an agreement scheduled to apply for five years.[72] The U.S. government would suspend all pending 256K memory dumping cases, and the government of

---

[67]"Japan Chip Makers in Crunch," *New York Times,* November 17, 1986, p. D1.

[68]The best history on this series of events is Flamm, *Mismanaged Trade?,* chap. 4. See also Flamm, "Semiconductor Dependency and Strategic Trade Policy," *Brookings Papers on Economic Activity,* 1993, no. 1, pp. 249–334.

[69]Flamm, *Mismanaged Trade?,* chap. 6.

[70]Compare p. 177 supra.

[71]See Flamm, "Strategic Arguments," pp. 311–312; and Andrew R. Dick, "Learning by Doing and Dumping in the Semiconductor Industry," *Journal of Law & Economics,* vol. 34 (April 1991), pp. 144–148.

[72]"U.S. and Japan Resolve Dispute on Microchips," *New York Times,* July 31, 1986, p. 1.

Japan would monitor the costs and prices of all relevant products exported to the United States and third-country markets "to prevent exports at prices less than company-specific fair value." "Fair value" in this sense meant "constructed value" as defined under U.S. trade law. To implement the agreement, MITI was to gather from all Japanese memory chip exporters data on their fully allocated costs of production by standard product for the previous quarter and forward the data to the U.S. Department of Commerce. The Department of Commerce would check actual import prices against the cost data and, if imports of any company's product occurred at less than the company's reported costs, infer that dumping had occurred. Because the reported costs were for the *previous* quarter, the constructed value triggers lagged current costs by three to six months. Because learning occurred and costs fell in the interim, the Japanese firms were required not only to price *at* fully allocated cost, but *above* it.

The initial round of 256K DRAM cost submissions, effective until October 15, 1986, ranged from $2.50 (for Nippon Electric) to $8.70 (allegedly for Fujitsu).[73] Prior to that time, large-volume buyers were purchasing DRAMs at approximately $2.40 per chip, whether (as one would expect in a reasonably competitive market) they came from a low-cost supplier or a high-cost firm. Following the agreement, prices rose to at least $5 per chip and perhaps to the cost floor of the high-cost producers.[74] The U.S. personal computer manufacturers were furious, because under the agreement their rivals in Japan could continue to purchase memories at competitive market prices. European governments were even angrier, because the Japanese government had agreed to monitor export prices to all nations, and not merely the United States, so prices to Europe were set on the basis of an accord from which the Europeans had been excluded. They complained to GATT, which in 1988 ruled that the agreement was illegal. Remedial action was delayed until 1989.[75] In the meantime, Japanese memory device producers enjoyed record-setting profits, in part because no U.S. DRAM producers reentered the market to compete with them.

As we have learned in previous chapters, the temptation to chisel on prices held high above marginal cost is strong. A million dollars' worth of integrated circuits can be packed into a modest-sized crate. Persons still

---

[73]See "The Chip Market Goes Haywire," *Business Week*, September 1, 1986, p. 25. See also Flamm, *Mismanaged Trade?*, chap. 4. For the last quarter of 1986, the range of prices was said to be between $2.50 and $4. "Japan Chip Values Set," *New York Times*, October 13, 1986, p. D3.

[74]"Chip Prices Skyrocket; Tokyo Accord Blamed," *New York Times*, September 9, 1986, p. D1.

[75]In June 1989, Japan agreed in response to the European Community's GATT case decision to cease monitoring exports to non-U.S. markets. Shortly thereafter Japan settled European dumping charges by instituting a cost-based reference price system similar to the one enforced for the United States.

unknown bought DRAMs at low prices on the uncontrolled Japanese market and smuggled them to Hong Kong and other southeast Asian entrepôts, whence they found their way to other world markets at prices below the reported "fair values." In March of 1987 President Reagan announced that the United States would retaliate against violations of the July 1986 agreement by levying 100 percent duties on Japanese electronic products (e.g., laptop computers, color television sets, and power tools) with an estimated total value of $300 million.[76] Some of the retaliatory tariffs remained in force until 1991. To correct the situation MITI intervened even more vigorously, adding 1M DRAMs to its control agenda, setting individual company quotas, and monitoring export shipments in detail to suppress gray-market transactions. The sanctions took hold. Production fell, prices rose, and as the demand for chips boomed again, computer makers had to cut back their output because the needed memory chips could not be obtained.[77]

Prices continued to be high and supplies tight even after MITI shifted in late 1987 from imposing individual company production quotas to "forecasting" demand in the forthcoming quarter, supposedly letting companies draw their own conclusions. One possible interpretation of the evidence is that MITI's "forecasts" served as a focal point for restricting industry output—in effect, creating the basis for an effective cartel.[78] An alternative explanation is that the Japanese semiconductor makers came to realize, as Texas Instruments did a few years before, that profits would be higher if they refrained from aggressive learning curve pricing. The evidence needed to distinguish between these alternatives remains elusive.

The high prices charged for DRAMs during the late 1980s facilitated the growth of formidable new competitors—the Korean semiconductor manufacturers.[79] By 1992, Samsung of Korea had displaced Toshiba as the world's leading DRAM producer.[80] Not surprisingly, charges of Korean dumping in the U.S. market accompanied the leadership change, but after announcing a 20 percent production cutback, low-cost producer Samsung was found to have set its prices below constructed value by only a trivial amount.[81] History repeats itself.

---

[76]"U.S. Will Retaliate Against Japanese in a Chips Dispute," *New York Times*, March 28, 1987, p. 1.

[77]"Shortage of Memory Chips Hurts Computer Industry," *New York Times*, March 12, 1988, p. 1.

[78]See Flamm, *Mismanaged Trade?*, chap. 4.

[79]On the entry of Korean producers, see Borrus, *Competing for Control*, pp. 206–209.

[80]See "Memory Chips: Welcome Korea," *The Economist*, February 4, 1989, p. 66; "In Korea, All Circuits Are Go," *Business Week*, July 9, 1990, pp. 69–71; and "Masters of the Clean Room," *Business Week*, September 27, 1993, pp. 107–108.

[81]Flamm, *Mismanaged Trade?*, chap. 4.

In 1991, the semiconductor trade agreement between the United States and Japan was extended for another three years.[82] Under the extension, the Japanese companies no longer submitted quarterly cost data to the U.S. Department of Commerce. Rather, they agreed to continue collecting the data, making them available only if new dumping allegations surfaced.

Left unsettled was a more controversial issue. The 1986 agreement stated that "the Government of Japan will impress upon the Japanese producers and users of semiconductors the need to aggressively take advantage of increased market access opportunities in Japan for foreign-based firms." A side letter mentioned 20 percent as a target for foreign firms' Japanese market share. As the new agreement was negotiated in 1981, U.S. companies' share had risen to 12.5 percent from 8.5 percent in 1985. There was dispute over whether the 20 percent figure was in fact a commitment or only a vague goal and how foreign firms' shares were to be measured—for example, whether the captive production of IBM plants in Japan was to be counted. The new agreement set in slightly less vague terms a 20 percent target for the end of 1992.[83] Market access was important to American semiconductor makers because an increased share of the large Japanese market meant additional progress down learning curves, and hence lower costs and greater competitiveness. As events transpired, the Japanese government redoubled its efforts to encourage U.S. chip purchases, and in the last quarter of 1992, the 20 percent target was attained. Purchases fell again and then rose above 20 percent in subsequent quarters.[84] Heated debate continued over whether quantitative import targets, with their implications of "managed trade," were compatible with the free trading regime advocated in principle by the U.S. government.

A more fundamental recurring question in the dispute over international semiconductor trade was whether it was vital for the United States to maintain a strong position producing DRAMs, or whether its chip users should simply buy from the least-cost sources, domestic or foreign. Advocates of protection or subsidies for domestic manufacturers argued that as products requiring the most demanding fabrication tolerances, DRAMs were "technology drivers" whose production helped U.S. firms master the techniques for making more complex application-specific and microprocessor chips. This claim appears in hindsight to have been fallacious, since U.S. companies continued to dominate the design and production of microprocessors, whose tol-

---

[82] "Chip Pact Set by U.S. and Japan," *New York Times*, June 4, 1991, p. D1.

[83] "Japan Sees Chip Pact as Success; U.S. Disagrees," *New York Times*, May 22, 1992, p. D3.

[84] "New U.S.-Japan Accord on Semiconductors," *New York Times*, June 5, 1992, p. D1; "Washington Says Japan Meets Goal on Chip Imports," *New York Times*, March 20, 1993, p. 37; "Chip Fight Persisting with Japan," *New York Times*, December 18, 1993, p. 37; and "Foreign Chips Gain in Japan," *New York Times*, December 17, 1994, p. 49.

erances are at least as stringent as those of DRAMs. Second, it is argued that having strong domestic sources gives U.S. computer designers the earliest possible access to the latest memory chip layouts and thereby facilitates technical leadership in the computer field. This "without a nail" argument is probably true for some key components, but it is unclear whether it holds for DRAM chips, whose interfaces with computers have been standardized, and for which lower-capacity chips provide a functional, even if not ideal, substitute. Third, if the United States lacks significant domestic DRAM production, its chip users could be forced to pay high prices for the devices sold by the cartelized producers of the dominant supplying nation.[85] The high prices paid for Japanese DRAMs during the late 1980s are cited as an example. But the example also implies a powerful counterargument, because Japanese producers were induced to quote high prices by U.S. demands that they do so, not because they chose voluntarily to cartelize. And if they did cartelize, new entry, either in the United States or from nations such as Korea, would sooner or later undermine their efforts. Thus, the rebuttal argument insists, free trade unencumbered inter alia by ill-considered antidumping actions is the best policy. The debate will continue.

THE U.S. INDUSTRIAL POLICY RESPONSE

The Japanese challenge to U.S. leadership in semiconductors spurred industry and governmental initiatives to strengthen U.S. producers' technological performance. Efforts were undertaken on several fronts.

In 1984, Congress passed a Semiconductor Chip Protection Act, which provided copyright protection for 10 years to the detailed circuitry layouts embodied in the photographic masks used in chip production.[86] It and a series of court rulings that allowed the computer code used in microprocessors to be copyrighted make it more expensive for rivals to imitate new chip designs.[87] Prior to these changes, imitators could slice away the microscopic deposition layers making up a chip, photograph them, and attempt to reproduce the layout for their own chips. With this form of imitation barred under the new law, would-be rivals must start with a chip's functional specifications and work out their own design embodiments, taking care to isolate their design team

---

[85]See Flamm, *Mismanaged Trade?*, chap. 7; and "Shortage of Memory Chips Hurts Computer Industry," *New York Times*, March 11, 1988, p. 1.

[86]"Piracy Ban Nears for Silicon Chips," *New York Times*, October 10, 1984, p. 1.

[87]See "A Trial with More at Stake Than a Copyright," *Business Week*, June 9, 1986, p. 35; and "The Uncertain Payoff from Intel's Landmark Case," *Business Week*, February 20, 1989, p. 35.

from any knowledge of the original chip's layout as a defense against charges of outright copying. Since the latter form of "reverse engineering" is more costly than the "slice and copy" approach, the original chip designer's head start advantage is enhanced.[88] The law does not prevent overseas rivals from copying chip layouts, but can be invoked to bar importation of infringing chips into the United States.

Recognizing that their leadership position depended upon continuing advances in semiconductor materials science and the ability to recruit outstanding new scientists and engineers, U.S. semiconductor makers jointly created the Semiconductor Research Corporation in 1982. Industry members pledged regular financial contributions to SRC, which in turn was charged with using the money to sponsor research and graduate student training at U.S. universities. In 1987, SRC's annual budget was $20 million.

As commercial uses of semiconductors proliferated during the 1970s, military support of industry research and development played a less important role than during the formative 1950s and 1960s. Between 1974 and 1977, the 16 to 18 large semiconductor producers reporting to the Federal Trade Commission's Line of Business survey together received federal government R&D contract support averaging $14 million per year.[89] This sum amounted to 11 percent of their total R&D expenditures in those years. Military support rose when the Department of Defense announced its VHSIC (Very High Speed Integrated Circuit) program, which planned to distribute $900 million over a 10-year period to develop high-performance integrated circuits specialized to an array of military applications.[90] The funds were to be apportioned among 14 U.S. companies, who were expected to cooperate in disseminating the results of their work to one another.

A more dramatic step was taken in direct response to the DRAM trade crisis of 1985–1986. In 1987 a new research and development consortium, Sematech, was created following an initiative by several industry members. The express motive for its founding was to restore the ability of U.S. chip makers to compete with their Japanese counterparts.[91] During its first five years of operation, 14 U.S. companies participated, contributing approximately $100 million per year of budgetary support, which was matched (after

---

[88]The logic of copyright protection is in this sense analogous to the logic of patent grants, which will be explored more thoroughly in Chapter 9.

[89]U.S. Federal Trade Commission, *Annual Line of Business Report*, various years, master table.

[90]See Langlois et al., *Microelectronics*, pp. 144–147.

[91]"U.S. Chip Makers Plan Huge Venture," *New York Times*, January 6, 1987, p. D1. A predecessor was the Microelectronics and Computer Technology Corporation (MCC), established in 1983 to perform cooperative research and development on a range of computer and semiconductor problems. There is near consensus that MCC's technical accomplishments were modest.

heated intragovernmental debate[92]) by Department of Defense money. Sematech established a laboratory and production facility in Austin, Texas, with 700 employees, one-third of whom had been transferred from the sponsoring companies. Sematech's original objective was to advance integrated circuit manufacturing technology by having its staff work cooperatively on producing state-of-the-art memory chips in near-commercial quantities. To initiate the work, IBM donated designs and manufacturing technology for the 4M DRAM it was about to begin producing in its own facilities, and AT&T made a similar contribution for 1M static random access memories. By working together on such projects, Sematech staff exchanged the "tricks" they brought from their home bases, and apparently, the accumulated know-how was complementary. Its dissemination is said to have facilitated the attainment of enhanced chip yields both in the consortium's laboratories and in the "fabs" of sponsoring companies.[93]

As the plan for Sematech evolved, however, another objective gained even higher priority. Memory chip makers in the United States fell behind Japan because they failed to invest sufficiently during the 1970s and early 1980s. The problem observed for steel in Chapter 5 began to reappear in semiconductors. Lagging investment translated into lagging demand for the output of companies who specialized in making semiconductor manufacturing equipment. Weak equipment demand in turn meant depleted profits and cutbacks in research and development on new equipment designs. Meanwhile, Japanese equipment makers advanced. In 1979, nine of the world's ten leading semiconductor equipment makers were based in the United States. By 1988, world sales leadership had been captured by three veterans of Japan's VLSI project.[94] The semiconductor equipment division of Perkin-Elmer, once the world's vanguard supplier of photolithographic "steppers," fell to eighth place, lapsed into unprofitability, and was offered for sale by its parent.[95] After the U.S. government voiced opposition to the division's purchase by Japan's Nikon, it was acquired by the Silicon Valley Group, with IBM financing an

---

[92]See "A Pentagon Study Urges U.S. Aid for the Embattled Chip Industry," *New York Times*, February 13, 1987, p. 1; and "Holding the Line Against an Industrial Policy," *Business Week*, February 5, 1990, p. 60.

[93]See "Sematech Starts To Make Progress," *New York Times*, April 19, 1991, p. D1; and "Chip Group Makes Ultra-Thin Chip in the US," *New York Times*, January 22, 1993, p. D4.

[94]"Pillar of Chip Industry Eroding," *New York Times*, March 3, 1989, p. D1.

[95]See "Nikon in Talks To Buy Key Perkin-Elmer Unit," *New York Times*, November 27, 1989, p. 1; and "Perkin Unit to Remain U.S. Owned," *New York Times*, May 16, 1990, p. D1.

On innovation more generally in "steppers" and substitute processes, see Rebecca Henderson, "Underinvestment and Incompetence as Responses to Radical Innovation: Evidence from the Photolithographic Alignment Equipment Industry," *RAND Journal of Economics*, vol. 24 (Summer 1993), pp. 248–270.

appreciable part of the acquisition. In 1993, the reconstituted Perkin-Elmer operation entered an extensive 10-year technology exchange arrangement with Canon of Japan. GCA, another leading U.S. stepper maker, experienced analogous setbacks and ownership changes.

Having gained technological leadership, the Japanese equipment makers were said to be delivering their new apparatus to Japanese semiconductor fabricators many months before it was made available to American companies, thereby putting the U.S. firms at a competitive disadvantage.[96] Concerned about this problem, Sematech moved from its initial emphasis on internal process development to emulate the Japanese VLSI approach, allocating a substantial fraction of its budget to support U.S. equipment makers' design efforts. Its staff began working closely with the equipment specialists' R&D teams. The U.S. equipment companies, including the reconstituted Perkin-Elmer and GCA organizations, developed superior new apparatus, regaining orders that had initially been earmarked for Japanese vendors.[97] GCA, however, won too few new orders to convince semiconductor fabricators that it would remain in business to service the machines it had installed. This precipitated a cessation of additional orders and a downward spiral that ended with GCA's liquidation.[98] Thus, Sematech's intervention in the equipment development field yielded only ambiguous success. And at least one other promising photolithographic machine was developed without Sematech support.[99] As doubts about the contributions Sematech might make in the future gained ground, the Department of Defense and Congress began considering whether the consortium's subsidies should be ended.[100]

Another cooperative venture died stillborn.[101] In June 1989, seven semiconductor and computer manufacturers joined to form U.S. Memories Inc. Its mission was to *produce*, not develop, 4-megabit DRAMs and memory chips of

---

[96]See "The Competition in Chip-making Equipment," *New York Times*, September 6, 1984, p. D6; "Silicon Valley Is Watching Its Worst Nightmare Unfold,' *Business Week*, September 4, 1989, pp. 63–67; and "Japanese Criticized by Chip Makers," *New York Times*, May 7, 1991, p. D4.

[97]"One Stepper Forward for Sematech," *Business Week*, June 8, 1992, p. 110; and "Chipping Away at Japan," *Business Week*, December 7, 1992, p. 120.

[98]See Lucien P. Randazzese, "GCA and Domestic Lithography: Managing Procurement Incentives in SEMATECH and Vertical Consortia," RAND Corporation report (Santa Monica, CA: 1995).

[99]"Jersey Company To Introduce Fast Chip-Making Machine," *New York Times*, May 22, 1990, p. D1.

[100]See "New Drive by Sematech for Funding," *New York Times*, December 19, 1991, p. D1; "U.S. Plans To Reduce Chip Funds," *New York Times*, August 18, 1992, p. D1; and "Environment Is a Mission at Sematech," *New York Times*, October 5, 1992, p. D1.

[101]"7 Makers Plan Chip Venture," *New York Times*, June 22, 1989, p. D1; and "'This Will Surely Come Back To Haunt Us,'" *Business Week*, January 29, 1990, pp. 72–73.

subsequent generations. The new enterprise was expected to undertake an initial capital investment of $1 billion. However, efforts to secure financing failed, in part because DRAM prices dropped unexpectedly with the onset of a recession and partly because U.S. chip users refused to commit themselves to placing the bulk of their orders with a new source whose reliability had not been established.

That neither government subsidies nor cooperative research guarantee success in the difficult business of integrated circuit design and production is suggested by the experience of Europe. During the 1950s and 1960s, companies whose home base is Europe fared well in producing discrete semiconductors.[102] But with weak computer industry demand, they lagged in the move to large-scale integrated circuits. The West German government was the first to launch an aggressive program to revitalize its national champions, allocating approximately $105 million of R&D subsidies between 1974 and 1978.[103] Government programs then proliferated in all of the major European industrial nations.[104] The British government committed approximately $300 million, 40 percent of which was for integrated circuit work, under its five-year Alvey program, initiated in 1983. Interfirm cooperation was a requirement for participation. France projected R&D subsidies of $5 billion over a five-year period under its Filière Electronique program, initiated in 1982. Semiconductor work was an important part of the effort. The Dutch and German governments together pledged a third of a billion dollars in 1983 for the megaproject, intended to bring national champions Philips and Siemens to the frontiers of semiconductor technology. The European Community initiated its ESPRIT[105] program in 1983, allocating more than $150 million per year for five years to support cooperative long-range research by industry and universities on information technologies, including semiconductors. In 1988 a more narrowly targeted Community program, JESSI (the Joint European Submicron Silicon Initiative), was announced. Governmental semiconductor R&D subsidies totaling $250 million per year over eight years were planned.[106]

Although more time must pass before the results of JESSI can be evaluated, the earlier programs quite clearly did not spawn the technology champions they sought to create. In 1988, only half of Europe's integrated circuit demands by one measure and 31 percent by another were satisfied from internal sources, and much of the internal production was by companies with a

---

[102]Tilton, *International Diffusion of Technology*, Chap. 5.

[103]Malerba, *The Semiconductor Business*, p. 191.

[104]See Langlois et al., *Microelectronics*, pp. 134–151; and Kenneth Flamm, "Semiconductors," in Gary C. Hufbauer, ed., *Europe 1992: An American Perspective* (Washington, DC: Brookings, 1990), pp. 281–284.

[105]European Strategic Program for Research in Information Technology.

[106]"Europe's High-Tech Titans Put Their Chips on JESSI," *Business Week*, November 14, 1988, p. 82.

U.S. or Japanese home base.[107] Only three enterprises at home in Europe remained among the world's top 20 merchant semiconductor vendors in 1989: Philips (tenth), SGS-Thomson of Italy and France (twelfth), and Siemens of Germany (fifteenth).[108] Philips and SGS-Thomson owed a considerable fraction of their integrated circuit sales to acquired U.S. subsidiaries. With their world market shares continuing to decline (see Figure 6.3), the leading European firms began withdrawing during the early 1990s from highly competitive chip lines and entering joint ventures to tap the know-how of companies such as IBM and Toshiba in new research and development efforts.[109]

FIGURE 6.3
Trends in World Semiconductor Sales Shares, by Companies' National Home Bases

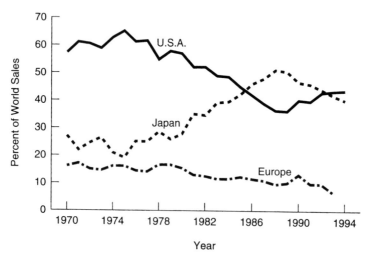

Sources: Adapted from Kenneth Flamm, *Mismanaged Trade? Strategic Policy and the Semiconductor Industry* (Washington, DC: Brookings Institution manuscript, 1993), Figure 1–5; based upon data whose source was Dataquest.

---

[107]Flamm, "Semiconductors," p. 271.

[108]Flamm, "Semiconductors," p. 264.

[109]See "Can Europe Survive the Chip Wars?" *Business Week,* December 21, 1992, pp. 56–57; "Europe's Electronics Rescue Plan," *New York Times,* September 5, 1991, p. D1; "European Research: Still Looking for the Answer," *The Economist,* June 22, 1991, pp. 73–74; "The Last Hurrah for European High Tech?" *Business Week,* April 29, 1991, pp. 44–46; and "Europe's Would-Be Champions," *The Economist,* August 27, 1994, p. 60.

A complete explanation of why massive R&D subsidies and cooperation were insufficient to save the day in Europe would probably overflow a 16-megabit memory chip. However, three provisional hypotheses can be advanced. First, Europe relied too heavily on bureaucratically encumbered national champion enterprises, whose leadership positions were retained inter alia through poorly digested mergers. The absence in Europe of aggressive start-up firms like those who grew to lead the U.S. market is noteworthy. Second, Europe's champions lacked the fierce determination to succeed so evident among their otherwise analogous broad-line electrical company counterparts in Japan. And third, Europe, unlike Japan, protected its national champions too long through tariffs and local procurement preferences, shielding them from the competitive pressures that drive semiconductor design and production teams to work overtime in their struggle to stay abreast.

EPILOGUE

As the decade of the 1990s dawned, U.S. semiconductor manufacturers began to regain strength. It is difficult to determine world market positions with pinpoint accuracy, because diverse sources differ in their handling of captive (nonmerchant) production, the attribution of nationality, the output of joint-venture offshore plants, and the like. Figure 6.3 covers merchant sales only (e.g., ignoring the output of IBM and AT&T), ascribing sales to the nation in which companies have their home base, wherever the production actually occurred. The decline of U.S. companies' combined world market share appears to have been stemmed by 1990.[110] Japanese manufacturers, having adopted less aggressive pricing and investment policies as a result of the 1985–1987 international trade disputes, exhibited indications of peaking, and in 1993, they lost their world sales leadership position to their U.S. counterparts.[111] U.S. companies were particularly strong in microprocessors (selling in a $100–$500 price range, with Intel and Motorola in dominant positions), and application-specific chips, while abandoning most of the commodity DRAM market (at $3–$12 per chip) to Korean and Japanese suppliers. Yet only one thing is certain: There will be more on which to report as the struggles continue.

---

[110]See "U.S. Again Leads in Computer Chips," *Washington Post*, November 20, 1992, p. A1; and "A Power Surge in Chips," *Business Week*, January 11, 1993, p. 80.

[111]"U.S. Surpasses Japan on Chips," *New York Times*, December 15, 1993, p. D2; and "Where the Chips May Fall Next," *New York Times*, April 17, 1995, p. D1. On investment patterns, see Flamm, *Mismanaged Trade?*, chap. 4, and "The Future of Silicon Valley," *Business Week*, February 5, 1990, pp. 55–56.

AFTERWORD

Pricing strategies take on new complexities when there are compelling dynamic economies of scale through learning by doing. Firms strive to dominate narrow product markets by being the first to offer technologically advanced designs and by setting their prices so aggressively that it is prohibitively costly for laggards to keep pace. When several producers play the same game, however, rivalry can become so fierce that all market participants end up with losses. When the rivalry spills across national borders, difficult problems are posed for national and supranational organizations responsible for enforcing international trading rules. Because a technological lead is so crucial in this environment, governments have intervened to subsidize the research and development efforts of their national champions. But subsidy policies alone have been insufficient to dictate market outcomes. Although semiconductor makers have apparently learned to shun hyperaggressive learning curve pricing strategies, the most successful firms have tended to combine a forced pace of innovation with pricing choices that afford latecomers at best meager profit-making options.

7

COMPUTERS

After a slow start, IBM gained a dominant position in the rapidly growing computer industry through superior salesmanship and vigorous cultivation of demand. It retained its high market share into the 1980s through a "fast second" strategy in research and new product development and through aggressive pricing responses to firms that attempted to enter market segments in which (partly through tied goods pricing strategies) it had initially commanded large price-cost margins. The legality of those responses and the meaning of "predatory pricing" were tested in a series of antitrust cases that clarified the scope of the earlier Standard Oil precedent. IBM's delayed recognition of the microcomputer revolution induced a "fast second" response, as a result of which IBM surrendered control of technological standards to Microsoft and integrated circuit maker Intel. That in turn opened the microcomputer manufacturing field to a host of competitive entrants. IBM's monopoly position was undermined; Microsoft's newly gained power was subjected to an antitrust challenge.

INTRODUCTION

In 1963, when the author of this book began to confront the mysteries of electronic computation, Princeton University's most powerful computer was an IBM 7094. Costing several million dollars, it filled a room of approximately 800 square feet. Its internal memory was 64,000 bytes. Nonrepetitive jobs were run one-by-one by reading in punched cards, which regularly jammed in the input mechanism. A relatively simple multiple regression analysis consumed about one minute of the computer's efforts, but because of batch traffic jams, the average waiting time was more than an hour, and when the computer crashed, as it did regularly, the queue extended to 24 hours or more. "Word processing" had not yet been invented. Thirty years later, this chapter was written on an already old-fashioned desktop computer whose acquisition cost, with high-resolution printer, was approximately $2200. Two million bytes of internal memory were available. The multiple regression that took a minute to run in 1963 required about a second in 1993, and the results were available immediately to the eager user.

This simple story encapsulates the furious pace of technological progress in computers. Kenneth Flamm estimates that during the two decades between 1957 and 1978, the price of computing capacity fell at an average rate of 28 percent per year.[1] Measuring the computer industry's productivity as the processing power delivered per hour of labor used in developing and manufacturing computers, government statistics show the rate of productivity growth between 1973 and 1988 to have been 23.1 percent *per year*. Such rapid productivity growth in a major industry poses problems for those who calculate gross national product. If GNP were reckoned in terms of the *physical volume* of output, the computer industry's output would have risen from 0.85 percent of the manufacturing sector total in 1973 to 43 percent in 1988.[2] But when industry outputs are aggregated to determine sector GNP, output is weighted by periodically updated product prices. Because the price of computing capacity has fallen so swiftly, the industry's reweighted share of manufacturing sector current-dollar output in 1988 was 2.34 percent.

EARLY HISTORY

The computer industry had long and complex origins.[3] Crude mechanical adding and multiplying machines were devised in the seventeenth century by mathematicians Blaise Pascal and Wilhelm von Leibniz. A mechanical "difference engine" anticipating many computer concepts was invented and constructed by Charles Babbage during the first half of the nineteenth century. Mechanical calculators were used to multiply and divide during the first half of the twentieth century. In the 1930s, the first analog computers (initially called "differential analyzers") came into widespread scientific use. They simulated differential equation trajectories, at first through the interaction of mechanical parts and later by varying the flow of current through electron tubes. As World War II broke out in 1939, it had become clear that a wider range of numeric computations could be accomplished at much greater speed by replacing mechanical with electronic components. During the war primi-

---

[1] Kenneth Flamm, *Targeting the Computer: Government Support and International Competition* (Washington, DC: Brookings, 1987), pp. 24–25.

[2] F. M. Scherer, "Lagging Productivity Growth: Measurement, Technology, and Shock Effects," *Empirica*, vol. 20 (1993), p. 10.

[3] For a highly readable history, see Joel Shurkin, *Engines of the Mind* (New York: Norton, 1984). A history closer in perspective to the approach taken here is Nancy Dorfman, *Innovation and Market Structure: Lessons from the Computer and Semiconductor Industries* (Cambridge: Ballinger, 1987).

tive computers combining electronic with mechanical components were built at Harvard University, MIT, and the National Cash Register Company to perform scientific calculations, simulate aircraft flight, and break codes. In England, increasingly sophisticated German codes were broken using the Mark II Colossus machines, which contained 2400 vacuum tubes and 800 electromechanical relays. The Mark II Colossus was by most criteria the first true electronic digital computer.[4] However, because the existence of Colossus was kept secret for three decades, the machine generally credited with ushering in the digital computer revolution was the ENIAC (Electronic Numerical Integrator and Computer), developed and built in the Engineering School of the University of Pennsylvania.

ENIAC was conceived in 1942 by J. Presper Eckert and John Mauchly. At the time, a sizeable team at the University of Pennsylvania was using mechanical calculators to compute precise artillery shell trajectories for the U.S. Army's Ballistic Research Laboratory. Mauchly, who had been fascinated by the idea of electronic computation, proposed an electronic digital computer to speed the effort. In 1943 the Army awarded a contract to support the ENIAC project. Building the machine, with 17,468 vacuum tubes and tens of thousands of other electronic and mechanical components, cost $800,000. Its operation required 174 kilowatts of electric power. It was not completed in time for war projects, but in late 1945 it passed its full-scale tests and was put to work on a variety of military tasks. One was to perform the first extraordinarily complex calculations testing the feasibility of Edward Teller's early concepts for a hydrogen bomb. ENIAC lacked the ability to store "programs" guiding its internal operations; each computational step had to be programmed by setting thousands of external switches and connecting a maze of wires. Because this took months for the hydrogen bomb problem, physicist Stanislaw Ulam conducted parallel computations using only a mechanical calculator (or in other versions of the story, a slide rule) and ingenious shortcuts. Ulam's result (showing Teller's approach to be infeasible) was almost identical to that from ENIAC, but Ulam reached the goal first.[5]

Eckert and Mauchly were well aware of ENIAC's limitations. In 1944 they began thinking about a more advanced computer with internal program storage and external memory. Collaboration with mathematician John von Neumann led to the articulation of a logical scheme that has guided the design of virtually

---

[4]See Kenneth Flamm, *Creating the Computer: Government, Industry, and High Technology* (Washington, DC Brookings, 1988), pp. 38–39.

[5]See Robert Jungk, *Brighter than a Thousand Suns* (New York: Harcourt, Brace, 1958), pp. 291–293; and Richard Rhodes, *The Making of the Atomic Bomb* (New York: Simon & Schuster, 1988), pp. 771–773. Although advances in computer programming eventually gave computers a decisive speed edge, another handicap persists. From his manual computations, Ulam realized why the Teller design would not work and conceived the germ of a new, ultimately effective design.

all subsequent general-purpose digital computers.[6] Because the University of Pennsylvania refused to cede patent rights to Eckert and Mauchly, they formed their own firm, the Eckert-Mauchly Computer Corporation, in 1946, moving into a loft that had previously served as a ballet studio. Financial support proved difficult to secure, and when the firm's principal backer (an executive in a company making racetrack betting odds calculators) died, Eckert and Mauchly sold their venture in February 1950 to Remington Rand (later Sperry Rand), an established maker of office equipment and electric shavers. Development work continued, and in March 1951, the first UNIVAC computer was delivered to the U.S. Census Bureau. UNIVAC's capabilities became widely recognized when the computer was programmed to project the outcome of the 1952 U.S. presidential election and did so successfully in its real-time election night television debut.

Numerous other companies entered the newly emerging computer business during the early postwar years, most of them responding to burgeoning government needs.[7] Some were founded de novo to pursue computer development opportunities, but, in contrast to the history of semiconductors, most start-ups sold out to become the nucleus of established companies' computer operations. Entry into the new industry was eased inter alia when a federal court ruled in October 1973 that a fundamental computer patent issued to Eckert and Mauchly was invalid because the claimed inventions had been anticipated by an Iowa engineer and because they had been in public use (through ENIAC) more than a year before the patent application was filed in 1947.[8] Among the significant early entrants into the new field were Raytheon (which sold its computer operations in 1957 to Honeywell), Northrop Aircraft (stressing military applications), Burroughs, National Cash Register, RCA, Philco (which ceased commercial computer work in 1963), and General Electric.

As the industry evolved, however, a much more important entrant was IBM—the International Business Machines Corporation. The predecessor of IBM had been organized in 1911 to market Hollerith[9] punched-card tabulating and accounting machines and the time clocks employees use to record their hours at work. Under the leadership of Thomas J. Watson, who learned high-pressure salesmanship methods at the National Cash Register Company, it soon achieved and retained a 90 percent share of card puncher and tabula-

---

[6]"How Von Neumann Showed the Way,"*Invention and Technology*, 1990, pp. 8–16.

[7]The crucial role of government support is emphasized in Flamm, *Targeting the Computer* and *Creating the Computer*.

[8]Honeywell, Inc. v. Sperry Rand Corp., 180 U.S.P.Q. 673; CCH 1974 Trade Cases para. 74, 874 (1973).

[9]The tabulating machine was invented by Herman Hollerith in the 1880s. The "H" in FORTRAN format statements, designating alphabetic characters, commemorates Hollerith's contribution.

tor sales. Until the 1960s, most large-scale business and government data processing was done using punched-card machines. IBM took an early interest in electronic computing. It supported the work of Howard Aiken at Harvard and constructed a gigantic half-electronic, half-mechanical Selective Sequence Electronic Calculator, which resided in its 57th Street Manhattan showrooms between 1948 and 1952 as a facility on which scientists could carry out large-scale computations at no charge. Most of IBM's top managers considered all-electronic computers to have little promise for their principal market, business data processing. But during the late 1940s Thomas J. Watson Jr. persuaded his father to expand IBM's electronics staff, and after the Korean War erupted, IBM began work on a general-purpose computer aimed at the defense and scientific markets. The new machine, introduced in early 1953, was at first named the Defense Calculator and later the IBM 701. Meanwhile, Remington Rand had taken the lead with UNIVAC. Thomas J. Watson Jr. reconstructs his thoughts upon learning that UNIVAC was displacing IBM tabulating machines at the Census Bureau as follows:[10]

> "My God, here we are trying to build Defense Calculators, while UNIVAC is smart enough to start taking all the civilian business away!" I was terrified.

IBM thereupon began working on a business-oriented computer, the 702, on which deliveries also commenced in 1953. In 1954 it introduced its model 650, which combined electronic circuitry with punched-card input-output for small-scale business data-processing applications. Improved 600 and 700 series models followed. By 1955, IBM led (newly renamed) Sperry Rand in sales, and in 1956 IBM's accumulated share of the general-purpose computers installed in the United States amounted to 75 percent, compared to 19 percent for Sperry Rand and 4 percent for third-ranked Burroughs. The IBM shares, variously measured, ranged between 65 and 80 percent during the next 15 years.[11]

The early IBM computers were inferior technologically to their UNIVAC counterparts. But in part through its contract from the U.S. Air Force for the SAGE (Semi-Automatic Ground Environment) command and control system, said by Thomas J. Watson Jr. to be "the most important sale of my career,"[12] IBM enhanced its computer know-how and began developing more advanced scientific and commercial computers. The highly successful 7090

---

[10]Thomas J. Watson Jr. (with Peter Petre), *Father, Son & Co.: My Life at IBM and Beyond* (New York: Bantam, 1990), p. 242.

[11]Gerald Brock, *The U.S. Computer Industry: A Study of Market Power* (Cambridge: Ballinger, 1975), pp. 1, 13–21; and Richard Thomas DeLamarter, *Big Blue: IBM's Use and Abuse of Power* (New York: Dodd, Mead, 1986), pp. 57 and 104.

[12]*Father, Son & Co.*, p. 245.

scientific model and 1401 business computer were introduced in 1959 and 1960 respectively.[13]

THE BASES OF IBM'S DOMINANCE

IBM's rapid rise to computer industry dominance was achieved despite a slow start and (for several years) a technological lag vis a vis rival corporations. How was this possible?

By far the most important initial factor was IBM's superior sales effort. Computers were new and mysterious to most business firms. Few knew how they worked or what they could accomplish. From their employer's dominant position in punched-card machines, IBM sales personnel understood the data-processing needs of most sizable U.S. business and governmental organizations. They carried into their computer sales efforts a tradition of not accepting "no" as an answer. Once IBM's top management recognized (belatedly) the potential of computers, it mounted a thoroughgoing program to educate its sales representatives in computer technology. The field sales force in turn showed customers how computers could be used, provided applications software, held their hands during the breaking-in period, and much else. As Thomas J. Watson Jr. explained in 1973:[14]

> Traditionally, we had a big share of the punch card accounting machine market. So we had a large field force of salesmen, repairmen and servicemen. They were perhaps the only people in America who understood how to put in an automated bookkeeping system. The invention [of the computer] was important. But the knowledge of how to put a great big system on line, how to make it run, and solve problems was probably four times as important.

IBM's rivals recognized much more slowly the nonscientific data-processing potential of computers and the need for hand-holding. Remington Rand in particular dissipated its lead by training and motivating its sales force poorly and by failing to resolve internal strategy quarrels between the Eckert-Mauchly group (located in Philadelphia) and another group based in Minneapolis. As one account reports, Remington engineers spent "20 percent of their time working on computers, and 80 percent of their time working on each other."[15]

Perceiving correctly that business firms lacked employees with computer knowledge, IBM strove to fill the gap, but with a distinct IBM bias. During the 1950s and early 1960s its computers were leased to educational institutions

---

[13]The 7094 computer on which the author cut his teeth was a 7090 mainframe combined with a 1401 for input-output control.

[14]DeLamarter, *Big Blue*, p. 29, quoting from *Nation's Business*, February 1973. See also Watson, *Father, Son & Co.*, pp. 257–258.

[15]Shurkin, *Engines of the Mind*, p. 258.

offering computer science courses at discounts of 60 percent for academic uses and 20 percent for administrative use. Some prestigious institutions received free computers. As a result, a generation of computer specialists entered business jobs after being trained on IBM machines. Their initial instinct, absent compelling evidence to the contrary, was to buy IBM. This plus IBM's more effective field sales effort gave IBM a substantial reputational advantage in the minds of computer purchasers. The comments of two companies in response to a 1966 questionnaire asking what factors they considered in buying new computers illustrate the problem IBM competitors faced:[16]

> We do write specifications and go out for bids, but this is really window-dressing. . . . Logical computer selection seems almost impossible.

> Selection has been: any computer as long as it is manufactured by IBM.

Among the executives responsible for computer purchases, it was conventional wisdom that, no matter how the subsequent implementation effort turned out, "You can't get fired for choosing IBM."

Because there was so much early uncertainty about what computers could do and even whether they would work at all, many companies were reluctant to invest in them. Under an antitrust mandate (based upon its punched-card market dominance) to lease its machines as well as selling them, IBM offered leases that could be canceled on 30 days' notice. Most business users in fact chose to lease. Other computer vendors were forced to follow suit, but Remington Rand probably lost orders because it tried to enhance its cash flow by stressing sales over leases.

Once IBM gained a dominant computer market share, its position was to some extent self-reinforcing. After installing IBM computers and developing at considerable expense the specialized applications programs needed to operate them, users were subject to "software lock-in." Rewriting the software for the incompatible operating system of another firm's computer would be costly in both effort and transitional data-processing disruptions. Thus, absent strong differences on other dimensions of the equation, the company offering a familiar, compatible computer was favored when replacement machines were being sought.[17] IBM attempted to reinforce this advantage by opposing government efforts to propagate uniform data format standards

---

[16]Brock, *The U.S. Computer Industry*, p. 47.

[17]Compare Brock, *The U.S. Computer Industry*, pp. 49–51; with Franklin Fisher, John J. McGowan, and Joen Greenwood, *Folded, Spindled, and Mutilated: Economic Analysis and U.S. v. IBM* (Cambridge: MIT Press, 1983), pp. 196–204. As consultants to IBM in its various antitrust cases, Fisher et al. provide the most careful argument in defense of IBM's practices. Thomas DeLamarter was a member of the U.S. government's antitrust prosecution team. His *Big Blue* is the best statement of the government's position.

FIGURE 7.1
Cost Curves of IBM with Automation and Rivals Using
Job Shop Methods

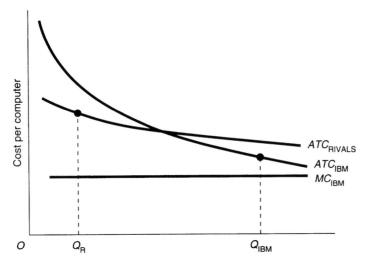

Number of computers assembled per year

(e.g., ASCII), maintaining instead its own incompatible formats and causing inconvenience to users migrating between different computer makes.[18]

Commanding a large market share also permitted IBM to take advantage of scale economies. The relationships were complex, and quantitative evidence is at best fragmentary, but several likely areas of benefit can be identified. In the assembly of computers, learning by doing definitely occurs. It seems unlikely that computer learning curve slopes were as steep as in semiconductors, and it is not clear what cumulative volume had to be attained before the learning opportunities were exhausted. Determining the importance of learning by doing is complicated by differences in production methods between IBM and its rivals. With a large output volume, IBM employed relatively highly automated assembly methods, which carried substantial fixed-investment and plant overhead burdens. Brock presents internal IBM studies showing that long-run average manufacturing costs for IBM 370/168 central processor units declined by approximately 11 percent as output rose from 300 to 700 units.[19] Marginal costs were believed to be constant. Using labor-intensive batch methods, IBM's rivals operated on a quite different long-run curve, as illustrated in Figure 7.1. At a low volume such as OQ_R, unit costs were much lower (and probably more susceptible to learning by doing)

---

[18]See Brock, *The U.S Computer Industry*, pp. 142–155; DeLamarter, *Big Blue*, pp. 257–263; and Dorfman, *Innovation and Market Structure*, p. 78.

[19]Brock, p. 29. It is unclear how much of the decline is attributable to fixed cost spreading and how much to learning by doing.

than they would be with automation, which is why the batch methods were adopted. But at the larger volume OQ_{IBM} attained by IBM, costs with automation were lower. It is uncertain how large the differences were.

IBM may have enjoyed a further advantage by being able to spread the costs of research and development over a larger number of computers sold. The computer industry is one of the most R&D–intensive manufacturing industries. Between 1974 and 1977, it placed second (after pharmaceuticals) out of 234 manufacturing lines in company-financed R&D expenditures as a percentage of sales, averaging 8.9 percent over the four years.[20] Constructing ENIAC cost roughly $800,000. The first IBM general-purpose computer, the 701, was estimated to require $3 million for initial designs and a prototype, and as much as $9 million for further engineering and perhaps tooling.[21] The development of RCA's Spectra computer series in the mid–1960s cost a reported $15 million.[22] The IBM System 360, a family of computers introduced during the mid–1960s, required R&D expenditures estimated at $500 million. The large difference between RCA's Spectra cost and IBM's System 360 outlays reveals a difficulty of comparing R&D costs between operations of varying size. With a very large customer base, IBM had to design numerous models and variants, solve more complex problems to achieve compatibility across models, and provide extensive software support. With a narrower base, rivals could target their R&D more precisely and avoid many complexities. What matters under these circumstances is the ratio of required R&D outlays relative to the volume of products that can be sold. A clue is provided by unusually disaggregated 1973 data on the computer operations of 14 major companies. The correlation between company-financed R&D outlays as a percentage of sales and the logarithm of computer sales was only +0.03, suggesting that smaller companies found themselves compelled to spend neither more nor less per sales dollar than industry leaders on research and development.[23]

A final scale economies domain also poses interpretational difficulties. The early computers broke down frequently, in part because they used failure-prone vacuum tubes rather than the much more reliable semiconductors

---

[20]Federal Trade Commission, *Statistical Report: Annual Line of Business Report,* (Washington, DC: various years). Unfortunately, later data broken down by line of business within diversified companies are not available.

[21]Watson, *Father, Son & Co.*, p. 216.

[22]Dorfman, *Innovation and Market Structure*, p. 66.

[23]Federal Trade Commission, *Statistical Report: Annual Line of Business Report: 1973* (Washington, DC: March 1979), p. 135. Similarly, using the less finely segmented 1991 R&D data reported in *Business Week*, June 29, 1992, p. 120, the correlation between R&D/sales ratios and sales for 26 computer industry companies with 1991 sales of $250 million or more was –0.087, which is not significantly different from zero. For a possible complication to this interpretation, see Wesley J. Cohen and Steven Klepper, "The Anatomy of Industry R&D Intensity Distributions," *American Economic Review*, vol. 82 (September 1992), pp. 773–799.

upon which modern computers are based. A random system "crash" when a company was processing its payroll could have dire consequences, so prompt repair service was essential. With thousands of its computers scattered throughout the United States, IBM could blanket the nation with service centers, from which a repair engineer could speed to the failure site. A firm maintaining only hundreds of computers faced a trade-off, especially in the less densely populated parts of the United States.[24] If it stationed a repair person, say, in Salt Lake City, its repair person was likely to be idle most of the time when the three or four of its computers in that area were functioning well. But if it centralized Mountain states repair staff in, say, Denver, its response time would be considerably longer than that of IBM, which could keep one or more Salt Lake City–based repair engineers busy nearly full time. Thus, with its extensive customer base, IBM could provide faster service, lower-cost service, or some preferred combination of the two.

What complicates this analysis is the fact that IBM "bundled" the price of repair service into the price of leasing or buying a computer. Thus, service was available to customers at an effective marginal price of zero. This situation made it difficult for independent computer service organizations to enter and survive, competing with IBM and others for service contracts. Had a viable independent computer service industry existed (as it did later for personal computers), the Salt Lake City branch might have serviced IBM computers, Burroughs computers, Honeywell computers, and others, although parts availability and the need for specialized training might have inhibited broad-line coverage. This arrangement would have reduced or eliminated the response time and cost disadvantage of smaller computer makers. Thus, the economies of scale IBM realized depended upon a specific pattern of service industry organization which in turn flowed at least in part from the bundled pricing strategy IBM chose.

The price advantages IBM enjoyed by virtue of software lock-in and other reputational factors plus the scale economies it tapped by virtue of its large market share permitted IBM to be much more profitable than its smaller mainframe computer rivals. DeLamarter estimated that between 1960 and 1972, IBM realized before-tax profits totaling $9.2 billion while eight rivals accumulated losses of nearly $1 billion.[25] Of the eight, only three, Honeywell, supercomputer maker Control Data, and minicomputer specialist Digital Equipment recorded substantial net profits from their computer operations. Because of persistent losses, many early entrants into the computer industry exited, usually by selling their computer operations to one of the survivors. Before that happened, however, they pursued diverse business strategies to gain an advantage, or at least to minimize their disadvantage vis à vis IBM. To those strategies we now turn.

---

[24]See Brock, *The U.S. Computer Industry*, pp. 33–37, who found maintenance economies to be second only to software cost-spreading economies as advantages IBM enjoyed relative to smaller rivals.

[25]*Big Blue*, p. 352.

THE LEAPFROG GAME

Among the companies manufacturing general-purpose business and scientific computers, a key dimension of rivalry was the introduction of new models, which, by incorporating the latest technological advances, offered performance substantially better than what one could achieve using earlier-generation machines. Typically, one company would lead off with a machine of advanced design, and others would soon respond with their own new models, often surpassing or "leapfrogging" the first mover's technology.[26] More often than not, IBM was not the first mover, but after overcoming the performance handicap it experienced for several years relative to UNIVAC during the mid–1950s, it was seldom far behind, and its new models frequently pushed out the technological frontier. Some illustrations will convey the flavor of the leapfrog dynamics.

Vacuum tubes were used by all manufacturers during the industry's early years because transistors had not yet become sufficiently reliable. After being overtaken by IBM, Sperry Rand attempted to come back by introducing its transistorized Solid State 80 computer in August 1958. In 1959, the 80 was modified to use punched cards identical to those adopted by IBM and to run software written for IBM's popular model 650. IBM responded with its transistorized model 7090 scientific computer in 1959 and, more directly against Sperry Rand's threat, with the highly successful transistorized model 1401 business computer in 1960. The 1401 provided better performance than the Solid State 80, and IBM retained its dominant market position.[27]

By the early 1960s, IBM computers had been adopted by so many users that compatibility with IBM software seemed essential if one sought to dislodge IBM's hold on the market. In July 1964, Honeywell began delivering its H–200 computer, which had four times as much memory as the IBM 1401 and memory access ten times as fast as with the 1401. Equally important, the H–200 came with an emulation program, appropriately named "the Liberator," which allowed H–200 users to run software written for the IBM 1401. In the six weeks following the H–200 announcement, Honeywell received 400 orders, many for 1401 replacements.[28] When IBM announced System 360 models leapfrogging the H–200, RCA sought to gain by introducing in 1965 its even more advanced Spectra–70 series, whose larger models were the first to incorporate monolithic integrated circuits. Like the H–200, the Spectra computers were designed to be compatible with IBM software. So closely to IBM standards did RCA conform that Spectra's operating manuals are said to have contained some of the same typographical errors as IBM's. But the Spectra

---

[26]Compare Tarun Khanna, "Technology Races, Spillovers, and Product Line Dynamics: Evidence from the High-End Computer Industry," working paper, Harvard Business School, November 1993; and Fisher et al., *Folded, Spindled, and Mutilated*, chap. 5.

[27]Brock, *The U.S. Computer Industry*, pp. 92–93.

[28]Ibid., pp. 93–94.

elicited only a weak market response, and when IBM introduced even more advanced System 370 designs in 1970, RCA concluded that the stakes were too high, selling its computer operations in 1971 to Sperry Rand.

Others chose to attack IBM not by offering compatibility at superior performance/price ratios, but by introducing unique new computer capabilities. General Electric was the first to market general-purpose computers with time-sharing capabilities—that is, computers on which multiple users could run their jobs simultaneously. The announcement of GE's time-sharing model 635 in 1964 induced IBM to develop its own time-sharing machines, but both companies encountered substantial technological difficulties. A more successful challenge came from Control Data Corporation (CDC), founded by expatriates from the strife-ridden Minneapolis branch of Sperry Rand. Control Data chose to focus its efforts on top-of-the-line scientific computers for sophisticated users able to write their own applications software. Its transistorized 1604 computer, introduced in 1960, was slightly slower but a good deal less expensive than the IBM 7090. A much more powerful computer, the CDC 6600, was introduced in 1964. It was judged to operate 15 times faster than the best alternative available at the time.[29]

Thus, by 1964, IBM was confronted with an array of threats to its dominant market position, some offering IBM compatibility with superior performance and others features IBM machines lacked. IBM had a further problem. Its 1401 and 7090 series used completely different and incompatible operating systems. As business and government organizations began to learn what they could do with computers, their demands expanded, and many sought to migrate upward from small (1401-family) computers to large (7090-type) machines. But their software had to be rewritten to make the change, and if the costs of change had to be borne, they might well switch to one of the high-performance machines offered by IBM's competitors. Something had to be done to address these multiple challenges.

IBM's System/360, whose broad concept was worked out in 1961, was the solution. As initially implemented, System 360 included five main models spanning a 25-fold range of processing performance capabilities.[30] Each was designed to be compatible with other members of the family, and through microcode emulators, each could run software written for both the 1401 and 7090 families. All had common interfaces into which add-on memory, disk and tape drives, and other peripherals could be connected. To achieve all this, a massive hardware and software development effort was required. As the project progressed, the competition from leapfrogging rivals became increas-

---

[29]See Brock, *The U.S. Computer Industry*, p. 96, citing Kenneth E. Knight, "Changes in Computer Performance," *Datamation*, vol. 12 (September 1966), pp. 40–54.

[30]Emerson W. Pugh, Lyle R. Johnson, and John H. Palmer, *IBM's 360 and Early 370 Systems* (Cambridge: MIT Press, 1991), pp. 635–640. The name "360" was chosen to indicate that the series covered the complete compass of data processing applications.

ingly intense, inducing IBM to announce the forthcoming availability of all the principal System/360 machines in April of 1964. Explaining this decision, IBM chairman Watson recalled:[31]

> Our original intent was to announce the first machines in April 1964 and gradually phase out the old product line by unveiling the rest over eighteen months. Unfortunately, we'd miscalculated how much time we had, and the flaws in our existing product line caught up with us a year or two sooner than we'd anticipated. By spring 1963 the old computers were obsolete. We did a technical study showing that while the 360s were going to be better than the latest computers from RCA, Burroughs, Honeywell, Univac, and General Electric, all those competitive machines were superior to our existing line. A number of them offered two to three times the performance of our computers for the same price. Our salesmen were hamstrung . . . they had nothing to tell customers. By the middle of 1963, sales offices were sending in panicky reports that they could no longer hold the line against the competition.

By announcing the full System/360 product spectrum at once, IBM convinced many customers to hold off ordering competitors' machines and wait until its new computers were available. This decision was enormously controversial both within IBM and outside, because some of the System/360 models had not yet been fully developed and tested, and numerous problems remained to be solved before they could be delivered. Although the first deliveries began in April 1965, serious programming and production problems were encountered, deliveries of some models slipped by a year, other models were canceled altogether, and the quality and performance of the early machines were below the standards IBM had set for itself.[32] Eventually, however, the problems were resolved, and System 360 turned out to be enormously successful. Among other things, it established a basic systems architecture that endured into the 1990s.

The original System 360 plan did not include a time-sharing computer. However, when General Electric announced its time-sharing model 635, designed in collaboration with Massachusetts Institute of Technology engineers, IBM hastened to announce in August 1964 that a time-sharing 360/67 model would be added to the 360 family. At the time many basic time-sharing problems remained unsolved, provoking an IBM staff member to complain within the company that the product would be "completely unserviceable in any manner that will result in customer satisfaction."[33] The 360/67 in fact fell considerably short of its goals, and some problems remained unresolved even

---

[31]*Father, Son & Co.*, p. 374.

[32]Ibid., pp. 375–384. Compare Fisher et al., *Folded, Spindled, and Mutilated,* pp. 290–296; and DeLamarter, *Big Blue*, pp. 54–66.

[33]DeLamarter, *Big Blue*, p. 93. Compare Fisher et al., *Folded, Spindled and Mutilated*, pp. 284–288, who insist that customers understood "the developmental nature of the program."

after System 370 improvements were introduced in 1970. General Electric's time-sharing effort was also problem-ridden, and when it became clear that massive investments would be required to match the IBM System 370 models, General Electric withdrew from the general-purpose computer business.

IBM's management was jolted even more severely by the announcement in August 1963 of Control Data Corporation's powerful model 6600, developed by a team that included only 16 engineers and programmers. Recalling that he was "furious" because IBM had nothing even remotely comparable in its product plan, IBM head Thomas Watson Jr. ordered the development of a counterpart:[34]

> Even though our engineering staff was overloaded, we tried to catch up with Control Data, and at the System/360 unveiling the following April, we said we would bring out a supercomputer at the top of the line that would leapfrog Control Data's machine. Control Data hadn't yet delivered its first 6600, and the effect of this announcement was to put a chill on its market: suddenly it became hard for their salesmen to close deals.

IBM's attempt to recoup was unsuccessful. Its System 360/91 was inferior to the 6600 in performance. Only 11 units were sold (compared to nearly 100 CDC 6600 and 6700 units), and it sustained large financial losses on the effort.[35] After being outgunned and outsold by CDC, IBM withdrew and ceded supercomputer leadership to Control Data.[36] Nevertheless, CDC filed an antitrust complaint against IBM's 360/91 marketing tactics. In January 1973, the case was settled out of court when IBM paid CDC $101 million and sold to CDC at book value its applications software subsidiary, the Service Bureau Corporation.

By the early 1970s, these events had transformed the computer industry's structure. Many early entrants had withdrawn or sold off their operations. IBM continued to dominate in general-purpose computers, with a market share variously estimated between 65 and 80 percent. Surviving "mainframe" rivals—notably, Sperry Rand, Burroughs, Honeywell, NCR, and Control Data—cultivated niches in the market through unique performance features

---

[34]*Father, Son & Co.*, p. 409.

[35]See Russell W. Pittman, "Predatory Investment: U.S. vs. IBM," *International Journal of Industrial Organization*, vol. 2 (December 1984), pp. 341–366; and Fisher et al., *Folded, Spindled, and Mutilated*, p. 278.

[36]Control Data in turn lost supercomputer leadership when the head of its development team, Seymour Cray, left to create his own company, Cray Research, in 1976. In 1989 Seymour Cray founded still another firm, Cray Computer, to develop a supercomputer using gallium arsenide integrated circuits. See "The Genius," *Business Week*, April 30, 1991, pp. 81–88. Cray Computer declared bankruptcy in 1995 before it had sold any computers.

or software lock-in, rather than attacking IBM head-to-head by offering compatible operating systems. In 1971 IBM began a major effort to consider what would come next. A radically different architecture was proposed by its FS (Future System) task force. But three and one half years later the project was terminated and a decision was made to continue the basic System 360 architecture in subsequent models through evolutionary improvements. To depart from what had become the industry standard was viewed as too risky, not only because of technical hurdles, but because customers satisfied with the existing 360 standards might defect to rivals who once again began stressing compatibility.[37]

INNOVATION AND THE "FAST SECOND" STRATEGY

There is a deeper economic rationale in the computer industry's technology leapfrogging history from the late 1950s onward. Companies that dominate their market often have weak incentives to take the lead in introducing technological innovations. In part, resistance to change comes from the natural propensity to stick with what has succeeded in pleasing existing customers.[38] But there are also more distinctly economic barriers to change, bolstered in computers by the widespread leasing, rather than outright sale, of mainframe computer hardware. When a new and superior machine was introduced, it cannibalized already existing lease base revenues, inducing customers to tender the required 30 days' notice, roll out the older machines, cease paying for them, and install the new variant. IBM was exquisitely sensitive to the lease base erosion problem. It tried to strike an optimal compromise between protecting existing lease base revenues on the one hand vs. remaining abreast of competitive technologies. Thus, when the Honeywell H–200 threatened, managers responsible for the IBM 1401 resisted moving to the new System 360 concept and proposed instead an upgraded version of the 1401. They were rebuffed in July 1963 by their group head:[39]

> The [System 360 Model 30] must be engineered and planned to impact solidly the 1401.... I know your reluctance to do this, but corporate policy is that you do it. It is obvious that in 1967 the 1401 will be as dead as a Dodo. Let's stop fighting this.

---

[37]Pugh et al., *IBM's 360*, pp. 538–551 and 633. See also DeLamarter, *Big Blue*, pp. 215–216.

[38]See Clayton M. Christensen, "Differences in the Innovative Behavior of Established and Entrant Firms," working paper, Harvard Business School, April 1992.

[39]Fisher et al., *Folded, Spindled, and Mutilated*, p. 135.

FIGURE 7.2
Brock's Analysis of IBM's Innovation Incentive

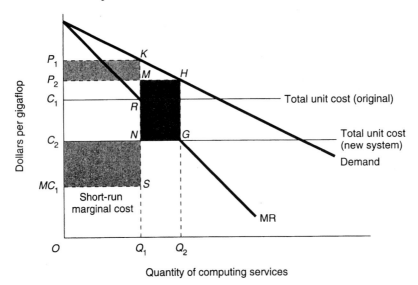

Source: Adapted from a mathematical model in Gerald W. Brock, *The U.S. Computer Industry* (Cambridge: Ballinger, 1975), pp. 211–215.

The drag an established lease base imposes upon incentives to innovate is illustrated in Figure 7.2, which adapts the approach of Gerald Brock.[40] The analysis begins with the demand for a particular class of computer services (measured in billions of floating-point operations, or gigaflops), for which the associated marginal revenue curve *MR* has been constructed. The existing generation of computers was installed at a long-run marginal cost of OC_1 per gigaflop. Given that marginal cost, a firm that dominates the market maximizes profits by installing computers sufficient to provide OQ_1 gigaflops of service at a price of OP_1. Once the machines have been installed, their manufacturing cost is sunk, and so the only costs that continue are the short-run marginal costs MC_1S associated with servicing the machines.[41] Now suppose a new generation, with long-run marginal cost of OC_2, becomes technically feasible. If it is introduced, the new profit-maximizing output will be OQ_2 and the price OP_2. The profits attributable to the expansion of output are measured by darkly shaded rectangle *MHGN*. Before introducing the new generation but after installing the old, the dominant firm was securing revenues in

---

[40]*The U.S. Computer Industry*, pp. 211–215.

[41]Brock assumes that all costs are sunk once old machines have been put in place.

excess of nonsunk costs equal to rectangle P_1KSMC_1. Of this, P_2MNC_2 is also realized as profit on the new machine, so that rectangle reflects neither gain nor loss to the incumbent. But by scrapping the old machines, which are assumed to have no salvage value, the dominant firm loses the surplus of new unit cost over old marginal cost (lightly shaded rectangle) C_2NSMC_1. In addition, by reducing its price to sell more computer services, it sacrifices lightly shaded profit rectangle P_1KMP_2. Thus, the dominant firm's gain from innovation is given by the darkly shaded rectangle *minus* the two lightly shaded rectangles. For an outsider with no established lease base, on the other hand, the profit gain from capturing the market with new machines is the surplus of price over full cost on *all* units—that is, rectangle P_2HGC_2. If the outsider can capture the whole market, its profit from innovation exceeds the dominant incumbent's profit, reduced as it must be by the loss from forgoing high prices on existing machines and the quasi rents it was realizing already due to the low nonsunk costs of existing machines. Even if it captures only a fraction—say, half—of the relevant market, the outsider is likely to anticipate higher incremental profits from innovation than will the incumbent. For the incumbent, any profit gain (before deduction of cannibalized surpluses) comes entirely from expanding the market. The more price-elastic demand is, the greater that gain will be. Thus, as Brock shows, dominant incumbents will have relatively strong incentives to innovate compared to outsiders when the elasticity of computer demand is high, and relatively weak incentives when the price elasticity is low (but above unity).

To be sure, if the incumbent lets outsiders capture the market it currently controls, it can no longer count rectangle P_1KSMC_1 as surplus it would enjoy even without innovating. Thus, once rival inroads are imminent, the whole new-generation profit P_2HGC_2 is at risk. An asymmetry exists. Before a rival threat materializes, the incumbent's incentive to innovate is attenuated by the potential loss of existing lease base surpluses, but after the rival threatens, the incumbent has at least as much to lose as the rivals have to gain. Thus, dominant incumbents have weak incentives to *beat* rivals to the market with an innovation, but they have strong incentives to *tie* them if by innovating simultaneously they can retain their existing customers and also win the sales from market expansion. Or more realistically, by announcing a new product in advance of actual deliveries, as IBM repeatedly did, the dominant incumbent can retain its existing customers even if it lags rivals slightly in product deliveries. Thus, it can play a "fast second" strategy and still retain its dominance.[42]

This fast second phenomenon exists even when old and new products are sold, rather than leased. Suppose the total amount of profit to be gained from

---

[42]The fast second strategy was named by W. L. Baldwin and G. L. Childs, "The Fast Second and Rivalry in Research and Development," *Southern Economic Journal*, vol. 36 (July 1969), pp. 18–24, who observe that by being second, the incumbent may also save R&D costs by learning from the first mover's errors.

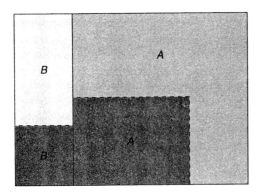

FIGURE 7.3
Profits Gained by Large and Small Innovators Through Technological Leadership

a new product is given by the rectangular area portrayed in Figure 7.3. How that profit is divided up depends upon the timing of innovation by firms Alpha and Beta and the incumbency advantages (e.g., software lock-in and long-standing relationships) each enjoys. Alpha is assumed to be dominant in related existing product lines; Beta is either a fringe rival or newcomer. If Alpha and Beta reach the market simultaneously with their new products, Alpha will win 75 percent of the sales and profits (i.e., areas *A* plus *A'*) by virtue of its established customer relationships, while Beta gains 25 percent (*B* plus *B'*). Now suppose that by leading its rival into the market by a year, either firm can capture one-third of the profits that would go to its rival in a tie situation. Thus, Alpha can capture darkly shaded *B'* from Beta by being first, while Beta can capture *A'* from Alpha by being first. Clearly, the gain from jumping out in front is less for dominant incumbent Alpha than for outsider Beta. Again, Beta has stronger incentives to lead the race in an attempt to capture *A'*, but Alpha will try to prevent such capture by pursuing a fast second strategy.

There is substantial evidence that IBM in fact tended to favor fast second strategies rather than forcing the pace of innovation. The qualitative illustrations offered previously support that inference. So also do quantitative tabulations of innovations. Thus, of 20 major computer industry innovations identified by Brock, IBM was the first mover on 29 percent (dividing ties fractionally among the contending companies).[43] On Kenneth Flamm's master list of "principal developments in computer technology," IBM accounted for seven innovations, other private sector companies nine, and universities and other nonprofit laboratories three.[44] On three more comprehensive innovation tabulations by Flamm, IBM's position was as follows:

---

[43]Brock, *The U.S. Computer Industry*, p. 204. One innovation contributed solely by a university group is excluded.

[44]*Creating the Computer*, pp. 260–261.

	IBM	Other Firms	Nonprofits
Computer hardware	10.5	11.5	9.0
Memory technology	12	5	3
Computer software	8	19	20

IBM's share of innovations was commensurate with its share of the computer market only in memory technology; in other realms it fell short. There is a likely economic explanation for its superior performance in memories. Business firms' demand for computers is probably much more sensitive to the ease of storing and retrieving masses of information—that is, to developments in memory technology—than to central processor speed and other advances in raw processing power. If sensitivity can be equated with the price elasticity of demand, this result is consistent with Brock's theory, which implies stronger innovative incentives for dominant incumbents when demand is highly price-elastic.[45]

IBM'S PRICING STRATEGY

As dominant seller during the computer industry's early decades, IBM was the price leader. Its pricing strategies were much more complex than any we have considered thus far.

At first the business firms that bought (or more often, leased) computers knew very little about the machines and what they could do, and therefore the business demand for computers was ill defined. IBM too had to grope its way to a policy. As a financial executive recalled:[46]

> We priced the 702 in error at $30,000 . . . expecting only 6 takers. We obtained 60 orders. This unplanned price (or value) test was useful, if embarrassing. It demonstrated that large users were willing to experiment with a potential escape from the unit record bind without assurance of cost displacement.
>
> We then withdrew the 702 and substituted the (only slightly modified) 705 at $45,000, *and retained most of our original takers*. This apparent absence of price elasticity led us to high functional pricing of improvements (such as expanded memories and faster tapes).

Before that time, IBM had priced its punched card machines on the basis of what it called *displaceable cost*—that is, the amount of data-processing cost

---

[45]There is reason to believe that IBM was also especially strong in printer technology—a field ignored by Brock and Flamm, but one quite important to business users. See Dorfman, *Innovation and Market Structure*, pp. 124–133.

[46]Memorandum by Hillary Faw to Frank Cary (later IBM chairman), December 10, 1971, p. 6 (emphasis in original), quoted in DeLamarter, *Big Blue*, p. 143.

FIGURE 7.4
Interdependent Pricing of Computers and Peripheral Equipment

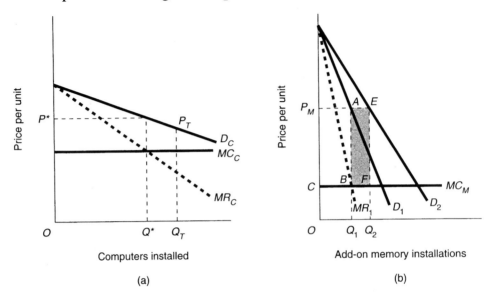

Computers installed

(a)

Add-on memory installations

(b)

saved by a new machine, with no particular relationship to the cost of providing the machine. It attempted to apply the concept to computers, but found that early users were willing to pay even more than displaceable cost to alleviate overwhelming paper (or card) processing burdens and, later, because it was prestigious to have computerized operations. From its pricing experiences a "new value (price) system had become established arbitrarily and artfully by IBM."[47] Later, more advanced, computers provided substantial savings over their predecessors, but prices remained more closely linked to the established value structure than to the costs of providing the new machines.

IBM's pricing strategy also recognized another important propensity. New computer customers systematically underestimated the extent to which their perceived needs would grow, and therefore the amount of rapid-access and long-term memory capacity they would eventually demand. But after the most eager customers adopted computers, the still untapped masses of potential computer users were quite sensitive to initial computer costs. IBM therefore saw to it that "bare-bones" machines were available at highly attractive prices. Once users were "hooked," they migrated upward to more elaborate installations whose additional capacity bore much higher price/cost margins. This was in effect a form of "tying." The bare-bones computer was the "tying" good; once it was installed, many computer users then leased or purchased additional quantities of memory—i.e., the "tied good." A simple case is illustrated in Figure 7.4. The relatively elastic demand function for

---

[47]Ibid., p. 143.

entry-level computers D_C and its related marginal revenue function MR_C are shown in Figure 7.4a. The monopoly profit-maximizing quantity of computers installed is OQ^* at price OP^*. With that price and quantity combination, IBM experienced relatively inelastic add-on memory demand, shown in Figure 7.4b, of D_1 and the corresponding marginal revenue MR_1. Profits on the tied good were maximized by setting the price OP_M, yielding a large surplus of revenues over production costs $P_M ABC$. If demand for the tied good increases (shifts to the right) as more bare-bones computers are installed, there is likely also to be an incentive to reduce the computer price below its myopic profit-maximizing level OP^* down to OP_T. This price reduction leads to additional computer installations, which shifts the demand for add-on memory from D_1 to D_2. Some profit is sacrificed on computer installations, but with the proper pricing choice, it is more than compensated by the extra profit $AEFB$ (shaded area) gained from additional memory installations. Using data subpoenaed from a government antitrust case, DeLamarter shows that profit margins on the 1401 and 360 systems rose dramatically with the amount of memory supplied.[48]

IBM also had to determine how computer leasing prices would relate to outright equipment sale prices. Under the rule of thumb it appears to have applied over its first two computer generations, the sales price of a computer equaled the revenue accumulated over approximately 52 months of leasing, which led most customers to favor leasing rather than purchasing. But its finances were strained by the enormous investments required to introduce System 360, so in September 1966 it implemented what came to be called the "3-by–3 tilt," reducing purchase prices by 3 percent and raising lease charges by 3 percent. As anticipated, there was a large movement toward purchasing, which brought in the desired cash. More surprising was the impetus the change gave to companies that purchased IBM computers and then leased them to users at rates more favorable than those quoted by IBM. When the tilt was effected, the leasing companies had a total computer inventory of $275 million. By the end of 1968, their inventory position had soared to $1.9 billion.[49] When IBM reversed the tilt on later 360 models and new System 370 models, leasing firms' profits were reduced, and their stock prices plummeted. A round of private antitrust cases followed.[50]

The leasing companies changed the character of computer industry competition in complex ways.[51] For one, they depreciated their machines over relatively long periods—for example, ten years, as compared to roughly five years for IBM. This meant that they were likely to be offering System 360

---

[48]*Big Blue*, pp. 49–52 and 77–80.

[49]Pretrial brief of the government in *U.S.* v. International Business Machines Corp., October 1974, p. 325.

[50]Brock, *The U.S. Computer Industry*, pp. 178–179; and *Greyhound Computer Corp.* v. *IBM*, 559 F. 2d 488 (1977).

[51]Compare DeLamarter, *Big Blue*, pp. 106–108 and 153–158; and Fisher et al., *Folded, Spindled, and Mutilated*, pp. 299–307.

model leases, perhaps at bargain prices, when improved System 370 models were introduced, thereby increasing the competitive pressure on System 370. Also, with large inventories at stake, they were unusually sophisticated computer buyers, sensitive to any opportunities to save money by substituting other firms' equipment for IBM's.

Their sensitivity to substitution possibilities interacted with the general pricing structure IBM had adopted and the common interface System 360 models provided for peripheral equipment. The high prices set for add-on memory, magnetic disk storage drives, and other "tied" goods were an inducement to competitive arbitrage. The top-to-bottom "plug compatibility" of System 360 models meant that competitors could develop substitute tape drives, disk drives, and add-on memory boxes of a standardized design, sell or lease them at prices well below IBM's price while still making a profit, and in effect plug them into the IBM machines. Compatibility was achieved by "reverse engineering" IBM's basic peripheral equipment designs and implementing characteristically modest performance improvements.[52] The large computer inventory in the hands of cost-conscious leasing companies constituted a market eager for such products, augmenting the demand of other sophisticated computer owners. The three phenomena together led during the late 1960s to the rapid growth of a new "PCM" (plug-compatible manufacturers) industry, including such companies as Potter Instrument, Telex, Memorex, California Computer Products, and Storage Technology.

IBM's management was distressed about this new competition, which in 1970 had captured 4 percent of IBM's disk storage base and 11 percent of its tape drive base, and was expected to grow rapidly unless countered.[53] At the time, disk and tape drives accounted for approximately 30 percent of the value of total IBM computer systems installations.[54] IBM commissioned detailed studies of the PCMs, examining their products, their stated goals, their likely unit costs, their financial structure, and points of vulnerability to competitive actions IBM might undertake. On the basis of these studies, IBM initiated a series of measures to counter the PCMs' threat to its enormous System 360 peripherals lease base and the placement of peripherals for the improved System 370, on which deliveries began in 1970.[55] We illustrate by focusing on disk drives. The actions taken with respect to tape drives were similar.

---

[52]Because the basic design parameters were set by IBM, which had achieved particularly important innovations in magnetic disk memory technology, the reverse-engineering peripheral manufacturers were viewed by IBM management as "parasites." See Watson, *Father, Son & Co.*, p. 405. The growth of PCMs was facilitated in part by personnel defections from IBM's San Jose development laboratories. See Pugh et al., *IBM's 360*, pp. 490–494 and 499.

[53]Brock, *The U.S. Computer Industry*, p. 113.

[54]Flamm, *Targeting the Computer*, p. 220.

[55]For various views, see Brock, *The U.S. Computer Industry*, chap. 8; DeLamarter, *Big Blue*, pp. 128–133 and 161–198; and Fisher et al., *Folded, Spindled, and Mutilated*, pp. 310–332.

The principal IBM disk drive units used with System 360 in 1970 were the 2311, first leased in 1964, and the much higher-capacity 2314, introduced in 1965. PCMs targeted their efforts mainly toward the newer 2314. To deter them, IBM introduced in December 1970 a new model, the 2319-B. It was manufactured by disassembling 2314 units returned to IBM by customers and repackaging them in new boxes with slightly modified electronics. The announced monthly rental price for three 2319-B spindles was $1000, compared to $1455 for three identically performing 2314 spindles. Price-sensitive customers who threatened to defect to less-expensive PCM disk drives were encouraged by IBM sales representatives to terminate their 2314 lease, wheel out the old drives, and install 2319-Bs. Less aggressive customers retained their 2314s and paid the higher lease rate. This strategy was in effect a subtle form of price discrimination that segregated customers according to their willingness to embrace competitive substitutes.

A somewhat more complex price discrimination scheme was adopted in 1970 for System 370 customers. Because new higher-performance disk drives were not expected to be available for small and intermediate 370 systems until 1973, 2314 drives had to fill the gap. But they were vulnerable to PCM competition. Price-sensitive customers could have IBM install an "integrated file adapter" (IFA) for $555 per month, replacing the controller (still available at $1420 per month) used to supervise the operation of 2314 drives. Unlike the separately packaged 2314 controller, the IFA was incompatible with PCM disk drive designs and was buried within the 370 computer central processor unit, where it was inaccessible to PCMs. To the new 2314-incompatible IFA, System 370 users could attach 2319-A drives, three of which were leased at $1000 per month, repackaged and rewired from returned 2314 drives, whose lease rate remained at $1455 per month. Customers who preferred to seize the price savings offered by PCMs had to pay IBM for the special controller that ran them; those who remained with IBM 2314s paid a double premium.

The PCMs reduced their prices in response to IBM's actions and continued to win new installations, albeit at lower profit rates. After continuing internal strategy debates, IBM announced in May 1971 a new program, the Fixed Term Plan, to hinder PCM expansion further. Up to that time, IBM lease contracts permitted cancellation on 30 days notice. This option was retained, but disk and tape drive customers who agreed to a one-year lease with substantial early cancellation penalties were given an 8 percent discount relative to the monthly rental rate, and those who accepted a two-year lease were accorded a 16 percent discount. Longer-term leases were new only for IBM; they were an accepted feature of PCMs' marketing strategy. But in adopting the Fixed Term Plan, IBM had more in mind than merely matching the practices of its rivals. Because the technology of disk storage was advancing rapidly, a particular model was likely to remain economically viable for somewhere between three and seven years. If IBM could lock the PCMs out through fixed-term leases during the first two years of a new disk drive model's life cycle, the PCMs had to anticipate shorter effective new model lives than IBM—for example, three years rather than five years for a unit expected to be in service for five years. With shorter effective unit lives, the

PCMs would have less revenue and hence less profit. As an IBM staff member wrote on a flip chart evaluating for his superiors the consequences of the Fixed Term Plan:[56]

PCM corporate revenues lower—no funds for mfg., eng.—dying company!

In the two days of trading after the Fixed Term Plan was announced, the common stock prices of PCM manufacturers fell by between 10 and 18 percent.[57] Further declines followed in the ensuing month.

IBM's internal analyses of possible reactions to the competition from PCMs continued under a program code-named, appropriately enough, SMASH. From SMASH came a set of interface and price changes similar to those implemented in 1970 for the 2319-A, but in this case targeted toward IBM's more advanced 3330 disk drive, introduced in 1970 for use with System 370. The original 3330 controller was packaged in a single box leased at $2400 per month. Under the SMASH attachment strategy, part of the reconfigured controller could be buried within the computer's central processor unit, where it was inaccessible to PCMs and where, with minor coding changes, the compatibility of PCM devices could be impaired. Controllers modified in this way were leased at lower rental rates—for example, between $700 and $2200, depending upon capacity—than stand-alone 3330 controllers.

The 2319 and SMASH pricing actions sacrificed IBM revenues in the short run, but by retarding the competitive inroads of PCMs, probably enhanced long-run sales and profits. However, as lower profit margins were accepted on disk drives, add-on memory, and other devices whose acquisition was tied to the choice of an IBM mainframe, the incentive for holding mainframe prices below the profit-maximizing level (i.e., at P_T rather than P^* in Figure 7.4a) to increase peripheral equipment installations was weakened. Two months after the Fixed Term Plan was implemented, IBM announced in July 1971 price *increases* on its System 360 and 370 central processor units (CPUs) that roughly offset expected Fixed Term Plan revenue losses.[58] From internal staff analyses carried out at the time, it would appear that IBM recognized that sustaining its overall profitability required raising price/cost margins on less vulnerable parts of the computer system. The best locus for such price increases appeared to be the CPU, to which large numbers of customers were now locked as a result of software and training investments.

---

[56]Brock, *The U.S. Computer Industry*, p. 121; and DeLamarter, *Big Blue*, p. 185. Although some did die, others struggled on, helped inter alia by mergers with mainframe computer makers, and new entry by domestic and Japanese firms occurred. See "EMC Shows Faster Data Storage System," *New York Times*, November 11, 1992, p. C3; and "The Midgets, the Mammoth, and the Mainframes," *Business Week*, June 7, 1993, p. 31.

[57]Brock, p. 122.

[58]Brock, *The U.S. Computer Industry*, pp. 123–124; and DeLamarter, *Big Blue*, pp. 186 and 208. Compare the strained rationalization in Fisher et al., *Folded, Spindled and Mutilated*, pp. 328–331.

Here too, however, IBM may have overstepped. The higher profits on CPUs made them an attractive target for rivals developing compatible CPUs—that is, processors with operating systems functionally identical to the IBM System 360 and 370 standards. The first significant rival to exploit this opportunity was the Amdahl Corporation, founded by Gene M. Amdahl, principal architect of IBM's System 360, who left IBM in 1970 to establish his own company.[59] In 1975 Amdahl Corporation introduced the Amdahl 470, featuring a CPU fully compatible with IBM's top-of-the-line System 370/168 processor, but operating 2.5 times faster and priced 8 to 12 percent lower. The Amdahl machine achieved higher performance through an innovative CPU design incorporating densely packed integrated circuits mounted on ceramic boards cooled by gold-plated fins. Through denser chip packing, internal data travel distances were minimized, thereby speeding information flow. The gold-plated cooling apparatus facilitated dense packing and eliminated the need for costly internal air-conditioning systems. To finance the $45 million of estimated development costs, Amdahl sold 41 percent of its common stock to Fujitsu of Japan. By 1978, several other companies had followed Amdahl's lead and challenged IBM with their own compatible CPUs.[60]

Experiencing new competition when it tried to sustain high prices on peripheral equipment and again when it raised its CPU prices, IBM tried still another strategy. In March 1977 it introduced a new and more powerful 3033 CPU offering higher performance at a lower price. Soon thereafter it reduced prices by 20 to 35 percent on its high-end System 370 CPUs and add-on memory boxes and by 15 percent on disk drives.[61] In 1979 it introduced a new 4300 line of small and intermediate computers, again pricing them extraordinarily aggressively compared to past precedents.[62] The internal analyses that underlay these changes are not available, since, unlike earlier IBM actions, they were not the object of antitrust litigation and document discovery. However, it seems reasonable to infer that, having learned that each segment of its computer business would induce competitive entry if prices were set too high, it adopted something closer to an across-the-board limit pricing strategy.

---

[59]See "A Tyro Challenges IBM in Big Computers," *Business Week*, May 12, 1975, pp. 65–67; and "Gene Amdahl Takes Aim at I.B.M.," *Fortune*, September 1977, pp. 106–120. Memorex was developing an IBM-compatible CPU during the early 1970s, but cash flow crises resulting from IBM's disk drive actions caused it to discontinue the effort.

[60]"The New Wave of Change Challenging IBM," *Business Week*, May 29, 1978, pp. 92–99.

[61]See "I.B.M. Foresees Benefits from Price Cuts," *New York Times*, April 26, 1977, p. 51; and "More Tumult for the Computer Industry," *Business Week*, May 30, 1977, pp. 58–66.

[62]"IBM Shocks the Plug-Compatibles," *Business Week*, June 18, 1979, p. 107. On later events, see "Why IBM Reversed Itself on Computer Pricing," *Business Week*, January 28, 1980, p. 84; and "IBM's Mimics Struggle to Keep Pace," *Business Week*, September 20, 1982, pp. 93–96.

ANTITRUST CHALLENGES

The aggressive product announcement and pricing practices of IBM drew a series of antitrust challenges from impacted rivals and the federal government during the late 1960s and early 1970s.

The first, as we have seen, came in December 1968 when Control Data Corporation charged that IBM's System 360/91 announcement was made without any basis in an effectively functioning machine, but which deflected orders from potential CDC customers who believed that such a machine was forthcoming. IBM settled with CDC on terms highly favorable to the latter.

IBM's pricing and interface actions with respect to plug-compatible manufacturers and leasing companies led to numerous antitrust actions, some litigated bitterly to final court decisions.[63] In all but one leasing company action, IBM was the ultimate winner. Whether these outcomes resulted because the facts and the logic of antitrust law favored IBM, or because of IBM's vastly superior legal resources, continues to be debated.

It is clear that IBM studied the operations of the PCMs, identified their points of vulnerability, and implemented strategies skillfully structured to threaten (and in some cases end) their survival. What *should* a dominant firm do when its business is challenged by new entrants? Plainly, it would not be good policy to have it remain passive, as the United States Steel Corporation did, holding a pricing umbrella over its rivals and watching its market share erode. IBM's behavior was closer to that of Standard Oil, keeping prices high when it could do so and reacting to entry with strategic price cuts. However, its "fighting brands" were offered under the IBM logo rather than under some pseudonym, and it did not acquire the assets of competitors against which it had directed its aggression. The *Standard Oil* case left unsettled in 1911 just how vigorously a market leader could retaliate against usurpers before its behavior was deemed "predatory." Nor did subsequent antitrust cases provide undisputed guidance. The advice antitrust experts offered was as schizophrenic as Tom Lehrer's football anthem, "Fight Fiercely, Harvard":

Let's try not to injure them,
But fight, fight, fight!
(Let's not be rough, though.)
Fight, fight, fight!

One school of thought stressed the relationship of prices to costs. Predation should not be inferred, Areeda and Turner argued, unless prices were set below marginal costs, or given the difficulty of measuring marginal cost in a

---

[63]Telex Corp. v. IBM, 367 F. Supp. 258 (1973), reversed at 510 F. 2d 894 (1975); California Computer Products v. IBM, 613 F. 2d 727 (1979); Memorex Corp. et al. v. IBM, 636 F. 2d 1188 (1980); Transamerica Computer Co. v. IBM, 698 F. 2d 1377 (1983); and Greyhound Computer Corp. v. IBM, 559 F. 2d 488 (1977).

litigation, average variable costs.[64] For the IBM peripherals cases, this was a generous standard indeed, since before plug-compatible competition materialized, the cost of actually producing the disk and tape drives in question was only about 20 percent of their sales price. By this criterion, IBM did not predate except in some anomalous and relatively unimportant instances.

Another school stressed the alleged predator's intent and the consequences of its actions for the future character of competition in the affected markets.[65] IBM's intent was clearly enough to undermine the profitability of its rivals, to halt their expansion, and arguably to create in the minds of new would-be competitors the fear that a similar fate would befall them if they entered. If it succeeded in deterring future entry, a force compelling IBM to reduce its prices and to speed the introduction of advanced technology would be eliminated, and computer users could be the losers.

Figure 7.5 illustrates the economic logic of the Areeda-Turner marginal cost rule.[66] Figure 7.5a reviews the conventional profit maximization calculus of a monopoly with demand curve D and (constant) marginal cost function MC. The short-run profit-maximizing price is OP_M. At that price, the dead-weight welfare loss is given by the area of triangle MCL. If the monopolist reduces its price to deter or repel entry, the dead-weight loss shrinks until, at the competitive equilibrium point C, it goes to zero. Price reductions *below* marginal cost and corresponding output increases lead to renewed dead-weight welfare losses—for example, if the price is forced to point G on the demand function, to a loss measured by triangle CHG. As shown in Figure 7.5b, these relationships are translated to a new kind of diagram, with the total dead-weight welfare loss measured on the vertical axis and with price *declining* as the monopolist moves to the right on the horizontal axis. The welfare losses, measured as areas in Figure 7.5a, are graphed in Figure 7.5b by the parabolic function $W(P)$, whose minimum value occurs, as in Figure 7.5a, at the competitive (marginal cost) price P_C. Clearly, as Areeda and Turner argued, price reductions down to marginal cost are welfare-enhancing, but cuts below marginal cost cause renewed dead-weight losses, the more so with deeper cuts.

---

[64]Phillip Areeda and Donald F. Turner, "Predatory Pricing and Related Practices under Section 2 of the Sherman Act," *Harvard Law Review*, vol. 88 (February 1975), pp. 697–733.

[65]See, for example, F. M. Scherer, "Predatory Pricing and the Sherman Act: A Comment," *Harvard Law Review*, vol. 89 (March 1976), pp. 869–890 and 901–903. Significant extensions include Oliver E. Williamson, "Predatory Pricing: A Strategic and Welfare Analysis," *Yale Law Journal*, vol. 87 (December 1977), pp. 284–340; William J. Baumol, "Quasi-Permanence of Price Reductions: A Policy for Preventing Predatory Pricing," *Yale Law Journal*, vol. 89 (November 1979), pp. 1–26; and Paul L. Joskow and Alvin K. Klevorick, "A Framework for Analyzing Predatory Pricing Policy," *Yale Law Journal*, vol. 89 (December 1979), pp. 213–270.

[66]It is drawn from Scherer, "Predatory Pricing," pp. 883–889.

FIGURE 7.5
Short-run Welfare Consequences of Price-Cutting by a Monopolist

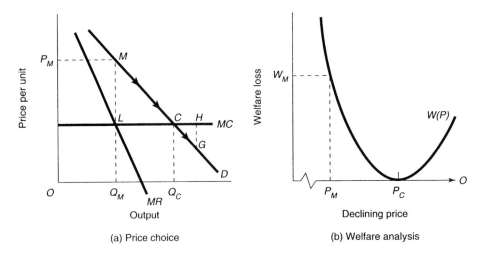

(a) Price choice

(b) Welfare analysis

FIGURE 7.6
Long-run Welfare Consequences of Predation by a Monopolist

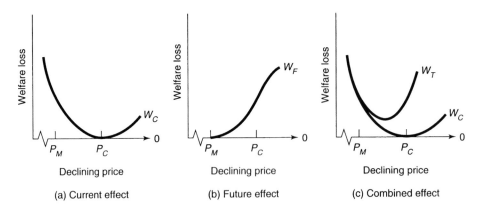

(a) Current effect

(b) Future effect

(c) Combined effect

However, this analysis takes into account only the short-run effects. If by cutting price today the monopolist can exclude competitors and therefore charge above-cost prices in the future, a richer analysis, presented in Figure 7.6, is required. Curve W_C (for current welfare loss) in Figure 7.6a replicates $W(P)$ in Figure 7.5b. The future welfare loss function W_F in Figure 7.6b assumes that the deeper today's price cuts are, the more future competition will be excluded, and hence the greater will be the discounted present value of future dead-weight losses as a larger wedge is sustained between prices and marginal costs. To evaluate the total welfare effect W_T of exclusionary price cutting, the curves in Figure 7.6a and b must be summed vertically, as in Figure 7.6c. There we see that the total welfare-loss-minimizing price is below the short-run monopoly-profit-maximizing price but above marginal cost. To the extent that these assumptions hold, the Areeda-Turner rule is too weak. On the other hand, if sharp price-cutting drove out inefficient fringe firms and thus reduced future production costs, the curve in Figure 7.6b might over some range be downward-sloping, in which case temporary price-cutting below marginal cost could maximize long-run welfare.

Crucial to the conclusion implied by Figure 7.6 is the assumption that IBM's price-cutting and other responses to competitive entry challenges succeeded in deterring would-be entrants. But was this true? And how could its truth be demonstrated in an antitrust proceeding? The author's own view as a participant (against IBM) in two antitrust cases was that IBM hoped to succeed but, in the end, failed. Technological change was so irrepressible that it continually opened up new opportunities for profiting from IBM's oversights and excesses, and there was no shortage of newcomers willing to ignore history and try their luck against the giant. As a result, computer users were well served. But this begs the more difficult question: Was the continuing stream of new entry inevitable, given IBM's strategies? And should the law accord the benefit of the doubt on the side of discouraging actions that intimidate would-be entrants?

On January 17, 1969, during the closing hours of the Lyndon Johnson presidency, the U.S. Department of Justice filed an antitrust complaint charging IBM with monopolizing general-purpose computer systems markets and asking unspecified structural reorganization. Incoming President Nixon referred to his Council of Economic Advisers the question of whether the government should pursue the case. The CEA recommended in favor, and a litigation of unprecedented ferocity and cost followed. Although the complaint was later amended to include actions taken by IBM against PCMs during the early 1970s, the case focused mainly on IBM's position in variously defined computer systems markets, the tactics by which it had ascended to market leadership, and its conduct in introducing System 360. Defining the market narrowly, the government claimed that IBM held a monopoly position—that is, under prior legal precedents, more than 65 percent of all installed general-purpose computers by value. Defining the market broadly to include military computers, peripherals, software services, and much else, IBM claimed a market share of 32 percent—too small for monopolization. Although it was proud to proclaim its superior profitability on Wall Street, IBM insisted in court that its profits did not reflect monopoly power. Allegations of abusive conduct were contested vigorously; for example, interface changes that made connection difficult for PCMs were arguably chosen to improve technical performance, not to inhibit competitive entry. And above all, IBM insisted that its technological performance was extraordinary, and that "IBM has earned its success through competition on the merits—new product innovation, superior service and price competition."[67] The government's legal team was badly outgunned. The presiding judge showed no inclination to focus the issues or expedite the presentation of evidence, which dragged on from 1975 to 1981. One government economist testified for 78 days. When Ronald Reagan assumed the U.S. presidency in 1981, his new assistant attorney general for antitrust conducted an independent review. In January 1982, he concluded that "continuing the case would be an expensive and ultimately futile endeavor."[68] The case was thereupon terminated.

Although IBM continually proclaimed its innocence in court, its chairman apparently held contrary views:[69]

> Looking back, I see a lot of sad irony in the whole affair. I think a lot of people would agree that at the outset the Justice Department's complaint had merit. IBM was clearly in a commanding position in the market, and some of our tactics had been harsh. We eliminated many of these practices ourselves, and our overall record during the case was pretty clean. . . . [T]he case stretched on unresolved for so long that before it was over history showed my argument . . . to have been right. IBM kept growing, but the computer industry grew even more, and the natural forces of technological change etched away whatever monopoly power we may have had.

Watson was right. By 1982, as we shall see in a moment, the character of competition in the computer industry had been transformed, and it was about to undergo even more radical change. The fundamental problem is that U.S. antitrust processes are unable to cope in a timely way with monopoly power in technologically dynamic markets, especially when a well-heeled company is determined to fight the government's efforts at every turn.

A much less ambitious antitrust challenge was brought against IBM in 1981 by the European Community competition policy authorities.[70] It evoked less furious resistance and, in the end, a mild but probably efficacious settlement.[71] IBM agreed to disclose within four months of new mainframe computer product announcements the detailed technical specifications required to effect interfaces. In this way, it allowed other companies developing devices compatible with IBM computers for the European market an earlier start toward designing their products than they would have if they waited until the actual IBM products were available for reverse engineering.

---

[67]IBM, Pretrial Brief, January 15, 1975, p. 374.

[68]Memorandum of William F. Baxter to the attorney general, January 6, 1982, p. 6.

[69]Watson, *Father, Son & Co.*, p. 415.

[70]"Europeans Aim Action at I.B.M.," *New York Times*, April 26, 1984, p. D1.

[71]"IBM Settles Antitrust Suit with Common Market, Rivals Welcome Concessions, But Hoped for More," *Wall Street Journal*, August 3, 1984, p. 2. The accord was terminated in 1994. "I.B.M. Ending '84 Pact," *New York Times*, July 8, 1994, p. 42.

There is a double irony in the European Community decree. For one, the agreed-upon remedy was similar to the main proposal of the U.S. Computer Industry Association in 1976 for an expedited settlement to the then-pending U.S. government case against IBM.[72] Also, it provided approbation on competition policy grounds for the early release of information on IBM compatibility standards. A Japanese compatible computer maker, Hitachi, considered such information so vital that it paid $622,000 to individuals offering to steal similar materials from IBM in June 1982. The would-be thieves turned out to be U.S. FBI agents. An embarrassed Hitachi caught *in flagrante delicto* agreed to pay to IBM a large but undisclosed sum for its transgressions.[73] To the extent that IBM sets industry standards, timely interface information is essential to the survival of compatible device makers. As a U.S. manufacturer of compatible CPUs observed, "timing is crucial—for every month you lose, you lose an incredible amount of opportunity."[74]

THE STRUGGLE CONTINUES

The challenges to computer industry leader IBM did not end with the leapfrog competitions precipitating System 360, the entry of plug-compatible peripheral manufacturers, and the antitrust cases in their wake. Competition continued to emerge on new fronts.

Minicomputers opened one of the fronts. IBM and its principal mainframe computer rivals had from the industry's early years included small computers in their product lines. But minicomputers were different in two principal respects. The conventional wisdom was that small computers were used primarily by relatively small business firms, which typically had little knowledge of how the machines worked. As minicomputer industry pioneer Kenneth Olsen described the prevailing philosophy, "IBM will say, 'We'll make your system work no matter how dumb you are.'"[75] In contrast, minicomputers were optimized to provide minimal bells, whistles, and hand-holding, offering instead substantial but not top computing performance at low prices. Second, and closely related, the minicomputer makers assumed that the individuals using their computers wanted to interact in real time with the machines, and not to submit batch jobs through the remote intermediation of a specialized operator. Thus, the user sat at a keyboard to provide inputs, and outputs were obtained immediately through a cathode-ray tube screen.

---

[72]*Antitrust and Trade Regulation Report*, March 30, 1976, p. A–25.

[73]See "Japanese Executives Charged in I.B.M. Theft Case," *New York Times*, June 23, 1982, pp. 1 and D6; and "Trade Ethics in Silicon Valley: Data Hunting Held Common," *New York Times*, June 25, 1982, p. D1.

[74]"IBM's Mimics Struggle to Keep Pace," *Business Week*, September 20, 1982, p. 96.

[75]"Minicomputers Challenge the Big Machines," *Business Week*, April 26, 1976, p. 60.

The minicomputer industry's genesis is attributed to the founding of Digital Equipment Corporation (DEC) in 1958 by Kenneth Olsen, previously involved in computer frontier-advancing work at the Massachusetts Institute of Technology. Digital Equipment was financed in part through a $70,000 investment by the American Research and Development Corporation, the prototype for high-technology venture capital funds in the United States. DEC grew rapidly with a series of PDP (programmed data processor) models, some for scientific work and some used in such specialized tasks as industrial process control and guiding numerically controlled machine tools. Important steps forward were its PDP–6 in 1964, the first commercial computer to provide time-sharing capabilities (i.e., before General Electric and IBM reached that goal), and in 1965 its PDP–8, offering substantial computing power at a price of only $18,000. By the end of the 1970s, DEC had grown to become the second-largest U.S. computer maker. Its approach to minicomputers was imitated by numerous new and established firms.[76] Among the newcomers were Scientific Data Systems (acquired in 1969 by Xerox Corporation), Data General, Wang Laboratories, Tandem, and Prime. When IBM introduced its first true minicomputer, the Series 1, in 1976, several dozen minicomputer makers were sustaining nearly a tenth of total computer industry equipment sales.

The Microcomputer Revolution

An even more important innovation was the microcomputer or, in its most familiar embodiment, the personal computer. By the mid–1970s, several lines of technological development had converged to prepare the ground for a major leap forward in computer design.

Two of these lines have been surveyed in Chapter 6: the microprocessor and the dynamic random-access memory chip (DRAM). Microprocessors were available by 1971 from Intel and other semiconductor producers. Soon called "the computer on a chip," they made it possible to compress central processing unit functions that had previously filled a box the size of a large refrigerator onto a thumbnail-size chip. DRAMs, first used for commercial mainframe computers in 1970, provided compact rapid-access internal memory capacity to complement the microprocessor.

A third necessity for practical microcomputers was a means of storing data inputs and outputs for longer periods. Magnetic tape drives, used inter alia with the first UNIVAC, were one possibility, but they were slow and unwieldy. Spinning magnetic disks proved to be superior, but they required a long period of technological development in which IBM was the pioneer.[77] The first commercial installation was IBM's RAMAC 650 (Random Access

---

[76]See, for example, Dorfman, *Innovation and Market Structure*, chap. 5.

[77]See Clayton M. Christensen, "The Rigid Disk Drive Industry: A History of Commercial and Technological Turbulence," *Business History Review*, vol. 67 (Winter 1993), pp. 533–535.

Method of Accounting and Control), introduced in 1956. The first RAMACs stacked 50 disks in a large box, each disk 24 inches in diameter, and each with its own magnetic reading and recording head. Painstaking research and development greatly increased the amount of information that could be stored per square inch, reduced head clearances and data access times, and, crucially for microcomputers, shrank the size of the disks—for example, from 24 inches for the first RAMACs to 14 inches in 1963, 8 inches (the first floppy disk) in 1971, 5.25 inches in 1979, and 3.5 inches in 1982. IBM led the way to the 8-inch generation. After that, each new architecture (i.e., "hard" vs. "floppy" configuration and size) was pioneered by a different company. Nearly all of the pioneering companies were founded by individuals who had worked in IBM's San Jose laboratories, or by persons who had worked in IBM spin-off firms (especially Shugart Associates).[78]

These technological developments intersected during the mid–1970s to spawn two new product lines—video games, led by Magnavox and Atari, which we shall ignore, and personal computers, whose genesis we trace.[79] The shot that presaged the personal computer revolution was the Altair 8800, a rudimentary box containing an Intel 8080 microprocessor and operated by toggle switches. It appealed to electronics hobbyists, including the Homebrew Computer Club of California, among whose members were Stephen Wozniak and Steven Jobs. Wozniak and Jobs crafted a much more accessible system, the Apple I, with keyboard input and television monitor output. When their employers (Hewlett-Packard and game maker Atari) expressed no interest, they founded their own company, Apple Computer, and in 1977 they began selling the improved Apple II, complete with a tape cassette storage device. In that same year Commodore introduced its PET personal computer and the Tandy Corporation, parent of the Radio Shack retail chain, launched its TRS–80 model I (whose design was so primitive that it was widely called the Trash–80). At first the new personal computers were suitable mainly for game-playing and educational computing (e.g., running a BASIC program that simulated 10,000 coin flips, generating 7869 heads).[80] However, applications software usable on the new computers began to appear—for example, the VisiCalc spreadsheet and WordStar word-processing programs, both introduced in Apple II versions during 1979. Output could be printed using either electric

---

[78]Christensen, "The Rigid Disk Drive Industry," p. 575. See also Josh Lerner, "Technological Racing in the Winchester Disk Drive Industry," working paper, Harvard University, April 1991.

[79]The definitive early histories are Paul Freiberger and Michael Swaine, *Fire in the Valley* (New York: Osborne/McGraw-Hill, 1984); and Michael Moritz, *The Little Kingdom: The Story of Apple Computer* (New York: Morrow, 1984). An excellent shorter history is Richard N. Langlois, "External Economies and Economic Progress: The Case of the Microcomputer Industry," *Business History Review*, vol. 66 (Spring 1992), pp. 1–50.

[80]The author judged an Apple II entry yielding that result at the Cook County Science Fair in 1979.

typewriters (for high quality, but slow) or faster but lower-quality dot matrix printers. The advent of 5.25 inch floppy disks facilitated storage. Personal computers were recognized to be more than a toy. Many more companies, old and new, began marketing personal computers of widely varying architecture and design.[81] In 1980, 371,000 devices classified as personal computers were shipped by U.S. manufacturers; in 1981, the count rose to 750,000.

By 1980 IBM's management recognized that a significant new branch of the computer business was emerging, and IBM was already three years behind the market leaders. A particularly rapid "fast second" response was necessary. It organized a new development team, freed the team from standard IBM procedures, and gave the team a one-year deadline to market its product. There was too little time to develop an operating system and components afresh, as was IBM's custom. Intel's 8088 chip was selected as the microprocessor. Negotiations with the company that had written the most popular personal computer operating system, CP/M, broke down, so IBM turned to a small software firm, Microsoft, which had originated a PC version of the BASIC programming language.[82] Microsoft's head, William Gates, bought 8088-compatible operating software from another small firm, adapted it, and licensed it to IBM as MS/DOS (Microsoft disk operating system), or PC/DOS in the IBM version. Tandon, a second-generation offshoot of IBM's San Jose laboratories, was chosen as the new computer's first floppy-disk-drive vendor. The resulting IBM PC was unveiled on August 12, 1981, and promoted heavily through network television advertisements featuring a humorous Charlie Chaplin look-alike.

The new computer was far more successful than IBM management had anticipated. Sales forecasts were exceeded by a factor of five. In 1982, IBM sold 180,000 PCs in the United States; in 1983, more than 400,000.[83] There were several reasons for this success. The PC's exterior styling was more classic and professional-looking than that of existing rivals. Unlike early versions of the TRS–80 and Apple II, the PC offered 80-column alphabetic and numeric readout on its high-resolution screen without requiring users to pay extra for 80-column circuitry. It was not cheap—more than $3300 with two floppy disks and a monitor—but alternative computers of comparable 64-kilobyte internal memory capacity were only a few hundred dollars less expensive, and the PC cost much less than a low-end minicomputer. The 16-bit microprocessor (with 8-bit bus) had more expansion potential than the 8-bit chips used by

[81]For a retrospective on the situation in 1980, see L. R. Shannon, "What a Difference a Decade Makes!" *New York Times*, September 1, 1992, p. B7.

[82]See James Wallace and Jim Erickson, *Hard Drive: Bill Gates and the Making of the Microsoft Empire* (Harper Business: 1993), pp. 165–190.

[83]"Personal Computers: And the Winner Is IBM," *Business Week*, October 3, 1983, p. 76.

most rivals. The architecture was flexible and widely publicized. Software programs were readily adapted to it, and an assortment of peripheral devices could be attached. The machine was widely available through specialty computer stores and Sears Roebuck. But most of all, it was IBM. This meant that it was a serious business machine, not a toy. Taken seriously in this way, it became the machine of choice for software writers. Applications programs proliferated, and with a wider array of software than any rival, the PC attracted more buyers in a snowball effect.

There was a flaw in the formula, however. By relying upon Microsoft for its operating system, IBM lost the proprietary position it had tried (not always successfully) to maintain on its mainframe computers. Microsoft retained the right to, and did, license MS/DOS to other computer manufacturers. IBM tried to differentiate its product by placing exclusive BIOS (basic input-output system) software on a read-only memory chip, but it was not hard to devise functional equivalents. Intel microprocessors were also available to others. Soon PC clones from both the United States and East Asia began to proliferate. The adoption of MS/DOS by clones strengthened that operating system as a standard and attracted still more software development activity. Companies such as Tandy and Kaypro that had initially chosen other operating systems switched to MS/DOS. Most who were reluctant to switch (such as Digital Equipment) saw their sales evaporate. In a replay of the early 1960s, IBM again faced the competition of compatible machines, but this time there were as many as 200 rivals, not two or three.

IBM tried to stay ahead by offering faster and more powerful computers, first in April 1983 with the XT (adding hard-disk capabilities) and then with the faster AT, embodying the Intel 80286 chip, in 1984. Its dollar share of the 6.75 million personal computers sold in the United States reached 40 percent in 1985.[84] But others were able to play the leapfrog game at least as well. Newcomer Compaq introduced a portable high-performance IBM-compatible computer in 1983 and adopted 32-bit technology using the Intel 80386 microprocessor in September 1986, seven months before IBM. Several personal computer makers announced new systems using the Intel 80486-SX chip on the day it was unveiled in 1991. IBM's attempt to market a budget-priced PC Jr. in 1984 failed because of faulty ergonomic design.[85] Toshiba led the way to laptop computers in 1986. IBM's analogous offering was poorly received; not until 1991 was a successful IBM laptop marketed.

IBM attempted to regain control of the standard when it introduced its 32-bit Personal System 2 (PS/2) in April 1987. Taking advantage of the 32-bit microprocessor architecture, the PS/2 incorporated a new operating system,

---

[84]See "The PC Wars: IBM vs. the Clones," *Business Week*, July 28, 1986, pp. 62–68.

[85]"How IBM Made 'Junior' an Underachiever," *Business Week*, June 25, 1984, pp. 106–107.

including in its more expensive models a "Micro Channel" data bus that permitted the computer to perform multiple tasks simultaneously. Patents and copyrights were expected to protect the Micro Channel and other features of the operating system from imitation. But within six months alternative versions of the PS/2 BIOS had been developed, and a group of nine IBM-compatible computer makers collaborated to develop their own "Extended Industry Standard Architecture" more compatible than PS/2 with earlier-vintage software.[86] When it became clear that the clones' growth would not be halted by PS/2, IBM announced a new patent licensing policy that made Micro Channel available to rivals at royalties ranging between 1 and 5 percent of the value of the computers using it.[87]

Acceptance of the original IBM PC architecture as a standard and the vast number of applications programs written for it led most personal computer manufacturers to adopt some version of MS/DOS. The most important exception in the United States was Apple. Even before IBM entered the personal computer market, Apple recognized that a superior alternative to the Apple II family technology would be needed. In 1979, it entered into a joint venture arrangement that permitted its technical staff to examine and utilize computer concepts developed at the Xerox Corporation's Palo Alto, California, research center, which was opened after Xerox acquired Scientific Data Systems in 1969. There Apple executives saw for the first time the Alto personal computer, with high-resolution graphics and pull-down menus operated by selecting among pictorial "icons" through a mouse-guided pointer.[88] Apple's Steven Jobs is said to have jumped around the room shouting, "Why aren't you doing anything about this? This is the greatest thing! This is revolutionary!"[89] Apple's first product incorporating the Xerox ideas, the Lisa computer, failed because of high prices and deficient performance. But Apple's second

---

[86]See "The Knockoffs Head for a Knockdown Fight with IBM," *Business Week*, December 21, 1987, pp. 112–113; "A Quandary for I.B.M. Over Its New PC Line," *New York Times*, April 7, 1988, p. D1; "If the PS/2 Is a Winner, Why Is IBM So Frustrated?" *Business Week*, April 11, 1988, pp. 82–83; "IBM's Micro Channel Gets a Little Respect," *Business Week*, March 20, 1989, pp. 156–158; and "Dispatches from the Bus Wars," *New York Times*, November 21, 1989, p. C10.

[87]"I.B.M. to Allow PS/2 Copies but Will Increase Royalties," *New York Times*, April 9, 1988, p. 37.

[88]Ten prototypes of Alto had been completed by 1974, but Xerox's management, preoccupied with problems in their copying business and believing that the Alto would be too high-priced to find a substantial market, thwarted its commercialization. See Douglas K. Smith and Robert C. Alexander, *Fumbling the Future: How Xerox Invented, then Ignored, the First Personal Computer* (New York: William Morrow, 1988).

[89]Jeffrey S. Young, *Steve Jobs: The Journey Is the Reward* (Glenview, IL: Scott, Foresman, 1988), pp. 174–175.

try, the Macintosh, was enthusiastically received following its introduction in early 1984. The graphics-oriented Macintosh approach soon became a second industry standard. Its proprietary operating system was more difficult to clone than MS/DOS. After introducing additional Macintosh models aimed at the business user market, Apple threatened to regain from IBM its leadership in U.S. personal computer unit sales.

The greater user-friendliness of Macintosh was recognized by Microsoft and IBM. Microsoft had introduced a mouse-driven user interface in 1983 following the appearance of Apple's Lisa. It achieved limited success. However, greatly improved Windows 3.0 and later versions emulated the Macintosh graphics approach more closely, survived a law suit by Apple alleging that their "look and feel" infringed Apple's copyright, and by the end of 1992 achieved cumulative sales of 20 million units. The success of Windows drove a wedge between Microsoft and IBM. Microsoft had collaborated with IBM to develop a new operating system, OS/2, introduced in 1987 eight months after the first IBM PS/2 computers for which it was designed.[90] OS/2 permitted greatly enhanced multitasking and networking capabilities and came with IBM's own graphical user interface, the Presentation Manager. But when acceptance of OS/2 as a standard proved disappointing, Microsoft shifted its marketing emphasis from OS/2 to Windows and announced that it was developing a competitor to OS/2, Windows NT, for use in multitasking environments.[91] IBM retaliated in 1991 by announcing that it would work jointly with Apple and Motorola, whose microprocessor the Macintosh computers used, to develop a completely new personal computer architecture that would run both IBM and Macintosh software without requiring Microsoft's operating systems or Intel's microprocessors.[92] The resulting Power PC chip, announced in late 1994, was based upon reduced instruction set chip (RISC) architecture, which had been used previously in small-scale supercomputers and work stations. Whether it will succeed in winning many computer users locked into Intel microprocessors and Microsoft software remains to be seen.

Other standards rivalries focused on still another operating system contender, Unix, and a different microprocessor approach to running diverse

---

[90]"I.B.M. Set to Ship New OS/2 System," *New York Times*, November 4, 1987, p. D5.

[91]See "Microsoft To Pitch a New Hardball," *New York Times*, November 12, 1990, p. D1; "Big Blue Makes a Big Commitment," *Business Week*, April 22, 1991, p. 33; and "Emerging Battlefronts in Software Strategy Wars," *New York Times*, May 17, 1993, p. D1. On the Windows NT software writing effort, see G. Pascal Zachary, *Show Stopper! The Breakneck Race To Create Windows NT and the Next Generation at Microsoft* (New York: Free Press, 1994).

[92]See "I.B.M. Now Apple's Main Ally," *New York Times*, October 3, 1991, p. D1; and "After 3 Years, a PC Alliance Is Ready To Fight," *New York Times*, November 4, 1994, p. D1.

operating systems, the reduced instruction set computing chip (RISC). During the 1980s Unix was the perennial bridesmaid, repeatedly identified as the operating system of the future but never securing sufficient unanimity to make the future happen.[93]

Throughout much of the 1980s, standard-setters IBM and Macintosh sold at premium prices yielding margins between manufacturing cost and whole-sale prices as large as 50 percent. As the competition from IBM-compatible machines intensified, however, the margins were squeezed. A portent of the new pricing regime materialized in early 1988, when IBM cut the prices of its more powerful new PS/2 computers because clone competition proved to be more rapid and tougher than it had anticipated. Even more important developments followed. As the number of chips needed to assemble a computer was reduced sharply and the chips (along with disk drives) became increasingly reliable, failure rates fell and consumers worried less about the risk of a serious system crash.[94] Consumers became better informed, realizing inter alia that they did not have to pay a premium price to obtain a high-quality machine.[95] Personal computers moved from being a highly differentiated product to near-commodity status. Price-competitive computer supermarkets proliferated and, even more importantly, consumers turned in large numbers to order-by-telephone vendors offering quick delivery of customized machines plus repair service at the user's home or office. A pioneer in the telephone order business was Dell Computer, which grew from Michael Dell's room as a student at the University of Texas in 1984 to sales of $2 billion in 1992. Losing market share rapidly to lower-priced rivals, IBM, Apple, and other premium-priced PC manufacturers such as Compaq and Nippon Electric were forced to compete much more aggressively. IBM introduced a line of "Value Point" fighting brands and began selling by telephone.[96] The price differential between IBM and less well-known PC-compatible brands narrowed into the $100-$200 range.[97] As the wave of price-cutting spread, higher-cost manufacturers plunged from profit to loss, and many exited from the industry.

---

[93]See "It's Goliath vs. Goliath for a $5 Billion Unix Market," *Business Week*, October 31, 1988, p. 27; "'The Unix War' Is Over — But the Fighting Goes On," *Business Week*, March 27, 1989, pp. 114–116; and "Computer Confusion," *Business Week*, June 10, 1991, pp. 72–77.

[94]See "If It Ain't Broke, Why Pay To Fix It?" *Business Week*, March 5, 1990, pp. 82–84.

[95]See "Behind the Price Cuts," *New York Times*, May 28, 1991, p. B8.

[96]See "In a Departure, I.B.M. To Sell Its PS/2 PC's by Telephone," *New York Times*, April 30, 1992, p. C3; "Big Blue Has a Clone of Its Own," *Business Week*, November 2, 1992, pp. 152–153; and "Computer Price Wars: Cut to the Quick," *The Economist*, March 21, 1992, p. 76.

[97]"PC Land's Little Guys Get Slaughtered," *Business Week*, February 15, 1993, pp. 105–106. On Apple, see "What Price Glory?" *The Economist*, August 24, 1991, pp. 61–62.

Rapid technological innovation and intensified price rivalry in personal computers had important repercussions for mainframe computers too. A standard 1988-vintage personnel computer had processing power and memory capacity equivalent to the most powerful general-purpose mainframe computers of a decade earlier, but was vastly less expensive. To be sure, the mainframes continued to advance technically, but personal computers captured many applications that would have been performed on mainframes or minicomputers during the late 1970s and early 1980s. Microcomputers linked together in massively parallel processing configurations threatened even the most powerful supercomputers.[98] Worldwide, mainframe revenues fell from 43 percent of all computer sales in 1983 to 27 percent in 1990 and continued to drop thereafter.[99] Mainframe computer manufacturers competed with unprecedented ferocity for the smaller volume of new orders.[100] Attempting to survive in a declining mainframe market, Burroughs acquired mainframe maker Sperry Rand in 1986 (changing the combined company's name to Unisys) and AT&T acquired NCR (once National Cash Register) in 1991. Other mainframe and (especially) minicomputer makers shrank to shadows of their former selves.

The IBM Corporation, which retained a 70 percent share of worldwide mainframe computer sales in 1983, was hit particularly hard by these developments. It reported a loss of $2.8 billion in 1991 — the first loss in its modern history. An even larger loss followed in 1992. Heads rolled. Between 1986 and 1992, IBM shed one-fourth of its work force. Research and development spending was cut. The average aggregate market value of its common stock plunged from $86 billion in 1986 to $31 billion in 1993. To overcome bureaucratic encrustation, it decentralized decision-making to 13 semiautonomous business units.[101] Its restructuring efforts reawakened old speculation: What would have happened if IBM had agreed to settle the antitrust charges against it by breaking itself into several parts?[102] It is arguable that at least one of the survivors would have entered the personal computer field earlier than the parent did and, by moving quickly and aggressively, established an operating system standard over which it could maintain control.

---

[98]See "The Hungry Pack Nipping at Cray's Heels," *Business Week*, October 26, 1987, pp. 110–111; and "Supercomputer Decline ??? Cray Computer," *New York Times*, March 25, 1995, p. 37.

[99]See "Pile 'em High, Sell 'em Cheap," *The Economist*, November 2, 1991, p. 60; and "Twilight of the Mainframes," *Business Week*, August 17, 1992, p. 33.

[100]"Mainframes Aren't All That Dead," *New York Times*, February 9, 1993, p. D1.

[101]"I.B.M. Announces a Sweeping Shift in Its Structure," *New York Times*, November 27, 1991, p. 1.

[102]See, for example, Allan Sloan, "Why Jumbo Has to Take Dance Lessons," *Boston Globe*, December 8, 1991, p. 98; "Breaking Up IBM," *Fortune*, July 27, 1992, p. 51; and "Too Big Blue," editorial, *The Economist*, May 22, 1993, p. 17.

Computer makers in the United States were not alone in their misery. During the 1980s Japanese computer makers reached the technological frontier and grew rapidly. Their progress in supercomputers was aided by government R&D grants and made-at-home preferences.[103] They were early entrants into personal computers and related equipment, especially PC-compatible printers.[104] They led the way to laptop computers, winning 38 percent of U.S. laptop sales during the late 1980s, in part on the basis of their virtually unchallenged dominance of flat-panel display production. Although total U.S. computer exports and imports were in rough balance at approximately 43 percent of domestic consumption, Japanese sources accounted for 37 percent of U.S. imports in 1990, while U.S.-based firms shipped to Japan 14 percent of their total computer exports.[105] However, the rising value of the yen made it increasingly difficult to sustain profitable U.S. sales from Japan.[106] The dollar's fall in turn induced companies such as Compaq and Dell to market their personal computers aggressively in Japan, precipitating a price war. Thus, Japanese companies, like their U.S. counterparts, saw their profits vanish during the early 1990s.[107]

Europe's computer industry fared even less well. Despite repeated rescue efforts, numerous joint ventures, and large R&D subsidies, the European Community nations failed to bring forward a successful national champion.[108] Sales leadership continued to be held by European branches of IBM, followed by other U.S. and Japanese firms.

As spreading competition undermined the profits of computer manufacturers, Intel and Microsoft continued to benefit from their dominant positions in the most widely accepted microprocessor and operating system standards. For 1992, Intel reported profits of $1.07 billion on sales of $5.8 billion; Microsoft had profits of $834 million on sales of $3.25 billion. By 1993, Microsoft had sold 100 million copies of MS/DOS and 25 million copies of Windows. Retaining a 28 percent common stock interest in what had become one of the world's great monopolies, Microsoft founder William Gates was

---

[103]See "The Battle of the Supercomputers," *Business Week*, October 17, 1983, pp. 156–162; and "Why Cray's Number Cruncher Got Crunched in Japan," *Business Week*, November 2, 1992, p. 154.

[104]"Computers: Japan Comes On Strong," *Business Week*, October 23, 1989, pp. 104–112.

[105]U.S. International Trade Administration, *U.S. Industrial Outlook: 1992* (Washington, DC: USGPO: January 1992), p. 27–3.

[106]"The Japanese Juggernaut That Isn't," *Business Week*, August 31, 1992, pp. 63–66.

[107]"NEC Computer Profits Fall, Hurt by U.S. Inroads," *New York Times*, November 20, 1993, p. D1.

[108]See, for example, "Spare the Rod and Spoil the Child," *The Economist*, April 20, 1991, p. 63; and "EC Panel Issues Plan To Research Supercomputers," *Wall Street Journal*, November 27, 1992, p. 1.

reported to be the wealthiest person in the United States, with an estimated net worth of $7 billion.[109]

In 1993, the Federal Trade Commission concluded a two-year-long investigation of Microsoft's practices with its commisioners deadlocked over corrective remedies. The Justice Department's Antitrust Division thereupon assumed jurisdiction for a further investigation. Subjected to scrutiny were Microsoft's pricing practices and the advantages its control of personal computer operating system specifications gave it over rival applications software writers. These included at least a head start in assuring compatibility with new operating systems and perhaps, it was alleged, the ability to appropriate ideas other firms disclosed in compatibility discussions or even to insert secret codes into its operating system to prevent rival applications programs from running smoothly. There were also charges that it tried to forestall the sales of rival programs by pre-announcing its own competing software before it was written (a phenomenon known as announcing "vaporware.")[110] Many of the allegations mirrored those leveled in earlier years against IBM. In July 1994, the Justice Department negotiated a settlement, under whose main provision Microsoft would cease charging its operating system licensees a royalty for the computers they shipped without Microsoft operating systems along with those in which Microsoft system software was loaded. However, when the consent order was presented before U.S. federal district court judge Stanley Sporkin for routine approval, Judge Sporkin disapproved the settlement and asked the Justice Department to impose more stringent restraints upon Microsoft's behavior.[111] Both the Justice Department and Microsoft filed appeals against Judge Sporkin's nearly unprecedented initiative, leading to reversal of the Sporkin order by an appellate court.

What renewed antitrust proceedings and, more generally, the forces of competition will bring remains uncertain. The most that can be said is that the struggle for monopoly positions in computers and allied technologies will continue, as will vigorous efforts to undermine those positions.

AFTERWORD

In its early decades of computer industry leadership, IBM pursued extraordinarily sophisticated pricing strategies, exploiting its advantages as standard setter to reap high profits, but responding aggressively when rivals sought to invade profitable product line niches. Evaluating these strategies posed new

---

[109]See "The Future of Microsoft: Today Windows, Tomorrow the World," *The Economist*, May 22, 1993, pp. 25–27.

[110]See Wallace and Erickson, *Hard Drive*, chap. 6.

[111]See "Microsoft Dilemma for Justice Dept.," *New York Times*, February 16, 1995, p. D1; and "Bill Gates, Uncensored," *Business Week*, April 10, 1995, pp. 132–134.

challenges for the formulation of antitrust policies toward dominant enterprises. IBM's behavior also illustrates the logic of "fast second" product development strategies. But when IBM lagged in recognizing new technological opportunities for supercomputers, minicomputers, and especially microcomputers, it squandered its position as standard setter and declined in size and profitability with breathtaking swiftness. Among the important questions to be answered in future years are whether the firms that seized IBM's leadership mantle will be able to learn from and avoid its mistakes and, if so, whether their pricing power will be reined in by the market or by the application of antitrust remedies.

8

AUTOMOBILES

Ford Motor Company surged to leadership of the U.S. automobile industry by rigidly standardizing its product and extending the frontiers of scale economies in assembly line manufacturing. General Motors captured the lead from Ford by offering a wide variety of models and changing model designs frequently, among other things exploiting economies of scale in the utilization of special tools required to produce each new model. As price leader in the automobile oligopoly, General Motors pursued a complex strategy including the use of a widely publicized formula, seeking higher profits on large cars than on small cars, and tying the profitable sale of luxury items and replacement parts to the less profitable sale of basic vehicles. Emphasis on large high-profit vehicles and cutting corners on the quality of small cars rendered the industry vulnerable to rapidly rising imports during the 1970s, which led to the imposition of import quotas by the U.S. government. The government also intervened to force improved gasoline mileage, reduced exhaust pollution, and enhanced car safety. We explore the market failures that led to these product design interventions.

INTRODUCTION

The automobile industry has a credible claim to being called the leading industry of the twentieth century. By most measures it continues to be the largest single manufacturing industry in prosperous nations. Its products have revolutionized notions of human mobility, precipitating radical changes in the spatial configuration of cities. Both in the United States and abroad, it has experienced alternating periods of structural stability and dramatic change. After a brief early interval, its structure became tightly oligopolistic.

FIGURE 8.1
Trends in Auto Manufacturers' U.S. Market Shares

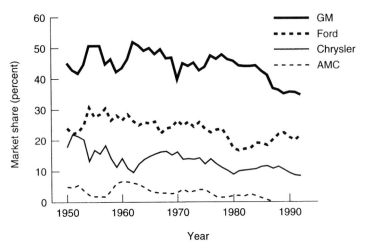

Sources: Lawrence J. White, *The Automobile Industry Since 1945* (Cambridge, MA: Harvard University Press, 1971), pp. 290–306 (for 1960–1967), drawing upon data from R. L. Polk & Co., *Automotive Industries, Annual Statistical Issue,* various years; and *Ward's Automotive Yearbook* (Southfield, MI), 1978 edition, pp. 92, 102–103, and 156; 1986 edition, p. 113; 1993 edition, p. 201.

In the United States, it has consistently been one of the most highly concentrated manufacturing industries. In 1987, for example, the four leading automobile assemblers originated 90 percent of the industry's domestic output by dollar value. Towering above other U.S. car makers through much of the period following World War II has been General Motors, with a share of U.S. passenger automobile unit sales (including imported cars) averaging 46 percent between 1950 and 1980. See Figure 8.1.[1] The number two producer, Ford, achieved roughly half of General Motors' share on average. Chrysler and

[1]The data cover passenger car registrations through 1975 and total U.S. sales thereafter. The calculated market shares include vehicles procured abroad and from foreign firm transplants in the United States, but sold under U.S. company nameplates. In recent years the line between passenger cars and trucks has become increasingly blurred because many consumers have chosen pickup trucks as a normal means of personal transportation. Although the number of passenger automobiles sold increased from 9.0 million in 1980 to 9.3 million in 1990, the number of trucks of less than 6,000 pounds weight (including utility trucks, vans, and minivans) rose from 985,000 in 1980 to 2.72 million in 1990. U.S. Bureau of the Census, *Statistical Abstract of the United States: 1993* (Washington, DC, USGPO, 1993), p. 617. Figure 8.1 and most of the data in this chapter refer for consistency to passenger cars only. See also "Why We Love Trucks," *Business Week,* December 5, 1994, pp. 70–81.

a changing assortment of other producers, domestic and foreign (e.g., Volkswagen, Toyota, Honda, and Nissan), occupied trailing positions, usually a considerable distance behind the leaders.

EARLY HISTORY

In its infant years the industry's structure was much more fragmented, and with more turbulent position shifts, than at present.[2] Although there were earlier prototypes, the first practical modern automobiles were introduced during the 1890s by such pioneering firms as Panhard & Levassor in France, Daimler and Benz in Germany, and Duryea in the United States. In the United States, and especially around Detroit, the idea of motor-propelled passenger vehicles caught on rapidly. By 1902 there were 12 American enterprises producing motor cars.[3] During the next two decades an estimated 169 firms entered the U.S. industry on a scale large enough to be called active auto manufacturers, but many failed quickly or merged with others. The most reliable tabulation shows 69 U.S. auto manufacturers to be operating in 1909 and 88 in 1921.[4] Of the roughly 4200 motor cars produced in 1900, more were propelled by steam or electric batteries than by gasoline-burning engines, but by 1910, gasoline propulsion had become the dominant design.

The first important transformation in the newly emerging industry's structure was wrought by the Ford Motor Company.[5] Founder Henry Ford began considering the idea of a gasoline-powered motor car in 1891, assembled his first full prototype in 1896, and brought in 11 other investors to incorporate the Ford Motor Company in 1903. Although roughly two-thirds of the 43,000 automobiles produced in the United States during 1907 were large models catering to the luxury market, Henry Ford from the beginning sought to design austere cars that could be produced and sold at modest prices to the vast majority of working-class Americans. After supplying a cumulative total of nearly 20,000 cars of diverse design between 1903 and 1908, Ford began delivering its revolutionary Model T in October 1908. Priced between $825

---

[2]Actually, the industry had two infancies. Steam-propelled carriages appeared in England during the 1820s but failed to have a lasting impact, partly because their use was opposed by the railways and other vested interests and partly because there was an insufficiently large middle class to create the demand for roads and other ancillary infrastructure. See David Beasley, *The Suppression of the Automobile: Skulduggery at the Crossroads* (Westport, CT: Greenwood, 1988).

[3]See Ralph C. Epstein, *The Automobile Industry: Its Economic and Commercial Development* (Wheaton, IL: Shaw, 1928), pp. 162–178.

[4]Ibid., pp. 176–177.

[5]The definitive history is Allan Nevins, *Ford: The Times, the Man, the Company* (New York: Scribner, 1954), on which this account draws.

and $1000, depending upon the accoutrements, the Model T was advertised with the claim, "No car under $2000 offers more, and no car over $2000 offers more except in trimmings." By rigidly standardizing interchangeable parts and overall vehicle configurations, by specializing his workers on narrowly subdivided tasks, and by embracing other mass production techniques culminating in the continuously moving assembly line at Highland Park, Michigan, in 1913, Ford squeezed cost out of his operations and offered consumers Model T cars at progressively declining prices—for the runabout version, $725 in 1910, $525 in 1912, $440 in 1914, and $345 in 1916.[6] Largely on the strength of the Model T, the Ford Motor Company's sales increased from 10,607 units in the fiscal year ending September 30, 1909, to 78,440 in 1912 and 472,350 in 1916.[7] Ford's share of total new-car output in the United States rose from 14 percent in (calendar year) 1909 to 48 percent in 1916 and a peak of 62 percent in 1921.[8]

Among the challenges the fledgling Ford Motor Company had to overcome was an allegation that its cars infringed a basic patent issued in 1895 to George B. Selden, who made broad claims to having "invented" the use of gasoline engines with transmissions to propel horseless carriages. Beginning in 1903, many of the leading auto manufacturers agreed to pay the association holding the Selden patent a royalty of 1.25 percent on the retail sales value of their cars. Henry Ford refused to submit, however, and a long, costly litigation followed. It ended only in 1911, when an appellate court severely restricted the scope of the Selden patent, thereupon finding that the cars offered by Ford (and other manufacturers) escaped its reach.[9]

The Ford Motor Company rose to industry dominance by exploiting scale economies and learning by doing to the maximum extent and setting prices aggressively to secure an increasing market share. Mergers (mainly, the acquisition of the Lincoln Motor Company, a luxury car maker) played only a minor role in its growth. The history of General Motors, ultimately the most successful challenger to Ford, was quite different. Its founder, William C. Durant, sought growth and success through merger. He began by acquiring and reorganizing the Buick Company, rebuilding it to a position of industry sales leadership in 1908 (i.e., before the sales of Ford's Model T accelerated).

---

[6]Nevins, *Ford*, pp. 646–647. See also James P. Womack, Daniel T. Jones, and Daniel Roos, *The Machine That Changed the World* (New York: HarperCollins, 1991), pp. 26–39; and Daniel Raff and Manuel Trajtenberg, "Quality-Adjusted Prices for the American Automobile Industry, 1906–1940," National Bureau of Economic Research Working Paper No. 5035 (February 1995).

[7]Nevins, *Ford*, p. 644.

[8]Simon N. Whitney, *Antitrust Policies* (New York: Twentieth Century Fund, 1958), vol. 1, p. 468. Slightly lower shares are recorded in Nevins, *Ford*, p. 488.

[9]Columbia Motor Car Co. et al. v. A. C. Duerr & Co. et al., 184 Fed. 893 (1911).

Between 1908 and 1910, he merged into his newly incorporated General Motors 25 other companies, including Olds, Cadillac, and Oakland (which later became the Pontiac Division). Durant had motives for an acquisition strategy beyond those evident in the creation of Standard Oil and United States Steel. At the time, it was not clear which technologies—gasoline vs. steam vs. electric, four-cycle vs. two-cycle gasoline engines, friction vs. sliding-gear transmissions, and so on—would eventually win market acceptance. He tried to cover the complete array of technological bets. Explaining his acquisition of the Carter Company in 1909, for example, he observed, "How was anyone to know Cartercar wasn't to be the thing? It had the friction drive and no other car had it. . . . I was for getting every kind of thing in sight, playing safe all along the line."[10] His acquisitions were flimsily financed, however, and in 1910 Durant was forced out by his bankers. He then proceeded to organize the Chevrolet Company, regaining control of General Motors by merging the two corporations in 1915.

In hindsight, the most spectacular of Durant's acquisitions was the one that got away. In 1908 Durant proposed to acquire the Ford Motor Company for $3 million. Henry Ford is said to have been receptive, but Durant could not raise the cash, and so the deal fell through. In 1909, Ford showed renewed interest in an $8 million acquisition offer by Durant, but again, Durant could not obtain the required cash, and so the two companies remained independent.[11]

When Chevrolet and General Motors were merged, the Du Pont Company began to take an interest in the automobile maker as a potential customer and diversification target. Du Pont sought diversification in part because its traditional gunpowder operations had been broken into three entities (creating two new companies, Hercules Powder and Atlas Powder) under an antitrust decree in 1912. In 1917 Du Pont invested some of its World War I contract profits in General Motors, and in 1919, it increased its stake to 23 percent of GM's common stock.[12] Despite this much-needed cash infusion, GM's finances lurched out of control again in 1920. Durant was once again ousted as chief executive officer and Pierre S. Du Pont became the new president.

Pierre Du Pont reorganized GM's management, among other things placing on its executive committee Alfred P. Sloan, who later guided the company throughout its rise to industry leadership. The new management proceeded to make several key strategic decisions. In addition to implementing the rigorous

---

[10]Epstein, *The Automobile Industry*, pp. 182–183. See also Alfred P. Sloan, Jr., *My Years with General Motors* (New York: Doubleday, 1963), p. 6.

[11]See Epstein, *The Automobile Industry*, p. 225; and Nevins, *Ford*, pp. 412–414.

[12]In a precedent-setting antitrust case, Du Pont was required in 1957 by the U.S. Supreme Court to divest its continuing General Motors stockholdings. U.S. v. E. I. Du Pont de Nemours et al., 353 U.S. 586 (1957).

financial controls needed to monitor decentralized operating units, it restructured the General Motors product lines. The market for automobiles was classified by price tiers. Chevrolet was designated to target the lowest price range (i.e., $450 to $800), developing a new offering to go head-to-head against Ford's Model T at the bottom of that range. Other assignments, in ascending price range order, went to Pontiac, Oldsmobile, Buick, and (in the $2500–$3500 range) Cadillac.[13] Another decision committed General Motors to continuous changes in engineering features and styling, but the principal changes were to be clustered in new models introduced annually.[14] The period from late August until the end of September was designated as the best time for new model introductions so as not to cause a decline in output during the peak spring selling months, but to enhance selling momentum as the fall and winter seasons opened.

These choices proved crucial in the struggle with Ford for market position. As he aged, Henry Ford became increasingly resistant to change. He insisted on emphasizing an essentially unaltered Model T into the 1920s, while consumer preferences shifted to closed bodies and other more luxurious features, and despite the increasing competition from used cars for the purchases of the low-income consumers to whom the Model T catered. As his market share ebbed, he then shut down Model T production entirely for nearly a year in 1927 to convert to the improved Model A. General Motors seized this opportunity to pull ahead of Ford, capturing 42 percent of the market in 1927 and 1928 against Ford's 15 percent. With its Model A, Ford regained the unit sales lead in 1929 and 1930. But through continuing design changes—for example, the introduction of a six-cylinder Chevrolet in 1929, a move matched by Ford only in 1937—General Motors surged ahead again in 1931, retaining and indeed widening its lead during the next six decades.

Ford Motor Company's fortunes deteriorated further as Henry Ford refused to surrender decision-making authority to his son Edsel, whose frustration probably contributed to his early death in 1943. Edsel's son Henry Ford II was then summoned back from military service and, with the support of his mother and grandmother to overcome his grandfather's reticence, he assumed the company's leadership in late 1945.[15] He brought in new operating managers (among others, the "Whiz Kids," who had cut their teeth managing military procurement operations during World War II), installed new systems of organization and control, and rescued the company from what would otherwise have been almost certain bankruptcy. The senior Henry Ford died at the age of 84 in 1947.

---

[13]Sloan, *My Years at General Motors*, pp. 71–74.

[14]Ibid., pp. 190–193 and 275–285.

[15]See, for example, David Halberstam, *The Reckoning* (New York: William Morrow, 1986), Chapter 5.

While General Motors grew, many other automobile producers dropped out of the running. Casualties during the depressed 1930s included Locomobile, Paige Detroit, Reo, Franklin, Stutz, Cord, Auburn, Hupp, and Kissel. The cessation of civilian auto production during World War II and the boom that followed helped the remaining smaller companies and two new entrants, Kaiser and Crosley, survive during the 1940s, but in the 1950s a further weeding-out occurred. Crosley ceased production in 1952. Nash and Hudson merged in 1954 to form American Motors, which later acquired military Jeep-maker Willys, which had absorbed the failing Kaiser Company in 1953. Studebaker and the erstwhile leading luxury car maker, Packard, merged in 1954, surviving until 1966. By 1967, the industry was reduced to a "Big Four" consisting of General Motors, Ford, Chrysler (shaped by Walter Chrysler through the merger of Maxwell, Dodge, and Chalmers during the 1920s), and American Motors. In 1987 American Motors ended a long but preponderantly losing struggle, submitting to acquisition by Chrysler after an alliance with Renault of France failed to reverse its fortunes.

Companies exited from the industry or merged with their peers largely because they were unprofitable. Even among the smaller survivors, profits were erratic but modest. Figure 8.2 traces the movement of after-tax profits as a percentage of common stockholders' equity for General Motors, Ford, and Chrysler between 1954 and 1978 (after which, we shall see, new patterns

FIGURE 8.2
Return on Stockholders' Equity for Three Leading Automobile Manufacturers, 1954–1978

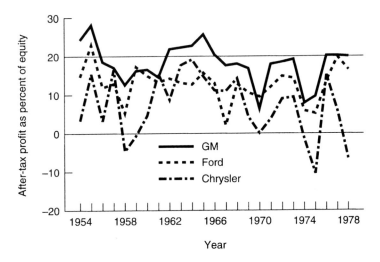

Source: Company Annual Reports

materialized). General Motors was almost consistently the most profitable of the three, with an average return on equity of 18.1 percent. Ford was second with an average of 12.6 percent and Chrysler third with 7.0 percent. American Motors is excluded because the extreme fluctuations in its profitability would have required a more encompassing, less easily interpreted graph. Its average return on equity over the 25-year period was 3.8 percent, with nine years of negative profits.

ECONOMIES OF SCALE

That General Motors, the largest U.S. auto maker, earned superior profits in most of the three decades following World War II suggests that it enjoyed some advantage relative to its smaller rivals. There are two main explanatory hypotheses: economies of large-scale operation, and pricing power associated with relative size. We explore each in turn, beginning with scale economies.

ASSEMBLY PLANTS

The automobile assembly plant epitomizes most observers' notion of scale economies. Henry Ford reduced the costs of his Model T by limiting each worker to a very narrow slice of the total assembly operation and then bringing one vehicle after another to workers on a moving assembly line. There are in fact substantial scale economies in auto assembly. But they peter out. The General Motors Lordstown, Ohio, assembly plant extended the frontiers of high-volume production during the early 1980s by having 100 vehicles pass down the assembly line per hour. The previous standard was 62 vehicles per hour.[16] One hundred vehicles per hour on conventional two-shift operation roughly 220 days per year (allowing time for model changeover) implies an assembly plant output of 350,000 vehicles per year. But the "speed-up" to 100 cars per hour triggered bitter protests from workers and product quality was unsatisfactory. Eventually General Motors cut back the pace.[17] In 1992 it adopted a new approach, moving to three ten-hour shifts per day four days per week, with an assembly line speed of 70 cars per hour. This made Lordstown the highest-volume assembly plant in the United States, with a total planned output of 450,000 cars per year.[18]

---

[16]See Lawrence J. White, *The Automobile Industry Since 1945* (Cambridge: Harvard University Press, 1971), p. 29; and U.S. Senate, Committee on the Judiciary, Subcommittee on Antitrust and Monopoly, Report, *Administered Prices: Automobiles* (Washington, DC: USGPO, 1958), pp. 14–15 (summarizing the testimony of American Motors president George Romney).

[17]See Emma Rothschild, "GM in More Trouble," *New York Review of Books*, March 23, 1972, pp. 18–25.

[18]"General Motors: Open All Night," *Business Week*, June 1, 1992, pp. 82–83.

What matters for market structure is the required scale of operations *relative to* total product demand. During the last five years of the 1980s, U.S. consumers purchased an average of 13.3 million passenger cars and small trucks per year. This means that the U.S. market could sustain 37 assembly plants operating under (optimistic) early 1970s Lordstown conditions or 30 plants under post–1992 Lordstown conditions. Actually, General Motors maintained 22 automobile and light truck assembly plants, Ford 15 plants, and Chrysler six plants in 1972, when total production was roughly 10 million units.[19] Thus, economies of scale *within* assembly plants are not nearly extensive enough to explain the concentration of production among a very few large companies.

There might be further economies of scale in assembling autos at more than one plant, giving a large multiplant company a cost advantage over single-plant operators.[20] Those that are known to exist are complex, changing over time, and probably modest in overall magnitude. Until the 1980s, General Motors and Ford tended to produce the same car model for the North American market at several geographically decentralized plants, sparing some cost of long-distance delivery (but adding to the cost of parts shipped from a central source). Lawrence J. White estimates the net transportation cost advantage from production in California as compared to Michigan at approximately 1.5 percent of the average passenger car price ex factory in 1963.[21] During the 1980s the industry reversed field, concentrating the production of a given model at a single plant in order to reduce manufacturing costs through greater specialization.[22] This change suggests that the main advantage from operating numerous assembly plants must have come from producing multiple models—a matter most conveniently taken up subsequently.

MAJOR COMPONENT PRODUCTION AND VERTICAL INTEGRATION

More pervasive scale economies are encountered in the production of major automobile components such as engines, transmissions, axles, fuel injectors, and air conditioners. In 1972 General Motors operated five U.S. transmission plants, two of them dedicated to manual (stick shift) types, and at least three engine plants. Ford had three of each.[23] This implies a required plant volume of at least a million transmissions or engines per year to achieve all scale

---

[19]Stanley E. Boyle, *A Reorganization of the U.S. Automobile Industry*, report printed by the U.S. Senate, Committee on the Judiciary, Subcommittee on Antitrust and Monopoly (Washington, DC: USGPO, 1974), pp. 58–65.

[20]See, for example, F. M. Scherer, Alan Beckenstein, Erich Kaufer, and R. D. Murphy, *The Economics of Multi-Plant Operation: An International Comparisons Study* (Cambridge: Harvard University Press, 1975).

[21]*The Automobile Industry Since 1945*, p. 43.

[22]See James M. Rubenstein, *The Changing U.S. Auto Industry: A Geographical Analysis* (Boston: Routledge, 1992).

[23]Boyle, *A Reorganization of the U.S. Automobile Industry*, pp. 102–114.

economies—an estimate consistent with interview evidence. If a company were to sell cars with both manual and automatic transmissions, or some cars with four-cylinder engines, some with six-cylinder engines, and so on, specialization of drive train manufacturing plants would require it to assemble 2 million or more units per year to utilize fully the output of efficient-sized component plants. Thus, an automobile assembler securing all economies of scale at the major component level would have to feed its components into four to six Lordstown-scale assembly plants, or nine plants assembling 62 cars per hour on two shifts per day. This range provides a crude approximation to the "least common multiple" number of assembly plants for dovetailing optimally with drive train component plants.

Here, however, we confront a fundamental question: Why must a company assembling automobiles make its own engines, transmissions, and other components? In other words, why must the assembler be vertically integrated into "upstream" component production? Why not buy the components from specialized vendors who secure maximum scale economies by producing for the entire market?[24] If that were feasible, there could be many assemblers, each of (relatively modest) efficient size, providing the benefits of competition without sacrificing economies of scale.

Some, indeed many, components are in fact purchased from outside specialists. But for important special-design components in whose production substantial scale economies exist, there are strong tendencies toward vertical integration, and hence toward relatively high least common assembly plant multiples.

The reason why is illustrated by a not atypical incident in the history of Ford Motor Company.[25] In 1939, General Motors offered the first automatic transmissions for high-volume passenger automobiles. Ford was impelled to follow suit. In the early years following World War II, Ford purchased its automatic transmissions from the Borg Warner Company. However, when Borg Warner announced a substantial price increase, Henry Ford II asked his finance staff to study the economics of building a vertically integrated automatic transmission plant. The finance staff reported that the full cost of internal transmission production was less than Borg Warner's price. Plans for the plant were thereupon finalized. When Borg Warner officials were informed of the impending change, they sharpened their pencil and submitted a new, lower price quotation. The proposal went back to Ford's finance staff, which concluded that the Borg Warner price was now less than Ford's projected internal unit cost and recommended that Ford continue purchasing from

---

[24]See George J. Stigler, "The Division of Labor Is Limited by the Extent of the Market," *Journal of Political Economy*, vol. 59 (June 1951), pp. 185–193.

[25]It is drawn from Paul W. Cherington, M. J. Peck, F. M. Scherer, et al., "New Product Decision-Making in the Ford Motor Company," unpublished report, Harvard Business School, 1958.

Ford rejected the recommendation and ordered that a

produce internally because Borg Warner had substantial
its relationship with Ford, and although it moderated its
to the threat of integration by Ford, that incident might be
.uture, and Borg Warner might repeatedly exploit its power
pportunistic price-raising attempts. Given the high required
nt transmission production, it was inevitable that there would
ansmission producers. Given General Motors' integration to pro-
y half of the U.S. market's transmission needs, the number of
t competing producers had to be even smaller—at most, two or
rg Warner, Eaton, and Dana). Each automobile assembler was likely
its own specialized transmission designs, requiring special tooling by
nsmission manufacturer. This design specificity essentially locked the
oler and the transmission manufacturer into a *bilateral monopoly* rela-
hip—that is, with a single (monopolistic) seller facing a single (monop-
istic) buyer for the specialized component.

The conflicts arising under bilateral monopoly are illustrated in Figure
5.3. The monopsonistic buyer's demand function is given by *MRP*—that is, the

FIGURE 8.3
Price and Output Preferences Under Bilateral Monopoly

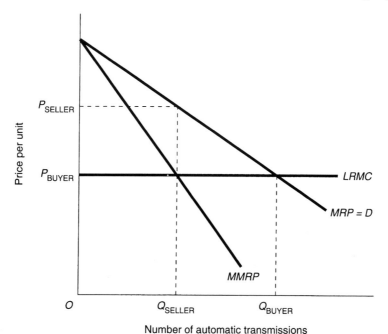

marginal revenue product of additional units.
reflecting the fact that buying more transmission
depresses the price at which the cars can be sold,
tional transmissions, and recognizing also that ma
substituted (on increasingly unfavorable price term
sions. Taking *MRP* to be the demand curve it faces,
mission vendor derives the curve marginal to it, obta
function *MMRP*. To maximize its profits, the *seller*
equal to its long-run production cost *LRMC* (assumed fo
stant regardless of volume),[26] offering output OQ_{SELLER} at
price of OP_{SELLER}. The monopsonistic buyer, on the oth
expand its purchases until its own marginal revenue produc
lowest possible price at which the transmission maker can su
OP_{BUYER}, which implies purchasing quantity OQ_{BUYER}. There
conflict between the price-quantity preferences of the buyer and
seller. Fearing that this conflict might under plausible future con
to his company's disadvantage, Henry Ford II decided to integrat
into transmission production, in which case he could equate his *MRP*
internal cost of production, which was only a bit above Borg Warner's

This "make vs. buy" scenario has been replayed countless times in th
tory of the automobile industry. In its early years, Ford Motor Company p
chased its transmissions, rear axles, and other drive train parts from th
Dodge Brothers. However, Ford often bargained for lower prices than those
preferred by the Dodges, and the Dodges apparently feared "that Ford might
suddenly cut off their contract and leave them stranded."[27] Therefore, in 1913
the two groups parted ways and Ford began producing for its own needs. Similar considerations led General Motors to acquire first a 60 percent ownership
share and then, in 1926, complete ownership in its principal body parts supplier, Fisher Body.[28]

The major automobile assemblers have never tried to integrate into producing *all* of their own component part needs. Outside purchase is more
likely, the less compelling scale economies are in the production of a component (permitting competition from multiple would-be vendors), the lower special tooling costs are, the less steep the component production learning curve
is (permitting easy shifts from one supplier to another), and the lower the
component's cost is relative to overall vehicle cost (making the impact of

---

[26]For the more complex upward-sloping marginal cost case, see F. M. Scherer and
David Ross, *Industrial Market Structure and Economic Performance*, 3rd ed. (Boston:
Houghton Mifflin, 1990), pp. 519–521.

[27]Nevins, *Ford*, p. 479.

[28]Sloan, *My Years with General Motors*, pp. 184–185.

opportunistic monopolistic pricing more tolerable).[29] General Motors has tended to be more completely integrated into component manufacturing than its smaller rivals because its higher assembly volume permitted it to exploit more fully the economies of high-scale component production. The sociological conditions facilitating or hampering conflict resolution also matter. Auto manufacturers in Japan have tended to be less integrated vertically than U.S.-based firms because they place more emphasis on sustaining harmonious long-term relationships with suppliers.

MODEL CHANGE AND TOOLING COSTS

General Motors initiated the practice of annual model changes during the 1920s. In the quarter century following World War II, this practice evolved into a fairly stable three-year cycle. The cycle began, usually in September, with the introduction of a completely new exterior body design, accompanied by internal engineering changes of varying degree. A "minor face-lift" followed at the beginning of the second year. That is, the front grille design, chrome strips, and other minor features were changed to distinguish the new offerings from their predecessors. At the beginning of the third year a "major facelift" ushered in more wide-ranging external styling changes without altering the basic shape of such key body parts as roof panels, fenders, hoods, and the like. At the start of the fourth year a thoroughgoing body redesign was brought forward, commencing a new cycle.

Most modern automobile bodies are made by welding and bolting together an array of contoured sheet metal parts stamped from cold-rolled steel.[30] The parts are manufactured in massive stamping presses, which smash a precut sheet of steel between two finely machined complementary steel dies to impart the desired curvature. To achieve the desired shape for more complex parts such as fenders, several stamping press stages may be required, each with its own set of dies: the first press gives the part its preliminary form, the second brings it near its final desired shape, and still another press rounds out the details. To avoid having factory floors and warehouses flooded with bulky stamped parts, stamping presses cycle regularly from making one part

---

[29] See, for example, Kirk Monteverde and David J. Teece, "Supplier Switching Costs and Vertical Integration in the Automobile Industry," *Bell Journal of Economics*, vol. 13 (Spring 1982), pp. 206–213; and Richard Langlois and Paul Robertson, "Explaining Vertical Integration: Lessons from the American Automobile Industry," *Journal of Economic History*, vol. 49 (June 1989), pp. 361–375.

[30] The still-definitive discussion of the economics of this process is John S. McGee, "Economies of Size in Auto Body Manufacture," *Journal of Law & Economics*, vol. 16 (October 1973), pp. 239–274. More recent developments in the methods by which dies are changed to make different parts are discussed in Womack et al., *The Machine That Changed the World*, pp. 51–53; and "Choreography on a Stamping Line," *New York Times*, December 24, 1988, pp. 35 and 37.

to others. With each such change, the appropriate new set of dies must be installed in the presses.

Tooling up for a new car model entails among other things designing and fabricating the complete set of dies with which body parts will be stamped. With proper care, many dies can be used to make as many as 10 million stamped parts. The dies require a large investment at the start of a model cycle. How large that investment is has been the subject of wildly varying estimates. Two authoritative estimates for the late 1960s and early 1970s delineate a range of $15 million to $46 million for a complete new body design.[31] However, estimates for new-model investment costs under 1990s conditions range from a minimum of $200 million[32] to $700 million for the 1994 Ford Mustang, $900 million for the Chrysler Cirrus and Stratus, $1.3 billion for Chrysler's Neon, and $1.9 billion for the 1995 Ford Taurus–Mercury Sable.[33] The higher estimates cover not only the cost of new dies for body stampings, but also design, fabrication and extensive testing of prototypes, tooling to produce new engines and other major drive train components, and in some cases investment in new plants. For less ambitious programs under 1990 conditions, the outlays for body stamping dies alone would approximate $250 million, and for a new drive train, another $250 million to $500 million. The cost of body stamping dies has escalated substantially above values cited for the late 1960s not only because of general inflation, but also because the tooling for unitized bodies, whose structural integrity is achieved through the stamped parts themselves, is much more expensive than for bodies placed upon an X-frame chassis, which was accepted practice before energy efficiency and low total weight were emphasized.

These new model tooling costs have important scale economy implications. The more cars one can produce during the life of a model, once the investment in tooling is sunk, the lower unit tooling costs per car will be. Assuming $250 million to be the required investment for a major body

---

[31]McGee, "Economies of Size," p. 253; and White, *The Automobile Industry Since 1945*, p. 36.

[32]"General Motors: The Next Move Is To Restore Each Division's Identity," *Business Week*, October 4, 1982, p. 76.

[33]See "There's Trouble Under Ford's Hood," *Business Week*, November 29, 1993, p. 67; "Chrysler's Neon," *Business Week*, May 3, 1993, pp. 116–126; "Following Chrysler," *The Economist*, April 23, 1994, pp. 66–67; and "'Tension and Tautness' in the Taurus— and at Ford," *Business Week*, January 9, 1995, p. 41.

The liqudity-constrained Chrysler Corporation projected new car program tooling expenditures averaging $569 million per year between 1979 and 1981. Power train program investments aded $373 million per year. The combined investments amounted to roughly $1000 per car actually sold by Chrysler in 1982–1984. "Chrysler Corporation Proposal for Government Assistance," unpublished memorandum submitted to the Chrysler loan guarantee board in 1979, Exhibit IV (kindly supplied by John Kwoka).

redesign alone and $700 million the investment for a wholly new car, including drive train, the average cost per car for diverse total model cycle production volumes is as follows:

Total Units Produced	Body Redesign Only	Complete New Vehicle
100,000	$2,500	$7,000
250,000	1,000	2,800
500,000	500	1,400
1,000,000	250	700
5,000,000	50	140

Plainly, if total model cycle sales number only in the hundreds of thousands, a severe cost penalty is incurred.[34] This was one of the most acute problems faced by the companies that exited from automobile production during the 1950s and 1960s. Producing at most a few hundred thousand units within a model cycle, they experienced much lower volumes and higher tooling costs than General Motors and Ford, which typically made millions of parts with a given set of dies. Some attempted to reduce this disadvantage by changing basic body designs less frequently than the standard three-year cycle, but then they commonly suffered from lower consumer acceptance by offering an unchanging design while their larger rivals fielded newer, more fashionable styling.[35]

The cost advantage derived by manufacturing a high volume of stamped parts from a set of expensive dies is so compelling that the major automobile companies exert much effort and ingenuity to achieve what they call "commonality" of body designs across their range of car offerings.[36] For a given basic body size (e.g., full-size, intermediate, compact, or subcompact),

[34]For very-low-volume cars, less costly tooling may be used or, as in the case of GM's Corvette, the body may be fabricated using low-investment-cost, high-marginal-cost fiberglass techniques.

[35]The Volkswagen Beetle was an important exception, attractive to some consumers precisely because of its invariant styling.

[36]It would be difficult to exaggerate the passion with which automobile makers pursued commonality. As an example, when he moved from the presidency of Ford Motor Company to becoming secretary of defense in 1961, Robert S. McNamara insisted that the U.S. Air Force and Navy achieve maximum commonality of new combat aircraft designs. The result of transplanting this Detroit practice to the quite different military environment was a fiasco. See Robert J. Art, *The TFX Decision: McNamara and the Military* (Boston: Little, Brown, 1968). Similarly, Volkswagen executives told the author in 1974 that the most serious error they had made in the early 1970s was proliferating models to replace their lagging "Beetle" without maintaining commonality among the dies.

General Motors attempted to have each of its car divisions design vehicles sufficiently alike that all can use the most complex and expensive dies in common. Bolsters were added to the dies to impart a slightly different fender shape, and minor parts such as the grille, chrome trim, and bumpers were customized so that, say, Buick's offerings appeared superficially different from those of Chevrolet, Pontiac, and Oldsmobile. With its substantially larger total volume across all divisions, General Motors was able during the 1950s and 1960s to sustain fuller utilization of body stamping dies even though its basic Chevrolet designs typically achieved roughly the same volumes as their Ford counterparts.[37]

After cost disadvantages attributable to design mandates contributed to the demise of smaller manufacturers, the three leading U.S. automakers moved away from a three-year cycle and toward much longer average model lives during the 1970s. One impetus was the rising cost of styling changes, especially for unitized bodies. There is reason to believe also that consumers became less fickle, attaching less value to driving the most up-to-date style, especially for their utilitarian compact cars. John Kwoka's research suggests that major styling changes had a strong positive effect on the sales of full-size and intermediate cars between 1960 and 1982, but that their impact on compact car sales was much smaller and statistically insignificant.[38]

With the introduction of new models, advertising outlays by auto producers (as distinguished from those of dealers) tend to escalate. On average during the mid–1970s, for which the best data exist, auto manufacturers' media advertising expenditures varied between 0.7 percent of factory sales (in boom years) and 0.9 percent (in a slump year).[39] That there are scale economies in national advertising is suggested by evidence that General Motors spent substantially less on average per car than its smaller rivals. Also, within compa-

---

[37] This advantage may have been frittered away by spending too much on tooling. See J. Patrick Wright (for John DeLorean), *On a Clear Day You Can See General Motors* (Grosse Pointe, MI: Wright Enterprises, 1979), p. 199; and White, *The Automobile Industry Since 1945*, p. 204. On the cost of extending dies to handle multiple models, see McGee, "Economies of Size," pp. 253–257.

General Motors probably carried its quest for commonality too far during the late 1970s and early 1980s by having divisional offerings that looked so much alike that the divisions lost much of their historical image differentiation. See "Can GM Solve Its Identity Crisis?" *Business Week*, January 23, 1984, pp. 32–33; and "G.M. Will Shed Some Models, Stressing Brand," *New York Times*, April 29, 1995, p. 35. It also suffered a reputation blow when someone neglected to change the label on Chevrolet engines installed in Oldsmobiles. "G.M. Calls Its Engine Swapping Innocent, But to the Brand-Faithful Buyer It's a Sin," *New York Times*, March 15, 1977, p. 51.

[38] John E. Kwoka, "The Sales and Competitive Effects of Styling and Advertising in the U.S. Auto Industry," *Review of Economics and Statistics*, vol. 75 (November 1993), pp. 649–656.

[39] Federal Trade Commission, *Annual Line of Business Report*, 1974 through 1977.

nies, the lower-volume brands had higher average advertising outlays per car than Chevrolet, Ford, and Plymouth.[40]

Launching new models that seek to capture the consumer's changing fancy is a risky endeavor. Costly mistakes are virtually inevitable, but they can be absorbed more easily by a large manufacturer with a broad portfolio of models than by a smaller, more specialized maker. Ford's Edsel—a name that has become the generic descriptor for a flop—led to losses of roughly $100 million, which constituted only a passing setback for a huge corporation that had regained its financial strength by 1958. Styling mistakes of similar gravity could and did spell fatal distress and/or a rush into merger for Kaiser, Stude-baker, Crosley, Nash, and other smaller makers. Ford and Chrysler also hedged their bets during the 1950s and 1960s by adhering fairly closely to the broad styling trends initiated by General Motors. In later decades, however, GM's ability to discern or shape consumer demands ebbed, and Ford and Chrysler have tended to pursue more independent styling approaches.

SALES THROUGH FRANCHISED DEALER NETWORKS

In the United States and most other industrialized nations, automobile manu-facturers sell their products through franchised dealers, which are in most respects independent businesses. Why this approach was chosen over direct vertical integration into retailing is explained by Alfred Sloan:

> When the used car came into the picture in a big way in the 1920s as a trade-in on a new car, the merchandising of automobiles became more a trading propo-sition than an ordinary selling proposition. Organizing and supervising the nec-essary thousands of complex trading institutions would have been difficult for the manufacturer; trading is a knack not easy to fit into the conventional type of a managerially controlled scheme of organization.

There are economies of scale in the operation of a dealership. Costly special diagnostic and repair machines are needed, as are minimum stocks of repair parts and specialists in sales, repairs, and diverse managerial functions. Peter Pashigian found that under late–1950s conditions, dealership costs per unit were minimized only when new car sales volumes of from 600 to 800 units per year were reached. A dealer selling 200 units per year experienced operating costs 25 to 35 percent higher per car sold than dealers achieving those higher volumes.[41] Since then, the minimum efficient scale has undoubtedly risen as cars have become more complex, requiring more expensive repair equipment and spare parts inventories, and as higher-power marketing methods have been adopted. As a result, the average number of new cars sold per dealer has

---

[40]White, *The Automobile Industry Since 1945*, p. 225; and Kwoka, "The Sales and Com-petitive Effects," p. 651.

[41]B. P. Pashigian, *The Distribution of Automobiles: An Economic Analysis of the Fran-chise System* (Englewood Cliffs, NJ: Prentice-Hall, 1961), p. 223.

risen and, at least since the 1950s, the number of new car dealers has shrunk—for example, from roughly 38,000 in 1958 to 30,800 in 1970; to 27,900 in 1980; to 24,725 in 1985; and to 22,451 in 1994.[42]

Dealership scale economies posed problems for smaller manufacturers in the smaller cities and towns of the United States. In a retail sales area serving a population of 40,000, approximately 2000 new cars might be sold in a typical year. The Chevrolet or Ford dealer's share of this volume would be sufficient to approach, even if not reach, Pashigian's 600-unit least-cost threshold. By "dualing" in the distribution of, say, Pontiacs and Cadillacs, other General Motors dealers could also come close. But for the manufacturer such as American Motors or Studebaker with at best a 5 percent market share, an exclusive dealer could expect to sell only 100 units per year—far too few to realize minimum costs. For this reason, dealers specializing in less-favored makes tended to be less profitable, and this situation in turn encouraged the most energetic dealers to seek Ford and General Motors franchises, strengthening those companies' retailing effectiveness.

To be sure, in the larger cities, even small manufacturers experienced little difficulty building dealerships reaching minimum efficient scales. But Americans are a mobile lot. When they buy a car, many realize that they might be living somewhere else—perhaps in a small town—before the time for a new purchase comes. And when they travel on business or vacation, they want to ensure that service will be available if their car breaks down, say, in rural Kansas. Manufacturers without dealerships throughout the nation, in large cities and small towns, were at a disadvantage vis à vis GM, Ford, and (less sharply) Chrysler in selling their cars. Recognizing this, Pashigian estimated that under late 1950s conditions, an automobile manufacturer needed to sell at least 600,000 units per year in order to maintain a strong network of franchised dealers, and he believed distributional advantages persisted out to annual volumes of 2 million units.[43]

Some important variables are left unaccounted for in this simple equation. For one, as the mechanical reliability of automobiles has risen over time, concern over the possibility of obtaining repair service in remote locations has ebbed, if not disappeared altogether. More significantly, as U.S. families became more affluent, in part by having multiple wage earners, many purchased second and even third cars. The "second car" was likely to be used only for local commuting, and so the purchaser could be much less concerned about obtaining service away from home. Recognition of this fact was central to Volkswagen's successful penetration of the U.S. market during the late 1950s. Volkswagen needed to emphasize only the creation of strong dealer-

---

[42]U.S. Bureau of the Census, *Statistical Abstract of the United States: 1993*, p. 779; and *Automotive News 1994 Data Book*, p. 107. See also Sloan, *My Years with General Motors*, p. 345; and White, *The Automobile Industry Since 1945*, p. 149. For a poignant account of one dealership's exit, see Ingrid Bengis, "My Father Sold Chryslers," *New York Times*, January 22, 1980, p. A21.

[43]Pashigian, *The Distribution of Automobiles*, pp. 234–238.

ships in the larger cities. A similar strategy was pursued by the Japanese automakers during the late 1960s and the 1970s. They established beachheads in larger cities, especially on the West Coast, and then expanded their networks as their sales grew to levels sufficient to support viable dealerships in smaller and more remote metropolitan areas.

Implicit in the discussion thus far is the assumption that manufacturers must sell their cars through *exclusive* dealerships. There is no legal reason why this need be so. U.S. antitrust law evolved precedents that made it hazardous for the Big Three, if not smaller manufacturers, to impose de jure exclusivity upon their franchised dealers.[44] However, the manufacturers had less formal means of persuading their dealers to focus their efforts exclusively on a single make or, in smaller cities, two or more brands from the same company. The dealer who strayed too far from the path of exclusivity was likely to experience difficulties getting "hot-selling" cars and cars that embodied special features. As a result, and because of specialization advantages, most dealers in fact elect not to take on the brands of competing manufacturers. In 1994, only 2.3 percent of the 17,893 dealers franchised to sell U.S. Big Three cars also carried the cars of competing corporations. However, among the 4558 dealerships specializing in imported cars, 22 percent carried competing brands.[45] There is reason to believe that dual distributorships became somewhat more common since the 1960s as dealers have won greater independence from their manufacturers, secured among other things by federal and state "dealer day in court" laws limiting the manufacturer's ability to cancel franchises arbitrarily.[46] This change is said to have helped Japanese producers gain a foothold in the United States.[47]

There is conflict between dealers and manufacturers over price-quantity relationships as well as over exclusivity. Especially in smaller towns and cities, the typical dealer enjoys a fair amount of customer loyalty. This makes the dealer a monopolistic competitor, facing a (mildly) downward-sloping demand curve. The profit-maximizing dealer under these conditions may (subject to qualifications raised later) restrict its output until marginal revenue equals marginal cost. The manufacturer also has monopoly power in selling its differentiated products. When two vertically related stages each try to equate marginal cost with (downward-sloping) marginal revenue, output is restricted more than it would be if the output decision were made by a single integrated

---

[44]For example, Hudson Sales Corp. v. Waldrip, 211 F. 2d 268 (1954).

[45]*Automotive News 1994 Data Book*, p. 107. See also Boyle, *A Reorganization of the U.S. Automobile Industry*, p. 196.

[46]See Richard L. Smith, "Franchise Regulation: An Economic Analysis of State Restrictions on Automobile Distribution," *Journal of Law & Economics*, vol. 25 (April 1982), pp. 125–157.

[47]Mitsuo Matsushita, "An International Comparison of Distribution and Trade Practices and Competition Policies," draft report, Tokyo (1986), p. 6.

firm,[48] just as a succession of independent principalities attempting to extract revenue-maximizing tolls at various points along the Rhine River virtually choked off boat traffic during the eighteenth and early nineteenth centuries. The auto manufacturers have attempted through persuasion, volume rebates, inventory-forcing, and the threat of franchise cancellation to induce their dealers to sell more cars than the dealers might otherwise prefer.[49] "Dealer day in court" laws were enacted in part to limit manufacturers' cancellation options when such conflicts arise.

SUMMARY

Because of scale economies in major drive train component production, metal stamping die and other new model investment costs, the maintenance of franchised dealer networks, and risk spreading, manufacturers selling less than a million cars per year operate at a distinct cost and product differentiation handicap relative to larger companies. There is reason to believe that advantages from large-scale operation persist even to the scale of General Motors, and this probably helps explain why GM was consistently more profitable than Ford and Chrysler from the 1950s through the 1970s.

Nevertheless, gigantic size is not unambiguously advantageous, even in automobiles. With it can come more complex decision making, bureaucratic rigidity, and inability to respond quickly to changing market conditions. Applying the organizational principles introduced by Du Pont and Sloan—combining decentralized decision making and incentives with strong central staff oversight—General Motors was remarkably successful in avoiding for many decades the disadvantages of massive size. Beginning in the late 1950s and accelerating in the 1960s, however, it began changing its approaches to organization and management, with consequences that will unfold in subsequent sections.[50]

PRICING

Scale economies, we shall see, provide much less than a full explanation of the superior profitability of General Motors. To comprehend the rest of the picture and set the stage for understanding how it changed in the 1980s, we must analyze with some care how automobile prices have been determined.

---

[48]For a proof, see Scherer and Ross, *Industrial Market Structure and Economic Performance*, pp. 537–539.

[49]Pashigian, *The Distribution of Automobiles*, pp. 52–60.

[50]Compare Peter F. Drucker, *The Concept of the Corporation* (New York: Day, 1946), especially Part II; and Alfred D. Chandler, *Strategy and Structure: Chapters in the History of the Industrial Enterprise* (Cambridge: MIT Press: 1962), chap. 3; with Wright, *On a Clear Day You Can See General Motors*. See also "GM Moves to Centralize All Operations," *Automotive News*, September 20, 1971, pp. 1 and 36–37.

PRICE LEADERSHIP

In the industry's early decades, Ford Motor Company strove to be the low-price seller, and others had to follow suit to the extent that the cost of their popularly priced cars allowed, or avoid competing with Ford by emphasizing more luxurious models. When Ford fell upon hard times, GM became the accepted industry price leader.

By the end of the automobile boom following World War II, a stylized and well-understood pattern of price leadership emerged. Each of the main producers attempted to offer cars in well defined price brackets, and car designs were arranged so that unit costs were in line with the price at which a model was expected to sell.[51] Suggested retail prices were announced once each year, in the fall, as new models were rolled out. Ford and Chrysler sought to match the prices of General Motors, except for small differentials reflecting differences in standard equipment and (in some years) Chrysler's willingness to sacrifice volume to cover its higher unit costs.[52] American Motors and the other smaller manufacturers pursued more independent pricing policies, correctly perceiving that their sales were too small to evoke retaliation from the Big Three. A complication intruded because in many years the requisites of inventory building caused General Motors to unveil its new models, and hence announce its prices, later than those of its rivals. Then Ford and Chrysler managers attempted to predict what prices General Motors would quote and make tentative announcements accordingly. When their guesses were on the high side, they announced within a few days' time revisions reducing their prices to parity with those of General Motors. When they guessed low, as in 1956, 1970, and 1974,[53] they might have used the price differential to gain volume at the expense of General Motors—provided that GM did not retaliate by reducing its own prices. But instead they revised their original announcements, following General Motors upward to parity. In this way, harmony among the oligopolists was maintained.

The pattern changed during the late 1970s. To ease the "sticker shock" resulting from large percentage price changes on September's new models in

---

[51]When unanticipated deviations from cost targets arose, last-minute adjustments in the quality of upholstery and the like were made to bring the costs into line. This was the case in 1958. See Cherington et al., "New Product Decision-Making." It remains true in the 1990s. See "Stuck! How Companies Cope When They Can't Raise Prices," *Business Week*, November 15, 1993, pp. 148–150.

[52]See the Senate Report, *Administered Prices*, pp. 52–76; White, *The Automobile Industry Since 1945*, pp. 109–116; Wright, *On a Clear Day You Can See General Motors*, pp. 224–225; and "Detroit's Dilemma on Prices," *Business Week*, January 20, 1975, pp. 82–83.

[53]*Administered Prices*, pp. 53–54 and 67–69; "Chrysler Increases Prices Again For '71, Following G.M. Pattern," *New York Times*, December 2, 1970, p. 35; and "Ford Motor Adds to Boost on '75 Models; Price Rise Will Near GM's Almost 10%," *Wall Street Journal*, August 21, 1974, p. 3.

that inflation-ridden period, General Motors announced a new policy of instituting list price changes roughly quarterly.[54] Ford and Chrysler followed suit. Other pricing strategy changes during that period were less consistent with follow-the-leader traditions. They will be examined when the necessary foundation has been laid.

FORMULA PRICING

General Motors was the leader, but to where should it lead? Part of the answer emerged in 1924, when GM's market share was still less than half Ford's. In a remarkable series of articles, the vice president for finance of General Motors articulated a formula for both price-setting and the allocation of GM's investible funds. As a basic principle, it stated:

> An acceptable theory of pricing must be to gain over a protracted period of time a margin of profit which represents the highest attainable return commensurate with capital turnover and the enjoyment of wholesale expansion. Thus the profit margin, translated into its salient characteristic rate of return on capital employed, is the logical yardstick by which to gage the price. . . .[55]

Clearly, this approach was oriented toward the long run. It might with some license be interpreted to mean that General Motors was embarking upon a limit pricing strategy.

To operationalize the concept, three quantitative variables were needed: the rate of return sought, the capital base to which it applied, and the relationship of sales volume to the capital base. The second and third were characterized in terms of *standard volume*—that is, sales at 80 percent of conservatively rated plant capacity, which in turn was linked to the amount of capital employed. General Motors then attempted to set prices that yielded a 20 percent after-tax return on capital at standard volume. During the 1920s it appears that this rate of return was to be achieved with respect to the total amount of capital used.[56] However, by the 1950s the formula had been modified so that GM realized at standard volume a return of 15 percent on total capital or, given the relationship of equity capital to other sources of capital, 20 percent on stockholders' equity.[57]

From the outset, it was recognized that actual sales might deviate from standard volume—above it in booms, below it in slumps—and that realized

---

[54]GM's New Price Strategy," *Automotive News*, May 8, 1978, p. 2; and "GM Conditions Buyers for Periodic Price Rises," *Chicago Tribune*, July 6, 1980, Section 5, p. 5.

[55]Donaldson Brown, "A Pricing Policy in Relation to Financial Control," *Management and Administration*, February 1924; reproduced in U.S. Senate, Select Committee on Small Business, Hearings, *Planning, Regulation, and Competition: Automobile Industry—1968* (Washington, DC: USGPO, 1968), p. 221.

[56]Brown, "Pricing Policy," *Management and Administration*, March 1924, reproduced in the Senate hearings, *Planning*, pp. 226–228.

[57]Senate Report, *Administered Prices*, pp. 104–105, citing testimony by Albert Bradley and Harlow Curtice of General Motors.

returns on investment would fluctuate accordingly. We return to Figure 8.2 to see how well General Motors fared in relation to its aspirations. Over the relatively normal postwar 1954–1978 period, its average return was 18.1 percent—a close approximation indeed to the target. In 18 of the 25 years, its actual return was within four percentage points of the target. It exceeded the target by more than four percentage points in two boom years, 1955 and 1965. It fell below in 1958, 1961, 1970, 1974, and 1975—in all of which U.S. real GNP growth was either negative or (in 1961) small.

PROFITABILITY AND MODEL SIZE

Although these results suggest close adherence to GM's broad pricing formula, the details were a good deal more complex. Most important, since at least the 1920s, there has been a marked tendency for automobile profit margins to rise disproportionately with vehicle weight, the traditional hallmark of luxury, or more recently, with the image of luxury a car projects. Figure 8.4

FIGURE 8.4
The Relationship of Prices and Costs to the Sizes of 1958–1960 Model Automobiles

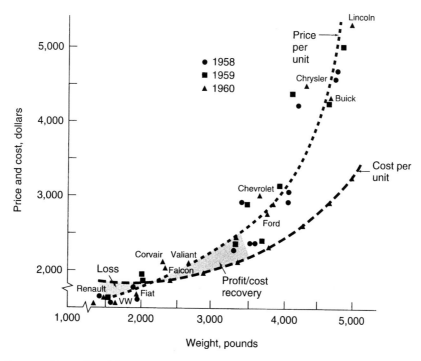

Source: Reproduced from National Academy of Engineering, *The Competitive Status of the U.S. Auto Industry* (Washington, DC: National Academy Press, 1982), p. 69, drawing upon data from *Consumer Reports*.

illustrates the relationships discernible in 1958–1960. Prices rise nonlinearly with vehicle weight. But vehicle costs rise less than proportionately with weight, because roughly the same number of stamping operations, boring machine cuts, welds, and the like are needed to assemble a large, heavy car as a smaller car.[58] As former GM Chevrolet Division head John DeLorean explains:

> American car customers, historically, have been willing to pay hundreds of dollars more for a few extra pounds and inches in their cars. The returns to the company are obvious. When I was with GM, a $300 to $400 difference between the building costs of a Chevrolet Caprice and a Cadillac DeVille, a bigger car, was small compared to a $3,800 difference in the sticker price.[59]

There are several explanations for this phenomenon. One is historical. As the automobile industry matured during the 1920s, the nonlinear relationship between price and weight gained solid acceptance in the market, bolstered among other things by General Motors' price line strategy decisions. But tradition alone cannot explain its persistence. A second reason, applicable mainly during the three decades following World War II, is that there were far fewer effective competitors—essentially, Cadillac, Packard (until 1957), Lincoln, and Chrysler Imperial—in the luxury car segment than there were for smaller cars, and as a result, price competition was sufficiently attenuated to sustain prices well above production costs. But the relationship remained even after the luxury segment was invaded by numerous foreign makes during the 1970s and 1980s. Berry et al. estimate that under 1990 conditions, the margin of price above marginal production cost (i.e., excluding fixed-cost allocations) was $801 for a subcompact Mazda 323, $1077 for a sub-compact Ford Escort, $2420 for a Buick Century, $7500 for a Cadillac Seville, and $10,975 for a BMW 735i.[60] It is possible that the gap between price and marginal cost rises with car size because the sales volume of more expensive mod-

---

[58] For supporting quantitative evidence, see *The Competitive Status of the U.S. Automobile Industry*, pp. 65–68; Marc Hagerman, *Automobile Marketing, Strategy, Pricing, and Product Planning*, U.S. Department of Transportation study HS 803–181: (1978), pp 14–23; Bernard A. Girod, Joseph Vinso, and H. Paul Root, "Profit Comparisons and Product Mix in the Automobile Industry," working paper no. 60, University of Michigan Graduate School of Business Administration, May 1972; U.S. House of Representatives, Committee on Banking, Housing and Urban Affairs, Subcommittee on Economic Stabilization, Report, *Findings of the Chrysler Loan Guarantee Board* (Washington, DC: USGPO, May 12, 1980), pp. 165 and 757; and "Small Car Blues at General Motors," *Business Week*, March 16, 1974, pp. 76–78. On changes in technology that reduced small-car costs in Europe, see "Small Cars, Big Comeback," *New York Times*, May 10, 1995, pp. D1 and D4.

[59] Wright, *On a Clear Day You Can See General Motors*, p. 177.

[60] Steven Berry, James Levinsohn, and Ariel Pakes, "Automobile Prices in Equilibrium," National Bureau of Economic Research, working paper no. 4264 (January 1993), part II, Table 10.

els is much smaller, and if the fixed costs specifically associated with those models were properly attributed, *net* profit returns would be equalized across sizes. But this conjecture is inconsistent with a vast amount of evidence (some to be reviewed in a moment) revealing auto executives' perception that luxury models have higher *net* profit returns. No such competitive equalization need occur if main-line producers can reduce costs by exploiting parts and design commonality in offering their luxury models, whereas marginal entrants into the luxury field (such as Rolls-Royce, Packard, Mercedes, and BMW) cannot. A final explanation is that the consumers who buy large and especially luxury cars impute at least part of their superior value to an image of exclusiveness, which in turn follows from paying a high price. It is significant that Packard, the leading U.S. luxury car of the 1910s and 1920s, lost its premium appeal when it chose to combat 1930s depression sales losses by offering look-alikes at much lower prices.[61] Cadillac, which stayed with a high-price strategy during the 1930s, thereupon displaced Packard as the U.S. luxury car of choice.[62]

Whatever the precise explanation, the superior profitability of larger cars had much to do with GM's ability to sustain a higher rate of return on invested capital than Ford, Chrysler, and other smaller rivals. Because of the broad-line strategy choice it made in the 1920s, it was particularly strong in the luxury and subluxury field following World War II. Thus, 18 percent of GM's unit sales between 1956 and 1960 were of high-priced Cadillacs and Buicks, whereas Chrysler derived 12 percent of its (much smaller) unit volume from Chryslers and Imperials, and only 2 percent of Ford's volume came from Lincolns and Continentals.[63] John DeLorean of GM observed flatly, "The profit advantage we had over Ford lay entirely in our dominance of the medium- and large-car segments."[64] Similarly, a quantitative study estimated that in 1969, 70 percent of General Motors' profit advantage over Ford in automotive operations came from its more profitable mix of luxury vehicles.[65]

Ford Motor Company was acutely aware of its disadvantage vis à vis General Motors. Its primary strategic objective during the late 1950s was to build

[61]Robert Sobel, "Ask the Man Who Owns One," *Audacity*, Winter 1994, pp. 14–27.

[62]Cadillac in turn failed to heed the lessons of history during the troubled 1980s, offering cars little differentiated from lower-price GM models and suffering severe image and market share erosion. See "Europe's Luxury Models Defy the Sales Slump," *Business Week*, August 9, 1982, p. 25; "A Generation Gap Hits Detroit," *Philadelphia Inquirer*, July 24, 1983; "Cadillac Seeks Sales to Match Its Image," *Advertising Age*, September 9, 1985, p. 10; "GM's New Luxury Cars: Why They're Not Selling," *Business Week*, January 19, 1987, pp. 94–98; and "Cadillac's Allante Struggles," *New York Times*, November 16, 1987, p. D1. Beginning in the late 1980s, Cadillac made a concerted effort to rebuild its image. See "Cadillac's Bid to Recapture Youth," *New York Times*, May 7, 1991, p. D1.

[63]White, *The Automobile Industry Since 1945*, pp. 294–295.

[64]Wright, *On a Clear Day You Can See General Motors*, p. 199.

[65]Girod et al., "Profit Comparisons and Product Mix," p. 40.

its position in what was then considered the medium-car segment (that is, where Mercury faced Buick, Oldsmobile, Pontiac, and Dodge), in which generous profits could be had on a substantial volume.[66] One manifestation was a compression of the model cycle to two years for Mercury; another was the ill-fated Edsel program. After these attempts failed, it saw a new opportunity when General Motors announced in 1974 that, responding to OPEC-induced gasoline price increases, it would undertake a massive downsizing program.[67] Ford chose not to follow suit, but to redouble its large car design and selling efforts.[68] For a while, the strategy was successful. Ford gained market share where it sought to, and in 1977, it reported record profits. See Figure 8.2. But this strategy left Ford unprepared for the Iranian oil crisis of 1979 and a sudden demand swerve to smaller, high-mileage cars. Ford plunged from high profits to losses totaling $3.5 billion (before tax adjustments) in the 1980–1982 period. It averted disaster in part by introducing in the fall of 1980 a new front-wheel drive "world car," named Escort in the Ford version and Lynx for the Mercury line, whose design evolved from the highly successsful Fiesta model produced by Ford's European subsidiary.[69]

Proclaiming that it could not survive on the thin profit margins small cars afforded, Chrysler also sought to rebuild its strength in luxury cars during the late 1970s.[70] However, it was temporarily restrained from doing so by U.S. government insistence that in exchange for federal loan guarantees to stave off its impending bankruptcy in 1980, it focus its entire effort on high-mileage cars. Later, freed from those constraints, it reentered the luxury segment.

The perception that small cars had low, indeed negative, profits underlay the more general reluctance of the leading U.S. automakers to produce them. During the 1950s, several smaller companies offered small cars, but except for American Motors' Rambler, they met with little success. In the later 1950s, imports of small cars from Europe increased dramatically. Led by the Volkswagen Beetle, whose U.S. sales rose from 50,000 units in 1956 to 120,442 units in 1959, imports experienced market share gains from 1.65 percent to 10.17 percent over the same interval.[71] The U.S. Big Three watched, waited, and planned. In early 1958 the president of General Motors told a congressional committee that "Thus far it has not been practical from the standpoint

---

[66]Cherington et al., "New Product Decision-Making in the Ford Motor Company."

[67]"GM Switching to Small Car for 'Gas-Conscious Era,'" *International Herald-Tribune*, March 23, 1974, and "GM's Juggernaut," *Business Week*, March 26, 1979, pp. 62–77.

[68]"Few Changes Mark 1977 Model Lineup Introduced by Ford," *New York Times*, September 8, 1976, p. 49. For a fuller account, see Halberstam, *The Reckoning*, pp. 510–543.

[69]See "Driving to Rebuild Ford for the Future," *Business Week*, August 4, 1980, p. 70.

[70]"Chrysler Set to Produce Luxury Line," *International Herald-Tribune*, September 27, 1979.

[71]White, *The Automobile Industry Since 1945*, p. 295.

of the economics to offer the small car, on the basis that because you take the value out so much more rapidly than you can take the cost out."[72] But in the fall of 1959 all three introduced compact models: General Motors the Corvair, Ford the Falcon, and Chrysler the Valiant/Dart. Lawrence J. White argues that they hesitated and then acted in parallel because they were reluctant to cannibalize higher-profit big car sales, feared that if one introduced a small car all would have to defend themselves by doing so, and waited until the market was large enough to accommodate offerings from all three.[73]

The availability of small cars from the Big Three cut imports by half, and plans to introduce even smaller versions were canceled. Instead, between 1960 and 1969 the Big Three increased their new small cars' size by an average of 3.7 inches in length and 360 pounds of weight.[74] Prices rose accordingly. When imports began climbing again, a new set of subcompacts was brought out: GM's Vega, Ford's Pinto, and American Motors' Gremlin, all in 1970. Chrysler, whose financial position was deteriorating, chose not to introduce its own new subcompact, instead filling out its line with a Colt model purchased from Mitsubishi in Japan. General Motors added an even smaller model, the Chevette, in 1975.

LIMIT PRICING?

The pricing strategy articulated by General Motors in 1925 was to achieve "the highest attainable return commensurate with capital turnover and the enjoyment of wholesale expansion." Prices that yielded it a 20 percent average return on stockholders' equity constrained much smaller companies lacking GM's economies of scale sufficiently that, one by one, they exited from the industry, leaving only Ford, Chrysler, and American Motors as domestic rivals.

Overseas competitors posed a different and more complex problem. Most specialized in cars smaller than the U.S. standard. After recovering from the devastation of World War II, foreign auto manufacturers had two advantages over U.S. producers in supplying small cars. With large and rapidly growing home market demand for small cars, they realized economies of scale, which increased as the market expanded and could be enhanced even more by exporting. Also, the wage rates in most industrialized European nations and in Japan were, at the exchange rates maintained under the Bretton Woods system until 1971, lower in dollar terms than those paid by U.S. automakers. Thus, the U.S.-based companies were at a cost disadvantage in offering small cars. This was one reason, but probably not the only one, why profit margins

---

[72]Ibid., p. 184, citing testimony of Harlow Curtice.

[73]Ibid., pp. 177–185.

[74]John E. Kwoka, "Market Power and Market Change in the U.S. Automobile Industry," *Journal of Industrial Economics*, vol. 32 (June 1984), p. 516.

on small cars in the United States were much lower than the margins on larger cars.

Dynamic limit pricing theory, we learned in Chapter 5, teaches that when a dominant group operates at a unit cost disadvantage relative to potential entrants—in this instance, foreign firms exporting to the United States—its long-run profits are maximized by setting prices above the level of potential entrants' costs and ceding market share to the entrants. A slow pace of entry (e.g., because distribution channels are not easily established) makes such a strategy all the more attractive.

The U.S. Big Three could not have been unaware of these considerations. But another factor favored a more aggressive defense against imports. A fringe benefit of the "cover all price ranges" strategy adopted by General Motors in the 1920s was the possibility of "moving up" consumers from low-priced to more profitable luxury cars as their life cycles evolved. The newly established family would buy an entry-level Chevrolet. As it prospered, it moved up to Oldsmobiles and Buicks, and if it became really affluent, it purchased a Cadillac, in the process raising its profit contribution to General Motors. For Ford and Chrysler, similar reasoning applied. Ceding the small-car market to foreign firms risked reducing the probability of later transitions to high-priced U.S. cars.

The U.S. manufacturers resolved this conflict by choosing to offer their own small cars, despite their low profitability. And from 1970 on, General Motors and Ford appear to have pursued a carefully calculated strategy of positioning one "stripped" subcompact model—that is, one lacking optional luxury features—at a price close to the prices quoted by the most popular imports. Thus, in early 1971, a stripped two-door Chevrolet Vega was priced at $2090 and a two-door Ford Pinto at $1919, compared to $1899 for a Volkswagen Beetle and $1798 for a two-door Toyota Corolla 1200.[75]

The U.S. firms offered these low-end models (and later the even smaller Chevette) in the spirit of limit pricing, but they would have preferred, if circumstances permitted, to "twist" the price curve of Figure 8.4 upward so that smaller cars yielded larger profit margins. As the energy price shocks of 1973–1974 caused an increasing number of U.S. consumers to buy smaller, more fuel-economical cars, the profit consequences of a twist became ever more pressing. An opportunity to twist the curve appeared when the United States withdrew from the gold standard in August 1971 and the value of the dollar floated downward. Between 1971 and late 1974, the West German mark rose by 42 percent and the Japanese yen by 15 percent relative to the dollar. This (plus quality improvements on Japanese cars) led producers of the lead-

---

[75]Lawrence J. White, "The Automobile Industry," in Walter Adams, ed., *The Structure of American Industry*, 6th ed. (New York: Macmillan, 1982), pp. 157–158. At the time, Toyota had not yet achieved the high quality levels that distinguished it later.

ing imported cars to announce substantial price increases. Then U.S. manufacturers raised their import-fighters' prices in tandem—by much higher proportions than the increases on their full-sized cars.[76]

The energy shocks led to a further complication. In 1975, the U.S. Congress passed a law setting minimum corporate average fuel economy (CAFE) standards for coming model years.[77] Passenger car producers were required to achieve an average new car fuel economy level of 18 miles per gallon in the 1978 model year, escalating in annual increments to 27.5 miles per gallon in 1985. At the time the law was passed, the average U.S.-produced new car was attaining 14.8 miles per gallon. Thus, a near doubling of fuel economy was contemplated. For each mile per gallon by which a domestic car producer's fleet fell below the model year target, a fine of $50 per car was to be levied. For General Motors, falling two miles per gallon below the target could mean paying the U.S. Treasury a fine of approximately $200 million and receiving considerable bad publicity.

In order to meet the CAFE standards, the automakers had to sell more small cars and improve the fuel efficiency of existing designs. To sell more small cars, they had to price those cars attractively relative to both imports and their larger domestic models. This mandate conflicted with their desire to *raise* the relative price of smaller cars and twist the small-car range of Figure 8.4's price curve upward.

Further macroeconomic developments did not eliminate this conflict. In the year following September 1977—that is, during the 1978 model year—the value of the Japanese yen soared by 40 percent relative to the U.S. dollar. This change forced Japanese producers to raise the prices of their cars, which had become the most popular imports into the U.S. market. In four discrete moves between December 1977 and August 1978, Toyota announced Corolla price increases cumulating to 15 percent.[78] Nissan followed Toyota upward with lags of no more than a week. The price increases were less than exchange rate movements because further increases were saved for new models appearing in September 1978, because the Japanese firms were raising their productivity at a fast pace, and probably also because they chose to sacrifice profit margins rather than volume. General Motors and Ford reacted to these changes in complex ways. With lags of four weeks (three cases) or five weeks (one case),

---

[76]Ibid.

[77]See U.S. House of Representatives, Committee on Government Operations, Subcommittee on the Environment et al., Report, *Automobile Fuel Economy: EPA's Performance* (Washington, DC: USGPO, May 1980); Robert W. Crandall, "Corporate Average Fuel Economy Standards," *Journal of Economic Perspectives*, vol. 6 (Spring 1992), pp. 171–179; and Robert W. Crandall and Pietro Nivola, *The Extra Mile* (New York: 20th Century Fund, 1985).

[78]Kwoka, "Market Power and Market Change," p. 514.

General Motors raised the prices of import-fighting Chevettes by somewhat smaller dollar amounts. Ford's Pinto followed three of these GM announcements. A finer – grained analysis reveals that GM and Ford raised prices by larger percentages on their upscale subcompacts, entering the 1979 model year with bottom-of-the-line car prices $600 lower on average than the most nearly equivalent (but better-outfitted) Japanese imports.[79] The basic prices of their import fighters rose by a much smaller proportion than those of full-size cars. Thus, GM and Ford took advantage of the yen's rise to toughen their limit pricing stance, at the same time ceding to Toyota the initiative of leading prices upward. Import retardation took priority over achieving a more favorable price-cost relationship for subcompact cars. On another dimension of the struggle, General Motors announced in September 1977 that Chevette prices would be $118 lower in seven western states, where Japanese penetration was highest, than in the rest of the United States. Ford quickly followed suit with its Pinto prices.

PRICE DISCRIMINATION THROUGH OPTIONS AND REPLACEMENT PARTS

Differences in the amount of optional as compared to "standard" equipment complicate comparisons of U.S. and foreign car prices or U.S. prices between two model years. The pricing of optional equipment is in turn a key dimension of the automakers' strategy.

As a rule, optional equipment is priced to carry much larger margins over manufacturing cost than the basic vehicle to which the equipment is appended. This practice is shown most clearly through data on the percentage by which wholesale prices of the 1966 Ford Galaxie 500 sedan and its optional equipment exceeded standard manufacturing costs:[80]

Percentage Markup	
Standard four-door six-cylinder vehicle	16.8
More powerful V–8 engine	293.3
Automatic transmission	143.4
Power steering	123.1
AM radio	84.7
Deluxe seatbelts	71.5
Air conditioning	57.8

[79] This analysis relies upon Keith Weigelt, "A Study of the U.S. Automotive Industry," term paper, Northwestern University, February 1981.

[80] From testimony of Ralph Nader in the House Select Committee on Small Business report, *Planning, Regulation, and Competition*, p. 330, with a comment from Ford vice president R. W. Markley, Jr., pp. 603–604. The standard manufacturing cost excludes allocations of general selling and administration, warranty, R&D, tool amortization, and capital costs.

The differences between the markups on optional equipment and the base vehicle price are exaggerated by an unknown amount, perhaps reaching 10 percentage points, because components transferred to the assembly plant from other Ford plants bore their own markups over cost, and in tallying *company* profit contributions, these margins would be added to the standard vehicle's stated 16.8 percent. Nevertheless, with any plausible adjustment, the markups on optional items were much higher than those on the standard vehicle.

The explanation is simple. Persuading the customer to take optional equipment is a subtle form of discriminating in price according to ability to pay. No automobile manufacturer, and no auto salesperson, wants to see the customer leave the showroom without buying a car. If the customer adheres to a low reservation price, he or she will be sold a stripped model yielding at least some margin over cost. But if possible, the salesperson attempts to "move the customer up" to a car loaded with options. In this way the salesperson gains a higher commission, and the manufacturer's profits rise more than proportionately because of the high margins on optional equipment.

This form of discrimination is also exercised more systematically with respect to especially "hot" styles. When the demand for a model proves to be unexpectedly strong so that production cannot keep pace, the only versions that reach the showrooms are fully loaded with options. In this way, and also by quoting smaller discounts off dealer list price, higher profit margins are realized. The customer who wants to buy a "stripped" car is asked to wait six months—or take a less-demanded model.

There is a different discriminatory rationale for the way special-design replacement parts are priced. The prices of such parts, purchased separately, typically aggregate to a large multiple of what it costs to buy them assembled. For instance, in 1981 a Mercury Lynx GL could be purchased at a dealer list price of $6504. If one were to buy all of the constituent parts individually, one would have paid $22,561—3.47 times the assembled price.[81] Assuming conservatively that assembly was costless and bore a zero profit margin, the implied profit margin on the separate parts turns out to 71 percent.

The theory explaining how auto parts are priced is a variant of the tying model first encountered in our analysis of computer peripheral equipment pricing. See Figure 7.4. The car itself is the tying good. Its purchase is attended by a considerable amount of competition from other models, limiting, perhaps severely, the extent to which prices can be elevated above production costs. Once the car is purchased, the consumer is more or less locked into the subsequent purchase of mechanical and body parts—the tied goods. The tie is weak for standard parts such as batteries, tires, and the like. But for body stampings, the original manufacturer enjoys a near-monopoly position because it already has the expensive dies with which the parts are made. A would-be competitor would have to duplicate that investment to stamp equivalent parts, amortizing the sum over a much smaller volume of spare parts

---

[81]The source of this estimate was the Alliance of American Insurers.

FIGURE 8.5
Tying of Auto Parts Sales to Original Car Purchase

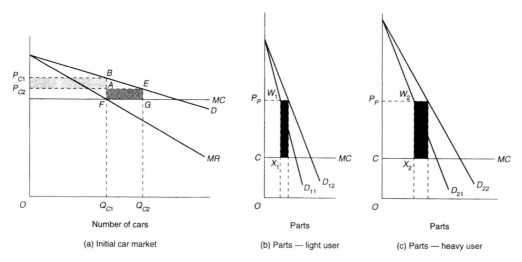

(a) Initial car market   (b) Parts — light user   (c) Parts — heavy user

production, and hence operating at a huge unit cost disadvantage. Similar considerations apply to special-design mechanical drive train components.

An additional opportunity for profitable price discrimination is introduced by the fact that some automobile owners drive their cars a lot, others very little. Heavy car users have stronger demand for automobile transportation than those who drive little, all else equal. Therefore the heavy user's demand curve for replacement parts lies farther to the right than that of the light user—for example, as with demand functions D_{21} as compared to D_{11} in parts (b) and (c) of Figure 8.5, assuming that the tying cars are sold at price OP_{C1} in the first panel. Exploiting the inelasticity of car purchasers' postpurchase parts demand by setting parts prices OP_p far above their marginal cost, the auto manufacturer realizes a tidy extra profit $P_p W_1 X_1 C$ from the light user and even more profit $P_p W_2 X_2 C$ from the heavy user. The sale of parts acts as a *meter* of demand, registering higher values, and permitting more profit extraction, from heavy than light users. Therefore, this form of price discrimination through tying is known as *metering*.[82]

Extracting additional profits from car buyers by metering their relatively inelastic postpurchase demands may be so attractive that the car manufacturer wants to enhance the effect by selling more cars, which is accomplished by reducing the original car price from OP_{C1} to, say, OP_{C2}. Now the quantity of

---

[82]On the theory, see Robert Crandall, "Vertical Integration and the Market for Repair Parts in the United States Automobile Industry," *Journal of Industrial Economics*, vol. 16 (July 1968), pp. 219–234. Crandall observes that GM's superior profitability is attributable partially to deeper vertical integration into the production of high-profit parts. Girod et al., "Profit Comparisons and Product Mix," concur.

cars sold increases by approximately 45 percent, and parts demand curves shift rightward commensurately to D_{12} and D_{22}. Profits from the sale of cars fall by the area of the lightly shaded rectangle $P_{C1}BAP_{C2}$ less rectangle $AEGF$. But profits from the sale of replacement parts rise by the more than offsetting darkly shaded (vertical) rectangles.

To be sure, the power of the auto manufacturers to profit from the sale of tied replacement parts is not unlimited. There are at least four inhibitions.

First, if replacement parts cost too much, some automobile owners will drive cars bearing fenders patched up with duct tape and bubble gum, or scrap them altogether. Second, when the car owner enters a repair shop for an expensive engine, transmission, or accident job, the shop owner may be able to obtain the needed parts less expensively from a junk yard. Frequently, however, it is not possible to find a junked car containing the right part. This difficulty has led to a third constraining, perhaps uniquely American, institution—the chop shop.[83] If an unquestioning body shop needs, say, a left front fender for a 1991 Buick LeSabre, it telephones a friendly junkyard, which calls a chop shop, which in turn commissions one of its agents to deliver the merchandise. The next day some erstwhile LeSabre owner is missing a car, which has been disassembled (chopped) in a matter of hours into a host of replacement parts that serve both the immediate demand and less predictable future demands. As a rough indicator of the size of this "industry," 1.3 million automobile thefts were reported in 1990; and a police sting operation in New York with no established reputation for reliable dealing netted 50 vehicles in four months.[84]

Finally, beginning in the late 1970s, technological advances made it possible for specialist "crash parts" producers, typically located in Taiwan and Mexico, to trace the contours of best-selling body parts, program milling machines to fabricate low-volume dies, and stamp out replacement copies at unit costs much lower than they would be if hard dies had to be produced by older methods. Automobile manufacturers fought this new price competition by advertising that the ersatz parts fit less well, required more installation labor, and rusted more quickly.[85] However, the offshore parts makers captured approximately 10 percent of the $2 billion annual crash parts market by 1990, causing U.S. auto manufacturers selectively to reduce the prices of parts

---

[83]See "Theft of Autos in New York Dominated by Professionals," *New York Times*, December 13, 1983, p. B4; and Richard Scheinin, "How Cars Disappear," *Philadelphia Inquirer Magazine*, February 17, 1985, pp. 20–31.

[84]"Police 'Chop Shop' Fools Car Thieves in Queens," *New York Times*, October 17, 1991, p. B3.

[85]See "Carmakers Fight Replacement Parts Made 'Offshore'," *Philadelphia Inquirer*, February 22, 1987, p. 1-F; "Car Makers Fight to Reclaim Market in Replacement Parts," *New York Times*, February 3, 1990, p. 35; and "Body-Part Heat: Ford vs. the Independents," *Business Week*, December 17, 1990, p. 30.

on which the new competition had emerged (i.e., usually those demanded in high volume).

RECAPITULATION

During the 1960s and 1970s it was commonly suggested by economists that the auto industry's high profitability, and especially the high profits of industry leader General Motors, implied monopolistic resource misallocation. This view was too simple. The standard monopoly resource allocation model assumes homogeneous products sold at uniform prices. Prices in automobiles are anything but uniform. Prices are elevated more above costs to consumers eager for the luxury of a big car and an abundance of optional equipment and for those demanding many replacement parts because of heavy usage or accident-proneness. A classic resource-misallocating monopoly chooses not to supply the marginal consumer—the person with a reservation price just above marginal cost. Auto producers do not behave in this way. They will sell a bottom-of-the-line stripped vehicle at a price close to marginal cost if they must. But they will extract surpluses on many other purchases. Figure 8.6 compares the standard monopoly model with an impressionistic view of what actually happens. In the standard model, marginal revenue and marginal cost are equalized, output is restricted to OQ_M, and profits (or rents) equal to the rectangular area P_MABM are gained. In the real world, rents denoted by the erratically bounded shaded area are captured as some customers pay prices higher than the uniform-price monopoly value, others pay less, and output is expanded to, or near, the competitive level for consumers buying bare-bones or entry-deterring economy cars. Pricing in automobiles is much more about transforming consumers' surplus into producer's surplus than about restricting output.

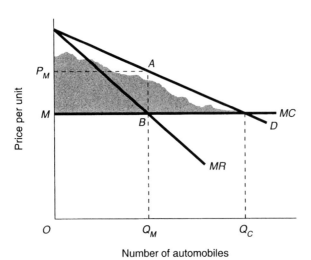

FIGURE 8.6
Surplus Capture Under Uniform-Price Monopoly and Discriminating Monopoly

FIGURE 8.7
Return on Stockholders' Equity for Three Leading
Automobile Manufacturers, 1954–1994

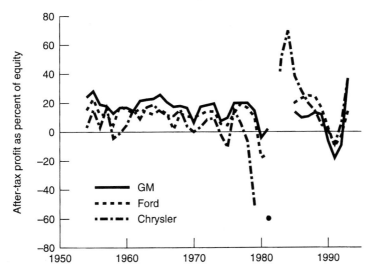

Source: Company Annual Reports.

THE OLD ORDER CHANGES

Beginning in the late 1970s and continuing through the 1980s, the automobile industry's structure, pricing, and profitability changed dramatically. Figure 8.7, which extends Figure 8.2, provides one indication. From 1950 through 1978, Big Three profit returns on stockholders' equity clustered in a relatively narrow band, with General Motors as the clear leader in nearly every year and with only Chrysler experiencing negative returns. In 1979, Chrysler led the shift to greater year-to-year variability. In 1980 all of the Big Four reported losses, totaling $4.2 billion. General Motors returned to profitability in 1981, but its three domestic rivals together lost a further $2.2 billion in 1981 and 1982. Chrysler's net worth was wiped out altogether, carrying the company to the brink of bankruptcy before it was rescued through a $1.5-billion U.S. government loan guarantee.[86]

---

[86]See Robert B. Reich and John Donahue, *New Deals: The Chrysler Revival and the American System* (New York: Times Books, 1985).

When stockholders' equity is negative, no meaningful return percentage can be computed—hence the two missing observations for Chrysler. When Chrysler and Ford began to rebuild their equity thereafter, the equity values, which are the denominator in return-on-equity calculations, were at first small, which explains in part why Chrysler and Ford pulled ahead of General Motors in returns on equity.

FIGURE 8.8
Passenger Car Imports as a Percentage of Total
U.S. Automobile Sales

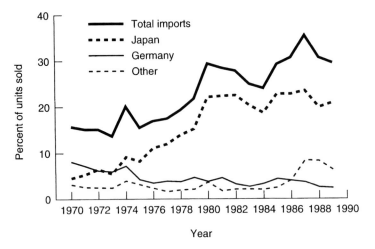

Sources: U.S. Bureau of the Census, *Statistical Abstract of the
United States,* various years; with gaps filled using data from *Ward's
Automotive Reports,* various years.

There were two proximate causes for the U.S. automakers' lapse into
financial distress. Passenger automobile and light truck sales dropped from
14.9 million units in 1978 to 13.5 million in 1979, 10.9 million in 1980, 10.3
million in 1981, and 10.0 million in 1982 as the Federal Reserve attempted to
suppress inflation by driving the prime interest rate from 9 percent in 1978 to
a peak of 20.5 percent in mid–1981. And second, of the depressed passenger
car demand remaining, imports captured a rapidly rising share, peaking temporarily at 29.5 percent in 1980. See Figure 8.8.[87] The sudden import jump
from 19.4 percent in 1978 was in turn precipitated by the 1979 Iranian oil crisis, which, combined with the phaseout of U.S. petroleum price controls, led
to rapidly rising gasoline prices and a lurch by consumers to buy smaller,
more-fuel-efficient cars that Ford and Chrysler were especially ill prepared to

---

[87]Imports from Canada are excluded because in 1965 the United States and Canada
ratified an automobile free-trade agreement, as a result of which the U.S. Big Three
assembled all of certain car models for the combined market in Canada and others in
the United States, cross-shipping to meet demands.

supply. Among the domestic cars sold, compacts and subcompacts rose from 38 percent in 1978 to 52 percent in 1981. The fact that smaller cars continued to bear more modest profit margins also contributed to declining profits.

COST-PUSH INFLATIONARY PRESSURES

Alongside these influences were a number of other more deep-seated problems. During the inflationary 1970s the automobile makers experienced intense pressure from rising costs. Steel was one of their most important inputs, and, as we recall from Chapter 5, its prices rose rapidly during the 1970s. Even more important, General Motors and the United Auto Workers had negotiated in 1948 a long-term bargaining relationship that contemplated automatic annual productivity increments plus unusually complete indexation of wages to increases in the cost of living.[88] That arrangement was emulated by the other leading auto manufacturers and retained in subsequent decades. When the consumer price index soared during the 1970s, autoworkers were protected more fully than other manufacturing workers. In 1971 the average production worker in automobile assembly plants enjoyed an hourly wage and fringe benefit premium of 62 percent relative to all other manufacturing workers. By 1980, the premium for autos had risen to 104 percent.[89] Because productivity growth did not keep pace with wage increases, the automakers' unit costs rose, which meant that prices had to rise, and/or profit margins would be squeezed.

General Motors was especially hard hit by rapidly rising labor costs. Historically, it had been more fully integrated vertically into manufacturing its own component parts than the other U.S automakers. Thus, White found that in 1966, 47 percent of the average General Motors sales dollar went to suppliers, compared to 57 percent for Ford and 58 percent for Chrysler.[90] Wages of the independent parts suppliers upon whom Ford and Chrysler relied more heavily were not as well indexed against inflation as those of the auto assemblers. Ford and Chrysler were also able to react by moving more of their outside parts purchase contracts to nonunionized suppliers in the southern

[88] See Sloan, *My Years at General Motors*, pp. 463–464. The General Motors agreement was precedent for the Experimental Negotiating Agreement accepted in 1973 by the steel industry and its union.

[89] U.S. Bureau of the Census, *Annual Survey of Manufactures*, "Statistics for Industry Groups and Industries," 1971 and 1980. The average wage premium, excluding fringe benefits, was 47 percent in 1971 and 72 percent in 1981.

[90] White, *The Automobile Industry Since 1945*, p. 86. See also Whitney, *Antitrust Policies*, p. 499; and the OECD staff report, *Globalisation of Industrial Activities: Four Case Studies* (Paris: OECD, 1992), p. 43.

United States and Mexico, whereas General Motors experienced severe conflicts with its union when it tried to shift parts production from inside its corporate framework to outside suppliers.[91] Thus, its more extensive vertical integration changed from being an advantage to a disadvantage, reducing GM's profits relative to those of Ford and Chrysler.

PRICES, QUALITY, AND IMPORT COMPETITION

Cost pressures led to substantial increases in car prices. Between 1972 and 1980, the average price of new passenger autos sold at retail in the United States increased in current-dollar terms from approximately $3600 to $7400.[92] As we have seen, the Big Three followed Japanese car prices upward when the yen's rising value induced import price increases, but they attempted to keep low-end model prices in roughly the same range as prices of the leading imports. Figure 8.9 shows how changing currency values raised the dollar

FIGURE 8.9
Dollar Cost of a Car Produced for 1 Million Yen

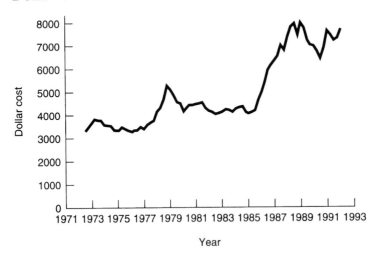

Source: *Economic Report of the President*, various years.

---

[91] See "The GM Settlement Is a Milestone for Both Sides," *Business Week*, October 8, 1984, p. 160.

[92] "Detroit Bows to Sticker Shock," *New York Times*, August 5, 1982, p. D1.

cost of a Japanese car whose factory cost was a constant 1 million yen.[93] The increase in dollar costs between 1977 and 1979 was not passed on fully in the form of higher prices for Japanese cars landed in the United States.[94] However, when high U.S. interest rates led to a decline in the relative value of the yen beginning in 1979 (and to even larger declines for leading European currencies), the pressure on importers to raise prices ebbed. This situation made it hazardous for U.S. producers to continue increasing their smaller-car prices, but domestic cost pressures forced the issue, especially for newly introduced small cars.[95] The U.S. companies continued, however, to keep stripped-model prices at what they hoped would be import-limiting levels.

This strategy proved to be seriously flawed. The perception in Detroit was that small cars were purchased because of their superior fuel economy and because they were inexpensive. The U.S. companies were reluctant at first to offer small cars and then to expand their range of compact models because, we have seen, they yielded minimal profits. The combination of these perceptions led to a philosophy that "small means cheap." The cars were therefore designed to sacrifice mechanical, "fit and finish," and other dimensions of quality to meet price targets while keeping manufacturing costs sufficiently low to provide some profit. Ford's 1960 Falcon was widely called the "Foulcan" because of the compromises it embodied. General Motors' 1960 Corvair was knowingly built with an unsafe rear suspension to save $15.[96] Quality sacrifices were ordered on GM's 1971 Vega, in John DeLorean's words, "to extract the last dime of profit from the car even if it meant hurting the car's image and our marketing program."[97] The parallel Ford Pinto also shaved costs, among other ways by placing its gas tank in a location that increased the probability of lethal fires following rear-end collisions. General Motors' front-wheel-drive X-line cars, introduced in 1979 as the definitive import

---

[93]It is computed by dividing one million yen by the number of yen that could be purchased with a dollar.

[94]See Richard C. Marston, "Price Behavior in Japanese and U.S. Manufacturing," in Paul R. Krugman, ed., *Trade with Japan: Has the Door Opened Wider?* (Chicago: University of Chicago Press, 1991), pp. 121–141; and Michael M. Knetter, "International Comparisons of Pricing-to-Market Behavior," *American Economic Review*, vol. 83 (June 1993), pp. 473–486.

[95]See "GM's X-Compact Prices Soaring, but Let the Buyer Beware," *Chicago Tribune*, April 13, 1980; "Detroit's New Sales Pitch," *Business Week*, September 22, 1980, pp. 78–85; "Detroit's High-Price Strategy Could Backfire," *Business Week*, November 24, 1980, pp. 109–111; and "G.M. Prices Its 'J' Cars To Compete with Japan," *New York Times*, May 16, 1981, p. 29.

[96]Wright, *On a Clear Day You Can See General Motors*, pp. 53–56. See also Ralph Nader, *Unsafe at Any Speed* (New York: Pocket Books, 1965), chap. 1.

[97]*On a Clear Day*, p. 165.

fighters, exhibited serious brake, transmission and electrical system problems shortly after their debut.[98]

Although small cars were especially afflicted, quality problems pervaded the whole array of U.S. automobiles. Surveys during the late 1970s and 1980s began to show with monotonous regularity that Japanese cars in particular came with fewer "fit and finish" defects, performed more reliably, and were in other respects of higher quality than their U.S. counterparts.[99] Many consumers turned to imported cars, and especially Japanese cars, because they were qualitatively superior, and not merely because they were inexpensive. Limit pricing an inferior product did not deter imports, whose share of the U.S. market nearly doubled between 1975 and 1980.

THE EROSION OF PRICE LEADERSHIP

Upward cost pressures, rising import competition, uncertainty over how to combat the import threat, and serious recessions in 1974–1975 and 1979–1982 combined to weaken General Motors' role as industry price leader. The first signs of erosion appeared during the 1974–1975 recession, when Chrysler began aggressively offering direct cash rebates to retail customers in order to unload a huge inventory overhang. Ford and General Motors followed suit, fighting a "rebate war" even while they abided by sticker prices that approximated actual transaction prices less and less closely.[100] A second rebate war followed at the trough of the 1981–1982 recession.[101] Rebating continued during the 1980s. In addition, de facto price competition broke out on another dimension when the automakers offered to finance consumers' purchases at interest rates as low as 2.9 percent at a time when the prime rate was 7.5 percent.[102] And in the late 1980s, the automakers began increasingly

[98]See "G.M. Head Criticizes Work on 'X' Cars," *New York Times*, April 14, 1981, p. 32; and "Wider Recall May Be Needed for G.M.'s '80 X-Cars," *New York Times*, January 5, 1983, p. B10.

[99]See, for example, National Academy of Engineering, *The Competitive Status of the U.S. Auto Industry*, pp. 95–99; Kwoka, "Market Power and Market Change," pp. 517–520; Womack et al., *The Machine That Changed the World*, pp. 84–91; and Fred Mannering and Clifford Winston, "Brand Loyalty and the Decline of American Automobile Firms," *Brookings Papers on Economic Activity:* Microeconomics, 1991, pp. 67–103.

[100]"Auto Rebates: A Financial Disaster for Detroit," *Business Week*, March 10, 1975, pp. 72–73.

[101]"Incentives Create Disarray in Car Pricing," *New York Times*, October 26, 1981, p. 26; and "Behind Detroit's 'Rebate War,' " *New York Times*, February 12, 1982, p. D1. On the aftermath, see "Rebates Are a Reason for Vehicle Price Increases by Big 3," *New York Times*, July 4, 1990, p. 44.

[102]"G.M. Confronts Harsh Reality," *New York Times*, August 29, 1986, p. D1.

to employ an even more subtle form of implicit price-shading—offering buyers medium-term leases and agreeing to take back the (possibly difficult-to-
sell) vehicle at the end of the lease.[103]

Price leadership under oligopoly conditions is more likely to bring collective profits near a maximum when the parameters of the pricing decision are
kept simple so that all sellers can understand and adhere. In crude oil, as we
saw, OPEC's discipline was repeatedly threatened by the difficulties of coordinating locational, sulfur content, and gravity differentials. In automobiles, the
complication of pricing decisions by differences in rebates, financing, and
leasing terms made it harder to discern the true prices at which cars were
being sold. As a result, Ford and Chrysler refused to follow some GM price
increases, and General Motors initiated unprecedented list price reductions to
offset its rivals' rebates.[104] These breaks in the industry's price discipline
undoubtedly contributed to reduced profitability.

IMPORT RESTRAINTS

In 1980, the hemorrhaging U.S. automakers turned to Washington for relief.
A petition by Ford Motor Co. and the United Auto Workers union for import
limitations was rejected in November 1980 by the U.S. International Trade
Commission, which ruled that protection under the U.S. trade law's "escape
clause" provisions was not warranted because imports were not the *principal*
cause of the auto industry's distress.[105] While Congress debated legislation that
would unilaterally restrict imports, the newly elected Reagan administration,
having pledged free trade, negotiated a settlement with Japan's Ministry of
Trade and Industry. On May 1, 1981, the parties announced that Japan would
"voluntarily" limit its exports to 1.68 million cars per year for at least two
years—a decrease from the 1.82 million cars exported in 1980.[106] Export quo-

---

[103]"Detroit Pushes Leasing But May Pay Later," *New York Times*, July 27, 1993, p. A1;
and "Auto-Makers' New Idea: Focus on Used-Car Sales," *New York Times*, July 28,
1994, p. 1; and "A Little Old Lady Drove It," *Business Week*, October 9, 1995, p. 8.

[104]"Chrysler Holds Prices Steady; Ford's Rise is Less than G.M.'s," *New York Times*,
January 7, 1981, p. D6; "Ford Won't Match G.M. Price Rise," *New York Times*, April
10, 1981, p. D5; "Major Price Restraints Announced by Chrysler," *New York Times*,
September 30, 1981, p. D1; "G.M. To Cut Prices of Some 1982 Cars by $500 to
$2,000," *New York Times*, January 30, 1982, p. 1; and "Chrysler Pricing," *New York
Times*, January 5, 1985, p. 29.

[105]"UAW and Ford Requests for Curbs on Imports Are Rejected by Panel," *Wall Street
Journal*, November 11, 1980, p. 3.

[106]"Tokyo's Car Curbs Hailed in U.S., But Japanese Makers Are Angered," *New York
Times*, May 2, 1981, p. 1. The European Union has imposed even more severe
restraints on Japanese imports and transplant production, first at the national and
then at the Community level. See "Japanese Agree to Limits on Car Exports to
Europe," *New York Times*, August 1, 1991, p. D2.

tas were in turn divided up among Japanese auto producers by MITI. As pro-posals for tighter restrictions continued to surface in Congress, the Japanese government retained the export limits, but raised the target to 1.85 million cars in 1984 and 2.3 million from 1985 through 1992, with a reduction to 1.65 million following thereafter.

Permitted to ship fewer cars to the United States than they were selling under free-market conditions, the Japanese auto manufacturers equated demand with constrained supply by raising their prices. Refer back to Figure 5.10, which describes the analogous situation in steel. In an econometric model that controls for changing product characteristics, Winston and Man-nering estimate that by 1983 Japanese auto prices were 20 percent higher than they would have been had there been no restraints on their exports.[107] Facing less intense competition, the U.S. auto manufacturers raised their average prices by 6 percent, in effect exploiting their advantage partly in the form of market share gains and partly in increased profits.

The auto trade restraints repeated the historical experience of steel in another respect. Up to 1981, the Japanese automakers were for the most part exporting relatively inexpensive subcompacts and compacts to the United States. With stringent limits on the number of cars they could ship, they raised the sales revenue and (disproportionately) profit realized per vehicle by increasing the size and luxury accoutrements of their exports.[108] By 1983, the models already offered had been upgraded, and new, larger models (such as the Nissan Maxima, the Toyota Cressida and Camry, and the Honda Prelude) were introduced. This upgrading was anticipated by Naohiro Amaya, MITI's principal negotiator, who had extensive experience in prior trade negotiations with the United States and insisted that no price or size limitations be included in the auto restraint agreement.[109] Thus, the agreement probably accelerated the transition by Japanese firms into the auto design classes from

[107]Clifford Winston et al., *Blind Intersection? Policy and the Automobile Industry* (Washington, DC; Brookings, 1987), p. 65. See also Robert C. Feenstra, "Measuring the Welfare Effect of Quality Change: Theory and Application to Japanese Autos," National Bureau of Economic Research working paper no. 4401 (July 1993). Another consequence of restricted supplies was bribery to obtain Japanese car dealerships and preferential car allocations. "Corruption Called Broad in Honda Case," *New York Times*, April 4, 1995, p. D1.

[108]In a five-month period, four of which followed the agreement, the average value of Japanese cars exported to the United States rose 23 percent relative to the same period a year earlier. See "Bigger Cars from Japan," *New York Times*, November 23, 1981, p. D2.

[109]Halberstam, *The Reckoning*, p. 614. See also Clyde Prestowitz, *Trading Places: How We Allowed Japan to Take the Lead* (New York: Basic Books, 1988), pp. 257–264 and 272–302, who decries the inexperience of U.S. trade negotiators compared to their Japanese counterparts.

which U.S. manufacturers derived most of their profits. During the second half of the 1980s, the Japanese auto companies continued that shift, introducing luxury models such as the Toyota Lexus, Honda Acura, and Nissan Infiniti, which provided strong competition to Cadillac and to such European cars as Mercedes and BMW.[110]

The Japanese companies began investigating another response to export restraints: establishing production operations in the United States. At first they were hesitant because they enjoyed cost and quality advantages by producing at home. Honda acted first, building upon its motorcycle production operations in Marysville, Ohio, to begin assembling its Accord model in 1982. Nissan followed suit, commencing pickup truck assembly at a U.S. plant in 1983 and adding automobiles in 1985. Toyota began full – scale U.S. production in 1988. At first, most of the parts were manufactured in Japan and shipped to U.S. plants for assembly. However, when the yen soared in value relative to the dollar in 1986 and 1987 (see again Figure 8.9), autoworker wages in Japan came to exceed U.S. wages in dollar terms. The Japanese companies thereupon expanded their U.S. plants' assembly volume and moved an increasing fraction of their components production to the United States.[111] To develop cars optimally suited to the American market, they also built up U.S. design studios, typically in style-setting California.[112] By 1992, they were assembling 1.16 million autos in the United States to supplement the 1.3 million cars exported under Japanese nameplates from their home plants. The growth of "transplant" production made the export quotas nonbinding and injected a stable new element of competition into the American market.

These changes did not, however, end trade conflict between Japan and the United States. On a visit to Japan in 1992, President George Bush intensified U.S. demands that the allegedly closed Japanese market for autos and auto parts be opened. Key drive train parts for Japanese-design autos assembled in the United States continued to be exported from Japan or (as the yen's value continued to rise) from Southeast Asian sources developed by Japanese manufacturers. Few new cars from U.S.-based firms made their way onto the Japanese market—in part because large cars were ill-suited to congested Japanese roads and because, given the low volumes, U.S. firms had not adapted their designs to right-side steering, but also because most retail distributors in Japan had exclusive links to their domestic suppliers. The overall U.S. deficit with Japan on automobile trade in 1994 was estimated to be $33 billion—$22 billion on cars per se and $11 billion on auto parts. Of the approximately $107 billion in auto parts purchased within Japan, only 2.4

---

[110]See "Gentility Loses in Luxury Car Fight," *New York Times*, August 30, 1994, p. D1.

[111]See "Honda: Is It an American Car?" *Business Week*, November 18, 1991, pp. 105–112.

[112]"Motor City for Japanese in California," *New York Times*, May 7, 1990, p. D1.

percent were imported.[113] In May 1995, the United States formally complained of unfair trading practices before the World Trade Organization and simultaneously threatened 100 percent tariffs on an array of Japanese imports, notably, luxury motor cars. Negotiations led in June 1995 to assurances that Japan would encourage more U.S. imports, but the terms of the understanding were vague, and further conflict seemed likely.

THE U.S. PRODUCERS RESTRUCTURE

The structural and profitability shocks that hit U.S. auto producers during the late 1970s and early 1980s induced dramatic behavioral changes. Prior to that period, the conventional wisdom in Detroit held that if there were problems, they stemmed mainly from government regulation and unfair foreign competition. By the early 1980s, Detroit inhabitants realized that the main faults lay nearer home.

A series of independent studies revealed that the sizable cost disadvantage of U.S. producers vis à vis Japanese rivals was attributable only in small measure to the lower wages paid abroad.[114] Instead, it was discovered, Japanese firms had during the 1970s quietly moved ahead of the U.S. industry in productivity. They used fewer labor hours to assemble vehicles, carried lower (*kanban*, or "just in time") inventories, designed new models more quickly, and were encumbered by much smaller managerial hierarchies. They also turned out vehicles of much higher quality. Underlying these differences were radical differences in approaches to organizing and managing the production of automobiles. The Japanese were found to emphasize philosophies that came later to be called "lean production."[115] Among the differences, the Japanese companies delegated to their workers much more responsibility for ensuring that high-quality vehicles rolled off the assembly lines. In Detroit, workers were supervised as if they were incapable of independent thought.[116] So regarded, they responded by exerting minimal quality control efforts and sometimes by deliberately sabotaging production quality.

---

[113]"U.S. Plans to Threaten Japan with Tariffs in Trade Dispute," *New York Times*, April 13, 1995, pp. 1 and D7; and U.S. Department of Commerce, *U.S. Industrial Outlook: 1994* (Washington, DC: January 1994), p. 35–14.

[114]See National Academy of Engineering, *The Competitive Status of the U.S. Auto Industry*, chap. 6; U.S. Department of Transportation, *The U.S. Automobile Industry, 1981* (Washington, DC: USGPO, 1982); "Autos: Studying the Japanese," *New York Times*, February 27, 1982, p. 29; Womack et al., *The Machine That Changed the World*, chaps. 3–8; and Melvin A. Fuss and Leonard Waverman, *Costs and Productivity in Automobile Production* (New York: Cambridge University Press: 1992).

[115]Womack et al., *The Machine That Changed the World*, chap. 3.

[116]For remarkably prescient interviews, see Studs Terkel, *Working* (Pantheon: 1971), pp. 159–154, who on p. 160 quotes a Ford welder, "They [management] give better care to that machine than they will to you."

The U.S. companies responded to their new self-realization with a series of changes. The first reaction was massive layoffs of both workers and managers along with numerous plant closures. In 18 months, Ford cut its fixed costs by $2.5 billion.[117] The layoffs were a credible threat to union members of more to come. As a result, first at Chrysler and then at the other major companies, contracts were renegotiated to eliminate automatic productivity increases, suspend cost-of-living increases, reduce paid vacation days, and reduce the pay of newly hired workers.[118] The wage reduction efforts appear to have had only fleeting success, however. In 1990, the hourly wages and fringe benefits of auto assembly workers exceeded those of other manufacturing workers by 96 percent—a reduction of only 6 percentage points relative to 1980.

Strenuous efforts were undertaken to improve the quality of U.S. autos, small and large. Ford proclaimed in its advertisements that "Quality is Job One." This was not mere puffery. Ford's managers made joint presentations with union leaders to tell plant workers that unless quality improved, job losses would continue. To convince skeptical consumers that the changes were real, product warranties were extended in time and scope. The result was a considerable reduction during the 1980s in mechanical and "fit and finish" defects, although by the early 1990s, the gap behind still-improving Japanese cars had not been eliminated.

Convinced that their efforts to produce small cars profitably were failing, the U.S. auto companies looked overseas for help. Beginning in 1982, General Motors entered joint ventures to procure small cars made by Isuzu and Suzuki in Japan, and in 1983 it announced a joint venture (NUMMI) with Toyota to produce front-wheel-drive Nova cars at a previously closed GM plant in Fremont, California.[119] In 1982, American Motors began producing in its Wisconsin plant the Alliance, designed by Renault of France. In 1985 Ford entered a joint venture to operate a Mexican plant assembling Mazda cars, and in 1987 it began taking 80 percent of the output from a new plant, with Mazda as majority owner, in Flat Rock, Michigan. Chrysler teamed with Mitsubishi to acquire small cars from Japan and then to operate jointly an assembly plant in Normal, Illinois. Through these joint ventures, the U.S. companies obtained better, less expensive small cars than they were able to produce

---

[117]Halberstam, *The Reckoning*, p. 593.

[118]See Reich and Donahue, *New Deals*, pp. 164–167 and 226–234; "Contract with Ford Is Backed by Board of U.A.W. Officers," *New York Times*, February 15, 1982, p. 1; "General Motors and Auto Workers Reach Settlement," *New York Times*, March 22, 1982, p. A1; and "The UAW Wants a Piece of the Action," *Business Week*, August 8, 1983, pp. 20–21.

[119]See John E. Kwoka, "International Joint Venture: General Motors and Toyota (1983)," in Kwoka and Lawrence J. White, eds., *The Antitrust Revolution*, 2nd ed. (New York: HarperCollins, 1994), pp. 46–75.

on their own. They also absorbed from their Japanese partners managerial know–how that could be transferred to their U.S. operations.

However, the joint ventures proved to be less than fully satisfactory. The rise of the yen relative to the dollar made it much less attractive to procure cars from Japan. The CAFE law required that American-made cars and imported cars be evaluated in separate categories, even when the imports were sold under U.S. nameplates. Consumers began shifting back to larger vehicles when oil and hence gasoline prices declined during the mid–1980s, and this swerve made it difficult for the U.S. companies to meet CAFE targets with the preponderantly large cars produced in their home plants. Consumers in the United States favored Japanese-nameplate cars from joint venture plants over the U.S. versions, and the U.S. companies' dealers marketed the joint venture cars with less than maximum enthusiasm. Thus, in the late 1980s, the U.S. companies reemphasized the development and production of their own smaller models—for example, Ford's Mondeo world car series, Chrysler's Neon, and General Motors' Saturn.

To rebuild their quality and styling capabilities, the major U.S. companies reduced the decision-making role of "bean counter" financial executives and resumed filling their top management ranks with "car guys"—that is, executives whose careers were in engineering and sales rather than finance.[120] Among other things, lean production methods were extended to new-car design. In the 1950s the standard new model's lead time—that is, the time span from acceptance of preliminary new design concepts to showroom availability—was 24 months, and on occasion new models were brought out in less than 20 months.[121] Through some process that has not been documented, bureaucracy and complexity proliferated in the intervening years, so that by the mid–1980s the average time taken to develop new models (excluding programs requiring new drive trains) had lengthened to 60 months.[122] This situation made it difficult among other things to respond to changing consumer preferences. Using lean design methods, Japanese auto producers were said to complete their development efforts in 46 months. Chastened by these comparisons, the U.S. companies reorganized their auto design teams to reduce both time and costs, with results that began to emerge in the early 1990s.

Greater size and more deeply encrusted bureaucracy made it more difficult for General Motors than its U.S. rivals to adapt to new ways of doing business. Despite what was learned through its joint venture with Toyota, its

---

[120]See Halberstam, *The Reckoning*, chap. 11, 13, 21, 28, 32, and 44.

[121]Sloan, *My Years at General Motors*, pp. 275–283; and Cherington et al., "New Product Decision-Making at Ford Motor Company."

[122]Womack et al., p. 118, summarizing Kim B. Clark, W. Bruce Chew, and Takahiro Fujimoto, "Product Development in the World Auto Industry," *Brookings Papers on Economic Activity*, no. 3 (Microeconomics), 1987, pp. 729–771. On the slow changeover of production lines, see "Motown's Struggle To Shift on the Fly," *Business Week*, July 11, 1994, pp. 111–112.

managers were slow to delegate greater responsibility to workers; indeed, it invested vast amounts in an unsuccessful attempt to solve its problems through automation.[123] To hurdle the barriers to change, a completely new Saturn division, with its own new dealer network, was created to design, produce, and sell small cars commencing from a clean slate.[124] Further evidence of difficulties led in 1992 to an unprecedented firing of GM's top two executives by outside board of directors members. Substantial improvements are said to have followed, although a return to its days of industry leadership remained improbable.[125]

The consequence of these many other changes was a revitalized, more efficient, more competitive U.S. automobile industry. By 1989, the assembly plants of U.S. companies had narrowed the gap between their average output per worker and that of Japanese plants. The best U.S. company plants had productivity equal to that of the best Japanese transplants in the United States. Some, however, continued to trail by a sizable margin.[126]

AUTOMOBILE TECHNOLOGY AND GOVERNMENT REGULATION

The design decisions of U.S. automakers and company efforts to advance technology have evoked so much critical concern that government authorities have intervened repeatedly to regulate technical choices and to force the pace at which new technologies have been implemented. Here we review the most important issues: the small car and fuel efficiency, pollution control, safety, and other technologies affecting car performance.

THE SMALL CAR AND FUEL EFFICIENCY

Making automobiles smaller is not the only way to achieve fuel efficiency; advances in engine technology and aerodynamic design also matter. But size

---

[123]See "General Motors: What Went Wrong," *Business Week*, March 16, 1987, pp. 102–110; "When GM's Robots Ran Amok," *The Economist*, August 10, 1991, pp. 64–65; and "General Motors' Productivity Trailing Domestic Rivals'," *New York Times*, October 6, 1992, p. D5.

[124]See "Saturn Shows What America Can Do Right," *Boston Globe*, July 10, 1994, p. A91.

[125]See "Can Jack Smith Fix GM?" *Business Week*, November 1, 1993, pp. 126–131; "A Great Showing for GM—Considering," *Business Week*, July 11, 1994, p. 6; and "Vapor Lock at GM," *Business Week*, November 7, 1994, pp. 28–29.

[126]Womack et al., *The Machine That Changed the World*, pp. 84–88.

and weight are important to miles-per-gallon performance.[127] Why Detroit has been reluctant to produce smaller cars, even in the wake of oil price shocks, is clear: small cars have traditionally been much less profitable than big cars. The rationale for government intervention is less transparent.

Somewhere in the human genome there appears to be a nearly universal DNA sequence that codes its carriers to believe that big, powerful means of personal transportation are better. Income and prices constrain the expression of this preference. But in all parts of the world, whether roads are narrow or broad, whether congestion is acute or not, people have migrated toward larger and more powerful cars as their real incomes have risen. To be sure, smaller vehicles are chosen more where gasoline costs $3 per gallon than where it costs $1, but, holding fuel prices constant, car size rises with income.

This propensity poses problems for government officials who advocate energy conservation in a wealthy nation like the United States. If consumer preferences are to be overridden, there must be some justification in a market failure. For automobile fuel efficiency, there are two plausible candidates, both associated with external diseconomies from burning petroleum-based automotive fuels. More fuel consumption means more carbon dioxide emissions, which in the very long run may cause adverse global warming consequences. We leave that controversial issue with no more than a mention. But second, consuming roughly one quarter of the world's petroleum products, the United States has a significant impact on the price of crude oil. There is a pecuniary externality to U.S. consumption decisions.

For reasons explored in Chapter 3, OPEC's discipline, and hence its ability to sustain high prices, tends to be stronger, the tighter is the balance between demand and the quantity of oil that can be supplied at a given price level. Excess capacity fosters chiseling and weak discipline. As the world's largest petroleum consumer, the United States collectively occupies the position of a (partial) monopsonist. The logic is illustrated in Figure 8.10. *SS'* is the supply curve for petroleum, taking into account the likelihood that with more supply, OPEC's discipline is firmer and prices are higher. If each consumer is but an atom in the universe of oil product purchasers, each will take the OPEC-derived prices as given. With such price-taking, the total quantity of petroleum consumed will be 16 million barrels per day and the price $20 per barrel. But if the government considers the collective impact of U.S. consumption decisions, it will realize that consuming more drives up the price, and so the *marginal supply cost* to the United States is given by the curve *MSC*. A monopsonist maximizes its welfare by equating its demand to marginal supply cost, restricting its consumption to 13.4 million barrels and paying the supplier the corresponding supply price (read off the supply curve) of $16.25.

To be sure, the U.S. government is not the sole purchaser in a decentralized market, but it can enforce the monopsony solution by levying a tax on petroleum products of *TM*, or $16.75, per barrel. The after-tax price rises to

---

[127]See Lester B. Lave, "Conflicting Objectives in Regulating the Automobile," *Science*, May 22, 1981, pp. 893–899.

FIGURE 8.10
Crude Oil Purchasing by the United States as a Monopsonist

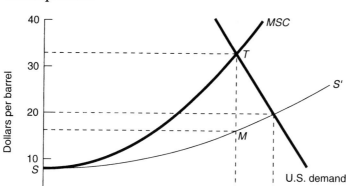

Million barrels per day

$33, the price realized by oil suppliers is $16.25, and the government collects tax revenue of approximately $82 billion per year, which it can redistribute back to consumers, more than compensating them for their higher outlays relative to the price-taking equilibrium.

The trouble with this scenario is that heavily taxing the products propelling America's automobiles and heating its homes requires political courage, which is a much scarcer commodity than crude petroleum. The miles-per-gallon law passed in 1975 can be interpreted as a second-best solution to the crude oil price externality problem, imposed in lieu of the first-best monopsony taxation solution.

As OPEC's pricing discipline crumbled during the mid 1980s and U.S. consumers began migrating back to larger cars, the auto manufacturers experienced increasing difficulty attaining their escalating CAFE miles-per-gallon targets. In 1986 the Reagan administration reduced the target from 27.5 mpg to 26 mpg, where it remained for three years until being raised again to 27.5.[128] In 1991 a bill was proposed in the U.S. Congress to raise the CAFE target from 27.5 mpg to 34 mpg in 1996 and 40 mpg in the year 2001. It was furiously opposed by the automobile industry and ultimately dropped from a bill containing other energy efficiency measures.[129] As an apparent conciliatory

---

[128]On the debate, see "Corporate Average Fuel Economy Standards," John F. Kennedy School of Government case study C16–86–670, Harvard University, 1986.

[129]See "Detroit's Assault on Mileage Bill," *New York Times,* May 11, 1991, p. 35; and "Energy Bill Is Limited but Offers a Beginning," *New York Times,* October 9, 1992, p. A16.

measure, President Clinton and the three leading U.S. auto manufacturers announced a program under which government laboratories would cooperate with the automakers to develop within ten years a passenger car capable of achieving 80 miles per gallon.[130] The presumption, subject of course to the will of Congress, was that the 27.5 mpg standard would remain intact. Whether the effort would achieve its intended goal was vigorously debated.

POLLUTION CONTROL

Exhaust pollution is the classic externality. As Cadwallader chugs down the street, smoke, nitrous oxides, and hydrocarbons are spewed out to foul the air for all adjacent inhabitants. Cadwallader himself receives at most a very small fraction of any benefit from the pollution control equipment he might install, so unless he is extraordinarily altruistic, he is reluctant to spend much money cleaning up his own exhaust. The selfish actions of individual car owners give rise to little demand for pollution control equipment.

The automobile manufacturers understand this market failure. Collectively, they could agree to remedy it by installing pollution control equipment, whether consumers demand it or not. But they are also acutely aware that pollution controls add to car costs, which means, if profits are to be maintained, that prices must be raised. And they know that even if everyone raises prices, they confront an industry demand curve with some price elasticity—ranging between −1 and −3, according to diverse statistical studies.[131] Assuming conservatively an elasticity of −1.5, the number of new cars demanded will fall by roughly 7.5 percent if pollution controls add five percent to vehicle prices. For each manufacturer this means less volume, a sacrifice of scale economies, higher unit costs, and a profit sacrifice probably exceeding 7.5 percent. It is not an attractive proposition. As a senior auto executive replied to the supervisor of Los Angeles County, inquiring in 1953 about possible auto industry help in combating the county's serious smog problem, "Well, Mr. Hahn, will that device sell more cars? . . . Will it look prettier, will it give us more horsepower? If not, we are not interested."[132]

Consequently, the U.S. automobile companies resisted the installation of pollution control equipment after research in the Los Angeles basin first iden-

---

[130]"Washington Joins Big 3 in Auto Venture," *New York Times*, September 29, 1993, p. D1. On the technological possibilities, see "Emerging Technologies for the Supercar," *Popular Science*, June 1994, pp. 95–101; John De Cicco and Marc Ross, "Improving Automotive Efficiency," *Scientific American*, December 1994, pp. 52–57; and "New Honda Engine a Threat to Natural Gas," *New York Times*, January 9, 1995, p. D1.

[131]See the statement of John Kwoka before the International Trade Commission hearing *In the matter of Minivans from Japan* (1992), Part II.

[132]Nader, *Unsafe at Any Speed*, p. 117.

tified automobiles as significant polluters. In the mid–1950s, the industry's trade association, the Automobile Manufacturers Association, responded to growing public pressure by organizing a cooperative industry research and development program, accompanied by patent cross-licensing agreements, on the alleged pollution problem.[133] Under the arrangement, participating companies agreed to cooperate in research on pollution control, not to publicize competitively any solutions to the problem (e.g., with individual companies, as distinguished from the whole industry, claiming credit), to adopt uniform dates for announcing the discovery of any pollution control devices, and to install devices only on agreed-upon dates.[134] A 1968–1969 government investigation revealed that the joint venture partners repeatedly suppressed information on auto pollution control possibilities, delayed the introduction of devices demanded by government authorities, and collectively refused to purchase and install devices developed by nonmembers. That providing nonsolutions was the venture's intent was discovered inadvertently by the author in the course of research at the Ford Motor Company in 1958.[135] Several R&D projects were studied. All but one were directed by engineers eager to make technical advances and see their work embodied in Ford cars. The pollution control project was the exception. It was headed by a public relations executive who lacked enthusiasm for any of the technologies under study.

Even after the formal collaborative mechanisms for resisting pollution controls were prohibited in 1969, industry and government continued to interact over the automobile pollution problem in a kind of minuet. Government officials, usually from California at first and then at the federal level, would demand solutions. The auto industry would respond by insisting that the solutions were technically infeasible, or that they would cost far too much.[136] Legislators would press forward nevertheless, enacting requirements opposed by industry, but that the automakers proved subsequently able to meet. Pressure to meet tough requirements repeatedly elicited technical solutions—first inexpensive crankcase blowby valves, then afterburner devices, then a host of carburetion and engine-tuning improvements, then gasoline fume control mecha-

---

[133]This account draws upon a U.S. Department of Justice staff memorandum reprinted in the *Congressional Record*, May 18, 1971, pp. H4063–H4074.

[134]Ibid., p. H4067.

[135]Cherington et al., "New Product Decision-Making in Ford Motor Company." The report was suppressed at the insistence of Henry Ford.

[136]For instance, Lee Iacocca of Ford said in 1970 that the National Air Quality Standards Act "could prevent continued production of automobiles after Jan. 1, 1975." "Detroit's Battle with Washington," *Business Week*, December 5, 1970, p. 28. David L. Kulp of Ford said in 1989 of the proposed 45-miles-per-gallon target and related pollution controls, "It's not realistic. . . . The family car as we know it would not exist." "Detroit's Big Worry for the 1990s: The Greenhouse Effect," *Business Week*, September 4, 1989, p. 103.

nisms, and then catalytic converters (which required the parallel reduction of tetraethyl lead in gasoline to avoid poisoning the catalysts, and thus in its own right greatly reduced atmospheric lead pollution). But because it was so difficult to elicit honest analyses from the automakers, there was a constant risk that requirements would be set which really did add more to costs than the value of the reduced emissions. The minuet continues as standards for 1998 and later years in California and several northeastern states tighten to levels that may be attained only through vehicles propelled by natural gas and/or electricity.[137]

SAFETY

The automobile industry's resistance to pollution controls was mirrored in its approach to incorporating features that make driving safer. Its attitude is at first glance curious. Although third parties are often injured, most of the consequences from driving an unsafe car fall directly upon car owners, their family, their employees, and others for whom they bear direct or (through insurance) indirect responsibility. The safety problem is not primarily one of externalities.

Rather, the industry's behavior was strongly affected by a perception that "safety doesn't sell." This belief was shaped among other things by a 1956 experience. In that year Ford aggressively marketed a "Lifeguard" design with new safety features such as doors that did not fly open in accidents, deep-dish steering wheels, and (as options) seat belts and padded dashboards and visors. Chevrolet meanwhile emphasized new styling and a "hot" V–8 engine. General Motors is said to have reacted to Ford's unprecedented safety campaign with "many an outraged telephone call . . . from the G.M. Building . . . to Ford headquarters."[138] But the market spoke louder. Chevrolet's cars outsold Ford's, and it became accepted wisdom in Detroit that "McNamara (head of the Ford car division) is selling safety, while Chevy is selling cars." Ford backed off from its safety campaign the following year, and for a long time to come safety was de-emphasized as a marketing variable.[139]

---

[137]"Clean-Air Laws Push Big 3 To Cooperate on Electric Car," *New York Times*, April 14, 1993, p. 1. See also the symposium, "Two Roads to Cleaner Air," *Issues in Science and Technology*, vol. 11 (Winter 1994–95), pp. 26–41; and the references in note 130 above.

[138]Dan Cordtz, "The Face in the Mirror at General Motors," *Fortune*, August 1966, p. 207.

[139]A decade later, after seat belt installation became standard, a Ford executive publicly advocated a coordination arrangement (like the one maintained for pollution devices) under which safety features would be introduced simultaneously by all manufacturers. "Safety Executive at Ford Asks End of 'One-Upmanship,'" *New York Times*, March 1, 1966 (early edition only).

It is unclear whether the automakers' perception that stressing safety actually impaired car sales was correct. What seems clear is that consumers were more interested in other design variables, and it is reasonable to suppose that many consumers preferred not to dwell on the potential lethality of the cars they purchased. This disposition in turn could have resulted from imperfect information on the ability of safety features to save lives and minimize injuries, or it might be shrugged off as irrational.[140] In either event, from it one might advance an argument for government intervention *in loco parentis*.

Intervention did come, in the Motor Vehicle Safety Act of 1966, which created a new agency, the National Highway Traffic Safety Administration (NHTSA), to draft and enforce rules setting minimum safety standards for automobiles.[141] The act's unanimous passage in both houses of Congress was precipitated in part by the publication of Ralph Nader's book, *Unsafe at Any Speed*,[142] documenting inter alia the defects of the 1969 Chevrolet Corvair, and by General Motors' blundering attempt to refute the book by assigning detectives to shadow Nader and catch him in some personal indiscretion. At first NHTSA mandated three-point seat and shoulder belts, padded instrument panels and the elimination of sharp protrusions from them, whiplash-reducing seatback extenders, improved door locks, collapsible steering columns, more permeable windshields, standardized bumper heights, and other equipment. Some of these features were offered under Ford's 1956 Lifeguard design, and most followed standards set in 1965 for autos purchased by federal government agencies. From there it moved to more stringent design standards, such as an ignition interlock system that prevented engine start–up unless seat belts were fastened, and to performance standards for occupant safety under specified crash conditions. The interlock standard was so unpopular with consumers that it was repealed by Congressional amendment in 1974.

NHSTA's effort to move beyond seat belts to passive occupant restraint systems is a metaphor on the interaction between government and industry over automobile safety. The basic problem was that the three-point seat belts mandated by NHSTA were fastened only 10 to 20 percent of the time, even though, it was estimated, their universal use could prevent as many as one-third of the 54,000 motor vehicle accident deaths that occurred in the United

---

[140]See, for example, Richard J. Arnould and Henry Grabowski, "Auto Safety Regulation: An Analysis of Market Failure," *Bell Journal of Economics*, vol. 12 (Spring 1981), pp. 27–48.

[141]See "The Crash Program That Is Changing Detroit," *Business Week*, February 27, 1971, pp. 78–84; Robert Crandall, Howard Gruenspecht, Theodore Keeler, and Lester Lave, *Regulating the Automobile* (Washington, DC: Brookings, 1986); and Jerry L. Mashaw and David L. Harfst, *The Struggle for Auto Safety* (Cambridge: Harvard University Press, 1990).

[142]See note 96 supra.

States during 1970 and reduce many additional serious injuries.[143] Since occupants would not protect themselves, NHSTA sought other means to protect them. In 1970 it proposed that by 1973, all new cars be equipped with passive systems—that is, devices that protected, whether or not the occupants took action to engage them. The main alternatives were air bags, developed during the 1950s, and harnesses that automatically engaged themselves. Automakers protested that the cost of compensating for occupant negligence in this way would be excessive. Wildly varying cost estimates were advanced.[144] Some economists argued that safety would not be enhanced in any event because, feeling more secure when belted, drivers would drive less carefully.[145] After protracted debate, NHSTA ruled in 1977 that either front-seat air bags or passive harnesses had to be installed in new cars beginning in 1982. The implementation lag provided an opportunity for the Reagan administration in 1981 to rescind the ruling. Passive-restraint advocates sued, and in 1983 the Supreme Court ruled that the administration's rescission had been "arbitrary and capricious."[146] The secretary of transportation revisited the issue and in 1984 announced a new policy holding that passive restraints would be required only if states containing three-fourths of the U.S. population failed by 1989 to pass mandatory seatbelt use laws. After further litigation concluding that the secretary's criterion would not be satisfied, passive restraints were mandated on 10 percent of the new cars sold in 1987, 25 percent in 1988, and 100 percent in 1990.

Meanwhile, many states began passing laws that encouraged seat belt usage by imposing fines upon motorists apprehended without using them and/or reducing the damage claims of persons injured when belts were unat-

---

[143]For an analysis concluding that the subjective costs to consumers of attaching seat belts exceeded probable benefits, see Winston et al., *Blind Intersection*, pp. 68–78. The authors reach their conclusion only by assuming what seems a wildly excessive monetary value for the time spent "hitching up"—estimated to be 2.97 seconds. A plausible alternative hypothesis from the author's comparison of U.S. with foreign belts is that, consistent with Detroit's philosophy of doing cheaply things it was forced unwillingly to do, the belts were poorly designed and manufactured.

[144]See "Don't Deflate Auto Safety," *New York Times*, September 23, 1981, p. A30, which asserts that internal company documents estimated the cost of front-seat air bags to be in the $100–$300 range while the industry stated publicly that they would cost $500 to $800.

[145]Sam Peltzman, "The Effects of Automobile Safety Regulation," *Journal of Political Economy*, vol. 83 (August 1975), pp. 677–725; H. Singh and M. Thayer, "Impact of Seat Belt Use on Driving Behavior," *Economic Inquiry*, vol. 30 (October 1992), pp. 649–658; and George Hoffer and Edward Millner, "Are Drivers' Behavioral Changes Negating the Efficacy of Mandated Safety Regulations?" *Regulation*, Summer 1992, pp. 15–17.

[146]Motor Vehicle Manufacturers Association of the United States et al. v. State Farm Mutual Automobile Insurance Co. et al., 463 U.S. 29 (June 1983).

tached. New York was the first, in 1984.[147] By 1986, 26 states and the District of Columbia had enacted such laws.[148] Whether for this reason or others, seat and shoulder belt usage rose—to an estimated 25 percent rate in 1985, when only two states had seat belt laws, and 50 percent in 1990.[149]

There is reason to believe that the laws were not the only causal factor. There have always been consumers—e.g., early Volvo and Mercedes buyers—who responded positively to safety enhancements. Their view of the trade-offs appears to have spread as the debate over safety progressed. In 1988, Chrysler led the way among U.S. manufacturers by making air bags standard equipment on several of its large and medium-size cars, stressing them as a feature more attractive than less costly automatic harnesses. In 1990 it made air bags standard in all models. Ford and General Motors followed suit in stages. In 1992, *Business Week* included a special 44-page section with advertisements proclaiming the safety features of several leading manufacturers' cars.[150] A new era seemed to be dawning.

The U.S. federal government's efforts to mandate safety improvements, reduce automobile exhaust pollution, and improve energy efficiency were not coordinated. Each responsible agency's actions took into account at best imperfectly the sacrifices it was imposing on other dimensions—for example, as pollution control and weight-raising safety mandates marginally increased gasoline consumption, or as miles-per-gallon targets forced reductions in car size, which, some argued, made the cars less safe.[151] Whether the right trade-offs have been struck will continue to be debated briskly.

AUTOMOBILE TECHNOLOGY MORE GENERALLY

Overcoming safety, pollution control, and fuel efficiency challenges does not always raise product cost. Sometimes goals can be achieved by implementing unambiguously superior technologies. But on this and on other facets of automobile technology, the U.S. industry lagged behind European and (later) Japanese manufacturers in introducing to passenger cars such important mechanical

---

[147]Several European nations had such mandates earlier and enforced them more vigorously than has been customary in the United States.

[148]"Panel Rejects a Challenge to U.S. Plan to Drop Air Bag Rules," *New York Times,* September 19, 1986, p. A20.

[149]"Poll Reports Increase in Wearing Seat Belts," *New York Times,* May 9, 1985, p. A13; and "Belts and Braces, Bags and Suits," *The Economist,* April 21, 1990, p. 31.

[150]"Safety First," *Business Week,* November 2, 1992. See also "Selling Autos by Selling Safety," *New York Times,* January 26, 1990, p. D1.

[151]Compare "Renewed Increase in Highway Fatalities Is Linked to More Small Cars," *New York Times,* May 26, 1981, p. 7; and "Cars Are Getting Smaller—But They're Also Getting Safer," *Business Week,* December 30, 1991, p. 26. See also, more generally, Lave, "Conflicting Objectives in Regulating the Automobile."

improvements as the diesel engine, fuel injection, the four-valve-per-cylinder engine, the stratified charge engine, disc brakes, automatic braking systems, front–wheel drive, radial tires, and much else. On the other hand, it has led the world in adding features that enhance driving ease and luxury such as the automatic transmission, power steering, air conditioning, and high-fidelity stereophonic radios. Were these differences merely accidental, or is there a more systematic explanation?

One hypothesis was advanced by William Abernathy.[152] He built upon the accepted wisdom that industries go through technological life cycles. In their early phases no single design concept is widely accepted, and product innovation flourishes. But as the industry matures, a dominant design emerges and the industry may evolve to a mass production stage at which there is much more stress on cost-saving (i.e., process) innovation than on product innovation. Indeed, Abernathy argued, mass production is hostile to product innovation because changes in product design interfere with the smooth flow of output in specialized, finely tuned mass production facilities. Because it placed so much stress on achieving high productivity, said Abernathy, the U.S. automobile industry was unresponsive to product technology opportunities.

Abernathy's thesis is hard to reconcile with the evidence of vigorous product innovation in Europe and more recently in Japan. The Japanese experience with "lean production" methods suggests that high-volume production and a flexible response to new product opportunities are not necessarily antithetical.[153] However, until they too began emulating Japanese approaches, most European automakers were committed to mass production methods very much like those used in America. Therefore, another explanation for the European record seems necessary.

The author's view, acquired from living near Detroit for ten years and in Europe for four, stresses a quite different phenomenon. Following the demise of Studebaker in 1966, the four enterprises that comprised the U.S. automobile assembly industry all had their headquarters in the Detroit metropolitan area. Their executives and engineers rotated employment among companies, they knew one another, they belonged to the same social clubs, and they shared a unique Detroit perspective on the world. European automobile manufacturers, in contrast, were nurtured in widely differing cultures. There were enormous differences in the way the automobile consumer was seen from the perspective of Fiat in fashion-conscious Torino, Peugeot (located in the shadow of the Ecole Polytechnique), Mercedes in the Stuttgart precision machinery center, BMW among Alpine road-racing Munich residents, Volks-

---

[152]William J. Abernathy, *The Productivity Dilemma: Roadblock to Innovation* (Baltimore: Johns Hopkins University Press, 1978).

[153]Womack et al., *The Machine That Changed the World.* The research at Massachusetts Institute of Technology that led to the "lean production" insight was influenced by Abernathy's work, and he probably would have altered his views had he not died prematurely.

wagen in less affluent Wolfsburg, and Volvo in conservative Göteborg. From the diversity of cultures came a diversity of technical approaches to automobile design, which in turn meant that a hundred flowers bloomed. As the European Common Market and European Free Trade Association reduced tariff barriers, these widely differing product concepts were forced to compete, leading sometimes to the selection of a single clearly dominant technology and in other instances to continuing diversity, with each product concept serving a differentiated demand niche. In the United States, on the other hand, the homogeneity of the Detroit culture limited the diversity of technical approaches and at the same time ensured that innovations made by one firm were rapidly imitated by others. Slower product innovation was a consequence.

With the establishment of new Japanese auto manufacturing centers in the south central United States and design studios in California, the homogeneity of the U.S. automobile industry has been shattered. That almost surely means that in the future the industry will be more receptive to opportunities for product innovation.

AFTERWORD

The automobile industry provides a classic illustration of how changes in technology and demand can undermine the stability of an oligopoly entrenched inter alia by massive scale economies. For half a century General Motors appeared to have found strategies that permitted it to rise to industry leadership, lead the way to highly profitable prices, and retain a dominant market position. But a pricing strategy under which profit margins rose with vehicle weight precipitated a crisis when oil price increases induced consumers and the government to demand energy-efficient cars and when foreign competitors came forward with high-quality designs that met these new requirements. Lulled into complacency by decades of success, the industry was slow to embrace improved product and process technologies pioneered overseas. Perceiving (no doubt correctly) little consumer demand for pollution control devices and safety-enhancing features, the U.S. automakers also provoked massive governmental intervention into their product design choices. The adaptation to these new challenges was painful for U.S. automakers, their workers, the locales in which their plants were concentrated, and their customers. The ultimate consequence of slow adjustment was forfeiture of a significant market share to foreign-based rivals.

9

PHARMACEUTICALS

The pharmaceuticals industry is extraordinarily research-intensive. Its R&D yields a stream of patented new drugs, which enjoy substantial monopoly power as a result of patients' and physicians' price insensitivity. Since 1962, the safety and efficacy of new drug entities have been subject to stringent regulations that contribute to high drug testing costs. The role of patent protection both domestically and internationally in this high-cost, high-risk environment is analyzed. Even after patents expire, price competition from generic drugs has tended to emerge only slowly because original branded drugs enjoy powerful first-mover advantages. Policy experiments provide insight into the conditions under which those advantages can be overcome. In recent years, the emergence of health maintenance organizations has begun to alter the balance of power between drug manufacturers and their customers. Proposals to change that balance further through government price controls are examined.

INTRODUCTION

All industries are different, but some are more different than others. The pharmaceutical (or ethical drug) industry fits the latter category. It is the most research-intensive U.S. manufacturing industry not dependent upon direct government contract support for its innovative activities. It has consistently been one of the most profitable industries. The quality of its products has been subjected to especially close regulation by government agencies—even more so than automobile quality. And as we shall elaborate, it has many related distinguishing features.

Rapid technological change makes it difficult to stake out distinct industry bounds. The U.S. Census Bureau counted 640 separate companies operating in 1987 and 585 during 1992 in the four-digit industry category, "pharmaceutical preparations." The largest four companies in 1987 accounted for 22 percent of the industry's recorded $32 billion sales; the largest 20, for 65 percent. Thus, the industry comprises a core of relatively large firms surrounded by a quite numerous fringe. Among fringe inhabitants not included in the Census industry category are scores of biotechnology firms whose drug products have not yet moved from development into production. More than 100 larger industry members belong to the principal industry trade association, the Pharmaceutical Manufacturers Association (PMA) (renamed in 1995 the Pharmaceutical Research and Manufacturers Association), upon whose statistical publications we draw on extensively here. The association's members had U.S. sales of $26.6 billion in 1987, rising to $51.3 billion in 1992.

The industry's products fill a vast array of differentiated needs. A standard source, *The Physician's Desk Reference*, listed 3900 distinct drug products in 1993, taking into account differences in chemical composition, source, and dosage form, but not package size variations. A company managing prescription drug insurance payments organized its 1993 formulary into 16 broad therapeutic groups (such as anti-infectives, cardiac drugs, neurological drugs, and respiratory preparations) and subdivided them into more than 100 categories, each specific to particular symptoms.[1] Drugs in one subcategory are unlikely to substitute for those in another. Approximately 40 of the subcategories contained three or fewer listed chemical entities. Thus, the industry is best described as a collection of differentiated oligopolies.

UNIQUE CHARACTERISTICS

Several of the industry's unique characteristics merit more extended discussion.

For one, most pharmaceutical products are available in the United States only under a physician's prescription.[2] In such cases, the consumer does not choose what he or she will consume; a third party does. Given this situation, it is customary to divide the industry's products into two broad groups: prescription or (slightly less accurately) ethical drugs, and proprietary or over-the-counter (OTC) drugs. The only government statistical source that achieves a clear distinction between these groups suggests that during the 1970s, prescription drugs accounted for slightly more than three-fourths of total U.S. pharmaceutical product sales.[3] There are, as we shall see, important behavioral differences between the two groups.

---

[1]PAID Prescripions, Inc., *The PAID National Formulary* (Fair Lawn, NJ: 1993).

[2]On the sudden shift to a regime of prescriptions during the 1930s without a clear congressional mandate, see Peter Temin, "The Origin of Compulsory Drug Prescriptions," *Journal of Law & Economics*, vol. 22 (April 1979), pp. 91–105.

[3]Federal Trade Commission, *Statistical Report: Annual Line of Business Report*, 1974 through 1977. (Washington, DC: 1981–1985).

Second, individuals suffering from some acute illness will commonly be willing to pay a very considerable sum for relief. What this means is that over a wide range of prices, the demand for an appropriate medicine tends to be quite price-inelastic. When, in addition, the number of relevant suppliers is small, the suppliers may possess considerable monopoly power.

Demand is made even more price-inelastic when drug purchases are reimbursed wholly or in part by insurance. In effect, insurance puts a wedge between the demand curve characterizing consumer behavior when the consumer is responsible for paying and the (higher) demand curve with insurance. The size of the wedge is greater, the higher the drug's price and the larger the reimbursement fraction. In 1987, an estimated 75 percent of the U.S. population under 65 years of age, and 45 percent of older individuals, had some insurance coverage for outpatient prescription drugs.[4] However, coverage was seldom complete. Taking into account the gaps, approximately 44 percent of Americans' total outpatient prescription drug charges were reimbursed by insurers in 1987. This represents a substantial increase over the share of charges reimbursed in 1977, estimated at 28 percent.[5] Further increases are likely if the federal and state governments begin mandating universal health insurance. OTC drugs are seldom reimbursed.

As suggested earlier, the pharmaceutical industry, and especially its prescription drugs component, is extraordinarily research-intensive. Perspective is gained by comparing company-financed research and development expenditures as a percentage of sales for the industries studied in this book (excluding agriculture). The latest year for which comparable and accurately segregated data are available is 1977:[6]

Crude petroleum	0.48%
Petroleum refining	0.26
Steel	0.42
Semiconductors	6.12
Computers	8.90
Automobiles	2.27
Prescription drugs	10.19
Over-the-counter drugs	2.90
Beer	0.45%

Pharmaceuticals not only lead the industries covered here, but had the highest ratio of company-financed R&D to sales among all 238 manufacturing

---

[4]U.S. Office of Technology Assessment, *Pharmaceutical R&D: Costs, Risks and Rewards* (Washington, DC: USGPO, February 1993), pp. 26–27 and 238–246.

[5]Ibid., p. 28.

[6]Federal Trade Commission, *Annual Line of Business Report: 1977.*

industries for which data were available. Computers ranked second. The OTC drug industry was twenty-fifth of 238.

Outlays for R&D in ethical drugs (the nomenclature adopted by the Pharmaceutical Manufacturers Association) rose after 1977 much more rapidly than sales, so that by 1992 they amounted to 16.4 percent of domestic sales (including export shipments).[7] Figure 9.1 traces the increase in PMA members' U.S. R&D expenditures, and also the number of new drug chemical entities (NCEs) approved for marketing in the United States, between 1960 and 1992. Outlays are measured in constant (1987) dollars on a logarithmic scale, so a constant percentage rate of growth would be indicated by a solid straight line. We observe that there was relatively rapid growth during the 1960s, retarded growth in the 1970s, and rapid growth again in the 1980s. During the 1980s, the real (i.e., constant-dollar) R&D growth rate was an astounding 10.6 percent per annum, compared to 4.3 percent for all U.S. industries tracked by the National Science Foundation.[8] Between 1960 and 1990, the average real growth rate for R&D outlays in ethical drugs was 6.92 percent, compared to 4.48 percent for all industries.

The pharmaceutical industry's R&D expenditures yielded an impressive stream of new products. The dashed line in Figure 9.1 traces the appearance of new chemical entities, excluding combinations and new applications of already existing chemical entities. Between 1940 and 1990, a total of 1265 such new drug entities were introduced into the U.S. market—60 percent of them originally developed in the United States.[9] After 1962, however, the number of NCE introductions fell to an average of 18 per year. The reasons for this change will be an important focus of later discussion.

Most of the new chemical entities emerging from drugmakers' R&D laboratories are protected, at least in their early years, by patents. Also, most new products are given trademarked brand names that are much easier to remember than the chemical names—for example, "Librium" rather than chlordiazepoxide, "Actifed" rather than pseudoephedrine/triprolidine, "Zantac" rather than ranitidine hydrochloride. Patents and the exclusive right to trademarks strengthen the monopoly power of their holders.

Product novelty, trademarking, and the difficulty consumers and prescribers have becoming informed about the efficacy of drug products interact to encourage unusually vigorous advertising and other promotional activity. Prescription drugs differ sharply from their OTC counterparts in this respect,

---

[7]Pharmaceutical Manufacturers Association, *Trends in U.S. Pharmaceutical Sales & R&D*, 1990–1993, Annual Survey Report (Washington, DC: PhRMA, 1993), p. 7.

[8]U.S. National Science Board, *Science & Engineering Indicators: 1993* (Washington, DC: USGPO, 1993), p. 332. The same GNP deflator is applied to both time series.

[9]Pharmaceutical Manufacturers Association, *Statistical Fact Book* (Washington, DC: PMA, September 1991), Table 2–8.

FIGURE 9.1
Trends in Drug R&D and Approved New Chemical Entities

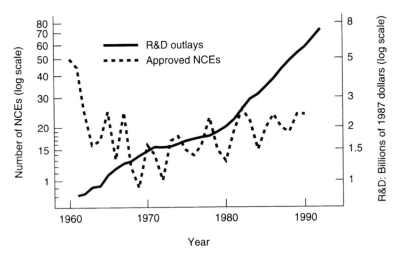

Source: Pharmaceutical Research and Manufacturers Association, *Prescription Drug Industry Fact Book: 1980* (Washington, DC: PMA, 1980), p. 23; *Statistical Fact Book* (September 1991), Figure 2–1 and Table 2–4; and *Trends in U.S. Pharmaceutical Sales and R&D* (Washington: PhRMA, 1993), p. 6.

as the following data on media advertising expenditures and "other promotional expenditures" as a percentage of 1977 industry sales show:[10]

	Media Advertising	*Other Promotional Expenditures*
Ethical drugs	4.0%	15.4%
OTC drugs	20.2%	15.4%

As anyone who has endured the headache and athlete's foot remedy ads on U.S. television might have suspected, OTC drug makers had the highest ratio of advertising to sales among the 238 industries into which the data are divided. Ethical drug firms ranked 28th in the intensity of their advertising, placed mainly in medical journals and directed toward prescribing physi-

---

[10] The source is Federal Trade Commission, *Annual Line of Business Report: 1977*, p. 31.

cians.[11] The two branches tied for fourteenth rank out of 238 in "other promotional expenditures" as a percentage of 1977 sales—a category that includes field sales representation, technical advisory functions, point-of-sale displays, the distribution of samples, and much else.

The ethical drugs industry is unique, however, in its use of "detailers"— salespersons who attempt regularly to visit each prescribing physician in their territory, providing brochures, free samples, and conversational give-and-take about the merits of their employer's products, especially the newest ones. Between 1968 and 1972, it is estimated, prescription drugmakers employed nearly 20,000 detailers to make a total of 17.4 million calls per year on their target audience of 200,000 U.S. physicians.[12] There is dispute over the value of this direct selling activity. Of the physicians queried in a 1966 survey, 57 percent said that detailers were their initial source of information on new drugs.[13] In another survey, 85 percent of general practitioners gave detailers "a strong vote of confidence" because of the valuable information they provided on new drugs and their ability to order drugs directly.[14] A governmental commission viewed the evidence more cautiously:[15]

> Whether such activities may be described as primarily promotional or primarily educational is difficult to determine. It is doubtful, however, that physicians can expect such detail men to give invariably unprejudiced and objective advice.

Whatever the merits, there is likely to be much less emphasis on the detailing of individual physicians as health care becomes concentrated in group care

---

[11]On the effectiveness of ethical drug advertising in increasing sales, see Keith B. Leffler, "Persuasion or Information? The Economics of Prescription Drug Advertising," *Journal of Law & Economics*, vol. 24 (April 1981), pp. 45–74. See also "Study Says Drug Ads in Medical Journals Frequently Mislead," *New York Times*, June 1, 1992, p. 1.

[12]U.S. Department of Health, Education, and Welfare, Task Force on Prescription Drugs, *Final Report* (Washington, DC: February 1969), p. 10; and David Schwartzman, *Innovation in the Pharmaceutical Industry* (Baltimore: Johns Hopkins University Press, 1976), p. 207.

[13]Task Force on Prescription Drugs, background paper, *The Drug Prescribers* (Washington, DC: December 1968), p. 14.

[14]Ibid. For similar views, see the Report of Great Britain's Sainsbury Committee, cited in Schwartzman, *Innovation in the Pharmaceutical Industry*, p. 188. A statistically significant impact of detailing on newly approved drug usage is reported by J. Howard Beales in "Marketing Information and Pharmaceuticals," in Robert J. Helms, ed., *Competitive Strategies in the Pharmaceutical Industry* (Washington, DC: American Enterprise Institute: 1995).

[15]Task Force on Prescription Drugs, *Final Report*, p. 10.

organizations with committees recommending appropriate prescription modalities.[16] More will be said on this subject later.

U.S. pharmaceutical manufacturers have compiled an extraordinary record of profitability. The industry held first or second rank in 24 out of 32 years between 1960 and 1991 on *Fortune* magazine's annual tabulation of median after-tax profit returns on stockholders' equity for the 500 largest U.S. industrial corporations, classified into 21 to 28 industry groups.[17] On average over the 32-year period, the reported rate of return on equity for pharmaceuticals was 18.4 percent, compared to 11.9 percent for all 500 industrials. This record has led to recurrent congressional complaints of monopoly prices and profiteering at the expense of consumers and taxpayers. There is a substantial counterliterature arguing that accountants' treatment of research and development outlays in conventional return-on-equity calculations overstates the industry's true profitability. The argument is valid, but after appropriate corrections are implemented, the most careful analyses continue to show above-average pharmaceutical industry profitability.[18]

The adverse international trade balances that have plagued many of the industries studied in this volume have not been a problem in pharmaceuticals. The industry's exports have consistently exceeded imports—for example, with exports averaging 3.2 percent of sales against 0.35 percent for imports between 1963 and 1986. The gap narrowed during the late 1980s and early 1990s.[19] This is only a part of the international trade picture, however. Like the auto companies, the pharmaceutical manufacturers recognized relatively early that in order to sell their products effectively in foreign markets, they needed to establish a presence there—that is, to become multinationals. In 1989, for example, U.S.-based members of the Pharmaceutical Manufacturers Association exported ethical drugs valued at $3.1 billion from their domestic plants, but reported additional foreign subsidiary sales of $13.7 billion.[20] Foreign subsidiaries performed 18 percent of the parents' worldwide research

---

[16]See "Next: Smaller, More Specialized Sales Forces," *Medical Marketing & Media*, March 1991, pp. 18–28.

[17]F. M. Scherer, "Pricing, Profits, and Technological Progress in the Pharmaceutical Industry," *Journal of Economic Perspectives*, vol. 7 (Summer 1993), p.98.

[18]For a thorough survey of the evidence and a careful reworking of the data, see Office of Technology Assessment, *Pharmaceutical R&D*, chap. 4. For an excellent analysis of the accounting theory problems, see Thomas R. Stauffer, "The Measurement of Corporate Rates of Return: A Generalized Formulation," *Bell Journal of Economics*, vol. 2 (Autumn 1971), pp. 434–469.

[19]The earlier data are from the author's data base used in *International High-Technology Competition* (Cambridge: Harvard University Press: 1992); the later data are from Pharmaceutical Manufacturers Association publications.

[20]Pharmaceutical Manufacturers Association, *Statistical Fact Book*, September 1991, Table 1–10.

and development expenditures. Foreign-based companies in turn had U.S. subsidiaries that accounted for approximately 30 percent of all ethical drug sales within the United States.[21]

THE PHARMACEUTICAL RESEARCH AND DEVELOPMENT PROCESS

Research and the development of new and improved products occupy a central role in the activities of modern pharmaceutical enterprises. This was not always so. There have been several revolutions in the way the ethical drugs business is conducted.

As late as the 1930s, the use of scientific methods to develop new medicaments was rare. Millennia of experience had identified many naturally occurring substances as having therapeutic properties, but quack medicines also abounded. Retail pharmacies' shelves were lined with bottles containing organic and inorganic chemicals which were compounded on the spot to satisfy either physicians' prescriptions or the patient's plea for the druggist's own preferred recipe to confer symptomatic relief. Until 1938, prescriptions were required in the United States only to obtain narcotic substances.

Gradually, however, modern chemistry began showing that there were better methods.[22] Aspirin was one of the early breakthroughs.[23] Since at least the time of Hippocrates, a substance from the bark of the white willow tree was used to relieve fever and pain. By the 1830s German and French chemists had extracted its active ingredient and then improved upon it, obtaining salicylic acid. But salicylic acid caused severe gastric distress and ulcers while relieving other symptoms. Seeking new markets for by-products of the synthetic organic dyes upon which its growth had depended, the German Bayer firm established in 1896 a laboratory devoted to creating and testing dyestuff derivatives for medicinal effects. Early successes led to the synthesis of improved molecular variants, of which acetylsalicylic acid was the safest,

---

[21]Ibid.; and Jeremy Holmes, "Factors Influencing the Location of Multinational Investment Decisions in the Pharmaceutical Industry," forthcoming in the proceedings of a U.K. Office of Health Economics symposium, June 1994. See also Robert Ballance, Janos Pogany, and Helmut Forstner, *The World's Pharmaceutical Industries* (Edward Elgar, 1992), chap. 1–3.

[22]Useful histories include Schwartzman, *Innovation in the Pharmaceutical Industry*, chap. 2; Joseph D. Cooper, "The Sources of Innovation," in Cooper, ed., *The Economics of Drug Innovation* (Washington, DC: American University, 1970), pp. 41–62; and Peter Temin, "Technology, Regulation, and Market Structure in the Modern Pharmaceutical Industry," *Bell Journal of Economics*, vol. 10 (Autumn 1979), pp. 429–446.

[23]See Charles C. Mann and Mark L. Plummer, *The Aspirin Wars* (Boston Harvard Business School Press, 1991), pp. 21–27.

most effective, and most profitable. Bayer recognized that catchy brand names could be marketed more effectively than complex chemical names, and so "aspirin" entered the world's vocabulary.

In the first decade of the twentieth century a German academician, Paul Ehrlich, formulated a conception of how small organic molecules interacted with proteins in the human body as keys do with locks. Ehrlich found many new chemicals with desirable therapeutic effects, including Salvarsan, the first drug effective against previously incurable syphilis. Later research at the laboratories of Bayer's merged successor, I. G. Farben, yielded in 1935 the discovery that a red dye derivative effectively combatted lethal streptococcal infections. The active ingredient was sulfanilamide, one of the first "wonder drugs." Numerous sulfa drug variants were synthesized and tested, leading to safer versions and the discovery of variants with diuretic (blood pressure–reducing) properties.

The antibacterial properties of a naturally occurring mold, penicillium notatum, were first observed accidentally in 1929 by Alexander Fleming in England. Fleming failed to follow through, but penicillin's therapeutic properties were identified by Howard Florey and Ernest Chain at Oxford University in time for that first antibiotic to play a lifesaving role in treating World War II casualties. Mass production methods using corn steep liquor as a fermentation medium were devised at a U.S. Department of Agriculture laboratory in Peoria, Illinois. Twenty U.S. companies participated in the top-priority wartime penicillin production program.[24]

The success of penicillin suggested to Selman Waksman of Rutgers University that other naturally occurring spores might have antibiotic effects. By screening and testing numerous soil samples during the early 1940s, he made two important discoveries: a specific new antibiotic, streptomycin, and even more important, a systematic method for finding new medicinal substances.

Waksman insisted that the patent he obtained on his purified form of streptomycin be licensed at modest royalties to all who applied, and so both the penicillin and streptomycin wonder drugs came to be produced by numerous firms in the years following World War II. Price competition was vigorous. The wholesale price of penicillin in commonly prescribed 300,000-unit doses dropped from $3 in 1945, after mass production was achieved, to $1 in 1948, 45 cents in 1949, 25 cents in 1950, and 10 cents in 1953.[25] Similar declines occurred for streptomycin. By 1953 the average producer was losing money on its sales after allocation of overhead costs.[26]

Nevertheless, in Waksman's screening methodology and the technique of synthesizing and testing numerous organic molecule variants, pioneered at

---

[24]Federal Trade Commission, *Economic Report on Antibiotics Manufacture* (Washington DC: June 1958), chaps. I and II.

[25]Ibid., pp. 166–171.

[26]Ibid., p. 211.

Bayer, drug producers found a powerful means of discovering additional therapeutic entities. And in most cases, if they played the game correctly, they could obtain patent protection on these new substances and market them without the competition experienced on penicillin and streptomycin. A new broad spectrum antibiotic, Aureomycin (chlortetracycline), was marketed by American Cyanamid in late 1948 as the first of these new patented wonder drugs. Chloromycetin (Parke Davis's chloramphenicol), Terramycin (Pfizer's oxytetracycline), and, in 1953, tetracycline (whose patent rights were shared by five firms) followed in close succession. Each was patented, each was sold at prices high in relation to production costs, and each proved to be highly profitable for its suppliers.

The lure of high profits in turn induced many other firms to try their hand at the game. U.S. pharmaceutical industry R&D outlays soared from an estimated $50 million in 1951 to $476 million in 1967—an average annual (current-dollar) growth rate of 14 percent.[27] The number of approved new chemical entities rose from an average of 19 per year during the 1940s to 45 per year during the 1950s.[28]

With few exceptions, the industry's approach to research and development during this period followed a "try every bottle on the shelf" approach reminiscent of Thomas A. Edison's earlier philosophy toward mechanical invention. In 1970 alone, U.S. pharmaceutical manufacturers members are said to have conducted 703,900 tests on newly synthesized and naturally occurring substances, out of which only a thousand proved sufficiently interesting to be carried into human tests.[29] The first stage in this process was a "broad screen" using cultured bacteria in vitro to test for antibiotic effects, earthworms to test for anesthetic and tranquilizer effects, and mice for still other effects. The average cost per individual test was on the order of $50.[30] Chemical entities with interesting effects at this first screening stage were moved into increasingly elaborate testing, at an average cost of $10,000, in higher animals such as guinea pigs, rabbits, dogs, and monkeys. The rare molecule that emerged from the "narrow screen" stage with persuasive indications of therapeutic action progressed into clinical testing—that is, on human beings. To the extent that this process was guided by systematic theory, it stemmed mainly from prior discoveries that certain molecules had recognized therapeutic effects, so chemists synthesized variants of those molecules to see whether they might work better.

---

[27] Task Force on Prescription Drugs, background paper, *The Drug Makers and the Drug Distributors* (Washington: D.C.: USGPO, 1968), p. 16.

[28] Pharmaceutical Manufacturers Association, *Fact Book: 1980*, p. 30.

[29] Schwartzman, *Innovation in the Pharmaceutical Industry*, p. 60.

[30] Harbridge House, Inc., "Drug Study," Task IV, *Patent Policy Study*, Pilot Case Studies for the U.S. Federal Council for Science and Technology, Committee on Government Patent Policy (Boston; Harbridge House, May 1967), p. IV–4.

As scientific knowledge has advanced, the industry has tended to move away from purely random screening to a process approximating what is called "rational drug design."[31] Extending the early insights of Paul Ehrlich, it is now known that each of the countless proteins in the human body has specific functions, and that the functioning or malfunctioning of those proteins is sensitive to the addition of chemicals at key receptor surfaces. The configuration of receptors can be gleaned through such methods as X-ray crystallography, and molecules can be designed to fit the receptors. Thus, the search is narrowed to specific classes of would-be therapeutic molecules. This seldom ends the quest, however. A good deal of trial and error, including animal and then human tests, is required to find the right molecule among many possibilities—that is, one that is effective without serious adverse side effects.

Also in its infancy, but with enormous potential, is the possibility of using biological gene-splicing and cloning methods to synthesize proteins that either regulate body mechanisms or correct for defects in existing regulating mechanisms. There is reason to believe that the genetic revolution will usher in a new golden era of pharmaceutical discovery.

FDA REGULATION

Further insight into drug research and development requires an understanding of how the process is regulated—in the United States, by an independent agency, the Food and Drug Administration (FDA).[32] The FDA is a child of scandal. Its predecessor organization resulted from Upton Sinclair's 1906 book, *The Jungle*, revealing the unsanitary conditions existing in Chicago's meat-packing houses, and from a series of articles in *Collier's* magazine on the patent medicine business. The Pure Food and Drug Act of 1906 prohibited the adulteration of foods and drugs sold in interstate commerce, including contamination and (for drugs) deviation from U.S. Pharmacopeia standards. It also imposed labeling standards. Its provisions had little impact on drug development, however, and it did not prevent an ingenious chemist from dissolving sulfanilamide in toxic diethylene glycol, as a result of which some hundred Americans came to an untimely end. To close the loophole, Congress passed the 1938 Food, Drug, and Cosmetic Act. One set of provisions prohibited the interstate sale of new drugs unless the FDA (created in 1930) had reviewed them to ensure that they were safe for use under the conditions stated on their

---

[31]Office of Technology Assessment, *Pharmaceutical R&D*, pp. 106–113.

[32]See, for example, Temin, "The Origin of Compulsory Drug Prescriptions;" and U.S. House of Representatives, Committee on Science and Technology, Report, *The Food and Drug Administration's Process for Approving New Drugs* (Washington: USGPO, November 1980), pp. 1–11.

labels. When the FDA found that those conditions were satisfied, it issued a "new drug approval" (NDA). However, if the FDA delayed its decision for more than 180 days after an application was filed, the drugmaker could begin legally marketing its new product without formal FDA approval.

This led to still another near-scandal. A U.S. firm applied to the FDA for approval of a new tranquilizer, thalidomide, which was already being sold widely in Germany, especially for use by women suffering from morning sickness. The responsible FDA staff member became suspicious in 1961 upon reading reports in a British medical journal of curious but mild side effects.[33] As a result, she repeatedly stalled approval and requested additional information. Before long it became clear that the drug's use led to the birth of approximately 8000 malformed babies in Europe. Because the drug's administration was confined to testing only in the United States, the casualty toll was held to nine. At the time Senator Estes Kefauver, unsuccessful candidate for the U.S. presidency in 1952 and 1956, was holding hearings on high prices and profits in the pharmaceutical industry. He seized the situation and introduced a new bill substantially enhancing the FDA's power over new drug testing and marketing. Among other things, the Kefauver-Harris Act of 1962 eliminated the delayed approval loophole and, more important, required the FDA to certify that new drugs were not only *safe*, but also *efficacious* (i.e., that they actually worked).

Up to that time, clinical drug testing tended to be a rather casual affair. Statistical sample design and tight experimental controls were seldom employed, placebo effects were not tested, and the efficacy of new drugs emerging from the process tended to be demonstrated through testimonials from physicians who might or might not have participated in the testing.

THE IND-NDA PROCESS

The 1962 statute and implementing rules adopted subsequently by the FDA introduced major changes. Before commencing human tests in the United States, companies must obtain from the FDA an "Investigation of New Drug" (IND) authorization. IND applicants must submit evidence that the drug's toxicity at anticipated dosage levels has been tested in higher animals (e.g., monkeys and dogs) and describe the sequence of human tests proposed, including measures that will ensure adequate experimental control and statistical validity. The FDA has 30 days from the IND application's submission to raise objections. When clinical testing begins, it usually follows an ordered time sequence encompassing three main phases (although on occasion the first two phases overlap). A précis of what happens in each phase, and the median

---

[33]See (on Dr. Frances Kelsey) "Still on Guard," *Philadelphia Inquirer*, May 8, 1988, p. I–1.

times and attrition rates (conditional on passing through the prior stage) for a sample of 93 clinical trials initiated between 1970 and 1982, is as follows:[34]

	Months (median)	*Attrition Rate*
Phase I: The drug is administered to a small number of healthy volunteers (often prisoners) to test for absorption, metabolism, and (by varying dosages) possible toxicity.	15.5	25%
Phase II: The drug is administered under carefully controlled conditions to a few and then dozens of patients with the disease to be treated.	24.3	52%
Phase III: The drug is administered in double-blind tests to at least two large samples (sometimes numbering in the thousands) of persons with the disease. Long-term toxicity tests are conducted in parallel.	36.0	36%

If the prognosis is still favorable as Phase III tests draw to a close, the company applies to the FDA for a new drug approval (NDA). The FDA may request additional information and more tests before making its decision. On average for the sample of 93 clinical trials summarized here, 23 percent of the substances that entered Phase I testing emerged with FDA approval.[35] For that sample, the median lag from application for an NDA to the FDA's decision was 30 months. Adjusting for overlapping phases, the median length of time from the start of clinical testing to NDA issuance was 98.9 months, or slightly more than eight years.

As experience was gained with this new testing regimen, the length of the phases increased. DiMasi et al. found that for self-originated new chemical entities—that is, excluding those licensed from other (e.g., foreign) companies—the average lag from the start of clinical testing to NDA approval on

---

[34]From Joseph A. DiMasi, Ronald W. Hansen, Henry G. Grabowski, and Louis Lasagna, "Cost of Innovation in the Pharmaceutical Industry," *Journal of Health Economics,* vol. 10 (July 1991), pp. 107–142. The attrition rates assume for the sake of simplicity that the phases are strictly sequential.

[35]The attrition rate at the FDA's decision-making stage is included in Phase III here.

successful applications was 4.7 years in the 1960s, 6.7 years in the 1970s, and 8.5 years in the 1980s.[36]

RISING COST, FEWER DRUGS

Costs rose commensurately, or even more. A benchmark is provided through Mansfield's study of 17 drug development projects in a U.S. company before the 1962 law took effect.[37] He found that on average, 37 percent of the new chemical entities entered into human tests received an NDA from the FDA. Adding the cost of failed tests to those of successful projects, the average success cost $1.05 million. The research vice president of a large drug company estimated that in 1969, after the new regulations were well understood, clinically testing a successful NDA, again counting the cost of failures, cost approximately $10.5 million.[38] For the 93 projects (mostly of 1970s and early 1980s vintage) whose times and attrition rates are summarized above, DiMasi et al. found the average cost, including clinical test failures, of a successful NDA to have risen further to $48 million (in 1987 dollars). When the costs of preclinical research and screening were added in, the average out-of-pocket cost for a successful NDA was found to double—that is, to $96 million.[39]

There has been much controversy over the extent to which the 1962 law and the FDA's implementing regulations were responsible for this 46-fold increase in drug testing costs. Plainly, the new regimen was not the only cause. Inflation occurred; the U.S. GNP deflator in 1978 was 2.4 times its 1956 value, reducing the *real* change to a factor of roughly 20. Attempting to pinpoint the role of regulation, Grabowski and colleagues took advantage of a natural experiment.[40] The British drug industry had a research orientation similar to that of the United States, but U.K. regulations advanced from reviewing safety

---

[36]Joseph DiMasi, Mark Seibring, and Louis Lasagna, "New Drug Development in the United States from 1963 to 1992," *Clinical Pharmacology & Therapeutics*, vol. 55 (June 1994), p. 615.

[37]Edwin Mansfield, Comment, in Cooper, ed., *The Economics of Drug Innovation*, p. 151.

[38]Harold A. Clymer, "The Changing Costs and Risks of Pharmaceutical Innovation," in Cooper, ed., *The Economics of Drug Innovation*, pp. 125–138.

[39]Cost estimates citing the DiMasi et al. study are typically more than twice this $98 million figure because the authors also account for the opportunity cost of invested funds, capitalizing out-of-pocket outlays to the date of product approval at an interest rate of 9 percent. Preclinical outlays eight or more years before the NDA date escalate considerably with capitalization.

[40]Henry G. Grabowski, John M. Vernon, and Lacy Glenn Thomas, "Estimating the Effects of Regulation on Innovation: An International Comparative Analysis," *Journal of Law & Economics*, vol. 21 (April 1978), pp. 133–163.

to requiring proof of efficacy only in 1971. Between 1960–1961 and 1966–1970, inflation-adjusted drug development costs in Great Britain rose by a factor of three, while in the United States they increased sixfold. This finding suggests that more stringent regulation in the United States was responsible for a twofold cost increase, while other influences accounted for a threefold rise. Included among the other influences was the recognition by drug companies that more extensive testing was required to avoid repeating the thalidomide disaster, with its enormous tort liability losses (especially in Europe),[41] and to accumulate evidence that will convince physicians of a new product's superiority over the numerous products already on the market. It is possible too that, in the wake of extensive prior searches, it became harder to find promising new chemical entities.[42] In a follow-up analysis, L.G. Thomas found that only small U.S. drugmakers, and not the larger firms, experienced significant drug-finding productivity declines relative to their British counterparts.[43]

Whether rooted in regulation or other influences, the soaring costs of drug discovery were mirrored by a sharp decline in the number of new drugs approved for marketing. Figure 9.2 tells the basic story. The dark solid line extends the Pharmaceutical Manufacturers Association's new chemical entity series presented in Figure 9.1. The dash-dash line tracks between 1950 and 1972 a similar Food and Drug Administration series entailing a slightly different, usually more expansive, NCE definition. Both reveal a precipitous decrease, already underway in 1960, in the number of new drugs approved for marketing. Critics of the FDA blame regulation for the much lower plateau at which NCE approvals stabilized.[44] Others insisted that the decline continuing through 1963 reflected the increasing difficulty of finding good new drugs.

In reply to critics, the FDA insisted that at least part of the decrease was intentional. What it had done by requiring more rigorous and costly testing, its head asserted, was mainly to discourage companies from developing "me

---

[41]Issuance of a new drug approval by the FDA does not immunize firms from tort liability. See Office of Technology Assessment, *Pharmaceutical R&D*, pp. 169–179.

[42]For a view skeptical of this hypothesis and supporting the "better experiments" hypothesis, see the comment of Dr. Louis Lasagna in Robert B. Helms, ed., *Drugs and Health: Economic Issues and Policy Objectives* (Washington, DC: American Enterprise Institute, 1981), pp. 317.

[43]L. G. Thomas, "Regulation and Firm Size: FDA Impact on Innovation," *RAND Journal of Economics*, vol. 21 (Winter 1990), pp. 497–517. Compare Steven N. Wiggins, "Product Quality Regulation and New Drug Introductions," *Review of Economics and Statistics*, vol. 63 (November 1981), pp. 615–619.

[44]See, for example, Sam Peltzman, "An Evaluation of Consumer Protection Legislation: The 1962 Drug Amendments," *Journal of Political Economy*, vol. 81 (September/October 1973), pp. 1049–1091. Peltzman's statistical methodology assumes that because there was a resurgence from the 1955 and 1958 slumps, an increase beginning in 1963 should also have occurred.

FIGURE 9.2
Trends in U.S. New Drug Approvals, 1940–1990

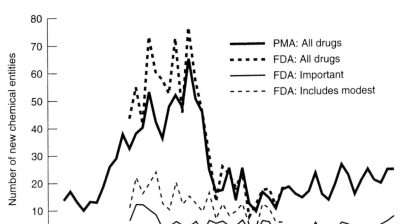

Sources: Pharmaceutical Research and Manufacturers Association, *Statistical Fact Book* (Washington, DC: PhRMA, September 1991), Table 2–4; Henry G. Grabowski, *Drug Regulation and Innovation* (Washington, DC: American Enterprise Institute), p. 22; and U.S. Congressional Budget Office, *How Health Care Reform Affects Pharmaceutical Research and Development* (Washington, DC: USGPO, 1994), p. 34.

too" variants adding little or nothing beyond the therapeutic effects of already existing drugs.[45] This was shown inter alia using the FDA's internal ratings of newly approved drugs according to their therapeutic novelty. The lowest (lighter solid) line tracks the appearance of drugs considered to offer important therapeutic gains; the next (light dash-dash) line those providing either important or modest, as distinguished from "little or no," gain. In the FDA's view, there was a surge of important discoveries as the drug-finding revolution took hold during the early 1950s. After that, however, the number of important new drug approvals was roughly constant, before and after the new law's bite. What had been weeded out by higher testing costs were mainly the drugs yielding little or no therapeutic gain. Industry executives conceded that testing had become too expensive to justify the deliberate development of "me

---

[45] Testimony of Commissioner Alexander Schmidt before the Senate Committee on Labor and Public Welfare, Subcommittee on Health, 1974, cited and drawn from Henry G. Grabowski, *Drug Regulation and Innovation* (Washington, DC: American Enterprise Institute, 1976), p. 22. The series for important new therapies has been extended from U.S. Congressional Budget Office compilations.

too" drugs through molecule manipulation. They argued nevertheless that the FDA had gone too far in its requirements and contested the FDA's evaluations of drug importance as biased.[46]

The debate then moved to a new plane. The escalation of drug testing costs led multinational pharmaceutical manufacturers to seek early returns on their investments by testing and then marketing their newest chemical entities in nations with less stringent regulations. As a result, there was a "drug lag" that let foreign consumers enjoy the benefits of new drugs earlier than U.S. consumers.[47] Some, to be sure, were available first in the United States, but that fraction declined appreciably after 1962. A General Accounting Office study singled out 13 important drugs introduced in the United States, mostly during the 1970s, that were available earlier in Europe or Canada.[48] On average, those drugs were available in at least one other nation 3.7 years before their U.S. introduction. As always, one can quarrel with the sample choice. Only three—beta blocker Inderal, antiulcer agent Tagamet, and antihypertensive Minipress–remained on the list of the 200 most prescribed drugs in the United States for 1986.[49]

The 2.5-year lag in the availability of Inderal and earlier beta blockers was singled out for special attention, since, it was estimated, their use could spare 10,000 to 20,000 heart attack victims per year from death through a second heart attack.[50] The FDA's hesitancy on beta blockers was not without explanation. The first such drug, practolol, caused blindness, peritonitis, and other side effects in 619 documented cases before being withdrawn from the European market in favor of the more benign Inderal.[51] But those reactions came from 250,000 patient years of experience with the drug—that is, in 2.5 cases per thousand patient years. The lives saved through early availability of the beta blockers, it was argued, more than justified the serious but much less frequent side effects.

---

[46]L. G. Thomas argues that the FDA's stringent test requirements *strengthened* U.S. firms' sales in world markets by forcing them to emphasize important new drugs. "Industrial Policy and International Competitiveness in the Pharmaceutical Industry," in Robert Helms, ed., *Competitive Strategies in the Pharmaceutical Industry.*

[47]See especially William Wardell and Louis Lasagna, *Regulation and Drug Development* (Washington, DC: American Enterprise Institute, 1975); and Henry Grabowski and John Vernon, "Consumer Protection Regulation in Ethical Drugs," *American Economic Review*, vol. 67 (February 1977), pp. 359–364.

[48]House Report, *The Food and Drug Administration's Process for Approving New Drugs*, p. 26.

[49]"31st Annual Prescription Survey," *Medical Advertising News*, April 1, 1987.

[50]Testimony of Dr. William Wardell, cited in *The Food and Drug Administration's Process*, p. 32. See also "Heart Ills Killed 930,477 in 1990," *New York Times*, January 19, 1993, p. C6.

[51]Ibid., p. 33.

THE DECISION-MAKING PROBLEM

Therein lies the central problem of drug regulation. Many drugs have adverse side effects. Sometimes they are lethal. Thousands have died from adverse reactions to penicillin. Millions have had ulcers, hemorrhages, or Reye's syndrome caused or aggravated by aspirin. But those and other potentially dangerous drugs have simultaneously conferred immense benefits upon the human race. How does one weigh the benefits against the risks?

There are incentives for regulatory agencies to place more emphasis on avoiding bad side effects than on accelerating the realization of good therapeutic effects. If a thalidomide or Oraflex (61 known deaths[52]) happens, regulators who let the drug be marketed are singled out for criticism. The press and legislators thrive on scapegoats. But a regulator is seldom if ever praised for approving a potentially dangerous drug that quietly provides widespread benefits. The penalties and rewards to regulators are asymmetric, and as a result, there is a tendency toward risk aversion.

Drug testing poses classic statistical decision theory problems. Sampling and a host of other more or less random influences make it difficult to measure effects with precision. The decision problem is usually set up in the form of a *null hypothesis:* that is, the drug is *not* safe or effective. In evaluating the data, decision-makers can make either of two errors:

Type I error.   The null hypothesis is rejected when it is true. The drug is deemed safe and effective when it really is not.

Type II error.   The null hypothesis is accepted when it is false. The drug is deemed unsafe or ineffective when it would in fact do good work.

Students are taught in statistics courses to put relatively heavy weight on avoiding Type I errors—that is, keeping their probability below .05 or even .01. For given sample size, this may mean a sizable probability of Type II error. This hews to the traditions of science, for much mischief can be done by accepting false theories, and if a hypothesis remains unproved but interesting, there will usually be more opportunities to test it. Because of the rewards and penalties asymmetry, regulators tend also to place heavy weight on avoiding Type I errors. But this may mean keeping good drugs off the market.

Thalidomide provides an illustration. In the United States, the drug was administered in uncontrolled tests to 3897 women of childbearing age, nine of whom gave birth to malformed children.[53] Suppose the probability of serious birth defects is in fact 0.0023. Suppose too that controlled tests are authorized

---

[52]See "The Miracle Drug That Became a Nightmare for Eli Lilly," *Business Week*, April 30, 1984, p. 104; and "Dangerous Drugs: Some Disasters of the Recent Past," *New York Times*, October 5, 1993, p. C3.

[53]House Report, *The Food and Drug Administration's Process*, p. 8.

using a sample of 100 childbearing women. Application of the binomial theorem yields the following distribution of observed side-effect incidence:

	Probability
Zero cases	.794
One case	.183
Two cases	.020
Three cases	.002

The probability of making a Type I error here is very high—nearly 0.8—unless the regulator just says "no" without supporting evidence. The only escape is to increase the sample size (e.g., to 1000), in which case the following distribution of outcomes is expected:

Defect cases	0	1	2	3	4	5	6	7
Probability	.100	.231	.265	.204	.117	.054	.021	.007

Now the Type I error probability is reduced to something approximating what scientists routinely require, but only by increasing greatly the cost of testing. Type II errors may still intrude—for example, if one or two malformed births would happen even without the use of thalidomide, or if the benefits from having thalidomide in physicians' medicine kits outweigh the costs of rare catastrophes.[54]

For another example, consider the case of drugs administered to dissolve blood clots in persons attended by emergency teams after the most common type of heart attack. In the early 1990s, two entities contended for that honor: a newcomer, genetically engineered TPA (tissue plasminogen activator) and an older drug, streptokinase (SKA).[55] Because TPA was challenging the accepted therapy, and also because it was expected to cost ten times as much per dose, the null hypothesis would be that TPA is less effective than, or no more effective than, SKA. Carefully structured trials were conducted, and it was found that 6.3 percent of the subjects died after being injected with TPA and heparin, while 7.4 percent died with SKA and heparin. One is inclined to reject the null hypothesis and conclude that TPA is better. But what is the risk

---

[54]Although its use by expectant mothers has been prohibited in all nations with FDA-like regulations, thalidomide is widely used to alleviate the pains of leprosy, and in 1994, it was being considered as a treatment for two leading causes of blindness. "Thalidomide May Be Used as a Treatment for Blindness," *Harvard Gazette,* April 29, 1994, p. 1.

[55]"A Costlier Heart Drug Also Proves Better," *New York Times,* May 1, 1993, p. 7.

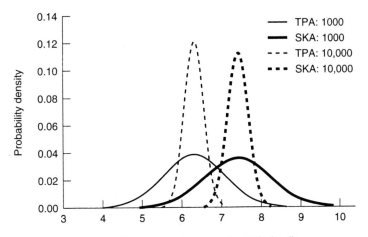

FIGURE 9.3
Testing TPA Against Streptokinase

Percentage of persons treated who die

of Type I error? We know only what we observe—that is, the proportion of
subjects dying. Taking that provisionally to be our best estimate of the true
proportion, assuming the relevant frequency distribution to be asymptotically
normal, and assuming for the moment that each drug was administered in
1000 cases, we plot the array of possible outcomes in Figure 9.3. The light
solid line traces the frequency distribution for TPA outcomes and the heavy
solid line the distribution for SKA. We see that the proportion of deaths with
TPA—that is, if we could replicate the experiment many times—*could have
been* as high as 8.5 percent, and the proportion with SKA could have been as
low as 5 percent. From the considerable overlap between the frequency distributions, it is clear that there is a substantial risk (one chance in three) of making a Type I error. One can accept that risk and favor TPA, or one can try to
reduce it by drawing larger samples. In fact, recognizing that it would be a
close call, TPA's maker chose to use samples of approximately 10,000 for each
contender—samples much larger than the FDA normally requires. The
tighter, taller dashed frequency distributions were the result. Now there is
very little overlap. Assuming further (an important *if*) that the experiments
are unbiased, the probability of concluding erroneously that TPA is superior
is reduced to less than one chance in 100.

REGULATORY REFORM

There is no way to escape tough decisions in such cases. Either errors are
risked, or the cost of testing escalates. The FDA has tended to err on the side
of more-extensive, higher-cost testing. We return to this point in a moment,
after asking whether the regulatory process might be improved in other ways.

One chronic complaint is that FDA decision making has been too slow—
requiring from the time of NDA application to approval an average of 2.4

years in the 1960s, 2.1 years in the 1970s, and 2.8 years in the 1980s.[56] Companies typically deliver to the FDA a truckload of data supporting their NDA application. But must it take two to three years to process the data, ask appropriate questions, and reach a decision? Quicker decision making would put health-improving new drugs in the hands of consumers sooner and allow companies to begin recouping their testing costs earlier.[57] After numerous procedural reforms put only a small dent in the problem,[58] Congress passed in 1992 a law permitting the FDA to levy fees on pharmaceutical companies and use the money to hire 600 additional NDA dossier examiners.[59] Whether increasing by 10 percent the size of an already large and bureaucratic regulatory agency will solve the problem remains to be seen.

Rigid procedures can inflict particularly high cost if they delay the availability of unique lifesaving drugs. To avoid this, the FDA has sought to accelerate its decision making on particularly vital drugs.[60] More important, it created special procedures (variously called "compassionate" and "treatment" INDs) under which drugs can be made widely available to physicians for the treatment of life-threatening diseases before receiving formal marketing approvals. And for drugs developed to combat AIDS, on which administering to randomly chosen subjects a placebo could be tantamount to a death sentence, standard experimental procedures were waived altogether.[61] One consequence was that it became harder to know which drugs were actually effective.[62]

---

[56]DiMasi et al., "New Drug Development," p. 615.

[57]Grabowski and Vernon estimate that cutting a year from FDA's average decision lag would increase the discounted present value of a new drug's lifetime cash flows by $23 to 40 million. "Returns to R&D on New Drug Introductions in the 1980s," in Helms, ed., *Competitive Strategies in the Pharmaceutical Industry*.

[58]For details on the process, see Office of Technology Assessment, *Pharmaceutical R&D*, pp. 138–163. See also Norman Dorsen, "Reforming Drug Laws," *New York Times*, November 2, 1979, p. A31; "A Guardian of U.S. Health Is Buckling Under Stress," *New York Times*, December 4, 1989, p. 1; and David A. Kessler and Karyn L. Feiden, "Faster Evaluation of Vital Drugs," *Scientific American*, March 1995, pp. 48–54.

[59]"Senate Passes Bill to Charge Makers for Drug Approval," *New York Times*, October 8, 1992, p. 1. On the incentive biases such a system could introduce, see the letter to the editor by Dr. Joseph Fins, *New York Times*, October 27, 1992, p. A22.

[60]See David Dranove and David Meltzer, "Does the FDA Accelerate or Delay the Approval of Important Drugs?" working paper, Northwestern University, December 1991.

[61]See "AIDS Drugs and FDA," *Medical Advertising News*, October 15, 1987, pp. 20–22; and "Radical New Method Is Proposed for Testing AIDS Drugs," *New York Times*, March 26, 1990, p. B8.

[62]See "New Study Questions the Use of AZT in Early Treatment of AIDS Virus," *New York Times*, April 2, 1993, p. 1.

The special procedures adopted in life-threatening cases suggest a range of further questions. Clearly, a scientific approach to drug testing is desirable when there are no overriding human considerations. Otherwise, the information needed to make good drug choices may not be forthcoming. But why shouldn't the FDA merely require that good testing procedures be used and that the results be published in an objective manner? Why should it decide which drugs may be marketed, and hence be available for medical use, and which may not? Is the market failure that justifies its activities at the information-gathering and disseminating level, or at the level of processing the information and deciding which drugs to use? Are there economies of scale in drug information processing that make the FDA better able than individual physicians (or groups of physicians) to choose which drugs are safe and efficacious, or should the FDA merely serve as an information-generating agency, leaving drug choices to be taken on a decentralized basis?

Having come this far, we take a step farther. Why should the law allow only physicians to choose which drugs to administer? In other words, why require prescriptions? Plainly, physicians have better scientific knowledge on average than patients. But patients know themselves better, and if they wish to inform themselves and assume the risk of choosing a particular drug, why not let them do so, among other things avoiding the cost of a physician visit? In many nations, prescriptions are not required, but it is hard to detect systematic adverse consequences in the form of higher poisoning or other mortality rates.[63] The requirement that all new drugs be dispensed only by prescription in the United States emerged with scant reasoned consideration by Congress, and the FDA chooses to waive that requirement for drugs it considers safe enough to warrant over-the-counter status.[64] These questions cannot be dodged if one seeks to design a sensible regulatory policy for pharmaceuticals.

THE PATENT SYSTEM AND PHARMACEUTICALS

Given the structure of FDA regulations, developing new drugs is costly and risky. Counting the cost of failures, the average cost of developing and testing an approved new chemical entity during the 1970s, we have seen, approximated $100 million. Since then, costs have continued to rise. We now ask, what incentives are there for drug companies to invest these large sums in the search for new drug products?

---

[63]Sam Peltzman, "The Health Effects of Mandatory Prescriptions," *Journal of Law & Economics*, vol. 30 (October 1987), pp. 207–238.

[64]Peter Temin, "Realized Benefits from Switching Drugs," *Journal of Law & Economics*, vol. 35 (October 1992), pp. 351–369. See also his earlier article, "The Origin of Compulsory Drug Prescriptions," note 2 supra.

Since its inception in medieval Europe, the patent system has been the classic means of providing incentives for invention and investment in the development of new technologies.[65] Patents have appeared incidentally in several of our industry studies. Now we focus the analytic spotlight on them.

A patent permits its holder to prevent (through appropriate legal action) others from using the covered invention for some specified period of time—in the United States, for 17 years from the date of patent issue, but in most industrialized nations, for 20 years from the date when an application for patent protection is filed.[66] The patent holder may choose to license one or more others to use the subject invention, charging them royalties in compensation for its waiver of exclusivity. To obtain a patent, one must show the Patent Office that the claimed invention, usually defined quite narrowly, is new—that is, not conceived by others or in the public domain for more than a year, and that it has actual or potential practical utility. During the 1980s, the number of invention patents issued annually by the U.S. Patent and Trademark Office averaged 71,000. Fewer than 10 percent went to unaffiliated individuals; most were assigned to corporations or other organizations. Thus, the modern patent system is a large-numbers operation that preponderantly serves organizations, not the lonely inventor toiling in her attic workshop. Fifty-nine percent of 1980s patents were issued to U.S.-owned corporations, individuals, and institutions calling the United States their home; the remaining 41 percent went to foreign-owned corporations and individuals.

Figure 9.4 lays out the patent system's basic theoretical rationale. A new product gives rise to a new demand curve D_N—one that would not have existed without the new product. The underlying R&D also engenders a production technology, embodied in the marginal cost curve MC. The developer introduces its product to the market as a monopolist, charging price OP_M and realizing profits (or more exactly, quasi-rents) measured by area $P_M ABC$. Despite the monopoly pricing, consumers also gain, because consumers' surplus triangle TAP_M has been created by the product's availability. If the investment in research, development, and testing is to be worthwhile for the firm, appropriately discounted quasi-rents must exceed, or at least equal, the value of that investment. But this may not happen if the new product is imitated quickly. When rivals begin marketing similar products, the original developer's demand curve shifts to the left—for example, to D_{N2}.[67] Ignoring some complications that will intrude later, the developer revises its price to OP_{M2} and sees its second-period quasi-rents shrink to $P_{M2}EFC$. With the price still exceeding production cost, more imitators may enter, shifting the developer's

---

[65]Erich Kaufer, *The Economics of the Patent System* (Chur, Switzerland: Harwood Academic Publishers, 1989).

[66]In June 1995, to harmonize its rules with world practice under the treaty of Marrakesh, the United States began issuing patents whose life was 20 years from the time of first patent application.

[67]This case is a simplification of the dominant-firm analysis underlying Figure 5.3 supra.

FIGURE 9.4
Erosion of Quasi-Rents Through Imitative Entry

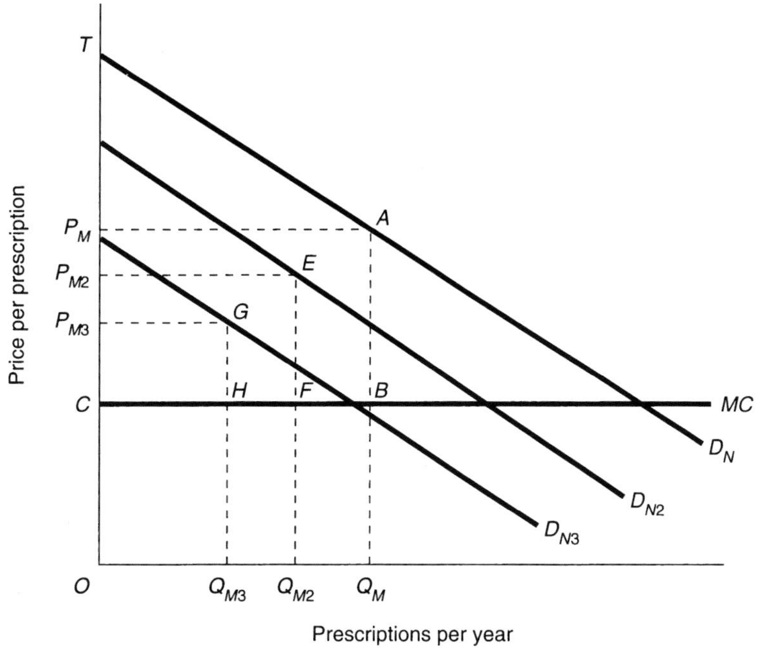

demand curve to D_{N3} and reducing quasi-rents to $P_{M3}GMC$, and so on. The imitative process may proceed so quickly that the discounted sum of the quasi-rent rectangles turns out to be less than the value of the developer's front-end R&D investment. If this erosion is anticipated, the would-be developer will refrain from making the investment, and no new product, with its attendant consumers' surplus, will be forthcoming. If rapid imitation is not anticipated but happens with some frequency, would-be product developers will learn their lesson and cease investing. The goose slows, or perhaps even ceases, its production of golden eggs.

OTHER BARRIERS TO IMITATION

Patents are granted by governments to retard imitation and thereby to make invention and the development of new products and processes more profitable, and hence more attractive, than they otherwise would be. However, other barriers to imitation often serve a function similar to that of patents, and if they are strong enough, patent rights may be redundant or, by entrenching monopoly power, they may provide more profit incentive than is necessary to call forth the required investment in innovation. The alternative barriers to imitation come in several flavors.

For one, an imitator may need to invest nearly as much money, and take as much time, developing its imitative product as the original innovator required.[68] Consider automobiles. One can spot a new car design racing around a rival test track six months before the car is introduced to the public. But to field an equivalent new model, rough and detailed designs must be executed, stamping dies must be fabricated, prototypes must be built and tested for strength and roadworthiness, production lines must be tooled, etc. All this takes, as we have seen, from two to five years, so the imitator incurs heavy costs, only to reach the market much later than the innovator. Or in integrated circuits, one can inspect and "reverse-engineer" a rival chip, but then photoresist masks have to be laid out, checked, and produced at considerable cost before one can begin moving down the learning curve, bearing for some time a cost handicap relative to the innovator, who has the advantage of a head start down the curve. And if the new chip requires more precise tolerances than earlier generations, time and money must be invested in outfitting a new fabrication facility.

With a head start into the market, the first mover will also be the first to acquaint consumers with the merits of its product. If the product is good, consumers may become attached physically (through investments in learning how to use it, or in complementary equipment) or psychologically to it. It may then be difficult for firms offering essentially the same thing to induce a switch away from the original product. For computers in particular, we saw that the "lock-in" advantages of commitments to complementary software conferred an enormous advantage. We shall learn more about the psychological dimension of first-mover advantages shortly.

In terms of the balance between innovation and imitation costs, pharmaceutical innovation is quite different from what transpires in most mechanical, electronic, and chemical fields. Most of the investment in new drug "research and development" is incurred to generate information—at the preclinical stage, information on what molecules have promise; and at the clinical test stage, information on whether the drug actually works in human beings and whether it is safe. Once the FDA confers its stamp of approval, all the world knows most of what the innovator knows—that the molecule provides the desired therapy. Most of the $100-million investment in screening and testing yields information as a pure public good, spilling over at close to zero cost to others. Absent product patents or something equivalent, a would-be imitator could hire a good chemical engineer, spend a few hundred thousand dollars developing a production process, and be in business with its knock-off substitute.

Drugs are also different, but somewhat less unique, in another respect. Most mechanical and electronic problems have multiple alternative solutions—some better, some worse. Unless the original inventor obtains an unusually broad patent (as with Jack Kilby's integrated circuit concept), clever imitators will find ways of "inventing around" the patent. But when one receives a patent on the unique quadruple benzene ring structure called chlortetracycline, no one else can produce and sell that molecule, and since

---

[68]See Edwin Mansfield et al., "Imitation Costs and Patents: An Empirical Study," *Economic Journal*, vol. 91 (December 1981), pp. 907–918.

other molecules might not work as well in human beings, a slight molecular variation must be tested all over again at high cost. Because the product's marketability depends upon having passed the specific molecule through testing, drug patents provide unusually tight protection.

It should not be surprising, therefore, that patents are considered important by drug manufacturers. On this we can be more precise. Richard Levin and associates administered a lengthy questionnaire to 650 U.S. research and development managers from 130 industries, in most of which technological innovation played a prominent role.[69] They asked their respondents inter alia to rate on a scale of 1 ("not at all effective") to 7 ("very effective") the effectiveness of several means of protecting the competitive advantages from technologically new products and processes. The alternative benefit appropriation instruments included patents to prevent duplication, keeping inventions secret, securing a lead-time advantage over rivals, moving quickly down one's learning curve, and mounting a more effective sales and service campaign. Among the 130 industries, only three had a higher score than the 6.5 average for drugs on the effectiveness of product patents, and two of those were possibly anomalous, the result of having only one executive responding.[70]

Table 9.1 summarizes the average scores for the seven industries studied in this volume on which data were available. Product patents were accorded far more significance in pharmaceuticals than in the other industries. They were considered *the* most effective means of appropriating the benefits from innovation in pharmaceuticals—the only industry in which that was true. Not surprisingly, being first on the market with a new product was the most effective benefits appropriating instrument in semiconductors, computers, and beer. Superior sales effort and providing superior service were most effective in three industries with mature technologies—petroleum refining, steel, and autos. Moving quickly down the learning curve to gain product and (especially) production process advantages over rivals received high weight from the semiconductor and computer makers and also from petroleum refiners.

These findings reinforce the results of earlier, more subjective, and perhaps therefore more error-prone, surveys. During the late 1960s Taylor and Silberston asked company executives in England to estimate the maximum amount by which their R&D outlays would be reduced if no effective patent

---

[69]Richard Levin, Alvin Klevorick, Richard R. Nelson, and Sidney Winter, "Appropriating the Returns from Industrial Research and Development," *Brookings Papers on Economic Activity*, Microeconomics (Washington, DC: Brookings, 1977) pp. 783–820. The analysis in this section also uses raw data provided by Professor Levin.

[70]For drugs, there were 17 respondents. Ahead of drugs with eight responses and a score of 6.88 was agricultural chemicals, which has characteristics strikingly similar to those of drugs. Most patents cover specific herbicide or pesticide molecules, each of which has to undergo extensive safety tests before being approved by the Environmental Protection Agency for commercial use. Many pharmaceutical companies also conduct agricultural chemical operations, since a newly synthesized molecule may turn out to be useful in either domain.

TABLE 9.1

Average Scores Evaluating the Effectiveness of Various Means of Appropriating the Benefits from Innovations[a]

Appropriation Method	Petroleum Refining	Steel	Semiconductors	Computers	Autos	Drugs	Beer
Number of Responses	10	10	10	21	4	17	2
For Product Inventions:							
Patents	4.33	5.10	4.50	3.43	5.00	6.53	2.00
Learning by doing	4.56	5.40	6.10	5.67	4.50	4.24	3.50
Lead time	3.78	5.40	6.20	6.33	4.50	5.47	6.50
Sales and service	5.44	5.50	6.00	5.48	5.25	5.59	6.00
For Process Inventions:							
Patents	4.90	3.50	3.20	3.33	4.50	4.88	2.00
Secrecy	3.70	4.00	4.70	4.95	3.75	4.29	5.00
Learning by doing	4.56	5.40	6.10	5.67	4.50	4.24	3.50

Source: The detailed computer file containing industry aggregates from a Yale University survey of 650 R&D executives. See note 69.

[a] 7.0 = very effective; 1.0 = not at all effective.

protection were available. The average across all industries was 8 percent; for pharmaceuticals, it was 64 percent.[71] Mansfield and associates asked the chief R&D executives of 100 U.S. corporations what fraction of the inventions they commercialized between 1981 and 1983 would not have been developed without patent protection.[72] The average for all industries was 14 percent; for pharmaceuticals, it was 60 percent. It should be clear now why a detailed discussion of the patent system has been saved for this chapter.

INTERNATIONAL PATENT POLICIES

Placing as much emphasis as they do on patents as means of protecting their investments in research, development, and testing, and with a strong orienta-

[71] C. T. Taylor and Z. A. Silberston, *The Economic Impact of the Patent System* (Cambridge, UK: Cambridge University Press: 1973), pp. 195–199.

[72] Edwin Mansfield, "Patents and Innovation: An Empirical Study," *Management Science*, vol. 32 (February 1986), p. 175.

tion toward selling their products throughout the world, pharmaceutical companies in the United States and Europe organized a powerful lobbying group to promote patent systems outside their home nations.[73] Many industrialized nations traditionally excluded foodstuffs and medicines from patentability on the assumption that such products were too important for consumer welfare to permit monopolies. Most less-developed nations followed this pattern and provided relatively weak patent protection more generally. For pharmaceutical manufacturers, this often meant that new products were subjected to early imitative competition, eroding profits. The drug companies made common cause with computer software developers, motion picture producers, and recording companies, persuading the U.S. government to threaten under Section 301 of the U.S. international trade law sanctions against nations with weak patent and copyright laws. They also succeeded in having the international harmonization of intellectual property laws given high priority during the Uruguay Round of multilateral trade negotiations. The agreement announced in December 1993 requires all GATT signatories to provide substantial patent protection for drugs and the like within ten years.

This provision has been bitterly controversial, especially in the less-developed countries (LDCs). Those nations typically cannot afford to mount ambitious new drug development efforts internally. They rely upon the products developed by multinational firms. Figure 9.5 illustrates the costs and benefits to them of providing patent protection.[74] If they grant drug patents, and assuming the LDC's demand function for a typical new drug to be D, the drug will be sold at monopoly price OP_M. If they do not, but a competitive knockoff industry exists either at home or abroad, the price will gravitate toward OP_C. Under patent monopoly, the medium-shaded triangle A will be dead-weight loss; the lightly shaded rectangle H will be profit to multinational drug companies (a clear gain from the firms' perspective); and the only benefit to the LDC citizens will be the darkly shaded consumers' surplus triangle B. Under competition, B, H, and A will all accrue to the LDC's citizens as consumers' surplus. By a convenient geometric property, when demand functions are linear, the marginal revenue function MR cuts MC halfway between zero output and the competitive output OQ_C. As a consequence, triangle B is congruent to triangle A, each of which has half the area of rectangle H. Thus, the surplus gained by LDC citizens under competition is four times their surplus under monopoly.

This does not necessarily mean that the LDCs are better off denying patent protection (ignoring industrialized nations' threats to retaliate against exports of *other* LDC industries). They might be better off if the extra profits (rectangle H) conveyed to drug firms led to the development of more new drugs, and hence to a multiplication of consumers' surplus triangle B.

---

[73]See Michael Santoro, "Pfizer: Protecting Intellectual Property in a Global Marketplace," Harvard Business School case study N9–392–072, February 1992.

[74]It is adapted from Alan V. Deardorff, "Welfare Effects of Global Patent Protection," *Economica*, vol. 59 (February 1992), pp. 35–51.

FIGURE 9.5
Impact of Patent Policy on LDC Welfare

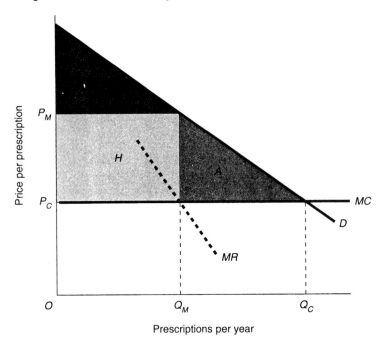

Prescriptions per year

Is this likely? For the LDC citizens to be as well off with patent protection as without, there would have to be at least *three* new drug products, each providing incremental consumers' surplus *B*, to compensate for the loss of surplus (*H* + *A*) from having existing products monopolized. Figure 9.6 conceptualizes the effect of LDC patent protection on the drug development efforts of multinational companies. The vertical axis measures the number of new chemical entities developed. The horizontal axis (scaled in dollars) measures both the amount of money spent on R&D and the quasi rents earned from drug sales all over the world. The curve RD(NCE) is a kind of "production function" showing the relationship between R&D inputs and the output of new drugs. It is drawn to imply diminishing marginal returns; each new drug costs more to develop than the one before it. The curve Q_1 shows the relationship between the number of new drugs marketed (vertical axis) and drug developers' quasi-rents (horizontal axis). The more drugs, the more quasi-rent, but with diminishing returns, since company decision makers will pursue the new chemical entities expected to be most lucrative before adding low-profit items to their portfolio. To maximize their profits, drug developers will seek to maximize the horizontal distance between RD(NCE) and Q_1. The profit-maximizing number of drugs is 15, yielding net profit (quasi-rents less R&D cost) of *YZ*.

FIGURE 9.6
Impact of Quasi-Rent Volume on NCE Development

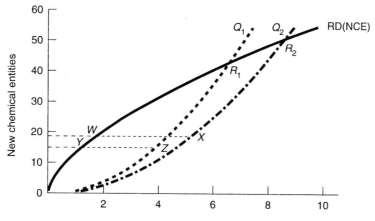

R&D outlays, quasi-rents (billion dollars per year)

If LDCs change their laws to provide patent protection for new drugs, the quasi-rent function will shift to the right, e.g., to Q_2. A shift of 20 percent is assumed, reflecting the fact that low-income nations account for only about one-fifth of world gross national product, so their purchasing power is not enormous, and the fact that multinational drug companies already have substantial operations in LDCs, many of which yield profits despite weak patent protection.[75] With enhanced quasi-rent potential, drug companies will reoptimize and develop more drugs. Under the conditions illustrated in Figure 9.6, they will develop 18 drugs instead of 15, leading to net profit WX. But this is far short of the threefold increase required to leave LDC citizens as well off. Indeed, assuming diminishing returns in either the production function or the quasi-rent function or both, it is difficult to imagine circumstances under which such a threefold increase could ensue. The opposition of LDC citizens to strong pharmaceutical patents becomes understandable.

There is an alternative model that may describe drug developers' behavior more realistically. The previous paragraph assumed that pharmaceutical companies can pick the R&D strategy that maximizes their collective profits. The alternative model assumes that, given patent protection, firms gain profits more or less closely approaching monopoly levels on the new drugs they succeed in marketing, but they compete in their R&D expenditures for being the first to develop potential new drugs and winning the patents that cover them. Indeed, they compete so vigorously that total R&D costs escalate to offset completely the monopoly quasi-rents gained from selling the drugs. In this

---

[75]See Ballance et al., *The World's Pharmaceutical Industries*, pp. 30–31 and 76.

case, which might be called Demsetz-Barzel competition,[76] the industry equilibrium with quasi-rent function Q_1 occurs at point R_1, where the quasi-rent function intersects the R&D cost function, leaving zero net profit. Demsetz-Barzel competition leads to much larger R&D expenditures and a higher yield of new products—that is, 42 NCEs–than does monopoly profit maximization in setting both R&D outlays *and* prices. If under these conditions profit opportunities expand because LDCs grant strong patents, the zero-net-profit industry equilibrium shifts to point R_2, where 50 NCEs are developed. Again, however, the change explicitly attributable to enhanced patent protection is far smaller than what is required to improve the welfare of LDC citizens.

DRUG PRICING

To round out the picture, we focus now on pharmaceutical firms' pricing decisions. We must consider cases in which patent protection confers a monopoly in the sale of a specific chemical entity, those in which the patent has expired and other firms begin producing chemically identical drugs (generic competition), and those that lie in between (notably, the differentiated oligopoly case). We also examine how pricing is affected by various government interventions.

THE PRICING OF ANTIBIOTICS

During the pharmaceutical industry's early formative years, we recall, numerous firms produced and sold penicillin, on which no effective patent protection existed. Price competition was intense, and profits were driven to zero and perhaps lower. The picture changed when new, patented, broad-spectrum antibiotics began entering the market.

Aureomycin, the first broad-spectrum antibiotic, was introduced by American Cyanamid in December 1948 at a wholesale price (i.e., the price retailer pharmacies paid) of $15 per bottle of 16 capsules in the standard 250-mg dosage form.[77] During the next 18 months the Aureomycin price was reduced in steps to $10, $8, and $6. Two of the three reductions were made just before the sale of new patented broad-spectrum antibiotics, Chloromycetin from Parke-Davis and Terramycin from Pfizer, began. With one brief exception, the three drugs were offered at identical prices. A 15 percent price reduction to $5.10 was initiated by Pfizer in September 1951 and matched by the other two sellers within four days. In 1951, the net profit mar-

---

[76]See Harold Demsetz, "Why Regulate Utilities?" *Journal of Law & Economics*, vol. 11 (April 1968), pp. 55–66; and Yoram Barzel, "Optimal Timing of Innovations," *Review of Economics and Statistics*, vol. 50 (August 1968), pp. 348–355.

[77]This account is drawn from Federal Trade Commission, *Economic Report on Antibiotics Manufacture*, pp. 190–197 and 210–215.

gin of the three broad-spectrum antibiotic producers, after deduction of allocated research and selling costs, averaged 50 percent of sales. During the next decade the three products' wholesale prices remained at $5.10. A fourth broad-spectrum antibiotic, tetracycline, was introduced by American Cyanamid in 1953 at $5.10. Within a year four other firms also began selling their own tetracycline brands, each at $5.10, persisting into 1961.[78]

There were five companies selling tetracycline because three firms (American Cyanamid, Pfizer, and Bristol Myers) had all filed patent applications for the same chemical molecule, engendering what is known as an "interference" in the Patent Office. Bristol Myers in turn had licensed Squibb and Upjohn under its prospective patent. The contending patent applicants, fearful that protracted litigation might lead to no patent at all and hence price competition echoing what they experienced on penicillin, agreed to settle their disputes by having the firm found to have harbored the true inventor license the others.[79] Eventually, Pfizer received the patent. There was no formal agreement that licenses would not be granted to other companies, but Pfizer denied licenses to other applicants, and so the club remained an oligopolistic five.

The identity of wholesale prices was mirrored, with occasional exceptions, in the pricing of antibiotics sold to local government hospitals and the federal government.[80] The companies' pricing behavior became a focus of government inquiry when all five responded on June 5, 1955, to a Veterans Administration request for 5640 bottles by bidding $19.1884 per 100-capsule bottle. All five quoted the $19.1884 price again in the next four VA procurements. The parallel quotation of such an odd number by five firms led antitrust authorities to infer collusion. But there was an alternative noncollusive explanation. The $19.1884 price was obtained by applying a series of round-number discounts to round-number prices: $19.1884 was the standard 2 percent trade discount off $19.58, which (after rounding) was 20 percent off the price to wholesalers of $24.48, which in turn was 20 percent off the price to retailers of $30.60, which was 40 percent off the retail list price of $51,

---

[78]Schwartzman, *Innovation in the Pharmaceutical Industry*, pp. 273–278.

[79]As the patent counsel for American Cyanamid wrote in 1954 to the responsible Patent Office examiner: "[A]s the interference is delayed . . . the selling price on the product will be lowered so that at the termination of the interference the profits which would normally accrue to Cyanamid or Pfizer, from which research funds come, will have been reduced to nothing. . . . Cyanamid would rather pay royalties to a bona fide patentee than see the pharmaceutical business in which it has a major interest ruined by irresponsible price cutting." Document no. 928 in the Federal Trade Commission antitrust case, In the Matter of American Cyanamid Co. et al., 63 F.T.C. 1747 (1963).

[80]This example is drawn from Scherer and Ross, *Industrial Market Structure and Economic Performance* (Boston: Houghton Mifflin, 1990), pp. 267–268, 307–308, and 343–345. The author was a consultant to Pfizer on one of the antitrust cases that followed.

which was 15 percent off the $60 price from which Pfizer announced a reduction in 1951. Uniform adherence to the $19.1884 price came only after the companies had quoted differing trade discounts in two earlier VA procurements. By adhering to round-number and round-number-discount "focal point prices," the oligopolists were in effect attempting to coordinate their behavior without actually meeting and colluding. However, when the temptation proved to be too great, their discipline broke. In October 1956, the Armed Services Medical Procurement Agency made its first tetracycline purchase, calling for 94,000 bottles. Two firms quoted $19.1884, but Bristol Myers undercut to $18.97 and American Cyanamid won the order at $11.00. Even at that low price, Cyamamid achieved in one fell swoop a contribution to profits of at least $750,000, since the marginal cost of producing 100 capsules was less than $3.00.

Getting together in a smoke-filled room and agreeing to quote uniform prices is a per se violation of the U.S. Sherman Act, Section 1. But what about the behavior of the broad-spectrum antibiotic manufacturers? In the flurry of antitrust cases that followed the events described above, company executives stated under oath that they had not met and agreed on either prices or on limiting the membership of the tetracycline club. Thus, their behavior fell into a gray area of U.S. law known as the *conscious parallelism* doctrine. Characterizing the law as it existed at the time of a federal criminal action against the tetracycline makers, District Judge Marvin Frankel instructed the jury:[81]

> [U]nlawful agreement may be shown if the proof establishes a concert of action, with all the parties working together understandingly with a single design for the accomplishment of a common purpose. . . . It is not sufficient to show that the parties acted uniformly or similarly or in ways that may seem to have been mutually beneficial. If such actions were taken independently as a matter of individual business judgment, without any agreement or arrangement or understanding among the parties, then there would be no conspiracy.

A key point of contention was whether the large and continuing disparity between tetracycline prices and production costs "exhibited qualities or peculiarities of a type that could be deemed evidence that such prices resulted from agreement rather than from competition."[82] The jury thought it did and found the companies guilty. But a 2–1 majority of the appellate court disapproved of the judge's instruction letting jurors consider such "inflammatory" issues as profits.[83] After further appeals, a different district court judge rehearing the evidence found the companies innocent. Thus, in one of the

---

[81]U.S. v. Charles Pfizer & Co. et al., S.D. New York (1967), from pp. 6200–6201 of the trial record.

[82]Ibid., p. 6271.

[83]437 F. 2d 957 (1970); affirmed on a 3–3 split within the Supreme Court, 404 U.S. 548 (1972); remanded and vacated at 367 F. Supp. 91 (1973).

most closely contested antitrust cases ever, the conscious parallelism doctrine was interpreted permissively toward the kind of pricing practiced by tetracycline suppliers.

DIFFERENTIATED PRODUCT PRICING

The early patented broad-spectrum antibiotics were priced at high levels relative to their production costs. The entry of new variants was accompanied by price reductions. Although tetracycline was preferred in many indications, the products were fairly close substitutes, and for more than a decade they were priced identically. Is this typical or atypical of new, patented drugs?

The most complete evidence comes from a statistical study by Lu and Comanor of 148 new branded chemical entities introduced into the U.S. market between 1978 and 1987.[84] All but 13 had at least one fairly close substitute in their principal therapeutic indications; the average number of substitutes was 1.86. The authors distinguished inter alia between drugs that offered an important therapeutic gain, as rated by the Food and Drug Administration (10 percent of the sample); those with modest gains (37 percent); and those with little or no therapeutic gain relative to substances already on the market. They found that drugs contributing important therapeutic gains were introduced at prices 3.2 times the level of substitute products in equivalent dosages; those making modest gains were priced at 2.17 times the average for substitutes; and those making little or no gain were priced at roughly the same level as preexisting substitutes. During the four years after introduction, prices of the important new drugs (adjusted for general inflation) tended to decline—by about 13 percent on average, whereas the prices of drugs making little or no therapeutic contribution tended to rise by 22 percent. Thus, over time, there was some convergence of prices within therapeutic classes. Introductory prices tended to be lower by 8 to 10 percent, all else equal, for each additional differentiated substitute available at the time of first marketing. The entry of additional substitute products had a significant negative impact on incumbents' prices, all else equal.

Superior drugs, it would appear, carry price premiums, and often very large premiums. As in the antibiotics history, new but not appreciably superior drugs tend to be priced near parity with their peers. More interbrand competition leads to somewhat lower prices, all else equal. Superior drugs tend initially to be priced above the level at which they will ultimately be marketed, perhaps because their makers misjudge the degree of superiority, or perhaps because pharmaceutical companies expect physicians to perceive high prices as signals for superiority. The most puzzling evidence, possibly

[84]Z. John Lu and William S. Comanor, "Strategic Pricing of New Pharmaceuticals," working paper, University of California, Santa Barbara (1994).

unique to the 1980s, which saw the Producer Price Index for prescription drugs rise at an average annual rate of 8.8 percent, was the tendency for me-too drug prices to increase during their early years on the market.[85]

GENERIC COMPETITION

As patents on the early wonder drugs began to expire, new competition from generic substitutes materialized. Generic competition commenced for tetracycline and another broad-spectrum antibiotic, ampicillin, even before patents expired as a result of antitrust challenges demanding patent licensing. The generic products came from two rather different sources: from companies, both domestic and foreign, that specialized in making generic copies; and from well-known ethical drug houses attempting to fill out their product lines with so-called "branded generics."

The wholesale prices of branded tetracycline and related broad-spectrum antibiotics were stable at $30.60 per hundred capsules between 1951 and 1961.[86] Squibb was the first of the original five tetracycline manufacturers to break discipline, beginning in 1962, with list price cuts and then special discounts. As it increased its sales share from less than 7 to 20 percent, others followed suit. In 1966, tetracycline could be obtained at wholesale prices (with discounts) ranging from $2.55 (from a generic house) to $16.52 per hundred capsules (from patent holder Pfizer). The price-cutting then escalated, so that by 1972 Pfizer was selling its branded tetracycline at $3.47. The prices of many other antibiotics were pulled down by the tetracycline price warfare.

Antibiotics, however, may have been atypical. Because of patent conflicts, branded tetracycline was available at early dates from five different companies, and ampicillin had two initial U.S. sources. The drugs were at least as well known by their chemical names as by brand names, which facilitated generic prescribing. On other drugs with multiple sources owing to patent expiration, there was little price competition.[87] Even in the "jungle" of antibiotics,[88] American Cyanamid, the first to sell tetracycline, commanded one-

---

[85]The official price indices have systematic biases overstating the true average rate of price increase. See Ernst Berndt, Zvi Griliches, and Joshua Rosett, "Auditing the Producer Price Index: Micro Evidence from Prescription Pharmaceutical Preparations," *Journal of Economics and Business Studies*, vol. 11 (July 1993), pp. 251–264; and Zvi Griliches and Iain Cockburn, "Generics and New Goods in Pharmaceutical Price Indexes," *American Economic Review*, vol. 84 (December 1994), pp. 1213–1232.

[86]A much fuller account is found in Schwartzman, *Innovation in the Pharmaceutical Industry*, pp. 273–287.

[87]See Schwartzman, *Innovation*, p. 287; and Meir Statman, "The Effect of Patent Expiration on the Market Position of Drugs," in Helms, ed., *Drugs and Health*, pp. 145–149.

[88]Schwartzman, *Innovation*, p. 251.

third of all tetracycline sales in 1973, and Bristol Myers retained one-fourth of the ampicillin market.

That the availability of low-price generics did not drive out high-price brands was shown through an illuminating Federal Trade Commission staff study.[89] It compared in detail the market shares, prices, and marketing outlays of producers in two therapeutic classes, oral diuretics (antihypertension drugs) and pentaerythritol tetranitrate (PETN), which was used as a substitute for nitroglycerin pills against attacks of angina pectoris. The first successful oral diuretic, Merck's patented Diuril, was introduced in 1958. Molecular variants that avoided Merck's patent could be found, however, and within two years, ten other firms were offering their own patented substitutes. PETN was introduced by Warner-Lambert in 1952 under the Peritrate brand name. The chemical was already in the public domain, so no patent could be obtained, and some hundred other firms began offering their own generic or differentiated PETN variants. Study authors Bond and Lean expected competition to erode the original product suppliers' prices and market shares much more with PETN, where there was no effective patent protection, than in diuretics, in which many patented products coexisted. However, they found remarkable similarity between the two markets. Thirteen years after launching Diuril, Merck retained a 33 percent share of the oral diuretic market even though its price was four times as high as Abbott Laboratories' chemically equivalent product. Two decades after introducing Peritrate, Warner-Lambert retained 30 percent of the antianginal market and commanded prices five to six times those of chemically identical substitutes.

The diuretic-antianginal study showed that being the innovator in some therapeutic category—in Merck's case by inventing and marketing a wholly new entity, but in Warner-Lambert's case by aggressively marketing a new application of an already existing substance—imparted a brand image advantage that permitted the pioneering firm to maintain high prices while retaining a sizable market share for many years thereafter. The image that followed from being a "first mover" also increased the productivity of advertising and direct selling efforts. Once their brands were established as the segment leaders, Merck and Warner-Lambert were able to sustain them through marketing outlays much lower per sales dollar than those of rival firms. In oral diuretics, the study showed further, the latecomer brands that captured the largest market shares tended to be those whose products first offered significant therapeutic advantages over the pioneers.

Additional research has shown that innovative leadership confers systematic brand image advantages in a much wider array of industries, although the manifestations are more compelling in consumer than in producers' good

---

[89]Ronald S. Bond and David F. Lean, *Sales, Promotion, and Product Differentiation in Two Prescription Drug Markets*, Federal Trade Commission staff report (Washington, DC: USGPO, February 1977).

industries.[90] There is theoretical and empirical support for inferring that consumer loyalty to first-moving brands is especially strong when it is difficult or costly to tell from inspection whether a follower brand is equal in quality to the first mover, when the costs or risks from consuming a brand of inferior quality are substantial,[91] and when (as in luxury automobiles) prestige is an important component of the utility consumers derive from their brand choices.

Pharmaceuticals represent an extreme on two of these dimensions—the difficulty of judging quality in advance of consumption, and the risk of bad choices—and as a result, first-mover brand image advantages significantly supplement patent protection as barriers to rapid imitation. There are thousands of drugs and hundreds of drug suppliers. Minor chemical composition variations could in principle alter the drug's efficacy, yet few prescribing physicians can take the time to do their own systematic experiments before administering new brands, nor can they master the vast literature on drug effects.[92] The risks of a bad choice can be serious indeed: for the patient, delayed recovery, adverse side effects, or in the extreme, death; for the physician, a possible malpractice suit. Thus, when they have had successful experience with a drug—usually, by administering the first mover when it is the only one of its kind on the market—physicians are reluctant to incur the risks and information-processing costs of prescribing substitutes, even when the substitutes are proclaimed to be chemically identical. On over-the-counter drugs, for which no prescription is required, consumers' lack of knowledge and the risks of a bad experience similarly allow first movers simultaneously to maintain price premiums and substantial market shares. Aspirin, for example, has been working its wonders for a century, but Bayer aspirin continues to sell at prices two to three times those of generic substitutes.[93]

This is the economic reality that affects drug pricing. But the chemical reality is relevant too. Are generic substitutes in fact inferior to the first-

---

[90]For a survey of the literature, see William T. Robinson, G. Kalyanaram, and Glen Urban, "First-Mover Advantages from Pioneering New Markets: A Survey of the Empirical Evidence," *Review of Industrial Organization*, vol. 9 (February 1994), pp. 1–24.

[91]See Richard Schmalensee, "Product Differentiation Advantages of Pioneering Brands," *American Economic Review*, vol. 72 (June 1982), pp. 349–365.

[92]See Peter Temin, "Physician Prescribing Behavior: Is There Learning By Doing?" and the comment by Michael Halberstam, in Helms, ed., *Drugs and Health* (1981), pp. 173–182 and 222–227; and Task Force on Prescription Drugs, *The Drug Prescribers*, pp. 8–9.

[93]See "Over-the-Counter Painkillers: How Do They Compare?" *New York Times*, July 13, 1994, p. C12.

moving branded products? On this, there has been impassioned debate.[94] Generic drugs are required by the FDA to contain the same active chemical entity (or entities) as the original branded drug. But they differ in terms of binders, fillers, preservatives, and the density of packing, which can affect *bioequivalence*—that is, the rate at which the active ingredient is absorbed into the bloodstream or other locus of therapeutic action. That in turn has been found to affect the therapeutic efficacy of drugs in rare cases.[95] In 1969 the governmental Task Force on Prescription Drugs concluded that "in certain instances the clinical effects may not be the same," but that "lack of clinical equivalency among chemical equivalents meeting all official standards has been grossly exaggerated as a major hazard to the public health."[96] Two decades later, the Food and Drug Administration reported that tests on 2566 generic drug samples showed 27, or 1.1 percent, to be below specifications—roughly the same rate of noncompliance found in branded-drug tests.[97] Nevertheless, fear of even rare deviations undoubtedly influences some physicians' prescribing decisions.

For these and other reasons to be considered shortly, the inroads of generic drugs were modest in most therapeutic classes, even after patents expired. In 1980, 69 percent of the prescriptions filled at retail in the United States were for multisource drugs—that is, those for which a substitute to the first mover's brand existed.[98] However, physicians wrote their prescriptions generically, rather than specifying a particular brand, in only 21 percent of those cases (half of which involved antibiotics). On another 4 percent of the multisource population, pharmacists substituted a generic product for the physician's designated brand. Thus, generic substitution occurred in at most 25 percent of the cases for which it was feasible.

---

[94]See, for example, the exchange of letters to the editors of the *New York Times* from Herman Weinreb and Leroy Schwartz (October 8, 1985), Allen Koplin and Laurence Lieberman (December 17, 1985); and Uriel Barzel, W. J. Blechman, Martin Surks, and Melvyn Kassenoff (August 31, 1987). All but two of the letter writers were medical doctors, one a pharmacist. See also "Generic Drugs: Are They As Good as the Original?" *New York Times*, October 12, 1989, p. B11; and "The Big Lie About Generic Drugs," *Consumer Reports*, August 1987, pp. 480–485.

[95]See Task Force on Prescription Drugs, *The Drug Prescribers*, pp. 35–36; and "Report of Generic Antiepileptic Failure May Be What Brandname Firms Are Looking For," *Medical Advertising News*, October 15, 1987, p. 4.

[96]*Final Report*, p. 31.

[97]"F.D.A. Chief Says Most Generics Meet Standards," *New York Times*, November 18, 1989, p. 28.

[98]Allison Masson and Robert L. Steiner, *Generic Substitution and Prescription Drug Prices*, Federal Trade Commission staff report (Washington, DC: 1985), p. 26.

CONGRESS CHANGES THE RULES

The possibilities for achieving competition after patents expire were limited further by oddities in the interpretation of the 1962 Kefauver-Harris law. For proposed generic substitutes to drugs that had been marketed prior to that law, the FDA maintained accelerated, low-cost approval procedures.[99] However, the FDA and, after a challenge, the Supreme Court interpreted the 1962 law to say that generic substitutes for post–1962 entities were also "new drugs." To receive an NDA, they had to prove safety and efficacy, just as the drugs with which they proposed to compete had.[100] Generic suppliers could not meet this burden by referencing the tests performed by the original drug developer, since the underlying data were kept secret. Although the FDA did not demand of generic applicants all the safety and efficacy tests it required for truly new drugs, the testing costs for generics were sufficiently high, given the characteristically low prices commanded by generic drugs and their small market shares, to discourage many would-be generic producers.

Meanwhile, the producers of branded drugs were airing quite different grievances. They apply for patent protection at the time a chemical entity shows interesting therapeutic effects in animals—typically, in the year before filing an IND proposal. Under normal conditions, patents are issued two to three years later—that is, when human testing is under way for one to two years. As the average period from IND issue to NDA issue lengthened to eight years, six to seven years of the patent's life ebbed away before the developer could begin to recoup its investment through sales. This left a patent-protected marketing period of only 10 or 11 years—too little, drug developers claimed, to recover the high costs of new drug testing.[101]

In the Waxman-Hatch Act of 1984, the U.S. Congress forged a grand compromise attempting to mitigate the problems of both generic and branded drug suppliers. For generic producers, new approval procedures were authorized. Generic drug applications can be approved by the FDA if the would-be producer proves that its active ingredient is chemically identical to that of the original branded drug, that the generic formulation is bioequivalent, and that the company follows good manufacturing practices. Bioequivalence is typically demonstrated by tests in 24 human subjects showing blood absorption levels within plus-or-minus 20 percent of the branded drug's norm—the standard to which the FDA also holds branded drugmakers.

---

[99]Commission on the Federal Drug Approval Process, *Final Report* (Washington, DC: USGPO, March 1982), pp. 93–97; and Edmund Kitch, "The Patent System and the New Drug Application," in Landau, ed., *Regulating New Drugs*, pp. 100–104.

[100]U.S. v. Generix Drug Corp. et al., 460 U.S. 453 (March 1983).

[101]See Henry G. Grabowski and John M. Vernon, *The Regulation of Pharmaceuticals* (Washington, DC: American Enterprise Institute; 1983), pp. 49–62.

For the developers of innovative drugs, the 1984 Act authorized patent life extensions of up to five years to compensate for regulatory delays, but the period of exclusive marketing cannot exceed 14 years. Thus, a patent issued after the first year of an eight-year clinical testing program, which would allow ten years of exclusivity without the new law, could be extended four years to protect 14 years of exclusive marketing. In addition, if new forms of existing drugs are developed and the FDA requires that they be tested for safety and efficacy, the 1984 law guarantees three years of exclusive marketing after an NDA is issued, whether or not patents remain in force.

Prior to the 1984 compromise on patent lives and generic drug testing, Congress enacted two other laws with important implications for property rights in new drugs. Perceiving that the high costs of drug testing were discouraging the development of drugs targeted toward diseases of low incidence, Congress passed in 1983 the Orphan Drug Act. It states that the first firm to receive FDA approval of a new orphan drug, defined as a drug treating symptoms affecting fewer than 200,000 persons in the United States, is entitled to market that drug exclusively during the first seven years after NDA approval, whether or not the drug has patent protection. In addition, it authorized special tax credits for expenditures on the clinical testing of orphan drugs and special financial grants from the federal government to help defray the costs of orphan drug research. The seven-year exclusivity provision was expected to be especially important for biological products that replicated substances occurring in the human body, whose patentability was uncertain. It appears to have been the most important of the orphan drug provisions, since only $5.4 million of tax credits and $3.9 million for direct research grants were authorized in 1987.[102] Between 1984 and September 1992, 494 chemical and biological entities received orphan drug designations (typically made at an early stage in clinical testing), and 79 orphan drugs emerged from the testing process with NDA approvals.[103] Only 37 percent of the orphan drug designations went to members of the Pharmaceutical Manufacturers Association, suggesting that the main beneficiaries of the law were relatively new, small firms—for example, biotechnology start-up companies.

In the Stevenson-Wydler Act of 1980, uniform policies toward inventions made with federal government research support were articulated, and cooperative research and development agreements (CRADAs), under which companies and government joined forces to accomplish research tasks, were authorized. Both were important to the pharmaceutical industry. In 1962, the Department of Health, Education, and Welfare implemented a policy ensuring that it could exercise residual patent rights in inventions made under HEW grants and contracts. Pharmaceutical manufacturers had previously

---

[102]Office of Technology Assessment, *Pharmaceutical R&D*, pp. 190–195 and 229.

[103]Ibid., pp. 226–227.

avoided direct research contracts with the government for fear of forfeiting patent rights. The new policy threatened patent rights on chemicals developed by university researchers with government grant support, and as a consequence, virtually all drugmakers abruptly ended arrangements under which they conducted therapeutic screening and clinical tests on new chemical entities discovered by academic grantees.[104] The Stevenson-Wydler Act permitted companies benefiting from government research support to retain exclusive patent rights. This change prompted drug companies to renew cooperative arrangements with academic investigators and to begin working with the National Institutes of Health. Dozens of pharmaceutical industry CRADAs, some leading to important new drugs such as AZT and Ceredase, ensued.[105]

THE GENERIC DRUG RENAISSANCE

The eased generic-drug-testing burden under the Waxman-Hatch Act, combined with the expiration of patents on many drugs, led to an explosion of generic-drug applications. In the first six months after the new law took effect, the FDA received 440 generic-drug applications.[106] By 1991, the FDA had approved more than 2000 generic applications.[107] The generic dispensing rate at retail pharmacies increased to 30 percent in 1989, up from 17 percent in 1980.[108] What did not happen, however, was anything resembling active two-way price rivalry between branded and generic drug suppliers. One study found that on average, branded-drug prices *rose* when generic competition materialized.[109] Another concluded that generic competition reduced incumbent brands' prices by just 2 percent on average, although there was more branded-drug price reduction, the larger the number of generic competitors.[110]

Figure 9.7 analyzes what happens when a drug moves from exclusive marketing to having generic competition. Its basic simplifying assumption is that there are two kinds of decision makers (an amalgam of the physician and the consumer) in drug choices: those who, because of risk aversion, imperfect information, and/or generous health insurance coverage, are insensitive to

---

[104]Harbridge House, *Drug Study,* Part I.

[105]Office of Technology Assessment, *Pharmaceutical R&D,* pp. 219–225.

[106]"Generics Grab More of the Drug Action," *Business Week,* May 13, 1985, p. 64.

[107]"The High Cost of Prescription Drugs," *Consumers' Research,* March 1991, p. 29.

[108]See Scherer, "Pricing, Profits, and Technological Progress in the Pharmaceutical Industry," p. 101, from which the remainder of this paragraph is drawn.

[109]Henry Grabowski and John Vernon, "Brand Loyalty, Entry, and Price Competition in Pharmaceuticals after the 1984 Drug Act," *Journal of Law & Economics,* vol. 35 (October 1992), pp. 331–350.

[110]Richard E. Caves, Michael Whinston, and Mark Hurwitz, "Patent Expiration, Entry, and Competition in the U.S. Pharmaceutical Industry," *Brookings Papers on Economic Activity,* Microeconomics: 1991, pp. 1–48.

FIGURE 9.7
Bifurcation of Market Following Generic Entry

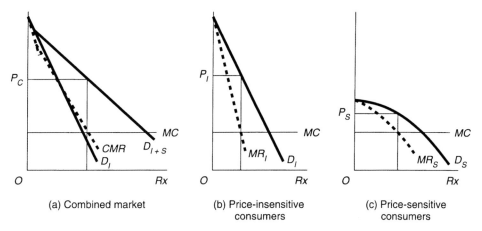

(a) Combined market (b) Price-insensitive (c) Price-sensitive
consumers consumers

generics' attractive prices (characterized by demand curve D_I in Figure 9.7a); and those who *are* price-sensitive (whose demand is given by the horizontal distance between D_I and combined demand curve D_{I+S}).[111] Before generics become available, even price-sensitive consumers must buy the branded drug (or a differentiated substitute), and so the demand curve confronting the branded drug producer is D_{I+S}. The potentially price-sensitive consumers' demand function has a choke price (i.e., vertical intercept) only slightly lower than that of price-insensitive consumers because the price-sensitive consumers evaluate differentiated substitute brands more carefully, but consider them inferior. The appropriate marginal revenue function *CMR* is derived, and the branded drugmaker sets monopoly price OP_C.

When generics become available, the market bifurcates. The demand curve of the price-insensitive consumers (Figure 9.7b) retains essentially the same shape as it had before there was generic competition, and so the branded drug supplier's profit-maximizing price OP_I differs insignificantly from the precompetition price. Or if the precompetition demand curve for the insensitive consumers was slightly less elastic than for sensitive consumers, as shown in Figure 9.7a, the postcompetition price to insensitive consumers may even rise. With attractive generic substitutes available, however, the branded drug demand curve for price-sensitive consumers becomes much more elastic, as shown in Figure 9.7c. To retain a sizable fraction of those consumers, the branded drugmaker must reduce its price to them to OP_S, which is much lower than the profit-maximizing price to insensitive consumers.

---

[111]For an algebraic version of this model, see Richard Frank and David Salkever, "Pricing, Patent Loss and the Market for Pharmaceuticals," *Southern Economic Journal*, vol. 59 (October 1992), pp. 165–179.

In principle, this two-price approach is a standard exercise in price discrimination. However, it is not easily pulled off. To discriminate in price, a firm must be able to segregate its customers. The price-sensitive class includes particularly well-informed retail consumers, patients of health maintenance organizations with policies favoring generics, and most hospital pharmacies. Using a "generic" label and charging lower prices is a plausible means of segregating consumers by demand elasticity. Many branded drug companies, we have seen, have chosen to produce generic versions of *rival* firms' drugs. But they have been reluctant to offer generic versions of their own drugs because of the price discriminator's scourge: arbitrage. If high-price consumers become aware that the original brand producer is selling a low-price copy of its own drug, they may defect in droves from the high-price market to the low-price market. Rather than risk this, the branded drug producers chose simply to abandon the price-sensitive market altogether and sell only at high prices. Or they pursued a high-price policy, but captured *some* of the price-sensitive customers by offering secret discounts to HMOs with particularly aggressive procurement policies, abandoning the other price-sensitive consumers to generic rivals.[112]

As generics made increasing inroads into branded drugs' sales during the 1990s, however, the loss of volume under "branded-only" policies became more compelling relative to the perceived risk of arbitrage under a "branded plus generic" strategy. In 1992 Merck, the largest U.S. pharmaceutical maker, announced that it would begin offering generic versions of its own branded drugs whose patents had expired.[113] To keep branded and generic products segregated as much as possible, the generic versions were sold under the label of Merck's West Point Pharma subsidiary. SmithKline Beecham followed suit in 1994 with a generic version of its antiulcer drug, Tagamet, expected to sell at $8 to $12 for a month's supply, compared to the $80 retail price commanded by branded Tagamet before its patent expired.[114] The generic cimetidine would bear the label of SmithKline's Penn Labs subsidiary.

These developments will probably change the dynamics of competition between branded and generic drugs. It is nevertheless useful to review several additional insights yielded by quantitative analyses of generic pricing following the 1984 law's passage. First, as noted previously, there was a weak tendency for more erosion of branded drugs' prices, the larger was the number of generic competitors.[115] Erosion was greater for drugs with particularly high

---

[112]Hospitals also received special discounts, but that was true even before generic competition escalated.

[113]"Merck Sets Generic Drug Sales," *New York Times*, September 8, 1992, p. D1.

[114]"SmithKline Will Produce Generic Version of Tagamet," *New York Times*, May 11, 1994, p. D5; and "New Drug Era Begins as Tagamet Patent Ends," *New York Times*, May 17, 1994, p. D5.

[115]Caves et al., "Patent Expiration," pp. 24–28; and Grabowski and Vernon, "Brand Loyalty," pp. 338–339.

sales to hospitals, which avidly embrace cost-saving opportunities through generic purchases, and for the subset of drugs taken by injection, whose use is preponderantly within hospitals. Second, as more firms tended to enter the generic sale of a given drug, the larger the branded drug's sales were and the higher was the ratio of the branded drug's price to its estimated marginal cost.[116] Third, branded drugmakers were more successful in defending their market positions against generic inroads through advertising and other promotional outlays on drugs taken to combat temporary illnesses than on long-term-therapy drugs.[117] For the latter, consumers are more price-sensitive and hence less responsive to promotional blandishments. Fourth, although branded drug prices were influenced little by the intensity of generic competition, generic drug prices varied greatly with the number of generic producers. Caves and associates found that with one generic producer, the generic product's price averaged 68 percent of the preentry branded product price. The average generic price dropped to 50 percent with three generic rivals, 29 percent with ten generics, and 17 percent with 20 generics.[118] In short, price competition worked much more powerfully *among* relatively undifferentiated generic products than *between* differentiated branded products and undifferentiated generics. Fifth, firms that began supplying a given drug generically early in the drug's postpatent history tended to retain larger generic market shares than latecomers.[119] Thus, generic first-mover advantages were realized both from the higher profit margins attainable before numerous generic suppliers begin competing and from larger long-term market shares.

Recognition that disproportionate profits flowed to generic first movers led generic drug producers to compete aggressively to be the first gaining FDA approval as branded drugs' patent expiration dates approached. Some tried to cut corners by bribing FDA officials to assign their applications priority and by submitting test results based on pills purchased from the branded supplier instead of those made in their own laboratories.[120] Companies apprehended doing so had their approvals rescinded, were fined, and were barred from

---

[116]Grabowski and Vernon, "Brand Loyalty," p. 344; and Fiona Scott Morton, "Barriers to Entry, Brand Advertising, and Generic Entry in the U.S. Pharmaceutical Industry," working paper, Massachusetts Institute of Technology, November 1993.

[117]Mark Hurwitz and Richard E. Caves, "Persuasion or Information? Promotion and the Shares of Brand Name and Generic Pharmaceuticals," *Journal of Law & Economics*, vol. 31 (October 1988), p. 315.

[118]Caves et al., "Patent Expiration," p. 36.

[119]Grabowski and Vernon, "Brand Loyalty," p. 346.

[120]See "How Far Has the Cancer Spread at the FDA?" *Business Week*, September 18, 1989, pp. 30–31; "More Charges Expected in Generic Drug Inquiry," *New York Times*, December 20, 1990, p. D1; "After the Storm," *Drug Topics*, June 17, 1991, pp. 40–44; and "Red Ink, Wiretaps, and Death Threats," *Business Week*, February 21, 1994, pp. 80–81.

submitting further generic applications. To combat such abuses, Congress mandated stringent new regulations in the Generic Drug Enforcement Act of 1992.

The original branded drug supplier has a natural first-mover advantage in marketing generic versions of its product. It can carry out the required tests and time its application to the FDA so that its product appears on the market a few days before its patent expires. In the future, one can expect original brand owners to win large market shares for the generic products they choose to launch alongside their branded products.

PUSHING GENERIC DRUGS

More can be said about the conditions under which generic drugs are substituted for higher-priced first-moving brands. The evidence from Canada is particularly informative. Between 1969 and 1987, Canada had a law under which generic suppliers could obtain licenses to import and/or produce drugs still covered by patents, paying a modest (4 percent) royalty for the privilege.[121] The law had two rationales: the desire to reduce expenditures under Canada's public medical insurance programs, leavened by evidence that ethical drugs were more expensive in Canada than in the United States; and the recognition that there was virtually no industry developing original drugs within Canada. Rejecting drugmakers' requests for higher royalties to motivate new drug development, the Exchequer Court stated:[122]

> It would . . . be unrealistic to think that the returns from the Canadian market have any important bearing on whether research on an international scale will go on or not.

Thus, as a nation with less than 1 percent of the world's population, Canada chose to be a free rider (or more precisely, cheap rider) on foreign nations' pharmaceutical R&D. By 1976, prices in Canada for a sample of 43 patented drugs were 21 percent lower on average than in the United States.[123]

Regulations governing the substitution of licensed generic drugs for branded drugs varied widely among the Canadian provinces, providing a natural experiment to discern the conditions under which generic use is most

---

[121]On the history, see Paul K. Gorecki, *Regulating the Price of Prescription Drugs in Canada*, Economic Council of Canada Technical Report No. 8 (Ottawa: ECC, May 1981). The drug patent licensing provisions were abandoned in anticipation of Canada's free trade treaties, first with the United States and then under the North American Free Trade Agreement.

[122]Merck & Co. Inc. v. Sherman & Ulster Ltd., 65 C.R.R. 99, 108–109 (1971).

[123]Office of Technology Assessment, *Pharmaceutical R&D*, p. 253.

likely.[124] All provinces permitted substitution, but in Quebec, only with the patient's explicit consent. Some provinces gave the pharmacist discretion in the matter, but Ontario and New Brunswick required that the lowest-cost substitute be dispensed when reimbursement from public funds would occur— notably, for persons older than 65 years and welfare recipients. In most provinces, pharmacists were freed from malpractice liability when they dispensed generic drugs listed on the province formulary, but in Quebec, no waiver was conferred. Some provinces, including Quebec, reimbursed the full cost of the drug dispensed, whereas others, including Saskatchewan and Ontario, reimbursed only the price of the lowest-cost generic or the price set in an annual competition.

For 21 drugs with multiple sources, the average shares of reimbursed purchases won during 1980 by generic drugs in three provinces analyzed by McRae and Tapon were as follows:

Ontario	82.5%
Saskatchewan	61.6%
Quebec	23.5%

Quebec, with very weak prosubstitution rules, had by far the lowest generic share. Both Saskatchewan and Ontario had strong prosubstitution rules. Saskatchewan's generic share was lower, partly because unusually many physicians exercised their mandate to prohibit generic use and perhaps also because pharmacies in small prairie towns commanded too little patronage to stock both branded drugs and generic substitutes. A key variable in the equation was revealed in 1982, when Quebec shifted from paying the full price of the drug dispensed to paying only the median price of available substitutes. The average generic share in seven important categories jumped in a year's time from 18.7 to 54.7 percent.

Newfoundland and Saskatchewan both had choice and cost reimbursement rules strongly favoring substitution in 1983. Both published formularies listing generic drugs considered by expert panels to be biologically equivalent. But the formularies differed between provinces, with a marked impact on generic choices, as a tabulation of reimbursed generic shares by Gorecki shows:

---

[124]This section is drawn from Scherer and Ross, *Industrial Market Structure and Economic Performance*, pp. 589–592, which in turn is based upon Paul Gorecki, "The Importance of Being First: The Case of Prescription Drugs in Canada," *International Journal of Industrial Organization*, vol. 4 (December 1986), pp. 371–396; and James J. McRae and Francis Tapon, "Some Empirical Evidence on Post-Patent Barriers to Entry in the Canadian Pharmaceutical Industry," *Journal of Health Economics*, vol. 4 (March 1985), pp. 43–61.

	Newfoundland	Saskatchewan
Four drugs listed as interchangeable in both provinces	76.0%	57.2%
Three drugs listed as interchangeable in Saskatchewan but not in Newfoundland	9.7%	59.2%

Not being listed on the formulary appears to have had a strongly negative effect on the three Saskatchewan drugs. Gorecki repeated his formulary analysis for New Brunswick and Nova Scotia, where pharmacists were not required to substitute the lowest-priced brands and the costs of high-priced brands were reimbursed. The generic drugs' reimbursed market shares were:

	New Brunswick	Nova Scotia
Three drugs listed as interchangeable in both provinces	5.1%	5.8%
Four drugs listed as interchangeable in Nova Scotia but not in New Brunswick	3.2%	13.9%

Although a formulary effect appears, what is most striking is the low share for all generics—the result of fully reimbursing branded drug prices and other weak substitution mandates.

In the United States, the use of generic drugs was at first inhibited by state laws preventing pharmacists from deviating generically or otherwise from physicians' exact prescriptions. With the initiation of the federal Medicaid and Medicare programs in 1966, the states assumed a cooperative role in reimbursing the costs of prescription drugs (for Medicare, in hospitals only, but for Medicaid, also on outpatient prescriptions). State legislators became more cost-conscious, and by 1984, all 50 states had passed laws permitting, and in some instances requiring, the substitution of generic drugs, when they existed, for the branded drugs named in prescriptions.[125]

Organizations lobbying on behalf of pharmacists provided support for the repeal of state antisubstitution laws. For this they probably had an economic

---

[125]Masson and Steiner, *Generic Substitution*, pp. 1 and 189–217.

motive. An analysis of 37 drugs' 1980 prices by Masson and Steiner showed the following average differences between branded and generic products:[126]

	Brands	*Generics*
Average retail price	$8.22	$6.22
Average wholesale price paid by retailer	$4.86	$2.65
Retailer dollar margin	$3.35	$3.57
Retailer percentage margin	41%	57%

On average, pharmacists realized higher dollar margins in dispensing generic drugs. If this were not true, and especially if margins were strictly proportional to the retail price, the incentive to dispense generics would be impaired. The relationship observed by Masson and Steiner appears to be typical in retailing more broadly: private-label goods carry lower retail prices but yield higher dollar margins than branded items.[127]

Since 1977, generic substitution on prescriptions reimbursed under U.S. government health insurance programs has been encouraged through Maximum Allowable Cost (MAC) rules. These state that when generic substitutes exist, and unless the prescribing physician explicitly prohibits substitution, retail pharmacies will be reimbursed no more than the published wholesale price of the lowest-priced approved drug—virtually always, a generic—plus a dispensing fee that varies from state to state.[128] Pharmacies supplying higher-priced brands in such cases bear the additional cost out of their own pockets.

Nongovernmental health care providers and insurers have also deployed an array of weapons to combat rising drug costs. Most hospitals and, to an increasing extent, many health maintenance organizations have adopted formularies that list drugs acceptable for diverse indications, emphasizing both generics when they exist and, among substitutable single-source branded

---

[126]Ibid., p. 36.

[127]National Commission on Food Marketing, Technical Study No. 10, *Private Label Products in Food Retailing* (Washington, DC: USGPO, June 1966), pp. 65–77. Private-label goods tend to turn over more slowly on retailers' shelves, so higher margins are required to induce the shelf space allocation.

[128]On the effects, see Masson and Steiner, *Generic Substitution*, pp. 52–55. The MAC provisions applied mainly to Medicaid recipients, who accounted for between 10 and 15 percent of U.S. prescription drug expenditures during the late 1980s. Office of Technology Assessment, *Pharmaceutical R&D*, p. 245, note 18.

drugs, the lowest-cost alternatives. The formularies are compiled by committees whose members can presumably devote more time to weighing safety and efficacy against cost than do individual physicians.[129] During the early 1990s, inclusion or exclusion from formularies was used by HMOs as a bargaining lever to extract price discounts from the manufacturers of high-priced drugs.[130] Many states have also published formularies, exclusion from which implies the denial of reimbursement from Medicaid and Medicare funds.[131]

To an increasing degree during the 1980s and 1990s, health insurance companies providing prescription drug benefits have attempted to combat insured consumers' price insensitivity and encourage generic drug usage by differentiating patient copayment rates–for example, under the Massachusetts HealthFlex Blue plan in 1994, $9 per prescription for branded drugs but only $3 for generic substitutes. Large employers have also made arrangements with mail order pharmacies and retail chains to supply drugs at a discount. Some mail order houses and retail prescription drug reimbursement organizations in turn develop the equivalent of formularies, telephoning physicians and asking them to save their clients money by prescribing lower-cost entities.[132] High-priced branded drugs were threatened with exclusion from the formularies, or an unfavorable ranking, unless they offered substantial price discounts.

---

[129]For various views, see Task Force on Prescription Drugs, *The Drug Prescribers*, pp. 12–13; Michael Weintraub, "The United States: Hospital Formularies," in William Wardell, ed., *Controlling the Use of Therapeutic Drugs* (Washington, DC: American Enterprise Institute, 1978), pp. 31–55; T. Donald Rucker and Gordon Schiff, "Drug Formularies: Myths-in-Formation," *Medical Care*, vol. 28 (October 1990), pp. 928–939; and Ronald Hansen, "Costs and Benefits of Cost-Benefit Analysis in Pharmaceutical Promotion and Utilization Decisions," in Helms, ed., *Competitive Strategies in the Phrmaceutical Industry*.

[130] These practices led to a suit against the pharmaceutical manufacturers by a group of retail pharmacists alleging illegal price discrimination. See "Seven Big Drug Makers Are Sued over Pricing," *New York Times*, October 15, 1993, p. D3; and "The Plots To Keep Drug Prices High,"*Fortune*, December 27, 1993, pp. 120–124.

[131]On the possibility that these restrictions led to increases in nondrug medical costs, see William J. Moore and Robert Newman, "Drug Formulary Restrictions as a Cost-Containment Policy in Medicaid Programs," *Journal of Law & Economics*, vol. 36 (April 1993), pp. 71–114.

[132]In 1993 Merck, the largest U.S. pharmaceutical company, acquired Medco, a leading mail order and retail prescription benefit management company. SmithKline Beecham thereupon acquired Diversified Pharmaceutical Services and Eli Lilly acquired PCS Health Systems, both rivals of Medco. The bandwagon effect implied by these three vertical mergers evoked charges that parents' drugs would be favored by the subsidiaries. See "Pharmacists Paid to Suggest Drugs," *New York Times*, July 29, 1994, p. 1.

FURTHER GOVERNMENTAL PRICE CONTROL MEASURES

These developments led to continuing increases in generic drugs' share of all prescriptions in the United States and to growing pressure on pharmaceutical makers' prices and profits. The companies and some outside observers warned that the loss of branded drug volume to generic alternatives and the concomitant diminution of profits would threaten the continuation of rapidly rising research and development expenditures. See again Figure 9.1.

However, other forces were in motion. The apparent failure of branded drug prices to decline significantly when generic drugs appeared, the impoverishing prices charged for new lifesaving drugs such as AZT and Factor VIII,[133] comparisons showing that identical branded drugs cost much more in the United States than in many foreign nations,[134] and the rapid inflation of branded drug prices during the 1980s (probably attributable in part to increased insurance coverage)[135] led to demands for additional governmental price suppression initiatives. Like unsuccessful presidential candidate Estes Kefauver 32 years earlier, successful candidate Bill Clinton singled out the drug companies for charges of profiteering at the expense of the public.[136]

The first skirmish in what would be a long war began during the late 1980s. In 1988, Congress extended the Medicare program to provide among other things reimbursement of outpatient drug costs for persons 65 or more years of age. Fearing that Medicare responsibility for drug cost reimbursement would lead to federal government price controls, some drug companies lobbied actively against the extension. That, and more importantly, citizen furor over rising taxes to cover the program led to its rescission in 1989. Some members of Congress were angry over the drug companies' role, and in 1990, they retaliated by inserting new drug price control measures into the Medicaid law.[137] The drugmakers were required to provide rebates to the government amounting to the difference between the lowest price at which they sold drugs to nongovernmental purchasers and the standard wholesale price to

---

[133]See, for example, "Burroughs Wellcome Reaps Profits, Outrage, from Its AIDS Drug," *Wall Street Journal*, September 15, 1989, p. 1; and "What Price Progress?" *Boston Globe*, December 20, 1992, p. A1.

[134]See "Why Drugs Cost More in U.S.," *New York Times*, May 24, 1991, p. D1; and U.S. General Accounting Office, Report, *Prescription Drugs: Companies Typically Charge More in the United States Than in the United Kingdom* (Washington, DC: January 1994).

[135]But see note 85 above.

[136]"President Assails 'Shocking' Prices of Drug Industry," *New York Times*, February 13, 1993, p. 1.

[137]See "Prescription Drug Prices," *CQ Researcher*, vol. 2 (July 17, 1992), pp. 607–608.

retailers, but not less than 12.5 or (later) 15 percent.[138] In addition, they were expected to keep increases in their prices below the rate at which the Consumer Price Index rose or refund the surplus of such price hikes on Medicaid purchases to the government. If drug companies did not comply with the rebate scheme, their branded products could be declared ineligible for federally supported cost reimbursement. An elaborate accounting system was created to enforce the new provisions.

Several other price control initiatives were proposed but not enacted. One would permit the drug companies to charge no more on government-reimbursed prescriptions than the lowest price they received anywhere in the world (e.g., in response to foreign price controls or compulsory licensing measures). Another would impose forfeiture of tax credits proportional to the difference between drug price index increases and the rise in the Consumer Price Index. Still another would have the National Institutes of Health intervene to ensure that the prices of drugs developed under CRADAs were "reasonable."[139] A fourth proposal would end orphan drug status for entities whose sales had accumulated to more than $200 million—a scheme that, if enacted, would in many cases induce drug companies to raise their prices to reduce sales and hence delay reaching the ceiling.

The universal health care proposal introduced by President Clinton in 1993, but rejected by the Congress, included still another approach.[140] An Advisory Council on Breakthrough Drugs would be charged with reviewing the prices of new drugs and singling out brands whose prices appeared "excessive," or that were marketed overseas at lower prices than in the United States. The president's task force rejected giving the National Health Board binding price control authority. Instead, it was proposed that the Board seek price rebates through moral suasion or "jawboning," subjecting the drug's manufacturer to adverse publicity, urging it to moderate its demands, and threatening to remove the drug from the list of those eligible for reimbursement.

Figure 9.8 shows why this approach to price regulation is simple administratively but dangerous. To construct it, Henry Grabowski and John Vernon gathered detailed sales data on 100 new chemical entities introduced into the United States between 1970 and 1979. Making complex but plausible assumptions about production and marketing cost ratios, overseas sales, the pattern of sales over time, taxes, and discount rates (9 percent in real terms), they estimated the discounted present value of net quasi-rents (in 1988 purchasing power) at the time of initial marketing. The products were grouped into

---

[138] See Office of Technology Assessment, *Pharmaceutical R&D*, pp. 247–249.

[139] But see "U.S. Gives Up Right to Control Prices," *New York Times*, April 12, 1995, p. A23.

[140] Congressional Budget Office, *How Health Care Reform Affects Pharmaceutical Research and Development*, pp. 29–39.

FIGURE 9.8
Discounted Present Value of 1970–1979 NCE Quasi-Rents and R&D Costs, by Deciles

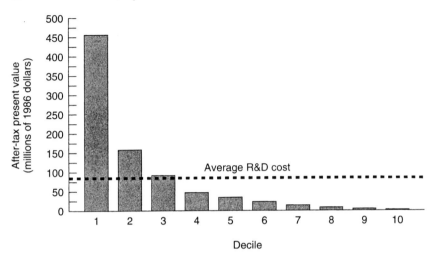

Source: Reproduced from Henry G. Grabowski and John M. Vernon, "A New Look at the Returns and Risks to Pharmaceutical R&D," *Management Science,* vol. 36 (July 1990), pp. 804–821.

deciles, giving rise to the highly skewed distribution shown in Figure 9.8. Quasi-rent returns are compared to the $81 million average capitalized cost of research and testing per new drug, assumed (for lack of more precise data) not to vary with returns.[141] Ten of the 100 products—the so-called "blockbusters"—yielded on average six times their average R&D investments. Their discounted quasi-rents summed to 55 percent of the sample total. Products in the second decile had returns nearly twice their R&D cost; those in the third decile fared slightly better than breaking even. The remaining seven deciles yielded quasi-rents lower than their R&D outlays.

Jawbone regulation under the Clinton proposal would target the few blockbuster drugs, proclaiming to the public how profitable they are and seeking to elicit price concessions. Administratively, nothing could be simpler. The strategy has been called "Willie Sutton regulation" after the 1930s antihero who, when eventually apprehended and asked why he robbed banks, replied, "Because that's where the money is." But suppose the jawboning is

---

[141]There are theoretical reasons for predicting higher development costs on drugs expected to be more lucrative, but no evidence of a close correlation between the two has been found. See Joseph A. DiMasi, Ronald Hansen, Henry Grabowski, and Louis Lasagna, "Research and Development Costs for New Drugs by Therapeutic Category," working paper, 1994.

successful in cutting the quasi-rents of the top decile by one-third. Then the discounted quasi-rents across *all* new chemical entities would move from being slightly higher than total R&D costs (i.e., yielding supranormal net profits) to being 17 percent lower than total R&D costs.[142] Whether one accepts the Demsetz-Barzel or monopoly profit maximization hypothesis concerning the determinants of research and development spending (see Figure 9.6), significant R&D cutbacks would almost surely be induced.[143] Whether the cutbacks would disproportionately involve the most important new drugs, which would bear the burden of Willie Sutton regulation but retain superior profits, or whether they would occur across the board, is uncertain.

There is reason to believe that the highly skewed distribution of returns is typical and not an anomaly. Grabowski and Vernon discovered a very similar distribution for new chemical entities introduced during the early 1980s.[144] Examining the 1972 sales of NCEs introduced during the 1960s by ten leading U.S. firms, Schwartzman found that four of the 38 products accounted for 74 percent of total sample revenues.[145] Only 15 of 132 biotechnology companies with securities traded publicly reported positive profits in 1993.[146] For other high-technology fields, there is similar evidence of highly skewed profit distributions.[147]

---

[142]Using different assumptions, the Office of Technology Assessment found the discounted quasi-rents of early 1980s NCEs to exceed R&D costs by an average amount translating to 3.4 percent of sales revenue. *Pharmaceutical R&D*, pp. 7–22.

[143]A statistical analysis of annual data for the years 1962 through 1991 suggests that U.S. pharmaceutical R&D outlays changed by about 0.6 percentage points with a 1-percentage-point change in lagged industry value added less payrolls, taking into account also a positive time trend. Where $\delta RD(t)$ is the percentage change in R&D from year $t-1$ to year t, $\delta CF(t)$ the corresponding change in cash flow, and T the year, the regression equation was:

$$\delta RD(t) = -1.43 + .365 \, \delta CF(t) + .104 \, \delta CF(t-1) + .143 \, \delta CF(t-2)$$
$$(2.42) \quad (2.83) \qquad\quad (0.84) \qquad\qquad\quad (1.11)$$
$$+ .00073 \, T \quad R^2 = 0.488$$
$$(2.45)$$

with *t*-ratios in parentheses.

[144]Henry Grabowski and John Vernon, "Returns to R&D on New Drug Introductions in the 1980s," forthcoming in Helms, ed., *Competitive Strategies in the Pharmaceutical Industry*.

[145]*Innovation in the Pharmaceutical Industry*, pp. 106–107. See also Ballance et al., *The World's Pharmaceutical Industries*, pp. 108--109.

[146]"Turning a Biotech Profit," *New York Times*, July 6, 1994, p. D3.

[147]See F. M. Scherer, "Firm Size, Market Structure, Opportunity, and the Output of Patented Inventions," *American Economic Review*, vol. 55 (December 1965), p. 1098; and the colloquy in *Brookings Papers on Economic Activity: Microeconomics*, 1989, pp. 314–317 and 402–410.

One basis for the claim that branded drug prices in the United States are excessive is evidence that prices are often lower, and sometimes much lower, overseas. In addition to exchange rate variations, there are two main reasons for the differentials: weaker patent protection in many nations, and governmental price controls.[148] National governments rationalize policies leading to low drug prices in part upon free-rider (or cheap-rider) grounds: the loss of profits on their small fraction of world demand will not significantly affect research spending and new drug development. The argument is less plausible in the United States, accounting for 20 percent of world pharmaceuticals consumption in 1990.[149] During the early 1990s the European Union Commission began efforts to harmonize widely varying member nation regulatory policies with respect to pharmaceutical prices and testing.[150] For the EU, originating an additional 24 percent of world demand, free-rider logic also falters.

Thus, it is important to choose the right trade-offs between price competition, regulation, and technological change. Willie Sutton regulation, targeting the early profits of the most successful new drugs, almost certainly gets the trade-off wrong. Strengthening generic competition after patents or orphan drug exclusivity periods end seems a more promising approach. Letting important new drugs realize high profits for a limited period of time, among other things compensating for the numerous losers, maintains incentives to invest in innovation. Vigorous generic competition means that companies can sustain high profitability only by continuing to innovate. To ensure that only the significant contributions yield large profit rewards and to focus the innovative process on achieving further breakthroughs, regulators and health care organizations must improve the information on which prescription decisions are based. With the right balance of carrots and sticks, the goose will continue to lay golden eggs.

AFTERWORD

Pharmaceutical producers enjoy substantial monopoly power in setting the prices of significant new products, in part because of patent and regulatory barriers to competitive entry and partly, after patents expire, because habit

---

[148]For a survey, see Office of Technology Assessment, *Pharmaceutical R&D,* pp. 250–262.

[149]Ballance et al., *The World's Pharmaceutical Industries,* pp. 30–31.

[150]See, for example, Sir Leon Brittan, "Making a Reality of the Single Market: Pharmaceutical Pricing and the EEC," speech delivered at the Institute of Economic Affairs, Health and Welfare Unit, Brussels, December 1992; and "New EU Drug Agency: Cure-All or Ill?" *International Herald-Tribune,* January 27, 1994, p. 9.

and the fear that generic copies will be less effective lead physicians to prescribe first-moving brands. In their research and development decision making, drugmakers must weigh the prospect of lucrative monopoly rewards against the high costs and risks of seeking successful new chemical entities, made higher by the insistence of regulators that both safety and efficacy be demonstrated through statistically valid clinical trials. The industry's history following World War II is a chronicle of attractive rewards stimulating ever-increasing R&D investments. But the rewards are highly skewed; only a minority of approved new drugs yield returns well in excess of R&D investments, taking into account also the funds spent on "dry holes." Policymakers must attempt to adjust the strength of patent protection, create incentives for generic substitution, alter regulatory hurdles, and take other measures so that there is enough price competition to ensure that consumers are well served with existing drugs, but not so much that research leading to significant new drugs is stifled. It is a weighty challenge.

10

BEER

Seller concentration in the brewing industry increased dramatically during the second half of the twentieth century. We explore the roots of those structural changes in historical accidents, first-mover "image" advantages reinforced through increasingly sophisticated advertising campaigns, economies of scale, economies of multiplant operation entailing trade-offs between plant scale economies and transportation costs, process technology changes, and the pricing strategies pursued by the leading brewers. Industry restructuring occurred in part through a wave of brewing company mergers, whose evaluation by antitrust authorities brought forward new market definition concepts.

INTRODUCTION

In April 1933 one remarkable experiment ended and another began. For 13 years the commercial production and sale of alcoholic beverages in the United States had been prohibited under the eighteenth amendment to the U.S. Constitution. On March 23, 1933, Prohibition was repealed following ratification of the twenty-first amendment. Within a few weeks, scores of breweries commenced the newly legal business of making and selling beer. Before the year ended, more than 500 commercial breweries had begun operation. No single firm supplied more than 4 percent of national demand.[1] A half century later, the four leading U.S. brewing companies originated 78 percent of national

---

[1] Anita M. McGahan, "The Emergence of the National Brewing Oligopoly: Competition in the American Market, 1933–1958," *Business History Review*, vol. 65 (Summer 1991), p. 230; and "Cooperation on Price and Capacity Commitments: The Case of Brewing After Repeal," working paper, June 1994.

output. Ten years after that, in 1993, the four leaders' share had risen to 88 percent.

How is it possible that a race in which all the participants left the starting line at the same time, and with no obvious handicaps, turned out so unequally? This chapter is mainly about the dynamics through which oligoplistic market structures evolve. Brewing is, of course, a consumer goods industry, and that orientation provides a second and interacting theme.

To say that all entrants started on identical terms in 1933 would be slightly inaccurate. Many companies that thrived in the pre-Prohibition brewing industry, some of whose names continue even today to be well known, remained in operation during Prohibition. Some produced legal but unpopular "near beers," with an alcoholic content of less than 0.5 percent, or turned to the bottling of soft drinks. Others, such as Anheuser-Busch of St. Louis, produced malt and malt syrup, which were in great demand as raw materials for the millions of consumers who (legally) took up home brewing. The output of barley, from which brewers' malt is made, declined by only 8 percent from 1915–1919 to 1922–1926.[2]

It would also be incorrect to say that commercial brewing ceased during Prohibition. In many parts of the United States, beer was abundantly available in "speakeasies" and other illicit outlets. To be sure, the product's illegality altered supply and demand relationships. Before Prohibition, one could buy beer in the Chicago area for approximately $10 per 31-gallon barrel. During Prohibition, the average going price for a barrel of bootleg beer from an estimated 30 breweries rose into the $55-to-$60 range, covering among other things the augmented risks of doing business and generous subventions to much of the Chicago police force.[3] With many citizens drinking illegally, respect for the rule of law more generally declined. The center of Chicago's brewing industry was a large plant in the Bridgeport area that, even in the 1970s, was a prominent landmark visible from the Dan Ryan expressway. Built in 1893, it was sold to the Chicago Mafia when the eighteenth amendment was ratified, had its name changed from Manhattan Brewing to Malt-Maid Products and then to Fort Dearborn Products, and came under the control of Al Capone. When Prohibition ended, it immediately began selling beer again on the open market and altered its name back to Manhattan Brewing.[4] Its long-time nominal owner was gunned down on a Chicago street corner in

---

[2]U.S. Bureau of the Census, *Historical Statistics of the United States: Colonial Times to 1957* (Washington, DC: USGPO, 1960), p. 297. In the 1980s, 42 percent of U.S. barley consumption was for alcoholic beverages and malt-based foods, as distinguished from animal feed. U.S. Department of Agriculture, *Agricultural Statistics: 1991*, p. 45.

[3]Richard La Susa, "Nevermore the Local Lagers," *Chicago Tribune Magazine*, April 24, 1977, pp. 50–51.

[4]Ibid., p. 68.

1955. In 1968, the competitive processes reshaping the brewing industry throughout the United States forced it, like dozens of other Chicago breweries, to shut down. Being a first mover with considerable momentum in 1933 did not save the day.

THE PREMIUM BEER STRATEGY

Much more important was a set of strategy choices whose long-term consequences could scarcely have been anticipated when they were made. Beer is heavy and bulky in relation to its value and, especially before pasteurization became widely accepted, difficult to transport long distances without jeopardizing quality. Among 101 four-digit manufacturing industries for which accurate 1963 data were available, only 14 (including refined petroleum products and steel) had a lower value per pound than beer.[5] Unless special media such as pipelines are available, a low value per pound limits the distance products can be shipped economically. Refer back to Figure 4.4 in Chapter 4. Indeed, up to 1919 and again after 1933, brewing was preponderantly a localized industry. Except in the South, where the lack of natural ice made brewing difficult until artificial refrigeration techniques were perfected, most cities of any size had several breweries that served local demands. The perceived high cost of shipping—at first by horse cart or rail, and during the 1930s in trucks small and inefficient by modern standards—led breweries to limit their sales to a relatively narrow (e.g., 30-mile) radius from their brewing site. Their products came to be known as "local" beers.

A few brewers such as Schlitz ("the beer that made Milwaukee famous"), Miller, Pabst, and Anheuser-Busch chose a different strategy. Their home bases were Milwaukee, which took advantage of Lake Michigan ice for brewing and shipping, and St. Louis, whose deep caves provided natural refrigeration for storing (lagering) the beer. Beginning in the closing decades of the nineteenth century, these so-called "shipping brewers" attempted to reach out to a wider constituency, at first within the region surrounding their brewing plants and then (after the repeal of Prohibition) through much of the nation.[6] Abundant ice and pasteurization solved much of the perishability problem;

---

[5] F. M. Scherer, Alan Beckenstein, Erich Kaufer, and R. D. Murphy, *The Economics of Multi-Plant Operation: An International Comparisons Study* (Cambridge: Harvard University Press, 1975), pp. 429–433.

[6] See McGahan, "The Emergence of the National Brewing Oligopoly," pp. 236–238 and 241–242. Anheuser-Busch sought a national presence almost immediately. When Prohibition was repealed, it delivered its first case of Budweiser to President Franklin D. Roosevelt by horse-drawn wagon. See "August A. Busch Jr. Dies at 90," *New York Times*, September 30, 1989, p. 29.

rail shipment to relatively distant warehouses made the best of high transportation costs.

But transportation costs remained a significant problem. Under 1963 conditions, the average cost of shipping packaged beer in one-way containers 350 miles from the brewing site added 7.8 percent to the ex-works price of the beer.[7] Shipping returnable bottles nearly doubled that figure.[8] Extending the one-way shipping radius from Milwaukee or St. Louis to the East Coast entailed shipping costs roughly 18 percent of the ex-works price; on West Coast shipments, the cost was approximately 30 percent.

The only way the shipping brewers could serve a larger market was to sell their beers as something special—as "premium" beers from midwestern brewing centers adhering consistently to old-world quality traditions, and hence commanding premium prices. The greater the shipping distance, the larger the price premium was, as the following 24-bottle case wholesale price data for the Budweiser beer of Anheuser-Busch (A-B) in January 1954 show:[9]

Delivery Location	Case Price	Percent Above St. Louis
St. Louis	$2.93	—
Chicago	3.29	12.3
Houston	3.55	21.2
New York City	3.53	20.5
Los Angeles	3.65	24.6

With prices high in relation to those of local or "popular-priced" beers, the shipping brewers had to be content with very small shares in the more distant urban markets. But because of the premium image they had cultivated, sales did not go to zero. A few other companies such as Milwaukee's Blatz ("the beer that made Milwaukee change its mind"), New York's Schaefer, and Washington State's Olympia, pursued similar but somewhat less ambitious

---

[7]Scherer et al., *The Economics of Multi-Plant Operation*, pp. 87–90.

[8]Canadian brewers minimized return trip costs by adopting standardized bottles that could be returned to the nearest brewery, regardless of (Canadian) origin.

[9]The source is the Supreme Court decision in Federal Trade Commission v. Anheuser-Busch Inc., 363 U.S. 536, 540, note 4. Previously A-B had raised prices by 15 cents per case to an apparently unsustainable level in all states but Wisconsin and Missouri, so 15 cents have been deducted here from all but the St. Louis price.

strategies, shipping their beer over a radius of several hundred miles and charging tapered "regional" prices above those of local beers but below those of the Milwaukee and St. Louis brewers.

NEW PLANT AND ADVERTISING STRATEGIES

By the early years following World War II, the leading midwestern companies were selling their products throughout much of the United States. But transportation costs remained a problem. Pabst was the first of the clear-cut national brewers to attempt a solution. In 1945 it reduced its transportation costs to the East Coast by acquiring a brewery in Newark, New Jersey.[10] It began producing its Blue Ribbon beer there a year later. In 1949 it moved to the West Coast with the acquisition of a Los Angeles brewery. Schlitz acquired a Brooklyn brewery in 1949 and opened a new Los Angeles area brewery in 1954. Having purchased a site in Newark during 1944, Anheuser-Busch delayed its commitment but began operations from a newly-constructed brewery there in 1951. In 1954, it opened a brewery in Los Angeles. Thus, by 1951, three major midwestern brewers had reduced their transportation costs to the East Coast, and by 1954, they had achieved similar status on the West Coast.

One other company deserves attention for pioneering an analogous plant decentralization strategy with less evident success.[11] In 1935 and 1936, Falstaff expanded from its St. Louis home base with the acquisition of breweries in Omaha and New Orleans. It followed Pabst to California in 1952 and also acquired small breweries in Fort Wayne, Indiana, and Galveston, Texas. However, there were significant differences between its strategy and those of Pabst, Schlitz, and Anheuser-Busch. Falstaff tried to achieve wider distribution quickly by acquiring small decentralized breweries rather than by shipping first and then buying or building. The acquired breweries then produced Falstaff beer as well as their traditional offerings. Falstaff also sought to build a nationwide image in a less conventional way. It bid aggressively for contracts to supply Cold War military base canteens, believing that when the troops returned home, they would reach for the familiar Falstaff label. Instead, most ex-GIs, anxious to distance themselves from their military lives, reached for anything but Falstaff, and so Falstaff's civilian sector sales were

---

[10]During the 1930s Pabst expanded brewing operations from its home base in Milwaukee to Peoria, Illinois, but that move had a much less dramatic impact on its transportation costs.

[11]See "How Falstaff Brews New Markets," *Business Week*, July 30, 1966, pp. 47–48.

TABLE 10.1

Media Advertising Outlays per Barrel Sold by Leading Brewers

Year	Pabst	A-B	Schlitz	Falstaff	Miller	Ballantine	Schaefer	Stroh	Schmidt
1949	$0.48	$0.26	$0.33	$0.21	$0.31	$0.24	$0.26	n.a.	n.a.
1950	0.63	0.30	0.34	0.17	0.32	0.22	0.20	$0.20	$0.22
1951	0.72	0.34	0.41	0.10	0.40	0.39	0.25	0.22	0.19
1952	0.73	0.28	0.37	0.34	0.40	0.61	0.36	0.31	0.17
1953	0.73	0.45	0.71	0.41	0.62	0.52	0.25	0.35	0.21
1954	1.18	1.17	1.35	0.83	1.64	0.73	0.61	0.62	0.28
1955	0.97	0.98	1.29	0.71	0.77	0.40	0.58	0.56	0.29
1956	1.99	1.16	1.45	1.13	1.64	0.86	0.82	0.68	0.41
1957	1.60	1.60	1.77	1.25	1.44	0.97	0.86	0.79	0.52
1958	1.26	1.48	1.31	1.16	1.45	0.83	1.19	1.03	0.60
1959	0.89	1.38	1.27	1.14	1.32	0.67	0.96	0.88	0.85
1960	1.08	1.40	1.77	1.10	1.59	0.72	0.74	0.80	0.99
1961	0.99	1.47	2.21	1.11	0.88	0.79	0.68	1.03	1.04
1962	1.17	1.46	2.07	1.53	0.98	0.98	0.77	1.38	1.24

Sources: Douglas F. Greer, "Product Differentiation and Concentration in the Brewing Industry," *Journal of Industrial Economics,* vol. 19 (July 1971), p. 214; and Charles F. Keithahn, *The Brewing Industry,* Federal Trade Commission staff report (Washington, DC: December 1978), pp. 77–78; both drawing upon original data published in *Advertising Age,* August 6, 1956; September 29, 1958; and January 2, 1967. The data exclude outlays for outdoor and point-of-purchase displays, which were used extensively in the early 1950s. Reprinted with permission of Blackwell Publishers.

disappointing. Since history is impatient with losers, we focus on Pabst, Schlitz, and A-B.[12]

ESCALATING ADVERTISING

Concurrent with the decentralization of those three firms' production operations, there were dramatic developments on the advertising front. During the early 1950s, the measured media advertising outlays of some, but not all, leading brewing companies rose sharply. Table 10.1 summarizes the data available from 1949 through 1962. Pabst, the first to pursue a decentralization strategy aggressively, had the highest outlays per barrel in 1949 and appears to have led the upward movement during the early 1950s, when it alone had a West Coast plant. Schlitz followed into the 70-cent range two years after Pabst, and all three, joined by Miller, crossed the $1.00 mark abreast in 1954.

---

[12]One should not, however, overlook a moral: that not all first movers succeed, and so in assessing the profits from innovation, one must measure the losses of the unsuccessful first movers along with the supranormal gains of the winners.

The regional brewers were slow to respond, and in some cases (e.g., New York-based Ballantine, the nation's third-largest brewer in 1950; Detroit's Stroh, and Philadelphia's Schmidt) their advertising outlays lagged far behind those of the leaders, despite the media invasion into their own backyards.

Two main hypotheses contend to explain the escalation of beer advertising expenditures during the early 1950s. One joins the history presented thus far with an important piece of economic theory called the Dorfman-Steiner (D-S) theorem.[13] D-S postulates that with differentiated products, sellers must solve two problems simultaneously: setting the profit-maximizing price, and setting the optimal level of sales-enhancing advertising expenditures.[14] The price-setting component is conventional: output is increased until marginal revenue equals marginal production plus distribution cost. The D-S advertising equation, which is based upon the plausible assumption that more advertising leads to more units sold, but with diminishing marginal returns, can be simplified to:[15]

$$\left(\frac{A}{S}\right)^* = e_A \left(\frac{P - MC}{P}\right)$$

where $(A/S)^*$ is the profit-maximizing ratio of advertising outlays to product sales, e_A is the elasticity of demand with respect to advertising outlays (i.e., the percentage change in quantity sold for a one percent change in advertising outlays); and $(P - MC)/P$ is a price-cost margin. The intuition is that as the margin between price and marginal cost widens, the incremental profit from selling one more unit rises, and so it is worth striving more vigorously for that extra sale by raising advertising or other promotional expenditures. The gain in units sold may come from taking business away from rivals, expanding the market by persuading more consumers to use the advertised product, or some combination of the two.

Suppose now that the shipping brewers were in approximate profit-maximizing equilibrium before they decentralized their production operations. Decentralization reduced transportation costs in serving East and West coast consumers and hence marginal cost MC. As a first approximation, prices remained unchanged, or at least, the premium traditionally charged to

---

[13] Robert Dorfman and Peter O. Steiner, "Optimal Advertising and Optimal Quality," *American Economic Review*, vol. 44 (December 1954), pp. 826–836. A dynamic extension is Marc Nerlove and Kenneth J. Arrow, "Optimal Advertising Policy under Dynamic Conditions," *Economica*, vol. 29 (May 1962), pp. 129–142. The further stimulating effect of rivalry among oligopolistic advertisers is analyzed theoretically in Michael Waterson, *Economic Theory of the Industry* (New York: Cambridge University Press, 1984), pp. 132–134.

[14] The theorem also applies to other sales-increasing outlays—for example, on research and development, product quality control, and providing specialized service.

[15] For a derivation, see F. M. Scherer and David J. Ross, *Industrial Market Structure and Economic Performance* (Boston: Houghton Mifflin: 1990), p. 593.

cover shipping costs was not significantly reduced. Thus, with decentralization, $P - MC$ rose, and so $(P - MC)/P$ rose, inducing, for a given e_A, an increase in the ratio of advertising outlays in relation to sales. There is reason to believe that consumers were responsive to beer advertising, and so e_A had an appreciable positive value.[16] Thus, eliminating transportation costs amounting to roughly 10 percent of sales should have raised the ratio of advertising to sales substantially. And that, of course, is what was observed.

As is not uncommon, other things were changing at the same time, giving rise to the second explanatory hypothesis. In particular, during the early 1950s television viewing was spreading rapidly. In 1950, 3.8 million U.S. households had television sets; by 1955, the new medium had penetrated 26 million households—two-thirds the number with radio sets.[17] A survey of 16 brewing company managers in 1954 elicited nearly unanimous agreement that television was the most effective advertising medium for selling beer.[18] A 1955 survey of mostly small and medium-size brewers showed that television advertising outlays rose from an average of 5 cents per barrel in 1950 to 31 cents per barrel in 1954.[19] Companies selling more than 500,000 barrels per year raised their television outlays by 46 cents per barrel—a penny more than their *total* advertising increase. In 1953, Anheuser-Busch was the first brewing company to purchase a baseball team, and in 1954, sponsorship of St. Louis Cardinals game radio and television broadcasting shifted from the Griesedieck Western Brewery Company, another St. Louis brewer, to A-B.[20]

The emergence of a powerful new advertising medium undoubtedly influenced the developments of the early 1950s, although in principle, the availability of a more efficient medium could have *reduced* total advertising outlays by displacing inefficient media, rather than increasing them. Plant decentralization and the Dorfman-Steiner effect led unambiguously to higher expenditures. The correct explanation of the advertising escalation probably comes from some combination of the two hypotheses.

Volume Consequences

At first, the multiplant posture of the shipping brewers and their intensified advertising had disappointing consequences. The combined market share of Pabst, Schlitz, and A-B rose from 16.1 percent in 1950 to just 18.3 percent in

---

[16]See Christina M. L. Kelton and W. David Kelton, "Advertising and Intraindustry Brand Shift in the U.S. Brewing Industry," *Journal of Industrial Economics*, vol. 30 (March 1982), pp. 293–304.

[17]U.S. Bureau of the Census, *Historical Statistics of the United States: Colonial Times to 1957*, p. 491.

[18]"Let's Take a Look at a TV Survey," *Modern Brewery Age*, April 1954, p. 44.

[19]"Brewery Advertising Outlays Show Constant Upward Curve," *Modern Brewery Age*, September 1955, p. 35.

[20]"Beer Teams Up with Baseball," *Business Week*, February 28, 1953, p. 32.

FIGURE 10.1
Trends in Leading Brewers' U.S. Market Shares

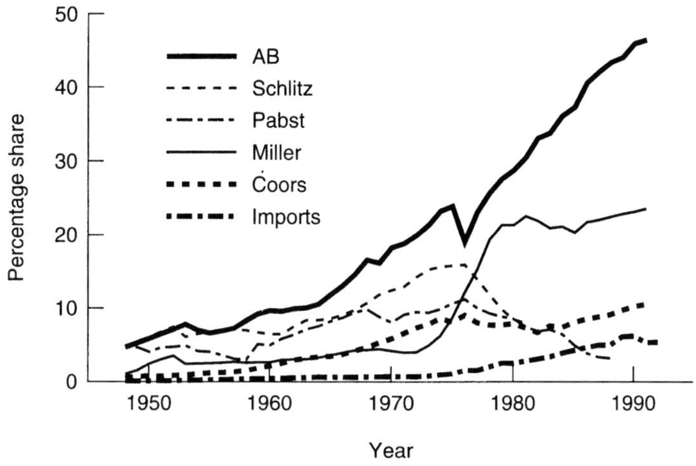

Sources: Charles F. Keithahn, *The Brewing Industry,* Federal Trade Commission staff report (Washington, DC: USGPO, December 1978), pp. 22–23; Anita M. McGahan, "The Emergence of the National Brewing Oligopoly," *Business History Review,* vol. 65 (Summer 1991), p. 265; *Brewers Almanac* (Washington, DC: Beer institute: various years); and *Modern Brewery Age Blue Book* (Norwalk, CT: various years).

1958. See Figure 10.1. Meanwhile, beer sales were stagnant, increasing from their 1950 level of 83.5 million 31-gallon barrels by only two million barrels before falling back to 83.9 million barrels in recession year 1958. Pabst, the leader of the advertising escalation, was unable to maintain its sales momentum, became overextended financially, and beginning in 1958, as Table 10.1 reveals, began spending much less on advertising per barrel than its national rivals.

But then the brewers' fortunes shifted. With changing demographics, attributable only in part to the maturing of 1940s "baby boomers" to drinking age, beer consumption rose briskly from 83.9 million barrels in 1958 to 96.2 million barrels in 1964 and 130.7 million barrels in 1972.[21] Compared to the 1950s, marked by two brief but sharp recessions, the 1960s were a period of unusually strong and consistent economic growth. Real disposable income per capita rose at an average rate of 1.25 percent between 1950 and 1958, but at twice that rate from 1958 to 1972. Tens of millions of Americans joined the prosperous middle class. As their general standards of living rose, they sought something better in their beer consumption too. They "moved up" to premium beers. The consumption of premium and "superpremium" (e.g., Anheuser-Busch's Michelob) beers rose from an estimated 20 percent of all brands by liquid volume in 1950 to 21

---

[21]On demographic influences, see Keithahn, *The Brewing Industry,* pp. 29–32.

percent in 1958 and 44 percent in 1972.[22] Since premium brands sold at higher prices, the revenue share increase was even larger. The traditional shipping brewers were major beneficiaries. Anheuser-Busch, Schlitz, and Pabst experienced a combined market share gain to 43.5 percent in 1972. See again Figure 10.1.

Quality and Premium Prices

The question must now be asked, were "premium" beers in fact superior to the offerings of local and regional brewers? Here we tread on dangerous ground, because economists by strong tradition accept that what the consumer *believes* is better must indeed be better. *De gustibus non est disputandum.* Yet adhering tautologically to that tradition also risks missing important insights.

Carefully structured double-blind studies and countless less formal (but more enjoyable!) experiments have revealed repeatedly that consumers, or at least 90 percent of all consumers, cannot tell one conventional lager beer from another and do not, among other things, systematically prefer premium brands over popular-priced brands when the labels are removed.[23] The Schlitz Company exploited this phenomenon through panel tests televised live at the halftime of sports events beginning with the 1980–1981 professional football playoffs. Television viewers were shown panels of 100 persons, each of whom had signed sworn affidavits that they normally drank Budweiser, Michelob, Miller, or some other rival beer. Each drank from two unmarked glasses, one containing Schlitz and one a rival beer. Each pressed a button indicating preference, and in real time the preferences were tallied on an electronic scoreboard. Invariably, as the binomial distribution implies for individuals who cannot distinguish between two objects, nearly half the panelists revealed a preference for Schlitz over their normal brand.[24]

Scientific tests also reveal that consumers are likely to prefer products with the label of a high-prestige beer, even when some other beer is inside the container. This is true not only in the United States, but also in other nations. Because of strong prohibitionist influences in Sweden, Swedish consumers tended to view the Carlsberg beer from fun-loving Copenhagen as superior to local offerings. Tests during the late 1960s by the leading Swedish brewer, Pripps, revealed that the most-preferred choice of Swedish consumer panels

---

[22]Estimates compiled by R. S. Weinberg and Associates, and introduced into merger filings before the U.S. Department of Justice during the 1980s.

[23]The best summary of the studies is Douglas F. Greer, *Industrial Organization and Public Policy,* (2nd ed. New York: Macmillan, 1984), pp. 76–78.

[24]If individuals were truly unable to distingish by taste among competing beers, the predicted number of Schlitz choices is 50, with a standard error of 5.

was Pripps' Three Towns beer with a Carlsberg label; the least-preferred choice was Carlsberg beer with a Three Towns label.[25]

The United States probably does differ, however, in an important respect. The taste for beer is an acquired taste. If a first-time beer sampler had to choose between America's Budweiser and the excellent Budwar beer from Bohemia's Budějovice, which the good soldier Švejk tried so diligently to reach,[26] he or she would most likely be repelled by the strongly hops-flavored Budwar and select America's Budweiser. Recognizing this, the leading U.S. premium brewers have deliberately chosen formulas sufficiently bland to win a mass following among relatively inexperienced consumers and (through repeat purchase) consumers acculturated to bland beers.[27] It is probably too much of an infringement on the *de gustibus* principle, but we say it anyway: U.S. premium beers are beers crafted for people who do not appreciate beer. The taste tests conducted by one leading U.S. brewer during the 1960s revealed that consumers in the South, where beer-drinking proclivities were less fully ingrained, preferred even blander beer than northern consumers. As a result, its "standard" formula was altered on the bland side for shipments to the South.

There remains the claim that U.S. "premium" beers maintained higher standards of uniformity than small local brewers, at least during the industry's formative post-Prohibition years.[28] There is some truth in this assertion. Despite much effort to develop continuous-flow processes (analogous to those found in petroleum refineries), beer brewing remains a batch process. Absent prohibitively costly "clean room" techniques like those used in the semiconductor industry, unfriendly bacteria or other contaminants can infiltrate the brew, and bad batches occur. In 1992, 7 percent of the beer produced in U.S. breweries went down the drain and not out the door, largely because of spillage in packaging but sometimes because it failed to meet quality control standards.[29] Some brewers were less scrupulous than others about discarding bad batches, and the very smallest breweries may have been unable to afford a chemist to ensure high-quality standards. Those who repeatedly sold bad beer are no longer in business.

---

[25]From an interview by the author in connection with Scherer et al., *The Economics of Multi-Plant Operation.*

[26]Jaroslav Hašek, *The Good Soldier Švejk,* translation by Cecil Parrott (New York: Penguin, 1973). The German word for Budwar is Budweiser.

[27]See "American Beer: How Changing Tastes Have Changed It," *New York Times,* May 12, 1982, pp. 23 and 27.

[28]See McGahan, "The Emergence," pp. 241–242, 258, and 270.

[29]Beer Institute, *Brewers Almanac: 1993,* p. 7.

However, it is questionable whether the quality control of the local and regional brewers who survived, selling at subpremium prices, was inferior to that of the premium brewers. And even large brewers fell victim to quality lapses. In Canada, Carling and its related beers held approximately 60 percent of the Dominion market during the 1950s until it was discovered that an additive used in Quebec was lethal when imbibed in large quantities. As a consequence of the ensuing publicity, Carling suffered severe market share losses. The Schlitz story is even more on point. During the 1960s Schlitz embraced more completely than other sizable companies new brewing techniques that accelerated the fermentation process, thereby reducing cost. The beer's "body" suffered by such a small amount that it went unnoticed by most consumers. During the 1970s, Schlitz reduced the fermentation time further and substituted inexpensive corn syrup for part of the more expensive malt.[30] Rival Anheuser-Busch launched an extensive pamphlet campaign to inform consumers of the quality sacrifices while touting its own offerings.[31] Whatever the exact cause, Schlitz's sales went into a steep dive. A new president hired away from A-B returned a full complement of malt to the formula, but the damage was done, and Schlitz was unable to reverse its decline.

It must also be recognized that there is probably a trade-off between formula consistency and other dimensions of quality. The most memorable beer the author has consumed in nearly half a century of beer connoisseurship was a German brew lagered a full year before sale. It was notoriously unstable, with a shelf life after bottling of at best three weeks. But it was always worth trying, and when it was good, it was nectar of the gods. As in pharmaceuticals, tradeoffs between Type I and Type II errors are difficult to avoid.

That premium image depends more upon pricing strategy than quality control is demonstrated by the history of Pabst. In 1962, the state of Michigan raised its tax on beer from 2.25 to 12 cents per sixpack of 12-ounce containers. When others passed the tax along to consumers through higher prices, Pabst decided to forgo the increase and move from premium to popular price status. Its Michigan market share rose from a approximately 2 percent to more than 20 percent. Pabst's leaders were so pleased with the results that they began charging popular prices in several other states. Again, they experienced appreciable market share gains. However, when they tried later to return Pabst Blue Ribbon prices to premium levels, they found that they were unable to do so without massive sales losses. Once sacrificed by the everyday quotation of

---

[30]"Schlitz Seeks to Brew Better Image, But Sales Are Still Lacking Gusto," *Wall Street Journal,* August 30, 1979, p. 1; and David A. Aaker, *Managing Brand Equity* (New York: Free Press, 1991), pp. 78–85.

[31]Lacking a sample, the author offers as a reward an autographed copy of this book to the first reader who can supply a copy of the A-B handbills.

popular prices, the image as a premium beer could not be regained. Later, as beers retaining premium images continued to expand their sales, Pabst entered a spiral of decline even at popular prices.

Rival premium brewers learned from the Pabst experience to defend their images by maintaining premium prices, departing from the rule at most two or three times a year for special price cuts of very short duration. When such "specials" are offered, the premium brewers are in effect saying, "Here is a particularly good deal. You can obtain our premium beer at popular prices for a short time only. Buy now, because next week we will be back at premium prices where we belong." In this way, they strive to encourage sampling by consumers, some of whom will be retained as repeat premium-price purchasers.

As rivalry in the brewing industry evolved, companies that carried premium images into the period following World War II and maintained them were able to realize more revenue from selling a barrel of beer than companies with local and regional images or companies like Pabst that had squandered their images. The following data on average 1980 revenue per 31-gallon barrel for six representative companies are illustrative:[32]

Anheuser-Busch	$60.49
Miller	59.19
Coors	55.01
Schlitz	54.69
Pabst	47.70
Genessee	41.78

With by far the largest superpremium beer market share through its Michelob brand and heavy emphasis on premium-priced Budweiser, A-B realized the most revenue per barrel. Coors and Miller (an early shipping brewer that lagged in decentralizing its brewing operations) sustained and built upon solid premium-price status. The unique features of their strategies will be discussed later. Schlitz's fading premium image is visible. The earlier shift to popular prices in many states by Pabst led to revenue realizations 20 percent below those of the leaders. Northern New York's Genessee was a particularly strong representative of the remaining regional brewers.

Because brewing costs varied little with image, the brewers with premium images had wider strategy options than less-well-endowed companies. They

---

[32]The data were compiled for the author in what became a series of antitrust inquiries concerning proposed brewing company mergers during the 1980s.

could spend more per barrel on advertising, take more profit per barrel, squeeze the margin between premium and local beer prices, or some combination thereof. To examine the choices made, however, additional background is needed.

SCALE ECONOMIES, COSTS, AND PRICING STRATEGY

Brewing beer is one of the most ancient technologies, traceable back at least five millennia.[33] Malt (and/or other grains) and hops (or extract of hops) are cooked in water; yeast is added to ferment the grain into alcohol and sugar; the brew is cooled and aged (or, from the German, "lagered") to complete fermentation, and solids are filtered out of the finished brew, which is then packaged. With a modest investment and scrupulous cleanliness, one can make one's own beer at home. One might suppose from this that economies of scale are unimportant. Early postwar U.S. studies accepted that supposition and implied that breweries producing 100,000 barrels per year were viable, even though unit costs were believed to continue declining out to volumes of 1.5 million barrels.[34] But subsequent technological and marketing changes made those estimates obsolete.[35]

Following the two-thirds rule, investment costs can be saved by scaling up brewing vessels. This is not a new phenomenon.[36] The participants in London's thriving eighteenth-century brewing industry recognized the cost advantages of larger vessels, especially for then-popular porter, which required a year's aging. The quest for scale economies led to ever larger storage vats (which we would now call tanks). But after 1784, according to the era's histo-

---

[33]See "The Beer That Made Sumerians Famous," *New York Times*, March 24, 1993, p. C4.

[34]See Ira Horowitz and Ann R. Horowitz, "Firms in a Declining Market: The Brewing Case," *Journal of Industrial Economics*, vol. 13 (March 1965), pp. 145–152; and Greer, "Product Differentiation and Concentration," p. 210 note.

[35]For more detailed analyses of brewing scale economies, see T. A. J. Cockerill, "Economies of Scale in the Brewing Industry: A Comparative Study of the United Kingdom and the United States of America," M.Phil. dissertation, University of Leeds, 1971; and F. M. Scherer, *Economies of Scale at the Plant and Multi-Plant Levels: Detailed Evidence* (manuscript deposited with several research libraries: September 1975).

[36]Compare McGahan, "The Emergence," p. 244.

rian, "it became a matter of prestige to boast the largest vat in London."[37] A "vat race" ensued. When the Griffin Brewery inaugurated the largest vat to date in 1790, places were set for 200 people to dine within it. Yet as often happens, the bounds of materials technology were overstepped, bringing the race to a halt. In 1809 the Horse Shoe Brewery's largest vat burst, sweeping away the brewery's walls, causing several adjacent tenements to collapse, and (perhaps apocryphally) killing eight people "by drowning, injury, poisoning by the porter fumes or drunkenness."[38]

Amplifying the advantages of scale-up, advances in technology during the 1960s made it possible to automate brewhouse functions. Using old methods, approximately 24 persons were required on each shift in a sizable brewhouse. By automating filling, ingredient dispensing, mixing, and cleaning operations, the number of persons per shift could be reduced to two. But to take advantage of those advances, a sizable brewery was required. Tapping mid–1970s data obtained from the Schlitz Company, Keithahn reported that the construction cost per barrel of capacity in modern breweries fell from $30 for a brewery of one million barrels per year capacity to $15 for a four-million-barrel plant.[39] As of 1967, only six out the 154 breweries operating in the United States had reached the four-million-barrel size threshold, and at least 120 had capacities of less than 1.5 million barrels. Thus, considerable structural adjustment was needed to exploit the new technology.

Even more compelling scale economies arise in the packaging house. In the first years after Prohibition ended, most beer was shipped to market in either kegs or 12-ounce bottles. Beginning in 1935, canned beer entered the picture rapidly. By 1970, marketing competition forced brewers to sell their products in 12-ounce cans, 12-ounce bottles, 16-ounce cans, a larger bottle, kegs, and perhaps 7-ounce cans or bottles. Meanwhile, advances in packaging technology were increasing canning and bottling machine speeds. In 1970 the fastest canning machine, which required only one operator, canned 1200 12-ounce cans, or 3.63 barrels, per minute. Later versions filled 2000 cans per minute. With two-shift operation, a 1200-can/minute line fills roughly 870,000 barrels of beer per year. Three-shift operation provides minor additional savings. Bottling machines were somewhat slower (750 per minute) in 1970, but altogether, machinery to package efficiently the six container sizes listed above using 1970-vintage technology required an output of at least four million barrels per year.

---

[37]Peter Mathias, *The Brewing Industry in England: 1700–1830* (Cambridge, UK: Cambridge University Press, 1959), p. 61.

[38]Ibid., p. 62.

[39]*The Brewing Industry*, p. 49.

FIGURE 10.2
Brewing Cost Functions Embodying Old and New Technologies, Late 1960s

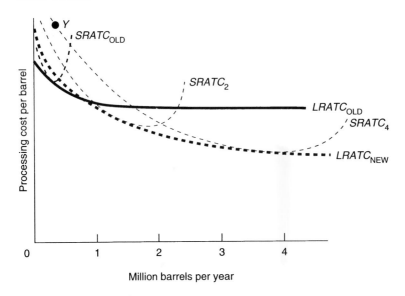

The brewing, packaging, and other in-plant cost conditions faced by brewers of varying size in the late 1960s are illustrated in Figure 10.2. The technology embodied in traditional breweries gave rise to a long-run unit cost (or planning) curve $LRATC_{OLD}$. Most economies of scale were exhausted at outputs of approximately one million barrels per year. A small plant already built using that technology had a short-run cost curve such as $SRATC_{OLD}$. The newer capital-intensive technology offered long-run unit cost curve $LRATC_{NEW}$. Costs were higher at small scale, but persistent scale economies allowed much lower-cost production at large scales, depending upon a firm's new-capacity investment decision and hence the short-run cost function selected.

Small and especially local brewers were caught in a Hobson's choice by this new situation. If they stayed with the old technology, they had much higher unit costs than modern breweries. If they jumped to a new brewery (e.g., with capacity of four million barrels per year) but operated it at only 300,000 barrels per year, their costs (at point Y on $SRATC_4$) would be even higher than with the old technology. Their inferior brand image made it difficult to charge prices high enough to cover their high costs (on which more later) or to expand their output enough to utilize a modern brewery fully. Their inferior brand image also left them with funds too meager to launch new products or to support volume-increasing advertising campaigns. They were trapped.

MULTIPLANT ECONOMIES OF SCALE

In addition to having the sales volume needed to build modern, large-scale plants, the principal national brewers also enjoyed modest advantages from operating multiple plants.

When many different beers were produced or special-shape bottles were offered, additional packaging machines had to be dedicated to those variants, or time was lost while machines were shut down, cleaned, and perhaps reconfigured for a new type or shape. However, multibrewery operators enjoyed an additional trade-off. They could assign the low-volume products to a centrally located brewery, shipping them to warehouses all over the nation and in effect saving production cost by accepting somewhat higher transportation costs. Anheuser-Busch pursued this approach inter alia for its Michelob, which was packaged in special bottles.

Anheuser-Busch also pursued with extraordinary finesse a dynamic strategy taking advantage of its multiplant posture.[40] As its volume rose, it expanded from its 1954 three-plant structure to additional new plants: Tampa in 1958; Houston in 1965; Columbus, Ohio, in 1968; Jacksonville in 1969; Merrimack, New Hampshire, in 1970; Williamsburg, Virginia (with a theme park) in 1971; and then to Syracuse (purchased in 1979 from a fading Schlitz before construction was completed); Fort Collins, Colorado; northern California; and northwestern Georgia. See Figure 10.3, which numbers the plants in order of initial construction. By 1990, all but two of these plants (Merrimack and Tampa) had capacities of 4 million barrels per year or more. Anheuser-Busch's original but somewhat high-cost St. Louis brewery, the largest in the system, served as a pivot point. When a large new plant came on stream, St. Louis would redirect its output away from the geographic area in which the new plant was built, at first taking up the slack through output reductions and then by shipping more beer toward areas where demand was growing until capacity expansions were implemented there too. In this way A-B was able to build larger new plants, or expand existing plants in larger increments, than it would if no such geographic output reallocation were possible. By the late 1960s, it had a sophisticated linear programming model to guide its plant construction phasing and output allocation.

The extent to which the large national shippers benefited from economies of scale in advertising is disputed and uncertain. It is difficult to draw simple inferences from the amounts companies spend, because first movers with strong brand images reinforce those images through advertising at lower cost

---

[40]For the mathematical theory, see Scherer et al., *The Economics of Multi-Plant Operation*, pp. 35–48 and chap. 8.

FIGURE 10.3
The Multiplant Structure of Anheuser-Busch in 1990

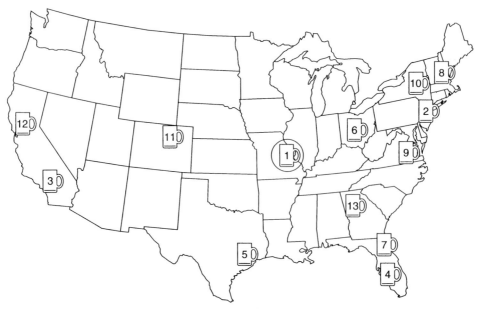

Source: Company Annual Reports.

than late movers.[41] Given that relationship, it should not be surprising, as we shall see shortly, that market leader A-B tends to spend less per barrel of sales than its smaller advertising-minded rivals.

There are two main reasons why larger firms might enjoy scale economies in advertising. It may be necessary to send some threshold number of messages to trigger consumer awareness. If so, the company with a large share of the target medium market can spread the virtually fixed cost of attaining the threshold over a larger sales base than smaller rivals. Also, network television advertising is feasible only for companies with national distribution, which in brewing (with one exception) means those with multiplant operations. Economists disagree on whether network advertising is more effective and/or less costly than spot messages.[42] Data for 1980–1982 presented to Pabst by an

[41]See Robert D. Buzzell and P. W. Farris, "Marketing Costs in Consumer Goods Industries," in Hans Thorelli, ed., *Strategy + Structure = Performance* (Bloomington: Indiana University Press, 1977), pp. 128–129.

[42]For a review of the evidence more generally, see Scherer and Ross, *Industrial Market Structure and Economic Performance*, p. 135.

advertising agency suggested that reaching men in the 18–49-year age category watching sports events costs only half as much per thousand viewers with television network advertising as with spot insertions.[43] However, the fact that the largest brewers use substantial fractions of *both* spot and network advertising suggests that there are limits (such as inflexibility of audience targeting) to the advantages of network ads. Altogether, the evidence suggests, large nationwide brewers derive at least some advantage from their size in advertising.

Most beer in the United States moves from the brewery to an independent wholesaler's warehouse, and from there to retail outlets—that is, to stores, restaurants, and taverns. Especially in smaller cities and the less-populated areas of the United States, economies of scale appear to limit the number of efficient beer wholesalers to three or four. A significant factor in the success of Anheuser-Busch was a nine-month trip August Busch took in 1955 to visit all his wholesalers, listening to their problems and assuring them that no other wholesaler would distribute Budweiser beer in their assigned territory.[44] As a result of this, analogous follow-up measures, and continuing suasion, A-B built a network of fiercely loyal and enthusiastic wholesalers, most of whom handle only A-B and affiliated foreign beers and who, as A-B gained market share (see Figure 10.1), were large enough to realize all scale economies. Typically, the second-best-selling brand in a city or county has more or less exclusive access to another wholesaler, whereas all other brands are distributed nonexclusively by the remaining middlemen. The result for the lower-volume brands is diffusion of merchandising "push," higher wholesaling cost, and, under the Dorfman-Steiner theorem, less expenditure by wholesalers on point-of-sale marketing. An internal analysis by a brewing company that must remain anonymous revealed that A-B wholesalers had net per-barrel operating margins (i.e., wholesaler commission less operating costs) four times those realized by wholesalers of the smaller firm, partly because A-B's higher product prices yielded more generous commissions and partly because the smaller firm's operating costs per barrel were 21 percent higher than those of A-B wholesalers.[45]

---

[43]Provided to the author in connection with the analysis of a merger.

[44]McGahan, "The Emergence of the National Brewing Oligopoly," pp. 277–278.

On the tendency for territorial exclusivity, sometimes supported by state laws, to raise beer prices to consumers by curbing intrabrand price competition, see W. P. Culbertson and David Bradford, "The Price of Beer: Some Evidence from Interstate Comparisons," *International Journal of Industrial Organization*, vol. 9 (June 1991), pp. 275–289; and Tim R. Sass and David S. Saurman, "Mandated Exclusive Territories and Economic Efficiency," *Journal of Law & Economics*, vol. 36 (April 1993), pp. 153–177.

On the legal implications, see "Abrams Begins Antitrust Inquiry to Examine Rising Price of Beer," *New York Times*, June 13, 1985, p. B7.

[45]From the documentation of 1980s merger proposals.

FIGURE 10.4
Trends in Beer Prices and Productivity, 1950–1987

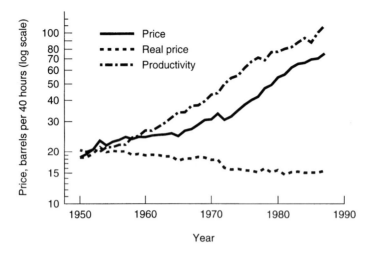

Source: U.S. Bureau of the Census, *Census of Manufactures,* various years; and *Brewers Almanac: 1993* (Washington, DC: *Beer Institute* 1994).

THE SQUEEZE

As the large national brewers and some regional brewers built sizable new breweries, they achieved a substantial cost advantage over smaller firms, who were unable to modernize because they could not sustain sufficient volume. The cost advantage of the multiplant brewers was enhanced by scale economies in advertising and, to a more limited degree, in wholesaling. The brewers with strong premium images also enjoyed a revenue-per-barrel advantage over traditional local and regional brands (excluding brands of the microbreweries that proliferated during the 1980s). Limit pricing theory teaches that when firms enjoy appreciable cost and product differentiation advantages, they may choose to set prices that squeeze out rival firms and systematically increase their own market shares. This is what happened in the brewing industry.

There was, as we have seen repeatedly in this volume, considerable general inflation in the United States during the decades following World War II. Unable to modernize but afflicted by increases in wages and other costs, the small breweries attempted to raise their prices. But the larger companies refused to cooperate. Figure 10.4 traces the concomitant trends. Between 1953 and 1965, the nominal average price per barrel of beer sold in the United States (solid line) rose by only 8 percent. After that, nominal beer prices rose more rapidly, but *fell* on average in real terms—that is, when adjusted for general inflation using the gross national product deflator (dashed line). The price conflict between small and expanding national brewers led among other things to a narrowing of the percentage price differential between premium and popular-priced brands.[46] The larger brewers were able to reduce inflation-adjusted prices without sacrificing sustained profitability because, through modernization and the exploitation of scale economies, they experienced rapid labor productivity growth (dot-dash line). As large efficient breweries displaced small inefficient units, average output (in barrels) per hour of labor input for the brewing industry as a whole rose at 5.03 percent per year between 1950 and 1987.[47]

The price-cost squeeze forced smaller brewing companies into unprofitability, and eventually into exiting from the industry. In 1947, according to the Census of Manufactures, 404 companies brewed and sold beer in the U. S. The number of brewing companies fell to 263 in 1954, 211 in 1958, 125 in 1967, 81 in 1977, and 67 in 1982.[48] Most companies exited by terminating their brewing operations altogether. Some merged with larger companies, who in many instances closed the small breweries and transferred the production of viable brands to their own breweries, thereby increasing capacity utilization and/or the ability to build plants of larger scale.[49] For companies such as Heileman, Falstaff, and National that grew by making multiple small acquisitions, some important handicaps accompanied the scale increases. The acquired brands typically had only local or regional brand images and hence commanded much lower prices than premium brands, and their modest volumes meant that added costs were incurred in resetting packaging machinery frequently.

FURTHER DEVELOPMENTS

To comprehend fully the dynamics that led to continuing increases in brewing industry concentration, several further developments must be considered.

ADVERTISING DE-ESCALATION

The brewers who rebuilt their industry after Prohibition pursued for the most part conservative, traditional approaches to marketing. One of the first

---

[46]Keithahn, *The Beer Industry*, p. 96.

[47]In this estimate, it was assumed that salaried employees worked a constant 2000 hours per year.

[48]U.S. Bureau of the Census, *1982 Census of Manufactures*, "Concentration Ratios in Manufacturing," MC82-S-7 (April 1986), p. 7–9.

[49]Similar trends occurred in other industrialized nations. See, for example, Juergen Mueller and Joachim Schwalbach, "Structural Change in West Germany's Brewing Industry," *Journal of Industrial Economics*, vol. 28 (June 1980), pp. 353–368; and Maria Brouwer, "Evolutionary Aspects of the European Brewing Industry," in H. W. de Jong, ed., *The Structure of European Industry*, 2nd. ed. (Dordrecht, Netherlands: Kluwer, 1988), pp. 163–165.

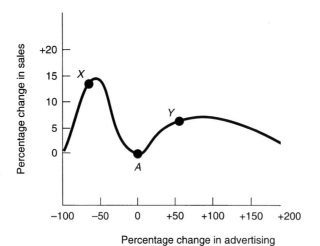

**FIGURE 10.5
Advertising Response
Function Observed by
Anheuser-Busch in
1963–1964**
Source: Adapted from Russell L. Ackoff and James R. Emshoff, "Advertising Research at Anheuser-Busch, Inc. (1968–74)," *Sloan Management Review*, vol. 16 (Winter 1975), p. 9.

companies to embrace new scientific management concepts was Anheuser-Busch. In 1959 it commissioned academic operations researchers Russell Ackoff and James Emshoff to undertake a series of studies that led in 1962 to a reassessment of advertising strategies.[50] They divided the United States into 18 regions and conducted a systematic year-long experiment, reducing advertising outlays from 1961 levels by 25 percent in some, holding them constant in others, and increasing them by 50 percent in still others. The results were perplexing: sales rose more in the territories with either *less* or *more* advertising than in those where it was held constant. In more elaborate 1963–1964 experiments, the "treatments" ranged more widely from –100 percent to +200 percent. What emerged was the bimodal response function reproduced in Figure 10.5. The first hump reflected the sensitive response of relatively heavy beer drinkers, the second hump the more sluggish response of those who drank beer less often. A-B's baseline advertising in 1961 apparently put the company at point *A* on the combined response function, whereas under the Dorfman-Steiner theorem, there would be two local profit-maximizing optima, one roughly at point *X* and another at point *Y*. As a result of these experiments and others showing that "pulsed" advertising was nearly as effective as continuous advertising, Budweiser advertising outlays were reduced from $1.89 per barrel in 1962 to $0.80 in 1968—that is, to point *X* on the response function.

Table 10.2 extends Table 10.1 by summarizing media advertising outlays per barrel averaged across time periods of several years for a group of

[50]See Ackoff and Emshoff, "Advertising Research at Anheuser-Busch, Inc. (1963–68)," *Sloan Management Review*, Winter 1975, pp. 1–14.

TABLE 10.2
Extension of Brewers' Media Advertising Trends

Company	*Dollars per Barrel in Period*						
	1950–54	1955–59	1960–64	1965–69	1970–75	1976–80	1985–88
A-B	$0.51	$1.31	$1.53	$1.02	$0.76	$1.47	$4.56
Schlitz	0.64	1.42	2.07	1.58	1.04	2.22	merged
Pabst	0.80	1.34	1.17	0.85	0.57	0.95	n.a.
Miller	0.68	1.31	1.24	1.80	1.89	2.02	5.25
Coors	n.a.	0.08	0.07	0.16	0.17	0.71	5.43
Falstaff	0.37	1.08	1.47	1.48	0.99	n.a.	merged
Stroh	0.38	0.79	1.01	1.49	1.03	1.57	2.42
Heileman	n.a.	n.a.	n.a.	n.a.	0.65	0.82	1.31
Schmidt	n.a.	0.53	1.03	0.88	0.87	0.84	merged

Sources: See Table 10.1 and note 51.

companies overlapping, but not identical to, those covered by Table 10.1.[51] The reduction of A-B's advertising in the wake of its 1962–1964 experiments is clearly evident. Other national brewers, with the exception of Miller, appear to have followed A-B down with a lag, some because they perceived that A-B had discovered a strategy yielding higher profits, and Pabst because it had lost its premium image in much of the nation. Schmidt serves as representative of regional brewers with relatively low revenues per barrel sold. The Coors anomaly will be addressed shortly.

THE MILLER STORY

Miller's advertising trajectory is an important exception to the 1965–1975 de-escalation pattern shown in Table 10.2. Miller sought national distribution as a premium brand during the 1930s and 1940s. It was tardy in decentralizing its brewing operations, but by 1969 it had million-barrel breweries near Los Angeles and Fort Worth along with its four-million-barrel home brewery at Milwaukee. Its principal brand, Miller High Life, was sold in clear bottles and advertised heavily as "the champagne of bottled beers." The upper-class image

---

[51]It is drawn from numerous sources, including those listed under Table 10.1, a compilation developed from *Leading National Advertisers* data for Pabst Company in 1982, and the leading National Advertisers *AD $ Summary* for 1985 through 1988. Overlapping reveals modest inconsistencies that do not change the basic picture.

projected by its marketing approach sustained premium prices, but total sales of only five million barrels and a market share of 4.2 percent in 1970.

In two steps between 1969 and 1970, the Miller Company was acquired by Philip Morris, Inc., at the time the fourth-largest U.S. cigarette producer. Philip Morris brought to the brewing industry the marketing strategies used aggressively in cigarettes. To discover unserved demand niches, it conducted psyche-probing research with consumer panels. What it found was not a niche, but a gaping hole. Eighty percent of beer consumption in the United States, it learned, was attributable to roughly 20 percent of the consumers. But those consumers had a problem. They loved to guzzle beer, but they were concerned about the weight gain to which their proclivities led. The challenge was, how to win their patronage?

In 1972 Miller purchased the brands of Chicago's Meister Brau company, whose breweries were closed. One of the acquired brands was a low-calorie beer, Meister Brau Lite. The Chicago company had targeted it toward calorie-conscious women, among other things promoting it by conducting a "Miss Lite" contest, but the target audience drank little beer and the campaign fell flat. Miller's marketers saw hidden potential in Lite. They altered its formula and in 1973 reintroduced it to the market as Miller Lite, pricing it at premium levels (even though it cost a bit less to produce than regular premium beer) and targeting it toward calorie-conscious heavy imbibers. Miller's advertising campaign, the most intensive in brewing industry history, did not mention corpulence. Rather, it featured a parade of famous athletes such as Dick Butkus, all-pro linebacker for the Chicago Bears, and Billy Martin, who alternated between widely publicized brawls and managing the New York Yankees, proclaiming that with Lite, they could drink all they wanted without feeling filled up. Miller Lite sales soared from 1.6 million barrels in 1974 to 4 million barrels in 1976, 13 million barrels in 1980, and 19 million barrels in 1986. Other brewers responded by introducing their own low-calorie formulations, and sales of all light beers exceeded 43 million barrels in 1986—23 percent of all U.S. beer consumption. Despite the imitative competition from others, Miller, the first mover, retained 44 percent of the light beer submarket in 1986.

Under the tutelage of Philip Morris, Miller also channeled massive advertising support to its other brands, leading the escalation of adverting expenditures evident in Table 10.2. Through advertising that portrayed workers enjoying the good life after a hard day at the oil field or shipyard, it repositioned its High Life brand from snob to working-class status. For the uppah-uppah who would have consumed High Life, it licensed the brand name from Löwenbräu of Munich, reformulated a pale imitation, and spent $15 to $30 per barrel on advertising proclaiming Lowenbrau as a superpremium beer. Meister Brau was rolled out as a popular-priced national brand in 1983 and advertised much more heavily ("Tastes as good as Budweiser at a better price") than was customary for regional beers. Milwaukee's Best was introduced nationally as a flanking budget-priced beer in 1984. The success of Miller Lite and the market share gains achieved (later, it appears, only temporarily) by Miller High Life propelled Miller's national market share to 21 percent in 1980. See again

Figure 10.1. Miller openly avowed its aspiration to overtake Anheuser-Busch as the nation's leading brewer—a challenge to which August Busch III replied, "Tell Miller to come right along, but tell them to bring lots of money."[52] For the brewers financially able to keep pace, an advertising war escalated.

THE COORS STORY

Coors stands out in Table 10.2 for its extraordinarily low media advertising outlays—at least, until the 1980s. From a single brewery in Golden, Colorado, it expanded after World War II to become the leading brand in the 11-state territory it served in the western United States. Its beer was sold unpasteurized, and to supply the huge California market, in which it held a 45 percent market share in 1972, it dispatched whole trainloads of beer in refrigerated cars. By the 1960s, it had become a kind of cult beer, spreading its fame not by advertising but by word of mouth, brewery tours for tourists visiting Colorado, and ubiquitous T-shirts bearing the Coors logo.[53] It capitalized on its limited distribution by prohibiting wholesalers from shipping into eastern markets, despite evident demand, thereby becoming a sort of forbidden fruit to easterners. Thus, although it was not nationally distributed, it had a national reputation—the "Coors mystique"—and sold at national premium prices.

A national premium reputation is a valuable asset upon which there are powerful incentives to capitalize. During the 1970s, Coors began expanding its marketing territory into Texas, Oklahoma, and then the Middle West. Having added a low-calorie beer to combat Miller Lite, it continued its expansion into the East during the 1980s, supporting state rollout campaigns for the first time with massive advertising. See the last column of Table 10.2. A key function of introductory advertising is to induce consumers to sample one's product, after which, it is hoped, they will be pleased and remain loyal.[54] Because of the reputation that preceded its entry and heavy advertising, it achieved unusually high trial rates. But because the reputation outshone the reality, repeat purchasing rates were much lower. Its sales share in eleven states east of the Mississippi in which it had operated for at least a year prior to 1985 averaged less than 6 percent. Nevertheless, its eastward expansion carried it to third place among U.S. brewers, trailing only Anheuser-Busch and Miller. See Figure 10.1.

Coors's invasion of the East was complicated by high transportation costs, which it attempted to mitigate by shipping rail tankcars of beer extract from

---

[52]See "Miller's Fast Growth Upsets the Beer Industry," *Business Week*, November 8, 1976, p. 58; and "Anheuser's Plan to Flatten Miller's Head," *Business Week*, April 21, 1980, pp. 171–172.

[53]See "The Brewery That Breaks All the Rules," *Business Week*, August 22, 1970, pp. 60–64.

[54]See Phillip Nelson, "Advertising as Information," *Journal of Political Economy*, vol. 82 (July/August 1974), pp. 729–754.

Colorado to a plant in Shenandoah, Virginia, where water was added and the reconstituted beer was packaged. This was attacked in Anheuser-Busch advertisements insisting that the new system contradicted Coors's traditional claim of brewing its beer from "pure Rocky Mountain spring water."[55] Coors sought but failed to obtain a federal court injunction against the A-B advertising.

BEER WARS

Beer consumption continued to expand briskly during the 1970s, from 122.6 million barrels (including imports) in 1970 to 181.9 million barrels in 1981. But then demand growth slowed. During the next ten years, the total demand increase was nine million barrels, of which one-third was satisfied by rising imports.

The retardation of growth on the demand side interacted with the rapid expansion of some brewers, notably Anheuser-Busch, Miller, and Coors, to cause widespread excess capacity. Finding its anticipated growth unexpectedly thwarted, Miller was forced to mothball a new brewery with 10.5 million barrels of capacity at Trenton, Ohio, between 1983 and 1990. Some smaller companies were operating at less than half of their rated capacities.

Anheuser-Busch continued to increase both its market share and its absolute volume, opening new breweries and expanding existing units to keep capacity and demand balanced. However, it altered the multiplant expansion pattern described previously. The St. Louis brewery continued to serve as a pivot point, channeling its output toward geographic areas in which demand had grown particularly rapidly. However, when large expansions came onstream—typically in chunks of four million barrels—St. Louis used its released capacity to churn out large quantities of A-B's popularly priced Busch brand. The flood of Busch beer had a particularly potent impact on brewers such as Heileman and Stroh, whose principal strength had been in the Midwest. Stroh retaliated with its Old Milwaukee, Heileman with Blatz and Carling Black Label, Miller with Meister Brau and Milwaukee's Best, and others with their own "fighting" brands. Coors joined the fray with new Keystone and Keystone Light popular-priced brands in 1989. In 1989 price discounting spread to the premium brands of Miller and Coors, inducing Anheuser-Busch to announce selective regional price cuts on its flagship Budweiser brand.[56] However, the announcements apparently had their intended

---

[55]"Coors Says Anheuser Pours Water on Reputation," *New York Times*, August 14, 1992, p. D1; and "Court Rejects Coors Bid to Block Ads by Busch," *New York Times*, August 20, 1992, p. D1.

[56]"Anheuser Cutting Its Beer Prices," *New York Times*, October 26, 1989, p. D1; and "Anheuser-Busch, Slugging It Out, Plans Beer Price Cuts," *Wall Street Journal*, October 26, 1989, p. B1.

disciplinary effect on rivals, whose price-cutting abated, inducing A-B to back off from its threat of more widespread premium price reductions.[57]

The "beer wars" of the 1980s had a devastating effect on the profits of major brewing companies that lacked the strength of A-B, Miller, and Coors in premium brands. They sought refuge in a complex series of mergers. There had been many earlier brewing industry mergers, but with few exceptions, they involved the acquisition of small, failing brewers by regional companies of intermediate size. Now, however, the merger wave reached to the top of the firm size distribution. To grasp its scope, it is helpful to review a list of the leading companies as of 1979, with their shares of domestic production (by barrelage):

Anheuser-Busch	27.5%
Miller	21.3%
Schlitz	9.8%
Pabst	8.8%
Coors	7.7%
G. W. Heileman	6.6%
Stroh	3.6%
Olympia	3.5%
C. Schmidt	2.3%
Schaefer	2.1%

The four leaders continued to be the companies that had sought national distribution in the 1930s, although Miller had displaced Schlitz (once the largest seller) and Pabst in the rank ordering. Heileman, Stroh, Olympia, Schmidt, and Schaefer were regional brewers that had expanded their geographic reach by acquiring smaller firms.

Schlitz, fading rapidly because of earlier product formulation problems, tried to avert financial disaster by selling its new, still unoccupied brewery at Syracuse, New York, to Anheuser-Busch in 1980. But that was insufficient to stem the tide. In 1981 it sought to merge with Heileman, but the attempt was rebuffed on antitrust grounds by the U.S. Department of Justice. In 1982 Stroh, which in 1980 had acquired tenth-ranked but nearly bankrupt Schaefer,[58] received governmental approval to acquire Schlitz. The Schlitz brand continued to lose volume after the merger.

Pabst attempted to stop its downward spiral by acquiring in 1982 the Olympia Brewing Company of Washington State, which in turn had acquired

---

[57]See "A Warning Shot from the King of Beers," *Business Week*, December 18, 1989, p. 124.

[58]"Schaefer Pins Hope on Stroh," *New York Times*, May 17, 1980, p. 29.

Hamms of Minnesota and Lone Star of Texas. But later that year Pabst became the target of a takeover attempt, one party to which was Paul Kalmanovitz, whose S&P holding company had previously acquired General Brewing Company of California and Pearl of Texas along with what was left of the Falstaff Company. To thwart the takeover, Pabst sold to Heileman its large modern brewery in Georgia and nine of the less-well-known Pabst brands. Pabst's finances continued to deteriorate, and in 1984 Pabst and Heileman agreed to a complete merger. The deal was approved by the Department of Justice but enjoined on antitrust grounds by a Detroit federal court in a suit brought by rivals Schmidt (which had previously sought to acquire Pabst) and Stroh.[59] In 1985 Kalmanovitz tried again and succeeded in acquiring Pabst. Mr. Kalmanovitz favored "harvest" or "bleed" business strategies, withdrawing advertising support from the brands he controlled, pocketing the larger resulting short-run profits, and letting the decline in their volume accelerate.[60] He also increased short-run profits by bypassing wholesalers, selling directly to retail chains and foregoing the tavern and other institutional sales facilitated by wholesalers.[61] There is reason to believe that advertising spending was reinstated after the death of Kalmanovitz in 1987.[62]

Having been rebuffed in its attempt to merge with Pabst, Heileman was acquired in 1987 (shortly before a stock market crash) by Australian entrepreneur Alan Bond, who hoped to use Heileman as a springboard to increase importation of his Foster's beers. Bond paid $1.4 billion for Heileman's equity, which was believed by insiders to be worth no more than $400 million, and financed the acquisition by borrowing $1.1 billion. Bond financed a doubling of Heileman's advertising outlays in 1988, but then plunged into financial crisis. In 1991 Heileman declared voluntary bankruptcy but continued to operate.[63]

In 1987 Detroit-based Stroh acquired Philadelphia's Schmidt Brewing Company. In 1989 Stroh reached a tentative agreement to be acquired by Coors. However, Coors became fearful of Stroh's deteriorating position and chose not to consummate the merger.

---

[59] The principal argument used to justify an injunction was that a strengthened Heileman-Pabst would receive priority over Stroh and Schmidt brands from the numerous wholesalers the firms shared.

[60] See Brown Brothers Harriman & Co., *Brewing Industry Basic Report*, August 9, 1985, p. 19; and "One Last Call for Fading Beer Brands," *Business Week*, October 16, 1989, p. 68.

[61] See "Existing Distributors Are Being Squeezed by Brewers, Retailers," *Wall Street Journal*, November 22, 1993, p. 1, which observes also that Heileman joined Kalmanovitz in bypassing California wholesalers.

[62] Letter of Hal Asher to the editors of *Business Week*, November 27, 1989, pp. 9–12.

[63] "Heileman in Chapter 11, But Upbeat," *New York Times*, January 25, 1991, p. D1.

Thus, of the ten leading U.S. brewers in 1979, only six continued to exist as recognizable entities in 1990. Two of those six were owned by outside interests, and four of the six had tried, or at least seriously considered, merging with others of the four. By 1993, the six accounted for 97 percent of the beer produced in the United States (i.e., excluding imports), with shares as follows:[64]

Anheuser-Busch	46.9%
Miller	23.7%
Coors	10.7%
Stroh	6.7%
Heileman	4.8%
Pabst (owned by S&P)	3.8%

Second-ranked Miller responded in 1992 to the cessation of its growth with a downsizing program, among other things closing its eight-million-barrel-capacity brewery near Syracuse, New York.[65] The main beneficiary of the smaller companies' decline was Anheuser-Busch. Its chairman is said to have set as a goal achieving a 50 percent share of the U.S. beer market. If that happens, optimal dynamic limit pricing suggests, one might expect it to cease holding prices down to gain market share and begin harvesting the benefits of its growth through higher prices and profits. Whether it does so will be of great interest to consumers and students of industrial strategy.

MERGER ANTITRUST POLICY

Mergers were for many companies an attempt to escape or remedy a deteriorating market position or to achieve volume they were unable to build with existing brands.[66] In effect, they were a second-best solution to problems encountered in the marketplace. The companies who succeeded best on their own merits resorted least to mergers. After being stopped by the government in its 1958 attempt to purchase a small Miami brewer, Anheuser-Busch constructed a green-field plant in Tampa. It then grew entirely by promoting its own beer brands and building new plants to produce them. Coors's growth was also entirely internal, ignoring its brief and inconclusive flirtation with Stroh. After receiving an infusion of marketing know-how and capital through

---

[64]*Modern Brewery Age Blue Book: 1994*, p. 283.

[65]"Now, It's Jack MacDonough Time," *Business Week*, December 7, 1992, pp. 94–95; and "Miller Closing New York State Plant," *New York Times*, December 2, 1993, p. D5.

[66]See Victor J. Tremblay and Carol Tremblay, "The Determinants of Horizontal Acquisitions: Evidence from the US Brewing Industry," *Journal of Industrial Economics*, vol. 37 (September 1988), pp. 21–45.

its acquisition by Philip Morris (a so-called *conglomerate* merger), Miller between 1970 and 1988 acquired only one brewing company, Meister Brau, whose closed Chicago brewery had a capacity at the time of 825,000 barrels per year.[67]

The brewing industry played a prominent role in the evolution of U.S. antitrust policy toward mergers. During the first half of the twentieth century, the antitrust laws had little power to stop mergers unless they were accompanied by abusive practices like those that led to the breakup of Standard Oil. In 1950, Congress sought to retard merger activity by passing the Celler-Kefauver amendment to the Clayton Act, declaring illegal mergers "where in any line of commerce in any section of the country . . . the effect . . . may be substantially to lessen competition, or to tend to create a monopoly."

The new law was vigorously enforced, with the action against Anheuser-Busch's Florida acquisition as one of the first warning shots. Another case filed a year later was appealed to the Supreme Court and contributed early precedents. In 1958 Pabst acquired its Milwaukee neighbor, Blatz. The government brought suit against the acquisition in 1959, arguing inter alia that it reduced competition in Wisconsin, where Pabst had an 11.1 percent sales share in 1957 while Blatz had a 12.8 percent share, and in the three-state market of Wisconsin, Illinois, and Michigan, where the two firms' combined premerger share was 11.3 percent. The Supreme Court held that these states represented valid markets and that, given the trend toward increased concentration in the brewing industry, the market shares involved were sufficient to threaten a substantial lessening of competition.[68] After further litigation, Pabst, having closed Blatz's Milwaukee brewery in the interim, sold to Heileman in 1969 the remaining assets—in the words of Heileman's advertising at the time, a triangle (the Blatz trademark), 32 trucks, and the Blatz marching band.

Another important precedent emerged from Falstaff's attempt to establish a national presence by acquiring regional brewers. In 1965 Falstaff acquired Narragansett Brewing Company, whose 20 percent share made it the leading marketer in New England. Prior to the merger, Falstaff sold beer in 32 states, but not in New England or New York. Its leaders testified that they would enter New England only by merger, and not by shipping or building their own plant. The district court dismissed the case, but on appeal, the Supreme Court articulated a "potential competition" rule that brought the merger into jeopardy:[69]

---

[67]In 1988 Miller acquired another small brewer, Jacob Leinenkugel, using its facilities to produce specialty beers.

[68]U.S. v. Pabst Brewing Co., 384 U.S. 546 (1966), reversing 233 F. Supp. 475 (1964). The Supreme Court in effect ignored the possibility that Anheuser-Busch, Hamms, Grain Belt, and other brewers in adjacent states could substantially increase their presence in Wisconsin and Illinois if Pabst tried to increase prices there.

[69]U.S. v. Falstaff Brewing Corp. et al., 410 U.S. 526, 533–534 (1973). The rehearing decision is at 383 F. Supp. 1020 (1974).

> The specific question . . . is not what Falstaff's internal company decisions were but whether, given its financial capabilities and conditions in the New England market, it would be reasonable to consider it a potential entrant into that market. . . . [I]f it would appear to rational beer merchants in New England that Falstaff might well build a new brewery to supply the northeastern market then its entry by merger becomes suspect. . . . The District Court should therefore . . . determine whether in any realistic sense Falstaff could be said to be a potential competitor . . . so positioned on the edge of the market that it exerted beneficial influence on conditions in that market.

On rehearing, the district court found that these conditions were not met, and so the merger was allowed to stand. But by that time Falstaff's profitability was deteriorating, in part because of the high costs incurred in small, old breweries such as Narragansett that had been the focus of its acquisition program.

Many mergers of the 1970s and especially the 1980s were much larger than these litigated brewing company acquisitions. But most survived antitrust scrutiny because of new developments. For one, new, more conservative appointments to the Supreme Court during the early 1970s led the Court to demand more careful analyses delineating economically meaningful geographic and product market boundaries. This demand was met in part by the issuance of new Merger Guidelines by the Department of Justice in 1982.[70] The guidelines for geographic market definition adopted concepts similar to those proposed in 1972 to show that the acquisition by Heileman of Detroit's Associated Brewing Company did not substantially reduce competition.[71] In tandem, the deregulation of rail and truck transportation during the late 1970s reduced shipping costs, permitting breweries to ship their output larger distances for a given fraction of the ex-works product price. Meaningfully defined geographic markets widened considerably.

The 1982 Merger Guidelines did not permit companies to defend their merger by showing that it enhanced efficiency. However, revised Guidelines in 1984 stated that the Justice Department would favorably consider "clear and convincing evidence" that merger is "reasonably necessary to achieve significant net efficiencies" such as economies of scale, better integration of plants, and lower transportation or distribution costs.[72] This change probably played a role in the Department's clearance of some large brewing company

---

[70]U.S. Department of Justice, Antitrust Division, *U.S. Department of Justice Merger Guidelines* (Washington, DC: USGPO, June 14, 1982).

[71]U.S. v. G. W. Heileman Co. et al., Eastern District of Michigan (1972), CCH 1973 Trade Cases Para. 74,550. Testifying for the companies were Kenneth Elzinga and the author. They argued that determining whether a postulated geographic territory was a "market" hinged upon the ability of companies within the territory to raise prices without drawing in from adjacent territories beer shipments that undermine the attempted price increase.

[72]U.S. Department of Justice, Antitrust Division. *U.S. Department of Justice Merger Guidelines* (June 14, 1984), p. 22.

mergers during the 1980s. In addition, early decisions interpreting the Celler-Kefauver Act of 1950 articulated a "failing-firm defense." The defense required proof that a merger partner faced imminent business failure without a possibility of financial reorganization, and that there were no alternative mergers solving the problem while impairing competition less severely. The test was interpreted stringently, but during the 1980s the condition of many brewing companies had deteriorated to such a state that the failing-firm criteria were satisfied.

MICROBREWERIES: BUCKING THE TREND

As the concentration process advanced during the 1980s, a diametrically opposite phenomenon materialized: the proliferation of microbreweries, commonly defined as operations producing less than 15,000 barrels of beer per year. By 1993, approximately 350 microbrewers in the United States had a combined output estimated at 450,000 barrels, or 0.25 percent of total U.S. consumption.[73] The genesis of the microbrewery movement is usually attributed to the Anchor Brewing Company of San Francisco, which emerged from a failing local brewery in 1970 and by 1985 had achieved sales of 36,000 barrels per year—too large to be classified by the standard sources as remaining in the "micro" category.[74]

Microbreweries fall far short of realizing the potential economies of scale. They compensate for the concomitant cost disadvantage in several ways. First, they produce full-bodied, flavorful, typically unpasteurized European-style beers—a market niche that for long had been ignored by the regional and national brewers.[75] Second, catering mainly to affluent consumers, they compensate for higher costs by charging superpremium prices. Thus, in Boston's best liquor supermarket during the summer of 1994, the leading local microbrews sold at $17.99 per case of 24 bottles, compared to $20.99 for well-known German and Dutch beers, $14.99 for Budweiser and the principal premium light beers, $9.99 for Old Milwaukee, and $8.29 for Meister Brau. Third, most of the microbrewers (Anchor and a few others excepted) save on transportation costs by limiting their distribution to nearby metropolitan areas. Like Coors in its early stages, they rely on brewery tours and word-of-mouth rather than heavy advertising to promote their products. Fourth, many saved money by buying used equipment from old breweries abandoned in the United States and Europe (where a

---

[73]*Modern Brewery Age Blue Book: 1994*, pp. 284–286 and 292.

[74]"Small-Time Brewers Are Putting the Kick Back into Beer," *Business Week*, January 20, 1986, pp. 90–91.

[75]Asked by the author in a 1971 interview why he did not produce a full-bodied European beer, the president of a regional company said that the American consumer simply wasn't interested, preferring instead light, unobtrusive brews.

similar concentration trend operated). Some occupied premises were left abandoned when old-fashioned local breweries were closed.

When this chapter was written, the number of microbreweries was increasing at a brisk pace. To defend themselves, the national brewers were beginning to offer their own more full-bodied specialty beers.[76]

How the trend will evolve, and whether some microbrewers will grow to challenge the national companies seriously, will be watched with interest. Meanwhile, it suffices to identify the implications for public policy of this latest brewing industry development: precisely none.

SOME CONCLUDING OBSERVATIONS

With the completion of our last industry case study, the logical structure of this book should now be fully apparent. We began with competitive market structures, moved on to analyze the efforts of sellers to relieve the pressures of competition through cartelization and the acquisition of monopoly positions, and then returned repeatedly from varying perspectives to the problem of price-setting under oligopoly, where outcomes depend upon the specific strategies chosen by consciously interdependent rivals. Our early investigations focused on products that are relatively homogeneous. We then advanced to cases in which product differentiation played an important role—sometimes through technological innovation affecting product characteristics; sometimes through more superficial design changes (notably, in autos); and sometimes by cultivating a favorable image in consumers' minds through having been a first mover, person-to-person selling effort, and clever advertising. Beer is the case in which success was attained through little more than advertising to reinforce first-mover advantages that initially seemed innocuous. Yet in the long run the combination proved formidable, supporting strategies that radically transformed the brewing industry's structure. The first-mover advantages that come from technological pioneering are commonly even more powerful, but they may also be more short-lived if new domestic or foreign rivals, exploiting the rapidly changing technological opportunities on which they were based, leapfrog ahead and seize the lead.

In the short run, we have seen, competition has frequently been restrained, thereby permitting elevated prices, wages, and other costs and (less frequently) lethargy toward new technological challenges. Over the longer run (on occasion, as in steel, after a very long run indeed), competition proved to be a potent disciplinarian, undermining prices and dominant positions and compelling the adoption of new technologies. Sometimes the

---

[76]"From the Microbrewers Who Brought You Bud, Coors . . .," *Business Week,* April 24, 1995, pp. 66–70.

reforming competition arises within an industry's domestic boundaries. During the past two decades, it has to an increasing extent hurdled national borders as imports and direct investment by foreign enterprises have forced sluggish domestic firms to accept new ideas, reduce organizational slack, and set prices closer to costs. Injections of competition from abroad are often painful, fostering cries for relief from government through the erection of import barriers. More often than not, at least in the industries we have studied, such protection has delayed needed adjustments and caused other adverse side effects. The intensification of competition from abroad has sometimes corrected problems left unsolved by clumsy or delayed implementation of antitrust remedies at home. Some of the pain experienced from rapidly rising import competition might have been alleviated if festering problems had been corrected at an early date through swift but effective action to invigorate domestic competition. In steel, autos, and (less clearly) computers, there is persuasive evidence to support this conjecture.

It is almost surely true also that strong domestic enterprises able to hold their own in the rough-and-tumble of international competition emerge through a kind of natural selection process under which the contenders are repeatedly challenged by vigorous rivals. Or to put the point negatively, no environment is less propitious to the development of strong competitors than one in which a dominant seller like United States Steel holds a price umbrella over its fellow enterprises and adopts a lackadaisical attitude toward new technology. To be sure, elements of monopoly power may have to be added to the policy mix, especially when sizable and risky investments in new technology must be made. But it is important to sustain competitive pressure, prodding firms to pare their costs, improve existing products, and embrace new product opportunities, or if they fail to do so, see any supranormal profits eliminated. On this there is a growing consensus based upon evidence that goes far beyond the scope of our case studies.[77]

---

[77]See, for example, Michael Porter, *The Competitive Advantage of Nations* (New York: Free Press, 1990), pp. 117–124, 594–598, and 662–673; Martin Baily and Hans Gersbach, "Efficiency in Manufacturing and the Nature of Competition," *Brookings Papers on Economic Activity:* Microeconomics (1995), pp. 307–358; William S. Comanor and F. M. Scherer, "Rewriting History: The Early Sherman Act Monopolization Cases," *International Journal of the Economics of Business,* vol. 2 (July 1995), pp. 263–289; and James M. MacDonald, "Does Import Competition Force Efficient Production?" *Review of Economics and Statistics,* vol. 76 (November 1994), pp. 721–727.

INDEX